TOPOLOGY
Second Edition

James Munkres

PEARSON

Original edition, entitled TOPOLOGY: PEARSON NEW INTERNATIONAL EDITION, 2nd Edition, by MUNKRES, JAMES, published by Pearson Education Limited, Copyright © 2013 by Pearson Education, Inc.

Indian edition published by Pearson India Education Services Pvt. Ltd. Copyright © 2015.

ISBN 978-93-325-4953-1

First Impression, 2015
Second Impression, 2016
Third Impression

This edition is manufactured in India and is authorized for sale only in India, Bangladesh, Bhutan, Pakistan, Nepal, Sri Lanka and the Maldives. Circulation of this edition outside of these territories is UNAUTHORIZED.

Published by Pearson India Education Services Pvt.Ltd, CIN: U72200TN2005PTC057128. Formerly known as TutorVista Global Pvt Ltd, licensees of Pearson Education in South Asia

Head Office: 7th Floor, Knowledge Boulevard, A-8(A), Sector-62, Noida – 201309, U.P, India.

Registered Office: Module G4, Ground Floor, Elnet Software City, TS-140,Block 2 and 9, Rajiv Gandhi Salai, Taramani, Chennai 600 113, Tamil Nadu, India.Fax: 080-30461003 ,Phone: 080-30461060, www.pearson.co.in, Email: companysecretary.india@pearson.com

Printed in India by Pushp Print Services.

Table of Contents

Chapter 1

Set Theory and Logic

We adopt, as most mathematicians do, the naive point of view regarding set theory. We shall assume that what is meant by a *set* of objects is intuitively clear, and we shall proceed on that basis without analyzing the concept further. Such an analysis properly belongs to the foundations of mathematics and to mathematical logic, and it is not our purpose to initiate the study of those fields.

Logicians have analyzed set theory in great detail, and they have formulated axioms for the subject. Each of their axioms expresses a property of sets that mathematicians commonly accept, and collectively the axioms provide a foundation broad enough and strong enough that the rest of mathematics can be built on them.

It is unfortunately true that careless use of set theory, relying on intuition alone, can lead to contradictions. Indeed, one of the reasons for the axiomatization of set theory was to formulate rules for dealing with sets that would avoid these contradictions. Although we shall not deal with the axioms explicitly, the rules we follow in dealing with sets derive from them. In this book, you will learn how to deal with sets in an "apprentice" fashion, by observing how we handle them and by working with them yourself. At some point of your studies, you may wish to study set theory more carefully and in greater detail; then a course in logic or foundations will be in order.

§1 Fundamental Concepts

Here we introduce the ideas of set theory, and establish the basic terminology and notation. We also discuss some points of elementary logic that, in our experience, are apt to cause confusion.

Basic Notation

Commonly we shall use capital letters A, B, ... to denote sets, and lowercase letters a, b, ... to denote the *objects* or *elements* belonging to these sets. If an object a belongs to a set A, we express this fact by the notation

$$a \in A.$$

If a does not belong to A, we express this fact by writing

$$a \notin A.$$

The equality symbol $=$ is used throughout this book to mean *logical identity*. Thus, when we write $a = b$, we mean that "a" and "b" are symbols for the same object. This is what one means in arithmetic, for example, when one writes $\frac{2}{4} = \frac{1}{2}$. Similarly, the equation $A = B$ states that "A" and "B" are symbols for the same set; that is, A and B consist of precisely the same objects.

If a and b are different objects, we write $a \neq b$; and if A and B are different sets, we write $A \neq B$. For example, if A is the set of all nonnegative real numbers, and B is the set of all positive real numbers, then $A \neq B$, because the number 0 belongs to A and not to B.

We say that A is a *subset* of B if every element of A is also an element of B; and we express this fact by writing

$$A \subset B.$$

Nothing in this definition requires A to be different from B; in fact, if $A = B$, it is true that both $A \subset B$ and $B \subset A$. If $A \subset B$ and A is different from B, we say that A is a *proper subset* of B, and we write

$$A \subsetneq B.$$

The relations $\subset$ and $\subsetneq$ are called *inclusion* and *proper inclusion*, respectively. If $A \subset B$, we also write $B \supset A$, which is read "B *contains* A."

How does one go about specifying a set? If the set has only a few elements, one can simply list the objects in the set, writing "A is the set consisting of the elements a, b, and c." In symbols, this statement becomes

$$A = \{a, b, c\},$$

where braces are used to enclose the list of elements.

The usual way to specify a set, however, is to take some set A of objects and some *property* that elements of A may or may not possess, and to form the set consisting of all elements of A having that property. For instance, one might take the set of real numbers and form the subset B consisting of all even integers. In symbols, this statement becomes

$$B = \{x \mid x \text{ is an even integer}\}.$$

Here the braces stand for the words "the set of," and the vertical bar stands for the words "such that." The equation is read "B is the set of all x such that x is an even integer."

The Union of Sets and the Meaning of "or"

Given two sets A and B, one can form a set from them that consists of all the elements of A together with all the elements of B. This set is called the ***union*** of A and B and is denoted by $A \cup B$. Formally, we define

$$A \cup B = \{x \mid x \in A \text{ or } x \in B\}.$$

But we must pause at this point and make sure exactly what we mean by the statement "$x \in A$ or $x \in B$."

In ordinary everyday English, the word "or" is ambiguous. Sometimes the statement "P or Q" means "P or Q, or both" and sometimes it means "P or Q, but not both." Usually one decides from the context which meaning is intended. For example, suppose I spoke to two students as follows:

> "Miss Smith, every student registered for this course has taken either a course in linear algebra or a course in analysis."

> "Mr. Jones, either you get a grade of at least 70 on the final exam or you will flunk this course."

In the context, Miss Smith knows perfectly well that I mean "everyone has had linear algebra or analysis, or both," and Mr. Jones knows I mean "either he gets at least 70 or he flunks, but not both." Indeed, Mr. Jones would be exceedingly unhappy if both statements turned out to be true!

In mathematics, one cannot tolerate such ambiguity. One has to pick just one meaning and stick with it, or confusion will reign. Accordingly, mathematicians have agreed that they will use the word "or" in the first sense, so that the statement "P or Q" always means "P or Q, or both." If one means "P or Q, but not both," then one has to include the phrase "but not both" explicitly.

With this understanding, the equation defining $A \cup B$ is unambiguous; it states that $A \cup B$ is the set consisting of all elements x that belong to A or to B or to both.

The Intersection of Sets, the Empty Set, and the Meaning of "If . . . Then"

Given sets A and B, another way one can form a set is to take the common part of A and B. This set is called the *intersection* of A and B and is denoted by $A \cap B$. Formally, we define

$$A \cap B = \{x \mid x \in A \text{ and } x \in B\}.$$

But just as with the definition of $A \cup B$, there is a difficulty. The difficulty is not in the meaning of the word "and"; it is of a different sort. It arises when the sets A and B happen to have no elements in common. What meaning does the symbol $A \cap B$ have in such a case?

To take care of this eventuality, we make a special convention. We introduce a special set that we call the *empty set*, denoted by $\varnothing$, which we think of as "the set having no elements."

Using this convention, we express the statement that A and B have no elements in common by the equation

$$A \cap B = \varnothing.$$

We also express this fact by saying that A and B are *disjoint*.

Now some students are bothered by the notion of an "empty set." "How," they say, "can you have a set with nothing in it?" The problem is similar to that which arose many years ago when the number 0 was first introduced.

The empty set is only a convention, and mathematics could very well get along without it. But it is a very convenient convention, for it saves us a good deal of awkwardness in stating theorems and in proving them. Without this convention, for instance, one would have to prove that the two sets A and B do have elements in common before one could use the notation $A \cap B$. Similarly, the notation

$$C = \{x \mid x \in A \text{ and } x \text{ has a certain property}\}$$

could not be used if it happened that no element x of A had the given property. It is much more convenient to agree that $A \cap B$ and C equal the empty set in such cases.

Since the empty set $\varnothing$ is merely a convention, we must make conventions relating it to the concepts already introduced. Because $\varnothing$ is thought of as "the set with no elements," it is clear we should make the convention that for each object x, the relation $x \in \varnothing$ does not hold. Similarly, the definitions of union and intersection show that for every set A we should have the equations

$$A \cup \varnothing = A \quad \text{and} \quad A \cap \varnothing = \varnothing.$$

The inclusion relation is a bit more tricky. Given a set A, should we agree that $\varnothing \subset A$? Once more, we must be careful about the way mathematicians use the English language. The expression $\varnothing \subset A$ is a shorthand way of writing the sentence, "Every element that belongs to the empty set also belongs to the set A." Or to put it more formally, "For every object x, if x belongs to the empty set, then x also belongs to the set A."

Is this statement true or not? Some might say "yes" and others say "no." You will never settle the question by argument, only by agreement. This is a statement of the form "If P, then Q," and in everyday English the meaning of the "if … then" construction is ambiguous. It always means that if P is true, then Q is true also. Sometimes that is all it means; other times it means something more: that if P is false, Q must be false. Usually one decides from the context which interpretation is correct.

The situation is similar to the ambiguity in the use of the word "or." One can reformulate the examples involving Miss Smith and Mr. Jones to illustrate the ambiguity. Suppose I said the following:

> "Miss Smith, if any student registered for this course has not taken a course in linear algebra, then he has taken a course in analysis."

> "Mr. Jones, if you get a grade below 70 on the final, you are going to flunk this course."

In the context, Miss Smith understands that if a student in the course has not had linear algebra, then he has taken analysis, but if he has had linear algebra, he may or may not have taken analysis as well. And Mr. Jones knows that if he gets a grade below 70, he will flunk the course, but if he gets a grade of at least 70, he will pass.

Again, mathematics cannot tolerate ambiguity, so a choice of meanings must be made. Mathematicians have agreed always to use "if … then" in the first sense, so that a statement of the form "If P, then Q" means that if P is true, Q is true also, but if P is false, Q may be either true or false.

As an example, consider the following statement about real numbers:

$$\text{If } x > 0, \text{ then } x^3 \neq 0.$$

It is a statement of the form, "If P, then Q," where P is the phrase "$x > 0$" (called the **hypothesis** of the statement) and Q is the phrase "$x^3 \neq 0$" (called the **conclusion** of the statement). This is a true statement, for in every case for which the hypothesis $x > 0$ holds, the conclusion $x^3 \neq 0$ holds as well.

Another true statement about real numbers is the following:

$$\text{If } x^2 < 0, \text{ then } x = 23;$$

in every case for which the hypothesis holds, the conclusion holds as well. Of course, it happens in this example that there are no cases for which the hypothesis holds. A statement of this sort is sometimes said to be **vacuously true**.

To return now to the empty set and inclusion, we see that the inclusion $\varnothing \subset A$ does hold for every set A. Writing $\varnothing \subset A$ is the same as saying, "If $x \in \varnothing$, then $x \in A$," and this statement is vacuously true.

Contrapositive and Converse

Our discussion of the "if ... then" construction leads us to consider another point of elementary logic that sometimes causes difficulty. It concerns the relation between a *statement*, its *contrapositive*, and its *converse*.

Given a statement of the form "If P, then Q," its **contrapositive** is defined to be the statement "If Q is not true, then P is not true." For example, the contrapositive of the statement

$$\text{If } x > 0, \text{ then } x^3 \neq 0,$$

is the statement

$$\text{If } x^3 = 0, \text{ then it is not true that } x > 0.$$

Note that both the statement and its contrapositive are true. Similarly, the statement

$$\text{If } x^2 < 0, \text{ then } x = 23,$$

has as its contrapositive the statement

$$\text{If } x \neq 23, \text{ then it is not true that } x^2 < 0.$$

Again, both are true statements about real numbers.

These examples may make you suspect that there is some relation between a statement and its contrapositive. And indeed there is; they are two ways of saying precisely the same thing. Each is true if and only if the other is true; they are *logically equivalent*.

This fact is not hard to demonstrate. Let us introduce some notation first. As a shorthand for the statement "If P, then Q," we write

$$P \Longrightarrow Q,$$

which is read "P implies Q." The contrapositive can then be expressed in the form

$$(\text{not } Q) \Longrightarrow (\text{not } P),$$

where "not Q" stands for the phrase "Q is not true."

Now the only way in which the statement "$P \Rightarrow Q$" can fail to be correct is if the hypothesis P is true and the conclusion Q is false. Otherwise it is correct. Similarly, the only way in which the statement $(\text{not } Q) \Rightarrow (\text{not } P)$ can fail to be correct is if the hypothesis "not Q" is true and the conclusion "not P" is false. This is the same as saying that Q is false and P is true. And this, in turn, is precisely the situation in which $P \Rightarrow Q$ fails to be correct. Thus, we see that the two statements are either both correct or both incorrect; they are logically equivalent. Therefore, we shall accept a proof of the statement "not $Q \Rightarrow$ not P" as a proof of the statement "$P \Rightarrow Q$."

There is another statement that can be formed from the statement $P \Rightarrow Q$. It is the statement

$$Q \Longrightarrow P,$$

which is called the ***converse*** of $P \Rightarrow Q$. One must be careful to distinguish between a statement's converse and its contrapositive. Whereas a statement and its contrapositive are logically equivalent, the truth of a statement says nothing at all about the truth or falsity of its converse. For example, the true statement

$$If\ x > 0,\ then\ x^3 \neq 0,$$

has as its converse the statement

$$If\ x^3 \neq 0,\ then\ x > 0,$$

which is false. Similarly, the true statement

$$If\ x^2 < 0,\ then\ x = 23,$$

has as its converse the statement

$$If\ x = 23,\ then\ x^2 < 0,$$

which is false.

If it should happen that both the statement $P \Rightarrow Q$ and its converse $Q \Rightarrow P$ are true, we express this fact by the notation

$$P \Longleftrightarrow Q,$$

which is read "P holds if and only if Q holds."

Negation

If one wishes to form the contrapositive of the statement $P \Rightarrow Q$, one has to know how to form the statement "not P," which is called the ***negation*** of P. In many cases, this causes no difficulty; but sometimes confusion occurs with statements involving the phrases "for every" and "for at least one." These phrases are called *logical quantifiers*.

To illustrate, suppose that X is a set, A is a subset of X, and P is a statement about the general element of X. Consider the following statement:

(∗)   *For every $x \in A$, statement P holds.*

How does one form the negation of this statement? Let us translate the problem into the language of sets. Suppose that we let B denote the set of all those elements x of X for which P holds. Then statement (∗) is just the statement that A is a subset of B. What is its negation? Obviously, the statement that A is *not* a subset of B; that is, the statement that there exists at least one element of A that does not belong to B. Translating back into ordinary language, this becomes

For at least one $x \in A$, statement P does not hold.

Therefore, to form the negation of statement (∗), one replaces the quantifier "for every" by the quantifier "for at least one," and one replaces statement P by *its* negation.

The process works in reverse just as well; the negation of the statement

>*For at least one $x \in A$, statement Q holds,*

is the statement

>*For every $x \in A$, statement Q does not hold.*

The Difference of Two Sets

We return now to our discussion of sets. There is one other operation on sets that is occasionally useful. It is the ***difference*** of two sets, denoted by $A - B$, and defined as the set consisting of those elements of A that are not in B. Formally,

$$A - B = \{x \mid x \in A \text{ and } x \notin B\}.$$

It is sometimes called the ***complement*** of B relative to A, or the complement of B *in* A.

Our three set operations are represented schematically in Figure 1.1.

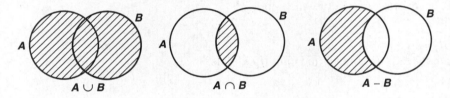

$$A \cup B \qquad\qquad A \cap B \qquad\qquad A - B$$

Figure 1.1

Rules of Set Theory

Given several sets, one may form new sets by applying the set-theoretic operations to them. As in algebra, one uses parentheses to indicate in what order the operations are to be performed. For example, $A \cup (B \cap C)$ denotes the union of the two sets A and $B \cap C$, while $(A \cup B) \cap C$ denotes the intersection of the two sets $A \cup B$ and C. The sets thus formed are quite different, as Figure 1.2 shows.

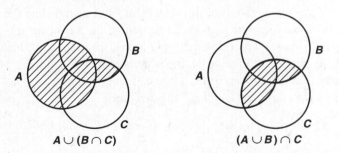

$$A \cup (B \cap C) \qquad\qquad (A \cup B) \cap C$$

Figure 1.2

Sometimes different combinations of operations lead to the same set; when that happens, one has a rule of set theory. For instance, it is true that for any sets A, B, and C the equation

$$A \cap (B \cup C) = (A \cap B) \cup (A \cap C)$$

holds. The equation is illustrated in Figure 1.3; the shaded region represents the set in question, as you can check mentally. This equation can be thought of as a "distributive law" for the operations $\cap$ and $\cup$.

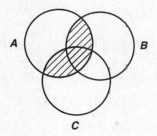

Figure 1.3

Other examples of set-theoretic rules include the second "distributive law,"

$$A \cup (B \cap C) = (A \cup B) \cap (A \cup C),$$

and *DeMorgan's laws*,

$$A - (B \cup C) = (A - B) \cap (A - C),$$
$$A - (B \cap C) = (A - B) \cup (A - C).$$

We leave it to you to check these rules. One can state other rules of set theory, but these are the most important ones. DeMorgan's laws are easier to remember if you verbalize them as follows:

The complement of the union equals the intersection of the complements.
The complement of the intersection equals the union of the complements.

Collections of Sets

The objects belonging to a set may be of any sort. One can consider the set of all even integers, and the set of all blue-eyed people in Nebraska, and the set of all decks of playing cards in the world. Some of these are of limited mathematical interest, we admit! But the third example illustrates a point we have not yet mentioned: namely, that the objects belonging to a set may *themselves* be sets. For a deck of cards is itself a set, one consisting of pieces of pasteboard with certain standard designs printed on them. The set of all decks of cards in the world is thus a set whose elements are themselves sets (of pieces of pasteboard).

We now have another way to form new sets from old ones. Given a set A, we can consider sets whose elements are subsets of A. In particular, we can consider the set of all subsets of A. This set is sometimes denoted by the symbol $\mathcal{P}(A)$ and is called the ***power set*** of A (for reasons to be explained later).

When we have a set whose elements are sets, we shall often refer to it as a ***collection*** of sets and denote it by a script letter such as $\mathcal{A}$ or $\mathcal{B}$. This device will help us in keeping things straight in arguments where we have to consider objects, and sets of objects, and collections of sets of objects, all at the same time. For example, we might use $\mathcal{A}$ to denote the collection of all decks of cards in the world, letting an ordinary capital letter A denote a deck of cards and a lowercase letter a denote a single playing card.

A certain amount of care with notation is needed at this point. We make a distinction between the object a, which is an *element* of a set A, and the one-element set $\{a\}$, which is a *subset* of A. To illustrate, if A is the set $\{a, b, c\}$, then the statements

$$a \in A, \quad \{a\} \subset A, \quad \text{and} \quad \{a\} \in \mathcal{P}(A)$$

are all correct, but the statements $\{a\} \in A$ and $a \subset A$ are not.

Arbitrary Unions and Intersections

We have already defined what we mean by the union and the intersection of two sets. There is no reason to limit ourselves to just two sets, for we can just as well form the union and intersection of arbitrarily many sets.

Given a collection $\mathcal{A}$ of sets, the ***union*** of the elements of $\mathcal{A}$ is defined by the equation

$$\bigcup_{A \in \mathcal{A}} A = \{x \mid x \in A \text{ for at least one } A \in \mathcal{A}\}.$$

The ***intersection*** of the elements of $\mathcal{A}$ is defined by the equation

$$\bigcap_{A \in \mathcal{A}} A = \{x \mid x \in A \text{ for every } A \in \mathcal{A}\}.$$

There is no problem with these definitions if one of the elements of $\mathcal{A}$ happens to be the empty set. But it is a bit tricky to decide what (if anything) these definitions mean if we allow $\mathcal{A}$ to be the empty collection. Applying the definitions literally, we see that no element x satisfies the defining property for the union of the elements of $\mathcal{A}$. So it is reasonable to say that

$$\bigcup_{A \in \mathcal{A}} A = \varnothing$$

if $\mathcal{A}$ is empty. On the other hand, every x satisfies (vacuously) the defining property for the intersection of the elements of $\mathcal{A}$. The question is, every x in what set? If one has a given large set X that is specified at the outset of the discussion to be one's "universe of discourse," and one considers only subsets of X throughout, it is reasonable to let

$$\bigcap_{A \in \mathcal{A}} A = X$$

when $\mathcal{A}$ is empty. Not all mathematicians follow this convention, however. To avoid difficulty, *we shall not define the intersection when $\mathcal{A}$ is empty.*

Cartesian Products

There is yet another way of forming new sets from old ones; it involves the notion of an "ordered pair" of objects. When you studied analytic geometry, the first thing you did was to convince yourself that after one has chosen an x-axis and a y-axis in the plane, every point in the plane can be made to correspond to a unique ordered pair (x, y) of real numbers. (In a more sophisticated treatment of geometry, the plane is more likely to be *defined* as the set of all ordered pairs of real numbers!)

The notion of ordered pair carries over to general sets. Given sets A and B, we define their cartesian product $A \times B$ to be the set of all ordered pairs (a, b) for which a is an element of A and b is an element of B. Formally,

$$A \times B = \{(a, b) \mid a \in A \text{ and } b \in B\}.$$

This definition assumes that the concept of "ordered pair" is already given. It can be taken as a primitive concept, as was the notion of "set"; or it can be given a definition in terms of the set operations already introduced. One definition in terms of set operations is expressed by the equation

$$(a, b) = \{\{a\}, \{a, b\}\};$$

it defines the ordered pair (a, b) as a collection of sets. If $a \neq b$, this definition says that (a, b) is a collection containing two sets, one of which is a one-element set and the other a two-element set. The *first coordinate* of the ordered pair is defined to be the element belonging to both sets, and the *second coordinate* is the element belonging to only one of the sets. If $a = b$, then (a, b) is a collection containing only one set $\{a\}$, since $\{a, b\} = \{a, a\} = \{a\}$ in this case. Its first coordinate and second coordinate both equal the element in this single set.

I think it is fair to say that most mathematicians think of an ordered pair as a primitive concept rather than thinking of it as a collection of sets!

Let us make a comment on notation. It is an unfortunate fact that the notation (a, b) is firmly established in mathematics with two entirely different meanings. One meaning, as an ordered pair of objects, we have just discussed. The other meaning is the one you are familiar with from analysis; if a and b are real numbers, the symbol (a, b) is used to denote the interval consisting of all numbers x such that $a < x < b$. Most of the time, this conflict in notation will cause no difficulty because the meaning will be clear from the context. Whenever a situation occurs where confusion is possible, we shall adopt a different notation for the ordered pair (a, b), denoting it by the symbol

$$a \times b$$

instead.

Exercises

1. Check the distributive laws for $\cup$ and $\cap$ and DeMorgan's laws.

2. Determine which of the following statements are true for all sets $A, B, C,$ and D. If a double implication fails, determine whether one or the other of the possible implications holds. If an equality fails, determine whether the statement becomes true if the "equals" symbol is replaced by one or the other of the inclusion symbols $\subset$ or $\supset$.
   (a) $A \subset B$ and $A \subset C \Leftrightarrow A \subset (B \cup C)$.
   (b) $A \subset B$ or $A \subset C \Leftrightarrow A \subset (B \cup C)$.
   (c) $A \subset B$ and $A \subset C \Leftrightarrow A \subset (B \cap C)$.
   (d) $A \subset B$ or $A \subset C \Leftrightarrow A \subset (B \cap C)$.
   (e) $A - (A - B) = B$.
   (f) $A - (B - A) = A - B$.
   (g) $A \cap (B - C) = (A \cap B) - (A \cap C)$.
   (h) $A \cup (B - C) = (A \cup B) - (A \cup C)$.
   (i) $(A \cap B) \cup (A - B) = A$.
   (j) $A \subset C$ and $B \subset D \Rightarrow (A \times B) \subset (C \times D)$.
   (k) The converse of (j).
   (l) The converse of (j), assuming that A and B are nonempty.
   (m) $(A \times B) \cup (C \times D) = (A \cup C) \times (B \cup D)$.
   (n) $(A \times B) \cap (C \times D) = (A \cap C) \times (B \cap D)$.
   (o) $A \times (B - C) = (A \times B) - (A \times C)$.
   (p) $(A - B) \times (C - D) = (A \times C - B \times C) - A \times D$.
   (q) $(A \times B) - (C \times D) = (A - C) \times (B - D)$.

3. (a) Write the contrapositive and converse of the following statement: "If $x < 0$, then $x^2 - x > 0$," and determine which (if any) of the three statements are true.
   (b) Do the same for the statement "If $x > 0$, then $x^2 - x > 0$."

4. Let A and B be sets of real numbers. Write the negation of each of the following statements:
   (a) For every $a \in A$, it is true that $a^2 \in B$.
   (b) For at least one $a \in A$, it is true that $a^2 \in B$.
   (c) For every $a \in A$, it is true that $a^2 \notin B$.
   (d) For at least one $a \notin A$, it is true that $a^2 \in B$.

5. Let $\mathcal{A}$ be a nonempty collection of sets. Determine the truth of each of the following statements and of their converses:
   (a) $x \in \bigcup_{A \in \mathcal{A}} A \Rightarrow x \in A$ for at least one $A \in \mathcal{A}$.
   (b) $x \in \bigcup_{A \in \mathcal{A}} A \Rightarrow x \in A$ for every $A \in \mathcal{A}$.
   (c) $x \in \bigcap_{A \in \mathcal{A}} A \Rightarrow x \in A$ for at least one $A \in \mathcal{A}$.
   (d) $x \in \bigcap_{A \in \mathcal{A}} A \Rightarrow x \in A$ for every $A \in \mathcal{A}$.

6. Write the contrapositive of each of the statements of Exercise 5.

7. Given sets A, B, and C, express each of the following sets in terms of A, B, and C, using the symbols $\cup$, $\cap$, and $-$.

$$D = \{x \mid x \in A \text{ and } (x \in B \text{ or } x \in C)\},$$
$$E = \{x \mid (x \in A \text{ and } x \in B) \text{ or } x \in C\},$$
$$F = \{x \mid x \in A \text{ and } (x \in B \Rightarrow x \in C)\}.$$

8. If a set A has two elements, show that $\mathscr{P}(A)$ has four elements. How many elements does $\mathscr{P}(A)$ have if A has one element? Three elements? No elements? Why is $\mathscr{P}(A)$ called the power set of A?

9. Formulate and prove DeMorgan's laws for arbitrary unions and intersections.

10. Let $\mathbb{R}$ denote the set of real numbers. For each of the following subsets of $\mathbb{R} \times \mathbb{R}$, determine whether it is equal to the cartesian product of two subsets of $\mathbb{R}$.
  (a) $\{(x, y) \mid x \text{ is an integer}\}$.
  (b) $\{(x, y) \mid 0 < y \leq 1\}$.
  (c) $\{(x, y) \mid y > x\}$.
  (d) $\{(x, y) \mid x \text{ is not an integer and } y \text{ is an integer}\}$.
  (e) $\{(x, y) \mid x^2 + y^2 < 1\}$.

§2   Functions

The concept of *function* is one you have seen many times already, so it is hardly necessary to remind you how central it is to all mathematics. In this section, we give the precise mathematical definition, and we explore some of the associated concepts.

A function is usually thought of as a *rule* that assigns to each element of a set A, an element of a set B. In calculus, a function is often given by a simple formula such as $f(x) = 3x^2 + 2$ or perhaps by a more complicated formula such as

$$f(x) = \sum_{k=1}^{\infty} x^k.$$

One often does not even mention the sets A and B explicitly, agreeing to take A to be the set of all real numbers for which the rule makes sense and B to be the set of all real numbers.

As one goes further in mathematics, however, one needs to be more precise about what a function is. Mathematicians *think* of functions in the way we just described, but the definition they use is more exact. First, we define the following:

Definition. A *rule of assignment* is a subset r of the cartesian product $C \times D$ of two sets, having the property that each element of C appears as the first coordinate of *at most one* ordered pair belonging to r.

Thus, a subset r of $C \times D$ is a rule of assignment if

$$[(c, d) \in r \text{ and } (c, d') \in r] \Longrightarrow [d = d'].$$

We think of r as a way of assigning, to the element c of C, the element d of D for which $(c, d) \in r$.

Given a rule of assignment r, the **domain** of r is defined to be the subset of C consisting of all first coordinates of elements of r, and the **image set** of r is defined as the subset of D consisting of all second coordinates of elements of r. Formally,

$$\text{domain } r = \{c \mid \text{there exists } d \in D \text{ such that } (c, d) \in r\},$$
$$\text{image } r = \{d \mid \text{there exists } c \in C \text{ such that } (c, d) \in r\}.$$

Note that given a rule of assignment r, its domain and image are entirely determined. Now we can say what a function is.

Definition. A *function* f is a rule of assignment r, together with a set B that contains the image set of r. The domain A of the rule r is also called the **domain** of the function f; the image set of r is also called the **image set** of f; and the set B is called the **range** of f.[†]

If f is a function having domain A and range B, we express this fact by writing

$$f : A \longrightarrow B,$$

which is read "f is a function from A to B," or "f is a mapping from A into B," or simply "f maps A into B." One sometimes visualizes f as a geometric transformation physically carrying the points of A to points of B.

If $f : A \to B$ and if a is an element of A, we denote by $f(a)$ the unique element of B that the rule determining f assigns to a; it is called the **value** of f at a, or sometimes the **image** of a under f. Formally, if r is the rule of the function f, then $f(a)$ denotes the unique element of B such that $(a, f(a)) \in r$.

Using this notation, one can go back to defining functions almost as one did before, with no lack of rigor. For instance, one can write (letting $\mathbb{R}$ denote the real numbers)

"Let f be the function whose rule is $\{(x, x^3 + 1) \mid x \in \mathbb{R}\}$ and whose range is $\mathbb{R}$,"

or one can equally well write

"Let $f : \mathbb{R} \to \mathbb{R}$ be the function such that $f(x) = x^3 + 1$."

Both sentences specify precisely the same function. But the sentence "Let f be the function $f(x) = x^3 + 1$" is no longer adequate for specifying a function because it specifies neither the domain nor the range of f.

[†]Analysts are apt to use the word "range" to denote what we have called the "image set" of f. They avoid giving the set B a name.

Definition.   If $f : A \to B$ and if A_0 is a subset of A, we define the **restriction** of f to A_0 to be the function mapping A_0 into B whose rule is

$$\{(a, f(a)) \mid a \in A_0\}.$$

It is denoted by $f | A_0$, which is read "f restricted to A_0."

EXAMPLE 1.   Let $\mathbb{R}$ denote the real numbers and let $\bar{\mathbb{R}}_+$ denote the nonnegative reals. Consider the functions

$$
\begin{array}{lll}
f : \mathbb{R} \longrightarrow \mathbb{R} & \text{defined by} & f(x) = x^2, \\
g : \bar{\mathbb{R}}_+ \longrightarrow \mathbb{R} & \text{defined by} & g(x) = x^2, \\
h : \mathbb{R} \longrightarrow \bar{\mathbb{R}}_+ & \text{defined by} & h(x) = x^2, \\
k : \bar{\mathbb{R}}_+ \longrightarrow \bar{\mathbb{R}}_+ & \text{defined by} & k(x) = x^2.
\end{array}
$$

The function g is different from the function f because their rules are different subsets of $\mathbb{R} \times \mathbb{R}$; it is the restriction of f to the set $\bar{\mathbb{R}}_+$. The function h is also different from f, even though their rules are the same set, because the range specified for h is different from the range specified for f. The function k is different from all of these. These functions are pictured in Figure 2.1.

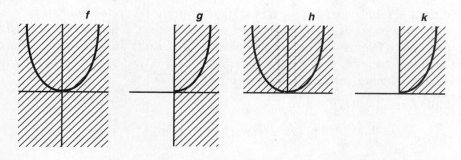

Figure 2.1

Restricting the domain of a function and changing its range are two ways of forming a new function from an old one. Another way is to form the composite of two functions.

Definition.   Given functions $f : A \to B$ and $g : B \to C$, we define the **composite** $g \circ f$ of f and g as the function $g \circ f : A \to C$ defined by the equation $(g \circ f)(a) = g(f(a))$.

Formally, $g \circ f : A \to C$ is the function whose rule is

$$\{(a, c) \mid \text{For some } b \in B, \ f(a) = b \text{ and } g(b) = c\}.$$

We often picture the composite $g \circ f$ as involving a physical movement of the point a to the point $f(a)$, and then to the point $g(f(a))$, as illustrated in Figure 2.2.

Note that $g \circ f$ is defined only when the range of f *equals* the domain of g.

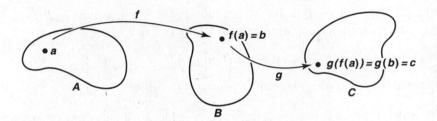

Figure 2.2

EXAMPLE 2.   The composite of the function $f : \mathbb{R} \to \mathbb{R}$ given by $f(x) = 3x^2 + 2$ and the function $g : \mathbb{R} \to \mathbb{R}$ given by $g(x) = 5x$ is the function $g \circ f : \mathbb{R} \to \mathbb{R}$ given by

$$(g \circ f)(x) = g(f(x)) = g(3x^2 + 2) = 5(3x^2 + 2).$$

The composite $f \circ g$ can also be formed in this case; it is the quite different function $f \circ g : \mathbb{R} \to \mathbb{R}$ given by

$$(f \circ g)(x) = f(g(x)) = f(5x) = 3(5x)^2 + 2.$$

Definition.   A function $f : A \to B$ is said to be *injective* (or *one-to-one*) if for each pair of distinct points of A, their images under f are distinct. It is said to be *surjective* (or f is said to map A *onto* B) if every element of B is the image of some element of A under the function f. If f is both injective and surjective, it is said to be *bijective* (or is called a *one-to-one correspondence*).

More formally, f is injective if

$$[f(a) = f(a')] \implies [a = a'],$$

and f is surjective if

$$[b \in B] \implies [b = f(a) \text{ for at least one } a \in A].$$

Injectivity of f depends only on the rule of f; surjectivity depends on the range of f as well. You can check that the composite of two injective functions is injective, and the composite of two surjective functions is surjective; it follows that the composite of two bijective functions is bijective.

If f is bijective, there exists a function from B to A called the *inverse* of f. It is denoted by f^{-1} and is defined by letting $f^{-1}(b)$ be that unique element a of A for which $f(a) = b$. Given $b \in B$, the fact that f is surjective implies that there *exists* such an element $a \in A$; the fact that f is injective implies that there is *only one* such element a. It is easy to see that if f is bijective, f^{-1} is also bijective.

EXAMPLE 3.   Consider again the functions f, g, h, and k of Figure 2.1. The function $f : \mathbb{R} \to \mathbb{R}$ given by $f(x) = x^2$ is neither injective nor surjective. Its restriction g to the nonnegative reals is injective but not surjective. The function $h : \mathbb{R} \to \bar{\mathbb{R}}_+$ obtained from f

by changing the range is surjective but not injective. The function $k : \bar{\mathbb{R}}_+ \to \bar{\mathbb{R}}_+$ obtained from f by restricting the domain *and* changing the range is both injective and surjective, so it has an inverse. Its inverse is, of course, what we usually call the *square-root function*.

A useful criterion for showing that a given function f is bijective is the following, whose proof is left to the exercises:

Lemma 2.1. *Let $f : A \to B$. If there are functions $g : B \to A$ and $h : B \to A$ such that $g(f(a)) = a$ for every a in A and $f(h(b)) = b$ for every b in B, then f is bijective and $g = h = f^{-1}$.*

Definition. Let $f : A \to B$. If A_0 is a subset of A, we denote by $f(A_0)$ the set of all images of points of A_0 under the function f; this set is called the *image* of A_0 under f. Formally,

$$f(A_0) = \{b \mid b = f(a) \text{ for at least one } a \in A_0\}.$$

On the other hand, if B_0 is a subset of B, we denote by $f^{-1}(B_0)$ the set of all elements of A whose images under f lie in B_0; it is called the *preimage* of B_0 under f (or the "counterimage," or the "inverse image," of B_0). Formally,

$$f^{-1}(B_0) = \{a \mid f(a) \in B_0\}.$$

Of course, there may be no points a of A whose images lie in B_0; in that case, $f^{-1}(B_0)$ is empty.

Note that if $f : A \to B$ is bijective and $B_0 \subset B$, we have two meanings for the notation $f^{-1}(B_0)$. It can be taken to denote the *preimage* of B_0 under the function f or to denote the *image* of B_0 under the function $f^{-1} : B \to A$. These two meanings give precisely the same subset of A, however, so there is, in fact, no ambiguity.

Some care is needed if one is to use the f and f^{-1} notation correctly. The operation f^{-1}, for instance, when applied to subsets of B, behaves very nicely; it preserves inclusions, unions, intersections, and differences of sets. We shall use this fact frequently. But the operation f, when applied to subsets of A, preserves only inclusions and unions. See Exercises 2 and 3.

As another situation where care is needed, we note that it is not in general true that $f^{-1}(f(A_0)) = A_0$ and $f(f^{-1}(B_0)) = B_0$. (See the following example.) The relevant rules, which we leave to you to check, are the following: If $f : A \to B$ and if $A_0 \subset A$ and $B_0 \subset B$, then

$$A_0 \subset f^{-1}(f(A_0)) \quad \text{and} \quad f(f^{-1}(B_0)) \subset B_0.$$

The first inclusion is an equality if f is injective, and the second inclusion is an equality if f is surjective.

EXAMPLE 4.   Consider the function $f : \mathbb{R} \to \mathbb{R}$ given by $f(x) = 3x^2 + 2$ (Figure 2.3). Let $[a, b]$ denote the closed interval $a \leq x \leq b$. Then

$$f^{-1}(f([0, 1])) = f^{-1}([2, 5]) = [-1, 1], \quad \text{and}$$
$$f(f^{-1}([0, 5])) = f([-1, 1]) = [2, 5].$$

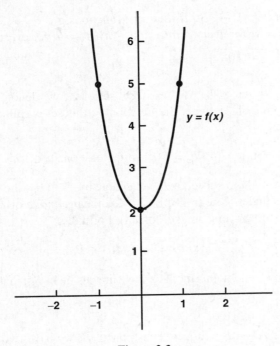

Figure 2.3

Exercises

1. Let $f : A \to B$. Let $A_0 \subset A$ and $B_0 \subset B$.
   (a) Show that $A_0 \subset f^{-1}(f(A_0))$ and that equality holds if f is injective.
   (b) Show that $f(f^{-1}(B_0)) \subset B_0$ and that equality holds if f is surjective.

2. Let $f : A \to B$ and let $A_i \subset A$ and $B_i \subset B$ for $i = 0$ and $i = 1$. Show that f^{-1} preserves inclusions, unions, intersections, and differences of sets:
   (a) $B_0 \subset B_1 \Rightarrow f^{-1}(B_0) \subset f^{-1}(B_1)$.
   (b) $f^{-1}(B_0 \cup B_1) = f^{-1}(B_0) \cup f^{-1}(B_1)$.
   (c) $f^{-1}(B_0 \cap B_1) = f^{-1}(B_0) \cap f^{-1}(B_1)$.
   (d) $f^{-1}(B_0 - B_1) = f^{-1}(B_0) - f^{-1}(B_1)$.
   Show that f preserves inclusions and unions only:
   (e) $A_0 \subset A_1 \Rightarrow f(A_0) \subset f(A_1)$.

(f) $f(A_0 \cup A_1) = f(A_0) \cup (A_1)$.

(g) $f(A_0 \cap A_1) \subset f(A_0) \cap f(A_1)$; show that equality holds if f is injective.

(h) $f(A_0 - A_1) \supset f(A_0) - f(A_1)$; show that equality holds if f is injective.

3. Show that (b), (c), (f), and (g) of Exercise 2 hold for arbitrary unions and inter-sections.

4. Let $f : A \to B$ and $g : B \to C$.

(a) If $C_0 \subset C$, show that $(g \circ f)^{-1}(C_0) = f^{-1}(g^{-1}(C_0))$.

(b) If f and g are injective, show that $g \circ f$ is injective.

(c) If $g \circ f$ is injective, what can you say about injectivity of f and g?

(d) If f and g are surjective, show that $g \circ f$ is surjective.

(e) If $g \circ f$ is surjective, what can you say about surjectivity of f and g?

(f) Summarize your answers to (b)–(e) in the form of a theorem.

5. In general, let us denote the **identity function** for a set C by i_C. That is, define $i_C : C \to C$ to be the function given by the rule $i_C(x) = x$ for all $x \in C$. Given $f : A \to B$, we say that a function $g : B \to A$ is a **left inverse** for f if $g \circ f = i_A$; and we say that $h : B \to A$ is a **right inverse** for f if $f \circ h = i_B$.

(a) Show that if f has a left inverse, f is injective; and if f has a right inverse, f is surjective.

(b) Give an example of a function that has a left inverse but no right inverse.

(c) Give an example of a function that has a right inverse but no left inverse.

(d) Can a function have more than one left inverse? More than one right inverse?

(e) Show that if f has both a left inverse g and a right inverse h, then f is bijective and $g = h = f^{-1}$.

6. Let $f : \mathbb{R} \to \mathbb{R}$ be the function $f(x) = x^3 - x$. By restricting the domain and range of f appropriately, obtain from f a bijective function g. Draw the graphs of g and g^{-1}. (There are several possible choices for g.)

§3 Relations

A concept that is, in some ways, more general than that of function is the concept of a *relation*. In this section, we define what mathematicians mean by a relation, and we consider two types of relations that occur with great frequency in mathematics: *equivalence relations* and *order relations*. Order relations will be used throughout the book; equivalence relations will not be used until §22.

Definition. A *relation* on a set A is a subset C of the cartesian product $A \times A$.

If C is a relation on A, we use the notation xCy to mean the same thing as $(x, y) \in C$. We read it "x is in the relation C to y."

A rule of assignment r for a function $f : A \to A$ is also a subset of $A \times A$. But it is a subset of a very special kind: namely, one such that each element of A appears as the first coordinate of an element of r exactly once. *Any* subset of $A \times A$ is a relation on A.

EXAMPLE 1.   Let P denote the set of all people in the world, and define $D \subset P \times P$ by the equation

$$D = \{(x, y) \mid x \text{ is a descendant of } y\}.$$

Then D is a relation on the set P. The statements "x is in the relation D to y" and "x is a descendant of y" mean precisely the same thing, namely, that $(x, y) \in D$. Two other relations on P are the following:

$$B = \{(x, y) \mid x \text{ has an ancestor who is also an ancestor of } y\},$$
$$S = \{(x, y) \mid \text{the parents of } x \text{ are the parents of } y\}.$$

We can call B the "blood relation" (pun intended), and we can call S the "sibling relation." These three relations have quite different properties. The blood relationship is symmetric, for instance (if x is a blood relative of y, then y is a blood relative of x), whereas the descendant relation is not. We shall consider these relations again shortly.

Equivalence Relations and Partitions

An *equivalence relation* on a set A is a relation C on A having the following three properties:

(1) (Reflexivity) xCx for every x in A.

(2) (Symmetry) If xCy, then yCx.

(3) (Transitivity) If xCy and yCz, then xCz.

EXAMPLE 2.   Among the relations defined in Example 1, the descendant relation D is neither reflexive nor symmetric, while the blood relation B is not transitive (I am not a blood relation to my wife, although my children are!) The sibling relation S is, however, an equivalence relation, as you may check.

There is no reason one must use a capital letter—or indeed a letter of any sort— to denote a relation, even though it *is* a set. Another symbol will do just as well. One symbol that is frequently used to denote an equivalence relation is the "tilde" symbol $\sim$. Stated in this notation, the properties of an equivalence relation become

(1) $x \sim x$ for every x in A.

(2) If $x \sim y$, then $y \sim x$.

(3) If $x \sim y$ and $y \sim z$, then $x \sim z$.

There are many other symbols that have been devised to stand for particular equivalence relations; we shall meet some of them in the pages of this book.

Given an equivalence relation $\sim$ on a set A and an element x of A, we define a certain subset E of A, called the *equivalence class* determined by x, by the equation

$$E = \{y \mid y \sim x\}.$$

Note that the equivalence class E determined by x contains x, since $x \sim x$. Equivalence classes have the following property:

Lemma 3.1.   *Two equivalence classes E and E' are either disjoint or equal.*

Proof.   Let E be the equivalence class determined by x, and let E' be the equivalence class determined by x'. Suppose that $E \cap E'$ is not empty; let y be a point of $E \cap E'$. See Figure 3.1. We show that $E = E'$.

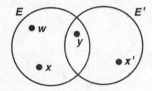

Figure 3.1

By definition, we have $y \sim x$ and $y \sim x'$. Symmetry allows us to conclude that $x \sim y$ and $y \sim x'$; from transitivity it follows that $x \sim x'$. If now w is any point of E, we have $w \sim x$ by definition; it follows from another application of transitivity that $w \sim x'$. We conclude that $E \subset E'$.

The symmetry of the situation allows us to conclude that $E' \subset E$ as well, so that $E = E'$.   ∎

Given an equivalence relation on a set A, let us denote by $\mathcal{E}$ the collection of all the equivalence classes determined by this relation. The preceding lemma shows that distinct elements of $\mathcal{E}$ are disjoint. Furthermore, the union of the elements of $\mathcal{E}$ equals all of A because every element of A belongs to an equivalence class. The collection $\mathcal{E}$ is a particular example of what is called a partition of A:

Definition.   A *partition* of a set A is a collection of disjoint nonempty subsets of A whose union is all of A.

Studying equivalence relations on a set A and studying partitions of A are really the same thing. Given any partition $\mathcal{D}$ of A, there is exactly one equivalence relation on A from which it is derived.

The proof is not difficult. To show that the partition $\mathcal{D}$ comes from some equivalence relation, let us define a relation C on A by setting xCy if x and y belong to the same element of $\mathcal{D}$. Symmetry of C is obvious; reflexivity follows from the fact that the union of the elements of $\mathcal{D}$ equals all of A; transitivity follows from the fact that distinct elements of $\mathcal{D}$ are disjoint. It is simple to check that the collection of equivalence classes determined by C is precisely the collection $\mathcal{D}$.

To show there is only one such equivalence relation, suppose that C_1 and C_2 are two equivalence relations on A that give rise to the same collection of equivalence classes $\mathcal{D}$. Given $x \in A$, we show that yC_1x if and only if yC_2x, from which we conclude that $C_1 = C_2$. Let E_1 be the equivalence class determined by x relative to the relation C_1; let E_2 be the equivalence class determined by x relative to the relation C_2. Then E_1 is an element of $\mathcal{D}$, so that it must equal the unique element D of $\mathcal{D}$ that contains x. Similarly, E_2 must equal D. Now by definition. E_1 consists of all y such that yC_1x; and E_2 consists of all y such that yC_2x. Since $E_1 = D = E_2$, our result is proved.

EXAMPLE 3.   Define two points in the plane to be equivalent if they lie at the same distance from the origin. Reflexivity, symmetry, and transitivity hold trivially. The collection $\mathcal{E}$ of equivalence classes consists of all circles centered at the origin, along with the set consisting of the origin alone.

EXAMPLE 4.   Define two points of the plane to be equivalent if they have the same y-coordinate. The collection of equivalence classes is the collection of all straight lines in the plane parallel to the x-axis.

EXAMPLE 5.   Let $\mathcal{L}$ be the collection of all straight lines in the plane parallel to the line $y = -x$. Then $\mathcal{L}$ is a partition of the plane, since each point lies on exactly one such line. The partition $\mathcal{L}$ comes from the equivalence relation on the plane that declares the points (x_0, y_0) and (x_1, y_1) to be equivalent if $x_0 + y_0 = x_1 + y_1$.

EXAMPLE 6.   Let $\mathcal{L}'$ be the collection of *all* straight lines in the plane. Then $\mathcal{L}'$ is not a partition of the plane, for distinct elements of $\mathcal{L}'$ are not necessarily disjoint; two lines may intersect without being equal.

Order Relations

A relation C on a set A is called an **order relation** (or a **simple order**, or a **linear order**) if it has the following properties:
  (1) (Comparability) For every x and y in A for which $x \neq y$, either xCy or yCx.
  (2) (Nonreflexivity) For no x in A does the relation xCx hold.
  (3) (Transitivity) If xCy and yCz, then xCz.
Note that property (1) does not by itself exclude the possibility that for some pair of elements x and y of A, both the relations xCy and yCx hold (since "or" means "one or the other, or both"). But properties (2) and (3) combined do exclude this possibility; for if both xCy and yCx held, transitivity would imply that xCx, contradicting nonreflexivity.

EXAMPLE 7.   Consider the relation on the real line consisting of all pairs (x, y) of real numbers such that $x < y$. It is an order relation, called the "usual order relation," on the real line. A less familiar order relation on the real line is the following: Define xCy if $x^2 < y^2$, or if $x^2 = y^2$ and $x < y$. You can check that this is an order relation.

EXAMPLE 8.   Consider again the relationships among people given in Example 1. The blood relation B satisfies none of the properties of an order relation, and the sibling relation S satisfies only (3). The descendant relation D does somewhat better, for it satisfies both (2) and (3); however, comparability still fails. Relations that satisfy (2) and (3) occur often enough in mathematics to be given a special name. They are called *strict partial order* relations; we shall consider them later (see §11).

As the tilde, $\sim$, is the generic symbol for an equivalence relation, the "less than" symbol, $<$, is commonly used to denote an order relation. Stated in this notation, the properties of an order relation become

(1) If $x \neq y$, then either $x < y$ or $y < x$.

(2) If $x < y$, then $x \neq y$.

(3) If $x < y$ and $y < z$, then $x < z$.

We shall use the notation $x \leq y$ to stand for the statement "either $x < y$ or $x = y$"; and we shall use the notation $y > x$ to stand for the statement "$x < y$." We write $x < y < z$ to mean "$x < y$ and $y < z$."

Definition. If X is a set and $<$ is an order relation on X, and if $a < b$, we use the notation (a, b) to denote the set

$$\{x \mid a < x < b\};$$

it is called an ***open interval*** in X. If this set is empty, we call a the ***immediate predecessor*** of b, and we call b the ***immediate successor*** of a.

Definition. Suppose that A and B are two sets with order relations $<_A$ and $<_B$ respectively. We say that A and B have the same ***order type*** if there is a bijective correspondence between them that preserves order; that is, if there exists a bijective function $f : A \rightarrow B$ such that

$$a_1 <_A a_2 \implies f(a_1) <_B f(a_2).$$

EXAMPLE 9.   The interval $(-1, 1)$ of real numbers has the same order type as the set $\mathbb{R}$ of real numbers itself, for the function $f : (-1, 1) \rightarrow \mathbb{R}$ given by

$$f(x) = \frac{x}{1 - x^2}$$

is an order-preserving bijective correspondence, as you can check. It is pictured in Figure 3.2.

EXAMPLE 10.   The subset $A = \{0\} \cup (1, 2)$ of $\mathbb{R}$ has the same order type as the subset

$$[0, 1) = \{x \mid 0 \leq x < 1\}$$

of $\mathbb{R}$. The function $f : A \rightarrow [0, 1)$ defined by

$$f(0) = 0,$$
$$f(x) = x - 1 \quad \text{for } x \in (1, 2)$$

is the required order-preserving correspondence.

One interesting way of defining an order relation, which will be useful to us later in dealing with some examples, is the following:

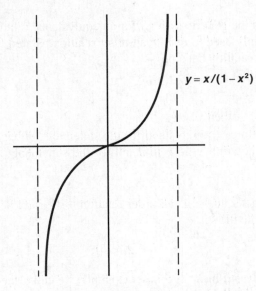

$y = x/(1-x^2)$

Figure 3.2

Definition. Suppose that A and B are two sets with order relations $<_A$ and $<_B$ respectively. Define an order relation $<$ on $A \times B$ by defining

$$a_1 \times b_1 < a_2 \times b_2$$

if $a_1 <_A a_2$, or if $a_1 = a_2$ and $b_1 <_B b_2$. It is called the ***dictionary order relation*** on $A \times B$.

Checking that this is an order relation involves looking at several separate cases; we leave it to you.

The reason for the choice of terminology is fairly evident. The rule defining $<$ is the same as the rule used to order the words in the dictionary. Given two words, one compares their first letters and orders the words according to the order in which their first letters appear in the alphabet. If the first letters are the same, one compares their second letters and orders accordingly. And so on.

EXAMPLE 11.   Consider the dictionary order on the plane $\mathbb{R} \times \mathbb{R}$. In this order, the point p is less than every point lying above it on the vertical line through p, and p is less than every point to the right of this vertical line.

EXAMPLE 12.   Consider the set $[0, 1)$ of real numbers and the set $\mathbb{Z}_+$ of positive integers, both in their usual orders; give $\mathbb{Z}_+ \times [0, 1)$ the dictionary order. This set has the same order type as the set of nonnegative reals; the function

$$f(n \times t) = n + t - 1$$

is the required bijective order-preserving correspondence. On the other hand, the set $[0, 1) \times \mathbb{Z}_+$ in the dictionary order has quite a different order type; for example, every element of this ordered set has an immediate successor. These sets are pictured in Figure 3.3.

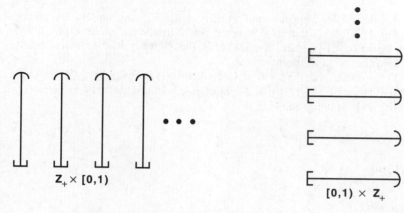

Figure 3.3

One of the properties of the real numbers that you may have seen before is the "least upper bound property." One can define this property for an arbitrary ordered set. First, we need some preliminary definitions.

Suppose that A is a set ordered by the relation $<$. Let A_0 be a subset of A. We say that the element b is the ***largest element*** of A_0 if $b \in A_0$ and if $x \leq b$ for every $x \in A_0$. Similarly, we say that a is the ***smallest element*** of A_0 if $a \in A_0$ and if $a \leq x$ for every $x \in A_0$. It is easy to see that a set has at most one largest element and at most one smallest element.

We say that the subset A_0 of A is ***bounded above*** if there is an element b of A such that $x \leq b$ for every $x \in A_0$; the element b is called an ***upper bound*** for A_0. If the set of all upper bounds for A_0 has a smallest element, that element is called the ***least upper bound***, or the ***supremum***, of A_0. It is denoted by $\sup A_0$; it may or may not belong to A_0. If it does, it is the largest element of A_0.

Similarly, A_0 is ***bounded below*** if there is an element a of A such that $a \leq x$ for every $x \in A_0$; the element a is called a ***lower bound*** for A_0. If the set of all lower bounds for A_0 has a largest element, that element is called the ***greatest lower bound***, or the ***infimum***, of A_0. It is denoted by $\inf A_0$; it may or may not belong to A_0. If it does, it is the smallest element of A_0.

Now we can define the least upper bound property.

Definition.   An ordered set A is said to have the ***least upper bound property*** if every nonempty subset A_0 of A that is bounded above has a least upper bound. Analogously, the set A is said to have the ***greatest lower bound property*** if every nonempty subset A_0 of A that is bounded below has a greatest lower bound.

We leave it to the exercises to show that A has the least upper bound property if and only if it has the greatest lower bound property.

EXAMPLE 13.   Consider the set $A = (-1, 1)$ of real numbers in the usual order. Assuming the fact that the real numbers have the least upper bound property, it follows that the set A has the least upper bound property. For, given any subset of A having an upper bound *in* A, it follows that its least upper bound (in the real numbers) must be in A. For example, the subset $\{-1/2n \mid n \in \mathbb{Z}_+\}$ of A, though it has no largest element, does have a least upper bound in A, the number 0.

On the other hand, the set $B = (-1, 0) \cup (0, 1)$ does not have the least upper bound property. The subset $\{-1/2n \mid n \in \mathbb{Z}_+\}$ of B is bounded above by any element of $(0, 1)$, but it has no least upper bound in B.

Exercises

Equivalence Relations

1. Define two points (x_0, y_0) and (x_1, y_1) of the plane to be equivalent if $y_0 - x_0^2 = y_1 - x_1^2$. Check that this is an equivalence relation and describe the equivalence classes.

2. Let C be a relation on a set A. If $A_0 \subset A$, define the **restriction** of C to A_0 to be the relation $C \cap (A_0 \times A_0)$. Show that the restriction of an equivalence relation is an equivalence relation.

3. Here is a "proof" that every relation C that is both symmetric and transitive is also reflexive: "Since C is symmetric, aCb implies bCa. Since C is transitive, aCb and bCa together imply aCa, as desired." Find the flaw in this argument.

4. Let $f : A \to B$ be a surjective function. Let us define a relation on A by setting $a_0 \sim a_1$ if

$$f(a_0) = f(a_1).$$

   (a) Show that this is an equivalence relation.
   (b) Let A^* be the set of equivalence classes. Show there is a bijective correspondence of A^* with B.

5. Let S and S' be the following subsets of the plane:

$$S = \{(x, y) \mid y = x + 1 \text{ and } 0 < x < 2\},$$
$$S' = \{(x, y) \mid y - x \text{ is an integer}\}.$$

   (a) Show that S' is an equivalence relation on the real line and $S' \supset S$. Describe the equivalence classes of S'.
   (b) Show that given any collection of equivalence relations on a set A, their intersection is an equivalence relation on A.
   (c) Describe the equivalence relation T on the real line that is the intersection of all equivalence relations on the real line that contain S. Describe the equivalence classes of T.

Order Relations

6. Define a relation on the plane by setting

$$(x_0, y_0) < (x_1, y_1)$$

if either $y_0 - x_0^2 < y_1 - x_1^2$, or $y_0 - x_0^2 = y_1 - x_1^2$ and $x_0 < x_1$. Show that this is an order relation on the plane, and describe it geometrically.

7. Show that the restriction of an order relation is an order relation.

8. Check that the relation defined in Example 7 is an order relation.

9. Check that the dictionary order is an order relation.

10. (a) Show that the map $f : (-1, 1) \to \mathbb{R}$ of Example 9 is order preserving.
  (b) Show that the equation $g(y) = 2y/[1 + (1 + 4y^2)^{1/2}]$ defines a function $g : \mathbb{R} \to (-1, 1)$ that is both a left and a right inverse for f.

11. Show that an element in an ordered set has at most one immediate successor and at most one immediate predecessor. Show that a subset of an ordered set has at most one smallest element and at most one largest element.

12. Let $\mathbb{Z}_+$ denote the set of positive integers. Consider the following order relations on $\mathbb{Z}_+ \times \mathbb{Z}_+$:
  (i) The dictionary order.
  (ii) $(x_0, y_0) < (x_1, y_1)$ if either $x_0 - y_0 < x_1 - y_1$, or $x_0 - y_0 = x_1 - y_1$ and $y_0 < y_1$.
  (iii) $(x_0, y_0) < (x_1, y_1)$ if either $x_0 + y_0 < x_1 + y_1$, or $x_0 + y_0 = x_1 + y_1$ and $y_0 < y_1$.
  In these order relations, which elements have immediate predecessors? Does the set have a smallest element? Show that all three order types are different.

13. Prove the following:
  Theorem. If an ordered set A has the least upper bound property, then it has the greatest lower bound property.

14. If C is a relation on a set A, define a new relation D on A by letting $(b, a) \in D$ if $(a, b) \in C$.
  (a) Show that C is symmetric if and only if $C = D$.
  (b) Show that if C is an order relation, D is also an order relation.
  (c) Prove the converse of the theorem in Exercise 13.

15. Assume that the real line has the least upper bound property.
  (a) Show that the sets

$$[0, 1] = \{x \mid 0 \le x \le 1\},$$
$$[0, 1) = \{x \mid 0 \le x < 1\}$$

have the least upper bound property.
  (b) Does $[0, 1] \times [0, 1]$ in the dictionary order have the least upper bound property? What about $[0, 1] \times [0, 1)$? What about $[0, 1) \times [0, 1]$?

§4   The Integers and the Real Numbers

Up to now we have been discussing what might be called the *logical foundations* for our study of topology—the elementary concepts of set theory. Now we turn to what we might call the *mathematical foundations* for our study—the integers and the real number system. We have already used them in an informal way in the examples and exercises of the preceding sections. Now we wish to deal with them more formally.

One way of establishing these foundations is to *construct* the real number system, using only the axioms of set theory—to build them with one's bare hands, so to speak. This way of approaching the subject takes a good deal of time and effort and is of greater logical than mathematical interest.

A second way is simply to assume a set of axioms for the real numbers and work from these axioms. In the present section, we shall sketch this approach to the real numbers. Specifically, we shall give a set of axioms for the real numbers and shall indicate how the familiar properties of real numbers and the integers are derived from them. But we shall leave most of the proofs to the exercises. If you have seen all this before, our description should refresh your memory. If not, you may want to work through the exercises in detail in order to make sure of your knowledge of the mathematical foundations.

First we need a definition from set theory.

Definition.   A *binary operation* on a set A is a function f mapping $A \times A$ into A.

When dealing with a binary operation f on a set A, we usually use a notation different from the standard functional notation introduced in §2. Instead of denoting the value of the function f at the point (a, a') by $f(a, a')$, we usually write the symbol for the function *between* the two coordinates of the point in question, writing the value of the function at (a, a') as afa'. Furthermore (just as was the case with relations), it is more common to use some symbol other than a letter to denote an operation. Symbols often used are the plus symbol $+$, the multiplication symbols $\cdot$ and $\circ$, and the asterisk $*$; however, there are many others.

Assumption

We assume there exists a set $\mathbb{R}$, called the set of *real numbers*, two binary operations $+$ and $\cdot$ on $\mathbb{R}$, called the addition and multiplication operations, respectively, and an order relation $<$ on $\mathbb{R}$, such that the following properties hold:

Algebraic Properties

(1) $(x + y) + z = x + (y + z)$,
$\quad\;\;(x \cdot y) \cdot z = x \cdot (y \cdot z)$ for all x, y, z in $\mathbb{R}$.

(2) $x + y = y + x$,
$\quad\;\;x \cdot y = y \cdot x$ for all x, y in $\mathbb{R}$.

(3) There exists a unique element of $\mathbb{R}$ called **zero**, denoted by 0, such that $x + 0 = x$ for all $x \in \mathbb{R}$.

There exists a unique element of $\mathbb{R}$ called **one**, different from 0 and denoted by 1, such that $x \cdot 1 = x$ for all $x \in \mathbb{R}$.

(4) For each x in $\mathbb{R}$, there exists a unique y in $\mathbb{R}$ such that $x + y = 0$.

For each x in $\mathbb{R}$ different from 0, there exists a unique y in $\mathbb{R}$ such that $x \cdot y = 1$.

(5) $x \cdot (y + z) = (x \cdot y) + (x \cdot z)$ for all $x, y, z \in \mathbb{R}$.

A Mixed Algebraic and Order Property

(6) If $x > y$, then $x + z > y + z$.

If $x > y$ and $z > 0$, then $x \cdot z > y \cdot z$.

Order Properties

(7) The order relation $<$ has the least upper bound property.

(8) If $x < y$, there exists an element z such that $x < z$ and $z < y$.

From properties (1)–(5) follow the familiar "laws of algebra." Given x, one denotes by $-x$ that number y such that $x + y = 0$; it is called the **negative** of x. One defines the **subtraction operation** by the formula $z - x = z + (-x)$. Similarly, given $x \neq 0$, one denotes by $1/x$ that number y such that $x \cdot y = 1$; it is called the **reciprocal** of x. One defines the **quotient** z/x by the formula $z/x = z \cdot (1/x)$. The usual laws of signs, and the rules for adding and multiplying fractions, follow as theorems. These laws of algebra are listed in Exercise 1 at the end of the section. We often denote $x \cdot y$ simply by xy.

When one adjoins property (6) to properties (1)–(5), one can prove the usual "laws of inequalities," such as the following:

$$\text{If } x > y \text{ and } z < 0, \text{ then } x \cdot z < y \cdot z.$$
$$-1 < 0 \text{ and } 0 < 1.$$

The laws of inequalities are listed in Exercise 2.

We define a number x to be **positive** if $x > 0$, and to be **negative** if $x < 0$. We denote the positive reals by $\mathbb{R}_+$ and the nonnegative reals (for reasons to be explained later) by $\bar{\mathbb{R}}_+$. Properties (1)–(6) are familiar properties in modern algebra. Any set with two binary operations satisfying (1)–(5) is called by algebraists a *field*; if the field has an order relation satisfying (6), it is called an **ordered field**.

Properties (7) and (8), on the other hand, are familiar properties in topology. They involve only the order relation; any set with an order relation satisfying (7) and (8) is called by topologists a **linear continuum**.

Now it happens that when one adjoins to the axioms for an ordered field [properties (1)–(6)] the axioms for a linear continuum [properties (7) and (8)], the resulting list contains some redundancies. Property (8), in particular, can be proved as a consequence of the others; given $x < y$ one can show that $z = (x + y)/(1 + 1)$ satisfies the requirements of (8). Therefore, in the standard treatment of the real numbers, properties (1)–(7) are taken as axioms, and property (8) becomes a theorem. We have included (8) in our list merely to emphasize the fact that it and the least upper bound property are the two crucial properties of the order relation for $\mathbb{R}$. From these two properties many of the topological properties of $\mathbb{R}$ may be derived, as we shall see in Chapter 3.

Now there is nothing in this list as it stands to tell us what an integer is. We now *define* the integers, using only properties (1)–(6).

Definition. A subset A of the real numbers is said to be ***inductive*** if it contains the number 1, and if for every x in A, the number $x+1$ is also in A. Let $\mathcal{A}$ be the collection of all inductive subsets of $\mathbb{R}$. Then the set $\mathbb{Z}_+$ of ***positive integers*** is defined by the equation

$$\mathbb{Z}_+ = \bigcap_{A \in \mathcal{A}} A.$$

Note that the set $\mathbb{R}_+$ of positive real numbers is inductive, for it contains 1 and the statement $x > 0$ implies the statement $x + 1 > 0$. Therefore, $\mathbb{Z}_+ \subset \mathbb{R}_+$, so the elements of $\mathbb{Z}_+$ are indeed positive, as the choice of terminology suggests. Indeed, one sees readily that 1 is the smallest element of $\mathbb{Z}_+$, because the set of all real numbers x for which $x \geq 1$ is inductive.

The basic properties of $\mathbb{Z}_+$, which follow readily from the definition, are the following:

(1) $\mathbb{Z}_+$ is inductive.

(2) (Principle of induction). If A is an inductive set of positive integers, then $A = \mathbb{Z}_+$.

We define the set $\mathbb{Z}$ of ***integers*** to be the set consisting of the positive integers $\mathbb{Z}_+$, the number 0, and the negatives of the elements of $\mathbb{Z}_+$. One proves that the sum, difference, and product of two integers are integers, but the quotient is not necessarily an integer. The set $\mathbb{Q}$ of quotients of integers is called the set of ***rational numbers***.

One proves also that, given the integer n, there is no integer a such that $n < a < n + 1$.

If n is a positive integer, we use the symbol S_n to denote the set of all positive integers less than n; we call it a ***section*** of the positive integers. The set S_1 is empty, and S_{n+1} denotes the set of positive integers between 1 and n, inclusive. We also use the notation

$$\{1, \ldots, n\} = S_{n+1}$$

for the latter set.

Now we prove two properties of the positive integers that may not be quite so familiar, but are quite useful. They may be thought of as alternative versions of the induction principle.

Theorem 4.1 (Well-ordering property). *Every nonempty subset of $\mathbb{Z}_+$ has a smallest element.*

Proof. We first prove that, for each $n \in \mathbb{Z}_+$, the following statement holds: *Every nonempty subset of* $\{1, \ldots, n\}$ *has a smallest element.*

Let A be the set of all positive integers n for which this statement holds. Then A contains 1, since if $n = 1$, the only nonempty subset of $\{1, \ldots, n\}$ is the set $\{1\}$ itself. Then, supposing A contains n, we show that it contains $n + 1$. So let C be a nonempty subset of the set $\{1, \ldots, n + 1\}$. If C consists of the single element $n + 1$, then that element is the smallest element of C. Otherwise, consider the set $C \cap \{1, \ldots, n\}$, which is nonempty. Because $n \in A$, this set has a smallest element, which will automatically be the smallest element of C also. Thus A is inductive, so we conclude that $A = \mathbb{Z}_+$; hence the statement is true for all $n \in \mathbb{Z}_+$.

Now we prove the theorem. Suppose that D is a nonempty subset of $\mathbb{Z}_+$. Choose an element n of D. Then the set $A = D \cap \{1, \ldots, n\}$ is nonempty, so that A has a smallest element k. The element k is automatically the smallest element of D as well. ∎

Theorem 4.2 (Strong induction principle). *Let A be a set of positive integers. Suppose that for each positive integer n, the statement $S_n \subset A$ implies the statement $n \in A$. Then $A = \mathbb{Z}_+$.*

Proof. If A does not equal all of $\mathbb{Z}_+$, let n be the smallest positive integer that is not in A. Then every positive integer less than n is in A, so that $S_n \subset A$. Our hypothesis implies that $n \in A$, contrary to assumption. ∎

Everything we have done up to now has used only the axioms for an ordered field, properties (1)–(6) of the real numbers. At what point do you need (7), the least upper bound axiom?

For one thing, you need the least upper bound axiom to prove that the set $\mathbb{Z}_+$ of positive integers has no upper bound in $\mathbb{R}$. This is the ***Archimedean ordering property*** of the real line. To prove it, we assume that $\mathbb{Z}_+$ has an upper bound and derive a contradiction. If $\mathbb{Z}_+$ has an upper bound, it has a least upper bound b. There exists $n \in \mathbb{Z}_+$ such that $n > b - 1$; for otherwise, $b - 1$ would be an upper bound for $\mathbb{Z}_+$ smaller than b. Then $n + 1 > b$, contrary to the fact that b is an upper bound for $\mathbb{Z}_+$.

The least upper bound axiom is also used to prove a number of other things about $\mathbb{R}$. It is used for instance to show that $\mathbb{R}$ has the greatest lower bound property. It is also used to prove the existence of a unique positive square root $\sqrt{x}$ for every positive real number. This fact, in turn, can be used to demonstrate the existence of real numbers that are not rational numbers; the number $\sqrt{2}$ is an easy example.

We use the symbol 2 to denote $1 + 1$, the symbol 3 to denote $2 + 1$, and so on through the standard symbols for the positive integers. It is a fact that this procedure assigns to each positive integer a unique symbol, but we never need this fact and shall not prove it.

Proofs of these properties of the integers and real numbers, along with a few other properties we shall need later, are outlined in the exercises that follow.

Exercises

1. Prove the following "laws of algebra" for $\mathbb{R}$, using only axioms (1)–(5):
   (a) If $x + y = x$, then $y = 0$.
   (b) $0 \cdot x = 0$. [*Hint:* Compute $(x + 0) \cdot x$.]
   (c) $-0 = 0$.
   (d) $-(-x) = x$.
   (e) $x(-y) = -(xy) = (-x)y$.
   (f) $(-1)x = -x$.
   (g) $x(y - z) = xy - xz$.
   (h) $-(x + y) = -x - y$; $-(x - y) = -x + y$.
   (i) If $x \neq 0$ and $x \cdot y = x$, then $y = 1$.
   (j) $x/x = 1$ if $x \neq 0$.
   (k) $x/1 = x$.
   (l) $x \neq 0$ and $y \neq 0 \Rightarrow xy \neq 0$.
   (m) $(1/y)(1/z) = 1/(yz)$ if $y, z \neq 0$.
   (n) $(x/y)(w/z) = (xw)/(yz)$ if $y, z \neq 0$.
   (o) $(x/y) + (w/z) = (xz + wy)/(yz)$ if $y, z \neq 0$.
   (p) $x \neq 0 \Rightarrow 1/x \neq 0$.
   (q) $1/(w/z) = z/w$ if $w, z \neq 0$.
   (r) $(x/y)/(w/z) = (xz)/(yw)$ if $y, w, z \neq 0$.
   (s) $(ax)/y = a(x/y)$ if $y \neq 0$.
   (t) $(-x)/y = x/(-y) = -(x/y)$ if $y \neq 0$.

2. Prove the following "laws of inequalities" for $\mathbb{R}$, using axioms (1)–(6) along with the results of Exercise 1:
   (a) $x > y$ and $w > z \Rightarrow x + w > y + z$.
   (b) $x > 0$ and $y > 0 \Rightarrow x + y > 0$ and $x \cdot y > 0$.
   (c) $x > 0 \Leftrightarrow -x < 0$.
   (d) $x > y \Leftrightarrow -x < -y$.
   (e) $x > y$ and $z < 0 \Rightarrow xz < yz$.
   (f) $x \neq 0 \Rightarrow x^2 > 0$, where $x^2 = x \cdot x$.
   (g) $-1 < 0 < 1$.
   (h) $xy > 0 \Leftrightarrow x$ and y are both positive or both negative.
   (i) $x > 0 \Rightarrow 1/x > 0$.
   (j) $x > y > 0 \Rightarrow 1/x < 1/y$.
   (k) $x < y \Rightarrow x < (x + y)/2 < y$.

3. (a) Show that if $\mathcal{A}$ is a collection of inductive sets, then the intersection of the elements of $\mathcal{A}$ is an inductive set.
   (b) Prove the basic properties (1) and (2) of $\mathbb{Z}_+$.

4. (a) Prove by induction that given $n \in \mathbb{Z}_+$, every nonempty subset of $\{1, \ldots, n\}$ has a largest element.
   (b) Explain why you cannot conclude from (a) that every nonempty subset of $\mathbb{Z}_+$ has a largest element.

5. Prove the following properties of $\mathbb{Z}$ and $\mathbb{Z}_+$:

    (a) $a, b \in \mathbb{Z}_+ \Rightarrow a + b \in \mathbb{Z}_+$. [*Hint:* Show that given $a \in \mathbb{Z}_+$, the set $X = \{x \mid x \in \mathbb{R} \text{ and } a + x \in \mathbb{Z}_+\}$ is inductive.]

    (b) $a, b \in \mathbb{Z}_+ \Rightarrow a \cdot b \in \mathbb{Z}_+$.

    (c) Show that $a \in \mathbb{Z}_+ \Rightarrow a - 1 \in \mathbb{Z}_+ \cup \{0\}$. [*Hint:* Let $X = \{x \mid x \in \mathbb{R} \text{ and } x - 1 \in \mathbb{Z}_+ \cup \{0\}\}$; show that X is inductive.]

    (d) $c, d \in \mathbb{Z} \Rightarrow c + d \in \mathbb{Z}$ and $c - d \in \mathbb{Z}$. [*Hint:* Prove it first for $d = 1$.]

    (e) $c, d \in \mathbb{Z} \Rightarrow c \cdot d \in \mathbb{Z}$.

6. Let $a \in \mathbb{R}$. Define inductively

$$a^1 = a,$$
$$a^{n+1} = a^n \cdot a$$

for $n \in \mathbb{Z}_+$. (See §7 for a discussion of the process of inductive definition.) Show that for $n, m \in \mathbb{Z}_+$ and $a, b \in \mathbb{R}$,

$$a^n a^m = a^{n+m},$$
$$(a^n)^m = a^{nm},$$
$$a^m b^m = (ab)^m.$$

These are called the *laws of exponents*. [*Hint:* For fixed n, prove the formulas by induction on m.]

7. Let $a \in \mathbb{R}$ and $a \neq 0$. Define $a^0 = 1$, and for $n \in \mathbb{Z}_+$, $a^{-n} = 1/a^n$. Show that the laws of exponents hold for $a, b \neq 0$ and $n, m \in \mathbb{Z}$.

8. (a) Show that $\mathbb{R}$ has the greatest lower bound property.

    (b) Show that $\inf\{1/n \mid n \in \mathbb{Z}_+\} = 0$.

    (c) Show that given a with $0 < a < 1$, $\inf\{a^n \mid n \in \mathbb{Z}_+\} = 0$. [*Hint:* Let $h = (1 - a)/a$, and show that $(1 + h)^n \geq 1 + nh$.]

9. (a) Show that every nonempty subset of $\mathbb{Z}$ that is bounded above has a largest element.

    (b) If $x \notin \mathbb{Z}$, show there is exactly one $n \in \mathbb{Z}$ such that $n < x < n + 1$.

    (c) If $x - y > 1$, show there is at least one $n \in \mathbb{Z}$ such that $y < n < x$.

    (d) If $y < x$, show there is a rational number z such that $y < z < x$.

10. Show that every positive number a has exactly one positive square root, as follows:

    (a) Show that if $x > 0$ and $0 \leq h < 1$, then

$$(x + h)^2 \leq x^2 + h(2x + 1),$$
$$(x - h)^2 \geq x^2 - h(2x).$$

    (b) Let $x > 0$. Show that if $x^2 < a$, then $(x + h)^2 < a$ for some $h > 0$; and if $x^2 > a$, then $(x - h)^2 > a$ for some $h > 0$.

   (c) Given $a > 0$, let B be the set of all real numbers x such that $x^2 < a$. Show that B is bounded above and contains at least one positive number. Let $b = \sup B$; show that $b^2 = a$.

   (d) Show that if b and c are positive and $b^2 = c^2$, then $b = c$.

11. Given $m \in \mathbb{Z}$, we say that m is ***even*** if $m/2 \in \mathbb{Z}$, and m is ***odd*** otherwise.

   (a) Show that if m is odd, $m = 2n + 1$ for some $n \in \mathbb{Z}$. [*Hint:* Choose n so that $n < m/2 < n + 1$.]

   (b) Show that if p and q are odd, so are $p \cdot q$ and p^n, for any $n \in \mathbb{Z}_+$.

   (c) Show that if $a > 0$ is rational, then $a = m/n$ for some $m, n \in \mathbb{Z}_+$ where not both m and n are even. [*Hint:* Let n be the smallest element of the set $\{x \mid x \in \mathbb{Z}_+ \text{ and } x \cdot a \in \mathbb{Z}_+\}$.]

   (d) *Theorem.* $\sqrt{2}$ *is irrational.*

§5   Cartesian Products

We have already defined what we mean by the cartesian product $A \times B$ of two sets. Now we introduce more general cartesian products.

Definition. Let $\mathcal{A}$ be a nonempty collection of sets. An ***indexing function*** for $\mathcal{A}$ is a surjective function f from some set J, called the ***index set***, to $\mathcal{A}$. The collection $\mathcal{A}$, together with the indexing function f, is called an ***indexed family of sets***. Given $\alpha \in J$, we shall denote the set $f(\alpha)$ by the symbol A_α. And we shall denote the indexed family itself by the symbol

$$\{A_\alpha\}_{\alpha \in J},$$

which is read "the family of all A_α, as α ranges over J." Sometimes we write merely $\{A_\alpha\}$, if it is clear what the index set is.

Note that although an indexing function is required to be surjective, it is not required to be *injective*. It is entirely possible for A_α and A_β to be the same set of $\mathcal{A}$, even though $\alpha \neq \beta$.

One way in which indexing functions are used is to give a new notation for arbitrary unions and intersections of sets. Suppose that $f : J \to \mathcal{A}$ is an indexing function for $\mathcal{A}$; let A_α denote $f(\alpha)$. Then we define

$$\bigcup_{\alpha \in J} A_\alpha = \{x \mid \text{for at least one } \alpha \in J, x \in A_\alpha\},$$

and

$$\bigcap_{\alpha \in J} A_\alpha = \{x \mid \text{for every } \alpha \in J, x \in A_\alpha\}.$$

These are simply new notations for previously defined concepts; one sees at once (using the surjectivity of the index function) that the first equals the union of all the elements of $\mathcal{A}$ and the second equals the intersection of all the elements of $\mathcal{A}$.

Two especially useful index sets are the set $\{1, \ldots, n\}$ of positive integers from 1 to n, and the set $\mathbb{Z}_+$ of all positive integers. For these index sets, we introduce some special notation. If a collection of sets is indexed by the set $\{1, \ldots, n\}$, we denote the indexed family by the symbol $\{A_1, \ldots, A_n\}$, and we denote the union and intersection, respectively, of the members of this family by the symbols

$$A_1 \cup \cdots \cup A_n \quad \text{and} \quad A_1 \cap \cdots \cap A_n.$$

In the case where the index set is the set $\mathbb{Z}_+$, we denote the indexed family by the symbol $\{A_1, A_2, \ldots\}$, and the union and intersection by the respective symbols

$$A_1 \cup A_2 \cup \cdots \quad \text{and} \quad A_1 \cap A_2 \cap \cdots.$$

Definition.   Let m be a positive integer. Given a set X, we define an ***m-tuple*** of elements of X to be a function

$$\mathbf{x} : \{1, \ldots, m\} \to X.$$

If $\mathbf{x}$ is an m-tuple, we often denote the value of $\mathbf{x}$ at i by the symbol x_i rather than $\mathbf{x}(i)$ and call it the ith ***coordinate*** of $\mathbf{x}$. And we often denote the function $\mathbf{x}$ itself by the symbol

$$(x_1, \ldots, x_m).$$

Now let $\{A_1, \ldots, A_m\}$ be a family of sets indexed with the set $\{1, \ldots, m\}$. Let $X = A_1 \cup \cdots \cup A_m$. We define the ***cartesian product*** of this indexed family, denoted by

$$\prod_{i=1}^{m} A_i \quad \text{or} \quad A_1 \times \cdots \times A_m,$$

to be the set of all m-tuples $(x_1, \ldots, x_m)$ of elements of X such that $x_i \in A_i$ for each i.

EXAMPLE 1.   We now have two definitions for the symbol $A \times B$. One definition is, of course, the one given earlier, under which $A \times B$ denotes the set of all ordered pairs (a, b) such that $a \in A$ and $b \in B$. The second definition, just given, defines $A \times B$ as the set of all functions $\mathbf{x} : \{1, 2\} \to A \cup B$ such that $\mathbf{x}(1) \in A$ and $\mathbf{x}(2) \in B$. There is an obvious bijective correspondence between these two sets, under which the ordered pair (a, b) corresponds to the function $\mathbf{x}$ defined by $\mathbf{x}(1) = a$ and $\mathbf{x}(2) = b$. Since we commonly denote this function $\mathbf{x}$ in "tuple notation" by the symbol (a, b), the notation itself suggests the correspondence. Thus for the cartesian product of two sets, the general definition of cartesian product reduces essentially to the earlier one.

EXAMPLE 2.   How does the cartesian product $A \times B \times C$ differ from the cartesian products $A \times (B \times C)$ and $(A \times B) \times C$? Very little. There are obvious bijective correspondences between these sets, indicated as follows:

$$(a, b, c) \longleftrightarrow (a, (b, c)) \longleftrightarrow ((a, b), c).$$

Definition.   Given a set X, we define an ***ω-tuple*** of elements of X to be a function

$$\mathbf{x} : \mathbb{Z}_+ \longrightarrow X;$$

we also call such a function a ***sequence***, or an ***infinite sequence***, of elements of X. If $\mathbf{x}$ is an ω-tuple, we often denote the value of $\mathbf{x}$ at i by x_i rather than $\mathbf{x}(i)$, and call it the ith ***coordinate*** of $\mathbf{x}$. We denote $\mathbf{x}$ itself by the symbol

$$(x_1, x_2, \ldots) \qquad \text{or} \qquad (x_n)_{n \in \mathbb{Z}_+}.$$

Now let $\{A_1, A_2, \ldots\}$ be a family of sets, indexed with the positive integers; let X be the union of the sets in this family. The ***cartesian product*** of this indexed family of sets, denoted by

$$\prod_{i \in \mathbb{Z}_+} A_i \qquad \text{or} \qquad A_1 \times A_2 \times \cdots,$$

is defined to be the set of all ω-tuples $(x_1, x_2, \ldots)$ of elements of X such that $x_i \in A_i$ for each i.

Nothing in these definitions requires the sets A_i to be different from one another. Indeed, they may all equal the same set X. In that case, the cartesian product $A_1 \times \cdots \times A_m$ is just the set of *all* m-tuples of elements of X, which we denote by X^m. Similarly, the product $A_1 \times A_2 \times \cdots$ is just the set of all ω-tuples of elements of X, which we denote by X^ω.

Later we will define the cartesian product of an *arbitrary* indexed family of sets.

EXAMPLE 3.   If $\mathbb{R}$ is the set of real numbers, then $\mathbb{R}^m$ denotes the set of all m-tuples of real numbers; it is often called ***euclidean m-space*** (although Euclid would never recognize it). Analogously, $\mathbb{R}^\omega$ is sometimes called "infinite-dimensional euclidean space"; it is the set of all ω-tuples $(x_1, x_2, \ldots)$ of real numbers, that is, the set of all functions $\mathbf{x} : \mathbb{Z}_+ \to \mathbb{R}$.

Exercises

1. Show there is a bijective correspondence of $A \times B$ with $B \times A$.

2. (a) Show that if $n > 1$ there is bijective correspondence of

$$A_1 \times \cdots \times A_n \qquad \text{with} \qquad (A_1 \times \cdots \times A_{n-1}) \times A_n.$$

   (b) Given the indexed family $\{A_1, A_2, \ldots\}$, let $B_i = A_{2i-1} \times A_{2i}$ for each positive integer i. Show there is bijective correspondence of $A_1 \times A_2 \times \cdots$ with $B_1 \times B_2 \times \cdots$.

3. Let $A = A_1 \times A_2 \times \cdots$ and $B = B_1 \times B_2 \times \cdots$.

   (a) Show that if $B_i \subset A_i$ for all i, then $B \subset A$. (Strictly speaking, if we are given a function mapping the index set $\mathbb{Z}_+$ into the union of the sets B_i, we must change its range before it can be considered as a function mapping $\mathbb{Z}_+$ into the union of the sets A_i. We shall ignore this technicality when dealing with cartesian products).

(b) Show the converse of (a) holds if B is nonempty.

(c) Show that if A is nonempty, each A_i is nonempty. Does the converse hold? (We will return to this question in the exercises of §19.)

(d) What is the relation between the set $A \cup B$ and the cartesian product of the sets $A_i \cup B_i$? What is the relation between the set $A \cap B$ and the cartesian product of the sets $A_i \cap B_i$?

4. Let $m, n \in \mathbb{Z}_+$. Let $X \neq \varnothing$.
    (a) If $m \leq n$, find an injective map $f : X^m \to X^n$.
    (b) Find a bijective map $g : X^m \times X^n \to X^{m+n}$.
    (c) Find an injective map $h : X^n \to X^\omega$.
    (d) Find a bijective map $k : X^n \times X^\omega \to X^\omega$.
    (e) Find a bijective map $l : X^\omega \times X^\omega \to X^\omega$.
    (f) If $A \subset B$, find an injective map $m : X^A \to X^B$.

5. Which of the following subsets of $\mathbb{R}^\omega$ can be expressed as the cartesian product of subsets of $\mathbb{R}$?
    (a) $\{\mathbf{x} \mid x_i \text{ is an integer for all } i\}$.
    (b) $\{\mathbf{x} \mid x_i \geq i \text{ for all } i\}$.
    (c) $\{\mathbf{x} \mid x_i \text{ is an integer for all } i \geq 100\}$.
    (d) $\{\mathbf{x} \mid x_2 = x_3\}$.

§6   Finite Sets

Finite sets and infinite sets, countable sets and uncountable sets, these are types of sets that you may have encountered before. Nevertheless, we shall discuss them in this section and the next, not only to make sure you understand them thoroughly, but also to elucidate some particular points of logic that will arise later on. First we consider finite sets.

Recall that if n is a positive integer, we use S_n to denote the set of positive integers less than n; it is called a *section* of the positive integers. The sets S_n are the prototypes for what we call the finite sets.

Definition.   A set is said to be *finite* if there is a bijective correspondence of A with some section of the positive integers. That is, A is finite if it is empty or if there is a bijection

$$f : A \longrightarrow \{1, \ldots, n\}$$

for some positive integer n. In the former case, we say that A has **cardinality 0**; in the latter case, we say that A has **cardinality n**.

For instance, the set $\{1, \ldots, n\}$ itself has cardinality n, for it is in bijective correspondence with itself under the identity function.

Now note carefully: *We have not yet shown that the cardinality of a finite set is uniquely determined by the set.* It is of course clear that the empty set must have cardinality zero. But as far as we know, there might exist bijective correspondences of a given nonempty set A with two different sets $\{1, \ldots, n\}$ and $\{1, \ldots, m\}$. The possibility may seem ridiculous, for it is like saying that it is possible for two people to count the marbles in a box and come out with two different answers, *both correct.* Our experience with counting in everyday life suggests that such is impossible, and in fact this is easy to prove when n is a small number such as 1, 2, or 3. But a direct proof when n is 5 million would be impossibly demanding.

Even empirical demonstration would be difficult for such a large value of n. One might, for instance, construct an experiment by taking a freight car full of marbles and hiring 10 different people to count them independently. If one thinks of the physical problems involved, it seems likely that the counters would not all arrive at the same answer. Of course, the conclusion one could draw is that at least one person made a mistake. But that would mean assuming the correctness of the result one was trying to demonstrate empirically. An alternative explanation could be that there do exist bijective correspondences between the given set of marbles and two different sections of the positive integers.

In real life, we accept the first explanation. We simply take it on faith that our experience in counting comparatively small sets of objects demonstrates a truth that holds for arbitrarily large sets as well.

However, in mathematics (as opposed to real life), one does not have to take this statement on faith. If it is formulated in terms of the existence of bijective correspondences rather than in terms of the physical act of counting, it is capable of mathematical proof. We shall prove shortly that if $n \neq m$, there do not exist bijective functions mapping a given set A onto both the sets $\{1, \ldots, n\}$ and $\{1, \ldots, m\}$.

There are a number of other "intuitively obvious" facts about finite sets that are capable of mathematical proof; we shall prove some of them in this section and leave the rest to the exercises. Here is an easy fact to start with:

Lemma 6.1.   *Let n be a positive integer. Let A be a set; let a_0 be an element of A. Then there exists a bijective correspondence f of the set A with the set $\{1, \ldots, n+1\}$ if and only if there exists a bijective correspondence g of the set $A - \{a_0\}$ with the set $\{1, \ldots, n\}$.*

Proof.   There are two implications to be proved. Let us first assume that there is a bijective correspondence

$$g : A - \{a_0\} \longrightarrow \{1, \ldots, n\}.$$

We then define a function $f : A \longrightarrow \{1, \ldots, n+1\}$ by setting

$$f(x) = g(x) \quad \text{for } x \in A - \{a_0\},$$
$$f(a_0) = n + 1.$$

One checks at once that f is bijective.

To prove the converse, assume there is a bijective correspondence

$$f : A \longrightarrow \{1, \ldots, n+1\}.$$

If f maps a_0 to the number $n+1$, things are especially easy; in that case, the restriction $f|A - \{a_0\}$ is the desired bijective correspondence of $A - \{a_0\}$ with $\{1, \ldots, n\}$. Otherwise, let $f(a_0) = m$, and let a_1 be the point of A such that $f(a_1) = n+1$. Then $a_1 \neq a_0$. Define a new function

$$h : A \longrightarrow \{1, \ldots, n+1\}$$

by setting

$$h(a_0) = n+1,$$
$$h(a_1) = m,$$
$$h(x) = f(x) \quad \text{for } x \in A - \{a_0\} - \{a_1\}.$$

See Figure 6.1. It is easy to check that h is a bijection.

Now we are back in the easy case; the restriction $h|A - \{a_0\}$ is the desired bijection of $A - \{a_0\}$ with $\{1, \ldots, n\}$. ∎

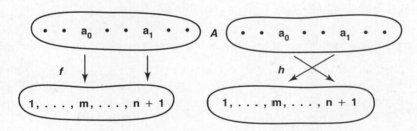

Figure 6.1

From this lemma a number of useful consequences follow:

Theorem 6.2. *Let A be a set; suppose that there exists a bijection $f : A \to \{1, \ldots, n\}$ for some $n \in \mathbb{Z}_+$. Let B be a proper subset of A. Then there exists no bijection $g : B \to \{1, \ldots, n\}$; but (provided $B \neq \varnothing$) there does exist a bijection $h : B \to \{1, \ldots, m\}$ for some $m < n$.*

Proof. The case in which $B = \varnothing$ is trivial, for there cannot exist a bijection of the empty set B with the nonempty set $\{1, \ldots, n\}$.

We prove the theorem "by induction." Let C be the subset of $\mathbb{Z}_+$ consisting of those integers n for which the theorem holds. We shall show that C is inductive. From this we conclude that $C = \mathbb{Z}_+$, so the theorem is true for all positive integers n.

First we show the theorem is true for $n = 1$. In this case A consists of a single element $\{a\}$, and its only proper subset B is the empty set.

Now assume that the theorem is true for n; we prove it true for $n + 1$. Suppose that $f : A \to \{1, \ldots, n + 1\}$ is a bijection, and B is a nonempty proper subset of A. Choose an element a_0 of B and an element a_1 of $A - B$. We apply the preceding lemma to conclude there is a bijection

$$g : A - \{a_0\} \longrightarrow \{1, \ldots, n\}.$$

Now $B - \{a_0\}$ is a proper subset of $A - \{a_0\}$, for a_1 belongs to $A - \{a_0\}$ and not to $B - \{a_0\}$. Because the theorem has been assumed to hold for the integer n, we conclude the following:

(1) There exists no bijection $h : B - \{a_0\} \to \{1, \ldots, n\}$.

(2) Either $B - \{a_0\} = \varnothing$, or there exists a bijection

$$k : B - \{a_0\} \longrightarrow \{1, \ldots, p\} \qquad \text{for some } p < n.$$

The preceding lemma, combined with (1), implies that there is no bijection of B with $\{1, \ldots, n + 1\}$. This is the first half of what we wanted to proved. To prove the second half, note that if $B - \{a_0\} = \varnothing$, there is a bijection of B with the set $\{1\}$; while if $B - \{a_0\} \neq \varnothing$, we can apply the preceding lemma, along with (2), to conclude that there is a bijection of B with $\{1, \ldots, p + 1\}$. In either case, there is a bijection of B with $\{1, \ldots, m\}$ for some $m < n + 1$, as desired. The induction principle now shows that the theorem is true for all $n \in \mathbb{Z}_+$. ∎

Corollary 6.3. *If A is finite, there is no bijection of A with a proper subset of itself.*

Proof. Assume that B is a proper subset of A and that $f : A \to B$ is a bijection. By assumption, there is a bijection $g : A \to \{1, \ldots, n\}$ for some n. The composite $g \circ f^{-1}$ is then a bijection of B with $\{1, \ldots, n\}$. This contradicts the preceding theorem. ∎

Corollary 6.4. $\mathbb{Z}_+$ *is not finite.*

Proof. The function $f : \mathbb{Z}_+ \to \mathbb{Z}_+ - \{1\}$ defined by $f(n) = n + 1$ is a bijection of $\mathbb{Z}_+$ with a proper subset of itself. ∎

Corollary 6.5. *The cardinality of a finite set A is uniquely determined by A.*

Proof. Let $m < n$. Suppose there are bijections

$$f : A \longrightarrow \{1, \ldots, n\},$$
$$g : A \longrightarrow \{1, \ldots, m\}.$$

Then the composite

$$g \circ f^{-1} : \{1, \ldots, n\} \longrightarrow \{1, \ldots, m\}$$

is a bijection of the finite set $\{1, \ldots, n\}$ with a proper subset of itself, contradicting the corollary just proved. ∎

Corollary 6.6. *If B is a subset of the finite set A, then B is finite. If B is a proper subset of A, then the cardinality of B is less than the cardinality of A.*

Corollary 6.7. *Let B be a nonempty set. Then the following are equivalent:*
(1) *B is finite.*
(2) *There is a surjective function from a section of the positive integers onto B.*
(3) *There is an injective function from B into a section of the positive integers.*

Proof. (1) $\Longrightarrow$ (2). Since B is nonempty, there is, for some n, a bijective function $f : \{1, \ldots, n\} \to B$.

(2) $\Longrightarrow$ (3). If $f : \{1, \ldots, n\} \to B$ is surjective, define $g : B \to \{1, \ldots, n\}$ by the equation

$$g(b) = \text{smallest element of } f^{-1}(\{b\}).$$

Because f is surjective, the set $f^{-1}\{(b)\}$ is nonempty; then the well-ordering property of $\mathbb{Z}_+$ tells us that $g(b)$ is uniquely defined. The map g is injective, for if $b \neq b'$, then the sets $f^{-1}(\{b\})$ and $f^{-1}(\{b'\})$ are disjoint, so their smallest elements must be different.

(3) $\Longrightarrow$ (1). If $g : B \to \{1, \ldots, n\}$ is injective, then changing the range of g gives a bijection of B with a subset of $\{1, \ldots, n\}$. It follows from the preceding corollary that B is finite. ∎

Corollary 6.8. *Finite unions and finite cartesian products of finite sets are finite.*

Proof. We first show that if A and B are finite, so is $A \cup B$. The result is trivial if A or B is empty. Otherwise, there are bijections $f : \{1, \ldots, m\} \to A$ and $g : \{1, \ldots, n\} \to B$ for some choice of m and n. Define a function $h : \{1, \ldots, m + n\} \to A \cup B$ by setting $h(i) = f(i)$ for $i = 1, 2, \ldots, m$ and $h(i) = g(i - m)$ for $i = m + 1, \ldots, m + n$. It is easy to check that h is surjective, from which it follows that $A \cup B$ is finite.

Now we show by induction that finiteness of the sets $A_1, \ldots, A_n$ implies finiteness of their union. This result is trivial for $n = 1$. Assuming it true for $n - 1$, we note that $A_1 \cup \cdots \cup A_n$ is the union of the two finite sets $A_1 \cup \cdots \cup A_{n-1}$ and A_n, so the result of the preceding paragraph applies.

Now we show that the cartesian product of two finite sets A and B is finite. Given $a \in A$, the set $\{a\} \times B$ is finite, being in bijective correspondence with B. The set $A \times B$ is the union of these sets; since there are only finitely many of them, $A \times B$ is a finite union of finite sets and thus finite.

To prove that the product $A_1 \times \cdots \times A_n$ is finite if each A_i is finite, one proceeds by induction. ∎

Exercises

1. (a) Make a list of all the injective maps

$$f : \{1, 2, 3\} \longrightarrow \{1, 2, 3, 4\}.$$

Show that none is bijective. (This constitutes a *direct* proof that a set A of cardinality three does not have cardinality four.)

(b) How many injective maps

$$f : \{1, \ldots, 8\} \longrightarrow \{1, \ldots, 10\}$$

are there? (You can see why one would not wish to try to prove *directly* that there is no bijective correspondence between these sets.)

2. Show that if B is not finite and $B \subset A$, then A is not finite.

3. Let X be the two-element set $\{0, 1\}$. Find a bijective correspondence between X^ω and a proper subset of itself.

4. Let A be a nonempty finite simply ordered set.
(a) Show that A has a largest element. [*Hint:* Proceed by induction on the cardinality of A.]
(b) Show that A has the order type of a section of the positive integers.

5. If $A \times B$ is finite, does it follow that A and B are finite?

6. (a) Let $A = \{1, \ldots, n\}$. Show there is a bijection of $\mathcal{P}(A)$ with the cartesian product X^n, where X is the two-element set $X = \{0, 1\}$.
(b) Show that if A is finite, then $\mathcal{P}(A)$ is finite.

7. If A and B are finite, show that the set of all functions $f : A \to B$ is finite.

§7 Countable and Uncountable Sets

Just as sections of the positive integers are the prototypes for the finite sets, the set of all the positive integers is the prototype for what we call the *countably infinite* sets. In this section, we shall study such sets; we shall also construct some sets that are neither finite nor countably infinite. This study will lead us into a discussion of what we mean by the process of "inductive definition."

Definition. A set A is said to be *infinite* if it is not finite. It is said to be *countably infinite* if there is a bijective correspondence

$$f : A \longrightarrow \mathbb{Z}_+.$$

EXAMPLE 1. The set $\mathbb{Z}$ of all integers is countably infinite. One checks easily that the function $f : \mathbb{Z} \to \mathbb{Z}_+$ defined by

$$f(n) = \begin{cases} 2n & \text{if } n > 0, \\ -2n + 1 & \text{if } n \le 0 \end{cases}$$

is a bijection.

EXAMPLE 2.   The product $\mathbb{Z}_+ \times \mathbb{Z}_+$ is countably infinite. If we represent the elements of the product $\mathbb{Z}_+ \times \mathbb{Z}_+$ by the integer points in the first quadrant, then the left-hand portion of Figure 7.1 suggests how to "count" the points, that is, how to put them in bijective correspondence with the positive integers. A picture is not a proof, of course, but this picture suggests a proof. First, we define a bijection $f : \mathbb{Z}_+ \times \mathbb{Z}_+ \to A$, where A is the subset of $\mathbb{Z}_+ \times \mathbb{Z}_+$ consisting of pairs (x, y) for which $y \leq x$, by the equation

$$f(x, y) = (x + y - 1, y).$$

Then we construct a bijection of A with the positive integers, defining $g : A \to \mathbb{Z}_+$ by the formula

$$g(x, y) = \frac{1}{2}(x - 1)x + y.$$

We leave it to you to show that f and g are bijections.
    Another proof that $\mathbb{Z}_+ \times \mathbb{Z}_+$ is countably infinite will be given later.

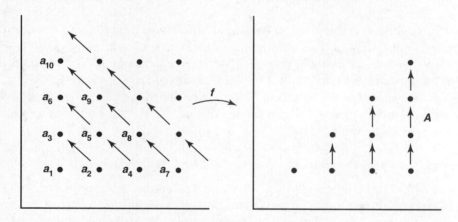

Figure 7.1

Definition.   A set is said to be ***countable*** if it is either finite or countably infinite. A set that is not countable is said to be ***uncountable***.

    There is a very useful criterion for showing that a set is countable. It is the following:

Theorem 7.1.   *Let B be a nonempty set. Then the following are equivalent:*
  (1) B is countable.
  (2) There is a surjective function $f : \mathbb{Z}_+ \to B$.
  (3) There is an injective function $g : B \to \mathbb{Z}_+$.

Proof.   (1) $\Longrightarrow$ (2). Suppose that B is countable. If B is countably infinite, there is a bijection $f : \mathbb{Z}_+ \to B$ by definition, and we are through. If B is finite, there is a bijection $h : \{1, \ldots, n\} \to B$ for some $n \geq 1$. (Recall that $B \neq \varnothing$.) We can extend h to a surjection $f : \mathbb{Z}_+ \to B$ by defining

$$f(i) = \begin{cases} h(i) & \text{for } 1 \leq i \leq n, \\ h(1) & \text{for } i > n. \end{cases}$$

(2) $\implies$ (3). Let $f : \mathbb{Z}_+ \to B$ be a surjection. Define $g : B \to \mathbb{Z}_+$ by the equation

$$g(b) = \text{smallest element of } f^{-1}(\{b\}).$$

Because f is surjective, $f^{-1}(\{b\})$ is nonempty; thus g is well defined. The map g is injective, for if $b \neq b'$, the sets $f^{-1}(\{b\})$ and $f^{-1}(\{b'\})$ are disjoint, so their smallest elements are different.

(3) $\implies$ (1). Let $g : B \to \mathbb{Z}_+$ be an injection; we wish to prove B is countable. By changing the range of g, we can obtain a bijection of B with a subset of $\mathbb{Z}_+$. Thus to prove our result, it suffices to show that every subset of $\mathbb{Z}_+$ is countable. So let C be a subset of $\mathbb{Z}_+$.

If C is finite, it is countable by definition. So what we need to prove is that every infinite subset C of $\mathbb{Z}_+$ is countably infinite. This statement is certainly plausible. For the elements of C can easily be arranged in an infinite sequence; one simply takes the set $\mathbb{Z}_+$ in its usual order and "erases" all the elements of $\mathbb{Z}_+$ that are not in C!

The plausibility of this argument may make one overlook its informality. Providing a formal proof requires a certain amount of care. We state this result as a separate lemma, which follows. ■

Lemma 7.2. *If C is an infinite subset of $\mathbb{Z}_+$, then C is countably infinite.*

Proof. We define a bijection $h : \mathbb{Z}_+ \to C$. We proceed by induction. Define $h(1)$ to be the smallest element of C; it exists because every nonempty subset C of $\mathbb{Z}_+$ has a smallest element. Then assuming that $h(1), \ldots, h(n-1)$ are defined, define

$$h(n) = \text{smallest element of } [C - h(\{1, \ldots, n-1\})].$$

The set $C - h(\{1, \ldots, n-1\})$ is not empty; for if it were empty, then $h : \{1, \ldots, n-1\} \to C$ would be surjective, so that C would be finite (by Corollary 6.7). Thus $h(n)$ is well defined. By induction, we have defined $h(n)$ for all $n \in \mathbb{Z}_+$.

To show that h is injective is easy. Given $m < n$, note that $h(m)$ belongs to the set $h(\{1, \ldots, n-1\})$, whereas $h(n)$, by definition, does not. Hence $h(n) \neq h(m)$.

To show that h is surjective, let c be any element of C; we show that c lies in the image set of h. First note that $h(\mathbb{Z}_+)$ cannot be contained in the finite set $\{1, \ldots, c\}$, because $h(\mathbb{Z}_+)$ is infinite (since h is injective). Therefore, there is an n in $\mathbb{Z}_+$, such that $h(n) > c$. Let m be the *smallest* element of $\mathbb{Z}_+$, such that $h(m) \geq c$. Then for all $i < m$, we must have $h(i) < c$. Thus, c does not belong to the set $h(\{1, \ldots, m-1\})$. Since $h(m)$ is defined as the smallest element of the set $C - h(\{1, \ldots, m-1\})$, we must have $h(m) \leq c$. Putting the two inequalities together, we have $h(m) = c$, as desired. ■

There is a point in the preceding proof where we stretched the principles of logic a bit. It occurred at the point where we said that "using the induction principle" we had defined the function h for all positive integers n. You may have seen arguments like this used before, with no questions raised concerning their legitimacy. We have already used such an argument ourselves, in the exercises of §4, when we defined a^n.

But there is a problem here. After all, the induction principle states only that if A is an inductive set of positive integers, then $A = \mathbb{Z}_+$. To use the principle to prove a theorem "by induction," one begins the proof with the statement "Let A be the set of all positive integers n for which the theorem is true," and then one goes ahead to prove that A is inductive, so that A must be all of $\mathbb{Z}_+$.

In the preceding theorem, however, we were not really proving a theorem by induction, but defining something by induction. How then should we start the proof? Can we start by saying, "Let A be the set of all integers n for which the function h is defined"? But that's silly; the symbol h has no *meaning* at the outset of the proof. It only takes on meaning in the course of the proof. So something more is needed.

What is needed is another principle, which we call the ***principle of recursive definition***. In the proof of the preceding theorem, we wished to assert the following:

Given the infinite subset C of $\mathbb{Z}_+$, there is a unique function $h : \mathbb{Z}_+ \to C$ satisfying the formula:

(∗)
$$h(1) = \text{smallest element of } C,$$
$$h(i) = \text{smallest element of } [C - h(\{1, \ldots, i - 1\})] \quad \text{for all } i > 1.$$

The formula (∗) is called a ***recursion formula*** for h; it defines the function h in *terms of itself.* A definition given by such a formula is called a ***recursive definition***.

Now one can get into logical difficulties when one tries to define something recursively. Not all recursive formulas make sense. The recursive formula

$$h(i) = \text{smallest element of } [C - h(\{1, \ldots, i + 1\})],$$

for example, is self-contradictory; although $h(i)$ necessarily is an element of the set $h(\{1, \ldots, i + 1\})$, this formula says that it does not belong to the set. Another example is the classic paradox:

> Let the barber of Seville shave every man of Seville who does not shave himself.
> Who shall shave the barber?

In this statement, the barber appears twice, once in the phrase "the barber of Seville" and once as an element of the set "men of Seville"; this definition of whom the barber shall shave is a recursive one. It also happens to be self-contradictory.

Some recursive formulas do make sense, however. Specifically, one has the following principle:

Principle of recursive definition.   *Let A be a set. Given a formula that defines $h(1)$ as a unique element of A, and for $i > 1$ defines $h(i)$ uniquely as an element of A in terms of the values of h for positive integers less than i, this formula determines a unique function $h : \mathbb{Z}_+ \to A$.*

This principle is the one we actually used in the proof of Lemma 7.2. You can simply accept it on faith if you like. It may however be proved rigorously, using the principle of induction. We shall formulate it more precisely in the next section and indicate how it is proved. Mathematicians seldom refer to this principle specifically. They are much more likely to write a proof like our proof of Lemma 7.2 above, a proof in which they invoke the "induction principle" to define a function when what they are really using is the principle of recursive definition. We shall avoid undue pedantry in this book by following their example.

Corollary 7.3. *A subset of a countable set is countable.*

Proof. Suppose $A \subset B$, where B is countable. There is an injection f of B into $\mathbb{Z}_+$; the restriction of f to A is an injection of A into $\mathbb{Z}_+$. ■

Corollary 7.4. *The set $\mathbb{Z}_+ \times \mathbb{Z}_+$ is countably infinite.*

Proof. In view of Theorem 7.1, it suffices to construct an injective map $f : \mathbb{Z}_+ \times \mathbb{Z}_+ \to \mathbb{Z}_+$. We define f by the equation

$$f(n, m) = 2^n 3^m.$$

It is easy to check that f is injective. For suppose that $2^n 3^m = 2^p 3^q$. If $n < p$, then $3^m = 2^{p-n} 3^q$, contradicting the fact that 3^m is odd for all m. Therefore, $n = p$. As a result, $3^m = 3^q$, Then if $m < q$, it follows that $1 = 3^{q-m}$, another contradiction. Hence $m = q$. ■

EXAMPLE 3.   The set $\mathbb{Q}_+$ of positive rational numbers is countably infinite. For we can define a surjection $g : \mathbb{Z}_+ \times \mathbb{Z}_+ \to \mathbb{Q}_+$ by the equation

$$g(n, m) = m/n.$$

Because $\mathbb{Z}_+ \times \mathbb{Z}_+$ is countable, there is a surjection $f : \mathbb{Z}_+ \to \mathbb{Z}_+ \times \mathbb{Z}_+$. Then the composite $g \circ f : \mathbb{Z}_+ \to \mathbb{Q}_+$ is a surjection, so that $\mathbb{Q}_+$ is countable. And, of course, $\mathbb{Q}_+$ is infinite because it contains $\mathbb{Z}_+$.

We leave it as an exercise to show the set $\mathbb{Q}$ of *all* rational numbers is countably infinite.

Theorem 7.5. *A countable union of countable sets is countable.*

Proof. Let $\{A_n\}_{n \in J}$ be an indexed family of countable sets, where the index set J is either $\{1, \ldots, N\}$ or $\mathbb{Z}_+$. Assume that each set A_n is nonempty, for convenience; this assumption does not change anything.

Because each A_n is countable, we can choose, for each n, a surjective function $f_n : \mathbb{Z}_+ \to A_n$. Similarly, we can choose a surjective function $g : \mathbb{Z}_+ \to J$. Now define

$$h : \mathbb{Z}_+ \times \mathbb{Z}_+ \to \bigcup_{n \in J} A_n$$

by the equation

$$h(k, m) = f_{g(k)}(m).$$

It is easy to check that h is surjective. Since $\mathbb{Z}_+ \times \mathbb{Z}_+$ is in bijective correspondence with $\mathbb{Z}_+$, the countability of the union follows from Theorem 7.1.   ∎

Theorem 7.6.   *A finite product of countable sets is countable.*

Proof.   First let us show that the product of two countable sets A and B is countable. The result is trivial if A or B is empty. Otherwise, choose surjective functions f : $\mathbb{Z}_+ \to A$ and $g : \mathbb{Z}_+ \to B$. Then the function $h : \mathbb{Z}_+ \times \mathbb{Z}_+ \to A \times B$ defined by the equation $h(n, m) = (f(n), g(m))$ is surjective, so that $A \times B$ is countable.

In general, we proceed by induction. Assuming that $A_1 \times \cdots \times A_{n-1}$ is countable if each A_i is countable, we prove the same thing for the product $A_1 \times \cdots \times A_n$. First, note that there is a bijective correspondence

$$g : A_1 \times \cdots \times A_n \longrightarrow (A_1 \times \cdots \times A_{n-1}) \times A_n$$

defined by the equation

$$g(x_1, \ldots, x_n) = ((x_1, \ldots, x_{n-1}), x_n).$$

Because the set $A_1 \times \cdots \times A_{n-1}$ is countable by the induction assumption and A_n is countable by hypothesis, the product of these two sets is countable, as proved in the preceding paragraph. We conclude that $A_1 \times \cdots \times A_n$ is countable as well.   ∎

It is very tempting to assert that countable products of countable sets should be countable; but this assertion is in fact not true:

Theorem 7.7.   *Let X denote the two element set $\{0, 1\}$. Then the set X^ω is uncountable.*

Proof.   We show that, given any function

$$g : \mathbb{Z}_+ \longrightarrow X^\omega,$$

g is not surjective. For this purpose, let us denote $g(n)$ as follows :

$$g(n) = (x_{n1}, x_{n2}, x_{n3}, \ldots x_{nm}, \ldots),$$

where each x_{ij} is either 0 or 1. Then we define an element $\mathbf{y} = (y_1, y_2, \ldots, y_n, \ldots)$ of X^ω by letting

$$y_n = \begin{cases} 0 & \text{if } x_{nn} = 1, \\ 1 & \text{if } x_{nn} = 0. \end{cases}$$

(If we write the numbers x_{ni} in a rectangular array, the particular elements x_{nn} appear as the diagonal entries in this array; we choose **y** so that its nth coordinate *differs* from the diagonal entry x_{nn}.)

Now **y** is an element of X^ω, and **y** does not lie in the image of g; given n, the point $g(n)$ and the point **y** differ in at least one coordinate, namely, the nth. Thus, g is not surjective. ∎

The cartesian product $\{0, 1\}^\omega$ is one example of an uncountable set. Another is the set $\mathcal{P}(\mathbb{Z}_+)$, as the following theorem implies:

Theorem 7.8. *Let A be a set. There is no injective map $f : \mathcal{P}(A) \to A$, and there is no surjective map $g : A \to \mathcal{P}(A)$.*

Proof. In general, if B is a nonempty set, the existence of an injective map $f : B \to C$ implies the existence of a surjective map $g : C \to B$; one defines $g(c) = f^{-1}(c)$ for each c in the image set of f, and defines g arbitrarily on the rest of C.

Therefore, it suffices to prove that given a map $g : A \to \mathcal{P}(A)$, the map g is not surjective. For each $a \in A$, the image $g(a)$ of a is a subset of A, which may or may not contain the point a itself. Let B be the subset of A consisting of all those points a such that $g(a)$ does not contain a;

$$B = \{a \mid a \in A - g(a)\}.$$

Now, B may be empty, or it may be all of A, but that does not matter. We assert that B is a subset of A that does not lie in the image of g. For suppose that $B = g(a_0)$ for some $a_0 \in A$. We ask the question: Does a_0 belong to B or not? By definition of B,

$$a_0 \in B \iff a_0 \in A - g(a_0) \iff a_0 \in A - B.$$

In either case, we have a contradiction. ∎

Now we have proved the existence of uncountable sets. But we have not yet mentioned the most familiar uncountable set of all—the set of real numbers. You have probably seen the uncountability of $\mathbb{R}$ demonstrated already. If one assumes that every real number can be represented uniquely by an infinite decimal (with the proviso that a representation ending in an infinite string of 9's is forbidden), then the uncountability of the reals can be proved by a variant of the diagonal procedure used in the proof of Theorem 7.7. But this proof is in some ways not very satisfying. One reason is that the infinite decimal representation of a real number is not at all an elementary consequence of the axioms but requires a good deal of labor to prove. Another reason is that the uncountability of $\mathbb{R}$ does not, in fact, depend on the infinite decimal expansion of $\mathbb{R}$ or indeed on any of the algebraic properties of $\mathbb{R}$; it depends on only the order properties of $\mathbb{R}$. We shall demonstrate the uncountability of $\mathbb{R}$, using only its order properties, in a later chapter.

Exercises

1. Show that $\mathbb{Q}$ is countably infinite.

2. Show that the maps f and g of Examples 1 and 2 are bijections.

3. Let X be the two-element set $\{0, 1\}$. Show there is a bijective correspondence between the set $\mathcal{P}(\mathbb{Z}_+)$ and the cartesian product X^ω.

4. (a) A real number x is said to be **algebraic** (over the rationals) if it satisfies some polynomial equation of positive degree
$$x^n + a_{n-1}x^{n-1} + \cdots + a_1 x + a_0 = 0$$
with rational coefficients a_i. Assuming that each polynomial equation has only finitely many roots, show that the set of algebraic numbers is countable.

   (b) A real number is said to be **transcendental** if it is not algebraic. Assuming the reals are uncountable, show that the transcendental numbers are uncountable. (It is a somewhat surprising fact that only two transcendental numbers are familiar to us: e and π. Even proving these two numbers transcendental is highly nontrivial.)

5. Determine, for each of the following sets, whether or not it is countable. Justify your answers.

   (a) The set A of all functions $f : \{0, 1\} \to \mathbb{Z}_+$.

   (b) The set B_n of all functions $f : \{1, \ldots, n\} \to \mathbb{Z}_+$.

   (c) The set $C = \bigcup_{n \in \mathbb{Z}_+} B_n$.

   (d) The set D of all functions $f : \mathbb{Z}_+ \to \mathbb{Z}_+$.

   (e) The set E of all functions $f : \mathbb{Z}_+ \to \{0, 1\}$.

   (f) The set F of all functions $f : \mathbb{Z}_+ \to \{0, 1\}$ that are "eventually zero." [We say that f is **eventually zero** if there is a positive integer N such that $f(n) = 0$ for all $n \geq N$.]

   (g) The set G of all functions $f : \mathbb{Z}_+ \to \mathbb{Z}_+$ that are eventually 1.

   (h) The set H of all functions $f : \mathbb{Z}_+ \to \mathbb{Z}_+$ that are eventually constant.

   (i) The set I of all two-element subsets of $\mathbb{Z}_+$.

   (j) The set J of all finite subsets of $\mathbb{Z}_+$.

6. We say that two sets A and B **have the same cardinality** if there is a bijection of A with B.

   (a) Show that if $B \subset A$ and if there is an injection
$$f : A \longrightarrow B,$$
then A and B have the same cardinality. [*Hint:* Define $A_1 = A$, $B_1 = B$, and for $n > 1$, $A_n = f(A_{n-1})$ and $B_n = f(B_{n-1})$. (Recursive definition again!) Note that $A_1 \supset B_1 \supset A_2 \supset B_2 \supset A_3 \supset \cdots$. Define a bijection $h : A \to B$ by the rule
$$h(x) = \begin{cases} f(x) & \text{if } x \in A_n - B_n \text{ for some } n, \\ x & \text{otherwise.} \end{cases}$$
]

(b) **Theorem** (Schroeder-Bernstein theorem).   *If there are injections $f : A \to$ C and $g : C \to A$, then A and C have the same cardinality.*

7. Show that the sets D and E of Exercise 5 have the same cardinality.

8. Let X denote the two-element set $\{0, 1\}$; let $\mathcal{B}$ be the set of *countable* subsets of X^ω. Show that X^ω and $\mathcal{B}$ have the same cardinality.

9. (a) The formula

$$(*) \qquad \begin{aligned} h(1) &= 1, \\ h(2) &= 2, \\ h(n) &= [h(n+1)]^2 - [h(n-1)]^2 \qquad \text{for } n \geq 2 \end{aligned}$$

is not one to which the principle of recursive definition applies. Show that nevertheless there does exist a function $h : \mathbb{Z}_+ \to \mathbb{R}$ satisfying this formula. [*Hint:* Reformulate $(*)$ so that the principle will apply and require h to be positive.]

(b) Show that the formula $(*)$ of part (a) does not determine h uniquely. [*Hint:* If h is a positive function satisfying $(*)$, let $f(i) = h(i)$ for $i \neq 3$, and let $f(3) = -h(3)$.]

(c) Show that there is no function $h : \mathbb{Z}_+ \to \mathbb{R}$ satisfying the formula

$$\begin{aligned} h(1) &= 1, \\ h(2) &= 2, \\ h(n) &= [h(n+1)]^2 + [h(n-1)]^2 \qquad \text{for } n \geq 2. \end{aligned}$$

*§8   The Principle of Recursive Definition

Before considering the general form of the principle of recursive definition, let us first prove it in a specific case, that of Lemma 7.2. That should make the underlying idea of the proof much clearer when we consider the general case.

So, given the infinite subset C of $\mathbb{Z}_+$, let us consider the following recursion formula for a function $h : \mathbb{Z}_+ \to C$:

$$(*) \qquad \begin{aligned} h(1) &= \text{smallest element of } C, \\ h(i) &= \text{smallest element of } [C - h(\{1, \ldots, i-1\})] \qquad \text{for } i > 1. \end{aligned}$$

We shall prove that there exists a unique function $h : \mathbb{Z}_+ \to C$ satisfying this recursion formula.

The first step is to prove that there exist functions defined on *sections* $\{1, \ldots, n\}$ of $\mathbb{Z}_+$ that satisfy $(*)$:

Lemma 8.1.   *Given $n \in \mathbb{Z}_+$, there exists a function*

$$f : \{1, \ldots, n\} \to C$$

that satisfies $(*)$ for all i in its domain.

Proof. The point of this lemma is that it is a statement that depends on n; therefore, it is capable of being proved by induction. Let A be the set of all n for which the lemma holds. We show that A is inductive. It then follows that $A = \mathbb{Z}_+$.

The lemma is true for $n = 1$, since the function $f : \{1\} \to C$ defined by the equation

$$f(1) = \text{smallest element of } C$$

satisfies $(*)$.

Supposing the lemma to be true for $n - 1$, we prove it true for n. By hypothesis, there is a function $f' : \{1, \ldots, n - 1\} \to C$ satisfying $(*)$ for all i in its domain. Define $f : \{1, \ldots, n\} \to C$ by the equations

$$f(i) = f'(i) \quad \text{for } i \in \{1, \ldots, n - 1\},$$
$$f(n) = \text{smallest element of } [C - f'(\{1, \ldots, n - 1\})].$$

Since C is infinite, f' is not surjective; hence the set $C - f'(\{1, \ldots, n - 1\})$ is not empty, and $f(n)$ is well defined. Note that this definition is an acceptable one; it does not define f in terms of *itself* but in terms of the given function f'.

It is easy to check that f satisfies $(*)$ for all i in its domain. The function f satisfies $(*)$ for $i \leq n - 1$ because it equals f' there. And f satisfies $(*)$ for $i = n$ because, by definition,

$$f(n) = \text{smallest element of } [C - f'(\{1, \ldots, n - 1\})]$$

and $f'(\{1, \ldots, n - 1\}) = f(\{1, \ldots, n - 1\})$. ∎

Lemma 8.2. *Suppose that $f : \{1, \ldots, n\} \to C$ and $g : \{1, \ldots, m\} \to C$ both satisfy $(*)$ for all i in their respective domains. Then $f(i) = g(i)$ for all i in both domains.*

Proof. Suppose not. Let i be the *smallest* integer for which $f(i) \neq g(i)$. The integer i is not 1, because

$$f(1) = \text{smallest element of } C = g(1),$$

by $(*)$. Now for all $j < i$, we have $f(j) = g(j)$. Because f and g satisfy $(*)$,

$$f(i) = \text{smallest element of } [C - f(\{1, \ldots, i - 1\})],$$
$$g(i) = \text{smallest element of } [C - g(\{1, \ldots, i - 1\})].$$

Since $f(\{1, \ldots, i - 1\}) = g(\{1, \ldots, i - 1\})$, we have $f(i) = g(i)$, contrary to the choice of i. ∎

Theorem 8.3.   *There exists a unique function $h : \mathbb{Z}_+ \to C$ satisfying (*) for all $i \in \mathbb{Z}_+$.*

Proof.   By Lemma 8.1, there exists for each n a function that maps $\{1, \ldots, n\}$ into C and satisfies (*) for all i in its domain. Given n, Lemma 8.2 shows that this function is unique; two such functions having the same domain must be equal. Let $f_n : \{1, \ldots, n\} \to C$ denote this unique function.

Now comes the crucial step. We define a function $h : \mathbb{Z}_+ \to C$ by defining its rule to be the *union* U of the rules of the functions f_n. The rule for f_n is a subset of $\{1, \ldots, n\} \times C$; therefore, U is a subset of $\mathbb{Z}_+ \times C$. We must show that U is the rule for a function $h : \mathbb{Z}_+ \to C$.

That is, we must show that each element i of $\mathbb{Z}_+$ appears as the first coordinate of exactly one element of U. This is easy. The integer i lies in the domain of f_n if and only if $n > i$. Therefore, the set of elements of U of which i is the first coordinate is precisely the set of all pairs of the form $(i, f_n(i))$, for $n \geq i$. Now Lemma 8.2 tells us that $f_n(i) = f_m(i)$ if $n, m \geq i$. Therefore, all these elements of U are equal; that is, there is only one element of U that has i as its first coordinate.

To show that h satisfies (*) is also easy; it is a consequence of the following facts:

$$h(i) = f_n(i) \quad \text{for } i \leq n,$$

f_n satisfies (*) for all i in its domain.

The proof of uniqueness is a copy of the proof of Lemma 8.2.   ∎

Now we formulate the general principle of recursive definition. There are no new ideas involved in its proof, so we leave it as an exercise.

Theorem 8.4 (Principle of recursive definition).   *Let A be a set; let a_0 be an element of A. Suppose ρ is a function that assigns, to each function f mapping a nonempty section of the positive integers into A, an element of A. Then there exists a unique function*

$$h : \mathbb{Z}_+ \to A$$

such that

(*)
$$\begin{aligned} h(1) &= a_0, \\ h(i) &= \rho(h|\{1, \ldots, i-1\}) \quad \text{for } i > 1. \end{aligned}$$

The formula (*) is called a ***recursion formula*** for h. It specifies $h(1)$, and it expresses the value of h at $i > 1$ in terms of the values of h for positive integers less than i.

EXAMPLE 1.   Let us show that Theorem 8.3 is a special case of this theorem. Given the infinite subset C of $\mathbb{Z}_+$, let a_0 be the smallest element of C, and define ρ by the equation

$$\rho(f) = \text{smallest element of } [C - (\text{image set of } f)].$$

Because C is infinite and f is a function mapping a finite set into C, the image set of f is not all of C; therefore, ρ is well defined. By Theorem 8.4 there exists a function $h : \mathbb{Z}_+ \to C$ such that $h(1) = a_0$, and for $i > 1$,

$$h(i) = \rho(h|\{1, \ldots, i-1\})$$
$$= \text{smallest element of } [C - (\text{image set of } h|\{1, \ldots, i-1\})]$$
$$= \text{smallest element of } [C - h(\{1 \ldots, i-1\})],$$

as desired.

EXAMPLE 2.   Given $a \in \mathbb{R}$, we "defined" a^n, in the exercises of §4, by the recursion formula

$$a^1 = a,$$
$$a^n = a^{n-1} \cdot a.$$

We wish to apply Theorem 8.4 to define a function $h : \mathbb{Z}_+ \to \mathbb{R}$ rigorously such that $h(n) = a^n$. To apply this theorem, let a_0 denote the element a of $\mathbb{R}$, and define ρ by the equation $\rho(f) = f(m) \cdot a$, where $f : \{1, \ldots, m\} \to \mathbb{R}$. Then there exists a unique function $h : \mathbb{Z}_+ \to \mathbb{R}$ such that

$$h(1) = a_0,$$
$$h(i) = \rho(h|\{1, \ldots, i-1\}) \quad \text{for } i > 1.$$

This means that $h(1) = a$, and $h(i) = h(i-1) \cdot a$ for $i > 1$. If we denote $h(i)$ by a^i, we have

$$a^1 = a,$$
$$a^i = a^{i-1} \cdot a,$$

as desired.

Exercises

1. Let $(b_1, b_2, \ldots)$ be an infinite sequence of real numbers. The sum $\sum_{k=1}^{n} b_k$ is defined by induction as follows :

$$\sum_{k=1}^{n} b_k = b_1 \qquad\qquad \text{for } n = 1,$$

$$\sum_{k=1}^{n} b_k = (\sum_{k=1}^{n-1} b_k) + b_n \qquad \text{for } n > 1.$$

Let A be the set of real numbers; choose ρ so that Theorem 8.4 applies to define this sum rigorously. We sometimes denote the sum $\sum_{k=1}^{n} b_k$ by the symbol $b_1 + b_2 + \cdots + b_n$.

2. Let $(b_1, b_2, \ldots)$ be an infinite sequence of real numbers. We define the product $\prod_{k=1}^{n} b_k$ by the equations

$$\prod_{k=1}^{1} b_k = b_1,$$

$$\prod_{k=1}^{n} b_k = (\prod_{k=1}^{n-1} b_k) \cdot b_n \qquad \text{for } n > 1.$$

Use Theorem 8.4 to define this product rigorously. We sometimes denote the product $\prod_{k=1}^{n} b_k$ by the symbol $b_1 b_2 \cdots b_n$.

3. Obtain the definitions of a^n and $n!$ for $n \in \mathbb{Z}_+$ as special cases of Exercise 2.

4. The *Fibonacci numbers* of number theory are defined recursively by the formula

$$\lambda_1 = \lambda_2 = 1,$$
$$\lambda_n = \lambda_{n-1} + \lambda_{n-2} \qquad \text{for } n > 2.$$

Define them rigorously by use of Theorem 8.4.

5. Show that there is a unique function $h : \mathbb{Z}_+ \to \mathbb{R}_+$ satisfying the formula

$$h(1) = 3,$$
$$h(i) = [h(i-1)+1]^{1/2} \qquad \text{for } i > 1.$$

6. (a) Show that there is no function $h : \mathbb{Z}_+ \to \mathbb{R}_+$ satisfying the formula

$$h(1) = 3,$$
$$h(i) = [h(i-1)-1]^{1/2} \qquad \text{for } i > 1.$$

Explain why this example does not violate the principle of recursive definition.

(b) Consider the recursion formula

$$h(1) = 3,$$
$$h(i) = \begin{cases} [h(i-1)-1]^{1/2} & \text{if } h(i-1) > 1 \\ 5 & \text{if } h(i-1) \leq 1 \end{cases} \qquad \text{for } i > 1.$$

Show that there exists a unique function $h : \mathbb{Z}_+ \to \mathbb{R}_+$ satisfying this formula.

7. Prove Theorem 8.4.

8. Verify the following version of the principle of recursive definition: Let A be a set. Let ρ be a function assigning, to every function f mapping a section S_n of $\mathbb{Z}_+$ into A, an element $\rho(f)$ of A. Then there is a unique function $h : \mathbb{Z}_+ \to A$ such that $h(n) = \rho(h|S_n)$ for each $n \in \mathbb{Z}_+$.

§9   Infinite Sets and the Axiom of Choice

We have already obtained several criteria for a set to be infinite. We know, for instance, that a set A is infinite if it has a countably infinite subset, or if there is a bijection of A with a proper subset of itself. It turns out that either of these properties is sufficient to characterize infinite sets. This we shall now prove. The proof will lead us into a discussion of a point of logic we have not yet mentioned—the axiom of choice.

Theorem 9.1. *Let A be a set. The following statements about A are equivalent:*

(1) *There exists an injective function $f : \mathbb{Z}_+ \to A$.*

(2) *There exists a bijection of A with a proper subset of itself.*

(3) *A is infinite.*

Proof.   We prove the implications $(1) \Rightarrow (2) \Rightarrow (3) \Rightarrow (1)$. To prove that $(1) \Rightarrow (2)$, we assume there is an injective function $f : \mathbb{Z}_+ \to A$. Let the image set $f(\mathbb{Z}_+)$ be denoted by B; and let $f(n)$ be denoted by a_n. Because f is injective, $a_n \neq a_m$ if $n \neq m$. Define

$$g : A \longrightarrow A - \{a_1\}$$

by the equations

$$g(a_n) = a_{n+1} \qquad \text{for } a_n \in B,$$
$$g(x) = x \qquad \text{for } x \in A - B.$$

The map g is indicated schematically in Figure 9.1; one checks easily that it is a bijection.

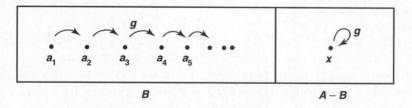

Figure 9.1

The implication $(2) \Rightarrow (3)$ is just the contrapositive of Corollary 6.3, so it has already been proved. To prove that $(3) \Rightarrow (1)$, we assume that A is infinite and construct "by induction" an injective function $f : \mathbb{Z}_+ \to A$.

First, since the set A is not empty, we can choose a point a_1 of A; define $f(1)$ to be the point so chosen.

Then, assuming that we have defined $f(1), \ldots, f(n-1)$, we wish to define $f(n)$. The set $A - f(\{1, \ldots, n-1\})$ is not empty; for if it were empty, the map $f : \{1, \ldots, n-1\} \to A$ would be a surjection and A would be finite. Hence, we can choose an element of the set $A - f(\{1, \ldots, n-1\})$ and define $f(n)$ to be this element. "Using the induction principle", we have defined f for all $n \in \mathbb{Z}_+$.

It is easy to see that f is injective. For suppose that $m < n$. Then $f(m)$ belongs to the set $f(\{1, \ldots, n-1\})$, whereas $f(n)$, by definition, does not. Therefore, $f(n) \neq f(m)$. ∎

Let us try to reformulate this "induction" proof more carefully, so as to make explicit our use of the principle of recursive definition.

Given the infinite set A, we attempt to define $f : \mathbb{Z}_+ \to A$ recursively by the formula

$$(*) \qquad \begin{aligned} f(1) &= a_1, \\ f(i) &= \text{an arbitrary element of } [A - f(\{1, \ldots, i-1\})] \qquad \text{for } i > 1. \end{aligned}$$

But this is not an acceptable recursion formula at all! For it does not define $f(i)$ *uniquely* in terms of $f|\{1, \ldots, i-1\}$.

In this respect this formula differs notably from the recursion formula we considered in proving Lemma 7.2. There we had an infinite subset C of $\mathbb{Z}_+$, and we defined h by the formula

$$\begin{aligned} h(1) &= \text{smallest element of } C, \\ h(i) &= \text{smallest element of } [C - h(\{1, \ldots, i-1\})] \qquad \text{for } i > 1. \end{aligned}$$

This formula does define $h(i)$ uniquely in terms of $h|\{1, \ldots, i-1\}$.

Another way of seeing that $(*)$ is not an acceptable recursion formula is to note that if it were, the principle of recursive definition would imply that there is a *unique* function $f : \mathbb{Z}_+ \to A$ satisfying $(*)$. But by no stretch of the imagination does $(*)$ specify f uniquely. In fact, this "definition" of f involves infinitely many arbitrary choices.

What we are saying is that the proof we have given for Theorem 9.1 is not actually a proof. Indeed, on the basis of the properties of set theory we have discussed up to now, it is not *possible* to prove this theorem. Something more is needed.

Previously, we described certain definite allowable methods for specifying sets:

(1) Defining a set by listing its elements, or by taking a given set A and specifying a subset B of it by giving a property that the elements of B are to satisfy.

(2) Taking unions or intersections of the elements of a given collection of sets, or taking the difference of two sets.

(3) Taking the set of all subsets of a given set.

(4) Taking cartesian products of sets.

Now the rule for the function f is really a set: a subset of $\mathbb{Z}_+ \times A$. Therefore, to prove the existence of the function f, we must construct the appropriate subset of $\mathbb{Z}_+ \times A$, using the allowed methods for forming sets. The methods already given simply are not adequate for this purpose. We need a new way of asserting the existence of a set. So, we add to the list of allowed methods of forming sets the following:

Axiom of choice.   *Given a collection $\mathcal{A}$ of disjoint nonempty sets, there exists a set C consisting of exactly one element from each element of $\mathcal{A}$; that is, a set C such that C is contained in the union of the elements of $\mathcal{A}$, and for each $A \in \mathcal{A}$, the set $C \cap A$ contains a single element.*

The set C can be thought of as having been obtained by choosing one element from each of the sets in $\mathcal{A}$.

The axiom of choice certainly seems an innocent-enough assertion. And, in fact, most mathematicians today accept it as part of the set theory on which they base their mathematics. But in years past a good deal of controversy raged around this particular assertion concerning set theory, for there are theorems one can prove with its aid that some mathematicians were reluctant to accept. One such is the well-ordering theorem, which we shall discuss shortly. For the present we shall simply use the choice axiom to clear up the difficulty we mentioned in the preceding proof. First, we prove an easy consequence of the axiom of choice:

Lemma 9.2 (Existence of a choice function).   *Given a collection $\mathcal{B}$ of nonempty sets (not necessarily disjoint), there exists a function*

$$c : \mathcal{B} \longrightarrow \bigcup_{B \in \mathcal{B}} B$$

such that $c(B)$ is an element of B, for each $B \in \mathcal{B}$.

The function c is called a ***choice function*** for the collection $\mathcal{B}$.

The difference between this lemma and the axiom of choice is that in this lemma the sets of the collection $\mathcal{B}$ are not required to be disjoint. For example, one can allow $\mathcal{B}$ to be the collection of *all* nonempty subsets of a given set.

Proof of the lemma.   Given an element B of $\mathcal{B}$, we define a set B' as follows:

$$B' = \{(B, x) \mid x \in B\}.$$

That is, B' is the collection of all ordered pairs, where the first coordinate of the ordered pair is the set B, and the second coordinate is an element of B. The set B' is a subset of the cartesian product

$$\mathcal{B} \times \bigcup_{B \in \mathcal{B}} B.$$

Because B contains at least one element x, the set B' contains at least the element (B, x), so it is nonempty.

Now we claim that if B_1 and B_2 are two different sets in $\mathcal{B}$, then the corresponding sets B_1' and B_2' are disjoint. For the typical element of B_1' is a pair of the form (B_1, x_1) and the typical element of B_2' is a pair of the form (B_2, x_2). No two such elements can be equal, for their first coordinates are different. Now let us form the collection

$$\mathcal{C} = \{B' \mid B \in \mathcal{B}\};$$

it is a collection of disjoint nonempty subsets of

$$\mathcal{B} \times \bigcup_{B \in \mathcal{B}} B.$$

By the choice axiom, there exists a set c consisting of exactly one element from each element of $\mathcal{C}$. Our claim is that c *is* the rule for the desired choice function.

In the first place, c is a subset of

$$\mathcal{B} \times \bigcup_{B \in \mathcal{B}} B.$$

In the second place, c contains exactly one element from each set B'; therefore, for each $B \in \mathcal{B}$, the set c contains exactly one ordered pair (B, x) whose first coordinate is B. Thus c is indeed the rule for a function from the collection $\mathcal{B}$ to the set $\bigcup_{B \in \mathcal{B}} B$. Finally, if $(B, x) \in c$, then x belongs to B, so that $c(B) \in B$, as desired.   ∎

A second proof of Theorem 9.1.   Using this lemma, one can make the proof of Theorem 9.1 more precise. Given the infinite set A, we wish to construct an injective function $f : \mathbb{Z}_+ \to A$. Let us form the collection $\mathcal{B}$ of all nonempty subsets of A. The lemma just proved asserts the existence of a choice function for $\mathcal{B}$; that is, a function

$$c : \mathcal{B} \longrightarrow \bigcup_{B \in \mathcal{B}} B = A$$

such that $c(B) \in B$ for each $B \in \mathcal{B}$. Let us now define a function $f : \mathbb{Z}_+ \to A$ by the recursion formula

$$(*) \qquad \begin{aligned} f(1) &= c(A), \\ f(i) &= c(A - f(\{1, \ldots, i-1\})) \quad \text{for } i > 1. \end{aligned}$$

Because A is infinite, the set $A - f(\{1, \ldots, i-1\})$ is nonempty; therefore, the right side of this equation makes sense. Since this formula defines $f(i)$ uniquely in terms of $f|\{1, \ldots, i-1\}$, the principle of recursive definition applies. We conclude that there exists a unique function $f : \mathbb{Z}_+ \to A$ satisfying $(*)$ for all $i \in \mathbb{Z}_+$. Injectivity of f follows as before.   ∎

Having emphasized that in order to construct a proof of Theorem 9.1 that is logically correct, one must make specific use of a choice function, we now backtrack and admit that in practice most mathematicians do no such thing. They go on with no qualms giving proofs like our first version, proofs that involve an infinite number of arbitrary choices. They know that they are really using the choice axiom; and they know that if it were necessary, they could put their proofs into a logically more satisfactory form by introducing a choice function specifically. But usually they do not bother.

And neither will we. You will find few further specific uses of a choice function in this book; we shall introduce a choice function only when the proof would become confusing without it. But there will be many proofs in which we make an infinite number of arbitrary choices, and in each such case we will actually be using the choice axiom implicitly.

Now we must confess that in an earlier section of this book there is a proof in which we constructed a certain function by making an infinite number of arbitrary choices. And we slipped that proof in without even mentioning the choice axiom. Our apologies for the deception. We leave it to you to ferret out which proof it was!

Let us make one final comment on the choice axiom. There are two forms of this axiom. One can be called the ***finite axiom of choice***; it asserts that given a *finite* collection $\mathcal{A}$ of disjoint nonempty sets, there exists a set C consisting of exactly one element from each element of $\mathcal{A}$. One needs this weak form of the choice axiom all the time; we have used it freely in the preceding sections with no comment. No mathematician has any qualms about the finite choice axiom; it is part of everyone's set theory. Said differently, no one has qualms about a proof that involves only finitely many arbitrary choices.

The stronger form of the axiom of choice, the one that applies to an *arbitrary* collection $\mathcal{A}$ of nonempty sets, is the one that is properly called "the axiom of choice." When a mathematician writes, "This proof depends on the choice axiom," it is invariably this stronger form of the axiom that is meant.

Exercises

1. Define an injective map $f : \mathbb{Z}_+ \to X^\omega$, where X is the two-element set $\{0, 1\}$, without using the choice axiom.

2. Find if possible a choice function for each of the following collections, without using the choice axiom:
   (a) The collection $\mathcal{A}$ of nonempty subsets of $\mathbb{Z}_+$.
   (b) The collection $\mathcal{B}$ of nonempty subsets of $\mathbb{Z}$.
   (c) The collection $\mathcal{C}$ of nonempty subsets of the rational numbers $\mathbb{Q}$.
   (d) The collection $\mathcal{D}$ of nonempty subsets of X^ω, where $X = \{0, 1\}$.

3. Suppose that A is a set and $\{f_n\}_{n \in \mathbb{Z}_+}$ is a given indexed family of injective functions

$$f_n : \{1, \ldots, n\} \longrightarrow A.$$

   Show that A is infinite. Can you define an injective function $f : \mathbb{Z}_+ \to A$ without using the choice axiom?

4. There was a theorem in §7 whose proof involved an infinite number of arbitrary choices. Which one was it? Rewrite the proof so as to make explicit the use of the choice axiom. (Several of the earlier exercises have used the choice axiom also.)

5. (a) Use the choice axiom to show that if $f : A \to B$ is surjective, then f has a right inverse $h : B \to A$.

   (b) Show that if $f : A \to B$ is injective and A is not empty, then f has a left inverse. Is the axiom of choice needed?

6. Most of the famous paradoxes of naive set theory are associated in some way or other with the concept of the "set of all sets." None of the rules we have given for forming sets allows us to consider such a set. And for good reason—the concept itself is self-contradictory. For suppose that $\mathscr{A}$ denotes the "set of all sets."

   (a) Show that $\mathscr{P}(\mathscr{A}) \subset \mathscr{A}$; derive a contradiction.

   (b) (*Russell's paradox.*) Let $\mathscr{B}$ be the subset of $\mathscr{A}$ consisting of all sets that are not elements of themselves;

$$\mathscr{B} = \{A \mid A \in \mathscr{A} \text{ and } A \notin A\}.$$

   (Of course, there may be *no* set A such that $A \in A$; if such is the case, then $\mathscr{B} = \mathscr{A}$.) Is $\mathscr{B}$ an element of itself or not?

7. Let A and B be two nonempty sets. If there is an injection of B into A, but no injection of A into B, we say that A has **greater cardinality** than B.

   (a) Conclude from Theorem 9.1 that every uncountable set has greater cardinality than $\mathbb{Z}_+$.

   (b) Show that if A has greater cardinality than B, and B has greater cardinality than C, then A has greater cardinality than C.

   (c) Find a sequence $A_1, A_2, \ldots$ of infinite sets, such that for each $n \in \mathbb{Z}_+$, the set A_{n+1} has greater cardinality than A_n.

   (d) Find a set that for every n has cardinality greater than A_n.

*8. Show that $\mathscr{P}(\mathbb{Z}_+)$ and $\mathbb{R}$ have the same cardinality. [*Hint:* You may use the fact that every real number has a decimal expansion, which is unique if expansions that end in an infinite string of 9's are forbidden.]

A famous conjecture of set theory, called the *continuum hypothesis*, asserts that there exists no set having greater cardinality than $\mathbb{Z}_+$ and lesser cardinality than $\mathbb{R}$. The *generalized continuum hypothesis* asserts that, given the infinite set A, there is no set having greater cardinality than A and lesser cardinality than $\mathscr{P}(A)$. Surprisingly enough, both of these assertions have been shown to be independent of the usual axioms for set theory. For a readable expository account, see [Sm].

§10   Well-Ordered Sets

One of the useful properties of the set $\mathbb{Z}_+$ of positive integers is the fact that each of its nonempty subsets has a smallest element. Generalizing this property leads to the concept of a well-ordered set.

Definition.   A set A with an order relation $<$ is said to be **well-ordered** if every nonempty subset of A has a smallest element.

EXAMPLE 1.   Consider the set $\{1, 2\} \times \mathbb{Z}_+$ in the dictionary ordering. Schematically, it can be represented as one infinite sequence followed by another infinite sequence:

$$a_1, a_2, a_3, \ldots; \; b_1, b_2, b_3, \ldots$$

with the understanding that each element is less than every element to the right of it. It is not difficult to see that every nonempty subset C of this ordered set has a smallest element: If C contains any one of the elements a_n, we simply take the smallest element of the intersection of C with the sequence $a_1, a_2, \ldots$; while if C contains no a_n, then it is a subset of the sequence $b_1, b_2, \ldots$ and as such has a smallest element.

EXAMPLE 2.   Consider the set $\mathbb{Z}_+ \times \mathbb{Z}_+$ in the dictionary order. Schematically, it can be represented as an infinite sequence of infinite sequences. We show that it is well-ordered. Let X be a nonempty subset of $\mathbb{Z}_+ \times \mathbb{Z}_+$. Let A be the subset of $\mathbb{Z}_+$ consisting of all *first coordinates* of elements of X. Now A has a smallest element; call it a_0. Then the collection

$$\{b \mid a_0 \times b \in X\}$$

is a nonempty subset of $\mathbb{Z}_+$; let b_0 be its smallest element. By definition of the dictionary order, $a_0 \times b_0$ is the smallest element of X. See Figure 10.1.

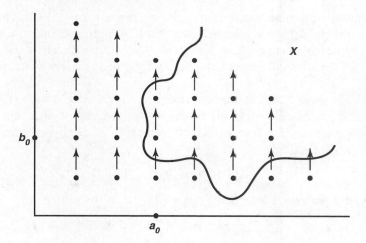

Figure 10.1

EXAMPLE 3.   The set of integers is not well-ordered in the usual order; the subset consisting of the negative integers has no smallest element. Nor is the set of real numbers in the interval $0 \leq x \leq 1$ well-ordered; the subset consisting of those x for which $0 < x < 1$ has no smallest element (although it has a greatest lower bound, of course).

There are several ways of constructing well-ordered sets. Two of them are the following:

(1) If A is a well-ordered set, then any subset of A is well-ordered in the restricted order relation.

(2) If A and B are well-ordered sets, then $A \times B$ is well-ordered in the dictionary order.

The proof of (1) is trivial; the proof of (2) follows the pattern given in Example 2.

It follows that the set $\mathbb{Z}_+ \times (\mathbb{Z}_+ \times \mathbb{Z}_+)$ is well-ordered in the dictionary order; it can be represented as an infinite sequence of infinite sequences of infinite sequences. Similarly, $(\mathbb{Z}_+)^4$ is well-ordered in the dictionary order. And so on. But if you try to generalize to an infinite product of $\mathbb{Z}_+$ with itself, you will run into trouble. We shall examine this situation shortly.

Now, given a set A without an order relation, it is natural to ask whether there exists an order relation for A that makes it into a well-ordered set. If A is finite, any bijection

$$f : A \longrightarrow \{1, \ldots, n\}$$

can be used to define an order relation on A; under this relation, A has the same order type as the ordered set $\{1, \ldots, n\}$. In fact, every order relation on a finite set can be obtained in this way:

Theorem 10.1. *Every nonempty finite ordered set has the order type of a section* $\{1, \ldots, n\}$ *of* $\mathbb{Z}_+$, *so it is well-ordered.*

Proof. This was given as an exercise in §6; we prove it here. First, we show that every finite ordered set A has a largest element. If A has one element, this is trivial. Supposing it true for sets having $n-1$ elements, let A have n elements and let $a_0 \in A$. Then $A - \{a_0\}$ has a largest element a_1, and the larger of $\{a_0, a_1\}$ is the largest element of A.

Second, we show there is an order-preserving bijection of A with $\{1, \ldots, n\}$ for some n. If A has one element, this fact is trivial. Suppose that it is true for sets having $n-1$ elements. Let b be the largest element of A. By hypothesis, there is an order-preserving bijection

$$f' : A - \{b\} \longrightarrow \{1, \ldots, n-1\}.$$

Define an order-preserving bijection $f : A \to \{1, \ldots, n\}$ by setting

$$f(x) = f'(x) \qquad \text{for } x \neq b,$$
$$f(b) = n. \qquad\qquad\qquad\quad \blacksquare$$

Thus, a finite ordered set has only one possible order type. For an infinite set, things are quite different. The well-ordered sets

$$\mathbb{Z}_+,$$
$$\{1, \ldots, n\} \times \mathbb{Z}_+,$$
$$\mathbb{Z}_+ \times \mathbb{Z}_+,$$
$$\mathbb{Z}_+ \times (\mathbb{Z}_+ \times \mathbb{Z}_+)$$

are all countably infinite, but they all have different order types, as you can check.

All the examples we have given of well-ordered sets are orderings of countable sets. It is natural to ask whether one can find a well-ordered uncountable set.

The obvious uncountable set to try is the countably infinite product

$$X = \mathbb{Z}_+ \times \mathbb{Z}_+ \times \cdots = (\mathbb{Z}_+)^\omega$$

of $\mathbb{Z}_+$ with itself. One can generalize the dictionary order to this set in a natural way, by defining

$$(a_1, a_2, \ldots) < (b_1, b_2, \ldots)$$

if for some $n \geq 1$,

$$a_i = b_i, \quad \text{for } i < n \text{ and } a_n < b_n.$$

This is, in fact, an order relation on the set X; but unfortunately it is not a well-ordering. Consider the set A of all elements $\mathbf{x}$ of X of the form

$$\mathbf{x} = (1, \ldots, 1, 2, 1, 1, \ldots),$$

where exactly one coordinate of $\mathbf{x}$ equals 2, and the others are all equal to 1. The set A clearly has no smallest element.

Thus, the dictionary order at least does not give a well-ordering of the set $(\mathbb{Z}_+)^\omega$. Is there some other order relation on this set that is a well-ordering? No one has ever constructed a specific well-ordering of $(\mathbb{Z}_+)^\omega$. Nevertheless, there is a famous theorem that says such a well-ordering exists:

Theorem (Well-ordering theorem).   *If A is a set, there exists an order relation on A that is a well-ordering.*

This theorem was proved by Zermelo in 1904, and it startled the mathematical world. There was considerable debate as to the correctness of the proof; the lack of any constructive procedure for well-ordering an arbitrary uncountable set led many to be skeptical. When the proof was analyzed closely, the only point at which it was found that there might be some question was a construction involving an infinite number of arbitrary choices, that is, a construction involving—the choice axiom.

Some mathematicians rejected the choice axiom as a result, and for many years a legitimate question about a new theorem was: Does its proof involve the choice axiom or not? A theorem was considered to be on somewhat shaky ground if one had to use the choice axiom in its proof. Present-day mathematicians, by and large, do not have such qualms. They accept the axiom of choice as a reasonable assumption about set theory, and they accept the well-ordering theorem along with it.

The proof that the choice axiom implies the well-ordering theorem is rather long (although not exceedingly difficult) and primarily of interest to logicians; we shall omit it. If you are interested, a proof is outlined in the supplementary exercises at the end of the chapter. Instead, we shall simply assume the well-ordering theorem whenever we need it. Consider it to be an additional axiom of set theory if you like!

We shall in fact need the full strength of this assumption only occasionally. Most of the time, all we need is the following weaker result:

Corollary.   *There exists an uncountable well-ordered set.*

We now use this result to construct a particular well-ordered set that will prove to be very useful.

Definition.   Let X be a well-ordered set. Given $\alpha \in X$, let S_α denote the set

$$S_\alpha = \{x \mid x \in X \text{ and } x < \alpha\}.$$

It is called the **section** of X by α.

Lemma 10.2.   *There exists a well-ordered set A having a largest element Ω, such that the section S_Ω of A by Ω is uncountable but every other section of A is countable.*

Proof.   We begin with an uncountable well-ordered set B. Let C be the well-ordered set $\{1, 2\} \times B$ in the dictionary order; then some section of C is uncountable. (Indeed, the section of C by any element of the form $2 \times b$ is uncountable.) Let Ω be the smallest element of C for which the section of C by Ω is uncountable. Then let A consist of this section along with the element Ω. ∎

Note that S_Ω is an uncountable well-ordered set every section of which is countable. Its order type is in fact uniquely determined by this condition. We shall call it a *minimal uncountable well-ordered set*. Furthermore, we shall denote the well-ordered set $A = S_\Omega \cup \{\Omega\}$ by the symbol $\bar{S}_\Omega$ (for reasons to be seen later).

The most useful property of the set S_Ω for our purposes is expressed in the following theorem:

Theorem 10.3.   *If A is a countable subset of S_Ω, then A has an upper bound in S_Ω.*

Proof.   Let A be a countable subset of S_Ω. For each $a \in A$, the section S_a is countable. Therefore, the union $B = \bigcup_{a \in A} S_a$ is also countable. Since S_Ω is uncountable, the set B is not all of S_Ω; let x be a point of S_Ω that is not in B. Then x is an upper bound for A. For if $x < a$ for some a in A, then x belongs to S_a and hence to B, contrary to choice. ∎

Exercises

1. Show that every well-ordered set has the least upper bound property.

2. (a) Show that in a well-ordered set, every element except the largest (if one exists) has an immediate successor.
   (b) Find a set in which every element has an immediate successor that is not well-ordered.

3. Both $\{1, 2\} \times \mathbb{Z}_+$ and $\mathbb{Z}_+ \times \{1, 2\}$ are well-ordered in the dictionary order. Do they have the same order type?

4. (a) Let $\mathbb{Z}_-$ denote the set of negative integers in the usual order. Show that a simply ordered set A fails to be well-ordered if and only if it contains a subset having the same order type as $\mathbb{Z}_-$.
   (b) Show that if A is simply ordered and every countable subset of A is well-ordered, then A is well-ordered.

5. Show the well-ordering theorem implies the choice axiom.

6. Let S_Ω be the minimal uncountable well-ordered set.
   (a) Show that S_Ω has no largest element.
   (b) Show that for every $\alpha \in S_\Omega$, the subset $\{x \mid \alpha < x\}$ is uncountable.
   (c) Let X_0 be the subset of S_Ω consisting of all elements x such that x has no immediate predecessor. Show that X_0 is uncountable.

7. Let J be a well-ordered set. A subset J_0 of J is said to be *inductive* if for every $\alpha \in J$,

$$(S_\alpha \subset J_0) \Longrightarrow \alpha \in J_0.$$

Theorem (The principle of transfinite induction).   *If J is a well-ordered set and J_0 is an inductive subset of J, then $J_0 = J$.*

8. (a) Let A_1 and A_2 be disjoint sets, well-ordered by $<_1$ and $<_2$, respectively. Define an order relation on $A_1 \cup A_2$ by letting $a < b$ either if $a, b \in A_1$ and $a <_1 b$, or if $a, b \in A_2$ and $a <_2 b$, or if $a \in A_1$ and $b \in A_2$. Show that this is a well-ordering.
   (b) Generalize (a) to an arbitrary family of disjoint well-ordered sets, indexed by a well-ordered set.

9. Consider the subset A of $(\mathbb{Z}_+)^\omega$ consisting of all infinite sequences of positive integers $\mathbf{x} = (x_1, x_2, \dots)$ that end in an infinite string of 1's. Give A the following order: $\mathbf{x} < \mathbf{y}$ if $x_n < y_n$ and $x_i = y_i$ for $i > n$. We call this the "antidictionary order" on A.
   (a) Show that for every n, there is a section of A that has the same order type as $(\mathbb{Z}_+)^n$ in the dictionary order.
   (b) Show A is well-ordered.

10. *Theorem.*   *Let J and C be well-ordered sets; assume that there is no surjective function mapping a section of J onto C. Then there exists a unique function $h : J \to C$ satisfying the equation*

(∗) $h(x) = \text{smallest} [C - h(S_x)]$

for each $x \in J$, where S_x is the section of J by x.

   Proof.

(a) If h and k map sections of J, or all of J, into C and satisfy (∗) for all x in their respective domains, show that $h(x) = k(x)$ for all x in both domains.

(b) If there exists a function $h : S_\alpha \to C$ satisfying (∗), show that there exists a function $k : S_\alpha \cup \{\alpha\} \to C$ satisfying (∗).

(c) If $K \subset J$ and for all $\alpha \in K$ there exists a function $h_\alpha : S_\alpha \to C$ satisfying (∗), show that there exists a function

$$k : \bigcup_{\alpha \in K} S_\alpha \longrightarrow C$$

satisfying (∗).

(d) Show by transfinite induction that for every $\beta \in J$, there exists a function $h_\beta : S_\beta \to C$ satisfying (∗). [*Hint:* If β has an immediate predecessor α, then $S_\beta = S_\alpha \cup \{\alpha\}$. If not, S_β is the union of all S_α with $\alpha < \beta$.]

(e) Prove the theorem.

11. Let A and B be two sets. Using the well-ordering theorem, prove that either they have the same cardinality, or one has cardinality greater than the other. [*Hint:* If there is no surjection $f : A \to B$, apply the preceding exercise.]

*§11   The Maximum Principle[†]

We have already indicated that the axiom of choice leads to the deep theorem that every set can be well-ordered. The axiom of choice has other consequences that are even more important in mathematics. Collectively referred to as "maximum principles," they come in many versions. Formulated independently by a number of mathematicians, including F. Hausdorff, K. Kuratowski, S. Bochner, and M. Zorn, during the years 1914–1935, they were typically proved as consequences of the well-ordering theorem. Later, it was realized that they were in fact *equivalent* to the well-ordering theorem. We consider several of them here.

First, we make a definition. Given a set A, a relation $\prec$ on A is called a **strict partial order** on A if it has the following two properties:

(1) (Nonreflexivity) The relation $a \prec a$ never holds.

(2) (Transitivity) If $a \prec b$ and $b \prec c$, then $a \prec c$.

These are just the second and third of the properties of a simple order (see §3); the comparability property is the one that is omitted. In other words, a strict partial order behaves just like a simple order except that it need not be true that for every pair of distinct points x and y in the set, either $x \prec y$ or $y \prec x$.

If $\prec$ is a strict partial order on a set A, it can easily happen that some subset B of A is simply ordered by the relation; all that is needed is for every pair of elements of B to be comparable under $\prec$.

[†]This section will be assumed in Chapter 5.

Now we can state the following principle, which was first formulated by Hausdorff in 1914.

Theorem (The maximum principle).   *Let A be a set; let $\prec$ be a strict partial order on A. Then there exists a maximal simply ordered subset B of A.*

Said differently, there exists a subset B of A such that B is simply ordered by $\prec$ and such that no subset of A that properly contains B is simply ordered by $\prec$.

EXAMPLE 1.   If $\mathcal{A}$ is any collection of sets, the relation "is a proper subset of" is a strict partial order on $\mathcal{A}$. Suppose that $\mathcal{A}$ is the collection of all circular regions (interiors of circles) in the plane. One maximal simply ordered subcollection of $\mathcal{A}$ consists of all circular regions with centers at the origin. Another maximal simply ordered subcollection consists of all circular regions bounded by circles tangent from the right to the y-axis at the origin. See Figure 11.1.

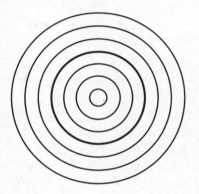 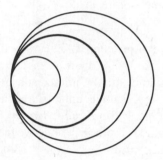

Figure 11.1

EXAMPLE 2.   If (x_0, y_0) and (x_1, y_1) are two points of the plane $\mathbb{R}^2$, define

$$(x_0, y_0) \prec (x_1, y_1)$$

if $y_0 = y_1$ and $x_0 < x_1$. This is a partial ordering of $\mathbb{R}^2$ under which two points are comparable only if they lie on the same horizontal line. The maximal simply ordered sets are the horizontal lines in $\mathbb{R}^2$.

One can give an intuitive "proof" of the maximum principle that is rather appealing. It involves a step-by-step procedure, which one can describe in physical terms as follows. Suppose we take a box, and put into it some of the elements of A according to the following plan: First we pick an arbitrary element of A and put it in the box. Then we pick another element of A. If it is comparable with the element in the box, we put it in the box too; otherwise, we throw it away. At the general step, we will have a collection of elements in the box and a collection of elements that have been tossed away. Take one of the remaining elements of A. If it is comparable with everything in the box, toss it in the box, too; otherwise, throw it away. Similarly continue. After you have checked all the elements of A, the elements you have in the box will be comparable with one another, and thus they will form a simply ordered set. Every element not in the box will be noncomparable with at least one element in the box, for that was why it was tossed away. Hence, the simply ordered set in the box is maximal, for no larger subset of A can satisfy the comparability condition.

Now of course the weak point in the preceding "proof" comes when we said, "After you have checked all the elements of A." How do you know you ever "get through" checking all the elements of A? If A should happen to be countable, it is not hard to make this intuitive proof into a real proof. Let us take the countably infinite case; the finite case is even easier. Index the elements of A bijectively with the positive integers, so that $A = \{a_1, a_2 \ldots\}$. This indexing gives a way of deciding what order to test the elements of A in, and how to know when one has tested them all.

Now we define a function $h : \mathbb{Z}_+ \to \{0, 1\}$, by letting it assign the value 0 to i if we "put a_i in the box," and the value 1 if we "throw a_i away." This means that $h(1) = 0$, and for $i > 1$, we have $h(i) = 0$ if and only if a_i is comparable with every element of the set

$$\{a_j \mid j < i \text{ and } h(j) = 0\}.$$

By the principle of recursive definition, this formula determines a unique function $h : \mathbb{Z}_+ \to \{0, 1\}$. It is easy to check that the set of those a_j for which $h(j) = 0$ is a maximal simply ordered subset of A.

If A is not countable, a variant of this procedure will work, *if we allow ourselves to use the well-ordering theorem.* Instead of indexing the elements of A with the set $\mathbb{Z}_+$, we index them (in a bijective fashion) with the elements of some well-ordered set J, so that $A = \{a_\alpha \mid \alpha \in J\}$. For this we need the well-ordering theorem, so that we know there is a bijection between A and some well-ordered set J. Then we can proceed as in the previous paragraph, letting α replace i in the argument. Strictly speaking, you need to generalize the principle of recursive definition to well-ordered sets as well, but that is not particularly difficult. (See the Supplementary Exercises.)

Thus, the well-ordering theorem implies the maximum principle.

Although the maximum principle of Hausdorff was the first to be formulated and is probably the simplest to understand, there is another such principle that is nowadays the one most frequently quoted. It is popularly called "Zorn's Lemma," although Kuratowski (1922) and Bochner (1922) preceded Zorn (1935) in enunciating and proving versions of it. For a history and discussion of the tangled history of these ideas, see [C] or [Mo]. To state this principle, we need some terminology.

Definition.   Let A be a set and let $\prec$ be a strict partial order on A. If B is a subset of A, an **upper bound** on B is an element c of A such that for every b in B, either $b = c$ or $b \prec c$. A **maximal element** of A is an element m of A such that for no element a of A does the relation $m \prec a$ hold.

Zorn's Lemma.   *Let A be a set that is strictly partially ordered. If every simply ordered subset of A has an upper bound in A, then A has a maximal element.*

Zorn's lemma is an easy consequence of the maximum principle: Given A, the maximum principle implies that A has a maximal simply ordered subset B. The hypothesis of Zorn's lemma tells us that B has an upper bound c in A. The element c is then automatically a maximal element of A. For if $c \prec d$ for some element d of A, then the set $B \cup \{d\}$, which properly contains B, is simply ordered because $b \prec d$ for every $b \in B$. This fact contradicts maximality of B.

It is also true that the maximum principle is an easy consequence of Zorn's lemma. See Exercises 5–7.

One final remark. We have defined what we mean by a strict partial order on a set, but we have not said what a partial order itself is. Let $\prec$ be a strict partial order on a set A. Suppose that we define $a \preceq b$ if either $a \prec b$ or $a = b$. Then the relation $\preceq$ is called a ***partial order*** on A. For example, the inclusion relation $\subset$ on a collection of sets is a partial order, whereas proper inclusion is a strict partial order.

Many authors prefer to deal with partial orderings rather than strict partial orderings; the maximum principle and Zorn's lemma are often expressed in these terms. Which formulation is used is simply a matter of taste and convenience.

Exercises

1. If a and b are real numbers, define $a \prec b$ if $b - a$ is positive and rational. Show this is a strict partial order on $\mathbb{R}$. What are the maximal simply ordered subsets?

2. (a) Let $\prec$ be a strict partial order on the set A. Define a relation on A by letting $a \preceq b$ if either $a \prec b$ or $a = b$. Show that this relation has the following properties, which are called the ***partial order axioms***:
   (i) $a \preceq a$ for all $a \in A$.
   (ii) $a \preceq b$ and $b \preceq a \Longrightarrow a = b$.
   (iii) $a \preceq b$ and $b \preceq c \Longrightarrow a \preceq c$.
   (b) Let P be a relation on A that satisfies properties (i)–(iii). Define a relation S on A by letting aSb if aPb and $a \neq b$. Show that S is a strict partial order on A.

3. Let A be a set with a strict partial order $\prec$; let $x \in A$. Suppose that we wish to find a maximal simply ordered subset B of A that contains x. One plausible way of attempting to define B is to let B equal the set of all those elements of A that are *comparable* with x;

$$B = \{y \mid y \in A \text{ and either } x \prec y \text{ or } y \prec x\}.$$

But this will not always work. In which of Examples 1 and 2 will this procedure succeed and in which will it not?

4. Given two points (x_0, y_0) and (x_1, y_1) of $\mathbb{R}^2$, define

$$(x_0, y_0) \prec (x_1, y_1)$$

if $x_0 < x_1$ and $y_0 \leq y_1$. Show that the curves $y = x^3$ and $y = 2$ are maximal simply ordered subsets of $\mathbb{R}^2$, and the curve $y = x^2$ is not. Find all maximal simply ordered subsets.

5. Show that Zorn's lemma implies the following:

   Lemma (Kuratowski). Let $\mathcal{A}$ be a collection of sets. Suppose that for every subcollection $\mathcal{B}$ of $\mathcal{A}$ that is simply ordered by proper inclusion, the union of the elements of $\mathcal{B}$ belongs to $\mathcal{A}$. Then $\mathcal{A}$ has an element that is properly contained in no other element of $\mathcal{A}$.

6. A collection $\mathcal{A}$ of subsets of a set X is said to be of *finite type* provided that a subset B of X belongs to $\mathcal{A}$ if and only if every finite subset of B belongs to $\mathcal{A}$. Show that the Kuratowski lemma implies the following:

   Lemma (Tukey, 1940). Let $\mathcal{A}$ be a collection of sets. If $\mathcal{A}$ is of finite type, then $\mathcal{A}$ has an element that is properly contained in no other element of $\mathcal{A}$.

7. Show that the Tukey lemma implies the Hausdorff maximum principle. [*Hint:* If $\prec$ is a strict partial order on A, let $\mathcal{A}$ be the collection of all subsets of A that are simply ordered by $\prec$. Show that $\mathcal{A}$ is of finite type.]

8. A typical use of Zorn's lemma in algebra is the proof that every vector space has a basis. Recall that if A is a subset of the vector space V, we say a vector belongs to the *span* of A if it equals a finite linear combination of elements of A. The set A is *independent* if the only finite linear combination of elements of A that equals the zero vector is the trivial one having all coefficients zero. If A is independent and if every vector in V belongs to the span of A, then A is a *basis* for V.

   (a) If A is independent and $v \in V$ does not belong to the span of A, show $A \cup \{v\}$ is independent.

   (b) Show the collection of all independent sets in V has a maximal element.

   (c) Show that V has a basis.

*Supplementary Exercises: Well-Ordering

In the following exercises, we ask you to prove the equivalence of the choice axiom, the well-ordering theorem, and the maximum principle. We comment that of these exercises, only Exercise 7 uses the choice axiom.

1. *Theorem (General principle of recursive definition). Let J be a well-ordered set; let C be a set. Let $\mathcal{F}$ be the set of all functions mapping sections of J into C. Given a function $\rho : \mathcal{F} \to C$, there exists a unique function $h : J \to C$ such that $h(\alpha) = \rho(h|S_\alpha)$ for each $\alpha \in J$.*

   [*Hint:* Follow the pattern outlined in Exercise 10 of §10.]

2. (a) Let J and E be well-ordered sets; let $h : J \to E$. Show the following two statements are equivalent:

   (i) h is order preserving and its image is E or a section of E.

(ii) $h(\alpha) = $ smallest $[E - h(S_\alpha)]$ for all α.

[*Hint:* Show that each of these conditions implies that $h(S_\alpha)$ is a section of E; conclude that it must be the section by $h(\alpha)$.]

(b) If E is a well-ordered set, show that no section of E has the order type of E, nor do two different sections of E have the same order type. [*Hint:* Given J, there is at most one order-preserving map of J into E whose image is E or a section of E.]

3. Let J and E be well-ordered sets; suppose there is an order-preserving map $k : J \to E$. Using Exercises 1 and 2, show that J has the order type of E or a section of E. [*Hint:* Choose $e_0 \in E$. Define $h : J \to E$ by the recursion formula

$$h(\alpha) = \text{smallest } [E - h(S_\alpha)] \quad \text{if} \quad h(S_\alpha) \neq E,$$

and $h(\alpha) = e_0$ otherwise. Show that $h(\alpha) \leq k(\alpha)$ for all α; conclude that $h(S_\alpha) \neq E$ for all α.]

4. Use Exercises 1–3 to prove the following:

(a) If A and B are well-ordered sets, then exactly one of the following three conditions holds: A and B have the same order type, or A has the order type of a section of B, or B has the order type of a section of A. [*Hint:* Form a well-ordered set containing both A and B, as in Exercise 8 of §10; then apply the preceding exercise.]

(b) Suppose that A and B are well-ordered sets that are uncountable, such that every section of A and of B is countable. Show A and B have the same order type.

5. Let X be a set; let $\mathcal{A}$ be the collection of all pairs $(A, <)$, where A is a subset of X and $<$ is a well-ordering of A. Define

$$(A, <) \prec (A', <')$$

if $(A, <)$ *equals* a section of $(A', <')$.

(a) Show that $\prec$ is a strict partial order on $\mathcal{A}$.

(b) Let $\mathcal{B}$ be a subcollection of $\mathcal{A}$ that is simply ordered by $\prec$. Define B' to be the union of the sets B, for all $(B, <) \in \mathcal{B}$; and define $<'$ to be the union of the relations $<$, for all $(B, <) \in \mathcal{B}$. Show that $(B', <')$ is a well-ordered set.

6. Use Exercises 1 and 5 to prove the following:

Theorem. The maximum principle is equivalent to the well-ordering theorem.

7. Use Exercises 1–5 to prove the following:

Theorem. The choice axiom is equivalent to the well-ordering theorem.

Proof. Let X be a set; let c be a fixed choice function for the nonempty subsets of X. If T is a subset of X and $<$ is a relation on T, we say that $(T, <)$ is a ***tower*** in X if $<$ is a well-ordering of T and if for each $x \in T$,

$$x = c(X - S_x(T)),$$

where $S_x(T)$ is the section of T by x.

(a) Let $(T_1, <_1)$ and $(T_2, <_2)$ be two towers in X. Show that either these two ordered sets are the same, or one equals a section of the other. [*Hint:* Switching indices if necessary, we can assume that $h : T_1 \to T_2$ is order preserving and $h(T_1)$ equals either T_2 or a section of T_2. Use Exercise 2 to show that $h(x) = x$ for all x.]

(b) If $(T, <)$ is a tower in X and $T \neq X$, show there is a tower in X of which $(T, <)$ is a section.

(c) Let $\{(T_k, <_k) | k \in K\}$ be the collection of all towers in X. Let

$$T = \bigcup_{k \in K} T_k \quad \text{and} \quad < = \bigcup_{k \in K} (<_k).$$

Show that $(T, <)$ is a tower in X. Conclude that $T = X$.

8. Using Exercises 1–4, construct an uncountable well-ordered set, as follows. Let $\mathcal{A}$ be the collection of all pairs $(A, <)$, where A is a subset of $\mathbb{Z}_+$ and $<$ is a well-ordering of A. (We allow A to be empty.) Define $(A, <) \sim (A', <')$ if $(A, <)$ and $(A', <')$ have the same order type. It is trivial to show this is an equivalence relation. Let $[(A, <)]$ denote the equivalence class of $(A, <)$; let E denote the collection of these equivalence classes. Define

$$[(A, <)] \ll [(A', <')]$$

if $(A, <)$ has the order type of a *section* of $(A', <')$.

(a) Show that the relation $\ll$ is well defined and is a simple order on E. Note that the equivalence class $[(\varnothing, \varnothing)]$ is the smallest element of E.

(b) Show that if $\alpha = [(A, <)]$ is an element of E, then $(A, <)$ has the same order type as the section $S_\alpha(E)$ of E by α. [*Hint:* Define a map $f : A \to E$ by setting $f(x) = [(S_x(A), \text{restriction of } <)]$ for each $x \in A$.]

(c) Conclude that E is well-ordered by $\ll$.

(d) Show that E is uncountable. [*Hint:* If $h : E \to \mathbb{Z}_+$ is a bijection, then h gives rise to a well-ordering of $\mathbb{Z}_+$.]

This same argument, with $\mathbb{Z}_+$ replaced by an arbitrary well-ordered set X, proves (without use of the choice axiom) the existence of a well-ordered set E whose cardinality is greater than that of X.

This exercise shows that one can construct an uncountable well-ordered set, and hence the minimal uncountable well-ordered set, by an explicit construction that does not use the choice axiom. However, this result is less interesting than it might appear. The crucial property of S_Ω, the one we use repeatedly, is the fact that every countable subset of S_Ω has an upper bound in S_Ω. That fact depends, in turn, on the fact that a countable union of countable sets is countable. And the proof of *that* result (if you examine it carefully) involves an infinite number of arbitrary choices—that is, it depends on the choice axiom.

Said differently, without the choice axiom we may be able to construct the minimal uncountable well-ordered set, but we can't use it for anything!

Chapter 2

Topological Spaces and Continuous Functions

The concept of topological space grew out of the study of the real line and euclidean space and the study of continuous functions on these spaces. In this chapter, we define what a topological space is, and we study a number of ways of constructing a topology on a set so as to make it into a topological space. We also consider some of the elementary concepts associated with topological spaces. Open and closed sets, limit points, and continuous functions are introduced as natural generalizations of the corresponding ideas for the real line and euclidean space.

§12   Topological Spaces

The definition of a topological space that is now standard was a long time in being formulated. Various mathematicians—Fréchet, Hausdorff, and others—proposed different definitions over a period of years during the first decades of the twentieth century, but it took quite a while before mathematicians settled on the one that seemed most suitable. They wanted, of course, a definition that was as broad as possible, so that it would include as special cases all the various examples that were useful in mathematics—euclidean space, infinite-dimensional euclidean space, and function spaces among them—but they also wanted the definition to be narrow enough that the standard theorems about these familiar spaces would hold for topological spaces in general. This is always the problem when one is trying to formulate a new mathematical concept, to decide how general its definition should be. The definition finally settled on may seem a bit abstract, but as you work through the various ways of constructing topological spaces, you will get a better feeling for what the concept means.

Definition.   A *topology* on a set X is a collection $\mathcal{T}$ of subsets of X having the following properties:

(1) $\varnothing$ and X are in $\mathcal{T}$.

(2) The union of the elements of any subcollection of $\mathcal{T}$ is in $\mathcal{T}$.

(3) The intersection of the elements of any finite subcollection of $\mathcal{T}$ is in $\mathcal{T}$.

A set X for which a topology $\mathcal{T}$ has been specified is called a *topological space*.

Properly speaking, a topological space is an ordered pair $(X, \mathcal{T})$ consisting of a set X and a topology $\mathcal{T}$ on X, but we often omit specific mention of $\mathcal{T}$ if no confusion will arise.

If X is a topological space with topology $\mathcal{T}$, we say that a subset U of X is an *open set* of X if U belongs to the collection $\mathcal{T}$. Using this terminology, one can say that a topological space is a set X together with a collection of subsets of X, called *open sets*, such that $\varnothing$ and X are both open, and such that arbitrary unions and finite intersections of open sets are open.

EXAMPLE 1.   Let X be a three-element set, $X = \{a, b, c\}$. There are many possible topologies on X, some of which are indicated schematically in Figure 12.1. The diagram in the upper right-hand corner indicates the topology in which the open sets are X, $\varnothing$, $\{a, b\}$, $\{b\}$, and $\{b, c\}$. The topology in the upper left-hand corner contains only X and $\varnothing$, while the topology in the lower right-hand corner contains every subset of X. You can get other topologies on X by permuting a, b, and c.

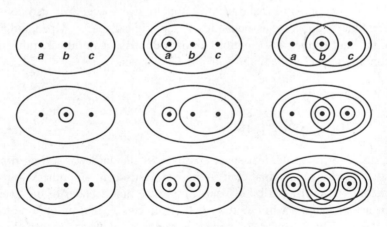

Figure 12.1

From this example, you can see that even a three-element set has many different topologies. But not every collection of subsets of X is a topology on X. Neither of the collections indicated in Figure 12.2 is a topology, for instance.

Figure 12.2

EXAMPLE 2.   If X is any set, the collection of *all* subsets of X is a topology on X; it is called the **discrete topology**. The collection consisting of X and $\varnothing$ only is also a topology on X; we shall call it the **indiscrete topology**, or the **trivial topology**.

EXAMPLE 3.   Let X be a set; let $\mathcal{T}_f$ be the collection of all subsets U of X such that $X - U$ either is finite or is all of X. Then $\mathcal{T}_f$ is a topology on X, called the **finite complement topology**. Both X and $\varnothing$ are in $\mathcal{T}_f$, since $X - X$ is finite and $X - \varnothing$ is all of X. If $\{U_\alpha\}$ is an indexed family of nonempty elements of $\mathcal{T}_f$, to show that $\bigcup U_\alpha$ is in $\mathcal{T}_f$, we compute

$$X - \bigcup U_\alpha = \bigcap (X - U_\alpha).$$

The latter set is finite because each set $X - U_\alpha$ is finite. If $U_1, \ldots, U_n$ are nonempty elements of $\mathcal{T}_f$, to show that $\bigcap U_i$ is in $\mathcal{T}_f$, we compute

$$X - \bigcap_{i=1}^{n} U_i = \bigcup_{i=1}^{n} (X - U_i).$$

The latter set is a finite union of finite sets and, therefore, finite.

EXAMPLE 4.   Let X be a set; let $\mathcal{T}_c$ be the collection of all subsets U of X such that $X - U$ either is countable or is all of X. Then $\mathcal{T}_c$ is a topology on X, as you can check.

Definition.   Suppose that $\mathcal{T}$ and $\mathcal{T}'$ are two topologies on a given set X. If $\mathcal{T}' \supset \mathcal{T}$, we say that $\mathcal{T}'$ is **finer** than $\mathcal{T}$; if $\mathcal{T}'$ *properly* contains $\mathcal{T}$, we say that $\mathcal{T}'$ is **strictly finer** than $\mathcal{T}$. We also say that $\mathcal{T}$ is **coarser** than $\mathcal{T}'$, or **strictly coarser**, in these two respective situations. We say $\mathcal{T}$ is **comparable** with $\mathcal{T}'$ if either $\mathcal{T}' \supset \mathcal{T}$ or $\mathcal{T} \supset \mathcal{T}'$.

This terminology is suggested by thinking of a topological space as being something like a truckload full of gravel—the pebbles and all unions of collections of pebbles being the open sets. If now we smash the pebbles into smaller ones, the collection of open sets has been enlarged, and the topology, like the gravel, is said to have been made finer by the operation.

Two topologies on X need not be comparable, of course. In Figure 12.1 preceding, the topology in the upper right-hand corner is strictly finer than each of the three topologies in the first column and strictly coarser than each of the other topologies in the third column. But it is not comparable with any of the topologies in the second column.

Other terminology is sometimes used for this concept. If $\mathcal{T}' \supset \mathcal{T}$, some mathematicians would say that $\mathcal{T}'$ is **larger** than $\mathcal{T}$, and $\mathcal{T}$ is **smaller** than $\mathcal{T}'$. This is certainly acceptable terminology, if not as vivid as the words "finer" and "coarser."

Many mathematicians use the words "weaker" and "stronger" in this context. Unfortunately, some of them (particularly analysts) are apt to say that $\mathcal{T}'$ is stronger than $\mathcal{T}$ if $\mathcal{T}' \supset \mathcal{T}$, while others (particularly topologists) are apt to say that $\mathcal{T}'$ is weaker than $\mathcal{T}$ in the same situation! If you run across the terms "strong topology" or "weak topology" in some book, you will have to decide from the context which inclusion is meant. We shall not use these terms in this book.

§13   Basis for a Topology

For each of the examples in the preceding section, we were able to specify the topology by describing the entire collection $\mathcal{T}$ of open sets. Usually this is too difficult. In most cases, one specifies instead a smaller collection of subsets of X and defines the topology in terms of that.

Definition.   If X is a set, a ***basis*** for a topology on X is a collection $\mathcal{B}$ of subsets of X (called ***basis elements***) such that

(1) For each $x \in X$, there is at least one basis element B containing x.

(2) If x belongs to the intersection of two basis elements B_1 and B_2, then there is a basis element B_3 containing x such that $B_3 \subset B_1 \cap B_2$.

If $\mathcal{B}$ satisfies these two conditions, then we define the ***topology $\mathcal{T}$ generated by*** $\mathcal{B}$ as follows: A subset U of X is said to be open in X (that is, to be an element of $\mathcal{T}$) if for each $x \in U$, there is a basis element $B \in \mathcal{B}$ such that $x \in B$ and $B \subset U$. Note that each basis element is itself an element of $\mathcal{T}$.

We will check shortly that the collection $\mathcal{T}$ is indeed a topology on X. But first let us consider some examples.

EXAMPLE 1.   Let $\mathcal{B}$ be the collection of all circular regions (interiors of circles) in the plane. Then $\mathcal{B}$ satisfies both conditions for a basis. The second condition is illustrated in Figure 13.1. In the topology generated by $\mathcal{B}$, a subset U of the plane is open if every x in U lies in some circular region contained in U.

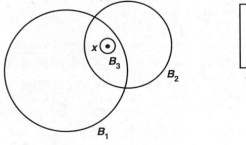

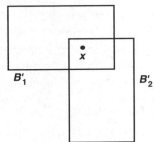

Figure 13.1   *Figure 13.2*

EXAMPLE 2.   Let $\mathscr{B}'$ be the collection of all rectangular regions (interiors of rectangles) in the plane, where the rectangles have sides parallel to the coordinate axes. Then $\mathscr{B}'$ satisfies both conditions for a basis. The second condition is illustrated in Figure 13.2; in this case, the condition is trivial, because the intersection of any two basis elements is itself a basis element (or empty). As we shall see later, the basis $\mathscr{B}'$ generates the same topology on the plane as the basis $\mathscr{B}$ given in the preceding example.

EXAMPLE 3.   If X is any set, the collection of all one-point subsets of X is a basis for the discrete topology on X.

Let us check now that the collection $\mathcal{T}$ generated by the basis $\mathscr{B}$ is, in fact, a topology on X. If U is the empty set, it satisfies the defining condition of openness vacuously. Likewise, X is in $\mathcal{T}$, since for each $x \in X$ there is some basis element B containing x and contained in X. Now let us take an indexed family $\{U_\alpha\}_{\alpha \in J}$, of elements of $\mathcal{T}$ and show that

$$U = \bigcup_{\alpha \in J} U_\alpha$$

belongs to $\mathcal{T}$. Given $x \in U$, there is an index α such that $x \in U_\alpha$. Since U_α is open, there is a basis element B such that $x \in B \subset U_\alpha$. Then $x \in B$ and $B \subset U$, so that U is open, by definition.

Now let us take *two* elements U_1 and U_2 of $\mathcal{T}$ and show that $U_1 \cap U_2$ belongs to $\mathcal{T}$. Given $x \in U_1 \cap U_2$, choose a basis element B_1 containing x such that $B_1 \subset U_1$; choose also a basis element B_2 containing x such that $B_2 \subset U_2$. The second condition for a basis enables us to choose a basis element B_3 containing x such that $B_3 \subset B_1 \cap B_2$. See Figure 13.3. Then $x \in B_3$ and $B_3 \subset U_1 \cap U_2$, so $U_1 \cap U_2$ belongs to $\mathcal{T}$, by definition.

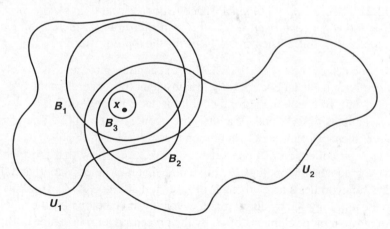

Figure 13.3

Finally, we show by induction that any finite intersection $U_1 \cap \cdots \cap U_n$ of elements of $\mathcal{T}$ is in $\mathcal{T}$. This fact is trivial for $n = 1$; we suppose it true for $n - 1$ and prove it for n. Now

$$(U_1 \cap \cdots \cap U_n) = (U_1 \cap \cdots \cap U_{n-1}) \cap U_n.$$

By hypothesis, $U_1 \cap \cdots \cap U_{n-1}$ belongs to $\mathcal{T}$; by the result just proved, the intersection of $U_1 \cap \cdots \cap U_{n-1}$ and U_n also belongs to $\mathcal{T}$.

Thus we have checked that collection of open sets generated by a basis $\mathcal{B}$ is, in fact, a topology.

Another way of describing the topology generated by a basis is given in the following lemma:

Lemma 13.1. *Let X be a set; let $\mathcal{B}$ be a basis for a topology $\mathcal{T}$ on X. Then $\mathcal{T}$ equals the collection of all unions of elements of $\mathcal{B}$.*

Proof. Given a collection of elements of $\mathcal{B}$, they are also elements of $\mathcal{T}$. Because $\mathcal{T}$ is a topology, their union is in $\mathcal{T}$. Conversely, given $U \in \mathcal{T}$, choose for each $x \in U$ an element B_x of $\mathcal{B}$ such that $x \in B_x \subset U$. Then $U = \bigcup_{x \in U} B_x$, so U equals a union of elements of $\mathcal{B}$. ∎

This lemma states that every open set U in X can be expressed as a union of basis elements. This expression for U is not, however, unique. Thus the use of the term "basis" in topology differs drastically from its use in linear algebra, where the equation expressing a given vector as a linear combination of basis vectors *is* unique.

We have described in two different ways how to go from a basis to the topology it generates. Sometimes we need to go in the reverse direction, from a topology to a basis generating it. Here is one way of obtaining a basis for a given topology; we shall use it frequently.

Lemma 13.2. *Let X be a topological space. Suppose that $\mathcal{C}$ is a collection of open sets of X such that for each open set U of X and each x in U, there is an element C of $\mathcal{C}$ such that $x \in C \subset U$. Then $\mathcal{C}$ is a basis for the topology of X.*

Proof. We must show that $\mathcal{C}$ is a basis. The first condition for a basis is easy: Given $x \in X$, since X is itself an open set, there is by hypothesis an element C of $\mathcal{C}$ such that $x \in C \subset X$. To check the second condition, let x belong to $C_1 \cap C_2$, where C_1 and C_2 are elements of $\mathcal{C}$. Since C_1 and C_2 are open, so is $C_1 \cap C_2$. Therefore, there exists by hypothesis an element C_3 in $\mathcal{C}$ such that $x \in C_3 \subset C_1 \cap C_2$.

Let $\mathcal{T}$ be the collection of open sets of X; we must show that the topology $\mathcal{T}'$ generated by $\mathcal{C}$ equals the topology $\mathcal{T}$. First, note that if U belongs to $\mathcal{T}$ and if $x \in U$, then there is by hypothesis an element C of $\mathcal{C}$ such that $x \in C \subset U$. It follows that U belongs to the topology $\mathcal{T}'$, by definition. Conversely, if W belongs to the topology $\mathcal{T}'$, then W equals a union of elements of $\mathcal{C}$, by the preceding lemma. Since each element of $\mathcal{C}$ belongs to $\mathcal{T}$ and $\mathcal{T}$ is a topology, W also belongs to $\mathcal{T}$. ∎

When topologies are given by bases, it is useful to have a criterion in terms of the bases for determining whether one topology is finer than another. One such criterion is the following:

Lemma 13.3.   *Let $\mathcal{B}$ and $\mathcal{B}'$ be bases for the topologies $\mathcal{T}$ and $\mathcal{T}'$, respectively, on X. Then the following are equivalent:*

(1) *$\mathcal{T}'$ is finer than $\mathcal{T}$.*

(2) *For each $x \in X$ and each basis element $B \in \mathcal{B}$ containing x, there is a basis element $B' \in \mathcal{B}'$ such that $x \in B' \subset B$.*

Proof.   (2) $\Rightarrow$ (1). Given an element U of $\mathcal{T}$, we wish to show that $U \in \mathcal{T}'$. Let $x \in U$. Since $\mathcal{B}$ generates $\mathcal{T}$, there is an element $B \in \mathcal{B}$ such that $x \in B \subset U$. Condition (2) tells us there exists an element $B' \in \mathcal{B}'$ such that $x \in B' \subset B$. Then $x \in B' \subset U$, so $U \in \mathcal{T}'$, by definition.

(1) $\Rightarrow$ (2). We are given $x \in X$ and $B \in \mathcal{B}$, with $x \in B$. Now B belongs to $\mathcal{T}$ by definition and $\mathcal{T} \subset \mathcal{T}'$ by condition (1); therefore, $B \in \mathcal{T}'$. Since $\mathcal{T}'$ is generated by $\mathcal{B}'$, there is an element $B' \in \mathcal{B}'$ such that $x \in B' \subset B$.   ∎

Some students find this condition hard to remember. "Which way does the inclusion *go?*" they ask. It may be easier to remember if you recall the analogy between a topological space and a truckload full of gravel. Think of the pebbles as the basis elements of the topology; after the pebbles are smashed to dust, the dust particles are the basis elements of the new topology. The new topology is finer than the old one, and each dust particle was contained inside a pebble, as the criterion states.

EXAMPLE 4.   One can now see that the collection $\mathcal{B}$ of all circular regions in the plane generates the same topology as the collection $\mathcal{B}'$ of all rectangular regions; Figure 13.4 illustrates the proof. We shall treat this example more formally when we study metric spaces.

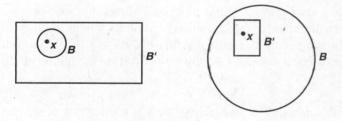

Figure 13.4

We now define three topologies on the real line $\mathbb{R}$, all of which are of interest.

Definition.   If $\mathcal{B}$ is the collection of all open intervals in the real line,

$$(a, b) = \{x \mid a < x < b\},$$

the topology generated by $\mathcal{B}$ is called the ***standard topology*** on the real line. Whenever we consider $\mathbb{R}$, we shall suppose it is given this topology unless we specifically state otherwise. If $\mathcal{B}'$ is the collection of all half-open intervals of the form

$$[a, b) = \{x \mid a \le x < b\},$$

where $a < b$, the topology generated by $\mathcal{B}'$ is called the ***lower limit topology*** on $\mathbb{R}$. When $\mathbb{R}$ is given the lower limit topology, we denote it by $\mathbb{R}_\ell$. Finally let K denote the set of all numbers of the form $1/n$, for $n \in \mathbb{Z}_+$, and let $\mathcal{B}''$ be the collection of all open intervals (a, b), along with all sets of the form $(a, b) - K$. The topology generated by $\mathcal{B}''$ will be called the ***K-topology*** on $\mathbb{R}$. When $\mathbb{R}$ is given this topology, we denote it by $\mathbb{R}_K$.

It is easy to see that all three of these collections are bases; in each case, the intersection of two basis elements is either another basis element or is empty. The relation between these topologies is the following:

Lemma 13.4. *The topologies of $\mathbb{R}_\ell$ and $\mathbb{R}_K$ are strictly finer than the standard topology on $\mathbb{R}$, but are not comparable with one another.*

Proof. Let $\mathcal{T}$, $\mathcal{T}'$, and $\mathcal{T}''$ be the topologies of $\mathbb{R}$, $\mathbb{R}_\ell$, and $\mathbb{R}_K$, respectively. Given a basis element (a, b) for $\mathcal{T}$ and a point x of (a, b), the basis element $[x, b)$ for $\mathcal{T}'$ contains x and lies in (a, b). On the other hand, given the basis element $[x, d)$ for $\mathcal{T}'$, there is no open interval (a, b) that contains x and lies in $[x, d)$. Thus $\mathcal{T}'$ is strictly finer than $\mathcal{T}$.

A similar argument applies to $\mathbb{R}_K$. Given a basis element (a, b) for $\mathcal{T}$ and a point x of (a, b), this same interval is a basis element for $\mathcal{T}''$ that contains x. On the other hand, given the basis element $B = (-1, 1) - K$ for $\mathcal{T}''$ and the point 0 of B, there is no open interval that contains 0 and lies in B.

We leave it to you to show that the topologies of $\mathbb{R}_\ell$ and $\mathbb{R}_K$ are not comparable. ∎

A question may occur to you at this point. Since the topology generated by a basis $\mathcal{B}$ may be described as the collection of arbitrary unions of elements of $\mathcal{B}$, what happens if you start with a given collection of sets and take finite intersections of them as well as arbitrary unions? This question leads to the notion of a subbasis for a topology.

Definition. A ***subbasis*** $\mathcal{S}$ for a topology on X is a collection of subsets of X whose union equals X. The ***topology generated by the subbasis*** $\mathcal{S}$ is defined to be the collection $\mathcal{T}$ of all unions of finite intersections of elements of $\mathcal{S}$.

We must of course check that $\mathcal{T}$ is a topology. For this purpose it will suffice to show that the collection $\mathcal{B}$ of all finite intersections of elements of $\mathcal{S}$ is a basis, for then the collection $\mathcal{T}$ of all unions of elements of $\mathcal{B}$ is a topology, by Lemma 13.1. Given $x \in X$, it belongs to an element of $\mathcal{S}$ and hence to an element of $\mathcal{B}$; this is the first condition for a basis. To check the second condition, let

$$B_1 = S_1 \cap \cdots \cap S_m \quad \text{and} \quad B_2 = S_1' \cap \cdots \cap S_n'$$

be two elements of $\mathcal{B}$. Their intersection

$$B_1 \cap B_2 = (S_1 \cap \cdots \cap S_m) \cap (S_1' \cap \cdots \cap S_n')$$

is also a finite intersection of elements of S, so it belongs to $\mathcal{B}$.

Exercises

1. Let X be a topological space; let A be a subset of X. Suppose that for each $x \in A$ there is an open set U containing x such that $U \subset A$. Show that A is open in X.

2. Consider the nine topologies on the set $X = \{a, b, c\}$ indicated in Example 1 of §12. Compare them; that is, for each pair of topologies, determine whether they are comparable, and if so, which is the finer.

3. Show that the collection $\mathcal{T}_c$ given in Example 4 of §12 is a topology on the set X. Is the collection

$$\mathcal{T}_\infty = \{U \mid X - U \text{ is infinite or empty or all of } X\}$$

a topology on X?

4. (a) If $\{\mathcal{T}_\alpha\}$ is a family of topologies on X, show that $\bigcap \mathcal{T}_\alpha$ is a topology on X. Is $\bigcup \mathcal{T}_\alpha$ a topology on X?

   (b) Let $\{\mathcal{T}_\alpha\}$ be a family of topologies on X. Show that there is a unique smallest topology on X containing all the collections $\mathcal{T}_\alpha$, and a unique largest topology contained in all $\mathcal{T}_\alpha$.

   (c) If $X = \{a, b, c\}$, let

   $$\mathcal{T}_1 = \{\varnothing, X, \{a\}, \{a, b\}\} \quad \text{and} \quad \mathcal{T}_2 = \{\varnothing, X, \{a\}, \{b, c\}\}.$$

   Find the smallest topology containing $\mathcal{T}_1$ and $\mathcal{T}_2$, and the largest topology contained in $\mathcal{T}_1$ and $\mathcal{T}_2$.

5. Show that if $\mathcal{A}$ is a basis for a topology on X, then the topology generated by $\mathcal{A}$ equals the intersection of all topologies on X that contain $\mathcal{A}$. Prove the same if $\mathcal{A}$ is a subbasis.

6. Show that the topologies of $\mathbb{R}_\ell$ and $\mathbb{R}_K$ are not comparable.

7. Consider the following topologies on $\mathbb{R}$:

   $\mathcal{T}_1 = $ the standard topology,
   $\mathcal{T}_2 = $ the topology of $\mathbb{R}_K$,
   $\mathcal{T}_3 = $ the finite complement topology,
   $\mathcal{T}_4 = $ the upper limit topology, having all sets $(a, b]$ as basis,
   $\mathcal{T}_5 = $ the topology having all sets $(-\infty, a) = \{x \mid x < a\}$ as basis.

   Determine, for each of these topologies, which of the others it contains.

8. (a) Apply Lemma 13.2 to show that the countable collection

   $$\mathcal{B} = \{(a, b) \mid a < b, \ a \text{ and } b \text{ rational}\}$$

is a basis that generates the standard topology on $\mathbb{R}$.

(b) Show that the collection

$$\mathcal{C} = \{[a, b) \mid a < b, a \text{ and } b \text{ rational}\}$$

is a basis that generates a topology different from the lower limit topology on $\mathbb{R}$.

§14   The Order Topology

If X is a simply ordered set, there is a standard topology for X, defined using the order relation. It is called the *order topology*; in this section, we consider it and study some of its properties.

Suppose that X is a set having a simple order relation $<$. Given elements a and b of X such that $a < b$, there are four subsets of X that are called the **intervals** determined by a and b. They are the following :

$$(a, b) = \{x \mid a < x < b\},$$
$$(a, b] = \{x \mid a < x \le b\},$$
$$[a, b) = \{x \mid a \le x < b\},$$
$$[a, b] = \{x \mid a \le x \le b\}.$$

The notation used here is familiar to you already in the case where X is the real line, but these are intervals in an arbitrary ordered set. A set of the first type is called an *open interval* in X, a set of the last type is called a **closed interval** in X, and sets of the second and third types are called **half-open intervals**. The use of the term "open" in this connection suggests that open intervals in X should turn out to be open sets when we put a topology on X. And so they will.

Definition.   Let X be a set with a simple order relation; assume X has more than one element. Let $\mathcal{B}$ be the collection of all sets of the following types:

(1) All open intervals (a, b) in X.

(2) All intervals of the form $[a_0, b)$, where a_0 is the smallest element (if any) of X.

(3) All intervals of the form $(a, b_0]$, where b_0 is the largest element (if any) of X.

The collection $\mathcal{B}$ is a basis for a topology on X, which is called the **order topology**.

If X has no smallest element, there are no sets of type (2), and if X has no largest element, there are no sets of type (3).

One has to check that $\mathcal{B}$ satisfies the requirements for a basis. First, note that every element x of X lies in at least one element of $\mathcal{B}$: The smallest element (if any) lies in all sets of type (2), the largest element (if any) lies in all sets of type (3), and every other element lies in a set of type (1). Second, note that the intersection of any two sets of the preceding types is again a set of one of these types, or is empty. Several cases need to be checked; we leave it to you.

EXAMPLE 1.   The standard topology on $\mathbb{R}$, as defined in the preceding section, is just the order topology derived from the usual order on $\mathbb{R}$.

EXAMPLE 2.   Consider the set $\mathbb{R} \times \mathbb{R}$ in the dictionary order; we shall denote the general element of $\mathbb{R} \times \mathbb{R}$ by $x \times y$, to avoid difficulty with notation. The set $\mathbb{R} \times \mathbb{R}$ has neither a largest nor a smallest element, so the order topology on $\mathbb{R} \times \mathbb{R}$ has as basis the collection of all open intervals of the form $(a \times b, c \times d)$ for $a < c$, and for $a = c$ and $b < d$. These two types of intervals are indicated in Figure 14.1. The subcollection consisting of only intervals of the second type is also a basis for the order topology on $\mathbb{R} \times \mathbb{R}$, as you can check.

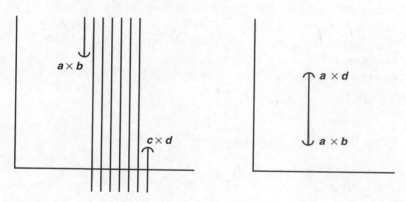

Figure 14.1

EXAMPLE 3.   The positive integers $\mathbb{Z}_+$ form an ordered set with a smallest element. The order topology on $\mathbb{Z}_+$ is the discrete topology, for every one-point set is open: If $n > 1$, then the one-point set $\{n\} = (n - 1, n + 1)$ is a basis element; and if $n = 1$, the one-point set $\{1\} = [1, 2)$ is a basis element.

EXAMPLE 4.   The set $X = \{1, 2\} \times \mathbb{Z}_+$ in the dictionary order is another example of an ordered set with a smallest element. Denoting $1 \times n$ by a_n and $2 \times n$ by b_n, we can represent X by

$$a_1, a_2, \ldots ; b_1, b_2, \ldots .$$

The order topology on X is *not* the discrete topology. Most one-point sets are open, but there is an exception—the one-point set $\{b_1\}$. Any open set containing b_1 must contain a basis element about b_1 (by definition), and any basis element containing b_1 contains points of the a_i sequence.

Definition.   If X is an ordered set, and a is an element of X, there are four subsets of X that are called the ***rays*** determined by a. They are the following:

$$(a, +\infty) = \{x \mid x > a\},$$
$$(-\infty, a) = \{x \mid x < a\},$$
$$[a, +\infty) = \{x \mid x \geq a\},$$
$$(-\infty, a] = \{x \mid x \leq a\}.$$

Sets of the first two types are called **open rays**, and sets of the last two types are called **closed rays**.

The use of the term "open" suggests that open rays in X are open sets in the order topology. And so they are. Consider, for example, the ray $(a, +\infty)$. If X has a largest element b_0, then $(a, +\infty)$ equals the basis element $(a, b_0]$. If X has no largest element, then $(a, +\infty)$ equals the union of all basis elements of the form (a, x), for $x > a$. In either case, $(a, +\infty)$ is open. A similar argument applies to the ray $(-\infty, a)$.

The open rays, in fact, form a subbasis for the order topology on X, as we now show. Because the open rays are open in the order topology, the topology they generate is contained in the order topology. On the other hand, every basis element for the order topology equals a finite intersection of open rays; the interval (a, b) equals the intersection of $(-\infty, b)$ and $(a, +\infty)$, while $[a_0, b)$ and $(a, b_0]$, if they exist, are themselves open rays. Hence the topology generated by the open rays contains the order topology.

§15   The Product Topology on $X \times Y$

If X and Y are topological spaces, there is a standard way of defining a topology on the cartesian product $X \times Y$. We consider this topology now and study some of its properties.

Definition.   Let X and Y be topological spaces. The **product topology** on $X \times Y$ is the topology having as basis the collection $\mathcal{B}$ of all sets of the form $U \times V$, where U is an open subset of X and V is an open subset of Y.

Let us check that $\mathcal{B}$ is a basis. The first condition is trivial, since $X \times Y$ is itself a basis element. The second condition is almost as easy, since the intersection of any two basis elements $U_1 \times V_1$ and $U_2 \times V_2$ is another basis element. For

$$(U_1 \times V_1) \cap (U_2 \times V_2) = (U_1 \cap U_2) \times (V_1 \cap V_2),$$

and the latter set is a basis element because $U_1 \cap U_2$ and $V_1 \cap V_2$ are open in X and Y, respectively. See Figure 15.1.

Note that the collection $\mathcal{B}$ is not a topology on $X \times Y$. The union of the two rectangles pictured in Figure 15.1, for instance, is not a product of two sets, so it cannot belong to $\mathcal{B}$; however, it is open in $X \times Y$.

Each time we introduce a new concept, we shall try to relate it to the concepts that have been previously introduced. In the present case, we ask: What can one say if the topologies on X and Y are given by bases? The answer is as follows:

Theorem 15.1.   *If $\mathcal{B}$ is a basis for the topology of X and $\mathcal{C}$ is a basis for the topology of Y, then the collection*

$$\mathcal{D} = \{B \times C \mid B \in \mathcal{B} \text{ and } C \in \mathcal{C}\}$$

is a basis for the topology of $X \times Y$.

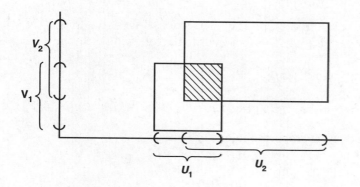

Figure 15.1

Proof. We apply Lemma 13.2. Given an open set W of $X \times Y$ and a point $x \times y$ of W, by definition of the product topology there is a basis element $U \times V$ such that $x \times y \in U \times V \subset W$. Because $\mathcal{B}$ and $\mathcal{C}$ are bases for X and Y, respectively, we can choose an element B of $\mathcal{B}$ such that $x \in B \subset U$, and an element C of $\mathcal{C}$ such that $y \in C \subset V$. Then $x \times y \in B \times C \subset W$. Thus the collection $\mathcal{D}$ meets the criterion of Lemma 13.2, so $\mathcal{D}$ is a basis for $X \times Y$. ∎

EXAMPLE 1.   We have a standard topology on $\mathbb{R}$: the order topology. The product of this topology with itself is called the **standard topology** on $\mathbb{R} \times \mathbb{R} = \mathbb{R}^2$. It has as basis the collection of all products of open sets of $\mathbb{R}$, but the theorem just proved tells us that the much smaller collection of all products $(a, b) \times (c, d)$ of open intervals in $\mathbb{R}$ will also serve as a basis for the topology of $\mathbb{R}^2$. Each such set can be pictured as the interior of a rectangle in $\mathbb{R}^2$. Thus the standard topology on $\mathbb{R}^2$ is just the one we considered in Example 2 of §13.

It is sometimes useful to express the product topology in terms of a subbasis. To do this, we first define certain functions called projections.

Definition.   Let $\pi_1 : X \times Y \to X$ be defined by the equation

$$\pi_1(x, y) = x;$$

let $\pi_2 : X \times Y \to Y$ be defined by the equation

$$\pi_2(x, y) = y.$$

The maps π_1 and π_2 are called the **projections** of $X \times Y$ onto its first and second factors, respectively.

We use the word "onto" because π_1 and π_2 are surjective (unless one of the spaces X or Y happens to be empty, in which case $X \times Y$ is empty and our whole discussion is empty as well!).

If U is an open subset of X, then the set $\pi_1^{-1}(U)$ is precisely the set $U \times Y$, which is open in $X \times Y$. Similarly, if V is open in Y, then

$$\pi_2^{-1}(V) = X \times V,$$

which is also open in $X \times Y$. The intersection of these two sets is the set $U \times V$, as indicated in Figure 15.2. This fact leads to the following theorem:

Theorem 15.2. *The collection*

$$S = \{\pi_1^{-1}(U) \mid U \ open \ in \ X\} \cup \{\pi_2^{-1}(V) \mid V \ open \ in \ Y\}$$

is a subbasis for the product topology on $X \times Y$.

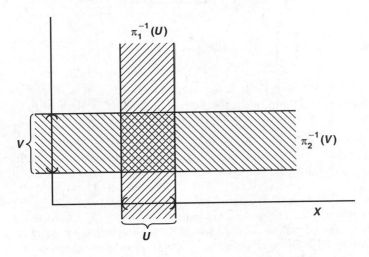

Figure 15.2

Proof. Let $\mathcal{T}$ denote the product topology on $X \times Y$; let $\mathcal{T}'$ be the topology generated by S. Because every element of S belongs to $\mathcal{T}$, so do arbitrary unions of finite intersections of elements of S. Thus $\mathcal{T}' \subset \mathcal{T}$. On the other hand, every basis element $U \times V$ for the topology $\mathcal{T}$ is a finite intersection of elements of S, since

$$U \times V = \pi_1^{-1}(U) \cap \pi_2^{-1}(V).$$

Therefore, $U \times V$ belongs to $\mathcal{T}'$, so that $\mathcal{T} \subset \mathcal{T}'$ as well.   ∎

§16   The Subspace Topology

Definition.   Let X be a topological space with topology $\mathcal{T}$. If Y is a subset of X, the collection

$$\mathcal{T}_Y = \{Y \cap U \mid U \in \mathcal{T}\}$$

is a topology on Y, called the **subspace topology**. With this topology, Y is called a **subspace** of X; its open sets consist of all intersections of open sets of X with Y.

It is easy to see that $\mathcal{T}_Y$ is a topology. It contains $\varnothing$ and Y because

$$\varnothing = Y \cap \varnothing \quad \text{and} \quad Y = Y \cap X,$$

where $\varnothing$ and X are elements of $\mathcal{T}$. The fact that it is closed under finite intersections and arbitrary unions follows from the equations

$$(U_1 \cap Y) \cap \cdots \cap (U_n \cap Y) = (U_1 \cap \cdots \cap U_n) \cap Y,$$

$$\bigcup_{\alpha \in J} (U_\alpha \cap Y) = (\bigcup_{\alpha \in J} U_\alpha) \cap Y.$$

Lemma 16.1. *If $\mathcal{B}$ is a basis for the topology of X then the collection*

$$\mathcal{B}_Y = \{B \cap Y \mid B \in \mathcal{B}\}$$

is a basis for the subspace topology on Y.

Proof. Given U open in X and given $y \in U \cap Y$, we can choose an element B of $\mathcal{B}$ such that $y \in B \subset U$. Then $y \in B \cap Y \subset U \cap Y$. It follows from Lemma 13.2 that $\mathcal{B}_Y$ is a basis for the subspace topology on Y. ∎

When dealing with a space X and a subspace Y, one needs to be careful when one uses the term "open set". Does one mean an element of the topology of Y or an element of the topology of X? We make the following definition : If Y is a subspace of X, we say that a set U is **open in Y** (or open *relative to Y*) if it belongs to the topology of Y; this implies in particular that it is a subset of Y. We say that U is **open in X** if it belongs to the topology of X.

There is a special situation in which every set open in Y is also open in X:

Lemma 16.2. *Let Y be a subspace of X. If U is open in Y and Y is open in X, then U is open in X.*

Proof. Since U is open in Y, $U = Y \cap V$ for some set V open in X. Since Y and V are both open in X, so is $Y \cap V$. ∎

Now let us explore the relation between the subspace topology and the order and product topologies. For product topologies, the result is what one might expect; for order topologies, it is not.

Theorem 16.3. *If A is a subspace of X and B is a subspace of Y, then the product topology on $A \times B$ is the same as the topology $A \times B$ inherits as a subspace of $X \times Y$.*

Proof. The set $U \times V$ is the general basis element for $X \times Y$, where U is open in X and V is open in Y. Therefore, $(U \times V) \cap (A \times B)$ is the general basis element for the subspace topology on $A \times B$. Now

$$(U \times V) \cap (A \times B) = (U \cap A) \times (V \cap B).$$

Since $U \cap A$ and $V \cap B$ are the general open sets for the subspace topologies on A and B, respectively, the set $(U \cap A) \times (V \cap B)$ is the general basis element for the product topology on $A \times B$.

The conclusion we draw is that the bases for the subspace topology on $A \times B$ and for the product topology on $A \times B$ are the same. Hence the topologies are the same. ∎

Now let X be an ordered set in the order topology, and let Y be a subset of X. The order relation on X, when restricted to Y, makes Y into an ordered set. However, *the resulting order topology on Y need not be the same as the topology that Y inherits as a subspace of X.* We give one example where the subspace and order topologies on Y agree, and two examples where they do not.

EXAMPLE 1.   Consider the subset $Y = [0, 1]$ of the real line $\mathbb{R}$, in the *subspace* topology. The subspace topology has as basis all sets of the form $(a, b) \cap Y$, where (a, b) is an open interval in $\mathbb{R}$. Such a set is of one of the following types:

$$(a, b) \cap Y = \begin{cases} (a, b) & \text{if } a \text{ and } b \text{ are in } Y, \\ [0, b) & \text{if only } b \text{ is in } Y, \\ (a, 1] & \text{if only } a \text{ is in } Y, \\ Y \text{ or } \varnothing & \text{if neither } a \text{ nor } b \text{ is in } Y. \end{cases}$$

By definition, each of these sets is open in Y. But sets of the second and third types are not open in the larger space $\mathbb{R}$.

Note that these sets form a basis for the *order* topology on Y. Thus, we see that in the case of the set $Y = [0, 1]$, its subspace topology (as a subspace of $\mathbb{R}$) and its order topology are the same.

EXAMPLE 2.   Let Y be the subset $[0, 1) \cup \{2\}$ of $\mathbb{R}$. In the subspace topology on Y the one-point set $\{2\}$ is open, because it is the intersection of the open set $(\frac{3}{2}, \frac{5}{2})$ with Y. But in the order topology on Y, the set $\{2\}$ is not open. Any basis element for the order topology on Y that contains 2 is of the form

$$\{x \mid x \in Y \text{ and } a < x \leq 2\}$$

for some $a \in Y$; such a set necessarily contains points of Y less than 2.

EXAMPLE 3.   Let $I = [0, 1]$. The dictionary order on $I \times I$ is just the restriction to $I \times I$ of the dictionary order on the plane $\mathbb{R} \times \mathbb{R}$. However, the dictionary order topology on $I \times I$ is not the same as the subspace topology on $I \times I$ obtained from the dictionary order topology on $\mathbb{R} \times \mathbb{R}$! For example, the set $\{1/2\} \times (1/2, 1]$ is open in $I \times I$ in the subspace topology, but not in the order topology, as you can check. See Figure 16.1.

The set $I \times I$ in the dictionary order topology will be called the ***ordered square***, and denoted by I_o^2.

The anomaly illustrated in Examples 2 and 3 does not occur for intervals or rays in an ordered set X. This we now prove.

Given an ordered set X, let us say that a subset Y of X is ***convex*** in X if for each pair of points $a < b$ of Y, the entire interval (a, b) of points of X lies in Y. Note that intervals and rays in X are convex in X.

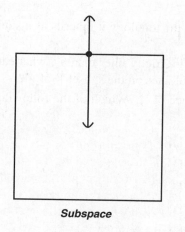

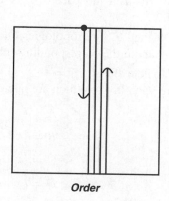

Subspace   Order

Figure 16.1

Theorem 16.4. *Let X be an ordered set in the order topology; let Y be a subset of X that is convex in X. Then the order topology on Y is the same as the topology Y inherits as a subspace of X.*

Proof. Consider the ray $(a, +\infty)$ in X. What is its intersection with Y? If $a \in Y$, then

$$(a, +\infty) \cap Y = \{x \mid x \in Y \text{ and } x > a\};$$

this is an open ray of the ordered set Y. If $a \notin Y$, then a is either a lower bound on Y or an upper bound on Y, since Y is convex. In the former case, the set $(a, +\infty) \cap Y$ equals all of Y; in the latter case, it is empty.

A similar remark shows that the intersection of the ray $(-\infty, a)$ with Y is either an open ray of Y, or Y itself, or empty. Since the sets $(a, +\infty) \cap Y$ and $(-\infty, a) \cap Y$ form a subbasis for the subspace topology on Y, and since each is open in the order topology, the order topology contains the subspace topology.

To prove the reverse, note that any open ray of Y equals the intersection of an open ray of X with Y, so it is open in the subspace topology on Y. Since the open rays of Y are a subbasis for the order topology on Y, this topology is contained in the subspace topology. ∎

To avoid ambiguity, let us agree that whenever X is an ordered set in the order topology and Y is a subset of X, *we shall assume that Y is given the subspace topology* unless we specifically state otherwise. If Y is convex in X, this is the same as the order topology on Y; otherwise, it may not be.

Exercises

1. Show that if Y is a subspace of X, and A is a subset of Y, then the topology A

inherits as a subspace of Y is the same as the topology it inherits as a subspace of X.

2. If $\mathcal{T}$ and $\mathcal{T}'$ are topologies on X and $\mathcal{T}'$ is strictly finer than $\mathcal{T}$, what can you say about the corresponding subspace topologies on the subset Y of X?

3. Consider the set $Y = [-1, 1]$ as a subspace of $\mathbb{R}$. Which of the following sets are open in Y? Which are open in $\mathbb{R}$?

$$A = \{x \mid \tfrac{1}{2} < |x| < 1\},$$
$$B = \{x \mid \tfrac{1}{2} < |x| \leq 1\},$$
$$C = \{x \mid \tfrac{1}{2} \leq |x| < 1\},$$
$$D = \{x \mid \tfrac{1}{2} \leq |x| \leq 1\},$$
$$E = \{x \mid 0 < |x| < 1 \text{ and } 1/x \notin \mathbb{Z}_+\}.$$

4. A map $f : X \to Y$ is said to be an **open map** if for every open set U of X, the set $f(U)$ is open in Y. Show that $\pi_1 : X \times Y \to X$ and $\pi_2 : X \times Y \to Y$ are open maps.

5. Let X and X' denote a single set in the topologies $\mathcal{T}$ and $\mathcal{T}'$, respectively; let Y and Y' denote a single set in the topologies $\mathcal{U}$ and $\mathcal{U}'$, respectively. Assume these sets are nonempty.
    (a) Show that if $\mathcal{T}' \supset \mathcal{T}$ and $\mathcal{U}' \supset \mathcal{U}$, then the product topology on $X' \times Y'$ is finer than the product topology on $X \times Y$.
    (b) Does the converse of (a) hold? Justify your answer.

6. Show that the countable collection

$$\{(a, b) \times (c, d) \mid a < b \text{ and } c < d, \text{ and } a, b, c, d \text{ are rational}\}$$

is a basis for $\mathbb{R}^2$.

7. Let X be an ordered set. If Y is a proper subset of X that is convex in X, does it follow that Y is an interval or a ray in X?

8. If L is a straight line in the plane, describe the topology L inherits as a subspace of $\mathbb{R}_\ell \times \mathbb{R}$ and as a subspace of $\mathbb{R}_\ell \times \mathbb{R}_\ell$. In each case it is a familiar topology.

9. Show that the dictionary order topology on the set $\mathbb{R} \times \mathbb{R}$ is the same as the product topology $\mathbb{R}_d \times \mathbb{R}$, where $\mathbb{R}_d$ denotes $\mathbb{R}$ in the discrete topology. Compare this topology with the standard topology on $\mathbb{R}^2$.

10. Let $I = [0, 1]$. Compare the product topology on $I \times I$, the dictionary order topology on $I \times I$, and the topology $I \times I$ inherits as a subspace of $\mathbb{R} \times \mathbb{R}$ in the dictionary order topology.

§17 Closed Sets and Limit Points

Now that we have a few examples at hand, we can introduce some of the basic concepts associated with topological spaces. In this section, we treat the notions of *closed set*, *closure* of a set, and *limit point*. These lead naturally to consideration of a certain axiom for topological spaces called the *Hausdorff axiom*.

Closed Sets

A subset A of a topological space X is said to be **closed** if the set $X - A$ is open.

EXAMPLE 1.   The subset $[a, b]$ of $\mathbb{R}$ is closed because its complement

$$\mathbb{R} - [a, b] = (-\infty, a) \cup (b, +\infty),$$

is open. Similarly, $[a, +\infty)$ is closed, because its complement $(-\infty, a)$ is open. These facts justify our use of the terms "closed interval" and "closed ray." The subset $[a, b)$ of $\mathbb{R}$ is neither open nor closed.

EXAMPLE 2.   In the plane $\mathbb{R}^2$, the set

$$\{x \times y \mid x \geq 0 \text{ and } y \geq 0\}$$

is closed, because its complement is the union of the two sets

$$(-\infty, 0) \times \mathbb{R} \quad \text{and} \quad \mathbb{R} \times (-\infty, 0),$$

each of which is a product of open sets of $\mathbb{R}$ and is, therefore, open in $\mathbb{R}^2$.

EXAMPLE 3.   In the finite complement topology on a set X, the closed sets consist of X itself and all finite subsets of X.

EXAMPLE 4.   In the discrete topology on the set X, every set is open; it follows that every set is closed as well.

EXAMPLE 5.   Consider the following subset of the real line:

$$Y = [0, 1] \cup (2, 3),$$

in the subspace topology. In this space, the set $[0, 1]$ is open, since it is the intersection of the open set $(-\frac{1}{2}, \frac{3}{2})$ of $\mathbb{R}$ with Y. Similarly, $(2, 3)$ is open as a subset of Y; it is even open as a subset of $\mathbb{R}$. Since $[0, 1]$ and $(2, 3)$ are complements in Y of each other, we conclude that both $[0, 1]$ and $(2, 3)$ are closed as subsets of Y.

These examples suggest that an answer to the mathematician's riddle: "How is a set different from a door?" should be: "A door must be either open or closed, and cannot be both, while a set can be open, or closed, or both, or neither!"

The collection of closed subsets of a space X has properties similar to those satisfied by the collection of open subsets of X:

Theorem 17.1.   *Let X be a topological space. Then the following conditions hold:*

(1) $\varnothing$ *and X are closed.*

(2) *Arbitrary intersections of closed sets are closed.*

(3) *Finite unions of closed sets are closed.*

Proof.   (1) $\varnothing$ and X are closed because they are the complements of the open sets X and $\varnothing$, respectively.

(2) Given a collection of closed sets $\{A_\alpha\}_{\alpha \in J}$, we apply DeMorgan's law,

$$X - \bigcap_{\alpha \in J} A_\alpha = \bigcup_{\alpha \in J} (X - A_\alpha).$$

Since the sets $X - A_\alpha$ are open by definition, the right side of this equation represents an arbitrary union of open sets, and is thus open. Therefore, $\bigcap A_\alpha$ is closed.

(3) Similarly, if A_i is closed for $i = 1, \ldots, n$, consider the equation

$$X - \bigcup_{i=1}^{n} A_i = \bigcap_{i=1}^{n} (X - A_i).$$

The set on the right side of this equation is a finite intersection of open sets and is therefore open. Hence $\bigcup A_i$ is closed.   ∎

Instead of using open sets, one could just as well specify a topology on a space by giving a collection of sets (to be called "closed sets") satisfying the three properties of this theorem. One could then define open sets as the complements of closed sets and proceed just as before. This procedure has no particular advantage over the one we have adopted, and most mathematicians prefer to use open sets to define topologies.

Now when dealing with subspaces, one needs to be careful in using the term "closed set." If Y is a subspace of X, we say that a set A is *closed in Y* if A is a subset of Y and if A is closed in the subspace topology of Y (that is, if $Y - A$ is open in Y). We have the following theorem:

Theorem 17.2.   *Let Y be a subspace of X. Then a set A is closed in Y if and only if it equals the intersection of a closed set of X with Y.*

Proof.   Assume that $A = C \cap Y$, where C is closed in X. (See Figure 17.1.) Then $X - C$ is open in X, so that $(X - C) \cap Y$ is open in Y, by definition of the subspace topology. But $(X - C) \cap Y = Y - A$. Hence $Y - A$ is open in Y, so that A is closed in Y. Conversely, assume that A is closed in Y. (See Figure 17.2.) Then $Y - A$ is open in Y, so that by definition it equals the intersection of an open set U of X with Y. The set $X - U$ is closed in X, and $A = Y \cap (X - U)$, so that A equals the intersection of a closed set of X with Y, as desired.   ∎

A set A that is closed in the subspace Y may or may not be closed in the larger space X. As was the case with open sets, there is a criterion for A to be closed in X; we leave the proof to you:

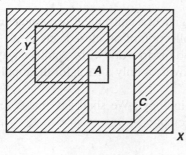

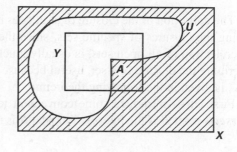

Figure 17.1   *Figure 17.2*

Theorem 17.3. *Let Y be a subspace of X. If A is closed in Y and Y is closed in X, then A is closed in X.*

Closure and Interior of a Set

Given a subset A of a topological space X, the *interior* of A is defined as the union of all open sets contained in A, and the *closure* of A is defined as the intersection of all closed sets containing A.

The interior of A is denoted by Int A and the closure of A is denoted by Cl A or by $\bar{A}$. Obviously Int A is an open set and $\bar{A}$ is a closed set; furthermore,

$$\text{Int } A \subset A \subset \bar{A}.$$

If A is open, $A = \text{Int } A$; while if A is closed, $A = \bar{A}$.

We shall not make much use of the interior of a set, but the closure of a set will be quite important.

When dealing with a topological space X and a subspace Y, one needs to exercise care in taking closures of sets. If A is a subset of Y, the closure of A in Y and the closure of A in X will in general be different. *In such a situation, we reserve the notation $\bar{A}$ to stand for the closure of A in X.* The closure of A in Y can be expressed in terms of $\bar{A}$, as the following theorem shows:

Theorem 17.4. *Let Y be a subspace of X; let A be a subset of Y; let $\bar{A}$ denote the closure of A in X. Then the closure of A in Y equals $\bar{A} \cap Y$.*

Proof. Let B denote the closure of A in Y. The set $\bar{A}$ is closed in X, so $\bar{A} \cap Y$ is closed in Y by Theorem 17.2. Since $\bar{A} \cap Y$ contains A, and since by definition B equals the intersection of *all* closed subsets of Y containing A, we must have $B \subset (\bar{A} \cap Y)$.

On the other hand, we know that B is closed in Y. Hence by Theorem 17.2, $B = C \cap Y$ for some set C closed in X. Then C is a closed set of X containing A; because $\bar{A}$ is the intersection of *all* such closed sets, we conclude that $\bar{A} \subset C$. Then $(\bar{A} \cap Y) \subset (C \cap Y) = B$.   ∎

The definition of the closure of a set does not give us a convenient way for actually finding the closures of specific sets, since the collection of all closed sets in X, like the collection of all open sets, is usually much too big to work with. Another way of describing the closure of a set, useful because it involves only a basis for the topology of X, is given in the following theorem.

First let us introduce some convenient terminology. We shall say that a set A *intersects* a set B if the intersection $A \cap B$ is not empty.

Theorem 17.5. *Let A be a subset of the topological space X.*

(a) Then $x \in \bar{A}$ if and only if every open set U containing x intersects A.

(b) Supposing the topology of X is given by a basis, then $x \in \bar{A}$ if and only if every basis element B containing x intersects A.

Proof. Consider the statement in (a). It is a statement of the form $P \Leftrightarrow Q$. Let us transform each implication to its contrapositive, thereby obtaining the logically equivalent statement (not P) $\Leftrightarrow$ (not Q). Written out, it is the following:

$x \notin \bar{A} \Longleftrightarrow$ there exists an open set U containing x that does not intersect A.

In this form, our theorem is easy to prove. If x is not in $\bar{A}$, the set $U = X - \bar{A}$ is an open set containing x that does not intersect A, as desired. Conversely, if there exists an open set U containing x which does not intersect A, then $X - U$ is a closed set containing A. By definition of the closure $\bar{A}$, the set $X - U$ must contain $\bar{A}$; therefore, x cannot be in $\bar{A}$.

Statement (b) follows readily. If every open set containing x intersects A, so does every basis element B containing x, because B is an open set. Conversely, if every basis element containing x intersects A, so does every open set U containing x, because U contains a basis element that contains x. ∎

Mathematicians often use some special terminology here. They shorten the statement "U is an open set containing x" to the phrase

"*U* is a ***neighborhood*** of *x*."

Using this terminology, one can write the first half of the preceding theorem as follows:

If A is a subset of the topological space X, then $x \in \bar{A}$ if and only if every neighborhood of x intersects A.

EXAMPLE 6.   Let X be the real line $\mathbb{R}$. If $A = (0, 1]$, then $\bar{A} = [0, 1]$, for every neighborhood of 0 intersects A, while every point outside $[0, 1]$ has a neighborhood disjoint from A. Similar arguments apply to the following subsets of X:

If $B = \{1/n \mid n \in \mathbb{Z}_+\}$, then $\bar{B} = \{0\} \cup B$. If $C = \{0\} \cup (1, 2)$, then $\bar{C} = \{0\} \cup [1, 2]$. If $\mathbb{Q}$ is the set of rational numbers, then $\bar{\mathbb{Q}} = \mathbb{R}$. If $\mathbb{Z}_+$ is the set of positive integers, then $\bar{\mathbb{Z}}_+ = \mathbb{Z}_+$. If $\mathbb{R}_+$ is the set of positive reals, then the closure of $\mathbb{R}_+$ is the set $\mathbb{R}_+ \cup \{0\}$. (This is the reason we introduced the notation $\bar{\mathbb{R}}_+$ for the set $\mathbb{R}_+ \cup \{0\}$, back in §2.)

EXAMPLE 7.   Consider the subspace $Y = (0, 1]$ of the real line $\mathbb{R}$. The set $A = (0, \frac{1}{2})$ is a subset of Y; its closure in $\mathbb{R}$ is the set $[0, \frac{1}{2}]$, and its closure in Y is the set $[0, \frac{1}{2}] \cap Y = (0, \frac{1}{2}]$.

Some mathematicians use the term "neighborhood" differently. They say that A is a neighborhood of x if A merely *contains* an open set containing x. We shall not follow this practice.

Limit Points

There is yet another way of describing the closure of a set, a way that involves the important concept of limit point, which we consider now.

If A is a subset of the topological space X and if x is a point of X, we say that x is a **limit point** (or "cluster point," or "point of accumulation") of A if every neighborhood of x intersects A in some point *other than x itself*. Said differently, x is a limit point of A if it belongs to the closure of $A - \{x\}$. The point x may lie in A or not; for this definition it does not matter.

EXAMPLE 8.   Consider the real line $\mathbb{R}$. If $A = (0, 1]$, then the point 0 is a limit point of A and so is the point $\frac{1}{2}$. In fact, every point of the interval $[0, 1]$ is a limit point of A, but no other point of $\mathbb{R}$ is a limit point of A.

If $B = \{1/n \mid n \in \mathbb{Z}_+\}$, then 0 is the only limit point of B. Every other point x of $\mathbb{R}$ has a neighborhood that either does not intersect B at all, or it intersects B only in the point x itself. If $C = \{0\} \cup (1, 2)$, then the limit points of C are the points of the interval $[1, 2]$. If $\mathbb{Q}$ is the set of rational numbers, every point of $\mathbb{R}$ is a limit point of $\mathbb{Q}$. If $\mathbb{Z}_+$ is the set of positive integers, no point of $\mathbb{R}$ is a limit point of $\mathbb{Z}_+$. If $\mathbb{R}_+$ is the set of positive reals, then every point of $\{0\} \cup \mathbb{R}_+$ is a limit point of $\mathbb{R}_+$.

Comparison of Examples 6 and 8 suggests a relationship between the closure of a set and the limit points of a set. That relationship is given in the following theorem:

Theorem 17.6. *Let A be a subset of the topological space X; let A' be the set of all limit points of A. Then*

$$\bar{A} = A \cup A'.$$

Proof.   If x is in A', every neighborhood of x intersects A (in a point different from x). Therefore, by Theorem 17.5, x belongs to $\bar{A}$. Hence $A' \subset \bar{A}$. Since by definition $A \subset \bar{A}$, it follows that $A \cup A' \subset \bar{A}$.

To demonstrate the reverse inclusion, we let x be a point of $\bar{A}$ and show that $x \in A \cup A'$. If x happens to lie in A, it is trivial that $x \in A \cup A'$; suppose that x does not lie in A. Since $x \in \bar{A}$, we know that every neighborhood U of x intersects A; because $x \notin A$, the set U must intersect A in a point different from x. Then $x \in A'$, so that $x \in A \cup A'$, as desired.   ∎

Corollary 17.7. *A subset of a topological space is closed if and only if it contains all its limit points.*

Proof. The set A is closed if and only if $A = \bar{A}$, and the latter holds if and only if $A' \subset A$. ∎

Hausdorff Spaces

One's experience with open and closed sets and limit points in the real line and the plane can be misleading when one considers more general topological spaces. For example, in the spaces $\mathbb{R}$ and $\mathbb{R}^2$, each one-point set $\{x_0\}$ closed. This fact is easily proved; every point different from x_0 has a neighborhood not intersecting $\{x_0\}$, so that $\{x_0\}$ is its own closure. But this fact is not true for arbitrary topological spaces. Consider the topology on the three-point set $\{a, b, c\}$ indicated in Figure 17.3. In this space, the one-point set $\{b\}$ is not closed, for its complement is *not* open.

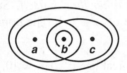

Figure 17.3

Similarly, one's experience with the properties of convergent sequences in $\mathbb{R}$ and $\mathbb{R}^2$ can be misleading when one deals with more general topological spaces. In an arbitrary topological space, one says that a sequence $x_1, x_2, \ldots$ of points of the space X *converges* to the point x of X provided that, corresponding to each neighborhood U of x, there is a positive integer N such that $x_n \in U$ for all $n \geq N$. In $\mathbb{R}$ and $\mathbb{R}^2$, a sequence cannot converge to more than one point, but in an arbitrary space, it can. In the space indicated in Figure 17.3, for example, the sequence defined by setting $x_n = b$ for all n converges not only to the point b, but also to the point a and to the point c!

Topologies in which one-point sets are not closed, or in which sequences can converge to more than one point, are considered by many mathematicians to be somewhat strange. They are not really very interesting, for they seldom occur in other branches of mathematics. And the theorems that one can prove about topological spaces are rather limited if such examples are allowed. Therefore, one often imposes an additional condition that will rule out examples like this one, bringing the class of spaces under consideration closer to those to which one's geometric intuition applies. The condition was suggested by the mathematician Felix Hausdorff, so mathematicians have come to call it by his name.

Definition. A topological space X is called a ***Hausdorff space*** if for each pair x_1, x_2 of distinct points of X, there exist neighborhoods U_1, and U_2 of x_1 and x_2, respectively, that are disjoint.

Theorem 17.8.   *Every finite point set in a Hausdorff space X is closed.*

Proof.   It suffices to show that every one-point set $\{x_0\}$ is closed. If x is a point of X different from x_0, then x and x_0 have disjoint neighborhoods U and V, respectively. Since U does not intersect $\{x_0\}$, the point x cannot belong to the closure of the set $\{x_0\}$. As a result, the closure of the set $\{x_0\}$ is $\{x_0\}$ itself, so that it is closed.   ∎

The condition that finite point sets be closed is in fact weaker than the Hausdorff condition. For example, the real line $\mathbb{R}$ in the finite complement topology is not a Hausdorff space, but it is a space in which finite point sets are closed. The condition that finite point sets be closed has been given a name of its own: it is called the **T_1 axiom**. (We shall explain the reason for this strange terminology in Chapter 4.) The T_1 axiom will appear in this book in a few exercises, and in just one theorem, which is the following:

Theorem 17.9.   *Let X be a space satisfying the T_1 axiom; let A be a subset of X. Then the point x is a limit point of A if and only if every neighborhood of x contains infinitely many points of A.*

Proof.   If every neighborhood of x intersects A in infinitely many points, it certainly intersects A in some point other than x itself, so that x is a limit point of A.

Conversely, suppose that x is a limit point of A, and suppose some neighborhood U of x intersects A in only finitely many points. Then U also intersects $A - \{x\}$ in finitely many points; let $\{x_1, \ldots, x_m\}$ be the points of $U \cap (A - \{x\})$. The set $X - \{x_1, \ldots, x_m\}$ is an open set of X, since the finite point set $\{x_1, \ldots, x_m\}$ is closed; then

$$U \cap (X - \{x_1, \ldots, x_m\})$$

is a neighborhood of x that intersects the set $A - \{x\}$ not at all. This contradicts the assumption that x is a limit point of A.   ∎

One reason for our lack of interest in the T_1 axiom is the fact that many of the interesting theorems of topology require not just that axiom, but the full strength of the Hausdorff axiom. Furthermore, most of the spaces that are important to mathematicians are Hausdorff spaces. The following two theorems give some substance to these remarks.

Theorem 17.10.   *If X is a Hausdorff space, then a sequence of points of X converges to at most one point of X.*

Proof.   Suppose that x_n is a sequence of points of X that converges to x. If $y \neq x$, let U and V be disjoint neighborhoods of x and y, respectively. Since U contains x_n for all but finitely many values of n, the set V cannot. Therefore, x_n cannot converge to y.   ∎

If the sequence x_n of points of the Hausdorff space X converges to the point x of X, we often write $x_n \to x$, and we say that x is the **limit** of the sequence x_n.

The proof of the following result is left to the exercises.

Theorem 17.11. *Every simply ordered set is a Hausdorff space in the order topology. The product of two Hausdorff spaces is a Hausdorff space. A subspace of a Hausdorff space is a Hausdorff space.*

The Hausdorff condition is generally considered to be a very mild extra condition to impose on a topological space. Indeed, in a first course in topology some mathematicians go so far as to impose this condition at the outset, refusing to consider spaces that are not Hausdorff spaces. We shall not go this far, but we shall certainly assume the Hausdorff condition whenever it is needed in a proof without having any qualms about limiting seriously the range of applications of the results.

The Hausdorff condition is one of a number of extra conditions one can impose on a topological space. Each time one imposes such a condition, one can prove stronger theorems, but one limits the class of spaces to which the theorems apply. Much of the research that has been done in topology since its beginnings has centered on the problem of finding conditions that will be strong enough to enable one to prove interesting theorems about spaces satisfying those conditions, and yet not so strong that they limit severely the range of applications of the results.

We shall study a number of such conditions in the next two chapters. The Hausdorff condition and the T_1 axiom are but two of a collection of conditions similar to one another that are called collectively the *separation axioms*. Other conditions include the *countability axioms*, and various *compactness* and *connectedness* conditions. Some of these are quite stringent requirements, as you will see.

Exercises

1. Let $\mathcal{C}$ be a collection of subsets of the set X. Suppose that $\varnothing$ and X are in $\mathcal{C}$, and that finite unions and arbitrary intersections of elements of $\mathcal{C}$ are in $\mathcal{C}$. Show that the collection

$$\mathcal{T} = \{X - C \mid C \in \mathcal{C}\}$$

   is a topology on X.

2. Show that if A is closed in Y and Y is closed in X, then A is closed in X.

3. Show that if A is closed in X and B is closed in Y, then $A \times B$ is closed in $X \times Y$.

4. Show that if U is open in X and A is closed in X, then $U - A$ is open in X, and $A - U$ is closed in X.

5. Let X be an ordered set in the order topology. Show that $\overline{(a, b)} \subset [a, b]$. Under what conditions does equality hold?

6. Let A, B, and A_α denote subsets of a space X. Prove the following:
  (a) If $A \subset B$, then $\bar{A} \subset \bar{B}$.
  (b) $\overline{A \cup B} = \bar{A} \cup \bar{B}$.
  (c) $\overline{\bigcup A_\alpha} \supset \bigcup \bar{A}_\alpha$; give an example where equality fails.

7. Criticize the following "proof" that $\overline{\bigcup A_\alpha} \subset \bigcup \bar{A}_\alpha$: if $\{A_\alpha\}$ is a collection of sets in X and if $x \in \overline{\bigcup A_\alpha}$, then every neighborhood U of x intersects $\bigcup A_\alpha$. Thus U must intersect some A_α, so that x must belong to the closure of some A_α. Therefore, $x \in \bigcup \bar{A}_\alpha$.

8. Let A, B, and A_α denote subsets of a space X. Determine whether the following equations hold; if an equality fails, determine whether one of the inclusions $\supset$ or $\subset$ holds.
  (a) $\overline{A \cap B} = \bar{A} \cap \bar{B}$.
  (b) $\overline{\bigcap A_\alpha} = \bigcap \bar{A}_\alpha$.
  (c) $\overline{A - B} = \bar{A} - \bar{B}$.

9. Let $A \subset X$ and $B \subset Y$. Show that in the space $X \times Y$,

$$\overline{A \times B} = \bar{A} \times \bar{B}.$$

10. Show that every order topology is Hausdorff.

11. Show that the product of two Hausdorff spaces is Hausdorff.

12. Show that a subspace of a Hausdorff space is Hausdorff.

13. Show that X is Hausdorff if and only if the ***diagonal*** $\Delta = \{x \times x \mid x \in X\}$ is closed in $X \times X$.

14. In the finite complement topology on $\mathbb{R}$, to what point or points does the sequence $x_n = 1/n$ converge?

15. Show the T_1 axiom is equivalent to the condition that for each pair of points of X, each has a neighborhood not containing the other.

16. Consider the five topologies on $\mathbb{R}$ given in Exercise 7 of §13.
  (a) Determine the closure of the set $K = \{1/n \mid n \in \mathbb{Z}_+\}$ under each of these topologies.
  (b) Which of these topologies satisfy the Hausdorff axiom? the T_1 axiom?

17. Consider the lower limit topology on $\mathbb{R}$ and the topology given by the basis $\mathcal{C}$ of Exercise 8 of §13. Determine the closures of the intervals $A = (0, \sqrt{2})$ and $B = (\sqrt{2}, 3)$ in these two topologies.

18. Determine the closures of the following subsets of the ordered square:

$$A = \{(1/n) \times 0 \mid n \in \mathbb{Z}_+\},$$
$$B = \{(1 - 1/n) \times \tfrac{1}{2} \mid n \in \mathbb{Z}_+\},$$
$$C = \{x \times 0 \mid 0 < x < 1\},$$
$$D = \{x \times \tfrac{1}{2} \mid 0 < x < 1\},$$
$$E = \{\tfrac{1}{2} \times y \mid 0 < y < 1\}.$$

19. If $A \subset X$, we define the **boundary** of A by the equation

$$\text{Bd } A = \bar{A} \cap \overline{(X - A)}.$$

    (a) Show that Int A and Bd A are disjoint, and $\bar{A} = \text{Int } A \cup \text{Bd } A$.
    (b) Show that Bd $A = \varnothing \Leftrightarrow A$ is both open and closed.
    (c) Show that U is open $\Leftrightarrow \text{Bd } U = \bar{U} - U$.
    (d) If U is open, is it true that $U = \text{Int}(\bar{U})$? Justify your answer.

20. Find the boundary and the interior of each of the following subsets of $\mathbb{R}^2$:
    (a) $A = \{x \times y \mid y = 0\}$
    (b) $B = \{x \times y \mid x > 0 \text{ and } y \neq 0\}$
    (c) $C = A \cup B$
    (d) $D = \{x \times y \mid x \text{ is rational}\}$
    (e) $E = \{x \times y \mid 0 < x^2 - y^2 \leq 1\}$
    (f) $F = \{x \times y \mid x \neq 0 \text{ and } y \leq 1/x\}$

*21. (Kuratowski) Consider the collection of all subsets A of the topological space X. The operations of closure $A \to \bar{A}$ and complementation $A \to X - A$ are functions from this collection to itself.
    (a) Show that starting with a given set A, one can form no more than 14 distinct sets by applying these two operations successively.
    (b) Find a subset A of $\mathbb{R}$ (in its usual topology) for which the maximum of 14 is obtained.

§18   Continuous Functions

The concept of continuous function is basic to much of mathematics. Continuous functions on the real line appear in the first pages of any calculus book, and continuous functions in the plane and in space follow not far behind. More general kinds of continuous functions arise as one goes further in mathematics. In this section, we shall formulate a definition of continuity that will include all these as special cases, and we shall study various properties of continuous functions. Many of these properties are direct generalizations of things you learned about continuous functions in calculus and analysis.

Continuity of a Function

Let X and Y be topological spaces. A function $f : X \to Y$ is said to be **continuous** if for each open subset V of Y, the set $f^{-1}(V)$ is an open subset of X.

    Recall that $f^{-1}(V)$ is the set of all points x of X for which $f(x) \in V$; it is empty if V does not intersect the image set $f(X)$ of f.

    Continuity of a function depends not only upon the function f itself, but also on the topologies specified for its domain and range. If we wish to emphasize this fact, we can say that f is continuous *relative* to specific topologies on X and Y.

Let us note that if the topology of the range space Y is given by a basis $\mathcal{B}$, then to prove continuity of f it suffices to show that the inverse image of every *basis element* is open: The arbitrary open set V of Y can be written as a union of basis elements

$$V = \bigcup_{\alpha \in J} B_\alpha.$$

Then

$$f^{-1}(V) = \bigcup_{\alpha \in J} f^{-1}(B_\alpha),$$

so that $f^{-1}(V)$ is open if each set $f^{-1}(B_\alpha)$ is open.

If the topology on Y is given by a subbasis $\mathcal{S}$, to prove continuity of f it will even suffice to show that the inverse image of each *subbasis* element is open: The arbitrary basis element B for Y can be written as a finite intersection $S_1 \cap \cdots \cap S_n$ of subbasis elements; it follows from the equation

$$f^{-1}(B) = f^{-1}(S_1) \cap \cdots \cap f^{-1}(S_n)$$

that the inverse image of every basis element is open.

EXAMPLE 1.   Let us consider a function like those studied in analysis, a "real-valued function of a real variable,"

$$f : \mathbb{R} \longrightarrow \mathbb{R}.$$

In analysis, one defines continuity of f via the "ϵ-δ definition," a bugaboo over the years for every student of mathematics. As one would expect, the ϵ-δ definition and ours are equivalent. To prove that our definition implies the ϵ-δ definition, for instance, we proceed as follows:

Given x_0 in $\mathbb{R}$, and given $\epsilon > 0$, the interval $V = (f(x_0) - \epsilon, f(x_0) + \epsilon)$ is an open set of the range space $\mathbb{R}$. Therefore, $f^{-1}(V)$ is an open set in the domain space $\mathbb{R}$. Because $f^{-1}(V)$ contains the point x_0, it contains some basis element (a, b) about x_0. We choose δ to be the smaller of the two numbers $x_0 - a$ and $b - x_0$. Then if $|x - x_0| < \delta$, the point x must be in (a, b), so that $f(x) \in V$, and $|f(x) - f(x_0)| < \epsilon$, as desired.

Proving that the ϵ-δ definition implies our definition is no harder; we leave it to you. We shall return to this example when we study metric spaces.

EXAMPLE 2.   In calculus one considers the property of continuity for many kinds of functions. For example, one studies functions of the following types:

$$f : \mathbb{R} \longrightarrow \mathbb{R}^2 \quad \text{(curves in the plane)}$$
$$f : \mathbb{R} \longrightarrow \mathbb{R}^3 \quad \text{(curves in space)}$$
$$f : \mathbb{R}^2 \longrightarrow \mathbb{R} \quad \text{(functions } f(x, y) \text{ of two real variables)}$$
$$f : \mathbb{R}^3 \longrightarrow \mathbb{R} \quad \text{(functions } f(x, y, z) \text{ of three real variables)}$$
$$f : \mathbb{R}^2 \longrightarrow \mathbb{R}^2 \quad \text{(vector fields } \mathbf{v}(x, y) \text{ in the plane).}$$

Each of them has a notion of continuity defined for it. Our general definition of continuity includes all these as special cases; this fact will be a consequence of general theorems we shall prove concerning continuous functions on product spaces and on metric spaces.

EXAMPLE 3.   Let $\mathbb{R}$ denote the set of real numbers in its usual topology, and let $\mathbb{R}_\ell$ denote the same set in the lower limit topology. Let

$$f : \mathbb{R} \longrightarrow \mathbb{R}_\ell$$

be the identity function; $f(x) = x$ for every real number x. Then f is not a continuous function; the inverse image of the open set $[a, b)$ of $\mathbb{R}_\ell$ equals itself, which is not open in $\mathbb{R}$. On the other hand, the identity function

$$g : \mathbb{R}_\ell \longrightarrow \mathbb{R}$$

is continuous, because the inverse image of (a, b) is itself, which is open in $\mathbb{R}_\ell$.

In analysis, one studies several different but equivalent ways of formulating the definition of continuity. Some of these generalize to arbitrary spaces, and they are considered in the theorems that follow. The familiar "ϵ-δ" definition and the "convergent sequence definition" do not generalize to arbitrary spaces; they will be treated when we study metric spaces.

Theorem 18.1.   *Let X and Y be topological spaces; let $f : X \to Y$. Then the following are equivalent:*

(1) *f is continuous.*

(2) *For every subset A of X, one has $f(\bar{A}) \subset \overline{f(A)}$.*

(3) *For every closed set B of Y, the set $f^{-1}(B)$ is closed in X.*

(4) *For each $x \in X$ and each neighborhood V of $f(x)$, there is a neighborhood U of x such that $f(U) \subset V$.*

If the condition in (4) holds for the point x of X, we say that f is ***continuous at the point*** x.

Proof.   We show that $(1) \Rightarrow (2) \Rightarrow (3) \Rightarrow (1)$ and that $(1) \Rightarrow (4) \Rightarrow (1)$.

$(1) \Rightarrow (2)$. Assume that f is continuous. Let A be a subset of X. We show that if $x \in \bar{A}$, then $f(x) \in \overline{f(A)}$. Let V be a neighborhood of $f(x)$. Then $f^{-1}(V)$ is an open set of X containing x; it must intersect A in some point y. Then V intersects $f(A)$ in the point $f(y)$, so that $f(x) \in \overline{f(A)}$, as desired.

$(2) \Rightarrow (3)$. Let B be closed in Y and let $A = f^{-1}(B)$. We wish to prove that A is closed in X; we show that $\bar{A} = A$. By elementary set theory, we have $f(A) = f(f^{-1}(B)) \subset B$. Therefore, if $x \in \bar{A}$,

$$f(x) \in f(\bar{A}) \subset \overline{f(A)} \subset \bar{B} = B,$$

so that $x \in f^{-1}(B) = A$. Thus $\bar{A} \subset A$, so that $\bar{A} = A$, as desired.

$(3) \Rightarrow (1)$. Let V be an open set of Y. Set $B = Y - V$. Then

$$f^{-1}(B) = f^{-1}(Y) - f^{-1}(V) = X - f^{-1}(V).$$

Now B is a closed set of Y. Then $f^{-1}(B)$ is closed in X by hypothesis, so that $f^{-1}(V)$ is open in X, as desired.

(1) $\Rightarrow$ (4). Let $x \in X$ and let V be a neighborhood of $f(x)$. Then the set $U = f^{-1}(V)$ is a neighborhood of x such that $f(U) \subset V$.

(4) $\Rightarrow$ (1). Let V be an open set of Y; let x be a point of $f^{-1}(V)$. Then $f(x) \in V$, so that by hypothesis there is a neighborhood U_x of x such that $f(U_x) \subset V$. Then $U_x \subset f^{-1}(V)$. It follows that $f^{-1}(V)$ can be written as the union of the open sets U_x, so that it is open.   ∎

Homeomorphisms

Let X and Y be topological spaces; let $f : X \to Y$ be a bijection. If both the function f and the inverse function

$$f^{-1} : Y \to X$$

are continuous, then f is called a ***homeomorphism***.

The condition that f^{-1} be continuous says that for each open set U of X, the inverse image of U under the map $f^{-1} : Y \to X$ is open in Y. But the *inverse image* of U under the map f^{-1} is the same as the *image* of U under the map f. See Figure 18.1. So another way to define a homeomorphism is to say that it is a bijective correspondence $f : X \to Y$ such that $f(U)$ is open if and only if U is open.

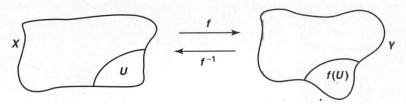

Figure 18.1

This remark shows that a homeomorphism $f : X \to Y$ gives us a bijective correspondence not only between X and Y but between the collections of open sets of X and of Y. As a result, any property of X that is entirely expressed in terms of the topology of X (that is, in terms of the open sets of X) yields, via the correspondence f, the corresponding property for the space Y. Such a property of X is called a ***topological property*** of X.

You may have studied in modern algebra the notion of an *isomorphism* between algebraic objects such as groups or rings. An isomorphism is a bijective correspondence that preserves the algebraic structure involved. The analogous concept in topology is that of *homeomorphism*; it is a bijective correspondence that preserves the topological structure involved.

Now suppose that $f : X \to Y$ is an injective continuous map, where X and Y are topological spaces. Let Z be the image set $f(X)$, considered as a subspace of Y; then the function $f' : X \to Z$ obtained by restricting the range of f is bijective. If f' happens to be a homeomorphism of X with Z, we say that the map $f : X \to Y$ is a ***topological imbedding***, or simply an ***imbedding***, of X in Y.

EXAMPLE 4.   The function $f : \mathbb{R} \to \mathbb{R}$ given by $f(x) = 3x + 1$ is a homeomorphism. See Figure 18.2. If we define $g : \mathbb{R} \to \mathbb{R}$ by the equation

$$g(y) = \frac{1}{3}(y - 1)$$

then one can check easily that $f(g(y)) = y$ and $g(f(x)) = x$ for all real numbers x and y. It follows that f is bijective and that $g = f^{-1}$; the continuity of f and g is a familiar result from calculus.

EXAMPLE 5.   The function $F : (-1, 1) \to \mathbb{R}$ defined by

$$F(x) = \frac{x}{1 - x^2}$$

is a homeomorphism. See Figure 18.3. We have already noted in Example 9 of §3 that F is a bijective order-preserving correspondence; its inverse is the function G defined by

$$G(y) = \frac{2y}{1 + (1 + 4y^2)^{1/2}}.$$

The fact that F is a homeomorphism can be proved in two ways. One way is to note that because F is order preserving and bijective, F carries a basis element for the order topology in $(-1, 1)$ onto a basis element for the order topology in $\mathbb{R}$ and vice versa. As a result, F is automatically a homeomorphism of $(-1, 1)$ with $\mathbb{R}$ (both in the order topology). Since the order topology on $(-1, 1)$ and the usual (subspace) topology agree, F is a homeomorphism of $(-1, 1)$ with $\mathbb{R}$.

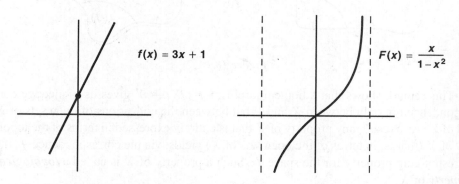

Figure 18.2   *Figure 18.3*

A second way to show F a homeomorphism is to use the continuity of the algebraic functions and the square-root function to show that both F and G are continuous. These are familiar facts from calculus.

EXAMPLE 6.   A bijective function $f : X \to Y$ can be continuous without being a homeomorphism. One such function is the identity map $g : \mathbb{R}_\ell \to \mathbb{R}$ considered in Example 3. Another is the following: Let S^1 denote the ***unit circle***,

$$S^1 = \{x \times y \mid x^2 + y^2 = 1\},$$

considered as a subspace of the plane $\mathbb{R}^2$, and let

$$F : [0, 1) \longrightarrow S^1$$

be the map defined by $f(t) = (\cos 2\pi t, \sin 2\pi t)$. The fact that f is bijective and continuous follows from familiar properties of the trigonometric functions. But the function f^{-1} is not continuous. The image under f of the open set $U = [0, \frac{1}{4})$ of the domain, for instance, is not open in S^1, for the point $p = f(0)$ lies in no open set V of $\mathbb{R}^2$ such that $V \cap S^1 \subset f(U)$. See Figure 18.4.

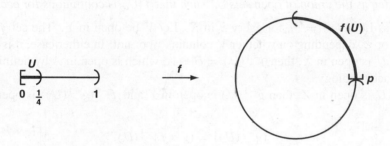

Figure 18.4

EXAMPLE 7.   Consider the function

$$g : [0, 1) \longrightarrow \mathbb{R}^2$$

obtained from the function f of the preceding example by expanding the range. The map g is an example of a continuous injective map that is not an imbedding.

Constructing Continuous Functions

How does one go about constructing continuous functions from one topological space to another? There are a number of methods used in analysis, of which some generalize to arbitrary topological spaces and others do not. We study first some constructions that do hold for general topological spaces, deferring consideration of the others until later.

Theorem 18.2 (Rules for constructing continuous functions).   *Let X, Y, and Z be topological spaces.*

(a) *(Constant function) If $f : X \to Y$ maps all of X into the single point y_0 of Y, then f is continuous.*

(b) *(Inclusion) If A is a subspace of X, the inclusion function $j : A \to X$ is continuous.*

(c) *(Composites) If $f : X \to Y$ and $g : Y \to Z$ are continuous, then the map $g \circ f : X \to Z$ is continuous.*

(d) (*Restricting the domain*) If $f : X \to Y$ is continuous, and if A is a subspace of X, then the restricted function $f|A : A \to Y$ is continuous.

(e) (*Restricting or expanding the range*) Let $f : X \to Y$ be continuous. If Z is a subspace of Y containing the image set $f(X)$, then the function $g : X \to Z$ obtained by restricting the range of f is continuous. If Z is a space having Y as a subspace, then the function $h : X \to Z$ obtained by expanding the range of f is continuous.

(f) (*Local formulation of continuity*) The map $f : X \to Y$ is continuous if X can be written as the union of open sets U_α such that $f|U_\alpha$ is continuous for each α.

Proof.   (a) Let $f(x) = y_0$ for every x in X. Let V be open in Y. The set $f^{-1}(V)$ equals X or $\varnothing$, depending on whether V contains y_0 or not. In either case, it is open.

(b) If U is open in X, then $j^{-1}(U) = U \cap A$, which is open in A by definition of the subspace topology.

(c) If U is open in Z, then $g^{-1}(U)$ is open in Y and $f^{-1}(g^{-1}(U))$ is open in X. But

$$f^{-1}(g^{-1}(U)) = (g \circ f)^{-1}(U),$$

by elementary set theory.

(d) The function $f|A$ equals the composite of the inclusion map $j : A \to X$ and the map $f : X \to Y$, both of which are continuous.

(e) Let $f : X \to Y$ be continuous. If $f(X) \subset Z \subset Y$, we show that the function $g : X \to Z$ obtained from f is continuous. Let B be open in Z. Then $B = Z \cap U$ for some open set U of Y. Because Z contains the entire image set $f(X)$,

$$f^{-1}(U) = g^{-1}(B),$$

by elementary set theory. Since $f^{-1}(U)$ is open, so is $g^{-1}(B)$.

To show $h : X \to Z$ is continuous if Z has Y as a subspace, note that h is the composite of the map $f : X \to Y$ and the inclusion map $j : Y \to Z$.

(f) By hypothesis, we can write X as a union of open sets U_α, such that $f|U_\alpha$, is continuous for each α. Let V be an open set in Y. Then

$$f^{-1}(V) \cap U_\alpha = (f|U_\alpha)^{-1}(V),$$

because both expressions represent the set of those points x lying in U_α for which $f(x) \in V$. Since $f|U$ is continuous, this set is open in U_α, and hence open in X. But

$$f^{-1}(V) = \bigcup_\alpha (f^{-1}(V) \cap U_\alpha),$$

so that $f^{-1}(V)$ is also open in X.   ■

Theorem 18.3 (The pasting lemma).   Let $X = A \cup B$, where A and B are closed in X. Let $f : A \to Y$ and $g : B \to Y$ be continuous. If $f(x) = g(x)$ for every $x \in A \cap B$, then f and g combine to give a continuous function $h : X \to Y$, defined by setting $h(x) = f(x)$ if $x \in A$, and $h(x) = g(x)$ if $x \in B$.

Proof.   Let C be a closed subset of Y. Now

$$h^{-1}(C) = f^{-1}(C) \cup g^{-1}(C),$$

by elementary set theory. Since f is continuous, $f^{-1}(C)$ is closed in A and, therefore, closed in X. Similarly, $g^{-1}(C)$ is closed in B and therefore closed in X. Their union $h^{-1}(C)$ is thus closed in X.   ∎

This theorem also holds if A and B are open sets in X; this is just a special case of the "local formulation of continuity" rule given in preceding theorem.

EXAMPLE 8.   Let us define a function $h : \mathbb{R} \to \mathbb{R}$ by setting

$$h(x) = \begin{cases} x & \text{for } x \le 0, \\ x/2 & \text{for } x \ge 0. \end{cases}$$

Each of the "pieces" of this definition is a continuous function, and they agree on the overlapping part of their domains, which is the one-point set $\{0\}$. Since their domains are closed in $\mathbb{R}$, the function h is continuous. One needs the "pieces" of the function to agree on the overlapping part of their domains in order to have a function at all. The equations

$$k(x) = \begin{cases} x - 2 & \text{for } x \le 0, \\ x + 2 & \text{for } x \ge 0, \end{cases}$$

for instance, do not define a function. On the other hand, one needs some limitations on the sets A and B to guarantee continuity. The equations

$$l(x) = \begin{cases} x - 2 & \text{for } x < 0, \\ x + 2 & \text{for } x \ge 0, \end{cases}$$

for instance, do define a function l mapping $\mathbb{R}$ into $\mathbb{R}$, and both of the pieces are continuous. But l is not continuous; the inverse image of the open set $(1, 3)$, for instance, is the nonopen set $[0, 1)$. See Figure 18.5.

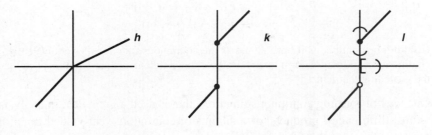

Figure 18.5

Theorem 18.4 (Maps into products).   *Let $f : A \to X \times Y$ be given by the equation*

$$f(a) = (f_1(a), f_2(a)).$$

Then f is continuous if and only if the functions

$$f_1 : A \longrightarrow X \quad \text{and} \quad f_2 : A \longrightarrow Y$$

are continuous.

The maps f_1 and f_2 are called the **coordinate functions** of f.

Proof.   Let $\pi_1 : X \times Y \to X$ and $\pi_2 : X \times Y \to Y$ be projections onto the first and second factors, respectively. These maps are continuous. For $\pi_1^{-1}(U) = U \times Y$ and $\pi_2^{-1}(V) = X \times V$, and these sets are open if U and V are open. Note that for each $a \in A$,

$$f_1(a) = \pi_1(f(a)) \quad \text{and} \quad f_2(a) = \pi_2(f(a)).$$

If the function f is continuous, then f_1 and f_2 are composites of continuous functions and therefore continuous. Conversely, suppose that f_1 and f_2 are continuous. We show that for each basis element $U \times V$ for the topology of $X \times Y$, its inverse image $f^{-1}(U \times V)$ is open. A point a is in $f^{-1}(U \times V)$ if and only if $f(a) \in U \times V$, that is, if and only if $f_1(a) \in U$ and $f_2(a) \in V$. Therefore,

$$f^{-1}(U \times V) = f_1^{-1}(U) \cap f_2^{-1}(V).$$

Since both of the sets $f_1^{-1}(U)$ and $f_2^{-1}(V)$ are open, so is their intersection.   ∎

There is no useful criterion for the continuity of a map $f : A \times B \to X$ whose *domain* is a product space. One might conjecture that f is continuous if it is continuous "in each variable separately," but this conjecture is not true. (See Exercise 12.)

EXAMPLE 9.   In calculus, a *parametrized curve* in the plane is defined to be a continuous map $f : [a, b] \to \mathbb{R}^2$. It is often expressed in the form $f(t) = (x(t), y(t))$; and one frequently uses the fact that f is a continuous function of t if both x and y are. Similarly, a *vector field* in the plane

$$\mathbf{v}(x, y) = P(x, y)\mathbf{i} + Q(x, y)\mathbf{j}$$
$$= (P(x, y), Q(x, y))$$

is said to be continuous if both P and Q are continuous functions, or equivalently, if $\mathbf{v}$ is continuous as a map of $\mathbb{R}^2$ into $\mathbb{R}^2$. Both of these statements are simply special cases of the preceding theorem.

One way of forming continuous functions that is used a great deal in analysis is to take sums, differences, products, or quotients of continuous real-valued functions. It is a standard theorem that if $f, g : X \to \mathbb{R}$ are continuous, then $f + g$, $f - g$, and $f \cdot g$ are continuous, and f/g is continuous if $g(x) \neq 0$ for all x. We shall consider this theorem in §21.

Yet another method for constructing continuous functions that is familiar from analysis is to take the limit of an infinite sequence of functions. There is a theorem to the effect that if a sequence of continuous real-valued functions of a real variable converges uniformly to a limit function, then the limit function is necessarily continuous. This theorem is called the *Uniform Limit Theorem*. It is used, for instance, to demonstrate the continuity of the trigonometric functions, when one defines these functions rigorously using the infinite series definitions of the sine and cosine. This theorem generalizes to a theorem about maps of an arbitrary topological space X into a metric space Y. We shall prove it in §21.

Exercises

1. Prove that for functions $f : \mathbb{R} \to \mathbb{R}$, the ϵ-δ definition of continuity implies the open set definition.

2. Suppose that $f : X \to Y$ is continuous. If x is a limit point of the subset A of X, is it necessarily true that $f(x)$ is a limit point of $f(A)$?

3. Let X and X' denote a single set in the two topologies $\mathcal{T}$ and $\mathcal{T}'$, respectively. Let $i : X' \to X$ be the identity function.
   (a) Show that i is continuous $\Leftrightarrow$ $\mathcal{T}'$ is finer than $\mathcal{T}$.
   (b) Show that i is a homeomorphism $\Leftrightarrow$ $\mathcal{T}' = \mathcal{T}$.

4. Given $x_0 \in X$ and $y_0 \in Y$, show that the maps $f : X \to X \times Y$ and $g : Y \to X \times Y$ defined by

$$f(x) = x \times y_0 \quad \text{and} \quad g(y) = x_0 \times y$$

   are imbeddings.

5. Show that the subspace (a, b) of $\mathbb{R}$ is homeomorphic with $(0, 1)$ and the subspace $[a, b]$ of $\mathbb{R}$ is homeomorphic with $[0, 1]$.

6. Find a function $f : \mathbb{R} \to \mathbb{R}$ that is continuous at precisely one point.

7. (a) Suppose that $f : \mathbb{R} \to \mathbb{R}$ is "continuous from the right," that is,

$$\lim_{x \to a^+} f(x) = f(a),$$

   for each $a \in \mathbb{R}$. Show that f is continuous when considered as a function from $\mathbb{R}_\ell$ to $\mathbb{R}$.
   (b) Can you conjecture what functions $f : \mathbb{R} \to \mathbb{R}$ are continuous when considered as maps from $\mathbb{R}$ to $\mathbb{R}_\ell$? As maps from $\mathbb{R}_\ell$ to $\mathbb{R}_\ell$? We shall return to this question in Chapter 3.

8. Let Y be an ordered set in the order topology. Let $f, g : X \to Y$ be continuous.
   (a) Show that the set $\{x \mid f(x) \le g(x)\}$ is closed in X.

(b) Let $h : X \to Y$ be the function

$$h(x) = \min\{f(x), g(x)\}.$$

Show that h is continuous. [*Hint:* Use the pasting lemma.]

9. Let $\{A_\alpha\}$ be a collection of subsets of X; let $X = \bigcup_\alpha A_\alpha$. Let $f : X \to Y$; suppose that $f|A_\alpha$, is continuous for each α.
    (a) Show that if the collection $\{A_\alpha\}$ is finite and each set A_α is closed, then f is continuous.
    (b) Find an example where the collection $\{A_\alpha\}$ is countable and each A_α is closed, but f is not continuous.
    (c) An indexed family of sets $\{A_\alpha\}$ is said to be *locally finite* if each point x of X has a neighborhood that intersects A_α for only finitely many values of α. Show that if the family $\{A_\alpha\}$ is locally finite and each A_α is closed, then f is continuous.

10. Let $f : A \to B$ and $g : C \to D$ be continuous functions. Let us define a map $f \times g : A \times C \to B \times D$ by the equation

$$(f \times g)(a \times c) = f(a) \times g(c).$$

Show that $f \times g$ is continuous.

11. Let $F \quad X \times Y \to Z$. We say that F is *continuous in each variable separately* if for each y_0 in Y, the map $h : X \to Z$ defined by $h(x) = F(x \times y_0)$ is continuous, and for each x_0 in X, the map $k : Y \to Z$ defined by $k(y) = F(x_0 \times y)$ is continuous. Show that if F is continuous, then F is continuous in each variable separately.

12. Let $F : \mathbb{R} \times \mathbb{R} \to \mathbb{R}$ be defined by the equation

$$F(x \times y) = \begin{cases} xy/(x^2 + y^2) & \text{if } x \times y \neq 0 \times 0. \\ 0 & \text{if } x \times y = 0 \times 0. \end{cases}$$

(a) Show that F is continuous in each variable separately.
(b) Compute the function $g : \mathbb{R} \to \mathbb{R}$ defined by $g(x) = F(x \times x)$.
(c) Show that F is not continuous.

13. Let $A \subset X$; let $f : A \to Y$ be continuous; let Y be Hausdorff. Show that if f may be extended to a continuous function $g : \bar{A} \to Y$, then g is uniquely determined by f.

§19   The Product Topology

We now return, for the remainder of the chapter, to the consideration of various methods for imposing topologies on sets.

Previously, we defined a topology on the product $X \times Y$ of two topological spaces. In the present section, we generalize this definition to more general cartesian products.

So let us consider the cartesian products

$$X_1 \times \cdots \times X_n \quad \text{and} \quad X_1 \times X_2 \times \cdots,$$

where each X_i is a topological space. There are two possible ways to proceed. One way is to take as basis all sets of the form $U_1 \times \cdots \times U_n$ in the first case, and of the form $U_1 \times U_2 \times \cdots$ in the second case, where U_i is an open set of X_i for each i. This procedure does indeed define a topology on the cartesian product; we shall call it the *box topology*.

Another way to proceed is to generalize the subbasis formulation of the definition, given in §15. In this case, we take as a subbasis all sets of the form $\pi_i^{-1}(U_i)$, where i is any index and U_i is an open set of X_i. We shall call this topology the *product topology*.

How do these topologies differ? Consider the typical basis element B for the second topology. It is a finite intersection of subbasis elements $\pi_i^{-1}(U_i)$, say for $i = i_1, \ldots, i_k$. Then a point $\mathbf{x}$ belongs to B if and only if $\pi_i(\mathbf{x})$ belongs to U_i for $i = i_1, \ldots, i_k$; there is no restriction on $\pi_i(x)$ for other values of i.

It follows that these two topologies agree for the finite cartesian product and differ for the infinite product. What is not clear is why we seem to prefer the second topology. This is the question we shall explore in this section.

Before proceeding, however, we shall introduce a more general notion of cartesian product. So far, we have defined the cartesian product of an indexed family of sets only in the cases where the index set was the set $\{1, \ldots, n\}$ or the set $\mathbb{Z}_+$. Now we consider the case where the index set is completely arbitrary.

Definition. Let J be an index set. Given a set X, we define a ***J-tuple*** of elements of X to be a function $\mathbf{x} : J \to X$. If α is an element of J, we often denote the value of $\mathbf{x}$ at α by x_α rather than $\mathbf{x}(\alpha)$; we call it the αth ***coordinate*** of $\mathbf{x}$. And we often denote the function $\mathbf{x}$ itself by the symbol

$$(x_\alpha)_{\alpha \in J},$$

which is as close as we can come to a "tuple notation" for an arbitrary index set J. We denote the set of all J-tuples of elements of X by X^J.

Definition. Let $\{A_\alpha\}_{\alpha \in J}$ be an indexed family of sets; let $X = \bigcup_{\alpha \in J} A_\alpha$. The ***cartesian product*** of this indexed family, denoted by

$$\prod_{\alpha \in J} A_\alpha,$$

is defined to be the set of all J-tuples $(x_\alpha)_{\alpha \in J}$ of elements of X such that $x_\alpha \in A_\alpha$ for each $\alpha \in J$. That is, it is the set of all functions

$$\mathbf{x} : J \to \bigcup_{\alpha \in J} A_\alpha$$

such that $\mathbf{x}(\alpha) \in A_\alpha$ for each $\alpha \in J$.

Occasionally we denote the product simply by $\prod A_\alpha$, and its general element by (x_α), if the index set is understood.

If all the sets A_α are equal to one set X, then the cartesian product $\prod_{\alpha \in J} A_\alpha$ is just the set X^J of *all* J-tuples of elements of X. We sometimes use "tuple notation" for the elements of X^J, and sometimes we use functional notation, depending on which is more convenient.

Definition. Let $\{X_\alpha\}_{\alpha \in J}$ be an indexed family of topological spaces. Let us take as a basis for a topology on the product space

$$\prod_{\alpha \in J} X_\alpha$$

the collection of all sets of the form

$$\prod_{\alpha \in J} U_\alpha,$$

where U_α is open in X_α, for each $\alpha \in J$. The topology generated by this basis is called the **box topology**.

This collection satisfies the first condition for a basis because $\prod X_\alpha$ is itself a basis element; and it satisfies the second condition because the intersection of any two basis elements is another basis element:

$$\left(\prod_{\alpha \in J} U_\alpha \right) \cap \left(\prod_{\alpha \in J} V_\alpha \right) = \prod_{\alpha \in J} (U_\alpha \cap V_\alpha).$$

Now we generalize the subbasis formulation of the definition. Let

$$\pi_\beta : \prod_{\alpha \in J} X_\alpha \to X_\beta$$

be the function assigning to each element of the product space its βth coordinate,

$$\pi_\beta((x_\alpha)_{\alpha \in J}) = x_\beta;$$

it is called the **projection mapping** associated with the index β.

Definition. Let $\mathcal{S}_\beta$ denote the collection

$$\mathcal{S}_\beta = \{\pi_\beta^{-1}(U_\beta) \mid U_\beta \text{ open in } X_\beta\},$$

and let $\mathcal{S}$ denote the union of these collections,

$$\mathcal{S} = \bigcup_{\beta \in J} \mathcal{S}_\beta.$$

The topology generated by the subbasis $\mathcal{S}$ is called the **product topology**. In this topology $\prod_{\alpha \in J} X_\alpha$ is called a **product space**.

To compare these topologies, we consider the basis $\mathcal{B}$ that $\mathcal{S}$ generates. The collection $\mathcal{B}$ consists of all finite intersections of elements of $\mathcal{S}$. If we intersect elements belonging to the same one of the sets $\mathcal{S}_\beta$, we do not get anything new, because

$$\pi_\beta^{-1}(U_\beta) \cap \pi_\beta^{-1}(V_\beta) = \pi_\beta^{-1}(U_\beta \cap V_\beta);$$

the intersection of two elements of $\mathcal{S}_\beta$, or of finitely many such elements, is again an element of $\mathcal{S}_\beta$. We get something new only when we intersect elements from different sets $\mathcal{S}_\beta$. The typical element of the basis $\mathcal{B}$ can thus be described as follows: Let β_1, $\ldots$, β_n be a finite set of distinct indices from the index set J, and let U_{β_i} be an open set in X_{β_i} for $i = 1, \ldots, n$. Then

$$B = \pi_{\beta_1}^{-1}(U_{\beta_1}) \cap \pi_{\beta_2}^{-1}(U_{\beta_2}) \cap \cdots \cap \pi_{\beta_n}^{-1}(U_{\beta_n})$$

is the typical element of $\mathcal{B}$.

Now a point $\mathbf{x} = (x_\alpha)$ is in B if and only if its β_1th coordinate is in U_{β_1}, its β_2th coordinate is in U_{β_2}, and so on. There is no restriction whatever on the αth coordinate of $\mathbf{x}$ if α is not one of the indices $\beta_1, \ldots, \beta_n$. As a result, we can write B as the product

$$B = \prod_{\alpha \in J} U_\alpha,$$

where U_α denotes the entire space X_α if $\alpha \neq \beta_1, \ldots, \beta_n$.

All this is summarized in the following theorem:

Theorem 19.1 (Comparison of the box and product topologies). *The box topology on $\prod X_\alpha$ has as basis all sets of the form $\prod U_\alpha$, where U_α is open in X_α for each α. The product topology on $\prod X_\alpha$ has as basis all sets of the form $\prod U_\alpha$, where U_α is open in X_α for each α and U_α equals X_α except for finitely many values of α.*

Two things are immediately clear. First, for finite products $\prod_{\alpha=1}^{n} X_\alpha$ the two topologies are precisely the same. Second, the box topology is in general finer than the product topology.

What is not so clear is why we prefer the product topology to the box topology. The answer will appear as we continue our study of topology. We shall find that a number of important theorems about finite products will also hold for arbitrary products if we use the product topology, but not if we use the box topology. As a result, the product topology is extremely important in mathematics. The box topology is not so important; we shall use it primarily for constructing counterexamples. Therefore, we make the following convention:

> *Whenever we consider the product $\prod X_\alpha$, we shall assume it is given the product topology unless we specifically state otherwise.*

Some of the theorems we proved for the product $X \times Y$ hold for the product $\prod X_\alpha$ no matter which topology we use. We list them here; most of the proofs are left to the exercises.

Theorem 19.2. *Suppose the topology on each space X_α is given by a basis $\mathcal{B}_\alpha$. The collection of all sets of the form*

$$\prod_{\alpha \in J} B_\alpha,$$

where $B_\alpha \in \mathcal{B}_\alpha$ for each α, will serve as a basis for the box topology on $\prod_{\alpha \in J} X_\alpha$.

The collection of all sets of the same form, where $B_\alpha \in \mathcal{B}_\alpha$ for finitely many indices α and $B_\alpha = X_\alpha$ for all the remaining indices, will serve as a basis for the product topology $\prod_{\alpha \in J} X_\alpha$.

> EXAMPLE 1.   Consider euclidean n-space $\mathbb{R}^n$. A basis for $\mathbb{R}$ consists of all open intervals in $\mathbb{R}$; hence a basis for the topology of $\mathbb{R}^n$ consists of all products of the form
>
> $$(a_1, b_1) \times (a_2, b_2) \times \cdots \times (a_n, b_n).$$
>
> Since $\mathbb{R}^n$ is a finite product, the box and product topologies agree. Whenever we consider $\mathbb{R}^n$, we will assume that it is given this topology, unless we specifically state otherwise.

Theorem 19.3. *Let A_α be a subspace of X_α, for each $\alpha \in J$. Then $\prod A_\alpha$ is a subspace of $\prod X_\alpha$ if both products are given the box topology, or if both products are given the product topology.*

Theorem 19.4. *If each space X_α is Hausdorff space, then $\prod X_\alpha$ is a Hausdorff space in both the box and product topologies.*

Theorem 19.5. *Let $\{X_\alpha\}$ be an indexed family of spaces; let $A_\alpha \subset X_\alpha$ for each α. If $\prod X_\alpha$ is given either the product or the box topology, then*

$$\prod \bar{A}_\alpha = \overline{\prod A_\alpha}.$$

Proof. Let $\mathbf{x} = (x_\alpha)$ be a point of $\prod \bar{A}_\alpha$; we show that $\mathbf{x} \in \overline{\prod A_\alpha}$. Let $U = \prod U_\alpha$ be a basis element for either the box or product topology that contains $\mathbf{x}$. Since $x_\alpha \in \bar{A}_\alpha$, we can choose a point $y_\alpha \in U_\alpha \cap A_\alpha$ for each α. Then $\mathbf{y} = (y_\alpha)$ belongs to both U and $\prod A_\alpha$. Since U is arbitrary, it follows that $\mathbf{x}$ belongs to the closure of $\prod A_\alpha$.

Conversely, suppose $\mathbf{x} = (x_\alpha)$ lies in the closure of $\prod A_\alpha$, in either topology. We show that for any given index β, we have $x_\beta \in \bar{A}_\beta$. Let V_β be an arbitrary open set of X_β containing x_β. Since $\pi_\beta^{-1}(V_\beta)$ is open in $\prod X_\alpha$ in either topology, it contains a point $\mathbf{y} = (y_\alpha)$ of $\prod A_\alpha$. Then y_β belongs to $V_\beta \cap A_\beta$. It follows that $x_\beta \in \bar{A}_\beta$. ∎

So far, no reason has appeared for preferring the product to the box topology. It is when we try to generalize our previous theorem about continuity of maps into product spaces that a difference first arises. Here is a theorem that does not hold if $\prod X_\alpha$ is given the box topology:

Theorem 19.6.   *Let $f : A \to \prod_{\alpha \in J} X_\alpha$ be given by the equation*

$$f(a) = (f_\alpha(a))_{\alpha \in J},$$

where $f_\alpha : A \to X_\alpha$ for each α. Let $\prod X_\alpha$ have the product topology. Then the function f is continuous if and only if each function f_α is continuous.

Proof.   Let π_β be the projection of the product onto its βth factor. The function π_β is continuous, for if U_β is open in X_β, the set $\pi_\beta^{-1}(U_\beta)$ is a subbasis element for the product topology on X_α. Now suppose that $f : A \to \prod X_\alpha$ is continuous. The function f_β equals the composite $\pi_\beta \circ f$; being the composite of two continuous functions, it is continuous.

Conversely, suppose that each coordinate function f_α is continuous. To prove that f is continuous, it suffices to prove that the inverse image under f of each subbasis element is open in A; we remarked on this fact when we defined continuous functions. A typical subbasis element for the product topology on $\prod X_\alpha$ is a set of the form $\pi_\beta^{-1}(U_\beta)$, where β is some index and U_β is open in X_β. Now

$$f^{-1}(\pi_\beta^{-1}(U_\beta)) = f_\beta^{-1}(U_\beta),$$

because $f_\beta = \pi_\beta \circ f$. Since f_β is continuous, this set is open in A, as desired.   ∎

Why does this theorem fail if we use the box topology? Probably the most convincing thing to do is to look at an example.

EXAMPLE 2.   Consider $\mathbb{R}^\omega$, the countably infinite product of $\mathbb{R}$ with itself. Recall that

$$\mathbb{R}^\omega = \prod_{n \in \mathbb{Z}_+} X_n,$$

where $X_n = \mathbb{R}$ for each n. Let us define a function $f : \mathbb{R} \to \mathbb{R}^\omega$ by the equation

$$f(t) = (t, t, t, \dots);$$

the nth coordinate function of f is the function $f_n(t) = t$. Each of the coordinate functions $f_n : \mathbb{R} \to \mathbb{R}$ is continuous; therefore, the function f is continuous if $\mathbb{R}^\omega$ is given the product topology. But f is not continuous if $\mathbb{R}^\omega$ is given the box topology. Consider, for example, the basis element

$$B = (-1, 1) \times (-\frac{1}{2}, \frac{1}{2}) \times (-\frac{1}{3}, \frac{1}{3}) \times \cdots$$

for the box topology. We assert that $f^{-1}(B)$ is not open in $\mathbb{R}$. If $f^{-1}(B)$ were open in $\mathbb{R}$, it would contain some interval $(-\delta, \delta)$ about the point 0. This would mean that $f((-\delta, \delta)) \subset B$, so that, applying π_n to both sides of the inclusion,

$$f_n((-\delta, \delta)) = (-\delta, \delta) \subset (-1/n, 1/n)$$

for all n, a contradiction.

Exercises

1. Prove Theorem 19.2.

2. Prove Theorem 19.3.

3. Prove Theorem 19.4.

4. Show that $(X_1 \times \cdots \times X_{n-1}) \times X_n$ is homeomorphic with $X_1 \times \cdots \times X_n$.

5. One of the implications stated in Theorem 19.6 holds for the box topology. Which one?

6. Let $\mathbf{x}_1, \mathbf{x}_2, \ldots$ be a sequence of the points of the product space $\prod X_\alpha$. Show that this sequence converges to the point $\mathbf{x}$ if and only if the sequence $\pi_\alpha(\mathbf{x}_1), \pi_\alpha(\mathbf{x}_2),$ $\ldots$ converges to $\pi_\alpha(\mathbf{x})$ for each α. Is this fact true if one uses the box topology instead of the product topology?

7. Let $\mathbb{R}^\infty$ be the subset of $\mathbb{R}^\omega$ consisting of all sequences that are "eventually zero," that is, all sequences $(x_1, x_2, \ldots)$ such that $x_i \neq 0$ for only finitely many values of i. What is the closure of $\mathbb{R}^\infty$ in $\mathbb{R}^\omega$ in the box and product topologies? Justify your answer.

8. Given sequences $(a_1, a_2, \ldots)$ and $(b_1, b_2, \ldots)$ of real numbers with $a_i > 0$ for all i, define $h : \mathbb{R}^\omega \to \mathbb{R}^\omega$ by the equation

$$h((x_1, x_2, \ldots)) = (a_1 x_1 + b_1, a_2 x_2 + b_2, \ldots).$$

Show that if $\mathbb{R}^\omega$ is given the product topology, h is a homeomorphism of $\mathbb{R}^\omega$ with itself. What happens if $\mathbb{R}^\omega$ is given the box topology?

9. Show that the choice axiom is equivalent to the statement that for any indexed family $\{A_\alpha\}_{\alpha \in J}$ of nonempty sets, with $J \neq 0$, the cartesian product

$$\prod_{\alpha \in J} A_\alpha$$

is not empty.

10. Let A be a set; let $\{X_\alpha\}_{\alpha \in J}$ be an indexed family of spaces; and let $\{f_\alpha\}_{\alpha \in J}$ be an indexed family of functions $f_\alpha : A \to X_\alpha$.

   (a) Show there is a unique coarsest topology $\mathcal{T}$ on A relative to which each of the functions f_α is continuous.

   (b) Let

$$S_\beta = \{f_\beta^{-1}(U_\beta) \mid U_\beta \text{ is open in } X_\beta\},$$

   and let $S = \bigcup S_\beta$. Show that S is a subbasis for $\mathcal{T}$.

   (c) Show that a map $g : Y \to A$ is continuous relative to $\mathcal{T}$ if and only if each map $f_\alpha \circ g$ is continuous.

   (d) Let $f : A \to \prod X_\alpha$ be defined by the equation

$$f(a) = (f_\alpha(a))_{\alpha \in J};$$

   let Z denote the subspace $f(A)$ of the product space $\prod X_\alpha$. Show that the image under f of each element of $\mathcal{T}$ is an open set of Z.

§20   The Metric Topology

One of the most important and frequently used ways of imposing a topology on a set is to define the topology in terms of a metric on the set. Topologies given in this way lie at the heart of modern analysis, for example. In this section, we shall define the metric topology and shall give a number of examples. In the next section, we shall consider some of the properties that metric topologies satisfy.

Definition.   A *metric* on a set X is a function

$$d : X \times X \longrightarrow R$$

having the following properties:
(1) $d(x, y) \geq 0$ for all $x, y \in X$; equality holds if and only if $x = y$.
(2) $d(x, y) = d(y, x)$ for all $x, y \in X$.
(3) (Triangle inequality) $d(x, y) + d(y, z) \geq d(x, z)$, for all $x, y, z \in X$.

Given a metric d on X, the number $d(x, y)$ is often called the **distance** between x and y in the metric d. Given $\epsilon > 0$, consider the set

$$B_d(x, \epsilon) = \{y \mid d(x, y) < \epsilon\}$$

of all points y whose distance from x is less than ϵ. It is called the **ϵ-ball centered at x**. Sometimes we omit the metric d from the notation and write this ball simply as $B(x, \epsilon)$, when no confusion will arise.

Definition.   If d is a metric on the set X, then the collection of all ϵ-balls $B_d(x, \epsilon)$, for $x \in X$ and $\epsilon > 0$, is a basis for a topology on X, called the **metric topology** induced by d.

The first condition for a basis is trivial, since $x \in B(x, \epsilon)$ for any $\epsilon > 0$. Before checking the second condition for a basis, we show that if y is a point of the basis element $B(x, \epsilon)$, then there is a basis element $B(y, \delta)$ *centered* at y that is contained in $B(x, \epsilon)$. Define δ to be the positive number $\epsilon - d(x, y)$. Then $B(y, \delta) \subset B(x, \epsilon)$, for if $z \in B(y, \delta)$, then $d(y, z) < \epsilon - d(x, y)$, from which we conclude that

$$d(x, z) \leq d(x, y) + d(y, z) < \epsilon.$$

See Figure 20.1.
Now to check the second condition for a basis, let B_1 and B_2 be two basis elements and let $y \in B_1 \cap B_2$. We have just shown that we can choose positive numbers δ_1 and δ_2 so that $B(y, \delta_1) \subset B_1$ and $B(y, \delta_2) \subset B_2$. Letting δ be the smaller of δ_1 and δ_2, we conclude that $B(y, \delta) \subset B_1 \cap B_2$.
Using what we have just proved, we can rephrase the definition of the metric topology as follows:

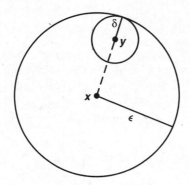

Figure 20.1

> *A set U is open in the metric topology induced by d if and only if for each*
> $y \in U$, *there is a* $\delta > 0$ *such that* $B_d(y, \delta) \subset U$.

Clearly this condition implies that U is open. Conversely, if U is open, it contains a basis element $B = B_d(x, \epsilon)$ containing y, and B in turn contains a basis element $B_d(y, \delta)$ centered at y.

EXAMPLE 1.   Given a set X, define

$$d(x, y) = 1 \quad \text{if } x \neq y,$$
$$d(x, y) = 0 \quad \text{if } x = y.$$

It is trivial to check that d is a metric. The topology it induces is the discrete topology; the basis element $B(x, 1)$, for example, consists of the point x alone.

EXAMPLE 2.   The standard metric on the real numbers $\mathbb{R}$ is defined by the equation

$$d(x, y) = |x - y|.$$

It is easy to check that d is a metric. The topology it induces is the same as the order topology: Each basis element (a, b) for the order topology is a basis element for the metric topology; indeed,

$$(a, b) = B(x, \epsilon),$$

where $x = (a + b)/2$ and $\epsilon = (b - a)/2$. And conversely, each ϵ-ball $B(x, \epsilon)$ equals an open interval: the interval $(x - \epsilon, x + \epsilon)$.

Definition.   If X is a topological space, X is said to be ***metrizable*** if there exists a metric d on the set X that induces the topology of X. A ***metric space*** is a metrizable space X together with a specific metric d that gives the topology of X.

Many of the spaces important for mathematics are metrizable, but some are not. Metrizability is always a highly desirable attribute for a space to possess, for the existence of a metric gives one a valuable tool for proving theorems about the space.

It is, therefore, a problem of fundamental importance in topology to find conditions on a topological space that will guarantee it is metrizable. One of our goals in Chapter 4 will be to find such conditions; they are expressed there in the famous theorem called *Urysohn's metrization theorem*. Further metrization theorems appear in Chapter 6. In the present section we shall content ourselves with proving merely that $\mathbb{R}^n$ and $\mathbb{R}^\omega$ are metrizable.

Although the metrizability problem is an important problem in topology, the study of metric spaces as such does not properly belong to topology as much as it does to analysis. Metrizability of a space depends only on the topology of the space in question, but properties that involve a specific metric for X in general do not. For instance, one can make the following definition in a metric space:

Definition.   Let X be a metric space with metric d. A subset A of X is said to be *bounded* if there is some number M such that

$$d(a_1, a_2) \leq M$$

for every pair a_1, a_2 of points of A. If A is bounded and nonempty, the *diameter* of A is defined to be the number

$$\operatorname{diam} A = \sup\{d(a_1, a_2) \mid a_1, a_2 \in A\}.$$

Boundedness of a set is not a topological property, for it depends on the particular metric d that is used for X. For instance, if X is a metric space with metric d, then there exists a metric $\bar{d}$ that gives the topology of X, relative to which *every* subset of X is bounded. It is defined as follows:

Theorem 20.1.   *Let X be a metric space with metric d. Define $\bar{d} : X \times X \to \mathbb{R}$ by the equation*

$$\bar{d}(x, y) = \min\{d(x, y), 1\}.$$

Then $\bar{d}$ is a metric that induces the same topology as d.

The metric $\bar{d}$ is called the *standard bounded metric* corresponding to d.

Proof.   Checking the first two conditions for a metric is trivial. Let us check the triangle inequality:

$$\bar{d}(x, z) \leq \bar{d}(x, y) + \bar{d}(y, z).$$

Now if either $d(x, y) \geq 1$ or $d(y, z) \geq 1$, then the right side of this inequality is at least 1; since the left side is (by definition) at most 1, the inequality holds. It remains to consider the case in which $d(x, y) < 1$ and $d(y, z) < 1$. In this case, we have

$$d(x, z) \leq d(x, y) + d(y, z) = \bar{d}(x, y) + \bar{d}(y, z).$$

Since $\bar{d}(x, z) \leq d(x, z)$ by definition, the triangle inequality holds for $\bar{d}$.

Now we note that in any metric space, the collection of ϵ-balls with $\epsilon < 1$ forms a basis for the metric topology , for every basis element containing x contains such an ϵ-ball centered at x. It follows that d and $\bar{d}$ induce the same topology on X, because the collections of ϵ-balls with $\epsilon < 1$ under these two metrics are the same collection. ∎

Now we consider some familiar spaces and show they are metrizable.

Definition.   Given $\mathbf{x} = (x_1, \ldots, x_n)$ in $\mathbb{R}^n$, we define the **norm** of $\mathbf{x}$ by the equation

$$\|x\| = (x_1^2 + \cdots + x_n^2)^{1/2};$$

and we define the **euclidean metric** d on $\mathbb{R}^n$ by the equation

$$d(\mathbf{x}, \mathbf{y}) = \|\mathbf{x} - \mathbf{y}\| = [(x_1 - y_1)^2 + \cdots + (x_n - y_n)^2]^{1/2}.$$

We define the **square metric** ρ by the equation

$$\rho(\mathbf{x}, \mathbf{y}) = \max\{|x_1 - y_1|, \ldots, |x_n - y_n|\}.$$

The proof that d is a metric requires some work; it is probably already familiar to you. If not, a proof is outlined in the exercises. We shall seldom have occasion to use this metric on $\mathbb{R}^n$.

To show that ρ is a metric is easier. Only the triangle inequality is nontrivial. From the triangle inequality for $\mathbb{R}$ it follows that for each positive integer i,

$$|x_i - z_i| \leq |x_i - y_i| + |y_i - z_i|.$$

Then by definition of ρ,

$$|x_i - z_i| \leq \rho(\mathbf{x}, \mathbf{y}) + \rho(\mathbf{y}, \mathbf{z}).$$

As a result

$$\rho(\mathbf{x}, \mathbf{z}) = \max\{|x_i - z_i|\} \leq \rho(\mathbf{x}, \mathbf{y}) + \rho(\mathbf{y}, \mathbf{z}),$$

as desired.

On the real line $\mathbb{R} = \mathbb{R}^1$, these two metrics coincide with the standard metric for $\mathbb{R}$. In the plane $\mathbb{R}^2$, the basis elements under d can be pictured as circular regions, while the basis elements under ρ can be pictured as square regions.

We now show that each of these metrics induces the usual topology on $\mathbb{R}^n$. We need the following lemma:

Lemma 20.2.   *Let d and d' be two metrics on the set X; let $\mathcal{T}$ and $\mathcal{T}'$ be the topologies they induce, respectively. Then $\mathcal{T}'$ is finer than $\mathcal{T}$ if and only if for each x in X and each $\epsilon > 0$, there exists a $\delta > 0$ such that*

$$B_{d'}(x, \delta) \subset B_d(x, \epsilon).$$

Proof. Suppose that $\mathcal{T}'$ is finer than $\mathcal{T}$. Given the basis element $B_d(x, \epsilon)$ for $\mathcal{T}$, there is by Lemma 13.3 a basis element B' for the topology $\mathcal{T}'$ such that $x \in B' \subset B_d(x, \epsilon)$. Within B' we can find a ball $B_{d'}(x, \delta)$ centered at x.

Conversely, suppose the δ-ϵ condition holds. Given a basis element B for $\mathcal{T}$ containing x, we can find within B a ball $B_d(x, \epsilon)$ centered at x. By the given condition, there is a δ such that $B_{d'}(x, \delta) \subset B_d(x, \epsilon)$. Then Lemma 13.3 applies to show $\mathcal{T}'$ is finer than $\mathcal{T}$. ∎

Theorem 20.3. *The topologies on $\mathbb{R}^n$ induced by the euclidean metric d and the square metric ρ are the same as the product topology on $\mathbb{R}^n$.*

Proof. Let $\mathbf{x} = (x_1, \ldots, x_n)$ and $\mathbf{y} = (y_1, \ldots, y_n)$ be two points of $\mathbb{R}^n$. It is simple algebra to check that

$$\rho(\mathbf{x}, \mathbf{y}) \le d(\mathbf{x}, \mathbf{y}) \le \sqrt{n}\rho(\mathbf{x}, \mathbf{y}).$$

The first inequality shows that

$$B_d(\mathbf{x}, \epsilon) \subset B_\rho(\mathbf{x}, \epsilon)$$

for all $\mathbf{x}$ and ϵ, since if $d(\mathbf{x}, \mathbf{y}) < \epsilon$, then $\rho(\mathbf{x}, \mathbf{y}) < \epsilon$ also. Similarly, the second inequality shows that

$$B_\rho(\mathbf{x}, \epsilon/\sqrt{n}) \subset B_d(\mathbf{x}, \epsilon)$$

for all $\mathbf{x}$ and ϵ. It follows from the preceding lemma that the two metric topologies are the same.

Now we show that the product topology is the same as that given by the metric ρ. First, let

$$B = (a_1, b_1) \times \cdots \times (a_n, b_n)$$

be a basis element for the product topology, and let $\mathbf{x} = (x_1, \ldots, x_n)$ be an element of B. For each i, there is an ϵ_i such that

$$(x_i - \epsilon_i, x_i + \epsilon_i) \subset (a_i, b_i);$$

choose $\epsilon = \min\{\epsilon_1, \ldots, \epsilon_n\}$. Then $B_\rho(\mathbf{x}, \epsilon) \subset B$, as you can readily check. As a result, the ρ-topology is finer than the product topology.

Conversely, let $B_\rho(\mathbf{x}, \epsilon)$ be a basis element for the ρ-topology. Given the element $\mathbf{y} \in B_\rho(\mathbf{x}, \epsilon)$, we need to find a basis element B for the product topology such that

$$\mathbf{y} \in B \subset B_\rho(\mathbf{x}, \epsilon).$$

But this is trivial, for

$$B_\rho(\mathbf{x}, \epsilon) = (x_1 - \epsilon, x_1 + \epsilon) \times \cdots \times (x_n - \epsilon, x_n + \epsilon)$$

is itself a basis element for the product topology. ∎

Now we consider the infinite cartesian product $\mathbb{R}^\omega$. It is natural to try to generalize the metrics d and ρ to this space. For instance, one can attempt to define a metric d on $\mathbb{R}^\omega$ by the equation

$$d(x, y) = \left[\sum_{i=1}^{\infty} (x_i - y_i)^2 \right]^{1/2}.$$

But this equation does not always make sense, for the series in question need not converge. (This equation does define a metric on a certain important subset of $\mathbb{R}^\omega$, however; see the exercises.)

Similarly, one can attempt to generalize the square metric ρ to $\mathbb{R}^\omega$ by defining

$$\rho(x, y) = \sup\{|x_n - y_n|\}.$$

Again, this formula does not always make sense. If however we replace the usual metric $d(x, y) = |x - y|$ on $\mathbb{R}$ by its bounded counterpart $\bar{d}(x, y) = \min\{|x - y|, 1\}$, then this definition *does* make sense; it gives a metric on $\mathbb{R}^\omega$ called the *uniform metric*.

The uniform metric can be defined more generally on the cartesian product $\mathbb{R}^J$ for arbitrary J, as follows:

Definition.   Given an index set J, and given points $\mathbf{x} = (x_\alpha)_{\alpha \in J}$ and $\mathbf{y} = (y_\alpha)_{\alpha \in J}$ of $\mathbb{R}^J$, let us define a metric $\bar{\rho}$ on $\mathbb{R}^J$ by the equation

$$\bar{\rho}(\mathbf{x}, \mathbf{y}) = \sup\{\bar{d}(x_\alpha, y_\alpha) \mid \alpha \in J\},$$

where $\bar{d}$ is the standard bounded metric on $\mathbb{R}$. It is easy to check that $\bar{\rho}$ is indeed a metric; it is called the **uniform metric** on $\mathbb{R}^J$, and the topology it induces is called the **uniform topology**.

The relation between this topology and the product and box topologies is the following:

Theorem 20.4.   *The uniform topology on $\mathbb{R}^J$ is finer than the product topology and coarser than the box topology; these three topologies are all different if J is infinite.*

Proof.   Suppose that we are given a point $\mathbf{x} = (x_\alpha)_{\alpha \in J}$ and a product topology basis element $\prod U_\alpha$ about $\mathbf{x}$. Let $\alpha_1, \ldots, \alpha_n$ be the indices for which $U_\alpha \neq \mathbb{R}$. Then for each i, choose $\epsilon_i > 0$ so that the ϵ_i-ball centered at x_{α_i} in the $\bar{d}$ metric is contained in U_{α_i}; this we can do because U_{α_i} is open in $\mathbb{R}$. Let $\epsilon = \min\{\epsilon_1, \ldots, \epsilon_n\}$; then the ϵ-ball centered at $\mathbf{x}$ in the $\bar{\rho}$ metric is contained in $\prod U_\alpha$. For if $\mathbf{z}$ is a point of $\mathbb{R}^J$ such that $\bar{\rho}(\mathbf{x}, \mathbf{z}) < \epsilon$, then $\bar{d}(x_\alpha, z_\alpha) < \epsilon$ for all α, so that $\mathbf{z} \in \prod U_\alpha$. It follows that the uniform topology is finer than the product topology.

On the other hand, let B be the ϵ-ball centered at $\mathbf{x}$ in the $\bar{\rho}$ metric. Then the box neighborhood

$$U = \prod (x_\alpha - \tfrac{1}{2}\epsilon, x_\alpha + \tfrac{1}{2}\epsilon)$$

of $\mathbf{x}$ is contained in B. For if $\mathbf{y} \in U$, then $\bar{d}(x_\alpha, y_\alpha) < \frac{1}{2}\epsilon$ for all α, so that $\bar{\rho}(\mathbf{x}, \mathbf{y}) \leq \frac{1}{2}\epsilon$.

Showing these three topologies are different if J is infinite is a task we leave to the exercises. ∎

In the case where J is infinite, we still have not determined whether $\mathbb{R}^J$ is metrizable in either the box or the product topology. It turns out that the only one of these cases where $\mathbb{R}^J$ is metrizable is the case where J is countable and $\mathbb{R}^J$ has the product topology. As we shall see.

Theorem 20.5. *Let $\bar{d}(a, b) = \min\{|a - b|, 1\}$ be the standard bounded metric on $\mathbb{R}$. If $\mathbf{x}$ and $\mathbf{y}$ are two points of $\mathbb{R}^\omega$, define*

$$D(\mathbf{x}, \mathbf{y}) = \sup\left\{\frac{\bar{d}(x_i, y_i)}{i}\right\}.$$

Then D is a metric that induces the product topology on $\mathbb{R}^\omega$.

Proof. The properties of a metric are satisfied trivially except for the triangle inequality, which is proved by noting that for all i,

$$\frac{\bar{d}(x_i, z_i)}{i} \leq \frac{\bar{d}(x_i, y_i)}{i} + \frac{\bar{d}(y_i, z_i)}{i} \leq D(\mathbf{x}, \mathbf{y}) + D(\mathbf{y}, \mathbf{z}),$$

so that

$$\sup\left\{\frac{\bar{d}(x_i, z_i)}{i}\right\} \leq D(\mathbf{x}, \mathbf{y}) + D(\mathbf{y}, \mathbf{z}).$$

The fact that D gives the product topology requires a little more work. First, let U be open in the metric topology and let $\mathbf{x} \in U$; we find an open set V in the product topology such that $\mathbf{x} \in V \subset U$. Choose an ϵ-ball $B_D(\mathbf{x}, \epsilon)$ lying in U. Then choose N large enough that $1/N < \epsilon$. Finally, let V be the basis element for the product topology

$$V = (x_1 - \epsilon, x_1 + \epsilon) \times \cdots \times (x_N - \epsilon, x_N + \epsilon) \times \mathbb{R} \times \mathbb{R} \times \cdots.$$

We assert that $V \subset B_D(\mathbf{x}, \epsilon)$: Given any $\mathbf{y}$ in $\mathbb{R}^\omega$,

$$\frac{\bar{d}(x_i, y_i)}{i} \leq \frac{1}{N} \quad \text{for } i \geq N.$$

Therefore,

$$D(\mathbf{x}, \mathbf{y}) \leq \max\left\{\frac{\bar{d}(x_1, y_1)}{1}, \cdots, \frac{\bar{d}(x_N, y_N)}{N}, \frac{1}{N}\right\}.$$

If $\mathbf{y}$ is in V, this expression is less than ϵ, so that $V \subset B_D(\mathbf{x}, \epsilon)$, as desired.

Conversely, consider a basis element

$$U = \prod_{i \in \mathbb{Z}_+} U_i$$

for the product topology, where U_i is open in $\mathbb{R}$ for $i = \alpha_1, \ldots, \alpha_n$ and $U_i = \mathbb{R}$ for all other indices i. Given $\mathbf{x} \in U$, we find an open set V of the metric topology such that $\mathbf{x} \in V \subset U$. Choose an interval $(x_i - \epsilon_i, x_i + \epsilon_i)$ in $\mathbb{R}$ centered about x_i and lying in U_i for $i = \alpha_1, \ldots, \alpha_n$; choose each $\epsilon_i \le 1$. Then define

$$\epsilon = \min\{\epsilon_i / i \mid i = \alpha_1, \ldots, \alpha_n\}.$$

We assert that

$$\mathbf{x} \in B_D(\mathbf{x}, \epsilon) \subset U.$$

Let $\mathbf{y}$ be a point of $B_D(\mathbf{x}, \epsilon)$. Then for all i,

$$\frac{\bar{d}(x_i, y_i)}{i} \le D(\mathbf{x}, \mathbf{y}) < \epsilon.$$

Now if $i = \alpha_1, \ldots, \alpha_n$, then $\epsilon \le \epsilon_i / i$, so that $\bar{d}(x_i, y_i) < \epsilon_i \le 1$; it follows that $|x_i - y_i| < \epsilon_i$. Therefore, $\mathbf{y} \in \prod U_i$, as desired. ∎

Exercises

1. (a) In $\mathbb{R}^n$, define

   $$d'(\mathbf{x}, \mathbf{y}) = |x_1 - y_1| + \cdots + |x_n - y_n|.$$

   Show that d' is a metric that induces the usual topology of $\mathbb{R}^n$. Sketch the basis elements under d' when $n = 2$.

   (b) More generally, given $p \ge 1$, define

   $$d'(\mathbf{x}, \mathbf{y}) = \left[\sum_{i=1}^{n} |x_i - y_i|^p \right]^{1/p}$$

   for $\mathbf{x}, \mathbf{y} \in \mathbb{R}^n$. Assume that d' is a metric. Show that it induces the usual topology on $\mathbb{R}^n$.

2. Show that $\mathbb{R} \times \mathbb{R}$ in the dictionary order topology is metrizable.

3. Let X be a metric space with metric d.
   (a) Show that $d : X \times X \to \mathbb{R}$ is continuous.
   (b) Let X' denote a space having the same underlying set as X. Show that if $d : X' \times X' \to \mathbb{R}$ is continuous, then the topology of X' is finer than the topology of X.

One can summarize the result of this exercise as follows: If X has a metric d, then the topology induced by d is the coarsest topology relative to which the function d is continuous.

4. Consider the product, uniform, and box topologies on $\mathbb{R}^\omega$.

   (a) In which topologies are the following functions from $\mathbb{R}$ to $\mathbb{R}^\omega$ continuous?

$$f(t) = (t, 2t, 3t, \dots),$$
$$g(t) = (t, t, t, \dots),$$
$$h(t) = (t, \tfrac{1}{2}t, \tfrac{1}{3}t, \dots).$$

   (b) In which topologies do the following sequences converge?

$$\mathbf{w}_1 = (1, 1, 1, 1, \dots), \qquad \mathbf{x}_1 = (1, 1, 1, 1, \dots),$$
$$\mathbf{w}_2 = (0, 2, 2, 2, \dots), \qquad \mathbf{x}_2 = (0, \tfrac{1}{2}, \tfrac{1}{2}, \tfrac{1}{2}, \dots),$$
$$\mathbf{w}_3 = (0, 0, 3, 3, \dots), \qquad \mathbf{x}_3 = (0, 0, \tfrac{1}{3}, \tfrac{1}{3} \dots),$$

$$\dots \qquad\qquad\qquad \dots$$

$$\mathbf{y}_1 = (1, 0, 0, 0, \dots), \qquad \mathbf{z}_1 = (1, 1, 0, 0, \dots),$$
$$\mathbf{y}_2 = (\tfrac{1}{2}, \tfrac{1}{2}, 0, 0, \dots), \qquad \mathbf{z}_2 = (\tfrac{1}{2}, \tfrac{1}{2}, 0, 0, \dots),$$
$$\mathbf{y}_3 = (\tfrac{1}{3}, \tfrac{1}{3}, \tfrac{1}{3}, 0, \dots), \qquad \mathbf{z}_3 = (\tfrac{1}{3}, \tfrac{1}{3}, 0, 0, \dots),$$

$$\dots \qquad\qquad\qquad \dots$$

5. Let $\mathbb{R}^\infty$ be the subset of $\mathbb{R}^\omega$ consisting of all sequences that are eventually zero. What is the closure of $\mathbb{R}^\infty$ in $\mathbb{R}^\omega$ in the uniform topology? Justify your answer.

6. Let $\bar\rho$ be the uniform metric on $\mathbb{R}^\omega$. Given $\mathbf{x} = (x_1, x_2, \dots) \in \mathbb{R}^\omega$ and given $0 < \epsilon < 1$, let

$$U(\mathbf{x}, \epsilon) = (x_1 - \epsilon, x_1 + \epsilon) \times \cdots \times (x_n - \epsilon, x_n + \epsilon) \times \cdots .$$

   (a) Show that $U(\mathbf{x}, \epsilon)$ is not equal to the ϵ-ball $B_{\bar\rho}(\mathbf{x}, \epsilon)$.
   (b) Show that $U(\mathbf{x}, \epsilon)$ is not even open in the uniform topology.
   (c) Show that

$$B_{\bar\rho}(\mathbf{x}, \epsilon) = \bigcup_{\delta < \epsilon} U(\mathbf{x}, \delta).$$

7. Consider the map $h : \mathbb{R}^\omega \to \mathbb{R}^\omega$ defined in Exercise 8 of §19; give $\mathbb{R}^\omega$ the uniform topology. Under what conditions on the numbers a_i and b_i is h continuous? a homeomorphism?

8. Let X be the subset of $\mathbb{R}^\omega$ consisting of all sequences $\mathbf{x}$ such that $\sum x_i^2$ converges. Then the formula

$$d(\mathbf{x}, \mathbf{y}) = \left[\sum_{i=1}^\infty (x_i - y_i)^2 \right]^{1/2}$$

defines a metric on X. (See Exercise 10.) On X we have the three topologies it inherits from the box, uniform, and product topologies on $\mathbb{R}^\omega$. We have also the topology given by the metric d, which we call the ℓ^2-*topology*. (Read "little ell two.")

(a) Show that on X, we have the inclusions

$$\text{box topology} \supset \ell^2\text{-topology} \supset \text{uniform topology}.$$

(b) The set $\mathbb{R}^\infty$ of all sequences that are eventually zero is contained in X. Show that the four topologies that $\mathbb{R}^\infty$ inherits as a subspace of X are all distinct.

(c) The set

$$H = \prod_{n \in \mathbb{Z}_+} [0, 1/n]$$

is contained in X; it is called the **Hilbert cube**. Compare the four topologies that H inherits as a subspace of X.

9. Show that the euclidean metric d on $\mathbb{R}^n$ is a metric, as follows: If $\mathbf{x}, \mathbf{y} \in \mathbb{R}^n$ and $c \in \mathbb{R}$, define

$$\mathbf{x} + \mathbf{y} = (x_1 + y_1, \ldots, x_n + y_n),$$
$$c\mathbf{x} = (cx_1, \ldots, cx_n),$$
$$\mathbf{x} \cdot \mathbf{y} = x_1 y_1 + \cdots + x_n y_n.$$

(a) Show that $\mathbf{x} \cdot (\mathbf{y} + \mathbf{z}) = (\mathbf{x} \cdot \mathbf{y}) + (\mathbf{x} \cdot \mathbf{z})$.

(b) Show that $|\mathbf{x} \cdot \mathbf{y}| \le \|\mathbf{x}\| \|\mathbf{y}\|$. [*Hint:* If $\mathbf{x}, \mathbf{y} \ne 0$, let $a = 1/\|\mathbf{x}\|$ and $b = 1/\|\mathbf{y}\|$, and use the fact that $\|a\mathbf{x} \pm b\mathbf{y}\| \ge 0$.]

(c) Show that $\|\mathbf{x} + \mathbf{y}\| \le \|\mathbf{x}\| + \|\mathbf{y}\|$. [*Hint:* Compute $(\mathbf{x} + \mathbf{y}) \cdot (\mathbf{x} + \mathbf{y})$ and apply (b).]

(d) Verify that d is a metric.

10. Let X denote the subset of $\mathbb{R}^\omega$ consisting of all sequences $(x_1, x_2, \ldots)$ such that $\sum x_i^2$ converges. (You may assume the standard facts about infinite series. In case they are not familiar to you, we shall give them in Exercise 11 of the next section.)

(a) Show that if $\mathbf{x}, \mathbf{y} \in X$, then $\sum |x_i y_i|$ converges. [*Hint:* Use (b) of Exercise 9 to show that the partial sums are bounded.]

(b) Let $c \in \mathbb{R}$. Show that if $\mathbf{x}, \mathbf{y} \in X$, then so are $\mathbf{x} + \mathbf{y}$ and $c\mathbf{x}$.

(c) Show that

$$d(\mathbf{x}, \mathbf{y}) = \left[\sum_{i=1}^{\infty} (x_i - y_i)^2 \right]^{1/2}$$

is a well-defined metric on X.

*11. Show that if d is a metric for X, then

$$d'(x, y) = d(x, y)/(1 + d(x, y))$$

is a bounded metric that gives the topology of X. [*Hint:* If $f(x) = x/(1+x)$ for $x > 0$, use the mean-value theorem to show that $f(a + b) - f(b) \leq f(a)$.]

§21 The Metric Topology (continued)

In this section, we discuss the relation of the metric topology to the concepts we have previously introduced.

Subspaces of metric spaces behave the way one would wish them to; if A is a subspace of the topological space X and d is a metric for X, then the restriction of d to $A \times A$ is a metric for the topology of A. This we leave to you to check.

About *order topologies* there is nothing to be said; some are metrizable (for instance, $\mathbb{Z}_+$ and $\mathbb{R}$), and others are not, as we shall see.

The *Hausdorff axiom* is satisfied by every metric topology. If x and y are distinct points of the metric space (X, d), we let $\epsilon = \frac{1}{2}d(x, y)$; then the triangle inequality implies that $B_d(x, \epsilon)$ and $B_d(y, \epsilon)$ are disjoint.

The *product topology* we have already considered in special cases; we have proved that the products $\mathbb{R}^n$ and $\mathbb{R}^\omega$ are metrizable. It is true in general that countable products of metrizable spaces are metrizable; the proof follows a pattern similar to the proof for $\mathbb{R}^\omega$, so we leave it to the exercises.

About *continuous functions* there is a good deal to be said. Consideration of this topic will occupy the remainder of the section.

When we study continuous functions on metric spaces, we are about as close to the study of calculus and analysis as we shall come in this book. There are two things we want to do at this point.

First, we want to show that the familiar "ϵ-δ definition" of continuity carries over to general metric spaces, and so does the "convergent sequence definition" of continuity.

Second, we want to consider two additional methods for constructing continuous functions, besides those discussed in §18. One is the process of taking sums, differences, products, and quotients of continuous real-valued functions. The other is the process of taking limits of uniformly convergent sequences of continuous functions.

Theorem 21.1. *Let $f : X \to Y$; let X and Y be metrizable with metrics d_X and d_Y, respectively. Then continuity of f is equivalent to the requirement that given $x \in X$ and given $\epsilon > 0$, there exists $\delta > 0$ such that*

$$d_X(x, y) \implies d_Y(f(x), f(y)) < \epsilon.$$

Proof. Suppose that f is continuous. Given x and ϵ, consider the set

$$f^{-1}(B(f(x), \epsilon)),$$

which is open in X and contains the point x. It contains some δ-ball $B(x, \delta)$ centered at x. If y is in this δ-ball, then $f(y)$ is in the ϵ-ball centered at $f(x)$, as desired.

Conversely, suppose that the ϵ-δ condition is satisfied. Let V be open in Y; we show that $f^{-1}(V)$ is open in X. Let x be a point of the set $f^{-1}(V)$. Since $f(x) \in V$, there is an ϵ-ball $B(f(x), \epsilon)$ centered at $f(x)$ and contained in V. By the ϵ-δ condition, there is a δ-ball $B(x, \delta)$ centered at x such that $f(B(x, \delta)) \subset B(f(x), \epsilon)$. Then $B(x, \delta)$ is a neighborhood of x contained in $f^{-1}(V)$, so that $f^{-1}(V)$ is open, as desired.   ∎

Now we turn to the convergent sequence definition of continuity. We begin by considering the relation between convergent sequences and closures of sets. It is certainly believable, from one's experience in analysis, that if x lies in the closure of a subset A of the space X, then there should exist a sequence of points of A converging to x. This is not true in general, but it is true for metrizable spaces.

Lemma 21.2 (The sequence lemma). *Let X be a topological space; let $A \subset X$. If there is a sequence of points of A converging to x, then $x \in \bar{A}$; the converse holds if X is metrizable.*

Proof. Suppose that $x_n \to x$, where $x_n \in A$. Then every neighborhood U of x contains a point of A, so $x \in \bar{A}$ by Theorem 17.5. Conversely, suppose that X is metrizable and $x \in \bar{A}$. Let d be a metric for the topology of X. For each positive integer n, take the neighborhood $B_d(x, 1/n)$ of radius $1/n$ of x, and choose x_n to be a point of its intersection with A. We assert that the sequence x_n converges to x: Any open set U containing x contains an ϵ-ball $B_d(x, \epsilon)$ centered at x; if we choose N so that $1/N < \epsilon$, then U contains x_i for all $i \geq N$.   ∎

Theorem 21.3. *Let $f : X \to Y$. If the function f is continuous, then for every convergent sequence $x_n \to x$ in X, the sequence $f(x_n)$ converges to $f(x)$. The converse holds if X is metrizable.*

Proof. Assume that f is continuous. Given $x_n \to x$, we wish to show that $f(x_n) \to f(x)$. Let V be a neighborhood of $f(x)$. Then $f^{-1}(V)$ is a neighborhood of x, and so there is an N such that $x_n \in f^{-1}(V)$ for $n \geq N$. Then $f(x_n) \in V$ for $n \geq N$.

To prove the converse, assume that the convergent sequence condition is satisfied. Let A be a subset of X; we show that $f(\bar{A}) \subset \overline{f(A)}$. If $x \in \bar{A}$, then there is a sequence x_n of points of A converging to x (by the preceding lemma). By assumption, the sequence $f(x_n)$ converges to $f(x)$. Since $f(x_n) \in f(A)$, the preceding lemma implies that $f(x) \in \overline{f(A)}$. (Note that metrizability of Y is not needed.) Hence $f(\bar{A}) \subset \overline{f(A)}$, as desired.   ∎

Incidentally, in proving Lemma 21.2 and Theorem 21.3 we did not use the full strength of the hypothesis that the space X is metrizable. All we really needed was the countable collection $B_d(x, 1/n)$ of balls about x. This fact leads us to make a new definition.

A space X is said to have a ***countable basis at the point*** x if there is a countable collection $\{U_n\}_{n \in \mathbb{Z}_+}$ of neighborhoods of x such that any neighborhood U of x contains *at* *least one* of the sets U_n. A space X that has a countable basis at each of its points is said to satisfy the *first countability axiom*.

If X has a countable basis $\{U_n\}$ at x, then the proof of Lemma 21.2 goes through; one simply replaces the ball $B_d(x, 1/n)$ throughout by the set

$$B_n = U_1 \cap U_2 \cap \cdots \cap U_n.$$

The proof of Theorem 21.3 goes through unchanged.

A metrizable space always satisfies the first countability axiom, but the converse is not true, as we shall see. Like the Hausdorff axiom, the first countability axiom is a requirement that we sometimes impose on a topological space in order to prove stronger theorems about the space. We shall study it in more detail in Chapter 4.

Now we consider additional methods for constructing continuous functions. We need the following lemma:

Lemma 21.4. *The addition, subtraction, and multiplication operations are continuous functions from $\mathbb{R} \times \mathbb{R}$ into $\mathbb{R}$; and the quotient operation is a continuous function from $\mathbb{R} \times (\mathbb{R} - \{0\})$ into $\mathbb{R}$.*

You have probably seen this lemma proved before; it is a standard "ϵ-δ argument." If not, a proof is outlined in Exercise 12 below; you should have no trouble filling in the details.

Theorem 21.5. *If X is a topological space, and if $f, g : X \to \mathbb{R}$ are continuous functions, then $f + g$, $f - g$, and $f \cdot g$ are continuous. If $g(x) \neq 0$ for all x, then f/g is continuous.*

Proof. The map $h : X \to \mathbb{R} \times \mathbb{R}$ defined by

$$h(x) = f(x) \times g(x)$$

is continuous, by Theorem 18.4. The function $f + g$ equals the composite of h and the addition operation

$$+ : \mathbb{R} \times \mathbb{R} \to \mathbb{R};$$

therefore $f + g$ is continuous. Similar arguments apply to $f - g$, $f \cdot g$, and f/g. ∎

Finally, we come to the notion of uniform convergence.

Definition. Let $f_n : X \to Y$ be a sequence of functions from the set X to the metric space Y. Let d be the metric for Y. We say that the sequence (f_n) *converges uniformly* to the function $f : X \to Y$ if given $\epsilon > 0$, there exists an integer N such that

$$d(f_n(x), f(x)) < \epsilon$$

for all $n > N$ and all x in X.

Uniformity of convergence depends not only on the topology of Y but also on its metric. We have the following theorem about uniformly convergent sequences:

Theorem 21.6 (Uniform limit theorem). *Let $f_n : X \to Y$ be a sequence of continuous functions from the topological space X to the metric space Y. If (f_n) converges uniformly to f, then f is continuous.*

Proof. Let V be open in Y; let x_0 be a point of $f^{-1}(V)$. We wish to find a neighborhood U of x_0 such that $f(U) \subset V$.

Let $y_0 = f(x_0)$. First choose ϵ so that the ϵ-ball $B(y_0, \epsilon)$ is contained in V. Then, using uniform convergence, choose N so that for all $n \geq N$ and all $x \in X$,

$$d(f_n(x), f(x)) < \epsilon/3.$$

Finally, using continuity of f_N, choose a neighborhood U of x_0 such that f_N carries U into the $\epsilon/3$ ball in Y centered at $f_N(x_0)$.

We claim that f carries U into $B(y_0, \epsilon)$ and hence into V, as desired. For this purpose, note that if $x \in U$, then

$$d(f(x), f_N(x)) < \epsilon/3 \quad \text{(by choice of } N\text{)},$$
$$d(f_N(x), f_N(x_0)) < \epsilon/3 \quad \text{(by choice of } U\text{)},$$
$$d(f_N(x_0), f(x_0)) < \epsilon/3 \quad \text{(by choice of } N\text{)}.$$

Adding and using the triangle inequality, we see that $d(f(x), f(x_0)) < \epsilon$, as desired. ∎

Let us remark that the notion of uniform convergence is related to the definition of the uniform metric, which we gave in the preceding section. Consider, for example, the space $\mathbb{R}^X$ of all functions $f : X \to \mathbb{R}$, in the uniform metric $\bar{\rho}$. It is not difficult to see that a sequence of functions $f_n : X \to \mathbb{R}$ converges uniformly to f if and only if the sequence (f_n) converges to f when they are considered as elements of the metric space $(\mathbb{R}^X, \bar{\rho})$. We leave the proof to the exercises.

We conclude the section with some examples of spaces that are not metrizable.

EXAMPLE 1. $\mathbb{R}^\omega$ *in the box topology is not metrizable.*

We shall show that the sequence lemma does not hold for $\mathbb{R}^\omega$. Let A be the subset of $\mathbb{R}^\omega$ consisting of those points all of whose coordinates are positive:

$$A = \{(x_1, x_2, \dots) \mid x_i > 0 \text{ for all } i \in \mathbb{Z}_+\}.$$

Let $\mathbf{0}$ be the "origin" in $\mathbb{R}^\omega$, that is, the point $(0, 0, \dots)$ each of whose coordinates is zero. In the box topology, $\mathbf{0}$ belongs to $\bar{A}$; for if

$$B = (a_1, b_1) \times (a_2, b_2) \times \cdots$$

is any basis element containing $\mathbf{0}$, then B intersects A. For instance, the point

$$(\tfrac{1}{2} b_1, \tfrac{1}{2} b_2 \dots)$$

belongs to $B \cap A$.

But we assert that there is no sequence of points of A converging to $\mathbf{0}$. For let $(\mathbf{a}_n)$ be a sequence of points of A, where

$$\mathbf{a}_n = (x_{1n}, x_{2n}, \dots, x_{in}, \dots).$$

Every coordinate x_{in} is positive, so we can construct a basis element B' for the box topology on $\mathbb{R}$ by setting

$$B' = (-x_{11}, x_{11}) \times (-x_{22}, x_{22}) \times \cdots .$$

Then B' contains the origin $\mathbf{0}$, but it contains no member of the sequence $(\mathbf{a}_n)$; the point $\mathbf{a}_n$ cannot belong to B' because its nth coordinate x_{nn} does not belong to the interval $(-x_{nn}, x_{nn})$. Hence the sequence $(\mathbf{a}_n)$ cannot converge to $\mathbf{0}$ in the box topology.

EXAMPLE 2.   *An uncountable product of $\mathbb{R}$ with itself is not metrizable.*
Let J be an uncountable index set; we show that $\mathbb{R}^J$ does not satisfy the sequence lemma (in the product topology).

Let A be the subset of $\mathbb{R}^J$ consisting of all points (x_α) such that $x_\alpha = 1$ for all but finitely many values of α. Let $\mathbf{0}$ be the "origin" in $\mathbb{R}^J$, the point each of whose coordinates is 0.

We assert that $\mathbf{0}$ belongs to the closure of A. Let $\prod U_\alpha$ be a basis element containing $\mathbf{0}$. Then $U_\alpha \neq \mathbb{R}$ for only finitely many values of α, say for $\alpha = \alpha_1, \ldots, \alpha_n$. Let (x_α) be the point of A defined by letting $x_\alpha = 0$ for $\alpha = \alpha_1, \ldots, \alpha_n$ and $x_\alpha = 1$ for all other values of α; then $(x_\alpha) \in A \cap \prod U_\alpha$, as desired.

But there is no sequence of points of A converging to $\mathbf{0}$. For let $\mathbf{a}_n$ be a sequence of points of A. Given n, let J_n denote the subset of J consisting of those indices α for which the αth coordinate of $\mathbf{a}_n$ is different from 1. The union of all the sets J_n is a countable union of finite sets and therefore countable. Because J itself is uncountable, there is an index in J, say β, that does not lie in any of the sets J_n. This means that for *each* of the points $\mathbf{a}_n$, its βth coordinate equals 1.

Now let U_β be the open interval $(-1, 1)$ in $\mathbb{R}$, and let U be the open set $\pi_\beta^{-1}(U_\beta)$ in $\mathbb{R}^J$. The set U is a neighborhood of $\mathbf{0}$ that contains none of the points $\mathbf{a}_n$; therefore, the sequence $\mathbf{a}_n$ cannot converge to $\mathbf{0}$.

Exercises

1. Let $A \subset X$. If d is a metric for the topology of X, show that $d|A \times A$ is a metric for the subspace topology on A.

2. Let X and Y be metric spaces with metrics d_X and d_Y, respectively. Let $f : X \to Y$ have the property that for every pair of points x_1, x_2 of X,

$$d_Y(f(x_1), f(x_2)) = d_X(x_1, x_2).$$

Show that f is an imbedding. It is called an **isometric imbedding** of X in Y.

3. Let X_n be a metric space with metric d_n, for $n \in \mathbb{Z}_+$.
   (a) Show that

$$\rho(x, y) = \max\{d_1(x_1, y_1), \ldots, d_n(x_n, y_n)\}$$

is a metric for the product space $X_1 \times \cdots \times X_n$.

(b) Let $\bar{d}_i = \min\{d_i, 1\}$. Show that

$$D(x, y) = \sup\{\bar{d}_i(x_i, y_i)/i\}$$

is a metric for the product space $\prod X_i$.

4. Show that $\mathbb{R}_\ell$ and the ordered square satisfy the first countability axiom. (This result does not, of course, imply that they are metrizable.)

5. **Theorem.** *Let $x_n \to x$ and $y_n \to y$ in the space $\mathbb{R}$. Then*

$$x_n + y_n \to x + y,$$
$$x_n - y_n \to x - y,$$
$$x_n y_n \to xy,$$

and provided that each $y_n \neq 0$ and $y \neq 0$,

$$x_n/y_n \to x/y.$$

[*Hint:* Apply Lemma 21.4; recall from the exercises of §19 that if $x_n \to x$ and $y_n \to y$, then $x_n \times y_n \to x \times y$.]

6. Define $f_n : [0, 1] \to \mathbb{R}$ by the equation $f_n(x) = x^n$. Show that the sequence $(f_n(x))$ converges for each $x \in [0, 1]$, but that the sequence (f_n) does not converge uniformly.

7. Let X be a set, and let $f_n : X \to \mathbb{R}$ be a sequence of functions. Let $\bar{\rho}$ be the uniform metric on the space $\mathbb{R}^X$. Show that the sequence (f_n) converges uniformly to the function $f : X \to \mathbb{R}$ if and only if the sequence (f_n) converges to f as elements of the metric space $(\mathbb{R}^X, \bar{\rho})$.

8. Let X be a topological space and let Y be a metric space. Let $f_n : X \to Y$ be a sequence of continuous functions. Let x_n be a sequence of points of X converging to x. Show that if the sequence (f_n) converges uniformly to f, then $(f_n(x_n))$ converges to $f(x)$.

9. Let $f_n : \mathbb{R} \to \mathbb{R}$ be the function

$$f_n(x) = \frac{1}{n^3[x - (1/n)]^2 + 1}.$$

See Figure 21.1. Let $f : \mathbb{R} \to \mathbb{R}$ be the zero function.
   (a) Show that $f_n(x) \to f(x)$ for each $x \in \mathbb{R}$.
   (b) Show that f_n does not converge uniformly to f. (This shows that the converse of Theorem 21.6 does not hold; the limit function f may be continuous even though the convergence is not uniform.)

10. Using the closed set formulation of continuity (Theorem 18.1), show that the following are closed subsets of $\mathbb{R}^2$:

$$A = \{x \times y \mid xy = 1\},$$
$$S^1 = \{x \times y \mid x^2 + y^2 = 1\},$$
$$B^2 = \{x \times y \mid x^2 + y^2 \leq 1\}.$$

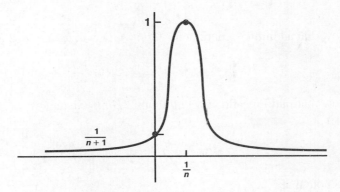

Figure 21.1

The set B^2 is called the (closed) **unit ball** in $\mathbb{R}^2$.

11. Prove the following standard facts about infinite series:

(a) Show that if (s_n) is a bounded sequence of real numbers and $s_n \leq s_{n+1}$ for each n, then (s_n) converges.

(b) Let (a_n) be a sequence of real numbers; define

$$s_n = \sum_{i=1}^{n} a_i.$$

If $s_n \to s$, we say that the **infinite series**

$$\sum_{i=1}^{\infty} a_i$$

converges to s also. Show that if $\sum a_i$ converges to s and $\sum b_i$ converges to t, then $\sum (ca_i + b_i)$ converges to $cs + t$.

(c) Prove the **comparison test** for infinite series: If $|a_i| \leq b_i$ for each i, and if the series $\sum b_i$ converges, then the series $\sum a_i$ converges. [*Hint:* Show that the series $\sum |a_i|$ and $\sum c_i$ converge, where $c_i = |a_i| + a_i$.]

(d) Given a sequence of functions $f_n : X \to \mathbb{R}$, let

$$s_n(x) = \sum_{i=1}^{n} f_i(x).$$

Prove the **Weierstrass M-test** for uniform convergence: If $|f_i(x)| \leq M_i$ for all $x \in X$ and all i, and if the series $\sum M_i$ converges, then the sequence (s_n) converges uniformly to a function s. [*Hint:* Let $r_n = \sum_{i=n+1}^{\infty} M_i$. Show that if $k > n$, then $|s_k(x) - s_n(x)| \leq r_n$; conclude that $|s(x) - s_n(x)| \leq r_n$.]

12. Prove continuity of the algebraic operations on $\mathbb{R}$, as follows: Use the metric $d(a, b) = |a - b|$ on $\mathbb{R}$ and the metric on $\mathbb{R}^2$ given by the equation

$$\rho((x, y), (x_0, y_0)) = \max\{|x - x_0|, |y - y_0|\}.$$

(a) Show that addition is continuous. [*Hint:* Given ϵ, let $\delta = \epsilon/2$ and note that

$$d(x + y, x_0 + y_0) \le |x - x_0| + |y - y_0|.]$$

(b) Show that multiplication is continuous. [*Hint:* Given (x_0, y_0) and $0 < \epsilon < 1$, let

$$3\delta = \epsilon/(|x_0| + |y_0| + 1)$$

and note that

$$d(xy, x_0 y_0) \le |x_0||y - y_0| + |y_0||x - x_0| + |x - x_0||y - y_0|.]$$

(c) Show that the operation of taking reciprocals is a continuous map from $\mathbb{R} - \{0\}$ to $\mathbb{R}$. [*Hint:* Show the inverse image of the interval (a, b) is open. Consider five cases, according as a and b are positive, negative, or zero.]

(d) Show that the subtraction and quotient operations are continuous.

*§22   The Quotient Topology[†]

Unlike the topologies we have already considered in this chapter, the quotient topology is not a natural generalization of something you have already studied in analysis. Nevertheless, it is easy enough to motivate. One motivation comes from geometry, where one often has occasion to use "cut-and-paste" techniques to construct such geometric objects as surfaces. The *torus* (surface of a doughnut), for example, can be constructed by taking a rectangle and "pasting" its edges together appropriately, as in Figure 22.1. And the *sphere* (surface of a ball) can be constructed by taking a disc and collapsing its entire boundary to a single point; see Figure 22.2. Formalizing these constructions involves the concept of quotient topology.

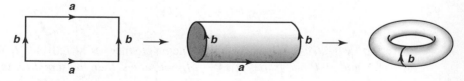

Figure 22.1

[†]This section will be used throughout Part II of the book. It also is referred to in a number of exercises of Part I.

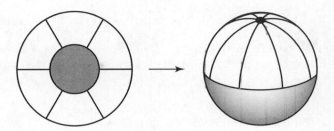

Figure 22.2

Definition.   Let X and Y be topological spaces; let $p : X \to Y$ be a surjective map. The map p is said to be a ***quotient map*** provided a subset U of Y is open in Y if and only if $p^{-1}(U)$ is open in X.

This condition is stronger than continuity; some mathematicians call it "strong continuity." An equivalent condition is to require that a subset A of Y be closed in Y if and only if $p^{-1}(A)$ is closed in X. Equivalence of the two conditions follows from equation

$$f^{-1}(Y - B) = X - f^{-1}(B).$$

Another way of describing a quotient map is as follows: We say that a subset C of X is ***saturated*** (with respect to the surjective map $p : X \to Y$) if C contains every set $p^{-1}(\{y\})$ that it intersects. Thus C is saturated if it equals the complete inverse image of a subset of Y. To say that p is a quotient map is equivalent to saying that p is continuous and p maps *saturated* open sets of X to open sets of Y (or saturated closed sets of X to closed sets of Y).

Two special kinds of quotient maps are the *open maps* and the *closed maps*. Recall that a map $f : X \to Y$ is said to be an ***open map*** if for each open set U of X, the set $f(U)$ is open in Y. It is said to be a ***closed map*** if for each closed set A of X, the set $f(A)$ is closed in Y. It follows immediately from the definition that if $p : X \to Y$ is a surjective continuous map that is either open or closed, then p is a quotient map. There are quotient maps that are neither open or closed. (See Exercise 3.)

EXAMPLE 1.   Let X be the subspace $[0, 1] \cup [2, 3]$ of $\mathbb{R}$, and let Y be the subspace $[0, 2]$ of $\mathbb{R}$. The map $p : X \to Y$ defined by

$$p(x) = \begin{cases} x & \text{for } x \in [0, 1], \\ x - 1 & \text{for } x \in [2, 3] \end{cases}$$

is readily seen to be surjective, continuous, and closed. Therefore it is a quotient map. It is not, however, an open map; the image of the open set $[0, 1]$ of X is not open in Y.

Note that if A is the subspace $[0, 1) \cup [2, 3]$ of X, then the map $q : A \to Y$ obtained by restricting p is continuous and surjective, but it is not a quotient map. For the set $[2, 3]$ is open in A and is saturated with respect to q, but its image is not open in Y.

EXAMPLE 2.   Let $\pi_1 : \mathbb{R} \times \mathbb{R} \to \mathbb{R}$ be projection onto the first coordinate; then π_1 is continuous and surjective. Furthermore, π_1 is an open map. For if $U \times V$ is a nonempty basis element for $\mathbb{R} \times \mathbb{R}$, then $\pi_1(U \times V) = U$ is open in $\mathbb{R}$; it follows that π_1 carries open sets of $\mathbb{R} \times \mathbb{R}$ to open sets of $\mathbb{R}$. However, π_1 is not a closed map. The subset

$$C = \{x \times y \mid xy = 1\}$$

of $\mathbb{R} \times \mathbb{R}$ is closed, but $\pi_1(C) = \mathbb{R} - \{0\}$, which is not closed in $\mathbb{R}$.

Note that if A is the subspace of $\mathbb{R} \times \mathbb{R}$ that is the union of C and the origin $\{0\}$, then the map $q : A \to \mathbb{R}$ obtained by restricting π_1 is continuous and surjective, but it is not a quotient map. For the one-point set $\{0\}$ is open in A and is saturated with respect to q, but its image is not open in $\mathbb{R}$.

Now we show how the notion of quotient map can be used to construct a topology on a set.

Definition.   If X is a space and A is a *set* and if $p : X \to A$ is a surjective map, then there exists exactly one topology $\mathcal{T}$ on A relative to which p is a quotient map; it is called the ***quotient topology*** induced by p.

The topology $\mathcal{T}$ is of course defined by letting it consist of those subsets U of A such that $p^{-1}(U)$ is open in X. It is easy to check that $\mathcal{T}$ is a topology. The sets $\varnothing$ and A are open because $p^{-1}(\varnothing) = \varnothing$ and $p^{-1}(A) = X$. The other two conditions follow from the equations

$$p^{-1}(\bigcup_{\alpha \in J} U_\alpha) = \bigcup_{\alpha \in J} p^{-1}(U_\alpha),$$

$$p^{-1}(\bigcap_{i=1}^{n} U_i) = \bigcap_{i=1}^{n} p^{-1}(U_i).$$

EXAMPLE 3.   Let p be the map of the real line $\mathbb{R}$ onto the three-point set $A = \{a, b, c\}$ defined by

$$p(x) = \begin{cases} a & \text{if } x > 0, \\ b & \text{if } x < 0, \\ c & \text{if } x = 0. \end{cases}$$

You can check that the quotient topology on A induced by p is the one indicated in Figure 22.3.

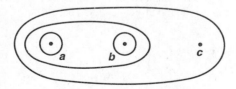

Figure 22.3

There is a special situation in which the quotient topology occurs particularly frequently. It is the following:

Definition. Let X be a topological space, and let X^* be a partition of X into disjoint subsets whose union is X. Let $p : X \to X^*$ be the surjective map that carries each point of X to the element of X^* containing it. In the quotient topology induced by p, the space X^* is called a ***quotient space*** of X.

Given X^*, there is an equivalence relation on X of which the elements of X^* are the equivalence classes. One can think of X^* as having been obtained by "identifying" each pair of equivalent points. For this reason, the quotient space X^* is often called an *identification space*, or a *decomposition space*, of the space X.

We can describe the topology of X^* in another way. A subset U of X^* is a collection of equivalence classes, and the set $p^{-1}(U)$ is just the union of the equivalence classes belonging to U. Thus the typical open set of X^* is a collection of equivalence classes whose *union* is an open set of X.

EXAMPLE 4.   Let X be the closed unit ball

$$\{x \times y \mid x^2 + y^2 \le 1\}$$

in $\mathbb{R}^2$, and let X^* be the partition of X consisting of all the one-point sets $\{x \times y\}$ for which $x^2 + y^2 < 1$, along with the set $S^1 = \{x \times y\} \mid x^2 + y^2 = 1\}$. Typical saturated open sets in X are pictured by the shaded regions in Figure 22.4. One can show that X^* is homeomorphic with the subspace of $\mathbb{R}^3$ called the ***unit 2-sphere***, defined by

$$S^2 = \{(x, y, z) \mid x^2 + y^2 + z^2 = 1\}.$$

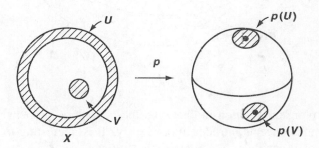

Figure 22.4

EXAMPLE 5.   Let X be the rectangle $[0, 1] \times [0, 1]$. Define a partition X^* of X as follows: It consists of all the one-point sets $\{x \times y\}$ where $0 < x < 1$ and $0 < y < 1$, the following types of two-point sets:

$$\{x \times 0, x \times 1\} \quad \text{where } 0 < x < 1,$$
$$\{0 \times y, 1 \times y\} \quad \text{where } 0 < y < 1,$$

and the four-point set

$$\{0 \times 0, 0 \times 1, 1 \times 0, 1 \times 1\}.$$

Typical saturated open sets in X are pictured by the shaded regions in Figure 22.5; each is an open set of X that equals a union of elements of X^*.

The image of each of these sets under p is an open set of X^*, as indicated in Figure 22.6. This description of X^* is just the mathematical way of saying what we expressed in pictures when we pasted the edges of a rectangle together to form a torus.

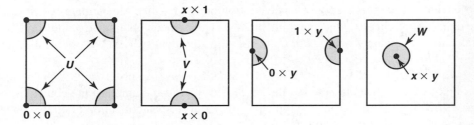

Figure 22.5

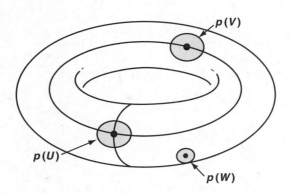

Figure 22.6

Now we explore the relationship between the notions of quotient map and quotient space and the concepts introduced previously. It is interesting to note that this relationship is not as simple as one might wish.

We have already noted that *subspaces* do not behave well; if $p : X \to Y$ is a quotient map and A is a subspace of X, then the map $q : A \to p(A)$ obtained by restricting p need not be a quotient map. One has, however, the following theorem:

Theorem 22.1. *Let $p : X \to Y$ be a quotient map; let A be a subspace of X that is saturated with respect to p; let $q : A \to p(A)$ be the map obtained by restricting p.*

(1) If A is either open or closed in X, then q is a quotient map.

(2) If p is either an open map or a closed map, then q is a quotient map.

Proof.   *Step 1.* We verify first the following two equations:

$$q^{-1}(V) = p^{-1}(V) \qquad \text{if } V \subset p(A);$$
$$p(U \cap A) = p(U) \cap p(A) \qquad \text{if } U \subset X.$$

To check the first equation, we note that since $V \subset p(A)$ and A is saturated, $p^{-1}(V)$ is contained in A. It follows that both $p^{-1}(V)$ and $q^{-1}(V)$ equal all points of A that are mapped by p into V. To check the second equation, we note that for any two subsets U and A of X, we have the inclusion

$$p(U \cap A) \subset p(U) \cap p(A).$$

To prove the reverse inclusion, suppose $y = p(u) = p(a)$, for $u \in U$ and $a \in A$. Since A is saturated, A contains the set $p^{-1}(p(a))$, so that in particular A contains u. Then $y = p(u)$, where $u \in U \cap A$.

Step 2. Now suppose A is open or p is open. Given the subset V of $p(A)$, we assume that $q^{-1}(V)$ is open in A and show that V is open in $p(A)$.

Suppose first that A is open. Since $q^{-1}(V)$ is open in A and A is open in X, the set $q^{-1}(V)$ is open in X. Since $q^{-1}(V) = p^{-1}(V)$, the latter set is open in X, so that V is open in Y because p is a quotient map. In particular, V is open in $p(A)$.

Now suppose p is open. Since $q^{-1}(V) = p^{-1}(V)$ and $q^{-1}(V)$ is open in A, we have $p^{-1}(V) = U \cap A$ for some set U open in X. Now $p(p^{-1}(V)) = V$ because p is surjective; then

$$V = p(p^{-1}(V)) = p(U \cap A) = p(U) \cap p(A).$$

The set $p(U)$ is open in Y because p is an open map; hence V is open in $p(A)$.

Step 3. The proof when A or p is closed is obtained by replacing the word "open" by the word "closed" throughout Step 2.   ∎

Now we consider other concepts introduced previously. *Composites of maps* behave nicely; it is easy to check that the composite of two quotient maps is a quotient map; this fact follows from the equation

$$p^{-1}(q^{-1}(U)) = (q \circ p)^{-1}(U).$$

On the other hand, *products of maps* do not behave well; the cartesian product of two quotient maps need not be a quotient map. See Example 7 following. One needs further conditions on either the maps or the spaces in order for this statement to be true. One such, a condition on the spaces, is called *local compactness*; we shall study it later. Another, a condition on the maps, is the condition that both the maps p and q be open maps. In that case, it is easy to see that $p \times q$ is also an open map, so it is a quotient map.

Finally, the *Hausdorff condition* does not behave well; even if X is Hausdorff, there is no reason that the quotient space X^* needs to be Hausdorff. There is a simple condition for X^* to satisfy the T_1 axiom; one simply requires that each element of the partition X^* be a closed subset of X. Conditions that will ensure X^* is Hausdorff are harder to find. This is one of the more delicate questions concerning quotient spaces; we shall return to it several times later in the book.

Perhaps the most important result in the study of quotient spaces has to do with the problem of constructing *continuous functions* on a quotient space. We consider that problem now. When we studied product spaces, we had a criterion for determining whether a map $f : Z \to \prod X_\alpha$ *into* a product space was continuous. Its counterpart in the theory of quotient spaces is a criterion for determining when a map $f : X^* \to Z$ *out of* a quotient space is continuous. One has the following theorem:

Theorem 22.2. *Let $p : X \to Y$ be a quotient map. Let Z be a space and let $g : X \to Z$ be a map that is constant on each set $p^{-1}(\{y\})$, for $y \in Y$. Then g induces a map $f : Y \to Z$ such that $f \circ p = g$. The induced map f is continuous if and only if g is continuous; f is a quotient map if and only if g is a quotient map.*

Proof.   For each $y \in Y$, the set $g(p^{-1}(\{y\}))$ is a one-point set in Z (since g is constant on $p^{-1}(\{y\})$). If we let $f(y)$ denote this point, then we have defined a map $f : Y \to Z$ such that for each $x \in X$, $f(p(x)) = g(x)$. If f is continuous, then $g = f \circ p$ is continuous. Conversely, suppose g is continuous. Given an open set V of Z, $g^{-1}(V)$ is open in X. But $g^{-1}(V) = p^{-1}(f^{-1}(V))$; because p is a quotient map, it follows that $f^{-1}(V)$ is open in Y. Hence f is continuous.

   If f is a quotient map, then g is the composite of two quotient maps and is thus a quotient map. Conversely, suppose that g is a quotient map. Since g is surjective, so is f. Let V be a subset of Z; we show that V is open in Z if $f^{-1}(V)$ is open in Y. Now the set $p^{-1}(f^{-1}(V))$ is open in X because p is continuous. Since this set equals $g^{-1}(V)$, the latter is open in X. Then because g is a quotient map, V is open in Z. ∎

Corollary 22.3. *Let $g : X \to Z$ be a surjective continuous map. Let X^* be the following collection of subsets of X:*

$$X^* = \{g^{-1}(\{z\}) \mid z \in Z\}.$$

Give X^* the quotient topology.

   (a) *The map g induces a bijective continuous map $f : X^* \to Z$, which is a homeomorphism if and only if g is a quotient map.*

   (b) *If Z is Hausdorff, so is X^*.*

Proof.   By the preceding theorem, g induces a continuous map $f : X^* \to Z$; it is clear that f is bijective. Suppose that f is a homeomorphism. Then both f and the projection map $p : X \to X^*$ are quotient maps, so that their composite q is a quotient map. Conversely, suppose that g is a quotient map. Then it follows from the preceding theorem that f is a quotient map. Being bijective, f is thus a homeomorphism.

Suppose Z is Hausdorff. Given distinct points of X^*, their images under f are distinct and thus possess disjoint neighborhoods U and V. Then $f^{-1}(U)$ and $f^{-1}(V)$ are disjoint neighborhoods of the two given points of X^*.   ∎

EXAMPLE 6.   Let X be the subspace of $\mathbb{R}^2$ that is the union of the line segments $[0, 1] \times \{n\}$, for $n \in \mathbb{Z}_+$, and let Z be the subspace of $\mathbb{R}^2$ consisting of all points of the form $x \times (x/n)$ for $x \in [0, 1]$ and $n \in \mathbb{Z}_+$. Then X is the union of countably many disjoint line segments, and Z is the union of countably many line segments having an end point in common. See Figure 22.7.

Define a map $g : X \to Z$ by the equation $g(x \times n) = x \times (x/n)$; then g is surjective and continuous. The quotient space X^* whose elements are the sets $g^{-1}(\{z\})$ is simply the space obtained from X by identifying the subset $\{0\} \times \mathbb{Z}_+$ to a point. The map g induces a bijective continuous map $f : X^* \to Z$. But f is *not* a homeomorphism.

To verify this fact, it suffices to show that g is not a quotient map. Consider the sequence of points $x_n = (1/n) \times n$ of X. The set $A = \{x_n\}$ is a closed subset of X because it has no limit points. Also, it is saturated with respect to g. On the other hand, the set $g(A)$ is not closed in Z, for it consists of the points $z_n = (1/n) \times (1/n^2)$; this set has the origin as a limit point.

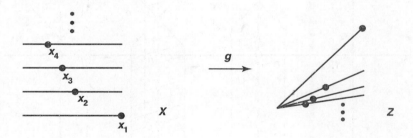

Figure 22.7

EXAMPLE 7.   *The product of two quotient maps need not be a quotient map.*

We give an example that involves non-Hausdorff spaces in the exercises. Here is another involving spaces that are nicer.

Let $X = \mathbb{R}$ and let X^* be the quotient space obtained from X by identifying the subset $\mathbb{Z}_+$ to a point b; let $p : X \to X^*$ be the quotient map. Let $\mathbb{Q}$ be the subspace of $\mathbb{R}$ consisting of the rational numbers; let $i : \mathbb{Q} \to \mathbb{Q}$ be the identity map. We show that

$$p \times i : X \times \mathbb{Q} \to X^* \times \mathbb{Q}$$

is not a quotient map.

For each n, let $c_n = \sqrt{2}/n$, and consider the straight lines in $\mathbb{R}^2$ with slopes 1 and -1, respectively, through the point $n \times c_n$. Let U_n consist of all points of $X \times \mathbb{Q}$ that lie above both of these lines or beneath both of them, and also between the vertical lines $x = n - 1/4$ and $x = n + 1/4$. Then U_n is open in $X \times \mathbb{Q}$; it contains the set $\{n\} \times \mathbb{Q}$ because c_n is not rational. See Figure 22.8.

Let U be the union of the sets U_n; then U is open in $X \times \mathbb{Q}$. It is saturated with respect to $p \times i$ because it contains the entire set $\mathbb{Z}_+ \times \{q\}$ for each $q \in \mathbb{Q}$. We assume that $U' = (p \times i)(U)$ is open in $X^* \times \mathbb{Q}$ and derive a contradiction.

Because U contains, in particular, the set $\mathbb{Z}_+ \times 0$, the set U' contains the point $b \times 0$. Hence U' contains an open set of the form $W \times I_\delta$, where W is a neighborhood of b in X^* and I_δ consists of all rational numbers y with $|y| < \delta$. Then

$$p^{-1}(W) \times I_\delta \subset U.$$

Choose n large enough that $c_n < \delta$. Then since $p^{-1}(W)$ is open in X and contains $\mathbb{Z}_+$, we can choose $\epsilon < 1/4$ so that the interval $(n - \epsilon, n + \epsilon)$ is contained in $p^{-1}(W)$. Then U contains the subset $V = (n - \epsilon, n + \epsilon) \times I_\delta$ of $X \times \mathbb{Q}$. But the figure makes clear that there are many points $x \times y$ of V that do not lie in U! (One such is the point $x \times y$, where $x = n + \frac{1}{2}\epsilon$ and y is a rational number with $|y - c_n| < \frac{1}{2}\epsilon$.)

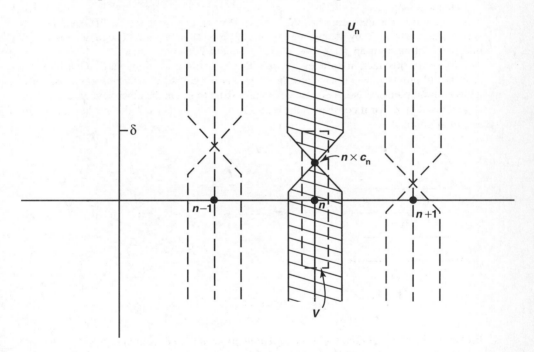

Figure 22.8

Exercises

1. Check the details of Example 3.

2. (a) Let $p : X \to Y$ be a continuous map. Show that if there is a continuous map $f : Y \to X$ such that $p \circ f$ equals the identity map of Y, then p is a quotient map.

   (b) If $A \subset X$, a **retraction** of X onto A is a continuous map $r : X \to A$ such that $r(a) = a$ for each $a \in A$. Show that a retraction is a quotient map.

3. Let $\pi_1 : \mathbb{R} \times \mathbb{R} \to \mathbb{R}$ be projection on the first coordinate. Let A be the subspace of $\mathbb{R} \times \mathbb{R}$ consisting of all points $x \times y$ for which either $x \geq 0$ or $y = 0$ (or both); let $q : A \to \mathbb{R}$ be obtained by restricting π_1. Show that q is a quotient map that is neither open nor closed.

4. (a) Define an equivalence relation on the plane $X = \mathbb{R}^2$ as follows:
$$x_0 \times y_0 \sim x_1 \times y_1 \quad \text{if } x_0 + y_0^2 = x_1 + y_1^2.$$

   Let X^* be the corresponding quotient space. It is homeomorphic to a familiar space; what is it? [*Hint:* Set $g(x \times y) = x + y^2$.]
   (b) Repeat (a) for the equivalence relation
$$x_0 \times y_0 \sim x_1 \times y_1 \quad \text{if } x_0^2 + y_0^2 = x_1^2 + y_1^2.$$

5. Let $p : X \to Y$ be an open map. Show that if A is open in X, then the map $q : A \to p(A)$ obtained by restricting p is an open map.

6. Recall that $\mathbb{R}_K$ denotes the real line in the K-topology. (See §13.) Let Y be the quotient space obtained from $\mathbb{R}_K$ by collapsing the set K to a point; let $p : \mathbb{R}_K \to Y$ be the quotient map.
   (a) Show that Y satisfies the T_1 axiom, but is not Hausdorff.
   (b) Show that $p \times p : \mathbb{R}_K \times \mathbb{R}_K \to Y \times Y$ is not a quotient map. [*Hint:* The diagonal is not closed in $Y \times Y$, but its inverse image is closed in $\mathbb{R}_K \times \mathbb{R}_K$.]

*Supplementary Exercises: Topological Groups

In these exercises we consider topological groups and some of their properties. The quotient topology gets its name from the special case that arises when one forms the quotient of a topological group by a subgroup.

A *topological group* G is a group that is also a topological space satisfying the T_1 axiom, such that the map of $G \times G$ into G sending $x \times y$ into $x \cdot y$, and the map of G into G sending x into x^{-1}, are continuous maps. Throughout the following exercises, let G denote a topological group.

1. Let H denote a group that is also a topological space satisfying the T_1 axiom. Show that H is a topological group if and only if the map of $H \times H$ into H sending $x \times y$ into $x \cdot y^{-1}$ is continuous.

2. Show that the following are topological groups:
   (a) $(\mathbb{Z}, +)$
   (b) $(\mathbb{R}, +)$
   (c) $(\mathbb{R}_+, \cdot)$
   (d) $(S^1, \cdot)$, where we take S^1 to be the space of all complex numbers z for which $|z| = 1$.

(e) The *general linear group* GL(n), under the operation of matrix multiplication. (GL(n) is the set of all nonsingular n by n matrices, topologized by considering it as a subset of euclidean space of dimension n^2 in the obvious way.)

3. Let H be a subspace of G. Show that if H is also a subgroup of G, then both H and $\bar{H}$ are topological groups.

4. Let α be an element of G. Show that the maps $f_\alpha, g_\alpha : G \to G$ defined by

$$f_\alpha(x) = \alpha \cdot x \quad \text{and} \quad g_\alpha(x) = x \cdot \alpha$$

are homeomorphisms of G. Conclude that G is a *homogeneous space*. (This means that for every pair x, y of points of G, there exists a homeomorphism of G onto itself that carries x to y.)

5. Let H be a subgroup of G. If $x \in G$, define $xH = \{x \cdot h \mid h \in H\}$; this set is called a **left coset** of H in G. Let G/H denote the collection of left cosets of H in G; it is a partition of G. Give G/H the quotient topology.
   (a) Show that if $\alpha \in G$, the map f_α of the preceding exercise induces a homeomorphism of G/H carrying xH to $(\alpha \cdot x)H$. Conclude that G/H is a homogeneous space.
   (b) Show that if H is a closed set in the topology of G, then one-point sets are closed in G/H.
   (c) Show that the quotient map $p : G \to G/H$ is open.
   (d) Show that if H is closed in the topology of G and is a normal subgroup of G, then G/H is a topological group.

6. The integers $\mathbb{Z}$ are a normal subgroup of $(\mathbb{R}, +)$. The quotient $\mathbb{R}/\mathbb{Z}$ is a familiar topological group; what is it?

7. If A and B are subsets of G, let $A \cdot B$ denote the set of all points $a \cdot b$ for $a \in A$ and $b \in B$. Let A^{-1} denote the set of all points a^{-1}, for $a \in A$.
   (a) A neighborhood V of the identity element e is said to be **symmetric** if $V = V^{-1}$. If U is a neighborhood of e, show there is a symmetric neighborhood V of e such that $V \cdot V \subset U$. [*Hint:* If W is a neighborhood of e, then $W \cdot W^{-1}$ is symmetric.]
   (b) Show that G is Hausdorff. In fact, show that if $x \neq y$, there is a neighborhood V of e such that $V \cdot x$ and $V \cdot y$ are disjoint.
   (c) Show that G satisfies the following separation axiom, which is called the **regularity axiom**: Given a closed set A and a point x not in A, there exist disjoint open sets containing A and x, respectively. [*Hint:* There is a neighborhood V of e such that $V \cdot x$ and $V \cdot A$ are disjoint.]
   (d) Let H be a subgroup of G that is closed in the topology of G; let $p : G \to G/H$ be the quotient map. Show that G/H satisfies the regularity axiom. [*Hint:* Examine the proof of (c) when A is saturated.]

Chapter 3

Connectedness
and Compactness

In the study of calculus, there are three basic theorems about continuous functions, and on these theorems the rest of calculus depends. They are the following:

Intermediate value theorem. If $f : [a, b] \to \mathbb{R}$ is continuous and if r is a real number between $f(a)$ and $f(b)$, then there exists an element $c \in [a, b]$ such that $f(c) = r$.

Maximum value theorem. If $f : [a, b] \to R$ is continuous, then there exists an element $c \in [a, b]$ such that $f(x) \le f(c)$ for every $x \in [a, b]$.

Uniform continuity theorem. If $f : [a, b] \to \mathbb{R}$ is continuous, then given $\epsilon > 0$, there exists $\delta > 0$ such that $|f(x_1) - f(x_2)| < \epsilon$ for every pair of numbers x_1, x_2 of $[a, b]$ for which $|x_1 - x_2| < \delta$.

These theorems are used in a number of places. The intermediate value theorem is used for instance in constructing inverse functions, such as $\sqrt[3]{x}$ and $\arcsin x$; and the maximum value theorem is used for proving the mean value theorem for derivatives, upon which the two *fundamental theorems of calculus* depend. The uniform continuity theorem is used, among other things, for proving that every continuous function is integrable.

We have spoken of these three theorems as theorems about continuous functions. But they can also be considered as theorems about the closed interval $[a, b]$ of real numbers. The theorems depend not only on the continuity of f but also on properties of the topological space $[a, b]$.

The property of the space $[a, b]$ on which the intermediate value theorem depends is the property called *connectedness*, and the property on which the other two depend is the property called *compactness*. In this chapter, we shall define these properties for arbitrary topological spaces, and shall prove the appropriate generalized versions of these theorems.

As the three quoted theorems are fundamental for the theory of calculus, so are the notions of connectedness and compactness fundamental in higher analysis, geometry, and topology—indeed, in almost any subject for which the notion of topological space itself is relevant.

§23   Connected Spaces

The definition of connectedness for a topological space is a quite natural one. One says that a space can be "separated" if it can be broken up into two "globs"—disjoint open sets. Otherwise, one says that it is connected. From this simple idea much follows.

Definition.   Let X be a topological space. A *separation* of X is a pair U, V of disjoint nonempty open subsets of X whose union is X. The space X is said to be *connected* if there does not exist a separation of X.

Connectedness is obviously a topological property, since it is formulated entirely in terms of the collection of open sets of X. Said differently, if X is connected, so is any space homeomorphic to X.

Another way of formulating the definition of connectedness is the following:

> *A space X is connected if and only if the only subsets of X that are both open and closed in X are the empty set and X itself.*

For if A is a nonempty proper subset of X that is both open and closed in X, then the sets $U = A$ and $V = X - A$ constitute a separation of X, for they are open, disjoint, and nonempty, and their union is X. Conversely, if U and V form a separation of X, then U is nonempty and different from X, and it is both open and closed in X.

For a subspace Y of a topological space X, there is another useful way of formulating the definition of connectedness:

Lemma 23.1.   *If Y is a subspace of X, a separation of Y is a pair of disjoint nonempty sets A and B whose union is Y, neither of which contains a limit point of the other. The space Y is connected if there exists no separation of Y.*

Proof.   Suppose first that A and B form a separation of Y. Then A is both open and closed in Y. The closure of A in Y is the set $\bar{A} \cap Y$ (where $\bar{A}$ as usual denotes the closure of A in X). Since A is closed in Y, $A = \bar{A} \cap Y$; or to say the same thing, $\bar{A} \cap B = \varnothing$. Since $\bar{A}$ is the union of A and its limit points, B contains no limit points of A. A similar argument shows that A contains no limit points of B.

Conversely, suppose that A and B are disjoint nonempty sets whose union is Y, neither of which contains a limit point of the other. Then $\bar{A} \cap B = \varnothing$ and $A \cap \bar{B} = \varnothing$;

therefore, we conclude that $\bar{A} \cap Y = A$ and $\bar{B} \cap Y = B$. Thus both A and B are closed in Y, and since $A = Y - B$ and $B = Y - A$, they are open in Y as well.   ∎

EXAMPLE 1.   Let X denote a two-point space in the indiscrete topology. Obviously there is no separation of X, so X is connected.

EXAMPLE 2.   Let Y denote the subspace $[-1, 0) \cup (0, 1]$ of the real line $\mathbb{R}$. Each of the sets $[-1, 0)$ and $(0, 1]$ is nonempty and open in Y (although not in $\mathbb{R}$); therefore, they form a separation of Y. Alternatively, note that neither of these sets contains a limit point of the other. (They do have a limit point 0 in common, but that does not matter.)

EXAMPLE 3.   Let X be the subspace $[-1, 1]$ of the real line. The sets $[-1, 0]$ and $(0, 1]$ are disjoint and nonempty, but they do not form a separation of X, because the first set is not open in X. Alternatively, note that the first set contains a limit point, 0, of the second. Indeed, there exists *no* separation of the space $[-1, 1]$. We shall prove this fact shortly.

EXAMPLE 4.   The rationals $\mathbb{Q}$ are not connected. Indeed, the only connected subspaces of $\mathbb{Q}$ are the one-point sets: If Y is a subspace of $\mathbb{Q}$ containing two points p and q, one can choose an irrational number a lying between p and q, and write Y as the union of the open sets

$$Y \cap (-\infty, a) \quad \text{and} \quad Y \cap (a, +\infty).$$

EXAMPLE 5.   Consider the following subset of the plane $\mathbb{R}^2$:

$$X = \{x \times y \mid y = 0\} \cup \{x \times y \mid x > 0 \text{ and } y = 1/x\}.$$

Then X is not connected; indeed, the two indicated sets form a separation of X because neither contains a limit point of the other. See Figure 23.1.

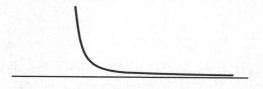

Figure 23.1

We have given several examples of spaces that are not connected. How can one construct spaces that *are* connected? We shall now prove several theorems that tell how to form new connected spaces from given ones. In the next section we shall apply these theorems to show that some specific spaces, such as intervals in $\mathbb{R}$, and balls and cubes in $\mathbb{R}^n$, are connected. First, a lemma:

Lemma 23.2.   *If the sets C and D form a separation of X, and if Y is a connected subspace of X, then Y lies entirely within either C or D.*

Proof.   Since C and D are both open in X, the sets $C \cap Y$ and $D \cap Y$ are open in Y. These two sets are disjoint and their union is Y; if they were both nonempty, they would constitute a separation of Y. Therefore, one of them is empty. Hence Y must lie entirely in C or in D.   ∎

Theorem 23.3. *The union of a collection of connected subspaces of X that have a point in common is connected.*

Proof. Let $\{A_\alpha\}$ be a collection of connected subspaces of a space X; let p be a point of $\bigcap A_\alpha$. We prove that the space $Y = \bigcup A_\alpha$ is connected. Suppose that $Y = C \cup D$ is a separation of Y. The point p is in one of the sets C or D; suppose $p \in C$. Since A_α is connected, it must lie entirely in either C or D, and it cannot lie in D because it contains the point p of C. Hence $A_\alpha \subset C$ for every α, so that $\bigcup A_\alpha \subset C$, contradicting the fact that D is nonempty. ∎

Theorem 23.4. *Let A be a connected subspace of X. If $A \subset B \subset \bar{A}$, then B is also connected.*

Said differently: If B is formed by adjoining to the connected subspace A some or all of its limit points, then B is connected.

Proof. Let A be connected and let $A \subset B \subset \bar{A}$. Suppose that $B = C \cup D$ is a separation of B. By Lemma 23.2, the set A must lie entirely in C or in D; suppose that $A \subset C$. Then $\bar{A} \subset \bar{C}$; since $\bar{C}$ and D are disjoint, B cannot intersect D. This contradicts the fact that D is a nonempty subset of B. ∎

Theorem 23.5. *The image of a connected space under a continuous map is connected.*

Proof. Let $f : X \rightarrow Y$ be a continuous map; let X be connected. We wish to prove the image space $Z = f(X)$ is connected. Since the map obtained from f by restricting its range to the space Z is also continuous, it suffices to consider the case of a continuous surjective map

$$g : X \rightarrow Z.$$

Suppose that $Z = A \cup B$ is a separation of Z into two disjoint nonempty sets open in Z. Then $g^{-1}(A)$ and $g^{-1}(B)$ are disjoint sets whose union is X; they are open in X because g is continuous, and nonempty because g is surjective. Therefore, they form a separation of X, contradicting the assumption that X is connected. ∎

Theorem 23.6. *A finite cartesian product of connected spaces is connected.*

Proof. We prove the theorem first for the product of two connected spaces X and Y. This proof is easy to visualize. Choose a "base point" $a \times b$ in the product $X \times Y$. Note that the "horizontal slice" $X \times b$ is connected, being homeomorphic with X, and each "vertical slice" $x \times Y$ is connected, being homeomorphic with Y. As a result, each "T-shaped" space

$$T_x = (X \times b) \cup (x \times Y)$$

is connected, being the union of two connected spaces that have the point $x \times b$ in common. See Figure 23.2. Now form the union $\bigcup_{x \in X} T_x$ of all these T-shaped spaces.

This union is connected because it is the union of a collection of connected spaces that have the point $a \times b$ in common. Since this union equals $X \times Y$, the space $X \times Y$ is connected.

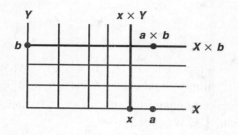

Figure 23.2

The proof for any finite product of connected spaces follows by induction, using the fact (easily proved) that $X_1 \times \cdots \times X_n$ is homeomorphic with $(X_1 \times \cdots \times X_{n-1}) \times X_n$. ∎

It is natural to ask whether this theorem extends to arbitrary products of connected spaces. The answer depends on which topology is used for the product, as the following examples show.

EXAMPLE 6.   Consider the cartesian product $\mathbb{R}^\omega$ in the box topology. We can write $\mathbb{R}^\omega$ as the union of the set A consisting of all bounded sequences of real numbers, and the set B of all unbounded sequences. These sets are disjoint, and each is open in the box topology. For if $\mathbf{a}$ is a point of $\mathbb{R}^\omega$, the open set

$$U = (a_1 - 1, a_1 + 1) \times (a_2 - 1, a_2 + 1) \times \cdots$$

consists entirely of bounded sequences if $\mathbf{a}$ is bounded, and of unbounded sequences if $\mathbf{a}$ if unbounded. Thus, even though $\mathbb{R}$ is connected (as we shall prove in the next section), $\mathbb{R}^\omega$ is not connected in the box topology.

EXAMPLE 7.   Now consider $\mathbb{R}^\omega$ in the product topology. Assuming that $\mathbb{R}$ is connected, we show that $\mathbb{R}^\omega$ is connected. Let $\tilde{\mathbb{R}}^n$ denote the subspace of $\mathbb{R}^\omega$ consisting of all sequences $\mathbf{x} = (x_1, x_2, \ldots)$ such that $x_i = 0$ for $i > n$. The space $\tilde{\mathbb{R}}^n$ is clearly homeomorphic to $\mathbb{R}^n$, so that it is connected, by the preceding theorem. It follows that the space $\mathbb{R}^\infty$ that is the union of the spaces $\tilde{\mathbb{R}}^n$ is connected, for these spaces have the point $\mathbf{0} = (0, 0, \ldots)$ in common. We show that the closure of $\mathbb{R}^\infty$ equals all of $\mathbb{R}^\omega$, from which it follows that $\mathbb{R}^\omega$ is connected as well.

Let $\mathbf{a} = (a_1, a_2, \ldots)$ be a point of $\mathbb{R}^\omega$. Let $U = \prod U_i$ be a basis element for the product topology that contains $\mathbf{a}$. We show that U intersects $\mathbb{R}^\infty$. There is an integer N such that $U_i = \mathbb{R}$ for $i > N$. Then the point

$$\mathbf{x} = (a_1, \ldots, a_n, 0, 0, \ldots)$$

of $\mathbb{R}^\infty$ belongs to U, since $a_i \in U_i$ for all i, and $0 \in U_i$ for $i > N$.

The argument just given generalizes to show that an arbitrary product of connected spaces is connected in the product topology. Since we shall not need this result, we leave the proof to the exercises.

Exercises

1. Let $\mathcal{T}$ and $\mathcal{T}'$ be two topologies on X. If $\mathcal{T}' \supset \mathcal{T}$, what does connectedness of X in one topology imply about connectedness in the other?

2. Let $\{A_n\}$ be a sequence of connected subspaces of X, such that $A_n \cap A_{n+1} \neq \varnothing$ for all n. Show that $\bigcup A_n$ is connected.

3. Let $\{A_\alpha\}$ be a collection of connected subspaces of X; let A be a connected subspace of X. Show that if $A \cap A_\alpha \neq \varnothing$ for all α, then $A \cup (\bigcup A_\alpha)$ is connected.

4. Show that if X is an infinite set, it is connected in the finite complement topology.

5. A space is ***totally disconnected*** if its only connected subspaces are one-point sets. Show that if X has the discrete topology, then X is totally disconnected. Does the converse hold?

6. Let $A \subset X$. Show that if C is a connected subspace of X that intersects both A and $X - A$, then C intersects Bd A.

7. Is the space $\mathbb{R}_\ell$ connected? Justify your answer.

8. Determine whether or not $\mathbb{R}^\omega$ is connected in the uniform topology.

9. Let A be a proper subset of X, and let B be a proper subset of Y. If X and Y are connected, show that

$$(X \times Y) - (A \times B)$$

is connected.

10. Let $\{X_\alpha\}_{\alpha \in J}$ be an indexed family of connected spaces; let X be the product space

$$X = \prod_{\alpha \in J} X_\alpha.$$

Let $\mathbf{a} = (a_\alpha)$ be a fixed point of X.
   (a) Given any finite subset K of J, let X_K denote the subspace of X consisting of all points $\mathbf{x} = (x_\alpha)$ such that $x_\alpha = a_\alpha$ for $\alpha \notin K$. Show that X_K is connected.
   (b) Show that the union Y of the spaces X_K is connected.
   (c) Show that X equals the closure of Y; conclude that X is connected.

11. Let $p : X \to Y$ be a quotient map. Show that if each set $p^{-1}(\{y\})$ is connected, and if Y is connected, then X is connected.

12. Let $Y \subset X$; let X and Y be connected. Show that if A and B form a separation of $X - Y$, then $Y \cup A$ and $Y \cup B$ are connected.

§24   Connected Subspaces of the Real Line

The theorems of the preceding section show us how to construct new connected spaces out of given ones. But where can we find some connected spaces to start with? The best place to begin is the real line. We shall prove that $\mathbb{R}$ is connected, and so are the intervals and rays in $\mathbb{R}$.

One application is the intermediate value theorem of calculus, suitably general-ized. Another is the result that such familiar spaces as balls and spheres in euclidean space are connected; the proof involves a new notion, called *path connectedness*, which we also discuss.

The fact that intervals and rays in $\mathbb{R}$ are connected may be familiar to you from analysis. We prove it again here, in generalized form. It turns out that this fact does not depend on the algebraic properties of $\mathbb{R}$, but only on its order properties. To make this clear, we shall prove the theorem for an arbitrary ordered set that has the order properties of $\mathbb{R}$. Such a set is called a *linear continuum*.

Definition.   A simply ordered set L having more than one element is called a ***linear continuum*** if the following hold:

(1) L has the least upper bound property.

(2) If $x < y$, there exists z such that $x < z < y$.

Theorem 24.1.   *If L is a linear continuum in the order topology, then L is connected, and so are intervals and rays in L.*

Proof.   Recall that a subspace Y of L is said to be *convex* if for every pair of points a, b of Y with $a < b$, the entire interval $[a, b]$ of points of L lies in Y. We prove that if Y is a convex subspace of L, then Y is connected.

So suppose that Y is the union of the disjoint nonempty sets A and B, each of which is open in Y. Choose $a \in A$ and $b \in B$; suppose for convenience that $a < b$. The interval $[a, b]$ of points of L is contained in Y. Hence $[a, b]$ is the union of the disjoint sets

$$A_0 = A \cap [a, b] \quad \text{and} \quad B_0 = B \cap [a, b],$$

each of which is open in $[a, b]$ in the subspace topology, which is the same as the order topology. The sets A_0 and B_0 are nonempty because $a \in A_0$ and $b \in B_0$. Thus, A_0 and B_0 constitute a separation of $[a, b]$.

Let $c = \sup A_0$. We show that c belongs neither to A_0 nor to B_0, which contradicts the fact that $[a, b]$ is the union of A_0 and B_0.

Case 1. Suppose that $c \in B_0$. Then $c \neq a$, so either $c = b$ or $a < c < b$. In either case, it follows from the fact that B_0 is open in $[a, b]$ that there is some interval of the form $(d, c]$ contained in B_0. If $c = b$, we have a contradiction at once, for d is a smaller upper bound on A_0 than c. If $c < b$, we note that $(c, b]$ does not intersect A_0

(because c is an upper bound on A_0). Then

$$(d, b] = (d, c] \cup (c, b]$$

does not intersect A_0. Again, d is a smaller upper bound on A_0 than c, contrary to construction. See Figure 24.1.

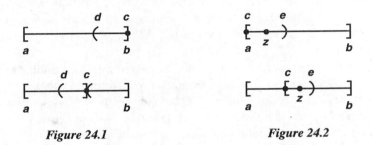

Figure 24.1	*Figure 24.2*

Case 2. Suppose that $c \in A_0$. Then $c \neq b$, so either $c = a$ or $a < c < b$. Because A_0 is open in $[a, b]$, there must be some interval of the form $[c, e)$ contained in A_0. See Figure 24.2. Because of order property (2) of the linear continuum L, we can choose a point z of L such that $c < z < e$. Then $z \in A_0$, contrary to the fact that c is an upper bound for A_0. ∎

Corollary 24.2. *The real line $\mathbb{R}$ is connected and so are intervals and rays in $\mathbb{R}$.*

As an application, we prove the intermediate value theorem of calculus, suitably generalized.

Theorem 24.3 (Intermediate value theorem). *Let $f : X \to Y$ be a continuous map, where X is a connected space and Y is an ordered set in the order topology. If a and b are two points of X and if r is a point of Y lying between $f(a)$ and $f(b)$, then there exists a point c of X such that $f(c) = r$.*

The intermediate value theorem of calculus is the special case of this theorem that occurs when we take X to be a closed interval in $\mathbb{R}$ and Y to be $\mathbb{R}$.

Proof. Assume the hypotheses of the theorem. The sets

$$A = f(X) \cap (-\infty, r) \quad \text{and} \quad B = f(X) \cap (r, +\infty)$$

are disjoint, and they are nonempty because one contains $f(a)$ and the other contains $f(b)$. Each is open in $f(X)$, being the intersection of an open ray in Y with $f(X)$. If there were no point c of X such that $f(c) = r$, then $f(X)$ would be the union of the sets A and B. Then A and B would constitute a separation of $f(X)$, contradicting the fact that the image of a connected space under a continuous map is connected. ∎

EXAMPLE 1.   One example of a linear continuum different from $\mathbb{R}$ is the ordered square. We check the least upper bound property. (The second property of a linear continuum is trivial to check.) Let A be a subset of $I \times I$; let $\pi_1 : I \times I \to I$ be projection on the first coordinate; let $b = \sup \pi_1(A)$. If $b \in \pi_1(A)$, then A intersects the subset $b \times I$ of $I \times I$. Because $b \times I$ has the order type of I, the set $A \cap (b \times I)$ will have a least upper bound $b \times c$, which will be the least upper bound of A. See Figure 24.3. If $b \notin \pi_1(A)$, then $b \times 0$ is the least upper bound of A; no element of the form $b' \times c$ with $b' < b$ can be an upper bound for A, for then b' would be an upper bound for $\pi_1(A)$.

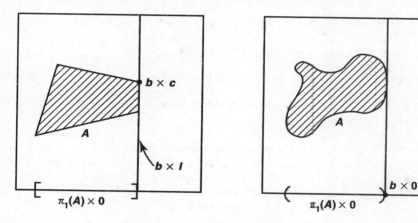

Figure 24.3

EXAMPLE 2.   If X is a well-ordered set, then $X \times [0, 1)$ is a linear continuum in the dictionary order; this we leave to you to check. This set can be thought of as having been constructed by "fitting in" a set of the order type of $(0, 1)$ immediately following each element of X.

Connectedness of intervals in $\mathbb{R}$ gives rise to an especially useful criterion for showing that a space X is connected; namely, the condition that every pair of points of X can be joined by a *path* in X:

Definition.   Given points x and y of the space X, a *path* in X from x to y is a continuous map $f : [a, b] \to X$ of some closed interval in the real line into X, such that $f(a) = x$ and $f(b) = y$. A space X is said to be *path connected* if every pair of points of X can be joined by a path in X.

It is easy to see that a path-connected space X is connected. Suppose $X = A \cup B$ is a separation of X. Let $f : [a, b] \to X$ be any path in X. Being the continuous image of a connected set, the set $f([a, b])$ is connected, so that it lies entirely in either A or B. Therefore, there is no path in X joining a point of A to a point of B, contrary to the assumption that X is path connected.

The converse does not hold; a connected space need not be path connected. See Examples 6 and 7 following.

EXAMPLE 3.   Define the ***unit ball*** B^n in $\mathbb{R}^n$ by the equation

$$B^n = \{\mathbf{x} \mid \|\mathbf{x}\| \le 1\},$$

where

$$\|\mathbf{x}\| = \|(x_1, \ldots, x_n)\| = (x_1^2 + \cdots + x_n^2)^{1/2}.$$

The unit ball is path connected; given any two points $\mathbf{x}$ and $\mathbf{y}$ of B^n, the straight-line path $f : [0, 1] \to \mathbb{R}^n$ defined by

$$f(t) = (1 - t)\mathbf{x} + t\mathbf{y}$$

lies in B^n. For if $\mathbf{x}$ and $\mathbf{y}$ are in B^n and t is in $[0, 1]$,

$$\|f(t)\| \le (1 - t)\|\mathbf{x}\| + t\|\mathbf{y}\| \le 1.$$

A similar argument shows that every open ball $B_d(\mathbf{x}, \epsilon)$ and every closed ball $\bar{B}_d(\mathbf{x}, \epsilon)$ in $\mathbb{R}^n$ is path connected.

EXAMPLE 4.   Define ***punctured euclidean space*** to be the space $\mathbb{R}^n - \{\mathbf{0}\}$, where $\mathbf{0}$ is the origin in $\mathbb{R}^n$. If $n > 1$, this space is path connected: Given $\mathbf{x}$ and $\mathbf{y}$ different from $\mathbf{0}$, we can join $\mathbf{x}$ and $\mathbf{y}$ by the straight-line path between them if that path does not go through the origin. Otherwise, we can choose a point $\mathbf{z}$ not on the line joining $\mathbf{x}$ and $\mathbf{y}$, and take the broken-line path from $\mathbf{x}$ to $\mathbf{z}$, and then from $\mathbf{z}$ to $\mathbf{y}$.

EXAMPLE 5.   Define the ***unit sphere*** S^{n-1} in $\mathbb{R}^n$ by the equation

$$S^{n-1} = \{\mathbf{x} \mid \|\mathbf{x}\| = 1\}.$$

If $n > 1$, it is path connected. For the map $g : \mathbb{R}^n - \{\mathbf{0}\} \to S^{n-1}$ defined by $g(\mathbf{x}) = \mathbf{x}/\|\mathbf{x}\|$ is continuous and surjective; and it is easy to show that the continuous image of a path-connected space is path connected.

EXAMPLE 6.   *The ordered square I_o^2 is connected but not path connected.*
Being a linear continuum, the ordered square is connected. Let $p = 0 \times 0$ and $q = 1 \times 1$. We suppose there is a path $f : [a, b] \to I_o^2$ joining p and q and derive a contradiction. The image set $f([a, b])$ must contain every point $x \times y$ of I_o^2, by the intermediate value theorem. Therefore, for each $x \in I$, the set

$$U_x = f^{-1}(x \times (0, 1))$$

is a nonempty subset of $[a, b]$; by continuity, it is open in $[a, b]$. See Figure 24.4. Choose, for each $x \in I$, a rational number q_x belonging to U_x. Since the sets U_x are disjoint, the map $x \to q_x$ is an injective mapping of I into $\mathbb{Q}$. This contradicts the fact that the interval I is uncountable (which we shall prove later).

EXAMPLE 7.   Let S denote the following subset of the plane.

$$S = \{x \times \sin(1/x) \mid 0 < x \le 1\}.$$

Because S is the image of the connected set $(0, 1]$ under a continuous map, S is connected. Therefore, its closure $\bar{S}$ in $\mathbb{R}^2$ is also connected. The set $\bar{S}$ is a classical example in topology

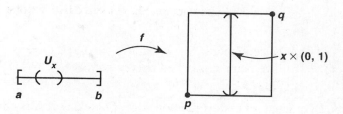

Figure 24.4

called the *topologist's sine curve*. It is illustrated in Figure 24.5; it equals the union of S and the vertical interval $0 \times [-1, 1]$. We show that $\bar{S}$ is not path connected.

Suppose there is a path $f : [a, c] \to \bar{S}$ beginning at the origin and ending at a point of S. The set of those t for which $f(t) \in 0 \times [-1, 1]$ is closed, so it has a largest element b. Then $f : [b, c] \to \bar{S}$ is a path that maps b into the vertical interval $0 \times [-1, 1]$ and maps the other points of $[b, c]$ to points of S.

Replace $[b, c]$ by $[0, 1]$ for convenience; let $f(t) = (x(t), y(t))$. Then $x(0) = 0$, while $x(t) > 0$ and $y(t) = \sin(1/x(t))$ for $t > 0$. We show there is a sequence of points $t_n \to 0$ such that $y(t_n) = (-1)^n$. Then the sequence $y(t_n)$ does not converge, contradicting continuity of f.

To find t_n, we proceed as follows: Given n, choose u with $0 < u < x(1/n)$ such that $\sin(1/u) = (-1)^n$. Then use the intermediate value theorem to find t_n with $0 < t_n < 1/n$ such that $x(t_n) = u$.

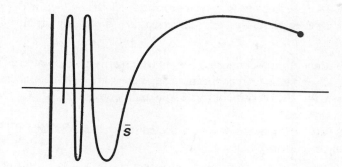

Figure 24.5

Exercises

1. (a) Show that no two of the spaces $(0, 1)$, $(0, 1]$, and $[0, 1]$ are homeomorphic. [*Hint:* What happens if you remove a point from each of these spaces?)]

(b) Suppose that there exist imbeddings $f : X \to Y$ and $g : Y \to X$. Show by means of an example that X and Y need not be homeomorphic.

(c) Show $\mathbb{R}^n$ and $\mathbb{R}$ are not homeomorphic if $n > 1$.

2. Let $f : S^1 \to \mathbb{R}$ be a continuous map. Show there exists a point x of S^1 such that $f(x) = f(-x)$.

3. Let $f : X \to X$ be continuous. Show that if $X = [0, 1]$, there is a point x such that $f(x) = x$. The point x is called a **fixed point** of f. What happens if X equals $[0, 1)$ or $(0, 1)$?

4. Let X be an ordered set in the order topology. Show that if X is connected, then X is a linear continuum.

5. Consider the following sets in the dictionary order. Which are linear continua?
   (a) $\mathbb{Z}_+ \times [0, 1)$
   (b) $[0, 1) \times \mathbb{Z}_+$
   (c) $[0, 1) \times [0, 1]$
   (d) $[0, 1] \times [0, 1)$

6. Show that if X is a well-ordered set, then $X \times [0, 1)$ in the dictionary order is a linear continuum.

7. (a) Let X and Y be ordered sets in the order topology. Show that if $f : X \to Y$ is order preserving and surjective, then f is a homeomorphism.
   (b) Let $X = Y = \bar{\mathbb{R}}_+$. Given a positive integer n, show that the function $f(x) = x^n$ is order preserving and surjective. Conclude that its inverse, the *nth root function*, is continuous.
   (c) Let X be the subspace $(-\infty, -1) \cup [0, \infty)$ of $\mathbb{R}$. Show that the function $f : X \to \mathbb{R}$ defined by setting $f(x) = x + 1$ if $x < -1$, and $f(x) = x$ if $x \geq 0$, is order preserving and surjective. Is f a homeomorphism? Compare with (a).

8. (a) Is a product of path-connected spaces necessarily path connected?
   (b) If $A \subset X$ and A is path connected, is $\bar{A}$ necessarily path connected?
   (c) If $f : X \to Y$ is continuous and X is path connected, is $f(X)$ necessarily path connected?
   (d) If $\{A_\alpha\}$ is a collection of path-connected subspaces of X and if $\bigcap A_\alpha \neq \varnothing$, is $\bigcup A_\alpha$ necessarily path connected?

9. Assume that $\mathbb{R}$ is uncountable. Show that if A is a countable subset of $\mathbb{R}^2$, then $\mathbb{R}^2 - A$ is path connected. [*Hint:* How many lines are there passing through a given point of $\mathbb{R}^2$?]

10. Show that if U is an *open* connected subspace of $\mathbb{R}^2$, then U is path connected. [*Hint:* Show that given $x_0 \in U$, the set of points that can be joined to x_0 by a path in U is both open and closed in U.]

11. If A is a connected subspace of X, does it follow that Int A and Bd A are connected? Does the converse hold? Justify your answers.

*12. Recall that S_Ω denotes the minimal uncountable well-ordered set. Let L denote the ordered set $S_\Omega \times [0, 1)$ in the dictionary order, with its smallest element deleted. The set L is a classical example in topology called the **long line**.

Theorem.   The long line is path connected and locally homeomorphic to $\mathbb{R}$, but it cannot be imbedded in $\mathbb{R}$.

(a) Let X be an ordered set; let $a < b < c$ be points of X. Show that $[a, c)$ has the order type of $[0, 1)$ if and only if both $[a, b)$ and $[b, c)$ have the order type of $[0, 1)$.

(b) Let X be an ordered set. Let $x_0 < x_1 < \cdots$ be an increasing sequence of points of X; suppose $b = \sup\{x_i\}$. Show that $[x_0, b)$ has the order type of $[0, 1)$ if and only if each interval $[x_i, x_{i+1})$ has the order type of $[0, 1)$.

(c) Let a_0 denote the smallest element of S_Ω. For each element a of S_Ω different from a_0, show that the interval $[a_0 \times 0, a \times 0)$ of $S_\Omega \times [0, 1)$ has the order type of $[0, 1)$. [*Hint:* Proceed by transfinite induction. Either a has an immediate predecessor in S_Ω, or there is an increasing sequence a_i in S_Ω with $a = \sup\{a_i\}$.]

(d) Show that L is path connected.

(e) Show that every point of L has a neighborhood homeomorphic with an open interval in $\mathbb{R}$.

(f) Show that L cannot be imbedded in $\mathbb{R}$, or indeed in $\mathbb{R}^n$ for any n. [*Hint:* Any subspace of $\mathbb{R}^n$ has a countable basis for its topology.]

*§25 Components and Local Connectedness[†]

Given an arbitrary space X, there is a natural way to break it up into pieces that are connected (or path connected). We consider that process now.

Definition.   Given X, define an equivalence relation on X by setting $x \sim y$ if there is a connected subspace of X containing both x and y. The equivalence classes are called the **components** (or the "connected components") of X.

Symmetry and reflexivity of the relation are obvious. Transitivity follows by noting that if A is a connected subspace containing x and y, and if B is a connected subspace containing y and z, then $A \cup B$ is a subspace containing x and z that is connected because A and B have the point y in common.

The components of X can also be described as follows:

Theorem 25.1.   *The components of X are connected disjoint subspaces of X whose union is X, such that each nonempty connected subspace of X intersects only one of them.*

Proof.   Being equivalence classes, the components of X are disjoint and their union is X. Each connected subspace A of X intersects only one of them. For if A intersects the components C_1 and C_2 of X, say in points x_1 and x_2, respectively, then $x_1 \sim x_2$ by definition; this cannot happen unless $C_1 = C_2$.

[†]This section will be assumed in Part II of the book.

To show the component C is connected, choose a point x_0 of C. For each point x of C, we know that $x_0 \sim x$, so there is a connected subspace A_x containing x_0 and x. By the result just proved, $A_x \subset C$. Therefore,

$$C = \bigcup_{x \in C} A_x.$$

Since the subspaces A_x are connected and have the point x_0 in common, their union is connected. ∎

Definition.   We define another equivalence relation on the space X by defining $x \sim y$ if there is a path in X from x to y. The equivalence classes are called the ***path components*** of X.

Let us show this is an equivalence relation. First we note that if there exists a path $f : [a, b] \to X$ from x to y whose domain is the interval $[a, b]$, then there is also a path g from x to y having the closed interval $[c, d]$ as its domain. (This follows from the fact that any two closed intervals in $\mathbb{R}$ are homeomorphic.) Now the fact that $x \sim x$ for each x in X follows from the existence of the constant path $f : [a, b] \to X$ defined by the equation $f(t) = x$ for all t. Symmetry follows from the fact that if $f : [0, 1] \to X$ is a path from x to y, then the "reverse path" $g : [0, 1] \to X$ defined by $g(t) = f(1 - t)$ is a path from y to x. Finally, transitivity is proved as follows: Let $f : [0, 1] \to X$ be a path from x to y, and let $g : [1, 2] \to X$ be a path from y to z. We can "paste f and g together" to get a path $h : [0, 2] \to X$ from x to z; the path h will be continuous by the "pasting lemma," Theorem 18.3.

One has the following theorem, whose proof is similar to that of the theorem preceding:

Theorem 25.2.   *The path components of X are path-connected disjoint subspaces of X whose union is X, such that each nonempty path-connected subspace of X intersects only one of them.*

Note that each component of a space X is closed in X, since the closure of a connected subspace of X is connected. If X has only finitely many components, then each component is also open in X, since its complement is a finite union of closed sets. But in general the components of X need not be open in X.

One can say even less about the path components of X, for they need be neither open nor closed in X. Consider the following examples:

EXAMPLE 1.   If $\mathbb{Q}$ is the subspace of $\mathbb{R}$ consisting of the rational numbers, then each component of $\mathbb{Q}$ consists of a single point. None of the components of $\mathbb{Q}$ are open in $\mathbb{Q}$.

EXAMPLE 2.   The "topologist's sine curve" $\bar{S}$ of the preceding section is a space that has a single component (since it is connected) and two path components. One path component is the curve S and the other is the vertical interval $V = 0 \times [-1, 1]$. Note that S is open in $\bar{S}$ but not closed, while V is closed but not open.

If one forms a space from $\bar{S}$ by deleting all points of V having rational second coordinate, one obtains a space that has only one component but uncountably many path components.

Connectedness is a useful property for a space to possess. But for some purposes, it is more important that the space satisfy a connectedness condition *locally*. Roughly speaking, local connectedness means that each point has "arbitrarily small" neighborhoods that are connected. More precisely, one has the following definition:

Definition.   A space X is said to be *locally connected at x* if for every neighborhood U of x, there is a connected neighborhood V of x contained in U. If X is locally connected at each of its points, it is said simply to be *locally connected*. Similarly, a space X is said to be *locally path connected at x* if for every neighborhood U of x, there is a path-connected neighborhood V of x contained in U. If X is locally path connected at each of its points, then it is said to be *locally path connected*.

> EXAMPLE 3.   Each interval and each ray in the real line is both connected and locally connected. The subspace $[-1, 0) \cup (0, 1]$ of $\mathbb{R}$ is not connected, but it is locally connected. The topologist's sine curve is connected but not locally connected. The rationals $\mathbb{Q}$ are neither connected nor locally connected.

Theorem 25.3.   *A space X is locally connected if and only if for every open set U of X, each component of U is open in X.*

Proof.   Suppose that X is locally connected; let U be an open set in X; let C be a component of U. If x is a point of C, we can choose a connected neighborhood V of x such that $V \subset U$. Since V is connected, it must lie entirely in the component C of U. Therefore, C is open in X.

Conversely, suppose that components of open sets in X are open. Given a point x of X and a neighborhood U of x, let C be the component of U containing x. Now C is connected; since it is open in X by hypothesis, X is locally connected at x.   ∎

A similar proof holds for the following theorem:

Theorem 25.4.   *A space X is locally path connected if and only if for every open set U of X, each path component of U is open in X.*

The relation between path components and components is given in the following theorem:

Theorem 25.5.   *If X is a topological space, each path component of X lies in a component of X. If X is locally path connected, then the components and the path components of X are the same.*

Proof.   Let C be a component of X; let x be a point of C; let P be the path component of X containing x. Since P is connected, $P \subset C$. We wish to show that if X is locally path connected, $P = C$. Suppose that $P \subsetneq C$. Let Q denote the union of all the path components of X that are different from P and intersect C; each of them necessarily lies in C, so that

$$C = P \cup Q.$$

Because X is locally path connected, each path component of X is open in X. Therefore, P (which is a path component) and Q (which is a union of path components) are open in X, so they constitute a separation of C. This contradicts the fact that C is connected.   ∎

Exercises

1. What are the components and path components of $\mathbb{R}_\ell$? What are the continuous maps $f : \mathbb{R} \to \mathbb{R}_\ell$?

2. (a) What are the components and path components of $\mathbb{R}^\omega$ (in the product topology)?
   (b) Consider $\mathbb{R}^\omega$ in the uniform topology. Show that $\mathbf{x}$ and $\mathbf{y}$ lie in the same component of $\mathbb{R}^\omega$ if and only if the sequence

   $$\mathbf{x} - \mathbf{y} = (x_1 - y_1, x_2 - y_2, \dots)$$

   is bounded. [*Hint:* It suffices to consider the case where $\mathbf{y} = \mathbf{0}$.]
   (c) Give $\mathbb{R}^\omega$ the box topology. Show that $\mathbf{x}$ and $\mathbf{y}$ lie in the same component of $\mathbb{R}^\omega$ if and only if the sequence $\mathbf{x} - \mathbf{y}$ is "eventually zero." [*Hint:* If $\mathbf{x} - \mathbf{y}$ is not eventually zero, show there is homeomorphism h of $\mathbb{R}^\omega$ with itself such that $h(\mathbf{x})$ is bounded and $h(\mathbf{y})$ is unbounded.]

3. Show that the ordered square is locally connected but not locally path connected. What are the path components of this space?

4. Let X be locally path connected. Show that every connected open set in X is path connected.

5. Let X denote the rational points of the interval $[0, 1] \times 0$ of $\mathbb{R}^2$. Let T denote the union of all line segments joining the point $p = 0 \times 1$ to points of X.
   (a) Show that T is path connected, but is locally connected only at the point p.
   (b) Find a subset of $\mathbb{R}^2$ that is path connected but is locally connected at none of its points.

6. A space X is said to be *weakly locally connected at x* if for every neighborhood U of x, there is a connected subspace of X contained in U that contains a neighborhood of x. Show that if X is weakly locally connected at each of its points, then X is locally connected. [*Hint:* Show that components of open sets are open.]

7. Consider the "infinite broom" X pictured in Figure 25.1. Show that X is not locally connected at p, but is weakly locally connected at p. [*Hint:* Any connected neighborhood of p must contain all the points a_i.]

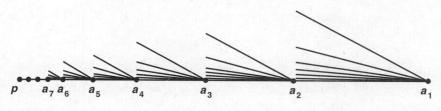

$$p \quad a_7\, a_6 \quad a_5 \quad a_4 \quad a_3 \quad a_2 \quad a_1$$

Figure 25.1

8. Let $p : X \to Y$ be a quotient map. Show that if X is locally connected, then Y is locally connected. [*Hint:* If C is a component of the open set U of Y, show that $p^{-1}(C)$ is a union of components of $p^{-1}(U)$.]

9. Let G be a topological group; let C be the component of G containing the identity element e. Show that C is a normal subgroup of G. [*Hint:* If $x \in G$, then xC is the component of G containing x.]

10. Let X be a space. Let us define $x \sim y$ if there is no separation $X = A \cup B$ of X into disjoint open sets such that $x \in A$ and $y \in B$.
    (a) Show this relation is an equivalence relation. The equivalence classes are called the ***quasicomponents*** of X.
    (b) Show that each component of X lies in a quasicomponent of X, and that the components and quasicomponents of X are the same if X is locally connected.
    (c) Let K denote the set $\{1/n \mid n \in \mathbb{Z}_+\}$ and let $-K$ denote the set $\{-1/n \mid n \in \mathbb{Z}_+\}$. Determine the components, path components, and quasicomponents of the following subspaces of $\mathbb{R}^2$:

    $A = (K \times [0, 1]) \cup \{0 \times 0\} \cup \{0 \times 1\}$.
    $B = A \cup ([0, 1] \times \{0\})$.
    $C = (K \times [0, 1]) \cup (-K \times [-1, 0]) \cup ([0, 1] \times -K) \cup ([-1, 0] \times K)$.

§26 Compact Spaces

The notion of compactness is not nearly so natural as that of connectedness. From the beginnings of topology, it was clear that the closed interval $[a, b]$ of the real line had a certain property that was crucial for proving such theorems as the maximum value theorem and the uniform continuity theorem. But for a long time, it was not clear how this property should be formulated for an arbitrary topological space. It used to be thought that the crucial property of $[a, b]$ was the fact that every infinite subset of $[a, b]$ has a limit point, and this property was the one dignified with the name of compactness. Later, mathematicians realized that this formulation does not lie at the heart of the matter, but rather that a stronger formulation, in terms of open coverings of the space, is more central. The latter formulation is what we now call compactness.

It is not as natural or intuitive as the former; some familiarity with it is needed before its usefulness becomes apparent.

Definition. A collection $\mathcal{A}$ of subsets of a space X is said to *cover* X, or to be a *covering* of X, if the union of the elements of $\mathcal{A}$ is equal to X. It is called an *open covering* of X if its elements are open subsets of X.

Definition. A space X is said to be *compact* if every open covering $\mathcal{A}$ of X contains a finite subcollection that also covers X.

EXAMPLE 1.   The real line $\mathbb{R}$ is not compact, for the covering of $\mathbb{R}$ by open intervals

$$\mathcal{A} = \{(n, n+2) \mid n \in \mathbb{Z}\}$$

contains no finite subcollection that covers $\mathbb{R}$.

EXAMPLE 2.   The following subspace of $\mathbb{R}$ is compact:

$$X = \{0\} \cup \{1/n \mid n \in \mathbb{Z}_+\}.$$

Given an open covering $\mathcal{A}$ of X, there is an element U of $\mathcal{A}$ containing 0. The set U contains all but finitely many of the points $1/n$; choose, for each point of X not in U, an element of $\mathcal{A}$ containing it. The collection consisting of these elements of $\mathcal{A}$, along with the element U, is a finite subcollection of $\mathcal{A}$ that covers X.

EXAMPLE 3.   Any space X containing only finitely many points is necessarily compact, because in this case every open covering of X is finite.

EXAMPLE 4.   The interval $(0, 1]$ is not compact; the open covering

$$\mathcal{A} = \{(1/n, 1] \mid n \in \mathbb{Z}_+\}$$

contains no finite subcollection covering $(0, 1]$. Nor is the interval $(0, 1)$ compact; the same argument applies. On the other hand, the interval $[0, 1]$ *is* compact; you are probably already familiar with this fact from analysis. In any case, we shall prove it shortly.

In general, it takes some effort to decide whether a given space is compact or not. First we shall prove some general theorems that show us how to construct new compact spaces out of existing ones. Then in the next section we shall show certain specific spaces are compact. These spaces include all closed intervals in the real line, and all closed and bounded subsets of $\mathbb{R}^n$.

Let us first prove some facts about subspaces. If Y is a subspace of X, a collection $\mathcal{A}$ of subsets of X is said to *cover* Y if the union of its elements *contains* Y.

Lemma 26.1.   *Let Y be a subspace of X. Then Y is compact if and only if every covering of Y by sets open in X contains a finite subcollection covering Y.*

Proof.   Suppose that Y is compact and $\mathcal{A} = \{A_\alpha\}_{\alpha \in J}$ is a covering of Y by sets open in X. Then the collection

$$\{A_\alpha \cap Y \mid \alpha \in J\}$$

is a covering of Y by sets open in Y; hence a finite subcollection

$$\{A_{\alpha_1} \cap Y, \dots, A_{\alpha_n} \cap Y\}$$

covers Y. Then $\{A_{\alpha_1}, \dots, A_{\alpha_n}\}$ is a subcollection of $\mathcal{A}$ that covers Y.

Conversely, suppose the given condition holds; we wish to prove Y compact. Let $\mathcal{A}' = \{A'_\alpha\}$ be a covering of Y by sets open in Y. For each α, choose a set A_α open in X such that

$$A'_\alpha = A_\alpha \cap Y.$$

The collection $\mathcal{A} = \{A_\alpha\}$ is a covering of Y by sets open in X. By hypothesis, some finite subcollection $\{A_{\alpha_1}, \dots, A_{\alpha_n}\}$ covers Y. Then $\{A'_{\alpha_1}, \dots, A'_{\alpha_n}\}$ is a subcollection of $\mathcal{A}'$ that covers Y.   ∎

Theorem 26.2.   *Every closed subspace of a compact space is compact.*

Proof.   Let Y be a closed subspace of the compact space X. Given a covering $\mathcal{A}$ of Y by sets open in X, let us form an open covering $\mathcal{B}$ of X by adjoining to $\mathcal{A}$ the single open set $X - Y$, that is,

$$\mathcal{B} = \mathcal{A} \cup \{X - Y\}.$$

Some finite subcollection of $\mathcal{B}$ covers X. If this subcollection contains the set $X - Y$, discard $X - Y$; otherwise, leave the subcollection alone. The resulting collection is a finite subcollection of $\mathcal{A}$ that covers Y.   ∎

Theorem 26.3.   *Every compact subspace of a Hausdorff space is closed.*

Proof.   Let Y be a compact subspace of the Hausdorff space X. We shall prove that $X - Y$ is open, so that Y is closed.

Let x_0 be a point of $X - Y$. We show there is a neighborhood of x_0 that is disjoint from Y. For each point y of Y, let us choose disjoint neighborhoods U_y and V_y of the points x_0 and y, respectively (using the Hausdorff condition). The collection $\{V_y \mid y \in Y\}$ is a covering of Y by sets open in X; therefore, finitely many of them $V_{y_1}, \dots, V_{y_n}$ cover Y. The open set

$$V = V_{y_1} \cup \cdots \cup V_{y_n}$$

contains Y, and it is disjoint from the open set

$$U = U_{y_1} \cap \cdots \cap U_{y_n}$$

formed by taking the intersection of the corresponding neighborhoods of x_0. For if z is a point of V, then $z \in V_{y_i}$ for some i, hence $z \notin U_{y_i}$ and so $z \notin U$. See Figure 26.1.

Then U is a neighborhood of x_0 disjoint from Y, as desired.   ∎

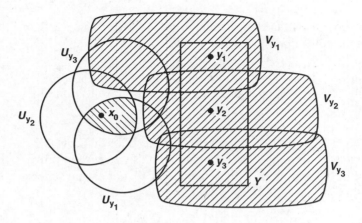

Figure 26.1

The statement we proved in the course of the preceding proof will be useful to us later, so we repeat it here for reference purposes:

Lemma 26.4. *If Y is a compact subspace of the Hausdorff space X and x_0 is not in Y, then there exist disjoint open sets U and V of X containing x_0 and Y, respectively.*

EXAMPLE 5.   Once we prove that the interval $[a, b]$ in $\mathbb{R}$ is compact, it follows from Theorem 26.2 that any closed subspace of $[a, b]$ is compact. On the other hand, it follows from Theorem 26.3 that the intervals $(a, b]$ and (a, b) in $\mathbb{R}$ cannot be compact (which we knew already) because they are not closed in the Hausdorff space $\mathbb{R}$.

EXAMPLE 6.   One needs the Hausdorff condition in the hypothesis of Theorem 26.3. Consider, for example, the finite complement topology on the real line. The only proper subsets of $\mathbb{R}$ that are closed in this topology are the finite sets. But *every* subset of $\mathbb{R}$ is compact in this topology, as you can check.

Theorem 26.5. *The image of a compact space under a continuous map is compact.*

Proof.   Let $f : X \to Y$ be continuous; let X be compact. Let $\mathcal{A}$ be a covering of the set $f(X)$ by sets open in Y. The collection

$$\{f^{-1}(A) \mid A \in \mathcal{A}\}$$

is a collection of sets covering X; these sets are open in X because f is continuous. Hence finitely many of them, say

$$f^{-1}(A_1), \ldots, f^{-1}(A_n),$$

cover X. Then the sets $A_1, \ldots, A_n$ cover $f(X)$.   ∎

One important use of the preceding theorem is as a tool for verifying that a map is a homeomorphism:

Theorem 26.6.   *Let $f : X \to Y$ be a bijective continuous function. If X is compact and Y is Hausdorff, then f is a homeomorphism.*

Proof.   We shall prove that images of closed sets of X under f are closed in Y; this will prove continuity of the map f^{-1}. If A is closed in X, then A is compact, by Theorem 26.2. Therefore, by the theorem just proved, $f(A)$ is compact. Since Y is Hausdorff, $f(A)$ is closed in Y, by Theorem 26.3.   ∎

Theorem 26.7.   *The product of finitely many compact spaces is compact.*

Proof.   We shall prove that the product of two compact spaces is compact; the theorem follows by induction for any finite product.

Step 1. Suppose that we are given spaces X and Y, with Y compact. Suppose that x_0 is a point of X, and N is an open set of $X \times Y$ containing the "slice" $x_0 \times Y$ of $X \times Y$. We prove the following:

> *There is a neighborhood W of x_0 in X such that N contains the entire set* $W \times Y$.

The set $W \times Y$ is often called a ***tube*** about $x_0 \times Y$.

First let us cover $x_0 \times Y$ by basis elements $U \times V$ (for the topology of $X \times Y$) lying in N. The space $x_0 \times Y$ is compact, being homeomorphic to Y. Therefore, we can cover $x_0 \times Y$ by finitely many such basis elements

$$U_1 \times V_1, \ldots, U_n \times V_n.$$

(We assume that each of the basis elements $U_i \times V_i$ actually intersects $x_0 \times Y$, since otherwise that basis element would be superfluous; we could discard it from the finite collection and still have a covering of $x_0 \times Y$.) Define

$$W = U_1 \cap \cdots \cap U_n.$$

The set W is open, and it contains x_0 because each set $U_i \times V_i$ intersects $x_0 \times Y$.

We assert that the sets $U_i \times V_i$, which were chosen to cover the slice $x_0 \times Y$, actually cover the tube $W \times Y$. Let $x \times y$ be a point of $W \times Y$. Consider the point $x_0 \times y$ of the slice $x_0 \times Y$ having the same y-coordinate as this point. Now $x_0 \times y$ belongs to $U_i \times V_i$ for some i, so that $y \in V_i$. But $x \in U_j$ for *every* j (because $x \in W$). Therefore, we have $x \times y \in U_i \times V_i$, as desired.

Since all the sets $U_i \times V_i$ lie in N, and since they cover $W \times Y$, the tube $W \times Y$ lies in N also. See Figure 26.2.

Step 2. Now we prove the theorem. Let X and Y be compact spaces. Let $\mathcal{A}$ be an open covering of $X \times Y$. Given $x_0 \in X$, the slice $x_0 \times Y$ is compact and may therefore be covered by finitely many elements $A_1, \ldots, A_m$ of $\mathcal{A}$. Their union $N = A_1 \cup \cdots \cup A_m$ is an open set containing $x_0 \times Y$; by Step 1, the open set N contains

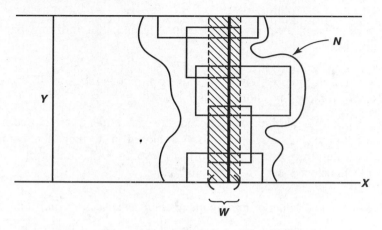

Figure 26.2

a tube $W \times Y$ about $x_0 \times Y$, where W is open in X. Then $W \times Y$ is covered by finitely many elements $A_1, \ldots, A_m$ of $\mathcal{A}$.

Thus, for each x in X, we can choose a neighborhood W_x of x such that the tube $W_x \times Y$ can be covered by finitely many elements of $\mathcal{A}$. The collection of all the neighborhoods W_x is an open covering of X; therefore by compactness of X, there exists a finite subcollection

$$\{W_1, \ldots, W_k\}$$

covering X. The union of the tubes

$$W_1 \times Y, \ldots, W_k \times Y$$

is all of $X \times Y$; since each may be covered by finitely many elements of $\mathcal{A}$, so may $X \times Y$ be covered. ∎

The statement proved in Step 1 of the preceding proof will be useful to us later, so we repeat it here as a lemma, for reference purposes:

Lemma 26.8 (The tube lemma).   *Consider the product space $X \times Y$, where Y is compact. If N is an open set of $X \times Y$ containing the slice $x_0 \times Y$ of $X \times Y$, then N contains some tube $W \times Y$ about $x_0 \times Y$, where W is a neighborhood of x_0 in X.*

EXAMPLE 7.   The tube lemma is certainly not true if Y is not compact. For example, let Y be the y-axis in $\mathbb{R}^2$, and let

$$N = \{x \times y; \ |x| < 1/(y^2 + 1)\}.$$

Then N is an open set containing the set $0 \times \mathbb{R}$, but it contains no tube about $0 \times \mathbb{R}$. It is illustrated in Figure 26.3.

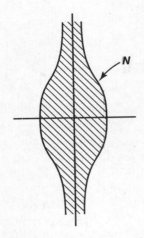

Figure 26.3

There is an obvious question to ask at this point. *Is the product of infinitely many compact spaces compact?* One would hope that the answer is "yes," and in fact it is. The result is important (and difficult) enough to be called by the name of the man who proved it; it is called the *Tychonoff theorem.*

In proving the fact that a cartesian product of connected spaces is connected, one proves it first for finite products and derives the general case from that. In proving that cartesian products of compact spaces are compact, however, there is no way to go directly from finite products to infinite ones. The infinite case demands a new approach, and the proof is a difficult one. Because of its difficulty, and also to avoid losing the main thread of our discussion in this chapter, we have decided to postpone it until later. However, you can study it now if you wish; the section in which it is proved (§37) can be studied immediately after this section without causing any disruption in continuity.

There is one final criterion for a space to be compact, a criterion that is formulated in terms of closed sets rather than open sets. It does not look very natural nor very useful at first glance, but it in fact proves to be useful on a number of occasions. First we make a definition.

Definition.   A collection $\mathcal{C}$ of subsets of X is said to have the *finite intersection property* if for every finite subcollection

$$\{C_1, \ldots, C_n\}$$

of $\mathcal{C}$, the intersection $C_1 \cap \cdots \cap C_n$ is nonempty.

Theorem 26.9.   *Let X be a topological space. Then X is compact if and only if for every collection $\mathcal{C}$ of closed sets in X having the finite intersection property, the intersection $\bigcap_{C \in \mathcal{C}} C$ of all the elements of $\mathcal{C}$ is nonempty.*

Proof. Given a collection $\mathcal{A}$ of subsets of X, let

$$\mathcal{C} = \{X - A \mid A \in \mathcal{A}\}$$

be the collection of their complements. Then the following statements hold:
(1) $\mathcal{A}$ is a collection of open sets if and only if $\mathcal{C}$ is a collection of closed sets.
(2) The collection $\mathcal{A}$ covers X if and only if the intersection $\bigcap_{C \in \mathcal{C}} C$ of all the elements of $\mathcal{C}$ is empty.
(3) The finite subcollection $\{A_1, \ldots, A_n\}$ of $\mathcal{A}$ covers X if and only if the intersection of the corresponding elements $C_i = X - A_i$ of $\mathcal{C}$ is empty.

The first statement is trivial, while the second and third follow from DeMorgan's law:

$$X - \left(\bigcup_{\alpha \in J} A_\alpha\right) = \bigcap_{\alpha \in J}(X - A_\alpha).$$

The proof of the theorem now proceeds in two easy steps: taking the *contrapositive* (of the theorem), and then the *complement* (of the sets)!

The statement that X is compact is equivalent to saying: "Given any collection $\mathcal{A}$ of open subsets of X, if $\mathcal{A}$ covers X, then some finite subcollection of $\mathcal{A}$ covers X." This statement is equivalent to its contrapositive, which is the following: "Given any collection $\mathcal{A}$ of open sets, if no finite subcollection of $\mathcal{A}$ covers X, then $\mathcal{A}$ does not cover X." Letting $\mathcal{C}$ be, as earlier, the collection $\{X - A \mid A \in \mathcal{A}\}$ and applying (1)–(3), we see that this statement is in turn equivalent to the following: "Given any collection $\mathcal{C}$ of closed sets, if every finite intersection of elements of $\mathcal{C}$ is nonempty, then the intersection of all the elements of $\mathcal{C}$ is nonempty." This is just the condition of our theorem. ∎

A special case of this theorem occurs when we have a ***nested sequence*** $C_1 \supset C_2 \supset \cdots \supset C_n \supset C_{n+1} \supset \ldots$ of closed sets in a compact space X. If each of the sets C_n is nonempty, then the collection $\mathcal{C} = \{C_n\}_{n \in \mathbb{Z}_+}$ automatically has the finite intersection property. Then the intersection

$$\bigcap_{n \in \mathbb{Z}_+} C_n$$

is nonempty.

We shall use the closed set criterion for compactness in the next section to prove the uncountability of the set of real numbers, in Chapter 5 when we prove the Tychonoff theorem, and again in Chapter 8 when we prove the Baire category theorem.

Exercises

1. (a) Let $\mathcal{T}$ and $\mathcal{T}'$ be two topologies on the set X; suppose that $\mathcal{T}' \supset \mathcal{T}$. What does compactness of X under one of these topologies imply about compactness under the other?

(b) Show that if X is compact Hausdorff under both $\mathcal{T}$ and $\mathcal{T}'$, then either $\mathcal{T}$ and $\mathcal{T}'$ are equal or they are not comparable.

2. (a) Show that in the finite complement topology on $\mathbb{R}$, every subspace is compact.

   (b) If $\mathbb{R}$ has the topology consisting of all sets A such that $\mathbb{R} - A$ is either countable or all of $\mathbb{R}$, is $[0, 1]$ a compact subspace?

3. Show that a finite union of compact subspaces of X is compact.

4. Show that every compact subspace of a metric space is bounded in that metric and is closed. Find a metric space in which not every closed bounded subspace is compact.

5. Let A and B be disjoint compact subspaces of the Hausdorff space X. Show that there exist disjoint open sets U and V containing A and B, respectively.

6. Show that if $f : X \to Y$ is continuous, where X is compact and Y is Hausdorff, then f is a closed map (that is, f carries closed sets to closed sets).

7. Show that if Y is compact, then the projection $\pi_1 : X \times Y \to X$ is a closed map.

8. *Theorem.* *Let $f : X \to Y$; let Y be compact Hausdorff. Then f is continuous if and only if the graph of f,*

$$G_f = \{x \times f(x) \mid x \in X\},$$

is closed in $X \times Y$. [*Hint:* If G_f is closed and V is a neighborhood of $f(x_0)$, then the intersection of G_f and $X \times (Y - V)$ is closed. Apply Exercise 7.]

9. Generalize the tube lemma as follows:

   Theorem. *Let A and B be subspaces of X and Y, respectively; let N be an open set in $X \times Y$ containing $A \times B$. If A and B are compact, then there exist open sets U and V in X and Y, respectively, such that*

$$A \times B \subset U \times V \subset N.$$

10. (a) Prove the following partial converse to the uniform limit theorem:

   Theorem. *Let $f_n : X \to \mathbb{R}$ be a sequence of continuous functions, with $f_n(x) \to f(x)$ for each $x \in X$. If f is continuous, and if the sequence f_n is monotone increasing, and if X is compact, then the convergence is uniform.* [We say that f_n is *monotone increasing* if $f_n(x) \leq f_{n+1}(x)$ for all n and x.]

   (b) Give examples to show that this theorem fails if you delete the requirement that X be compact, or if you delete the requirement that the sequence be monotone. [*Hint:* See the exercises of §21.]

11. *Theorem.* *Let X be a compact Hausdorff space. Let $\mathcal{A}$ be a collection of closed connected subsets of X that is simply ordered by proper inclusion. Then*

$$Y = \bigcap_{A \in \mathcal{A}} A$$

is connected. [*Hint:* If $C \cup D$ is a separation of Y, choose disjoint open sets U and V of X containing C and D, respectively, and show that

$$\bigcap_{A \in \mathcal{A}} (A - (U \cup V))$$

is not empty.]

12. Let $p : X \to Y$ be a closed continuous surjective map such that $p^{-1}(\{y\})$ is compact, for each $y \in Y$. (Such a map is called a **perfect map**.) Show that if Y is compact, then X is compact. [*Hint:* If U is an open set containing $p^{-1}(\{y\})$, there is a neighborhood W of y such that $p^{-1}(W)$ is contained in U.]

13. Let G be a topological group.

   (a) Let A and B be subspaces of G. If A is closed and B is compact, show $A \cdot B$ is closed. [*Hint:* If c is not in $A \cdot B$, find a neighborhood W of c such that $W \cdot B^{-1}$ is disjoint from A.]

   (b) Let H be a subgroup of G; let $p : G \to G/H$ be the quotient map. If H is compact, show that p is a closed map.

   (c) Let H be a compact subgroup of G. Show that if G/H is compact, then G is compact.

§27 Compact Subspaces of the Real Line

The theorems of the preceding section enable us to construct new compact spaces from existing ones, but in order to get very far we have to find some compact spaces to start with. The natural place to begin is the real line; we shall prove that every closed interval in $\mathbb{R}$ is compact. Applications include the extreme value theorem and the uniform continuity theorem of calculus, suitably generalized. We also give a characterization of all compact subspaces of $\mathbb{R}^n$, and a proof of the uncountability of the set of real numbers.

It turns out that in order to prove every closed interval in $\mathbb{R}$ is compact, we need only *one* of the order properties of the real line—the least upper bound property. We shall prove the theorem using only this hypothesis; then it will apply not only to the real line, but to well-ordered sets and other ordered sets as well.

Theorem 27.1. *Let X be a simply ordered set having the least upper bound property. In the order topology, each closed interval in X is compact.*

Proof. *Step 1.* Given $a < b$, let $\mathcal{A}$ be a covering of $[a, b]$ by sets open in $[a, b]$ in the subspace topology (which is the same as the order topology). We wish to prove the existence of a finite subcollection of $\mathcal{A}$ covering $[a, b]$. First we prove the following: If x is a point of $[a, b]$ different from b, then there is a point $y > x$ of $[a, b]$ such that the interval $[x, y]$ can be covered by at most two elements of $\mathcal{A}$.

If x has an immediate successor in X, let y be this immediate successor. Then $[x, y]$ consists of the two points x and y, so that it can be covered by at most two elements of $\mathcal{A}$. If x has no immediate successor in X, choose an element A of $\mathcal{A}$ containing x. Because $x \neq b$ and A is open, A contains an interval of the form $[x, c)$, for some c in $[a, b]$. Choose a point y in (x, c); then the interval $[x, y]$ is covered by the single element A of $\mathcal{A}$.

Step 2. Let C be the set of all points $y > a$ of $[a, b]$ such that the interval $[a, y]$ can be covered by finitely many elements of $\mathcal{A}$. Applying Step 1 to the case $x = a$, we see that there exists at least one such y, so C is not empty. Let c be the least upper bound of the set C; then $a < c \leq b$.

Step 3. We show that c belongs to C; that is, we show that the interval $[a, c]$ can be covered by finitely many elements of $\mathcal{A}$. Choose an element A of $\mathcal{A}$ containing c; since A is open, it contains an interval of the form $(d, c]$ for some d in $[a, b]$. If c is not in C, there must be a point z of C lying in the interval (d, c), because otherwise d would be a smaller upper bound on C than c. See Figure 27.1. Since z is in C, the interval $[a, z]$ can be covered by finitely many, say n, elements of $\mathcal{A}$. Now $[z, c]$ lies in the single element A of $\mathcal{A}$, hence $[a, c] = [a, z] \cup [z, c]$ can be covered by $n + 1$ elements of $\mathcal{A}$. Thus c is in C, contrary to assumption.

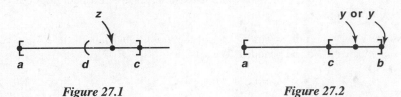

Figure 27.1   *Figure 27.2*

Step 4. Finally, we show that $c = b$, and our theorem is proved. Suppose that $c < b$. Applying Step 1 to the case $x = c$, we conclude that there exists a point $y > c$ of $[a, b]$ such that the interval $[c, y]$ can be covered by finitely many elements of $\mathcal{A}$. See Figure 27.2. We proved in Step 3 that c is in C, so $[a, c]$ can be covered by finitely many elements of $\mathcal{A}$. Therefore, the interval

$$[a, y] = [a, c] \cup [c, y]$$

can also be covered by finitely many elements of $\mathcal{A}$. This means that y is in C, contradicting the fact that c is an upper bound on C. ∎

Corollary 27.2. *Every closed interval in $\mathbb{R}$ is compact.*

Now we characterize the compact subspaces of $\mathbb{R}^n$:

Theorem 27.3. *A subspace A of $\mathbb{R}^n$ is compact if and only if it is closed and is bounded in the euclidean metric d or the square metric ρ.*

Proof. It will suffice to consider only the metric ρ; the inequalities

$$\rho(x, y) \leq d(x, y) \leq \sqrt{n}\rho(x, y)$$

imply that A is bounded under d if and only if it is bounded under ρ.

Suppose that A is compact. Then, by Theorem 26.3, it is closed. Consider the collection of open sets

$$\{B_\rho(\mathbf{0}, m) \mid m \in \mathbb{Z}_+\},$$

whose union is all of $\mathbb{R}^n$. Some finite subcollection covers A. It follows that $A \subset B_\rho(\mathbf{0}, M)$ for some M. Therefore, for any two points x and y of A, we have $\rho(x, y) \leq 2M$. Thus A is bounded under ρ.

Conversely, suppose that A is closed and bounded under ρ; suppose that $\rho(x, y) \leq N$ for every pair x, y of points of A. Choose a point x_0 of A, and let $\rho(x_0, \mathbf{0}) = b$. The triangle inequality implies that $\rho(x, \mathbf{0}) \leq N + b$ for every x in A. If $P = N + b$, then A is a subset of the cube $[-P, P]^n$, which is compact. Being closed, A is also compact. ∎

Students often remember this theorem as stating that the collection of compact sets in a *metric space* equals the collection of closed and bounded sets. This statement is clearly ridiculous as it stands, because the question as to which sets are bounded depends for its answer on the metric, whereas which sets are compact depends only on the topology of the space.

EXAMPLE 1.   The unit sphere S^{n-1} and the closed unit ball B^n in $\mathbb{R}^n$ are compact because they are closed and bounded. The set

$$A = \{x \times (1/x) \mid 0 < x \leq 1\}$$

is closed in $\mathbb{R}^2$, but it is not compact because it is not bounded. The set

$$S = \{x \times (\sin(1/x)) \mid 0 < x \leq 1\}$$

is bounded in $\mathbb{R}^2$, but it is not compact because it is not closed.

Now we prove the extreme value theorem of calculus, in suitably generalized form.

Theorem 27.4 (Extreme value theorem).   *Let $f : X \to Y$ be continuous, where Y is an ordered set in the order topology. If X is compact, then there exist points c and d in X such that $f(c) \leq f(x) \leq f(d)$ for every $x \in X$.*

The extreme value theorem of calculus is the special case of this theorem that occurs when we take X to be a closed interval in $\mathbb{R}$ and Y to be $\mathbb{R}$.

Proof.   Since f is continuous and X is compact, the set $A = f(X)$ is compact. We show that A has a largest element M and a smallest element m. Then since m and M belong to A, we must have $m = f(c)$ and $M = f(d)$ for some points c and d of X.

If A has no largest element, then the collection

$$\{(-\infty, a) \mid a \in A\}$$

forms an open covering of A. Since A is compact, some finite subcollection

$$\{(-\infty, a_1), \ldots, (-\infty, a_n)\}$$

covers A. If a_i is the largest of the elements $a_1, \ldots a_n$, then a_i belongs to none of these sets, contrary to the fact that they cover A.

A similar argument shows that A has a smallest element. ∎

Now we prove the uniform continuity theorem of calculus. In the process, we are led to introduce a new notion that will prove to be surprisingly useful, that of a *Lebesgue number* for an open covering of a metric space. First, a preliminary notion:

Definition.   Let (X, d) be a metric space; let A be a nonempty subset of X. For each $x \in X$, we define the **distance from x to A** by the equation

$$d(x, A) = \inf\{d(x, a) \mid a \in A\}.$$

It is easy to show that for fixed A, the function $d(x, A)$ is a continuous function of x: Given $x, y \in X$, one has the inequalities

$$d(x, A) \leq d(x, a) \leq d(x, y) + d(y, a),$$

for each $a \in A$. It follows that

$$d(x, A) - d(x, y) \leq \inf d(y, a) = d(y, A),$$

so that

$$d(x, A) - d(y, A) \leq d(x, y).$$

The same inequality holds with x and y interchanged; continuity of the function $d(x, A)$ follows.

Now we introduce the notion of Lebesgue number. Recall that the *diameter* of a bounded subset A of a metric space (X, d) is the number

$$\sup\{d(a_1, a_2) \mid a_1, a_2 \in A\}.$$

Lemma 27.5 (The Lebesgue number lemma).   *Let A be an open covering of the metric space (X, d). If X is compact, there is a $\delta > 0$ such that for each subset of X having diameter less than δ, there exists an element of A containing it.*

The number δ is called a **Lebesgue number** for the covering A.

Proof.   Let A be an open covering of X. If X itself is an element of A, then any positive number is a Lebesgue number for A. So assume X is not an element of A.

Choose a finite subcollection $\{A_1, \ldots, A_n\}$ of A that covers X. For each i, set $C_i = X - A_i$, and define $f : X \to \mathbb{R}$ by letting $f(x)$ be the average of the numbers $d(x, C_i)$. That is,

$$f(x) = \frac{1}{n} \sum_{i=1}^{n} d(x, C_i).$$

We show that $f(x) > 0$ for all x. Given $x \in X$, choose i so that $x \in A_i$. Then choose ϵ so the ϵ-neighborhood of x lies in A_i. Then $d(x, C_i) \geq \epsilon$, so that $f(x) \geq \epsilon/n$.

Since f is continuous, it has a minimum value δ; we show that δ is our required Lebesgue number. Let B be a subset of X of diameter less than δ. Choose a point x_0 of B; then B lies in the δ-neighborhood of x_0. Now

$$\delta \le f(x_0) \le d(x_0, C_m),$$

where $d(x_0, C_m)$ is the largest of the numbers $d(x_0, C_i)$. Then the δ-neighborhood of x_0 is contained in the element $A_m = X - C_m$ of the covering $\mathcal{A}$. ∎

Definition. A function f from the metric space (X, d_X) to the metric space (Y, d_Y) is said to be ***uniformly continuous*** if given $\epsilon > 0$, there is a $\delta > 0$ such that for every pair of points x_0, x_1 of X,

$$d_X(x_0, x_1) < \delta \implies d_Y(f(x_0), f(x_1)) < \epsilon.$$

Theorem 27.6 (Uniform continuity theorem). *Let $f : X \to Y$ be a continuous map of the compact metric space (X, d_X) to the metric space (Y, d_Y). Then f is uniformly continuous.*

Proof. Given $\epsilon > 0$, take the open covering of Y by balls $B(y, \epsilon/2)$ of radius $\epsilon/2$. Let $\mathcal{A}$ be the open covering of X by the inverse images of these balls under f. Choose δ to be a Lebesgue number for the covering $\mathcal{A}$. Then if x_1 and x_2 are two points of X such that $d_X(x_1, x_2) < \delta$, the two-point set $\{x_1, x_2\}$ has diameter less than δ, so that its image $\{f(x_1), f(x_2)\}$ lies in some ball $B(y, \epsilon/2)$. Then $d_Y(f(x_1), f(x_2)) < \epsilon$, as desired. ∎

Finally, we prove that the real numbers are uncountable. The interesting thing about this proof is that it involves no algebra at all—no decimal or binary expansions of real numbers or the like—just the order properties of $\mathbb{R}$.

Definition. If X is a space, a point x of X is said to be an ***isolated point*** of X if the one-point set $\{x\}$ is open in X.

Theorem 27.7. *Let X be a nonempty compact Hausdorff space. If X has no isolated points, then X is uncountable.*

Proof. Step 1. We show first that given any nonempty open set U of X and any point x of X, there exists a nonempty open set V contained in U such that $x \notin \bar{V}$.

Choose a point y of U different from x; this is possible if x is in U because x is not an isolated point of X and it is possible if x is not in U simply because U is nonempty. Now choose disjoint open sets W_1 and W_2 about x and y, respectively. Then the set $V = W_2 \cap U$ is the desired open set; it is contained in U, it is nonempty because it contains y, and its closure does not contain x. See Figure 27.3.

Step 2. We show that given $f : \mathbb{Z}_+ \to X$, the function f is not surjective. It follows that X is uncountable.

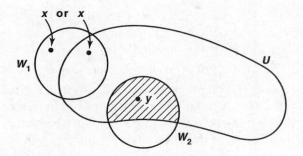

Figure 27.3

Let $x_n = f(n)$. Apply Step 1 to the nonempty open set $U = X$ to choose a nonempty open set $V_1 \subset X$ such that $\bar{V}_1$ does not contain x_1. In general, given V_{n-1} open and nonempty, choose V_n to be a nonempty open set such that $V_n \subset V_{n-1}$ and $\bar{V}_n$ does not contain x_n. Consider the nested sequence

$$\bar{V}_1 \supset \bar{V}_2 \supset \cdots$$

of nonempty closed sets of X. Because X is compact, there is a point $x \in \bigcap \bar{V}_n$, by Theorem 26.9. Now x cannot equal x_n for any n, since x belongs to $\bar{V}_n$ and x_n does not. ■

Corollary 27.8. *Every closed interval in $\mathbb{R}$ is uncountable.*

Exercises

1. Prove that if X is an ordered set in which every closed interval is compact, then X has the least upper bound property.

2. Let X be a metric space with metric d; let $A \subset X$ be nonempty.
   (a) Show that $d(x, A) = 0$ if and only if $x \in \bar{A}$.
   (b) Show that if A is compact, $d(x, A) = d(x, a)$ for some $a \in A$.
   (c) Define the ϵ-*neighborhood* of A in X to be the set

   $$U(A, \epsilon) = \{x \mid d(x, A) < \epsilon\}.$$

   Show that $U(A, \epsilon)$ equals the union of the open balls $B_d(a, \epsilon)$ for $a \in A$.
   (d) Assume that A is compact; let U be an open set containing A. Show that some ϵ-neighborhood of A is contained in U.
   (e) Show the result in (d) need not hold if A is closed but not compact.

3. Recall that $\mathbb{R}_K$ denotes $\mathbb{R}$ in the K-topology.
   (a) Show that $[0, 1]$ is not compact as a subspace of $\mathbb{R}_K$.

(b) Show that $\mathbb{R}_K$ is connected. [*Hint:* $(-\infty, 0)$ and $(0, \infty)$ inherit their usual topologies as subspaces of $\mathbb{R}_K$.]

(c) Show that $\mathbb{R}_K$ is not path connected.

4. Show that a connected metric space having more than one point is uncountable.

5. Let X be a compact Hausdorff space; let $\{A_n\}$ be a countable collection of closed sets of X. Show that if each set A_n has empty interior in X, then the union $\bigcup A_n$ has empty interior in X. [*Hint:* Imitate the proof of Theorem 27.7.]

   This is a special case of the *Baire category theorem*, which we shall study in Chapter 8.

6. Let A_0 be the closed interval $[0, 1]$ in $\mathbb{R}$. Let A_1 be the set obtained from A_0 by deleting its "middle third" $(\frac{1}{3}, \frac{2}{3})$. Let A_2 be the set obtained from A_1 by deleting its "middle thirds" $(\frac{1}{9}, \frac{2}{9})$ and $(\frac{7}{9}, \frac{8}{9})$. In general, define A_n by the equation

$$A_n = A_{n-1} - \bigcup_{k=0}^{\infty} \left(\frac{1 + 3k}{3^n}, \frac{2 + 3k}{3^n} \right).$$

The intersection

$$C = \bigcap_{n \in \mathbb{Z}_+} A_n$$

is called the ***Cantor set***; it is a subspace of $[0, 1]$.

(a) Show that C is totally disconnected.

(b) Show that C is compact.

(c) Show that each set A_n is a union of finitely many disjoint closed intervals of length $1/3^n$; and show that the end points of these intervals lie in C.

(d) Show that C has no isolated points.

(e) Conclude that C is uncountable.

§28 Limit Point Compactness

As indicated when we first mentioned compact sets, there are other formulations of the notion of compactness that are frequently useful. In this section we introduce one of them. Weaker in general than compactness, it coincides with compactness for metrizable spaces.

Definition. A space X is said to be ***limit point compact*** if every infinite subset of X has a limit point.

In some ways this property is more natural and intuitive than that of compactness. In the early days of topology, it was given the name "compactness," while the open covering formulation was called "bicompactness." Later, the word "compact" was shifted to apply to the open covering definition, leaving this one to search for a new name. It still has not found a name on which everyone agrees. On historical grounds, some call it "Fréchet compactness"; others call it the "Bolzano-Weierstrass property." We have invented the term "limit point compactness." It seems as good a term as any; at least it describes what the property is about.

Theorem 28.1. *Compactness implies limit point compactness, but not conversely.*

Proof. Let X be a compact space. Given a subset A of X, we wish to prove that if A is infinite, then A has a limit point. We prove the contrapositive—if A has no limit point, then A must be finite.

So suppose A has no limit point. Then A contains all its limit points, so that A is closed. Furthermore, for each $a \in A$ we can choose a neighborhood U_a of a such that U_a intersects A in the point a alone. The space X is covered by the open set $X - A$ and the open sets U_a; being compact, it can be covered by finitely many of these sets. Since $X - A$ does not intersect A, and each set U_a contains only one point of A, the set A must be finite. ∎

EXAMPLE 1.   Let Y consist of two points; give Y the topology consisting of Y and the empty set. Then the space $X = \mathbb{Z}_+ \times Y$ is limit point compact, for *every* nonempty subset of X has a limit point. It is not compact, for the covering of X by the open sets $U_n = \{n\} \times Y$ has no finite subcollection covering X.

EXAMPLE 2.   Here is a less trivial example. Consider the minimal uncountable well-ordered set S_Ω, in the order topology. The space S_Ω is not compact, since it has no largest element. However, it is limit point compact: Let A be an infinite subset of S_Ω. Choose a subset B of A that is countably infinite. Being countable, the set B has an upper bound b in S_Ω; then B is a subset of the interval $[a_0, b]$ of S_Ω, where a_0 is the smallest element of S_Ω. Since S_Ω has the least upper bound property, the interval $[a_0, b]$ is compact. By the preceding theorem, B has a limit point x in $[a_0, b]$. The point x is also a limit point of A. Thus S_Ω is limit point compact.

We now show these two versions of compactness coincide for metrizable spaces; for this purpose, we introduce yet another version of compactness called *sequential compactness*. This result will be used in Chapter 7.

Definition.   Let X be a topological space. If (x_n) is a sequence of points of X, and if

$$n_1 < n_2 < \cdots < n_i < \cdots$$

is an increasing sequence of positive integers, then the sequence (y_i) defined by setting $y_i = x_{n_i}$ is called a **subsequence** of the sequence (x_n). The space X is said to be **sequentially compact** if every sequence of points of X has a convergent subsequence.

*Theorem 28.2.   *Let X be a metrizable space. Then the following are equivalent:*
  (1) X *is compact.*
  (2) X *is limit point compact.*
  (3) X *is sequentially compact.*

Proof. We have already proved that (1) $\Rightarrow$ (2). To show that (2) $\Rightarrow$ (3), assume that X is limit point compact. Given a sequence (x_n) of points of X, consider the set $A = \{x_n \mid n \in \mathbb{Z}_+\}$. If the set A is finite, then there is a point x such that $x = x_n$ for infinitely many values of n. In this case, the sequence (x_n) has a subsequence that is constant, and therefore converges trivially. On the other hand, if A is infinite, then A has a limit point x. We define a subsequence of (x_n) converging to x as follows: First choose n_1 so that

$$x_{n_1} \in B(x, 1).$$

Then suppose that the positive integer n_{i-1} is given. Because the ball $B(x, 1/i)$ intersects A in infinitely many points, we can choose an index $n_i > n_{i-1}$ such that

$$x_{n_i} \in B(x, 1/i).$$

Then the subsequence $x_{n_1}, x_{n_2}, \ldots$ converges to x.

Finally, we show that (3) $\Rightarrow$ (1). This is the hardest part of the proof.

First, we show that if X is sequentially compact, then the Lebesgue number lemma holds for X. (This would follow from compactness, but compactness is what we are trying to prove!) Let $\mathcal{A}$ be an open covering of X. We assume that there is no $\delta > 0$ such that each set of diameter less than δ has an element of $\mathcal{A}$ containing it, and derive a contradiction.

Our assumption implies in particular that for each positive integer n, there exists a set of diameter less than $1/n$ that is not contained in any element of $\mathcal{A}$; let C_n be such a set. Choose a point $x_n \in C_n$, for each n. By hypothesis, some subsequence (x_{n_i}) of the sequence (x_n) converges, say to the point a. Now a belongs to some element A of the collection $\mathcal{A}$; because A is open, we may choose an $\epsilon > 0$ such that $B(a, \epsilon) \subset A$. If i is large enough that $1/n_i < \epsilon/2$, then the set C_{n_i} lies in the $\epsilon/2$-neighborhood of x_{n_i}; if i is also chosen large enough that $d(x_{n_i}, a) < \epsilon/2$, then C_{n_i} lies in the ϵ-neighborhood of a. But this means that $C_{n_i} \subset A$, contrary to hypothesis.

Second, we show that if X is sequentially compact, then given $\epsilon > 0$, there exists a finite covering of X by open ϵ-balls. Once again, we proceed by contradiction. Assume that there exists an $\epsilon > 0$ such that X cannot be covered by finitely many ϵ-balls. Construct a sequence of points x_n of X as follows: First, choose x_1 to be any point of X. Noting that the ball $B(x_1, \epsilon)$ is not all of X (otherwise X could be covered by a single ϵ-ball), choose x_2 to be a point of X not in $B(x_1, \epsilon)$. In general, given $x_1, \ldots, x_n$, choose x_{n+1} to be a point not in the union

$$B(x_1, \epsilon) \cup \cdots \cup B(x_n, \epsilon),$$

using the fact that these balls do not cover X. Note that by construction $d(x_{n+1}, x_i) \geq \epsilon$ for $i = 1, \ldots, n$. Therefore, the sequence (x_n) can have no convergent subsequence; in fact, any ball of radius $\epsilon/2$ can contain x_n for at most *one* value of n.

Finally, we show that if X is sequentially compact, then X is compact. Let $\mathcal{A}$ be an open covering of X. Because X is sequentially compact, the open covering $\mathcal{A}$ has a Lebesgue number δ. Let $\epsilon = \delta/3$; use sequential compactness of X to find a finite covering of X by open ϵ-balls. Each of these balls has diameter at most $2\delta/3$, so it lies in an element of $\mathcal{A}$. Choosing one such element of $\mathcal{A}$ for each of these ϵ-balls, we obtain a finite subcollection of $\mathcal{A}$ that covers X.   ∎

EXAMPLE 3.   Recall that $\bar{S}_\Omega$ denotes the minimal uncountable well-ordered set S_Ω with the point Ω adjoined. (In the order topology, Ω is a limit point of S_Ω, which is why we introduced the notation $\bar{S}_\Omega$ for $S_\Omega \cup \{\Omega\}$, back in §10.) It is easy to see that the space $\bar{S}_\Omega$ is not metrizable, for it does not satisfy the sequence lemma: The point Ω is a limit point of S_Ω; but it is not the limit of a sequence of points of S_Ω, for any sequence of points of S_Ω has an upper bound in S_Ω. The space S_Ω, on the other hand, does satisfy the sequence lemma, as you can readily check. Nevertheless, S_Ω is not metrizable, for it is limit point compact but not compact.

Exercises

1. Give $[0, 1]^\omega$ the uniform topology. Find an infinite subset of this space that has no limit point.

2. Show that $[0, 1]$ is not limit point compact as a subspace of $\mathbb{R}_\ell$.

3. Let X be limit point compact.
   (a) If $f : X \to Y$ is continuous, does it follow that $f(X)$ is limit point compact?
   (b) If A is a closed subset of X, does it follow that A is limit point compact?
   (c) If X is a subspace of the Hausdorff space Z, does it follow that X is closed in Z?

   We comment that it is not in general true that the product of two limit point compact spaces is limit point compact, even if the Hausdorff condition is assumed. But the examples are fairly sophisticated. See [S-S], Example 112.

4. A space X is said to be **countably compact** if every countable open covering of X contains a finite subcollection that covers X. Show that for a T_1 space X, countable compactness is equivalent to limit point compactness. [*Hint:* If no finite subcollection of U_n covers X, choose $x_n \notin U_1 \cup \cdots \cup U_n$, for each n.]

5. Show that X is countably compact if and only if every nested sequence $C_1 \supset C_2 \supset \cdots$ of closed nonempty sets of X has a nonempty intersection.

6. Let (X, d) be a metric space. If $f : X \to X$ satisfies the condition

$$d(f(x), f(y)) = d(x, y)$$

for all $x, y \in X$, then f is called an **isometry** of X. Show that if f is an isometry and X is compact, then f is bijective and hence a homeomorphism. [*Hint:* If $a \notin f(X)$, choose ϵ so that the ϵ-neighborhood of a is disjoint from $f(X)$. Set $x_1 = a$, and $x_{n+1} = f(x_n)$ in general. Show that $d(x_n, x_m) \geq \epsilon$ for $n \neq m$.]

7. Let (X, d) be a metric space. If f satisfies the condition

$$d(f(x), f(y)) < d(x, y)$$

for all $x, y \in X$ with $x \neq y$, then f is called a **shrinking map**. If there is a number $\alpha < 1$ such that

$$d(f(x), f(y)) \leq \alpha d(x, y)$$

for all $x, y \in X$, then f is called a **contraction**. A *fixed point* of f is a point x such that $f(x) = x$.

(a) If f is a contraction and X is compact, show f has a unique fixed point. [*Hint:* Define $f^1 = f$ and $f^{n+1} = f \circ f^n$. Consider the intersection A of the sets $A_n = f^n(X)$.]

(b) Show more generally that if f is a shrinking map and X is compact, then f has a unique fixed point. [*Hint:* Let A be as before. Given $x \in A$, choose x_n so that $x = f^{n+1}(x_n)$. If a is the limit of some subsequence of the sequence $y_n = f^n(x_n)$, show that $a \in A$ and $f(a) = x$. Conclude that $A = f(A)$, so that diam $A = 0$.]

(c) Let $X = [0, 1]$. Show that $f(x) = x - x^2/2$ maps X into X and is a shrinking map that is not a contraction. [*Hint:* Use the mean-value theorem of calculus.]

(d) The result in (a) holds if X is a complete metric space, such as $\mathbb{R}$; see the exercises of §43. The result in (b) does not: Show that the map $f : \mathbb{R} \to \mathbb{R}$ given by $f(x) = [x + (x^2 + 1)^{1/2}]/2$ is a shrinking map that is not a contraction and has no fixed point.

§29 Local Compactness

In this section we study the notion of local compactness, and we prove the basic theorem that any locally compact Hausdorff space can be imbedded in a certain compact Hausdorff space that is called its *one-point compactification*.

Definition. A space X is said to be *locally compact at x* if there is some compact subspace C of X that contains a neighborhood of x. If X is locally compact at each of its points, X is said simply to be *locally compact*.

Note that a compact space is automatically locally compact.

EXAMPLE 1. The real line $\mathbb{R}$ is locally compact. The point x lies in some interval (a, b), which in turn is contained in the compact subspace $[a, b]$. The subspace $\mathbb{Q}$ of rational numbers is not locally compact, as you can check.

EXAMPLE 2. The space $\mathbb{R}^n$ is locally compact; the point x lies in some basis element $(a_1, b_1) \times \cdots \times (a_n, b_n)$, which in turn lies in the compact subspace $[a_1, b_1] \times \cdots \times [a_n, b_n]$. The space $\mathbb{R}^\omega$ is not locally compact; *none* of its basis elements are contained in compact subspaces. For if

$$B = (a_1, b_1) \times \cdots \times (a_n, b_n) \times \mathbb{R} \times \cdots \times \mathbb{R} \times \cdots$$

were contained in a compact subspace, then its closure

$$\bar{B} = [a_1, b_1] \times \cdots \times [a_n, b_n] \times \mathbb{R} \times \cdots$$

would be compact, which it is not.

EXAMPLE 3.   Every simply ordered set X having the least upper bound property is locally compact: Given a basis element for X, it is contained in a closed interval in X, which is compact.

Two of the most well-behaved classes of spaces to deal with in mathematics are the metrizable spaces and the compact Hausdorff spaces. Such spaces have many useful properties, which one can use in proving theorems and making constructions and the like. If a given space is not of one of these types, the next best thing one can hope for is that it is a subspace of one of these spaces. Of course, a subspace of a metrizable space is itself metrizable, so one does not get any new spaces in this way. But a subspace of a compact Hausdorff space need not be compact. Thus arises the question: Under what conditions is a space homeomorphic with a subspace of a compact Hausdorff space? We give one answer here. We shall return to this question in Chapter 5 when we study compactifications in general.

Theorem 29.1.   *Let X be a space. Then X is locally compact Hausdorff if and only if there exists a space Y satisfying the following conditions:*

(1) X is a subspace of Y.

(2) The set $Y - X$ consists of a single point.

(3) Y is a compact Hausdorff space.

If Y and Y' are two spaces satisfying these conditions, then there is a homeomorphism of Y with Y' that equals the identity map on X.

Proof.   Step 1. We first verify uniqueness. Let Y and Y' be two spaces satisfying these conditions. Define $h : Y \to Y'$ by letting h map the single point p of $Y - X$ to the point q of $Y' - X$, and letting h equal the identity on X. We show that if U is open in Y, then $h(U)$ is open in Y'. Symmetry then implies that h is a homeomorphism.

First, consider the case where U does not contain p. Then $h(U) = U$. Since U is open in Y and is contained in X, it is open in X. Because X is open in Y', the set U is also open in Y', as desired.

Second, suppose that U contains p. Since $C = Y - U$ is closed in Y, it is compact as a subspace of Y. Because C is contained in X, it is a compact subspace of X. Then because X is a subspace of Y', the space C is also a compact subspace of Y'. Because Y' is Hausdorff, C is closed in Y', so that $h(U) = Y' - C$ is open in Y', as desired.

Step 2. Now we suppose X is locally compact Hausdorff and construct the space Y. Step 1 gives us an idea how to proceed. Let us take some object that is not a point of X, denote it by the symbol ∞ for convenience, and adjoin it to X, forming the set $Y = X \cup \{\infty\}$. Topologize Y by defining the collection of open sets of Y to consist of (1) all sets U that are open in X, and (2) all sets of the form $Y - C$, where C is a compact subspace of X.

We need to check that this collection is, in fact, a topology on Y. The empty set is a set of type (1), and the space Y is a set of type (2). Checking that the intersection of two open sets is open involves three cases:

$$U_1 \cap U_2 \qquad \text{is of type (1).}$$
$$(Y - C_1) \cap (Y - C_2) = Y - (C_1 \cup C_2) \qquad \text{is of type (2).}$$
$$U_1 \cap (Y - C_1) = U_1 \cap (X - C_1) \qquad \text{is of type (1),}$$

because C_1 is closed in X. Similarly, one checks that the union of any collection of open sets is open:

$$\bigcup U_\alpha = U \qquad \text{is of type (1).}$$
$$\bigcup (Y - C_\beta) = Y - (\bigcap C_\beta) = Y - C \qquad \text{is of type (2).}$$
$$(\bigcup U_\alpha) \cup (\bigcup (Y - C_\beta)) = U \cup (Y - C) = Y - (C - U),$$

which is of type (2) because $C - U$ is a closed subspace of C and therefore compact.

Now we show that X is a subspace of Y. Given any open set of Y, we show its intersection with X is open in X. If U is of type (1), then $U \cap X = U$; if $Y - C$ is of type (2), then $(Y - C) \cap X = X - C$; both of these sets are open in X. Conversely, any set open in X is a set of type (1) and therefore open in Y by definition.

To show that Y is compact, let $\mathcal{A}$ be an open covering of Y. The collection $\mathcal{A}$ must contain an open set of type (2), say $Y - C$, since none of the open sets of type (1) contain the point ∞. Take all the members of $\mathcal{A}$ different from $Y - C$ and intersect them with X; they form a collection of open sets of X covering C. Because C is compact, finitely many of them cover C; the corresponding finite collection of elements of $\mathcal{A}$ will, along with the element $Y - C$, cover all of Y.

To show that Y is Hausdorff, let x and y be two points of Y. If both of them lie in X, there are disjoint sets U and V open in X containing them, respectively. On the other hand, if $x \in X$ and $y = \infty$, we can choose a compact set C in X containing a neighborhood U of x. Then U and $Y - C$ are disjoint neighborhoods of x and ∞, respectively, in Y.

Step 3. Finally, we prove the converse. Suppose a space Y satisfying conditions (1)–(3) exists. Then X is Hausdorff because it is a subspace of the Hausdorff space Y. Given $x \in X$, we show X is locally compact at x. Choose disjoint open sets U and V of Y containing x and the single point of $Y - X$, respectively. Then the set $C = Y - V$ is closed in Y, so it is a compact subspace of Y. Since C lies in X, it is also compact as a subspace of X; it contains the neighborhood U of x. ∎

If X itself should happen to be compact, then the space Y of the preceding theorem is not very interesting, for it is obtained from X by adjoining a single isolated point. However, if X is not compact, then the point of $Y - X$ is a limit point of X, so that $\bar{X} = Y$.

Definition. If Y is a compact Hausdorff space and X is a proper subspace of Y whose closure equals Y, then Y is said to be a ***compactification*** of X. If $Y - X$ equals a single point, then Y is called the ***one-point compactification*** of X.

We have shown that X has a one-point compactification Y if and only if X is a locally compact Hausdorff space that is not itself compact. We speak of Y as "the" one-point compactification because Y is uniquely determined up to a homeomorphism.

> EXAMPLE 4.   The one-point compactification of the real line $\mathbb{R}$ is homeomorphic with the circle, as you may readily check. Similarly, the one-point compactification of $\mathbb{R}^2$ is homeomorphic to the sphere S^2. If $\mathbb{R}^2$ is looked at as the space $\mathbb{C}$ of complex numbers, then $\mathbb{C} \cup \{\infty\}$ is called the *Riemann sphere*, or the *extended complex plane*.

In some ways our definition of local compactness is not very satisfying. Usually one says that a space X satisfies a given property "locally" if every $x \in X$ has "arbitrarily small" neighborhoods having the given property. Our definition of local compactness has nothing to do with "arbitrarily small" neighborhoods, so there is some question whether we should call it local compactness at all.

Here is another formulation of local compactness, one more truly "local" in nature; it is equivalent to our definition when X is Hausdorff.

Theorem 29.2. *Let X be a Hausdorff space. Then X is locally compact if and only if given x in X, and given a neighborhood U of x, there is a neighborhood V of x such that $\bar{V}$ is compact and $\bar{V} \subset U$.*

Proof. Clearly this new formulation implies local compactness; the set $C = \bar{V}$ is the desired compact set containing a neighborhood of x. To prove the converse, suppose X is locally compact; let x be a point of X and let U be a neighborhood of x. Take the one-point compactification Y of X, and let C be the set $Y - U$. Then C is closed in Y, so that C is a compact subspace of Y. Apply Lemma 26.4 to choose disjoint open sets V and W containing x and C, respectively. Then the closure $\bar{V}$ of V in Y is compact; furthermore, $\bar{V}$ is disjoint from C, so that $\bar{V} \subset U$, as desired.   ∎

Corollary 29.3. *Let X be locally compact Hausdorff; let A be a subspace of X. If A is closed in X or open in X, then A is locally compact.*

Proof. Suppose that A is closed in X. Given $x \in A$, let C be a compact subspace of X containing the neighborhood U of x in X. Then $C \cap A$ is closed in C and thus compact, and it contains the neighborhood $U \cap A$ of x in A. (We have not used the Hausdorff condition here.)

Suppose now that A is open in X. Given $x \in A$, we apply the preceding theorem to choose a neighborhood V of x in X such that $\bar{V}$ is compact and $\bar{V} \subset A$. Then $C = \bar{V}$ is a compact subspace of A containing the neighborhood V of x in A.   ∎

Corollary 29.4. *A space X is homeomorphic to an open subspace of a compact Hausdorff space if and only if X is locally compact Hausdorff.*

Proof. This follows from Theorem 29.1 and Corollary 29.3.   ∎

Exercises

1. Show that the rationals $\mathbb{Q}$ are not locally compact.

2. Let $\{X_\alpha\}$ be an indexed family of nonempty spaces.
    (a) Show that if $\prod X_\alpha$ is locally compact, then each X_α is locally compact and X_α is compact for all but finitely many values of α.
    (b) Prove the converse, assuming the Tychonoff theorem.

3. Let X be a locally compact space. If $f : X \to Y$ is continuous, does it follow that $f(X)$ is locally compact? What if f is both continuous and open? Justify your answer.

4. Show that $[0, 1]^\omega$ is not locally compact in the uniform topology.

5. If $f : X_1 \to X_2$ is a homeomorphism of locally compact Hausdorff spaces, show f extends to a homeomorphism of their one-point compactifications.

6. Show that the one-point compactification of $\mathbb{R}$ is homeomorphic with the circle S^1.

7. Show that the one-point compactification of S_Ω is homeomorphic with $\bar{S}_\Omega$.

8. Show that the one-point compactification of $\mathbb{Z}_+$ is homeomorphic with the subspace $\{0\} \cup \{1/n \mid n \in \mathbb{Z}_+\}$ of $\mathbb{R}$.

9. Show that if G is a locally compact topological group and H is a subgroup, then G/H is locally compact.

10. Show that if X is a Hausdorff space that is locally compact at the point x, then for each neighborhood U of x, there is a neighborhood V of x such that $\bar{V}$ is compact and $\bar{V} \subset U$.

*11. Prove the following:
    (a) *Lemma.   If $p : X \to Y$ is a quotient map and if Z is a locally compact Hausdorff space, then the map*

    $$\pi = p \times i_Z : X \times Z \longrightarrow Y \times Z$$

    is a quotient map.

    [*Hint:* If $\pi^{-1}(A)$ is open and contains $x \times y$, choose open sets U_1 and V with $\bar{V}$ compact, such that $x \times y \in U_1 \times V$ and $U_1 \times \bar{V} \subset \pi^{-1}(A)$. Given $U_i \times \bar{V} \subset \pi^{-1}(A)$, use the tube lemma to choose an open set U_{i+1} containing $p^{-1}(p(U_i))$ such that $U_{i+1} \times \bar{V} \subset \pi^{-1}(A)$. Let $U = \bigcup U_i$; show that $U \times V$ is a saturated neighborhood of $x \times y$ that is contained in $\pi^{-1}(A)$.]

    An entirely different proof of this result will be outlined in the exercises of §46.

    (b) *Theorem.   Let $p : A \to B$ and $q : C \to D$ be quotient maps. If B and C are locally compact Hausdorff spaces, then $p \times q : A \times C \to B \times D$ is a quotient map.*

*Supplementary Exercises: Nets

We have already seen that sequences are "adequate" to detect limit points, continuous functions, and compact sets in metrizable spaces. There is a generalization of the notion of sequence, called a *net*, that will do the same thing for an arbitrary topological space. We give the relevant definitions here, and leave the proofs as exercises. Recall that a relation $\preceq$ on a set A is called a *partial order* relation if the following conditions hold:

(1) $\alpha \preceq \alpha$ for all α.

(2) If $\alpha \preceq \beta$ and $\beta \preceq \alpha$, then $\alpha = \beta$.

(3) If $\alpha \preceq \beta$ and $\beta \preceq \gamma$, then $\alpha \preceq \gamma$.

Now we make the following definition:

A **directed set** J is a set with a partial order $\preceq$ such that for each pair α, β of elements of J, there exists an element γ of J having the property that $\alpha \preceq \gamma$ and $\beta \preceq \gamma$.

1. Show that the following are directed sets:
   (a) Any simply ordered set, under the relation $\leq$.
   (b) The collection of all subsets of a set S, partially ordered by inclusion (that is, $A \preceq B$ if $A \subset B$).
   (c) A collection $\mathcal{A}$ of subsets of S that is closed under finite intersections, partially ordered by reverse inclusion (that is $A \preceq B$ if $A \supset B$).
   (d) The collection of all closed subsets of a space X, partially ordered by inclusion.

2. A subset K of J is said to be **cofinal** in J if for each $\alpha \in J$, there exists $\beta \in K$ such that $\alpha \preceq \beta$. Show that if J is a directed set and K is cofinal in J, then K is a directed set.

3. Let X be a topological space. A **net** in X is a function f from a directed set J into X. If $\alpha \in J$, we usually denote $f(\alpha)$ by x_α. We denote the net f itself by the symbol $(x_\alpha)_{\alpha \in J}$, or merely by (x_α) if the index set is understood.

   The net (x_α) is said to **converge** to the point x of X (written $x_\alpha \to x$) if for each neighborhood U of x, there exists $\alpha \in J$ such that

   $$\alpha \preceq \beta \Longrightarrow x_\beta \in U.$$

   Show that these definitions reduce to familiar ones when $J = \mathbb{Z}_+$.

4. Suppose that

   $$(x_\alpha)_{\alpha \in J} \longrightarrow x \text{ in } X \quad \text{and} \quad (y_\alpha)_{\alpha \in J} \longrightarrow y \text{ in } Y.$$

   Show that $(x_\alpha \times y_\alpha) \longrightarrow x \times y$ in $X \times Y$.

5. Show that if X is Hausdorff, a net in X converges to at most one point.

6. **Theorem.** Let $A \in X$. Then $x \in \bar{A}$ if and only if there is a net of points of A converging to x.

   [*Hint:* To prove the implication $\Rightarrow$, take as index set the collection of all neighborhoods of x, partially ordered by reverse inclusion.]

7. Theorem.   Let $f : X \to Y$. Then f is continuous if and only if for every convergent net (x_α) in X, converging to x, say, the net $(f(x_\alpha))$ converges to $f(x)$.

8. Let $f : J \to X$ be a net in X; let $f(\alpha) = x_\alpha$. If K is a directed set and $g : K \to J$ is a function such that
   (i) $i \preceq j \Rightarrow g(i) \preceq g(j)$,
   (ii) $g(K)$ is cofinal in J,
   then the composite function $f \circ g : K \to X$ is called a *subnet* of (x_α). Show that if the net (x_α) converges to x, so does any subnet.

9. Let $(x_\alpha)_{\alpha \in J}$ be a net in X. We say that x is an *accumulation point* of the net (x_α) if for each neighborhood U of x, the set of those α for which $x_\alpha \in U$ is cofinal in J.
   Lemma.   The net (x_α) has the point x as an accumulation point if and only if some subnet of (x_α) converges to x.
   [*Hint:* To prove the implication $\Rightarrow$, let K be the set of all pairs (α, U) where $\alpha \in J$ and U is a neighborhood of x containing x_α. Define $(\alpha, U) \preceq (\beta, V)$ if $\alpha \preceq \beta$ and $V \subset U$. Show that K is a directed set and use it to define the subnet.]

10. Theorem. X is compact if and only if every net in X has a convergent subnet.
    [*Hint:* To prove the implication $\Rightarrow$, let $B_\alpha = \{x_\beta \mid \alpha \preceq \beta\}$ and show that $\{B_\alpha\}$ has the finite intersection property. To prove $\Leftarrow$, let $\mathcal{A}$ be a collection of closed sets having the finite intersection property, and let $\mathcal{B}$ be the collection of all finite intersections of elements of $\mathcal{A}$, partially ordered by reverse inclusion.]

11. Corollary.   Let G be a topological group; let A and B be subsets of G. If A is closed in G and B is compact, then $A \cdot B$ is closed in G.
    [*Hint:* First give a proof using sequences, assuming that G is metrizable.]

12. Check that the preceding exercises remain correct if condition (2) is omitted from the definition of *directed set*. Many mathematicians use the term "directed set" in this more general sense.

Chapter 4

Countability and Separation Axioms

The concepts we are going to introduce now, unlike compactness and connectedness, do not arise naturally from the study of calculus and analysis. They arise instead from a deeper study of topology itself. Such problems as imbedding a given space in a metric space or in a compact Hausdorff space are basically problems of topology rather than analysis. These particular problems have solutions that involve the countability and separation axioms.

We have already introduced the first countability axiom; it arose in connection with our study of convergent sequences in §21. We have also studied one of the separation axioms—the Hausdorff axiom, and mentioned another—the T_1 axiom. In this chapter we shall introduce other, and stronger, axioms like these and explore some of their consequences. Our basic goal is to prove the *Urysohn metrization theorem*. It says that if a topological space X satisfies a certain countability axiom (the second) and a certain separation axiom (the regularity axiom), then X can be imbedded in a metric space and is thus metrizable.

Another imbedding theorem, important to geometers, appears in the last section of the chapter. Given a space that is a compact manifold (the higher-dimensional analogue of a surface), we show that it can be imbedded in some finite-dimensional euclidean space.

§30   The Countability Axioms

Recall the definition we gave in §21.

Definition.   A space X is said to have a *countable basis at x* if there is a countable collection $\mathcal{B}$ of neighborhoods of x such that each neighborhood of x contains at least one of the elements of $\mathcal{B}$. A space that has a countable basis at each of its points is said to satisfy the *first countability axiom*, or to be *first-countable*.

We have already noted that every metrizable space satisfies this axiom; see §21.

The most useful fact concerning spaces that satisfy this axiom is the fact that in such a space, convergent sequences are adequate to detect limit points of sets and to check continuity of functions. We have noted this before; now we state it formally as a theorem:

Theorem 30.1.   *Let X be a topological space.*

(a) *Let A be a subset of X. If there is a sequence of points of A converging to x, then $x \in \bar{A}$; the converse holds if X is first-countable.*

(b) *Let $f : X \to Y$. If f is continuous, then for every convergent sequence $x_n \to x$ in X, the sequence $f(x_n)$ converges to $f(x)$. The converse holds if X is first-countable.*

The proof is a direct generalization of the proof given in §21 under the hypothesis of metrizability, so it will not be repeated here.

Of much greater importance than the first countability axiom is the following:

Definition.   If a space X has a countable basis for its topology, then X is said to satisfy the *second countability axiom*, or to be *second-countable*.

Obviously, the second axiom implies the first: if $\mathcal{B}$ is a countable basis for the topology of X, then the subset of $\mathcal{B}$ consisting of those basis elements containing the point x is a countable basis at x. The second axiom is, in fact, much stronger than the first; it is so strong that not even every metric space satisfies it.

Why then is this second axiom interesting? Well, for one thing, many familiar spaces do satisfy it. For another, it is a crucial hypothesis used in proving such theorems as the Urysohn metrization theorem, as we shall see.

EXAMPLE 1.   The real line $\mathbb{R}$ has a countable basis—the collection of all open intervals (a, b) with rational end points. Likewise, $\mathbb{R}^n$ has a countable basis—the collection of all products of intervals having rational end points. Even $\mathbb{R}^\omega$ has a countable basis—the collection of all products $\prod_{n \in \mathbb{Z}_+} U_n$, where U_n is an open interval with rational end points for finitely many values of n, and $U_n = \mathbb{R}$ for all other values of n.

EXAMPLE 2.   In the uniform topology, $\mathbb{R}^\omega$ satisfies the first countability axiom (being metrizable). However, it does not satisfy the second. To verify this fact, we first show that if X is a space having a countable basis $\mathcal{B}$, then any discrete subspace A of X must be countable. Choose, for each $a \in A$, a basis element B_a that intersects A in the point a

alone. If a and b are distinct points of A, the sets B_a and B_b are different, since the first contains a and the second does not. It follows that the map $a \to B_a$ is an injection of A into $\mathscr{B}$, so A must be countable.

Now we note that the subspace A of $\mathbb{R}^\omega$ consisting of all sequences of 0's and 1's is uncountable; and it has the discrete topology because $\bar{\rho}(a, b) = 1$ for any two distinct points a and b of A. Therefore, in the uniform topology $\mathbb{R}^\omega$ does not have a countable basis.

Both countability axioms are well behaved with respect to the operations of taking subspaces or countable products:

Theorem 30.2. *A subspace of a first-countable space is first-countable, and a countable product of first-countable spaces is first-countable. A subspace of a second-countable space is second-countable, and a countable product of second-countable spaces is second-countable.*

Proof. Consider the second countability axiom. If $\mathscr{B}$ is a countable basis for X, then $\{B \cap A \mid B \in \mathscr{B}\}$ is a countable basis for the subspace A of X. If $\mathscr{B}_i$ is a countable basis for the space X_i, then the collection of all products $\prod U_i$, where $U_i \in \mathscr{B}_i$ for finitely many values of i and $U_i = X_i$ for all other values of i, is a countable basis for $\prod X_i$.

The proof for the first countability axiom is similar.   ∎

Two consequences of the second countability axiom that will be useful to us later are given in the following theorem. First, a definition:

Definition. A subset A of a space X is said to be **dense** in X if $\bar{A} = X$.

Theorem 30.3. *Suppose that X has a countable basis. Then:*
 (a) Every open covering of X contains a countable subcollection covering X.
 (b) There exists a countable subset of X that is dense in X.

Proof. Let $\{B_n\}$ be a countable basis for X.

(a) Let $\mathscr{A}$ be an open covering of X. For each positive integer n for which it is possible, choose an element A_n of $\mathscr{A}$ containing the basis element B_n. The collection $\mathscr{A}'$ of the sets A_n is countable, since it is indexed with a subset J of the positive integers. Furthermore, it covers X: Given a point $x \in X$, we can choose an element A of $\mathscr{A}$ containing x. Since A is open, there is a basis element B_n such that $x \in B_n \subset A$. Because B_n lies in an element of $\mathscr{A}$, the index n belongs to the set J, so A_n is defined; since A_n contains B_n, it contains x. Thus $\mathscr{A}'$ is a countable subcollection of $\mathscr{A}$ that covers X.

(b) From each nonempty basis element B_n, choose a point x_n. Let D be the set consisting of the points x_n. Then D is dense in X: Given any point x of X, every basis element containing x intersects D, so x belongs to $\bar{D}$.   ∎

The two properties listed in Theorem 30.3 are sometimes taken as alternative countability axioms. A space for which every open covering contains a countable subcovering is called a ***Lindelöf space***. A space having a countable dense subset is often said to be ***separable*** (an unfortunate choice of terminology).[†] Weaker in general than the second countability axiom, each of these properties is equivalent to the second countability axiom when the space is metrizable (see Exercise 5). They are less important than the second countability axiom, but you should be aware of their existence, for they are sometimes useful. It is often easier, for instance, to show that a space X has a countable dense subset than it is to show that X has a countable basis. If the space is metrizable (as it usually is in analysis), it follows that X is second-countable as well.

We shall not use these properties to prove any theorems, but one of them—the Lindelöf condition—will be useful in dealing with some examples. They are not as well behaved as one might wish under the operations of taking subspaces and cartesian products, as we shall see in the examples and exercises that follow.

EXAMPLE 3.   *The space $\mathbb{R}_\ell$ satisfies all the countability axioms but the second.*

Given $x \in \mathbb{R}_\ell$, the set of all basis elements of the form $[x, x + 1/n)$ is a countable basis at x. And it is easy to see that the rational numbers are dense in $\mathbb{R}_\ell$.

To see that $\mathbb{R}_\ell$ has no countable basis, let $\mathcal{B}$ be a basis for $\mathbb{R}_\ell$. Choose for each x, an element B_x of $\mathcal{B}$ such that $x \in B_x \subset [x, x + 1)$. If $x \neq y$, then $B_x \neq B_y$, since $x = \inf B_x$ and $y = \inf B_y$. Therefore, $\mathcal{B}$ must be uncountable.

To show that $\mathbb{R}_\ell$ is Lindelöf requires more work. It will suffice to show that every open covering of $\mathbb{R}_\ell$ by basis elements contains a countable subcollection covering $\mathbb{R}_\ell$. (You can check this.) So let

$$\mathcal{A} = \{[a_\alpha, b_\alpha)\}_{\alpha \in J}$$

be a covering of $\mathbb{R}$ by basis elements for the lower limit topology. We wish to find a countable subcollection that covers $\mathbb{R}$.

Let C be the set

$$C = \bigcup_{\alpha \in J} (a_\alpha, b_\alpha),$$

which is a subset of $\mathbb{R}$. We show the set $\mathbb{R} - C$ is countable.

Let x be a point of $\mathbb{R} - C$. We know that x belongs to no open interval (a_α, b_α); therefore $x = a_\beta$ for some index β. Choose such a β and then choose q_x to be a rational number belonging to the interval (a_β, b_β). Because (a_β, b_β) is contained in C, so is the interval $(a_\beta, q_x) = (x, q_x)$. It follows that if x and y are two points of $\mathbb{R} - C$ with $x < y$, then $q_x < q_y$. (For otherwise, we would have $x < y < q_y \leq q_x$, so that y would lie in the interval (x, q_x) and hence in C.) Therefore the map $x \to q_x$ of $\mathbb{R} - C$ into $\mathbb{Q}$ is injective, so that $\mathbb{R} - C$ is countable.

Now we show that some countable subcollection of $\mathcal{A}$ covers $\mathbb{R}$. To begin, choose for each element of $\mathbb{R} - C$ an element of $\mathcal{A}$ containing it; one obtains a countable subcollection $\mathcal{A}'$ of $\mathcal{A}$ that covers $\mathbb{R} - C$. Now take the set C and topologize it as a subspace of $\mathbb{R}$; in this topology, C satisfies the second countability axiom. Now C is covered by the sets (a_α, b_α), which are open in $\mathbb{R}$ and hence open in C. Then some countable subcollection

---
[†]This is a good example of how a word can be overused. We have already defined what we mean by a *separation* of a space; and we shall discuss the *separation* axioms shortly.

covers C. Suppose this subcollection consists of the elements (a_α, b_α) for $\alpha = \alpha_1, \alpha_2, \ldots$. Then the collection

$$\mathscr{A}'' = \{[a_\alpha, b_\alpha) \mid \alpha = \alpha_1, \alpha_2, \ldots\}$$

is a countable subcollection of $\mathscr{A}$ that covers the set C, and $\mathscr{A}' \cup \mathscr{A}''$ is a countable subcollection of $\mathscr{A}$ that covers $\mathbb{R}_\ell$.

EXAMPLE 4.   *The product of two Lindelöf spaces need not be Lindelöf.* Although the space $\mathbb{R}_\ell$ is Lindelöf, we shall show that the product space $\mathbb{R}_\ell \times \mathbb{R}_\ell = \mathbb{R}_\ell^2$ is not. The space $\mathbb{R}_\ell^2$ is an extremely useful example in topology called the **Sorgenfrey plane**.

The space $\mathbb{R}_\ell^2$ has as basis all sets of the form $[a, b) \times [c, d)$. To show it is not Lindelöf, consider the subspace

$$L = \{x \times (-x) \mid x \in \mathbb{R}_\ell\}.$$

It is easy to check that L is closed in $\mathbb{R}_\ell^2$. Let us cover $\mathbb{R}_\ell^2$ by the open set $\mathbb{R}_\ell^2 - L$ and by all basis elements of the form

$$[a, b) \times [-a, d).$$

Each of these open sets intersects L in at most one point. Since L is uncountable, no countable subcollection covers $\mathbb{R}_\ell^2$. See Figure 30.1.

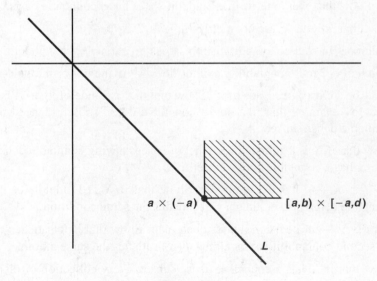

$a \times (-a)$ $[a,b) \times [-a,d)$

L

Figure 30.1

EXAMPLE 5.   *A subspace of a Lindelöf space need not be Lindelöf.* The ordered square I_o^2 is compact; therefore it is Lindelöf, trivially. However, the subspace $A = I \times (0, 1)$ is not Lindelöf. For A is the union of the disjoint sets $U_x = \{x\} \times (0, 1)$, each of which is open in A. This collection of sets is uncountable, and no proper subcollection covers A.

Exercises

1. (a) A G_δ *set* in a space X is a set A that equals a countable intersection of open sets of X. Show that in a first-countable T_1 space, every one-point set is a G_δ set.

   (b) There is a familiar space in which every one-point set is a G_δ set, which nevertheless does not satisfy the first countability axiom. What is it?

   The terminology here comes from the German. The "G" stands for "Gebiet," which means "open set," and the "δ" for "Durchschnitt," which means "intersection."

2. Show that if X has a countable basis $\{B_n\}$, then every basis C for X contains a countable basis for X. [*Hint:* For every pair of indices n, m for which it is possible, choose $C_{n,m} \in C$ such that $B_n \subset C_{n,m} \subset B_m$.]

3. Let X have a countable basis; let A be an uncountable subset of X. Show that uncountably many points of A are limit points of A.

4. Show that every compact metrizable space X has a countable basis. [*Hint:* Let A_n be a finite covering of X by $1/n$-balls.]

5. (a) Show that every metrizable space with a countable dense subset has a countable basis.

   (b) Show that every metrizable Lindelöf space has a countable basis.

6. Show that $\mathbb{R}_\ell$ and I_o^2 are not metrizable.

7. Which of our four countability axioms does S_Ω satisfy? What about $\bar{S}_\Omega$?

8. Which of our four countability axioms does $\mathbb{R}^\omega$ in the uniform topology satisfy?

9. Let A be a closed subspace of X. Show that if X is Lindelöf, then A is Lindelöf. Show by example that if X has a countable dense subset, A need not have a countable dense subset.

10. Show that if X is a countable product of spaces having countable dense subsets, then X has a countable dense subset.

11. Let $f : X \to Y$ be continuous. Show that if X is Lindelöf, or if X has a countable dense subset, then $f(X)$ satisfies the same condition.

12. Let $f : X \to Y$ be a continuous open map. Show that if X satisfies the first or the second countability axiom, then $f(X)$ satisfies the same axiom.

13. Show that if X has a countable dense subset, every collection of disjoint open sets in X is countable.

14. Show that if X is Lindelöf and Y is compact, then $X \times Y$ is Lindelöf.

15. Give $\mathbb{R}^I$ the uniform metric, where $I = [0, 1]$. Let $C(I, \mathbb{R})$ be the subspace consisting of continuous functions. Show that $C(I, \mathbb{R})$ has a countable dense subset, and therefore a countable basis. [*Hint:* Consider those continuous functions whose graphs consist of finitely many line segments with rational end points.]

16. (a) Show that the product space $\mathbb{R}^I$, where $I = [0, 1]$, has a countable dense subset.

(b) Show that if J has cardinality greater than $\mathcal{P}(\mathbb{Z}_+)$, then the product space $\mathbb{R}^J$ does not have a countable dense subset. [*Hint:* If D is dense in $\mathbb{R}^J$, define $f : J \to \mathcal{P}(D)$ by the equation $f(\alpha) = D \cap \pi_\alpha^{-1}((a, b))$, where (a, b) is a fixed interval in $\mathbb{R}$.]

*17. Give $\mathbb{R}^\omega$ the box topology. Let $\mathbb{Q}^\infty$ denote the subspace consisting of sequences of rationals that end in an infinite string of 0's. Which of our four countability axioms does this space satisfy?

*18. Let G be a first-countable topological group. Show that if G has a countable dense subset, or is Lindelöf, then G has a countable basis. [*Hint:* Let $\{B_n\}$ be a countable basis at e. If D is a countable dense subset of G, show the sets $d B_n$, for $d \in D$, form a basis for G. If G is Lindelöf, choose for each n a countable set C_n such that the sets $c B_n$, for $c \in C_n$, cover G. Show that as n ranges over $\mathbb{Z}_+$, these sets form a basis for G.]

§31   The Separation Axioms

In this section, we introduce three separation axioms and explore some of their properties. One you have already seen—the Hausdorff axiom. The others are similar but stronger. As always when we introduce new concepts, we shall examine the relationship between these axioms and the concepts introduced earlier in the book.

Recall that a space X is said to be *Hausdorff* if for each pair x, y of distinct points of X, there exist disjoint open sets containing x and y, respectively.

Definition.   Suppose that one-point sets are closed in X. Then X is said to be *regular* if for each pair consisting of a point x and a closed set B disjoint from x, there exist disjoint open sets containing x and B, respectively. The space X is said to be *normal* if for each pair A, B of disjoint closed sets of X, there exist disjoint open sets containing A and B, respectively.

It is clear that a regular space is Hausdorff, and that a normal space is regular. (We need to include the condition that one-point sets be closed as part of the definition of regularity and normality in order for this to be the case. A two-point space in the indiscrete topology satisfies the other part of the definitions of regularity and normality, even though it is not Hausdorff.) For examples showing the regularity axiom stronger than the Hausdorff axiom, and normality stronger than regularity, see Examples 1 and 3.

These axioms are called separation axioms for the reason that they involve "separating" certain kinds of sets from one another by disjoint open sets. We have used the word "separation" before, of course, when we studied connected spaces. But in that case, we were trying to find disjoint open sets *whose union was the entire space*.

The present situation is quite different because the open sets need not satisfy this condition.

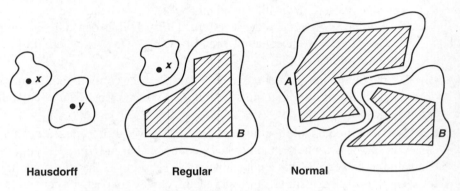

Hausdorff   **Regular**   **Normal**

Figure 31.1

The three separation axioms are illustrated in Figure 31.1.

There are other ways to formulate the separation axioms. One formulation that is sometimes useful is given in the following lemma:

Lemma 31.1. *Let X be a topological space. Let one-point sets in X be closed.*

(a) X is regular if and only if given a point x of X and a neighborhood U of x, there is a neighborhood V of x such that $\bar{V} \subset U$.

(b) X is normal if and only if given a closed set A and an open set U containing A, there is an open set V containing A such that $\bar{V} \subset U$.

Proof. (a) Suppose that X is regular, and suppose that the point x and the neighborhood U of x are given. Let $B = X - U$; then B is a closed set. By hypothesis, there exist disjoint open sets V and W containing x and B, respectively. The set $\bar{V}$ is disjoint from B, since if $y \in B$, the set W is a neighborhood of y disjoint from V. Therefore, $\bar{V} \subset U$, as desired.

To prove the converse, suppose the point x and the closed set B not containing x are given. Let $U = X - B$. By hypothesis, there is a neighborhood V of x such that $\bar{V} \subset U$. The open sets V and $X - \bar{V}$ are disjoint open sets containing x and B, respectively. Thus X is regular.

(b) This proof uses exactly the same argument; one just replaces the point x by the set A throughout.   ∎

Now we relate the separation axioms with the concepts previously introduced.

Theorem 31.2. *(a) A subspace of a Hausdorff space is Hausdorff; a product of Hausdorff spaces is Hausdorff.*

(b) A subspace of a regular space is regular; a product of regular spaces is regular.

Proof.   (a) This result was an exercise in §17. We provide a proof here. Let X be Hausdorff. Let x and y be two points of the subspace Y of X. If U and V are disjoint neighborhoods in X of x and y, respectively, then $U \cap Y$ and $V \cap Y$ are disjoint neighborhoods of x and y in Y.

Let $\{X_\alpha\}$ be a family of Hausdorff spaces. Let $\mathbf{x} = (x_\alpha)$ and $\mathbf{y} = (y_\alpha)$ be distinct points of the product space $\prod X_\alpha$. Because $\mathbf{x} \neq \mathbf{y}$, there is some index β such that $x_\beta \neq y_\beta$. Choose disjoint open sets U and V in X_β containing x_β and y_β, respectively. Then the sets $\pi_\beta^{-1}(U)$ and $\pi_\beta^{-1}(V)$ are disjoint open sets in $\prod X_\alpha$ containing $\mathbf{x}$ and $\mathbf{y}$, respectively.

(b) Let Y be a subspace of the regular space X. Then one-point sets are closed in Y. Let x be a point of Y and let B be a closed subset of Y disjoint from x. Now $\bar{B} \cap Y = B$, where $\bar{B}$ denotes the closure of B in X. Therefore, $x \notin \bar{B}$, so, using regularity of X, we can choose disjoint open sets U and V of X containing x and $\bar{B}$, respectively. Then $U \cap Y$ and $V \cap Y$ are disjoint open sets in Y containing x and B, respectively.

Let $\{X_\alpha\}$ be a family of regular spaces; let $X = \prod X_\alpha$. By (a), X is Hausdorff, so that one-point sets are closed in X. We use the preceding lemma to prove regularity of X. Let $\mathbf{x} = (x_\alpha)$ be a point of X and let U be a neighborhood of $\mathbf{x}$ in X. Choose a basis element $\prod U_\alpha$ about $\mathbf{x}$ contained in U. Choose, for each α, a neighborhood V_α of x_α in X_α such that $\bar{V}_\alpha \subset U_\alpha$; if it happens that $U_\alpha = X_\alpha$, choose $V_\alpha = X_\alpha$. Then $V = \prod V_\alpha$ is a neighborhood of x in X. Since $\bar{V} = \prod \bar{V}_\alpha$ by Theorem 19.5, it follows at once that $\bar{V} \subset \prod U_\alpha \subset U$, so that X is regular.   ∎

There is no analogous theorem for normal spaces, as we shall see shortly, in this section and the next.

EXAMPLE 1.   *The space $\mathbb{R}_K$ is Hausdorff but not regular.* Recall that $\mathbb{R}_K$ denotes the reals in the topology having as basis all open intervals (a, b) and all sets of the form $(a, b) - K$, where $K = \{1/n \mid n \in \mathbb{Z}_+\}$. This space is Hausdorff, because any two distinct points have disjoint open intervals containing them.

But it is not regular. The set K is closed in $\mathbb{R}_K$, and it does not contain the point 0. Suppose that there exist disjoint open sets U and V containing 0 and K, respectively. Choose a basis element containing 0 and lying in U. It must be a basis element of the form $(a, b) - K$, since each basis element of the form (a, b) containing 0 intersects K. Choose n large enough that $1/n \in (a, b)$. Then choose a basis element about $1/n$ contained in V; it must be a basis element of the form (c, d). Finally, choose z so that $z < 1/n$ and $z > \max\{c, 1/(n + 1)\}$. Then z belongs to both U and V, so they are not disjoint. See Figure 31.2.

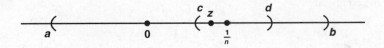

Figure 31.2

EXAMPLE 2. *The space* $\mathbb{R}_\ell$ *is normal.* It is immediate that one-point sets are closed in $\mathbb{R}_\ell$, since the topology of $\mathbb{R}_\ell$ is finer than that of $\mathbb{R}$. To check normality, suppose that A and B are disjoint closed sets in $\mathbb{R}_\ell$. For each point a of A choose a basis element $[a, x_a)$ not intersecting B; and for each point b of B choose a basis element $[b, x_b)$ not intersecting A. The open sets

$$U = \bigcup_{a \in A} [a, x_a) \quad \text{and} \quad V = \bigcup_{b \in B} [b, x_b)$$

are disjoint open sets about A and B, respectively.

EXAMPLE 3. *The Sorgenfrey plane* $\mathbb{R}_\ell^2$ *is not normal.*

The space $\mathbb{R}_\ell$ is regular (in fact, normal), so the product space $\mathbb{R}_\ell^2$ is also regular. Thus this example serves two purposes. It shows that a regular space need not be normal, and it shows that the product of two normal spaces need not be normal.

We suppose $\mathbb{R}_\ell^2$ is normal and derive a contradiction. Let L be the subspace of $\mathbb{R}_\ell^2$ consisting of all points of the form $x \times (-x)$. Then L is closed in $\mathbb{R}_\ell^2$, and L has the discrete topology. Hence every subset A of L, being closed in L, is closed in $\mathbb{R}_\ell^2$. Because $L - A$ is also closed in $\mathbb{R}_\ell^2$, this means that for every nonempty proper subset A of L, one can find disjoint open sets U_A and V_A containing A and $L - A$, respectively.

Let D denote the set of points of $\mathbb{R}_\ell^2$ having rational coordinates; it is dense in $\mathbb{R}_\ell^2$. We define a map θ that assigns, to each subset of the line L, a subset of the set D, by setting

$$\theta(A) = D \cap U_A \quad \text{if } \varnothing \subsetneqq A \subsetneqq L,$$
$$\theta(\varnothing) = \varnothing,$$
$$\theta(L) = D.$$

We show that $\theta : \mathscr{P}(L) \to \mathscr{P}(D)$ is injective.

Let A be a proper nonempty subset of L. Then $\theta(A) = D \cap U_A$ is neither empty (since U_A is open and D is dense in $\mathbb{R}_\ell^2$) nor all of D (since $D \cap V_A$ is nonempty). It remains to show that if B is another proper nonempty subset of L, then $\theta(A) \neq \theta(B)$.

One of the sets A, B contains a point not in the other; suppose that $x \in A$ and $x \notin B$. Then $x \in L - B$, so that $x \in U_A \cap V_B$; since the latter set is open and nonempty, it must contain points of D. These points belong to U_A and not to U_B; therefore, $D \cap U_A \neq D \cap U_B$, as desired. Thus θ is injective.

Now we show there exists an injective map $\phi : \mathscr{P}(D) \to L$. Because D is countably infinite and L has the cardinality of $\mathbb{R}$, it suffices to define an injective map ψ of $\mathscr{P}(\mathbb{Z}_+)$ into $\mathbb{R}$. For that, we let ψ assign to the subset S of $\mathbb{Z}_+$ the infinite decimal $.a_1 a_2 \ldots$, where $a_i = 0$ if $i \in S$ and $a_i = 1$ if $i \notin S$. That is,

$$\psi(S) = \sum_{i=1}^{\infty} a_i / 10^i.$$

Now the composite

$$\mathscr{P}(L) \xrightarrow{\theta} \mathscr{P}(D) \xrightarrow{\psi} L$$

is an injective map of $\mathscr{P}(L)$ into L. But Theorem 7.8 tells us such a map does not exist! Thus we have reached a contradiction.

This proof that $\mathbb{R}_\ell^2$ is not normal is in some ways not very satisfying. We showed only that there must exist some proper nonempty subset A of L such that the sets A and $B = L - A$ are not contained in disjoint open sets of $\mathbb{R}_\ell^2$. But we did not actually find such a set A. In fact, the set A of points of L having rational coordinates is such a set, but the proof is not easy. It is left to the exercises.

Exercises

1. Show that if X is regular, every pair of points of X have neighborhoods whose closures are disjoint.

2. Show that if X is normal, every pair of disjoint closed sets have neighborhoods whose closures are disjoint.

3. Show that every order topology is regular.

4. Let X and X' denote a single set under two topologies $\mathcal{T}$ and $\mathcal{T}'$, respectively; assume that $\mathcal{T}' \supset \mathcal{T}$. If one of the spaces is Hausdorff (or regular, or normal), what does that imply about the other?

5. Let $f, g : X \to Y$ be continuous; assume that Y is Hausdorff. Show that $\{x \mid f(x) = g(x)\}$ is closed in X.

6. Let $p : X \to Y$ be a closed continuous surjective map. Show that if X is normal, then so is Y. [*Hint:* If U is an open set containing $p^{-1}(\{y\})$, show there is a neighborhood W of y such that $p^{-1}(W) \subset U$.]

7. Let $p : X \to Y$ be a closed continuous surjective map such that $p^{-1}(\{y\})$ is compact for each $y \in Y$. (Such a map is called a *perfect map*.)
   (a) Show that if X is Hausdorff, then so is Y.
   (b) Show that if X is regular, then so is Y.
   (c) Show that if X is locally compact, then so is Y.
   (d) Show that if X is second-countable, then so is Y. [*Hint:* Let $\mathcal{B}$ be a countable basis for X. For each finite subset J of $\mathcal{B}$, let U_J be the union of all sets of the form $p^{-1}(W)$, for W open in Y, that are contained in the union of the elements of J.]

8. Let X be a space; let G be a topological group. An ***action*** of G on X is a continuous map $\alpha : G \times X \to X$ such that, denoting $\alpha(g \times x)$ by $g \cdot x$, one has:
   (i) $e \cdot x = x$ for all $x \in X$.
   (ii) $g_1 \cdot (g_2 \cdot x) = (g_1 \cdot g_2) \cdot x$ for all $x \in X$ and $g_1, g_2 \in G$.
   Define $x \sim g \cdot x$ for all x and g; the resulting quotient space is denoted X/G and called the ***orbit space*** of the action α.
   Theorem. *Let G be a compact topological group; let X be a topological space; let α be an action of G on X. If X is Hausdorff, or regular, or normal, or locally compact, or second-countable, so is X/G.*
   [*Hint:* See Exercise 13 of §26.]

*9. Let A be the set of all points of $\mathbb{R}^2_{\ell}$ of the form $x \times (-x)$, for x rational; let B be the set of all points of this form for x irrational. If V is an open set of $\mathbb{R}^2_{\ell}$ containing B, show there exists no open set U containing A that is disjoint from V, as follows:

(a) Let K_n consist of all irrational numbers x in $[0, 1]$ such that $[x, x + 1/n) \times [-x, -x + 1/n)$ is contained in V. Show $[0, 1]$ is the union of the sets K_n and countably many one-point sets.

(b) Use Exercise 5 of §27 to show that some set $\bar{K}_n$ contains an open interval (a, b) of $\mathbb{R}$.

(c) Show that V contains the open parallelogram consisting of all points of the form $x \times (-x + \epsilon)$ for which $a < x < b$ and $0 < \epsilon < 1/n$.

(d) Conclude that if q is a rational number with $a < q < b$, then the point $q \times (-q)$ of $\mathbb{R}^2_{\ell}$ is a limit point of V.

§32   Normal Spaces

Now we turn to a more thorough study of spaces satisfying the normality axiom. In one sense, the term "normal" is something of a misnomer, for normal spaces are not as well-behaved as one might wish. On the other hand, most of the spaces with which we are familiar do satisfy this axiom, as we shall see. Its importance comes from the fact that the results one can prove under the hypothesis of normality are central to much of topology. The Urysohn metrization theorem and the Tietze extension theorem are two such results; we shall deal with them later in this chapter.

We begin by proving three theorems that give three important sets of hypotheses under which normality of a space is assured.

Theorem 32.1.   *Every regular space with a countable basis is normal.*

Proof.   Let X be a regular space with a countable basis $\mathcal{B}$. Let A and B be disjoint closed subsets of X. Each point x of A has a neighborhood U not intersecting B. Using regularity, choose a neighborhood V of x whose closure lies in U; finally, choose an element of $\mathcal{B}$ containing x and contained in V. By choosing such a basis element for each x in A, we construct a countable covering of A by open sets whose closures do not intersect B. Since this covering of A is countable, we can index it with the positive integers; let us denote it by $\{U_n\}$.

Similarly, choose a countable collection $\{V_n\}$ of open sets covering B, such that each set $\bar{V}_n$ is disjoint from A. The sets $U = \bigcup U_n$ and $V = \bigcup V_n$ are open sets containing A and B, respectively, but they need not be disjoint. We perform the following simple trick to construct two open sets that *are* disjoint. Given n, define

$$U'_n = U_n - \bigcup_{i=1}^{n} \bar{V}_i \quad \text{and} \quad V'_n = V_n - \bigcup_{i=1}^{n} \bar{U}_i.$$

Note that each set U'_n is open, being the difference of an open set U_n and a closed set $\bigcup_{i=1}^{n} \bar{V}_i$. Similarly, each set V'_n is open. The collection $\{U'_n\}$ covers A, because each x in A belongs to U_n for some n, and x belongs to *none* of the sets $\bar{V}_i$. Similarly, the collection $\{V'_n\}$ covers B. See Figure 32.1.

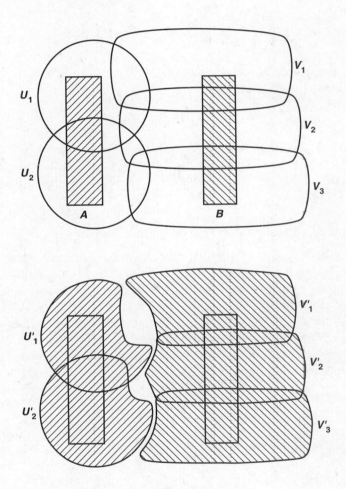

Figure 32.1

Finally, the open sets

$$U' = \bigcup_{n \in \mathbb{Z}_+} U'_n \quad \text{and} \quad V' = \bigcup_{n \in \mathbb{Z}_+} V'_n$$

are disjoint. For if $x \in U' \cap V'$, then $x \in U'_j \cap V'_k$ for some j and k. Suppose that $j \leq k$. It follows from the definition of U'_j that $x \in U_j$; and since $j \leq k$ it follows from the definition of V'_k that $x \notin \bar{U}_j$. A similar contradiction arises if $j \geq k$.   ∎

Theorem 32.2.   *Every metrizable space is normal.*

Proof.   Let X be a metrizable space with metric d. Let A and B be disjoint closed subsets of X. For each $a \in A$, choose ϵ_a so that the ball $B(a, \epsilon_a)$ does not intersect B. Similarly, for each b in B, choose ϵ_b so that the ball $B(b, \epsilon_b)$ does not intersect A. Define

$$U = \bigcup_{a \in A} B(a, \epsilon_a/2) \quad \text{and} \quad V = \bigcup_{b \in B} B(b, \epsilon_b/2).$$

Then U and V are open sets containing A and B, respectively; we assert they are disjoint. For if $z \in U \cap V$, then

$$z \in B(a, \epsilon_a/2) \cap B(b, \epsilon_b/2)$$

for some $a \in A$ and some $b \in B$. The triangle inequality applies to show that $d(a, b) < (\epsilon_a + \epsilon_b)/2$. If $\epsilon_a \leq \epsilon_b$, then $d(a, b) < \epsilon_b$, so that the ball $B(b, \epsilon_b)$ contains the point a. If $\epsilon_b \leq \epsilon_a$, then $d(a, b) < \epsilon_a$, so that the ball $B(a, \epsilon_a)$ contains the point b. Neither situation is possible. ∎

Theorem 32.3.   *Every compact Hausdorff space is normal.*

Proof.   Let X be a compact Hausdorff space. We have already essentially proved that X is regular. For if x is a point of X and B is a closed set in X not containing x, then B is compact, so that Lemma 26.4 applies to show there exist disjoint open sets about x and B, respectively.

Essentially the same argument as given in that lemma can be used to show that X is normal: Given disjoint closed sets A and B in X, choose, for each point a of A, disjoint open sets U_a and V_a containing a and B, respectively. (Here we use regularity of X.) The collection $\{U_a\}$ covers A; because A is compact, A may be covered by finitely many sets $U_{a_1}, \ldots, U_{a_m}$. Then

$$U = U_{a_1} \cup \cdots \cup U_{a_m} \quad \text{and} \quad V = V_{a_1} \cap \cdots \cap V_{a_m}$$

are disjoint open sets containing A and B, respectively. ∎

Here is a further result about normality that we shall find useful in dealing with some examples.

Theorem 32.4.   *Every well-ordered set X is normal in the order topology.*

It is, in fact, true that *every* order topology is normal (see Example 39 of [S-S]); but we shall not have occasion to use this stronger result.

Proof.   Let X be a well-ordered set. We assert that every interval of the form $(x, y]$ is open in X: If X has a largest element and y is that element, $(x, y]$ is just a basis element about y. If y is not the largest element of X, then $(x, y]$ equals the open set (x, y'), where y' is the immediate successor of y.

Now let A and B be disjoint closed sets in X; assume for the moment that neither A nor B contains the smallest element a_0 of X. For each $a \in A$, there exists a basis element about a disjoint from B; it contains some interval of the form $(x, a]$. (Here is where we use the fact that a is not the smallest element of X.) Choose, for each $a \in A$, such an interval $(x_a, a]$ disjoint from B. Similarly, for each $b \in B$, choose an interval $(y_b, b]$ disjoint from A. The sets

$$U = \bigcup_{a \in A} (x_a, a] \quad \text{and} \quad V = \bigcup_{b \in B} (y_b, b]$$

are open sets containing A and B, respectively; we assert they are disjoint. For suppose that $z \in U \cap V$. Then $z \in (x_a, a] \cap (y_b, b]$ for some $a \in A$ and some $b \in B$. Assume that $a < b$. Then if $a \le y_b$, the two intervals are disjoint, while if $a > y_b$, we have $a \in (y_b, b]$, contrary to the fact that $(y_b, b]$ is disjoint from A. A similar contradiction occurs if $b < a$.

Finally, assume that A and B are disjoint closed sets in X, and A contains the smallest element a_0 of X. The set $\{a_0\}$ is both open and closed in X. By the result of the preceding paragraph, there exist disjoint open sets U and V containing the closed sets $A - \{a_0\}$ and B, respectively. Then $U \cup \{a_0\}$ and V are disjoint open sets containing A and B, respectively. ∎

EXAMPLE 1.   *If J is uncountable, the product space $\mathbb{R}^J$ is not normal.* The proof is fairly difficult; we leave it as a challenging exercise (see Exercise 9).

This example serves three purposes. It shows that a regular space $\mathbb{R}^J$ need not be normal. It shows that a subspace of a normal space need not be normal, for $\mathbb{R}^J$ is homeomorphic to the subspace $(0, 1)^J$ of $[0, 1]^J$, which (assuming the Tychonoff theorem) is compact Hausdorff and therefore normal. And it shows that an uncountable product of normal spaces need not be normal. It leaves unsettled the question as to whether a finite or a countable product of normal spaces might be normal.

EXAMPLE 2.   *The product space $S_\Omega \times \bar{S}_\Omega$ is not normal.*[†]

Consider the well-ordered set $\bar{S}_\Omega$, in the order topology, and consider the subset S_Ω, in the subspace topology (which is the same as the order topology). Both spaces are normal, by Theorem 32.4. We shall show that the product space $S_\Omega \times \bar{S}_\Omega$ is not normal.

This example serves three purposes. First, it shows that a regular space need not be normal, for $S_\Omega \times \bar{S}_\Omega$ is a product of regular spaces and therefore regular. Second, it shows that a subspace of a normal space need not be normal, for $S_\Omega \times \bar{S}_\Omega$ is a subspace of $\bar{S}_\Omega \times \bar{S}_\Omega$, which is a compact Hausdorff space and therefore normal. Third, it shows that the product of two normal spaces need not be normal.

First, we consider the space $\bar{S}_\Omega \times \bar{S}_\Omega$, and its "diagonal" $\Delta = \{x \times x \mid x \in \bar{S}_\Omega\}$. Because $\bar{S}_\Omega$ is Hausdorff, Δ is closed in $\bar{S}_\Omega \times \bar{S}_\Omega$: If U and V are disjoint neighborhoods of x and y, respectively, then $U \times V$ is a neighborhood of $x \times y$ that does not intersect Δ.

Therefore, in the subspace $S_\Omega \times \bar{S}_\Omega$, the set

$$A = \Delta \cap (S_\Omega \times \bar{S}_\Omega) = \Delta - \{\Omega \times \Omega\}$$

[†]Kelley [K] attributes this example to J. Dieudonné and A. P. Morse independently.

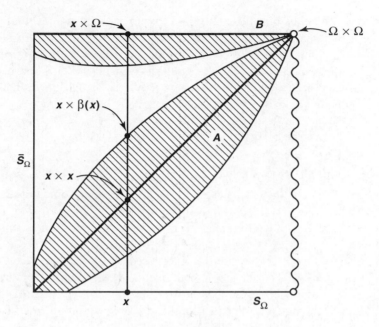

Figure 32.2

is closed. Likewise, the set

$$B = S_\Omega \times \{\Omega\}$$

is closed in $S_\Omega \times \bar{S}_\Omega$, being a "slice" of this product space. The sets A and B are disjoint. We shall assume there exist disjoint open sets U and V of $S_\Omega \times \bar{S}_\Omega$ containing A and B, respectively, and derive a contradiction. See Figure 32.2.

Given $x \in S_\Omega$, consider the vertical slice $x \times \bar{S}_\Omega$. We assert that there is some point β with $x < \beta < \Omega$ such that $x \times \beta$ lies outside U. For if U contained all points $x \times \beta$ for $x < \beta < \Omega$, then the top point $x \times \Omega$ of the slice would be a limit point of U, which it is not because V is an open set disjoint from U containing this top point.

Choose $\beta(x)$ to be such a point; just to be definite, let $\beta(x)$ be the *smallest* element of S_Ω such that $x < \beta(x) < \Omega$ and $x \times \beta(x)$ lies outside U. Define a sequence of points of S_Ω as follows: Let x_1 be any point of S_Ω. Let $x_2 = \beta(x_1)$, and in general, $x_{n+1} = \beta(x_n)$. We have

$$x_1 < x_2 < \dots,$$

because $\beta(x) > x$ for all x. The set $\{x_n\}$ is countable and therefore has an upper bound in S_Ω; let $b \in S_\Omega$ be its least upper bound. Because the sequence is increasing, it must converge to its least upper bound; thus $x_n \to b$. But $\beta(x_n) = x_{n+1}$, so that $\beta(x_n) \to b$ also. Then

$$x_n \times \beta(x_n) \longrightarrow b \times b$$

in the product space. See Figure 32.3. Now we have a contradiction, for the point $b \times b$ lies in the set A, which is contained in the open set U; and U contains *none* of the points $x_n \times \beta(x_n)$.

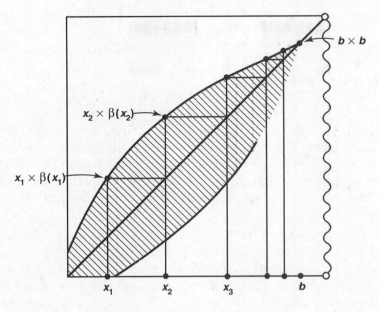

Figure 32.3

Exercises

1. Show that a closed subspace of a normal space is normal.

2. Show that if $\prod X_\alpha$ is Hausdorff, or regular, or normal, then so is X_α. (Assume that each X_α is nonempty.)

3. Show that every locally compact Hausdorff space is regular.

4. Show that every regular Lindelöf space is normal.

5. Is $\mathbb{R}^\omega$ normal in the product topology? In the uniform topology?

   It is not known whether $\mathbb{R}^\omega$ is normal in the box topology. Mary-Ellen Rudin has shown that the answer is affirmative if one assumes the continuum hypothesis [RM]. In fact, she shows it satisfies a stronger condition called *paracompactness*.

6. A space X is said to be *completely normal* if every subspace of X is normal. Show that X is completely normal if and only if for every pair A, B of separated sets in X (that is, sets such that $\bar{A} \cap B = \varnothing$ and $A \cap \bar{B} = \varnothing$), there exist disjoint open sets containing them. [*Hint:* If X is completely normal, consider $X - (\bar{A} \cap \bar{B})$.]

7. Which of the following spaces are completely normal? Justify your answers.
   (a) A subspace of a completely normal space.
   (b) The product of two completely normal spaces.
   (c) A well-ordered set in the order topology.
   (d) A metrizable space.

(e) A compact Hausdorff space.

(f) A regular space with a countable basis.

(g) The space $\mathbb{R}_\ell$.

*8. Prove the following:

Theorem.   Every linear continuum X is normal.

(a) Let C be a nonempty closed subset of X. If U is a component of $X - C$, show that U is a set of the form (c, c') or (c, ∞) or $(-\infty, c)$, where $c, c' \in C$.

(b) Let A and B be closed disjoint subsets of X. For each component W of $X - A \cup B$ that is an open interval with one end point in A and the other in B, choose a point c_W of W. Show that the set C of the points c_W is closed.

(c) Show that if V is a component of $X - C$, then V does not intersect both A and B.

*9. Prove the following:

Theorem.   If J is uncountable, then $\mathbb{R}^J$ is not normal.

Proof. (This proof is due to A. H. Stone, as adapted in [S-S].) Let $X = (\mathbb{Z}_+)^J$; it will suffice to show that X is not normal, since X is a closed subspace of R^J. We use functional notation for the elements of X, so that the typical element of X is a function $\mathbf{x} : J \to \mathbb{Z}_+$.

(a) If $\mathbf{x} \in X$ and if B is a finite subset of J, let $U(\mathbf{x}, B)$ denote the set consisting of all those elements $\mathbf{y}$ of X such that $\mathbf{y}(\alpha) = \mathbf{x}(\alpha)$ for $\alpha \in B$. Show the sets $U(\mathbf{x}, B)$ are a basis for X.

(b) Define P_n to be the subset of X consisting of those $\mathbf{x}$ such that on the set $J - \mathbf{x}^{-1}(n)$, the map $\mathbf{x}$ is injective. Show that P_1 and P_2 are closed and disjoint.

(c) Suppose U and V are open sets containing P_1 and P_2, respectively. Given a sequence $\alpha_1, \alpha_2, \ldots$ of distinct elements of J, and a sequence

$$0 = n_0 < n_1 < n_2 < \cdots$$

of integers, for each $i \geq 1$ let us set

$$B_i = \{\alpha_1, \cdots, \alpha_{n_i}\}$$

and define $\mathbf{x}_i \in X$ by the equations

$$\mathbf{x}_i(\alpha_j) = j \quad \text{for } 1 \leq j \leq n_{i-1},$$
$$\mathbf{x}_i(\alpha) = 1 \quad \text{for all other values of } \alpha.$$

Show that one can choose the sequences α_j and n_j so that for each i, one has the inclusion

$$U(\mathbf{x}_i, B_i) \subset U.$$

[*Hint:* To begin, note that $\mathbf{x}_1(\alpha) = 1$ for all α; now choose B_1 so that $U(\mathbf{x}_1, B_1) \subset U$.]

(d) Let A be the set $\{\alpha_1, \alpha_2, \ldots\}$ constructed in (c). Define $\mathbf{y} : J \to \mathbb{Z}_+$ by the equations

$$\mathbf{y}(\alpha_j) = j \quad \text{for } \alpha_j \in A,$$
$$\mathbf{y}(\alpha) = 2 \quad \text{for all other values of } \alpha.$$

Choose B so that $U(\mathbf{y}, B) \subset V$. Then choose i so that $B \cap A$ is contained in the set B_i. Show that

$$U(\mathbf{x}_{i+1}, B_{i+1}) \cap U(\mathbf{y}, B)$$

is not empty.

10. Is every topological group normal?

§33   The Urysohn Lemma

Now we come to the first deep theorem of the book, a theorem that is commonly called the "Urysohn lemma." It asserts the existence of certain real-valued continuous functions on a normal space X. It is the crucial tool used in proving a number of important theorems. We shall prove three of them—the Urysohn metrization theorem, the Tietze extension theorem, and an imbedding theorem for manifolds—in succeeding sections of this chapter.

Why do we call the Urysohn lemma a "deep" theorem? Because its proof involves a really original idea, which the previous proofs did not. Perhaps we can explain what we mean this way: By and large, one would expect that if one went through this book and deleted all the proofs we have given up to now and then handed the book to a bright student who had not studied topology, that student ought to be able to go through the book and work out the proofs independently. (It would take a good deal of time and effort, of course; and one would not expect the student to handle the trickier examples.) But the Urysohn lemma is on a different level. It would take considerably more originality than most of us possess to prove this lemma unless we were given copious hints!

Theorem 33.1 (Urysohn lemma). *Let X be a normal space; let A and B be disjoint closed subsets of X. Let $[a, b]$ be a closed interval in the real line. Then there exists a continuous map*

$$f : X \longrightarrow [a, b]$$

such that $f(x) = a$ for every x in A, and $f(x) = b$ for every x in B.

Proof.   We need consider only the case where the interval in question is the interval $[0, 1]$; the general case follows from that one. The first step of the proof is to construct, using normality, a certain family U_p of open sets of X, indexed by the rational numbers. Then one uses these sets to define the continuous function f.

Step 1. Let P be the set of all rational numbers in the interval $[0, 1]$.[†] We shall define, for each p in P, an open set U_p of X, in such a way that whenever $p < q$, we have

$$\bar{U}_p \subset U_q.$$

Thus, the sets U_p will be simply ordered by inclusion in the same way their subscripts are ordered by the usual ordering in the real line.

Because P is countable, we can use induction to define the sets U_p (or rather, the principle of recursive definition). Arrange the elements of P in an infinite sequence in some way; for convenience, let us suppose that the numbers 1 and 0 are the first two elements of the sequence.

Now define the sets U_p, as follows: First, define $U_1 = X - B$. Second, because A is a closed set contained in the open set U_1, we may by normality of X choose an open set U_0 such that

$$A \subset U_0 \quad \text{and} \quad \bar{U}_0 \subset U_1.$$

In general, let P_n denote the set consisting of the first n rational numbers in the sequence. Suppose that U_p is defined for all rational numbers p belonging to the set P_n, satisfying the condition

$$(*) \qquad\qquad p < q \Longrightarrow \bar{U}_p \subset U_q.$$

Let r denote the next rational number in the sequence; we wish to define U_r.

Consider the set $P_{n+1} = P_n \cup \{r\}$. It is a finite subset of the interval $[0, 1]$, and, as such, it has a simple ordering derived from the usual order relation $<$ on the real line. In a finite simply ordered set, every element (other than the smallest and the largest) has an immediate predecessor and an immediate successor. (See Theorem 10.1.) The number 0 is the smallest element, and 1 is the largest element, of the simply ordered set P_{n+1}, and r is neither 0 nor 1. So r has an immediate predecessor p in P_{n+1} and an immediate successor q in P_{n+1}. The sets U_p and U_q are already defined, and $\bar{U}_p \subset U_q$ by the induction hypothesis. Using normality of X, we can find an open set U_r of X such that

$$\bar{U}_p \subset U_r \quad \text{and} \quad \bar{U}_r \subset U_q.$$

We assert that $(*)$ now holds for every pair of elements of P_{n+1}. If both elements lie in P_n, $(*)$ holds by the induction hypothesis. If one of them is r and the other is a point s of P_n, then either $s \leq p$, in which case

$$\bar{U}_s \subset \bar{U}_p \subset U_r,$$

or $s \geq q$, in which case

$$\bar{U}_r \subset U_q \subset U_s.$$

[†]Actually, any countable dense subset of $[0, 1]$ will do, providing it contains the points 0 and 1.

Thus, for every pair of elements of P_{n+1}, relation $(*)$ holds.

By induction, we have U_p defined for all $p \in P$.

To illustrate, let us suppose we started with the standard way of arranging the elements of P in an infinite sequence:

$$P = \{1, 0, \tfrac{1}{2}, \tfrac{1}{3}, \tfrac{2}{3}, \tfrac{1}{4}, \tfrac{3}{4}, \tfrac{1}{5}, \tfrac{2}{5}, \tfrac{3}{5}, \ldots\}$$

After defining U_0 and U_1, we would define $U_{1/2}$ so that $\bar{U}_0 \subset U_{1/2}$ and $\bar{U}_{1/2} \subset U_1$. Then we would fit in $U_{1/3}$ between U_0 and $U_{1/2}$; and $U_{2/3}$ between $U_{1/2}$ and U_1. And so on. At the eighth step of the proof we would have the situation pictured in Figure 33.1. And the ninth step would consist of choosing an open set $U_{2/5}$ to fit in between $U_{1/3}$ and $U_{1/2}$. And so on.

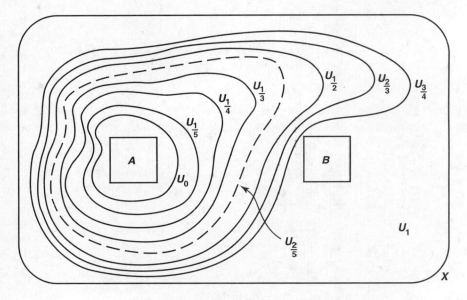

Figure 33.1

Step 2. Now we have defined U_p for all rational numbers p in the interval $[0, 1]$. We extend this definition to all rational numbers p in $\mathbb{R}$ by defining

$$U_p = \varnothing \quad \text{if } p < 0,$$
$$U_p = X \quad \text{if } p > 1.$$

It is still true (as you can check) that for any pair of rational numbers p and q,

$$p < q \implies \bar{U}_p \subset U_q.$$

Step 3. Given a point x of X, let us define $\mathbb{Q}(x)$ to be the set of those rational numbers p such that the corresponding open sets U_p contain x:

$$\mathbb{Q}(x) = \{p \mid x \in U_p\}.$$

This set contains no number less than 0, since no x is in U_p for $p < 0$. And it contains every number greater than 1, since every x is in U_p for $p > 1$. Therefore, $\mathbb{Q}(x)$ is bounded below, and its greatest lower bound is a point of the interval $[0, 1]$. Define

$$f(x) = \inf \mathbb{Q}(x) = \inf\{p \mid x \in U_p\}.$$

Step 4. We show that f is the desired function. If $x \in A$, then $x \in U_p$ for every $p \ge 0$, so that $\mathbb{Q}(x)$ equals the set of all nonnegative rationals, and $f(x) = \inf \mathbb{Q}(x) = 0$. Similarly, if $x \in B$, then $x \in U_p$ for no $p \le 1$, so that $\mathbb{Q}(x)$ consists of all rational numbers greater than 1, and $f(x) = 1$.

All this is easy. The only hard part is to show that f is continuous. For this purpose, we first prove the following elementary facts:

(1) $x \in \bar{U}_r \Rightarrow f(x) \le r$.

(2) $x \notin U_r \Rightarrow f(x) \ge r$.

To prove (1), note that if $x \in \bar{U}_r$, then $x \in U_s$ for every $s > r$. Therefore, $\mathbb{Q}(x)$ contains all rational numbers greater than r, so that by definition we have

$$f(x) = \inf \mathbb{Q}(x) \le r.$$

To prove (2), note that if $x \notin U_r$, then x is not in U_s for any $s < r$. Therefore, $\mathbb{Q}(x)$ contains no rational numbers less than r, so that

$$f(x) = \inf \mathbb{Q}(x) \ge r.$$

Now we prove continuity of f. Given a point x_0 of X and an open interval (c, d) in $\mathbb{R}$ containing the point $f(x_0)$, we wish to find a neighborhood U of x_0 such that $f(U) \subset (c, d)$. Choose rational numbers p and q such that

$$c < p < f(x_0) < q < d.$$

We assert that the open set

$$U = U_q - \bar{U}_p$$

is the desired neighborhood of x_0. See Figure 33.2.

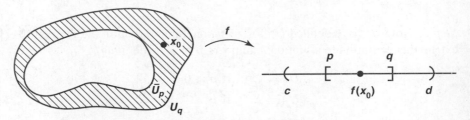

Figure 33.2

First, we note that $x_0 \in U$. For the fact that $f(x_0) < q$ implies by condition (2) that $x_0 \in U_q$, while the fact that $f(x_0) > p$ implies by (1) that $x_0 \notin \bar{U}_p$.

Second, we show that $f(U) \subset (c, d)$. Let $x \in U$. Then $x \in U_q \subset \bar{U}_q$, so that $f(x) \le q$, by (1). And $x \notin \bar{U}_p$, so that $x \notin U_p$ and $f(x) \ge p$, by (2). Thus, $f(x) \in [p, q] \subset (c, d)$, as desired. ∎

Definition.   If A and B are two subsets of the topological space X, and if there is a continuous function $f : X \to [0, 1]$ such that $f(A) = \{0\}$ and $f(B) = \{1\}$, we say that A and B *can be separated by a continuous function*.

The Urysohn lemma says that if every pair of disjoint closed sets in X can be separated by disjoint open sets, then each such pair can be separated by a continuous function. The converse is trivial, for if $f : X \to [0, 1]$ is the function, then $f^{-1}([0, \frac{1}{2}))$ and $f^{-1}((\frac{1}{2}, 1])$ are disjoint open sets containing A and B, respectively.

This fact leads to a question that may already have occurred to you: Why cannot the proof of the Urysohn lemma be generalized to show that in a regular space, where you can separate points from closed sets by disjoint open sets, you can also separate points from closed sets by continuous functions?

At first glance, it seems that the proof of the Urysohn lemma should go through. You take a point a and a closed set B not containing a, and you begin the proof just as before by defining $U_1 = X - B$ and choosing U_0 to be an open set about a whose closure is contained in U_1 (using regularity of X). But at the very next step of the proof, you run into difficulty. Suppose that p is the next rational number in the sequence after 0 and 1. You want to find an open set U_p such that $\bar{U}_0 \subset U_p$ and $\bar{U}_p \subset U_1$. For this, regularity is not enough.

Requiring that one be able to separate a point from a closed set by a continuous function is, in fact, a stronger condition than requiring that one can separate them by disjoint open sets. We make this requirement into a new separation axiom:

Definition.   A space X is *completely regular* if one-point sets are closed in X and if for each point x_0 and each closed set A not containing x_0, there is a continuous function $f : X \to [0, 1]$ such that $f(x_0) = 1$ and $f(A) = \{0\}$.

A normal space is completely regular, by the Urysohn lemma, and a completely regular space is regular, since given f, the sets $f^{-1}([0, \frac{1}{2}))$ and $f^{-1}((\frac{1}{2}, 1])$ are disjoint open sets about A and x_0, respectively. As a result, this new axiom fits in between regularity and normality in the list of separation axioms. Note that in the definition one could just as well require the function to map x_0 to 0, and A to $\{1\}$, for $g(x) = 1 - f(x)$ satisfies this condition. But our definition is at times a bit more convenient.

In the early years of topology, the separation axioms, listed in order of increasing strength, were labelled T_1, T_2 (Hausdorff), T_3 (regular), T_4 (normal), and T_5 (completely normal), respectively. The letter "T" comes from the German "Trennungsaxiom," which means "separation axiom." Later, when the notion of complete regularity was introduced, someone suggested facetiously that it should be called the "T-$3\frac{1}{2}$ axiom," since it lies between regularity and normality. This terminology is in fact sometimes used in the literature!

Unlike normality, this new separation axiom is nicely behaved with regard to subspaces and products:

Theorem 33.2.   *A subspace of a completely regular space is completely regular. A product of completely regular spaces is completely regular.*

Proof. Let X be completely regular; let Y be a subspace of X. Let x_0 be a point of Y, and let A be a closed set of Y disjoint from x_0. Now $A = \bar{A} \cap Y$, where $\bar{A}$ denotes the closure of A in X. Therefore, $x_0 \notin \bar{A}$. Since X is completely regular, we can choose a continuous function $f : X \to [0, 1]$ such that $f(x_0) = 1$ and $f(\bar{A}) = \{0\}$. The restriction of f to Y is the desired continuous function on Y.

Let $X = \prod X_\alpha$ be a product of completely regular spaces. Let $\mathbf{b} = (b_\alpha)$ be a point of X and let A be a closed set of X disjoint from $\mathbf{b}$. Choose a basis element $\prod U_\alpha$ containing $\mathbf{b}$ that does not intersect A; then $U_\alpha = X_\alpha$ except for finitely many α, say $\alpha = \alpha_1, \ldots, \alpha_n$. Given $i = 1, \ldots, n$, choose a continuous function

$$f_i : X_{\alpha_i} \to [0, 1]$$

such that $f_i(b_{\alpha_i}) = 1$ and $f_i(X - U_{\alpha_i}) = \{0\}$. Let $\phi_i(\mathbf{x}) = f_i(\pi_{\alpha_i}(\mathbf{x}))$; then ϕ_i maps X continuously into $\mathbb{R}$ and vanishes outside $\pi_{\alpha_i}^{-1}(U_{\alpha_i})$. The product

$$f(\mathbf{x}) = \phi_1(\mathbf{x}) \cdot \phi_2(\mathbf{x}) \cdot \cdots \cdot \phi_n(\mathbf{x})$$

is the desired continuous function on X, for it equals 1 at $\mathbf{b}$ and vanishes outside $\prod U_\alpha$. ∎

EXAMPLE 1.   The spaces $\mathbb{R}_\ell^2$ and $S_\Omega \times \bar{S}_\Omega$ are completely regular but not normal. For they are products of spaces that are completely regular (in fact, normal).

A space that is regular but not completely regular is much harder to find. Most of the examples that have been constructed for this purpose are difficult, and require considerable familiarity with cardinal numbers. Fairly recently, however, John Thomas [T] has constructed a much more elementary example, which we outline in Exercise 11.

Exercises

1. Examine the proof of the Urysohn lemma, and show that for given r,

$$f^{-1}(r) = \bigcap_{p>r} U_p - \bigcup_{q<r} U_q,$$

p, q rational.

2. (a) Show that a connected normal space having more than one point is uncountable.
   (b) Show that a connected regular space having more than one point is uncountable.[†] [*Hint:* Any countable space is Lindelöf.]

3. Give a direct proof of the Urysohn lemma for a metric space (X, d) by setting

$$f(x) = \frac{d(x, A)}{d(x, A) + d(x, B)}.$$

[†]Surprisingly enough, there does exist a connected *Hausdorff* space that is countably infinite. See Example 75 of [S-S].

4. Recall that A is a "G_δ set" in X if A is the intersection of a countable collection of open sets of X.

   Theorem. *Let X be normal. There exists a continuous function $f : X \to [0, 1]$ such that $f(x) = 0$ for $x \in A$, and $f(x) > 0$ for $x \notin A$, if and only if A is a closed G_δ set in X.*

   A function satisfying the requirements of this theorem is said to **vanish precisely on A**.

5. Prove:

   Theorem *(Strong form of the Urysohn lemma). Let X be a normal space. There is a continuous function $f : X \to [0, 1]$ such that $f(x) = 0$ for $x \in A$, and $f(x) = 1$ for $x \in B$, and $0 < f(x) < 1$ otherwise, if and only if A and B are disjoint closed G_δ sets in X.*

6. A space X is said to be **perfectly normal** if X is normal and if every closed set in X is a G_δ set in X.
   (a) Show that every metrizable space is perfectly normal.
   (b) Show that a perfectly normal space is completely normal. For this reason the condition of perfect normality is sometimes called the "T_6 axiom." [*Hint:* Let A and B be separated sets in X. Choose continuous functions $f, g : X \to [0, 1]$ that vanish precisely on $\bar{A}$ and $\bar{B}$, respectively. Consider the function $f - g$.]
   (c) There is a familiar space that is completely normal but not perfectly normal. What is it?

7. Show that every locally compact Hausdorff space is completely regular.

8. Let X be completely regular; let A and B be disjoint closed subsets of X. Show that if A is compact, there is a continuous function $f : X \to [0, 1]$ such that $f(A) = \{0\}$ and $f(B) = \{1\}$.

9. Show that $\mathbb{R}^J$ in the box topology is completely regular. [*Hint:* Show that it suffices to consider the case where the box neighborhood $(-1, 1)^J$ is disjoint from A and the point is the origin. Then use the fact that a function continuous in the uniform topology is also continuous in the box topology.]

*10. Prove the following:

   Theorem. *Every topological group is completely regular.*

   Proof. Let V_0 be a neighborhood of the identity element e, in the topological group G. In general, choose V_n to be a neighborhood of e such that $V_n \cdot V_n \subset V_{n-1}$. Consider the set of all dyadic rationals p, that is, all rational numbers of the form $k/2^n$, with k and n integers. For each dyadic rational p in $(0, 1]$, define an open set $U(p)$ inductively as follows: $U(1) = V_0$ and $U(\frac{1}{2}) = V_1$. Given n, if $U(k/2^n)$ is defined for $0 < k/2^n \le 1$, define

   $$U(1/2^{n+1}) = V_{n+1},$$
   $$U((2k + 1)/2^{n+1}) = V_{n+1} \cdot U(k/2^n)$$

for $0 < k < 2^n$. For $p \leq 0$, let $U(p) = \varnothing$; and for $p > 1$, let $U(p) = G$. Show that

$$V_n \cdot U(k/2^n) \subset U((k+1)/2^n)$$

for all k and n. Proceed as in the Urysohn lemma.

This exercise is adapted from [M-Z], to which the reader is referred for further results on topological groups.

*11. Define a set X as follows: For each even integer m, let L_m denote the line segment $m \times [-1, 0]$ in the plane. For each odd integer n and each integer $k \geq 2$, let $C_{n,k}$ denote the union of the line segments $(n + 1 - 1/k) \times [-1, 0]$ and $(n - 1 + 1/k) \times [-1, 0]$ and the semicircle

$$\{x \times y \mid (x - n)^2 + y^2 = (1 - 1/k)^2 \text{ and } y \geq 0\}$$

in the plane. Let $p_{n,k}$ denote the topmost point $n \times (1 - 1/k)$ of this semicircle. Let X be the union of all the sets L_m and $C_{n,k}$, along with two extra points a and b. Topologize X by taking sets of the following four types as basis elements:

   (i) The intersection of X with a horizontal open line segment that contains none of the points $p_{n,k}$.

   (ii) A set formed from one of the sets $C_{n,k}$ by deleting finitely many points.

   (iii) For each even integer m, the union of $\{a\}$ and the set of points $x \times y$ of X for which $x < m$.

   (iv) For each even integer m, the union of $\{b\}$ and the set of points $x \times y$ of X for which $x > m$.

   (a) Sketch X; show that these sets form a basis for a topology on X.

   (b) Let f be a continuous real-valued function on X. Show that for any c, the set $f^{-1}(c)$ is a G_δ set in X. (This is true for any space X.) Conclude that the set $S_{n,k}$ consisting of those points p of $C_{n,k}$ for which $f(p) \neq f(p_{n,k})$ is countable. Choose $d \in [-1, 0]$ so that the line $y = d$ intersects none of the sets $S_{n,k}$. Show that for n odd,

$$f((n-1) \times d) = \lim_{k \to \infty} f(p_{n,k}) = f((n+1) \times d).$$

   Conclude that $f(a) = f(b)$.

   (c) Show that X is regular but not completely regular.

§34   The Urysohn Metrization Theorem

Now we come to the major goal of this chapter, a theorem that gives us conditions under which a topological space is metrizable. The proof weaves together a number of strands from previous parts of the book; it uses results on metric topologies from Chapter 2 as well as facts concerning the countability and separation axioms proved in the present chapter. The basic construction used in the proof is a simple one, but very useful. You will see it several times more in this book, in various guises.

There are two versions of the proof, and since each has useful generalizations that will appear subsequently, we present both of them here. The first version generalizes to give an imbedding theorem for completely regular spaces. The second version will be generalized in Chapter 6 when we prove the Nagata-Smirnov metrization theorem.

Theorem 34.1 (Urysohn metrization theorem).   *Every regular space X with a countable basis is metrizable.*

Proof.   We shall prove that X is metrizable by imbedding X in a metrizable space Y; that is, by showing X homeomorphic with a subspace of Y. The two versions of the proof differ in the choice of the metrizable space Y. In the first version, Y is the space $\mathbb{R}^\omega$ in the product topology, a space that we have previously proved to be metrizable (Theorem 20.5). In the second version, the space Y is also $\mathbb{R}^\omega$, but this time in the topology given by the uniform metric $\bar{\rho}$ (see §20). In each case, it turns out that our construction actually imbeds X in the subspace $[0, 1]^\omega$ of $\mathbb{R}^\omega$.

Step 1. We prove the following: *There exists a countable collection of continuous functions $f_n : X \to [0, 1]$ having the property that given any point x_0 of X and any neighborhood U of x_0, there exists an index n such that f_n is positive at x_0 and vanishes outside U.*

It is a consequence of the Urysohn lemma that, given x_0 and U, there exists such a function. However, if we choose one such function for each pair (x_0, U), the resulting collection will not in general be countable. Our task is to cut the collection down to size. Here is one way to proceed:

Let $\{B_n\}$ be a countable basis for X. For each pair n, m of indices for which $\bar{B}_n \subset B_m$, apply the Urysohn lemma to choose a continuous function $g_{n,m} : X \to [0, 1]$ such that $g_{n,m}(\bar{B}_n) = \{1\}$ and $g_{n,m}(X - B_m) = \{0\}$. Then the collection $\{g_{n,m}\}$ satisfies our requirement: Given x_0 and given a neighborhood U of x_0, one can choose a basis element B_m containing x_0 that is contained in U. Using regularity, one can then choose B_n so that $x_0 \in B_n$ and $\bar{B}_n \subset B_m$. Then n, m is a pair of indices for which the function $g_{n,m}$ is defined; and it is positive at x_0 and vanishes outside U. Because the collection $\{g_{n,m}\}$ is indexed with a subset of $\mathbb{Z}_+ \times \mathbb{Z}_+$, it is countable; therefore it can be reindexed with the positive integers, giving us the desired collection $\{f_n\}$.

Step 2 (First version of the proof). Given the functions f_n of Step 1, take $\mathbb{R}^\omega$ in the product topology and define a map $F : X \to \mathbb{R}^\omega$ by the rule

$$F(x) = (f_1(x), f_2(x), \ldots).$$

We assert that F is an imbedding.

First, F is continuous because $\mathbb{R}^\omega$ has the product topology and each f_n is continuous. Second, F is injective because given $x \neq y$, we know there is an index n such that $f_n(x) > 0$ and $f_n(y) = 0$; therefore, $F(x) \neq F(y)$.

Finally, we must prove that F is a homeomorphism of X onto its image, the subspace $Z = F(X)$ of $\mathbb{R}^\omega$. We know that F defines a continuous bijection of X with Z, so we need only show that for each open set U in X, the set $F(U)$ is open in Z. Let z_0 be a point of $F(U)$. We shall find an open set W of Z such that

$$z_0 \in W \subset F(U).$$

Let x_0 be the point of U such that $F(x_0) = z_0$. Choose an index N for which $f_N(x_0) > 0$ and $f_N(X - U) = \{0\}$. Take the open ray $(0, +\infty)$ in $\mathbb{R}$, and let V be the open set

$$V = \pi_N^{-1}((0, +\infty))$$

of $\mathbb{R}^\omega$. Let $W = V \cap Z$; then W is open in Z, by definition of the subspace topology. See Figure 34.1. We assert that $z_0 \in W \subset F(U)$. First, $z_0 \in W$ because

$$\pi_N(z_0) = \pi_N(F(x_0)) = f_N(x_0) > 0.$$

Second, $W \subset F(U)$. For if $z \in W$, then $z = F(x)$ for some $x \in X$, and $\pi_N(z) \in (0, +\infty)$. Since $\pi_N(z) = \pi_N(F(x)) = f_N(x)$, and f_N vanishes outside U, the point x must be in U. Then $z = F(x)$ is in $F(U)$, as desired.

Thus F is an imbedding of X in $\mathbb{R}^\omega$.

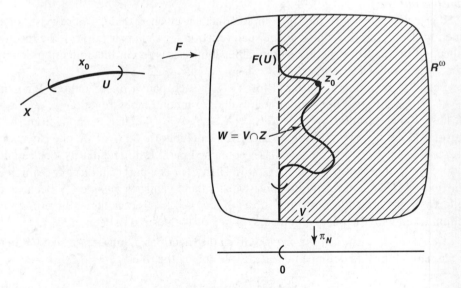

Figure 34.1

Step 3 (Second version of the proof). In this version, we imbed X in the metric space $(\mathbb{R}^\omega, \bar{\rho})$. Actually, we imbed X in the subspace $[0, 1]^\omega$, on which $\bar{\rho}$ equals the metric

$$\rho(\mathbf{x}, \mathbf{y}) = \sup\{|x_i - y_i|\}.$$

We use the countable collection of functions $f_n : X \to [0, 1]$ constructed in Step 1. But now we impose the additional condition that $f_n(x) \leq 1/n$ for all x. (This condition is easy to satisfy; we can just divide each function f_n by n.)

Define $F : X \to [0, 1]^\omega$ by the equation

$$F(x) = (f_1(x), f_2(x), \ldots)$$

as before. We assert that F is now an imbedding relative to the metric ρ on $[0, 1]^\omega$. We know from Step 2 that F is injective. Furthermore, we know that if we use the *product* topology on $[0, 1]^\omega$, the map F carries open sets of X onto open sets of the subspace $Z = F(X)$. This statement remains true if one passes to the finer (larger) topology on $[0, 1]^\omega$ induced by the metric ρ.

The one thing left to do is to prove that F is continuous. This does not follow from the fact that each component function is continuous, for we are not using the product topology on $\mathbb{R}^\omega$ now. Here is where the assumption $f_n(x) \leq 1/n$ comes in.

Let x_0 be a point of X, and let $\epsilon > 0$. To prove continuity, we need to find a neighborhood U of x_0 such that

$$x \in U \implies \rho(F(x), F(x_0)) < \epsilon.$$

First choose N large enough that $1/N \leq \epsilon/2$. Then for each $n = 1, \ldots, N$ use the continuity of f_n to choose a neighborhood U_n of x_0 such that

$$|f_n(x) - f_n(x_0)| \leq \epsilon/2$$

for $x \in U_n$. Let $U = U_1 \cap \cdots \cap U_N$; we show that U is the desired neighborhood of x_0. Let $x \in U$. If $n \leq N$,

$$|f_n(x) - f_n(x_0)| \leq \epsilon/2$$

by choice of U. And if $n > N$, then

$$|f_n(x) - f_n(x_0)| < 1/N \leq \epsilon/2$$

because f_n maps X into $[0, 1/n]$. Therefore for all $x \in U$,

$$\rho(F(x), F(x_0)) \leq \epsilon/2 < \epsilon,$$

as desired.   ■

In Step 2 of the preceding proof, we actually proved something stronger than the result stated there. For later use, we state it here:

Theorem 34.2 (Imbedding theorem). *Let X be a space in which one-point sets are closed. Suppose that $\{f_\alpha\}_{\alpha \in J}$ is an indexed family of continuous functions $f_\alpha : X \to \mathbb{R}$ satisfying the requirement that for each point x_0 of X and each neighborhood U of x_0, there is an index α such that f_α is positive at x_0 and vanishes outside U. Then the function $F : X \to \mathbb{R}^J$ defined by*

$$F(x) = (f_\alpha(x))_{\alpha \in J}$$

is an imbedding of X in $\mathbb{R}^J$. If f_α maps X into $[0, 1]$ for each α, then F imbeds X in $[0, 1]^J$.

The proof is almost a copy of Step 2 of the preceding proof; one merely replaces n by α, and $\mathbb{R}^\omega$ by $\mathbb{R}^J$, throughout. One needs one-point sets in X to be closed in order to be sure that, given $x \neq y$, there is an index α such that $f_\alpha(x) \neq f_\alpha(y)$.

A family of continuous functions that satisfies the hypotheses of this theorem is said to *separate points from closed sets* in X. The existence of such a family is readily seen to be equivalent, for a space X in which one-point sets are closed, to the requirement that X be completely regular. Therefore one has the following immediate corollary:

Theorem 34.3. *A space X is completely regular if and only if it is homeomorphic to a subspace of $[0, 1]^J$ for some J.*

Exercises

1. Give an example showing that a Hausdorff space with a countable basis need not be metrizable.

2. Give an example showing that a space can be completely normal, and satisfy the first countability axiom, the Lindelöf condition, and have a countable dense subset, and still not be metrizable.

3. Let X be a compact Hausdorff space. Show that X is metrizable if and only if X has a countable basis.

4. Let X be a locally compact Hausdorff space. Is it true that if X has a countable basis, then X is metrizable? Is it true that if X is metrizable, then X has a countable basis?

5. Let X be a locally compact Hausdorff space. Let Y be the one-point compactification of X. Is it true that if X has a countable basis, then Y is metrizable? Is it true that if Y is metrizable, then X has a countable basis?

6. Check the details of the proof of Theorem 34.2.

7. A space X is **locally metrizable** if each point x of X has a neighborhood that is metrizable in the subspace topology. Show that a compact Hausdorff space X is metrizable if it is locally metrizable. [*Hint:* Show that X is a finite union of open subspaces, each of which has a countable basis.]

8. Show that a regular Lindelöf space is metrizable if it is locally metrizable. [*Hint:* A closed subspace of a Lindelöf space is Lindelöf.] Regularity is essential; where do you use it in the proof?

9. Let X be a compact Hausdorff space that is the union of the closed subspaces X_1 and X_2. If X_1 and X_2 are metrizable, show that X is metrizable. [*Hint:* Construct a countable collection $\mathcal{A}$ of open sets of X whose intersections with X_i form a basis for X_i, for $i = 1, 2$. Assume $X_1 - X_2$ and $X_2 - X_1$ belong to $\mathcal{A}$. Let $\mathcal{B}$ consist of finite intersections of elements of $\mathcal{A}$.]

*§35   The Tietze Extension Theorem[†]

One immediate consequence of the Urysohn lemma is the useful theorem called the Tietze extension theorem. It deals with the problem of extending a continuous real-valued function that is defined on a subspace of a space X to a continuous function defined on all of X. This theorem is important in many of the applications of topology.

Theorem 35.1 (Tietze extension theorem). *Let X be a normal space; let A be a closed subspace of X.*

(a) Any continuous map of A into the closed interval $[a, b]$ of $\mathbb{R}$ may be extended to a continuous map of all of X into $[a, b]$.

(b) Any continuous map of A into $\mathbb{R}$ may be extended to a continuous map of all of X into $\mathbb{R}$.

Proof.   The idea of the proof is to construct a sequence of continuous functions s_n defined on the entire space X, such that the sequence s_n converges uniformly, and such that the restriction of s_n to A approximates f more and more closely as n becomes large. Then the limit function will be continuous, and its restriction to A will equal f.

Step 1. The first step is to construct a particular function g defined on all of X such that g is not too large, and such that g approximates f on the set A to a fair degree of accuracy. To be more precise, let us take the case $f : A \to [-r, r]$. We assert that there exists a continuous function $g : X \to \mathbb{R}$ such that

$$|g(x)| \le \tfrac{1}{3}r \qquad \text{for all } x \in X,$$
$$|g(a) - f(a)| \le \tfrac{2}{3}r \qquad \text{for all } a \in A.$$

The function g is constructed as follows:

Divide the interval $[r, r]$ into three equal intervals of length $\tfrac{2}{3}r$:

$$I_1 = \left[-r, -\tfrac{1}{3}r\right], \qquad I_2 = \left[-\tfrac{1}{3}r, \tfrac{1}{3}r\right], \qquad I_3 = \left[\tfrac{1}{3}r, r\right].$$

Let B and C be the subsets

$$B = f^{-1}(I_1) \quad \text{and} \quad C = f^{-1}(I_3)$$

of A. Because f is continuous, B and C are closed disjoint subsets of A. Therefore, they are closed in X. By the Urysohn lemma, there exists a continuous function

$$g : X \longrightarrow \left[-\tfrac{1}{3}r, \tfrac{1}{3}r\right]$$

having the property that $g(x) = -\tfrac{1}{3}r$ for each x in B, and $g(x) = \tfrac{1}{3}r$ for each x in C.

Then $|g(x)| \le \tfrac{1}{3}r$ for all x. We assert that for each a in A,

$$|g(a) - f(a)| \le \tfrac{2}{3}r.$$

[†]This section will be assumed in §62. It is also used in a number of exercises.

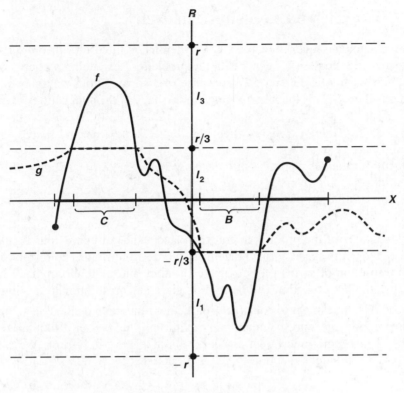

Figure 35.1

There are three cases. If $a \in B$, then both $f(a)$ and $g(a)$ belong to I_1. If $a \in C$, then $f(a)$ and $g(a)$ are in I_3. And if $a \notin B \cup C$, then $f(a)$ and $g(a)$ are in I_2. In each case, $|g(a) - f(a)| \leq \frac{2}{3}r$. See Figure 35.1.

Step 2. We now prove part (a) of the Tietze theorem. Without loss of generality, we can replace the arbitrary closed interval $[a, b]$ of $\mathbb{R}$ by the interval $[-1, 1]$.

Let $f : X \to [-1, 1]$ be a continuous map. Then f satisfies the hypotheses of Step 1, with $r = 1$. Therefore, there exists a continuous real-valued function g_1, defined on all of X, such that

$$|g_1(x)| \leq 1/3 \quad \text{for } x \in X,$$
$$|f(a) - g_1(a)| \leq 2/3 \quad \text{for } a \in A.$$

Now consider the function $f - g_1$. This function maps A into the interval $[-2/3, 2/3]$, so we can apply Step 1 again, letting $r = 2/3$. We obtain a real-valued function g_2

defined on all of X such that

$$|g_2(x)| \le \frac{1}{3}\left(\frac{2}{3}\right) \qquad \text{for } x \in X,$$

$$|f(a) - g_1(a) - g_2(a)| \le \left(\frac{2}{3}\right)^2 \qquad \text{for } a \in A.$$

Then we apply Step 1 to the function $f - g_1 - g_2$. And so on.

At the general step, we have real-valued functions $g_1, \ldots, g_n$ defined on all of X such that

$$|f(a) - g_1(a) - \cdots - g_n(a)| \le \left(\frac{2}{3}\right)^n$$

for $a \in A$. Applying Step 1 to the function $f - g_1 - \cdots - g_n$, with $r = \left(\frac{2}{3}\right)^n$, we obtain a real-valued function g_{n+1} defined on all of X such that

$$|g_{n+1}(x)| \le \frac{1}{3}\left(\frac{2}{3}\right)^n \qquad \text{for } x \in X,$$

$$|f(a) - g_1(a) - \cdots - g_{n+1}(a)| \le \left(\frac{2}{3}\right)^{n+1} \qquad \text{for } a \in A.$$

By induction, the functions g_n are defined for all n.

We now define

$$g(x) = \sum_{n=1}^{\infty} g_n(x)$$

for all x in X. Of course, we have to know that this infinite series converges. But that follows from the comparison theorem of calculus; it converges by comparison with the geometric series

$$\frac{1}{3}\sum_{n=1}^{\infty}\left(\frac{2}{3}\right)^{n-1}.$$

To show that g is continuous, we must show that the sequence s_n converges to g uniformly. This fact follows at once from the "Weierstrass M-test" of analysis. Without assuming this result, one can simply note that if $k > n$, then

$$|s_k(x) - s_n(x)| = \left|\sum_{i=n+1}^{k} g_i(x)\right|$$

$$\le \frac{1}{3}\sum_{i=n+1}^{k}\left(\frac{2}{3}\right)^{i-1}$$

$$< \frac{1}{3}\sum_{i=n+1}^{\infty}\left(\frac{2}{3}\right)^{i-1} = \left(\frac{2}{3}\right)^n.$$

Holding n fixed and letting $k \to \infty$, we see that

$$|g(x) - s_n(x)| \leq \left(\frac{2}{3}\right)^n$$

for all $x \in X$. Therefore, s_n converges to g uniformly.

We show that $g(a) = f(a)$ for $a \in A$. Let $s_n(x) = \sum_{i=1}^{n} g_i(x)$, the nth partial sum of the series. Then $g(x)$ is by definition the limit of the infinite sequence $s_n(x)$ of partial sums. Since

$$|f(a) - \sum_{i=1}^{n} g_i(a)| = |f(a) - s_n(a)| \leq \left(\frac{2}{3}\right)^n$$

for all a in A, it follows that $s_n(a) \to f(a)$ for all $a \in A$. Therefore, we have $f(a) = g(a)$ for $a \in A$.

Finally, we show that g maps X into the interval $[-1, 1]$. This condition is in fact satisfied automatically, since the series $(1/3) \sum (2/3)^n$ converges to 1. However, this is just a lucky accident rather than an essential part of the proof. If all we knew was that g mapped X into $\mathbb{R}$, then the map $r \circ g$, where $r : \mathbb{R} \to [-1, 1]$ is the map

$$r(y) = y \qquad \text{if } |y| \leq 1,$$
$$r(y) = y/|y| \quad \text{if } |y| \geq 1,$$

would be an extension of f mapping X into $[-1, 1]$.

Step 3. We now prove part (b) of the theorem, in which f maps A into $\mathbb{R}$. We can replace $\mathbb{R}$ by the open interval $(-1, 1)$, since this interval is homeomorphic to $\mathbb{R}$.

So let f be a continuous map from A into $(-1, 1)$. The half of the Tietze theorem already proved shows that we can extend f to a continuous map $g : X \to [-1, 1]$ mapping X into the *closed* interval. How can we find a map h carrying X into the *open* interval?

Given g, let us define a subset D of X by the equation

$$D = g^{-1}(\{-1\}) \cup g^{-1}(\{1\}).$$

Since g is continuous, D is a closed subset of X. Because $g(A) = f(A)$, which is contained in $(-1, 1)$, the set A is disjoint from D. By the Urysohn lemma, there is a continuous function $\phi : X \to [0, 1]$ such that $\phi(D) = \{0\}$ and $\phi(A) = \{1\}$. Define

$$h(x) = \phi(x)g(x).$$

Then h is continuous, being the product of two continuous functions. Also, h is an extension of f, since for a in A,

$$h(a) = \phi(a)g(a) = 1 \cdot g(a) = f(a).$$

Finally, h maps all of X into the open interval $(-1, 1)$. For if $x \in D$, then $h(x) = 0 \cdot g(x) = 0$. And if $x \notin D$, then $|g(x)| < 1$; it follows that $|h(x)| \leq 1 \cdot |g(x)| < 1$. ∎

Exercises

1. Show that the Tietze extension theorem implies the Urysohn lemma.

2. In the proof of the Tietze theorem, how essential was the clever decision in Step 1 to divide the interval $[-r, r]$ into three equal pieces? Suppose instead that one divides this interval into the three intervals

$$I_1 = [-r, -ar], \qquad I_2 = [-ar, ar], \qquad I_3 = [ar, r],$$

for some a with $0 < a < 1$. For what values of a other than $a = 1/3$ (if any) does the proof go through?

3. Let X be metrizable. Show that the following are equivalent:
    (i) X is bounded under every metric that gives the topology of X.
    (ii) Every continuous function $\phi : X \to \mathbb{R}$ is bounded.
    (iii) X is limit point compact.
    [*Hint:* If $\phi : X \to \mathbb{R}$ is a continuous function, then $F(x) = x \times \phi(x)$ is an imbedding of X in $X \times \mathbb{R}$. If A is an infinite subset of X having no limit point, let ϕ be a surjection of A onto $\mathbb{Z}_+$.]

4. Let Z be a topological space. If Y is a subspace of Z, we say that Y is a **retract** of Z if there is a continuous map $r : Z \to Y$ such that $r(y) = y$ for each $y \in Y$.
    (a) Show that if Z is Hausdorff and Y is a retract of Z, then Y is closed in Z.
    (b) Let A be a two-point set in $\mathbb{R}^2$. Show that A is not a retract of $\mathbb{R}^2$.
    (c) Let S^1 be the unit circle in $\mathbb{R}^2$; show that S^1 is a retract of $\mathbb{R}^2 - \{\mathbf{0}\}$, where $\mathbf{0}$ is the origin. Can you conjecture whether or not S^1 is a retract of $\mathbb{R}^2$?

5. A space Y is said to have the **universal extension property** if for each triple consisting of a normal space X, a closed subset A of X, and a continuous function $f : A \to Y$, there exists an extension of f to a continuous map of X into Y.
    (a) Show that $\mathbb{R}^J$ has the universal extension property.
    (b) Show that if Y is homeomorphic to a retract of $\mathbb{R}^J$, then Y has the universal extension property.

6. Let Y be a normal space. Then Y is said to be an **absolute retract** if for every pair of spaces (Y_0, Z) such that Z is normal and Y_0 is a closed subspace of Z homeomorphic to Y, the space Y_0 is a retract of Z.
    (a) Show that if Y has the universal extension property, then Y is an absolute retract.
    (b) Show that if Y is an absolute retract and Y is compact, then Y has the universal extension property. [*Hint:* Assume the Tychonoff theorem, so you know $[0, 1]^J$ is normal. Imbed Y in $[0, 1]^J$.]

7. (a) Show the logarithmic spiral

$$C = \{0 \times 0\} \cup \{e^t \cos t \times e^t \sin t \mid t \in \mathbb{R}\}$$

is a retract of $\mathbb{R}^2$. Can you define a specific retraction $r : \mathbb{R}^2 \to C$?

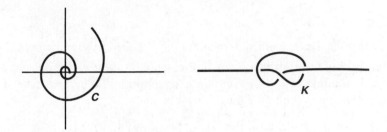

Figure 35.2

(b) Show that the "knotted x-axis" K of Figure 35.2 is a retract of $\mathbb{R}^3$.

*8. Prove the following:
  Theorem. *Let Y be a normal space. Then Y is an absolute retract if and only if Y has the universal extension property.*
  [*Hint:* If X and Y are disjoint normal spaces, A is closed in X, and $f : A \to Y$ is a continuous map, define the ***adjunction space*** Z_f to be the quotient space obtained from $X \cup Y$ by identifying each point a of A with the point $f(a)$ and with all the points of $f^{-1}(\{f(a)\})$. Using the Tietze theorem, show that Z_f is normal. If $p : X \cup Y \to Z_f$ is the quotient map, show that $p|Y$ is a homeomorphism of Y with a closed subspace of Z_f.]

9. Let $X_1 \subset X_2 \subset \cdots$ be a sequence of spaces, where X_i is a closed subspace of X_{i+1} for each i. Let X be the union of the X_i; let us topologize X by declaring a set U to be open in X if $U \cap X_i$ is open in X for each i.
  (a) Show that this is a topology on X and that each space X_i is a subspace (in fact, a closed subspace) of X in this topology. This topology is called the topology ***coherent*** with the subspaces X_i.
  (b) Show that $f : X \to Y$ is continuous if $f|X_i$ is continuous for each i.
  (c) Show that if each space X_i is normal, then X is normal. [*Hint:* Given disjoint closed sets A and B in X, set f equal to 0 on A and 1 on B, and extend f successively to $A \cup B \cup X_i$ for $i = 1, 2, \ldots$.]

*§36 Imbeddings of Manifolds[†]

We have shown that every regular space with a countable basis can be imbedded in the "infinite-dimensional" euclidean space $\mathbb{R}^\omega$. It is natural to ask under what conditions a space X can be imbedded in some finite-dimensional euclidean space $\mathbb{R}^N$. One answer to this question is given in this section. A more general answer will be obtained in Chapter 8, when we study dimension theory.

[†]This section will be assumed when we study paracompactness in §41 and when we study dimension theory in §50.

Definition. An *m-manifold* is a Hausdorff space X with a countable basis such that each point x of X has a neighborhood that is homeomorphic with an open subset of $\mathbb{R}^m$.

A 1-manifold is often called a *curve*, and a 2-manifold is called a *surface*. Manifolds form a very important class of spaces; they are much studied in differential geometry and algebraic topology.

We shall prove that if X is a compact manifold, then X can be imbedded in a finite-dimensional euclidean space. The theorem holds without the assumption of compactness, but the proof is a good deal harder.

First, we need some terminology.

If $\phi : X \to \mathbb{R}$, then the *support* of ϕ is defined to be the closure of the set $\phi^{-1}(\mathbb{R} - \{0\})$. Thus if x lies outside the support of ϕ, there is some neighborhood of x on which ϕ vanishes.

Definition. Let $\{U_1, \ldots, U_n\}$ be a finite indexed open covering of the space X. An indexed family of continuous functions

$$\phi_i : X \longrightarrow [0, 1] \quad \text{for } i = 1, \ldots, n,$$

is said to be a *partition of unity* dominated by $\{U_i\}$ if:

(1) (support ϕ_i) $\subset U_i$ for each i.
(2) $\sum_{i=1}^{n} \phi_i(x) = 1$ for each x.

Theorem 36.1 (Existence of finite partitions of unity). *Let $\{U_1, \ldots, U_n\}$ be a finite open covering of the normal space X. Then there exists a partition of unity dominated by $\{U_i\}$.*

Proof. Step 1. First, we prove that one can "shrink" the covering $\{U_i\}$ to an open covering $\{V_1, \ldots, V_n\}$ of X such that $\bar{V}_i \subset U_i$ for each i.

We proceed by induction. First, note that the set

$$A = X - (U_2 \cup \cdots \cup U_n)$$

is a closed subset of X. Because $\{U_1, \ldots, U_n\}$ covers X, the set A is contained in the open set U_1. Using normality, choose an open set V_1 containing A such that $\bar{V}_1 \subset U_1$. Then the collection $\{V_1, U_2, \ldots, U_n\}$ covers X.

In general, given open sets $V_1, \ldots, V_{k-1}$ such that the collection

$$\{V_1, \ldots, V_{k-1}, U_k, U_{k+1}, \ldots, U_n\}$$

covers X, let

$$A = X - (V_1 \cup \cdots \cup V_{k-1}) - (U_{k+1} \cup \cdots \cup U_n).$$

Then A is a closed subset of X which is contained in the open set U_k. Choose V_k to be an open set containing A such that $\bar{V}_k \subset U_k$. Then $\{V_1, \ldots, V_{k-1}, V_k, U_{k+1}, \ldots, U_n\}$ covers X. At the nth step of the induction, our result is proved.

Step 2. Now we prove the theorem. Given the open covering $\{U_1, \ldots, U_n\}$ of X, choose an open covering $\{V_1, \ldots, V_n\}$ of X such that $\bar{V}_i \subset U_i$ for each i. Then choose an open covering $\{W_1, \ldots, W_n\}$ of X such that $\overline{W}_i \subset V_i$ for each i. Using the Urysohn lemma, choose for each i a continuous function

$$\psi_i : X \longrightarrow [0, 1]$$

such that $\psi_i(\overline{W}_i) = \{1\}$ and $\psi_i(X - V_i) = \{0\}$. Since $\psi_i^{-1}(R - \{0\})$ is contained in V_i, we have

$$(\text{support } \psi_i) \subset \bar{V}_i \subset U_i.$$

Because the collection $\{W_i\}$ covers X, the sum $\Psi(x) = \sum_{i=1}^n \psi_i(x)$ is positive for each x. Therefore, we may define, for each j,

$$\phi_j(x) = \frac{\psi_j(x)}{\Psi(x)}.$$

It is easy to check that the functions $\phi_1, \ldots, \phi_n$ form the desired partition of unity. ∎

There is a comparable notion of *partition of unity* when the open covering and the collection of functions are not finite, nor even countable. We shall consider this matter in Chapter 6, when we study paracompactness.

Theorem 36.2.   *If X is a compact m-manifold, then X can be imbedded in $\mathbb{R}^N$ for some positive integer N.*

Proof.   Cover X by finitely many open sets $\{U_1, \ldots, U_n\}$, each of which may be imbedded in $\mathbb{R}^m$. Choose imbeddings $g_i : U_i \to \mathbb{R}^m$ for each i. Being compact and Hausdorff, X is normal. Let $\phi_1, \ldots, \phi_n$ be a partition of unity dominated by $\{U_i\}$; let $A_i = \text{support } \phi_i$. For each $i = 1, \ldots, n$, define a function $h_i : X \to \mathbb{R}^m$ by the rule

$$h_i(x) = \begin{cases} \phi_i(x) \cdot g_i(x) & \text{for } x \in U_i, \\ \mathbf{0} = (0, \ldots, 0) & \text{for } x \in X - A_i. \end{cases}$$

[Here $\phi_i(x)$ is a real number c and $g_i(x)$ is a point $\mathbf{y} = (y_1, \ldots, y_m)$ of $\mathbb{R}^m$; the product $c \cdot \mathbf{y}$ denotes of course the point $(cy_1, \ldots, cy_m)$ of $\mathbb{R}^m$.] The function h_i is well defined because the two definitions of h_i agree on the intersection of their domains, and h_i is continuous because its restrictions to the open sets U_i and $X - A_i$ are continuous.

Now define

$$F : X \longrightarrow (\underbrace{\mathbb{R} \times \cdots \times \mathbb{R}}_{n \text{ times}} \times \underbrace{\mathbb{R}^m \times \cdots \times \mathbb{R}^m}_{n \text{ times}})$$

by the rule

$$F(x) = (\phi_1(x), \ldots, \phi_n(x), h_1(x), \ldots, h_n(x)).$$

Clearly, F is continuous. To prove that F is an imbedding we need only to show that F is injective (because X is compact). Suppose that $F(x) = F(y)$. Then $\phi_i(x) = \phi_i(y)$ and $h_i(x) = h_i(y)$ for all i. Now $\phi_i(x) > 0$ for some i [since $\sum \phi_i(x) = 1$]. Therefore, $\phi_i(y) > 0$ also, so that $x, y \in U_i$. Then

$$\phi_i(x) \cdot g_i(x) = h_i(x) = h_i(y) = \phi_i(y) \cdot g_i(y).$$

Because $\phi_i(x) = \phi_i(y) > 0$, we conclude that $g_i(x) = g_i(y)$. But $g_i : U_i \to \mathbb{R}^m$ is injective, so that $x = y$, as desired.   ∎

In many applications of partitions of unity, such as the one just given, all one needs to know is that the sum $\sum \phi_i(x)$ is positive for each x. In others, however, one needs the stronger condition that that $\sum \phi_i(x) = 1$. See §50.

Exercises

1. Prove that every manifold is regular and hence metrizable. Where do you use the Hausdorff condition?

2. Let X be a compact Hausdorff space. Suppose that for each $x \in X$, there is a neighborhood U of x and a positive integer k such that U can be imbedded in $\mathbb{R}^k$. Show that X can be imbedded in $\mathbb{R}^N$ for some positive integer N.

3. Let X be a Hausdorff space such that each point of X has a neighborhood that is homeomorphic with an open subset of $\mathbb{R}^m$. Show that if X is compact, then X is an m-manifold.

4. An indexed family $\{A_\alpha\}$ of subsets of X is said to be a *point-finite indexed family* if each $x \in X$ belongs to A_α for only finitely many values of α.
   Lemma (The shrinking lemma). Let X be a normal space; let $\{U_1, U_2, \ldots\}$ be a point-finite indexed open covering of X. Then there exists an indexed open covering $\{V_1, V_2, \ldots\}$ of X such that $\bar{V}_n \subset U_n$ for each n.

5. The Hausdorff condition is an essential part of the definition of a manifold; it is not implied by the other parts of the definition. Consider the following space: Let X be the union of the set $\mathbb{R} - \{0\}$ and the two-point set $\{p, q\}$. Topologize X by taking as basis the collection of all open intervals in $\mathbb{R}$ that do not contain 0, along with all sets of the form $(-a, 0) \cup \{p\} \cup (0, a)$ and all sets of the form $(-a, 0) \cup \{q\} \cup (0, a)$, for $a > 0$. The space X is called the *line with two origins*.
   (a) Check that this is a basis for a topology.
   (b) Show that each of the spaces $X - \{p\}$ and $X - \{q\}$ is homeomorphic to $\mathbb{R}$.
   (c) Show that X satisfies the T_1 axiom, but is not Hausdorff.
   (d) Show that X satisfies all the conditions for a 1-manifold except for the Hausdorff condition.

*Supplementary Exercises: Review of the Basics

Consider the following properties a space may satisfy:

(1) connected
(2) path connected
(3) locally connected
(4) locally path connected
(5) compact
(6) limit point compact
(7) locally compact Hausdorff
(8) Hausdorff
(9) regular
(10) completely regular
(11) normal
(12) first-countable
(13) second-countable
(14) Lindelöf
(15) has a countable dense subset
(16) locally metrizable
(17) metrizable

1. For each of the following spaces, determine (if you can) which of these properties it satisfies. (Assume the Tychonoff theorem if you need it.)
   (a) S_Ω
   (b) $\bar{S}_\Omega$
   (c) $S_\Omega \times \bar{S}_\Omega$
   (d) The ordered square
   (e) $\mathbb{R}_\ell$
   (f) $\mathbb{R}_\ell^2$
   (g) $\mathbb{R}^\omega$ in the product topology
   (h) $\mathbb{R}^\omega$ in the uniform topology
   (i) $\mathbb{R}^\omega$ in the box topology
   (j) $\mathbb{R}^I$ in the product topology, where $I = [0, 1]$
   (k) $\mathbb{R}_K$

2. Which of these properties does a metric space necessarily have?

3. Which of these properties does a compact Hausdorff space have?

4. Which of these properties are preserved when one passes to a subspace? To a closed subspace? To an open subspace?

5. Which of these properties are preserved under finite products? Countable products? Arbitrary products?

6. Which of these properties are preserved by continuous maps?

7. After studying Chapters 6 and 7, repeat Exercises 1–6 for the following properties:

(18) paracompact

(19) topologically complete

   You should be able to answer all but one of the 340 questions involved in Exercises 1–6, and all but one of the 40 questions involved in Exercise 7. These two are unsolved; see the remark in Exercise 5 of §32.

Chapter 5

The Tychonoff Theorem

We now return to a problem we left unresolved in Chapter 3. We shall prove the Tychonoff theorem, to the effect that arbitrary products of compact spaces are compact. The proof makes use of Zorn's Lemma (see §11). An alternate proof, which relies instead on the well-ordering theorem, is outlined in the exercises.

The Tychonoff theorem is of great usefulness to analysts (less so to geometers). We apply it in §38 to construct the Stone-Čech compactification of a completely regular space, and in §47 in proving the general version of Ascoli's theorem.

§37 The Tychonoff Theorem

Like the Urysohn lemma, the Tychonoff theorem is what we call a "deep" theorem. Its proof involves not one but several original ideas; it is anything but straightforward. We shall discuss the crucial ideas of the proof in some detail before turning to the proof itself.

In Chapter 3, we proved the product $X \times Y$ of two compact spaces to be compact. For that proof the open covering formulation of compactness was quite satisfactory. Given an open covering of $X \times Y$ by basis elements, we covered each slice $x \times Y$ by finitely many of them, and proceeded from that to construct a finite covering of $X \times Y$.

It is quite tricky to make this approach work for an arbitrary product of compact spaces; one must well-order the index set and use transfinite induction. (See

Exercise 5.) An alternate approach is to abandon open coverings and to approach the problem by applying the closed set formulation of compactness, using Zorn's lemma.

To see how this idea might work, let us consider first the simplest possible case: the product of two compact spaces $X_1 \times X_2$. Suppose that $\mathcal{A}$ is a collection of closed subsets of $X_1 \times X_2$ that has the finite intersection property. Consider the projection map $\pi_1 : X_1 \times X_2 \to X_1$. The collection

$$\{\pi_1(A) \mid A \in \mathcal{A}\}$$

of subsets of X_1 also has the finite intersection property, and so does the collection of their closures $\overline{\pi_1(A)}$. Compactness of X_1 guarantees that the intersection of all the sets $\overline{\pi_1(A)}$ is nonempty. Let us choose a point x_1 belonging to this intersection. Similarly, let us choose a point x_2 belonging to all the sets $\overline{\pi_2(A)}$. The obvious conclusion we would like to draw is that the point $x_1 \times x_2$ lies in $\bigcap_{A \in \mathcal{A}} A$, for then our theorem would be proved.

But that is unfortunately not true. Consider the following example, in which $X_1 = X_2 = [0, 1]$ and the collection $\mathcal{A}$ consists of all closed elliptical regions bounded by ellipses that have the points $p = (\frac{1}{3}, \frac{1}{3})$ and $q = (\frac{1}{2}, \frac{2}{3})$ as their foci. See Figure 37.1. Certainly $\mathcal{A}$ has the finite intersection property. Now let us pick a point x_1 in the intersection of the sets $\{\overline{\pi_1(A)} \mid A \in \mathcal{A}\}$. Any point of the interval $[\frac{1}{3}, \frac{1}{2}]$ will do; suppose we choose $x_1 = \frac{1}{2}$. Similarly, choose a point x_2 in the intersection of the sets $\{\overline{\pi_2(A)} \mid A \in \mathcal{A}\}$. Any point of the interval $[\frac{1}{3}, \frac{2}{3}]$ will do; suppose we pick $x_2 = \frac{1}{2}$. This proves to be an unfortunate choice, for the point

$$x_1 \times x_2 = \tfrac{1}{2} \times \tfrac{1}{2}$$

does not lie in the intersection of the sets A.

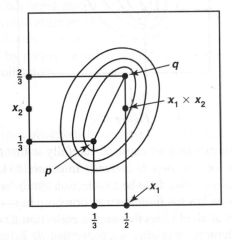

Figure 37.1

"Aha!" you say, "you made a bad choice. If after choosing $x_1 = \frac{1}{2}$ you had chosen $x_2 = \frac{2}{3}$, *then* you would have found a point in $\bigcap_{A \in \mathcal{A}} A$." The difficulty with our

Lemma 37.2. *Let X be a set; let $\mathcal{D}$ be a collection of subsets of X that is maximal with respect to the finite intersection property. Then:*

(a) *Any finite intersection of elements of $\mathcal{D}$ is an element of $\mathcal{D}$.*

(b) *If A is a subset of X that intersects every element of $\mathcal{D}$, then A is an element of $\mathcal{D}$.*

Proof. (a) Let B equal the intersection of finitely many elements of $\mathcal{D}$. Define a collection $\mathcal{E}$ by adjoining B to $\mathcal{D}$, so that $\mathcal{E} = \mathcal{D} \cup \{B\}$. We show that $\mathcal{E}$ has the finite intersection property; then maximality of $\mathcal{D}$ implies that $\mathcal{E} = \mathcal{D}$, so that $B \in \mathcal{D}$ as desired.

Take finitely many elements of $\mathcal{E}$. If none of them is the set B, then their intersection is nonempty because $\mathcal{D}$ has the finite intersection property. If one of them is the set B, then their intersection is of the form

$$D_1 \cap \cdots \cap D_m \cap B.$$

Since B equals a finite intersection of elements of $\mathcal{D}$, this set is nonempty.

(b) Given A, define $\mathcal{E} = \mathcal{D} \cup \{A\}$. We show that $\mathcal{E}$ has the finite intersection property, from which we conclude that A belongs to $\mathcal{D}$. Take finitely many elements of $\mathcal{E}$. If none of them is the set A, their intersection is automatically nonempty. Otherwise, it is of the form

$$D_1 \cap \cdots \cap D_n \cap A.$$

Now $D_1 \cap \cdots \cap D_n$ belongs to $\mathcal{D}$, by (a); therefore, this intersection is nonempty, by hypothesis. ∎

Theorem 37.3 (Tychonoff theorem). *An arbitrary product of compact spaces is compact in the product topology.*

Proof. Let

$$X = \prod_{\alpha \in J} X_\alpha,$$

where each space X_α is compact. Let $\mathcal{A}$ be a collection of subsets of X having the finite intersection property. We prove that the intersection

$$\bigcap_{A \in \mathcal{A}} \bar{A}$$

is nonempty. Compactness of X follows.

Applying Lemma 37.1, choose a collection $\mathcal{D}$ of subsets of X such that $\mathcal{D} \supset \mathcal{A}$ and $\mathcal{D}$ is maximal with respect to the finite intersection property. It will suffice to show that the intersection $\bigcap_{D \in \mathcal{D}} \bar{D}$ is nonempty.

Given $\alpha \in J$, let $\pi_\alpha : X \to X_\alpha$ be the projection map, as usual. Consider the collection

$$\{\pi_\alpha(D) \mid D \in \mathcal{D}\}$$

of subsets of X_α. This collection has the finite intersection property because $\mathcal{D}$ does. By compactness of X_α, we can for each α choose a point x_α of X_α such that

$$x_\alpha \in \bigcap_{D \in \mathcal{D}} \overline{\pi_\alpha(D)}.$$

Let $\mathbf{x}$ be the point $(x_\alpha)_{\alpha \in J}$ of X. We shall show that $\mathbf{x} \in \bar{D}$ for every $D \in \mathcal{D}$; then our proof will be finished.

First we show that if $\pi_\beta^{-1}(U_\beta)$ is any subbasis element (for the product topology on X) containing $\mathbf{x}$, then $\pi_\beta^{-1}(U_\beta)$ intersects every element of $\mathcal{D}$. The set U_β is a neighborhood of x_β in X_β. Since $x_\beta \in \overline{\pi_\beta(D)}$ by definition, U_β intersects $\pi_\beta(D)$ in some point $\pi_\beta(\mathbf{y})$, where $\mathbf{y} \in D$. Then it follows that $\mathbf{y} \in \pi_\beta^{-1}(U_\beta) \cap D$.

It follows from (b) of Lemma 37.2 that every subbasis element containing $\mathbf{x}$ *belongs* to $\mathcal{D}$. And then it follows from (a) of the same lemma that every *basis* element containing $\mathbf{x}$ belongs to $\mathcal{D}$. Since $\mathcal{D}$ has the finite intersection property, this means that every basis element containing $\mathbf{x}$ intersects every element of $\mathcal{D}$; hence $\mathbf{x} \in \bar{D}$ for every $D \in \mathcal{D}$ as desired.   ∎

Exercises

1. Let X be a space. Let $\mathcal{D}$ be a collection of subsets of X that is maximal with respect to the finite intersection property.
   (a) Show that $x \in \bar{D}$ for every $D \in \mathcal{D}$ if and only if every neighborhood of x belongs to $\mathcal{D}$. Which implication uses maximality of $\mathcal{D}$?
   (b) Let $D \in \mathcal{D}$. Show that if $A \supset D$, then $A \in \mathcal{D}$.
   (c) Show that if X satisfies the T_1 axiom, there is at most one point belonging to $\bigcap_{D \in \mathcal{D}} \bar{D}$.

2. A collection $\mathcal{A}$ of subsets of X has the ***countable intersection property*** if every countable intersection of elements of $\mathcal{A}$ is nonempty. Show that X is a Lindelöf space if and only if for every collection $\mathcal{A}$ of subsets of X having the countable intersection property,

$$\bigcap_{A \in \mathcal{A}} \bar{A}$$

   is nonempty.

3. Consider the three statements:
      (i) If X is a set and $\mathcal{A}$ is a collection of subsets of X having the countable intersection property, then there is a collection $\mathcal{D}$ of subsets of X such that $\mathcal{D} \supset \mathcal{A}$ and $\mathcal{D}$ is maximal with respect to the countable intersection property.

We call Y the compactification ***induced*** by the imbedding h.

Proof. Given h, let X_0 denote the subspace $h(X)$ of Z, and let Y_0 denote its closure in Z. Then Y_0 is a compact Hausdorff space and $\bar{X}_0 = Y_0$; therefore, Y_0 is a compactification of X_0.

We now construct a space Y containing X such that the pair (X, Y) is homeomorphic to the pair (X_0, Y_0). Let us choose a set A disjoint from X that is in bijective correspondence with the set $Y_0 - X_0$ under some map $k : A \to Y_0 - X_0$. Define $Y = X \cup A$, and define a bijective correspondence $H : Y \to Y_0$ by the rule

$$H(x) = h(x) \quad \text{for } x \in X,$$
$$H(a) = k(a) \quad \text{for } a \in A.$$

Then topologize Y by declaring U to be open in Y if and only if $H(U)$ is open in Y_0. The map H is automatically a homeomorphism; and the space X is a subspace of Y because H equals the homeomorphism h when restricted to the subspace X of Y. By expanding the range of H, we obtain the required imbedding of Y into Z.

Now suppose Y_i is a compactification of X and that $H_i : Y_i \to Z$ is an imbedding that is an extension of h, for $i = 1, 2$. Now H_i maps X onto $h(X) = X_0$. Because H_i is continuous, it must map Y_i into $\bar{X}_0$; because $H_i(Y_i)$ contains X_0 and is closed (being compact), it contains $\bar{X}_0$. Hence $H_i(Y_i) = \bar{X}_0$, and $H_2^{-1} \circ H_1$ defines a homeomorphism of Y_1 with Y_2 that equals the identity on X. ∎

In general, there are many different ways of compactifying a given space X. Consider for instance the following compactifications of the open interval $X = (0, 1)$:

EXAMPLE 1.   Take the unit circle S^1 in $\mathbb{R}^2$ and let $h : (0, 1) \to S^1$ be the map

$$h(t) = (\cos 2\pi t) \times (\sin 2\pi t).$$

The compactification induced by the imbedding h is equivalent to the one-point compactification of X.

EXAMPLE 2.   Let Y be the space $[0, 1]$. Then Y is a compactification of X; it is obtained by "adding one point at each end of $(0, 1)$."

EXAMPLE 3.   Consider the square $[-1, 1]^2$ in $\mathbb{R}^2$ and let $h : (0, 1) \to [-1, 1]^2$ be the map

$$h(x) = x \times \sin(1/x).$$

The space $Y_0 = \overline{h(X)}$ is the topologist's sine curve (see Example 7 of §24). The imbedding h gives rise to a compactification of $(0, 1)$ quite different from the other two. It is obtained by adding one point at the right-hand end of $(0, 1)$, and an entire line segment of points at the left-hand end!

A basic problem that occurs in studying compactifications is the following:

> *If Y is a compactification of X, under what conditions can a continuous real-valued function f defined on X be extended continuously to Y?*

The function f will have to be bounded if it is to be extendable, since its extension will carry the compact space Y into $\mathbb{R}$ and will thus be bounded. But boundedness is not enough, in general. Consider the following example:

EXAMPLE 4.   Let $X = (0, 1)$. Consider the one-point compactification of X given in Example 1. A bounded continuous function $f : (0, 1) \to \mathbb{R}$ is extendable to this compactification if and only if the limits

$$\lim_{x \to 0+} f(x) \quad \text{and} \quad \lim_{x \to 1-} f(x)$$

exist and are equal.

For the "the two-point compactification" of X considered in Example 2, the function f is extendable if and only if both these limits simply exist.

For the compactification of Example 3, extensions exist for a still broader class of functions. It is easy to see that f is extendable if both the above limits exist. But the function $f(x) = \sin(1/x)$ is also extendable to this compactification: Let H be the imbedding of Y in $\mathbb{R}^2$ that equals h on the subspace X. Then the composite map

$$Y \xrightarrow{\ H\ } \mathbb{R} \times \mathbb{R} \xrightarrow{\ \pi_2\ } \mathbb{R}$$

is the desired extension of f. For if $x \in X$, then $H(x) = h(x) = x \times \sin(1/x)$, so that $\pi_2(H(x)) = \sin(1/x)$, as desired.

There is something especially interesting about this last compactification. We constructed it by choosing an imbedding

$$h : (0, 1) \longrightarrow \mathbb{R}^2$$

whose component functions were the functions x and $\sin(1/x)$. Then we found that both the functions x and $\sin(1/x)$ could be extended to the compactification. This suggests that if we have a whole *collection* of bounded continuous functions defined on $(0, 1)$, we might use them as component functions of an imbedding of $(0, 1)$ into $\mathbb{R}^J$ for some J, and thereby obtain a compactification for which every function in the collection is extendable.

This idea is the basic idea behind the Stone-Čech compactification. It is defined as follows:

Theorem 38.2. *Let X be a completely regular space. There exists a compactification Y of X having the property that every bounded continuous map $f : X \to \mathbb{R}$ extends uniquely to a continuous map of Y into $\mathbb{R}$.*

Proof.   Let $\{f_\alpha\}_{\alpha \in J}$ be the collection of *all* bounded continuous real-valued functions on X, indexed by some index set J. For each $\alpha \in J$, choose a closed interval I_α in $\mathbb{R}$ containing $f_\alpha(X)$. To be definite, choose

$$I_\alpha = [\inf f_\alpha(X), \sup f_\alpha(X)].$$

Then define $h : X \to \prod_{\alpha \in J} I_\alpha$ by the rule

$$h(x) = (f_\alpha(x))_{\alpha \in J}.$$

By the Tychonoff theorem, $\prod I_\alpha$ is compact. Because X is completely regular, the collection $\{f_\alpha\}$ separates points from closed sets in X. Therefore, by Theorem 34.2, the map h is an imbedding.

Let Y be the compactification of X induced by the imbedding h. Then there is an imbedding $H : Y \to \prod I_\alpha$ that equals h when restricted to the subspace X of Y. Given a bounded continuous real-valued function f on X, we show it extends to Y. The function f belongs to the collection $\{f_\alpha\}_{\alpha\in J}$, so it equals f_β for some index β. Let $\pi_\beta : \prod I_\alpha \to I_\beta$ be the projection mapping. Then the continuous map $\pi_\beta \circ H : Y \to I_\beta$ is the desired extension of f. For if $x \in X$, we have

$$\pi_\beta(H(x)) = \pi_\beta(h(x)) = \pi_\beta((f_\alpha(x))_{\alpha\in J}) = f_\beta(x).$$

Uniqueness of the extension is a consequence of the following lemma. ∎

Lemma 38.3. *Let $A \subset X$; let $f : A \to Z$ be a continuous map of A into the Hausdorff space Z. There is at most one extension of f to a continuous function $g : \bar{A} \to Z$.*

Proof. This lemma was given as an exercise in §18; we give a proof here. Suppose that $g, g' : \bar{A} \to X$ are two different extensions of f; choose x so that $g(x) \neq g'(x)$. Let U and U' be disjoint neighborhoods of $g(x)$ and $g'(x)$, respectively. Choose a neighborhood V of x so that $g(V) \subset U$ and $g'(V) \subset U'$. Now V intersects A in some point y; then $g(y) \in U$ and $g'(y) \in U'$. But since $y \in A$, we have $g(y) = f(y)$ and $g'(y) = f(y)$. This contradicts the fact that U and U' are disjoint. ∎

Theorem 38.4. *Let X be a completely regular space; let Y be a compactification of X satisfying the extension property of Theorem 38.2. Given any continuous map $f : X \to C$ of X into a compact Hausdorff space C, the map f extends uniquely to a continuous map $g : Y \to C$.*

Proof. Note that C is completely regular, so that it can be imbedded in $[0, 1]^J$ for some J. So we may as well assume that $C \subset [0, 1]^J$. Then each component function f_α of the map f is a bounded continuous real-valued function on X; by hypothesis, f_α can be extended to a continuous map g_α of Y into $\mathbb{R}$. Define $g : Y \to \mathbb{R}^J$ by setting $g(y) = (g_\alpha(y))_{\alpha\in J}$; then g is continuous because $\mathbb{R}^J$ has the product topology. Now in fact g maps Y into the subspace C of $\mathbb{R}^J$. For continuity of g implies that

$$g(Y) = g(\bar{X}) \subset \overline{g(X)} = \overline{f(X)} \subset \bar{C} = C.$$

Thus g is the desired extension of f. ∎

Theorem 38.5. *Let X be a completely regular space. If Y_1 and Y_2 are two compactifications of X satisfying the extension property of Theorem 38.2, then Y_1 and Y_2 are equivalent.*

Proof. Consider the inclusion mapping $j_2 : X \to Y_2$. It is a continuous map of X into the compact Hausdorff space Y_2. Because Y_1 has the extension property, we may, by the preceding theorem, extend j_2 to a continuous map $f_2 : Y_1 \to Y_2$. Similarly, we may extend the inclusion map $j_1 : X \to Y_1$ to a continuous map $f_1 : Y_2 \to Y_1$ (because Y_2 has the extension property and Y_1 is compact Hausdorff).

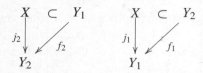

The composite $f_1 \circ f_2 : Y_1 \to Y_1$ has the property that for every $x \in X$, one has $f_1(f_2(x)) = x$. Therefore, $f_1 \circ f_2$ is a continuous extension of the identity map $i_X : X \to X$. But the identity map of Y_1 is also a continuous extension of i_X. By uniqueness of extensions (Lemma 38.3), $f_1 \circ f_2$ must equal the identity map of Y_1. Similarly, $f_2 \circ f_1$ must equal the identity map of Y_2. Thus f_1 and f_2 are homeomorphisms. $\blacksquare$

Definition. For each completely regular space X, let us choose, once and for all, a compactification of X satisfying the extension condition of Theorem 38.2. We will denote this compactification of X by $\beta(X)$ and call it the ***Stone-Čech compactification*** of X. It is characterized by the fact that any continuous map $f : X \to C$ of X into a compact Hausdorff space C extends uniquely to a continuous map $g : \beta(X) \to C$.

Exercises

1. Verify the statements made in Example 4.

2. Show that the bounded continuous function $g : (0, 1) \to \mathbb{R}$ defined by $g(x) = \cos(1/x)$ cannot be extended to the compactification of Example 3. Define an imbedding $h : (0, 1) \to [0, 1]^3$ such that the functions x, $\sin(1/x)$, and $\cos(1/x)$ are all extendable to the compactification induced by h.

3. Under what conditions does a metrizable space have a metrizable compactification?

4. Let Y be an arbitrary compactification of X; let $\beta(X)$ be the Stone-Čech compactification. Show there is a continuous surjective closed map $g : \beta(X) \to Y$ that equals the identity on X.

   [This exercise makes precise what we mean by saying that $\beta(X)$ is the "maximal" compactification of X. It shows that every compactification of X is equivalent to a quotient space of $\beta(X)$.]

5. (a) Show that every continuous real-valued function defined on S_Ω is "eventually constant." [*Hint:* First prove that for each ϵ, there is an element α of S_Ω

such that $|f(\beta) - f(\alpha)| < \epsilon$ for all $\beta > \alpha$. Then let $\epsilon = 1/n$ for $n \in \mathbb{Z}_+$ and consider the corresponding points α_n.]

(b) Show that the one-point compactification of S_Ω and the Stone-Čech compactification are equivalent.

(c) Conclude that every compactification of S_Ω is equivalent to the one-point compactification.

6. Let X be completely regular. Show that X is connected if and only if $\beta(X)$ is connected. [*Hint:* If $X = A \cup B$ is a separation of X, let $f(x) = 0$ for $x \in A$ and $f(x) = 1$ for $x \in B$.]

7. Let X be a discrete space; consider the space $\beta(X)$.

(a) Show that if $A \subset X$, then $\bar{A}$ and $\overline{X - A}$ are disjoint, where the closures are taken in $\beta(X)$.

(b) Show that if U is open in $\beta(X)$, then $\bar{U}$ is open in $\beta(X)$.

(c) Show that $\beta(X)$ is totally disconnected.

8. Show that $\beta(\mathbb{Z}_+)$ has cardinality at least as great as I^I, where $I = [0, 1]$. [*Hint:* The space I^I has a countable dense subset.]

9. (a) If X is normal and y is a point of $\beta(X) - X$, show that y is not the limit of a sequence of points of X.

(b) Show that if X is completely regular and noncompact, then $\beta(X)$ is not metrizable.

10. We have constructed a correspondence $X \to \beta(X)$ that assigns, to each completely regular space, its Stone-Čech compactification. Now let us assign, to each continuous map $f : X \to Y$ of completely regular spaces, the unique continuous map $\beta(f) : \beta(X) \to \beta(Y)$ that extends the map $i \circ f$, where $i : Y \to \beta(Y)$ is the inclusion map. Verify the following:

(i) If $1_X : X \to X$ is the identity map of X, then $\beta(1_X)$ is the identity map of $\beta(X)$.

(ii) If $f : X \to Y$ and $g : Y \to Z$, then $\beta(g \circ f) = \beta(g) \circ \beta(f)$.

These properties tell us that the correspondence we have constructed is what is called a *functor*; it is a functor from the "category" of completely regular spaces and continuous maps of such spaces, to the "category" of compact Hausdorff spaces and continuous maps of such spaces. You will see these properties again in Part II of the book; they are fundamental in algebra and in algebraic topology.

Chapter 6

Metrization Theorems
and Paracompactness

The Urysohn metrization theorem of Chapter 4 was the first step—a giant one—toward an answer to the question: When is a topological space metrizable? It gives conditions under which a space X is metrizable: that it be regular and have a countable basis. But mathematicians are never satisfied with a theorem if there is some hope of proving a stronger one. In the present case, one can hope to strengthen the theorem by finding conditions on X that are both necessary and sufficient for X to be metrizable, that is, conditions that are *equivalent* to metrizability.

We know that the regularity hypothesis in the Urysohn metrization theorem is a necessary one, but the countable basis condition is not. So the obvious thing to do is try to replace the countable basis condition by something weaker. Finding such condition is a delicate task. The condition has to be strong enough to imply metrizability, and yet weak enough that all metrizable spaces satisfy it. In a situation like this, discovering the right hypothesis is more than half the battle.

The condition that was eventually formulated, by J. Nagata and Y. Smirnov inde-pendently, involves a new notion, that of local finiteness. We say that a collection $\mathcal{A}$ of subsets of a space X is *locally finite* if every point of X has a neighborhood that intersects only finitely many elements of $\mathcal{A}$.

Now one way of expressing the condition that the basis $\mathcal{B}$ is countable is to say that $\mathcal{B}$ can be expressed in the form

$$\mathcal{B} = \bigcup_{n \in \mathbb{Z}_+} \mathcal{B}_n,$$

Lemma 39.2.   *Let X be a metrizable space. If A is an open covering of X, then there is an open covering $\mathcal{E}$ of X refining A that is countably locally finite.*

Proof.   We shall use the well-ordering theorem in proving this theorem. Choose a well-ordering $<$ for the collection A. Let us denote the elements of A generically by the letters $U, V, W, \ldots$.

Choose a metric for X. Let n be a positive integer, fixed for the moment. Given an element U of A, let us define $S_n(U)$ to be the subset of U obtained by "shrinking" U a distance of $1/n$. More precisely, let

$$S_n(U) = \{x \mid B(x, 1/n) \subset U\}.$$

(It happens that $S_n(U)$ is a closed set, but that is not important for our purposes.) Now we use the well-ordering $<$ of A to pass to a still smaller set. For each U in A, define

$$T_n(U) = S_n(U) - \bigcup_{V<U} V.$$

The situation where A consists of the three sets $U < V < W$ is pictured in Figure 39.1. Just as the figure suggests, the sets we have formed are disjoint.

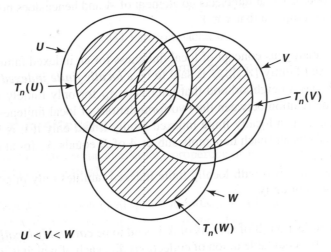

Figure 39.1

In fact, they are separated by a distance of at least $1/n$. This means that if V and W are distinct elements of A, then $d(x, y) \geq 1/n$ whenever $x \in T_n(V)$ and $y \in T_n(W)$.

To prove this fact, assume the notation has been so chosen that $V < W$. Since x is in $T_n(V)$, then x is in $S_n(V)$, so the $1/n$-neighborhood of x lies in V. On the other hand, since $V < W$ and y is in $T_n(W)$, the definition of the latter set tells us that y is not in V. It follows that y is not in the $1/n$-neighborhood of x.

The sets $T_n(U)$ are not yet the ones we want, for we do not know that they are open sets. (In fact, they are closed.) So let us expand each of them slightly to obtain an open set $E_n(U)$. Specifically, let $E_n(U)$ be the $1/3n$-neighborhood of $T_n(U)$; that is, let $E_n(U)$ be the union of the open balls $B(x, 1/3n)$, for $x \in T_n(U)$.

In the case $U < V < W$, we have the situation pictured in Figure 39.2. As the figure suggests, the sets we have formed are disjoint. Indeed, if V and W are distinct elements of $\mathcal{A}$, we assert that $d(x, y) \geq 1/3n$ whenever $x \in E_n(V)$ and $y \in E_n(W)$; this fact follows at once from the triangle inequality. Note that for each $V \in \mathcal{A}$, the set $E_n(V)$ is contained in V.

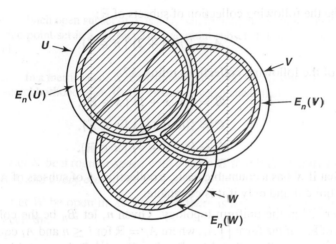

Figure 39.2

Now let us define

$$\mathcal{E}_n = \{E_n(U) \mid U \in \mathcal{A}\}.$$

We claim that $\mathcal{E}_n$ is a locally finite collection of open sets that refines $\mathcal{A}$. The fact that $\mathcal{E}_n$ refines $\mathcal{A}$ comes from the fact that $E_n(V) \subset V$ for each $V \in \mathcal{A}$. The fact that $\mathcal{E}_n$ is locally finite comes from the fact that for any x in X, the $1/6n$-neighborhood of x can intersect at most *one* element of $\mathcal{E}_n$.

Of course, the collection $\mathcal{E}_n$, will not cover X. (Figure 39.2 illustrates that fact.) But we assert that the collection

$$\mathcal{E} = \bigcup_{n \in \mathbb{Z}_+} \mathcal{E}_n$$

does cover X.

Let x be a point of X. The collection $\mathcal{A}$ with which we began covers X; let us choose U to be the first element of $\mathcal{A}$ (in the well-ordering $<$) that contains x. Since U is open, we can choose n so that $B(x, 1/n) \subset U$. Then, by definition, $x \in S_n(U)$. Now because U is the first element of $\mathcal{A}$ that contains x, the point x belongs to $T_n(U)$. Then x also belongs to the element $E_n(U)$ of $\mathcal{E}_n$, as desired. ∎

so that C equals a countable intersection of open sets of X.

Step 3. We show X is normal. Let C and D be disjoint closed sets in X. Applying Step 1 to the open set $X - D$, we construct a countable collection $\{U_n\}$ of open sets such that $\bigcup U_n = \bigcup \bar{U}_n = X - D$. Then $\{U_n\}$ covers C and each set $\bar{U}_n$ is disjoint from D. Similarly, there is a countable covering $\{V_n\}$ of D by open sets whose closures are disjoint from C.

Now we are back in the situation that arose in the proof that a regular space with a countable basis is normal (Theorem 32.1). We can repeat that proof *verbatim*. Define

$$ U_n' = U_n - \bigcup_{i=1}^{n} \bar{V}_i \quad \text{and} \quad V_n' = V_n - \bigcup_{i=1}^{n} \bar{U}_i. $$

Then the sets

$$ U' = \bigcup_{n \in \mathbb{Z}_+} U_n' \quad \text{and} \quad V' = \bigcup_{n \in \mathbb{Z}_+} V_n' $$

are disjoint open sets about C and D, respectively. ∎

Lemma 40.2. *Let X be normal; let A be a closed G_δ set in X. Then there is a continuous function $f : X \to [0, 1]$ such that $f(x) = 0$ for $x \in A$ and $f(x) > 0$ for $x \notin A$.*

Proof. We gave this as an exercise in §33; we provide a proof here. Write A as the intersection of the open sets U_n, for $n \in \mathbb{Z}_+$. For each n, choose a continuous function $f_n : X \to [0, 1]$ such that $f(x) = 0$ for $x \in A$ and $f(x) = 1$ for $x \in X - U_n$. Define $f(x) = \sum f_n(x)/2^n$. The series converges uniformly, by comparison with $\sum 1/2^n$, so that f is continuous. Also, f vanishes on A and is positive on $X - A$. ∎

Theorem 40.3 (Nagata-Smirnov metrization theorem). *A space X is metrizable if and only if X is regular and has a basis that is countably locally finite.*

Proof. *Step 1.* Assume X is regular with a countably locally finite basis $\mathcal{B}$. Then X is normal, and every closed set in X is a G_δ set in X. We shall show that X is metrizable by imbedding X in the metric space $(\mathbb{R}^J, \bar{\rho})$ for some J.

Let $\mathcal{B} = \bigcup \mathcal{B}_n$, where each collection $\mathcal{B}_n$ is locally finite. For each positive integer n, and each basis element $B \in \mathcal{B}_n$, choose a continuous function

$$ f_{n,B} : X \longrightarrow [0, 1/n] $$

such that $f_{n,B}(x) > 0$ for $x \in B$ and $f_{n,B}(x) = 0$ for $x \notin B$. The collection $\{f_{n,B}\}$ separates points from closed sets in X: Given a point x_0 and a neighborhood U of x_0, there is a basis element B such that $x_0 \in B \subset U$. Then $B \in \mathcal{B}_n$ for some n, so that $f_{n,B}(x_0) > 0$ and $f_{n,B}$ vanishes outside U.

Let J be the subset of $\mathbb{Z}_+ \times \mathcal{B}$ consisting of all pairs (n, B) such that B is an element of $\mathcal{B}_n$. Define

$$ F : X \longrightarrow [0, 1]^J $$

by the equation

$$F(x) = (f_{n,B}(x))_{(n,b) \in J}.$$

Relative to the product topology on $[0, 1]^J$, the map F is an imbedding, by Theorem 34.2.

Now we give $[0, 1]^J$ the topology induced by the uniform metric and show that F is an imbedding relative to this topology as well. Here is where the condition $f_{n,B}(x) < 1/n$ comes in. The uniform topology is finer (larger) than the product topology. Therefore, relative to the uniform metric, the map F is injective and carries open sets of X onto open sets of the image space $Z = F(X)$. We must give a separate proof that F is continuous.

Note that on the subspace $[0, 1]^J$ of $\mathbb{R}^J$, the uniform metric equals the metric

$$\rho((x_\alpha), (y_\alpha)) = \sup\{|x_\alpha - y_\alpha|\}.$$

To prove continuity, we take a point x_0 of X and a number $\epsilon > 0$, and find a neighborhood W of x_0 such that

$$x \in W \implies \rho(F(x), F(x_0)) < \epsilon.$$

Let n be fixed for the moment. Choose a neighborhood U_n of x_0 that intersects only finitely many elements of the collection $\mathcal{B}_n$. This means that as B ranges over $\mathcal{B}_n$, all but finitely many of the functions $f_{n,B}$ are identically equal to zero on U_n. Because each function $f_{n,B}$ is continuous, we can now choose a neighborhood V_n of x_0 contained in U_n on which each of the remaining functions $f_{n,B}$, for $B \in \mathcal{B}_n$, varies by at most $\epsilon/2$.

Choose such a neighborhood V_n of x_0 for each $n \in \mathbb{Z}_+$. Then choose N so that $1/N \leq \epsilon/2$, and define $W = V_1 \cap \cdots \cap V_N$. We assert that W is the desired neighborhood of x_0. Let $x \in W$. If $n \leq N$, then

$$|f_{n,B}(x) - f_{n,B}(x_0)| \leq \epsilon/2$$

because the function $f_{n,B}$ either vanishes identically or varies by at most $\epsilon/2$ on W. If $n > N$, then

$$|f_{n,B}(x) - f_{n,B}(x_0)| \leq 1/n < \epsilon/2$$

because $f_{n,B}$ maps X into $[0, 1/n]$. Therefore,

$$\rho(F(x), F(x_0)) \leq \epsilon/2 < \epsilon,$$

as desired.

Step 2. Now we prove the converse. Assume X is metrizable. We know X is regular; let us show that X has a basis that is countably locally finite.

Choose a metric for X. Given m, let $\mathcal{A}_m$ be the covering of X by all open balls of radius $1/m$. By Lemma 39.2, there is an open covering $\mathcal{B}_m$ of X refining $\mathcal{A}_m$ such that $\mathcal{B}_m$ is countably locally finite. Note that each element of $\mathcal{B}_m$ has diameter at most $2/m$. Let $\mathcal{B}$ be the union of the collections $\mathcal{B}_m$, for $m \in \mathbb{Z}_+$. Because each collection $\mathcal{B}_m$ is countably locally finite, so is $\mathcal{B}$. We show that $\mathcal{B}$ is a basis for X.

Given $x \in X$ and given $\epsilon > 0$, we show that there is an element B of $\mathcal{B}$ containing x that is contained in $B(x, \epsilon)$. First choose m so that $1/m < \epsilon/2$. Then, because $\mathcal{B}_m$ covers X, we can choose an element B of $\mathcal{B}_m$ that contains x. Since B contains x and has diameter at most $2/m < \epsilon$, it is contained in $B(x, \epsilon)$, as desired. ■

Exercises

1. Check the details of Examples 1 and 2.

2. A subset W of X is said to be an "F_σ set" in X if W equals a countable union of closed sets of X. Show that W is an F_σ set in X if and only if $X - W$ is a G_δ set in X.

   [The terminology comes from the French. The "F" stands for "fermé," which means "closed," and the "σ" for "somme," which means "union."]

3. Many spaces have *countable* bases; but no T_1 space has a *locally finite* basis unless it is discrete. Prove this fact.

4. Find a nondiscrete space that has a countably locally finite basis but does not have a countable basis.

5. A collection $\mathcal{A}$ of subsets of X is said to be **locally discrete** if each point of X has a neighborhood that intersects at most one element of $\mathcal{A}$. A collection $\mathcal{B}$ is **countably locally discrete** (or "σ-locally discrete") if it equals a countable union of locally discrete collections. Prove the following:

   Theorem (Bing metrization theorem). *A space X is metrizable if and only if it is regular and has a basis that is countably locally discrete.*

§41   Paracompactness

The concept of paracompactness is one of the most useful generalizations of compactness that has been discovered in recent years. It is particularly useful for applications in topology and differential geometry. We shall give just one application, a metrization theorem that we prove in the next section.

Many of the spaces that are familiar to us already are paracompact. For instance, every compact space is paracompact; this will be an immediate consequence of the definition. It is also true that every metrizable space is paracompact; this is a theorem due to A. H. Stone, which we shall prove. Thus the class of paracompact spaces includes the two most important classes of spaces we have studied. It includes many other spaces as well.

To see how paracompactness generalizes compactness, we recall the definition of compactness: A space X is said to be *compact* if every open covering $\mathcal{A}$ of X contains a finite subcollection that covers X. An equivalent way of saying this is the following:

> *A space X is compact if every open covering $\mathcal{A}$ of X has a finite open refinement $\mathcal{B}$ that covers X.*

This definition is equivalent to the usual one; given such a refinement $\mathcal{B}$, one can choose for each element of $\mathcal{B}$ an element of $\mathcal{A}$ containing it; in this way one obtains a finite subcollection of $\mathcal{A}$ that covers X.

This new formulation of compactness is an awkward one, but it suggests a way to generalize:

Definition. A space X is ***paracompact*** if every open covering $\mathcal{A}$ of X has a locally finite open refinement $\mathcal{B}$ that covers X.

Many authors, following the lead of Bourbaki, include as part of the definition of the term *paracompact* the requirement that the space be Hausdorff. (Bourbaki also includes the Hausdorff condition as part of the definition of the term *compact*.) We shall not follow this convention.

> EXAMPLE 1.   *The space $\mathbb{R}^n$ is paracompact.* Let $X = \mathbb{R}^n$. Let $\mathcal{A}$ be an open covering of X. Let $B_0 = \varnothing$, and for each positive integer m, let B_m denote the open ball of radius m centered at the origin. Given m, choose finitely many elements of $\mathcal{A}$ that cover $\bar{B}_m$ and intersect each one with the open set $X - \bar{B}_{m-1}$; let this finite collection of open sets be denoted $\mathcal{C}_m$. Then the collection $\mathcal{C} = \bigcup \mathcal{C}_m$ is a refinement of $\mathcal{A}$. It is clearly locally finite, for the open set B_m intersects only finitely many elements of $\mathcal{C}$, namely those elements belonging to the collection $\mathcal{C}_1 \cup \cdots \cup \mathcal{C}_m$. Finally, $\mathcal{C}$ covers X. For, given x, let m be the smallest integer such that $x \in \bar{B}_m$. Then x belongs to an element of $\mathcal{C}_m$, by definition.

Some of the properties of a paracompact space are similar to those of a compact space. For instance, a subspace of a paracompact space is not necessarily paracompact; but a closed subspace is paracompact. Also, a paracompact Hausdorff space is normal. In other ways, a paracompact space is not similar to a compact space; in particular, the product of two paracompact spaces need not be paracompact. We shall verify these facts shortly.

Theorem 41.1.   *Every paracompact Hausdorff space X is normal.*

Proof.   The proof is somewhat similar to the proof that a compact Hausdorff space is normal.

First one proves regularity. Let a be a point of X and let B be a closed set of X disjoint from a. The Hausdorff condition enables us to choose, for each b in B, an open set U_b about b whose closure is disjoint from a. Cover X by the open sets U_b, along with the open set $X - B$; take a locally finite open refinement $\mathcal{C}$ that covers X. Form the subcollection $\mathcal{D}$ of $\mathcal{C}$ consisting of every element of $\mathcal{C}$ that intersects B. Then $\mathcal{D}$

covers B. Furthermore, if $D \in \mathcal{D}$, then $\bar{D}$ is disjoint from a. For D intersects B, so it lies in some set U_b, whose closure is disjoint from a. Let

$$V = \bigcup_{D \in \mathcal{D}} D;$$

then V is an open set in X containing B. Because $\mathcal{D}$ is locally finite,

$$\bar{V} = \bigcup_{D \in \mathcal{D}} \bar{D},$$

so that $\bar{V}$ is disjoint from a. Thus regularity is proved.

To prove normality, one merely repeats the same argument, replacing a by the closed set A throughout and replacing the Hausdorff condition by regularity.   ■

Theorem 41.2. *Every closed subspace of a paracompact space is paracompact.*

Proof. Let Y be a closed subspace of the paracompact space X; let $\mathcal{A}$ be a covering of Y by sets open in Y. For each $A \in \mathcal{A}$, choose an open set A' of X such that $A' \cap Y = A$. Cover X by the open sets A', along with the open set $X - Y$. Let $\mathcal{B}$ be a locally finite open refinement of this covering that covers X. The collection

$$\mathcal{C} = \{B \cap Y \mid B \in \mathcal{B}\}$$

is the required locally finite open refinement of $\mathcal{A}$.   ■

> EXAMPLE 2.   *A paracompact subspace of a Hausdorff space X need not be closed in X.* Indeed, the open interval $(0, 1)$ is paracompact, being homeomorphic to $\mathbb{R}$, but it is not closed in $\mathbb{R}$.

> EXAMPLE 3.   *A subspace of a paracompact space need not be paracompact.* The space $\bar{S}_\Omega \times \bar{S}_\Omega$ is compact and, therefore, paracompact. But the subspace $S_\Omega \times \bar{S}_\Omega$ is not paracompact, for it is Hausdorff but not normal.

To prove the important theorem that every metrizable space is paracompact, we need the following lemma, due to E. Michael, which is also useful for other purposes:

Lemma 41.3. *Let X be regular. Then the following conditions on X are equivalent:*
    Every open covering of X has a refinement that is:
(1) An open covering of X and countably locally finite.
(2) A covering of X and locally finite.
(3) A closed covering of X and locally finite.
(4) An open covering of X and locally finite.

Proof. It is trivial that $(4) \Rightarrow (1)$. What we need to prove our theorem is the converse. In order to prove the converse, we must go through the steps $(1) \Rightarrow (2) \Rightarrow (3) \Rightarrow (4)$ anyway, so we have for convenience listed these conditions in the statement of the lemma.

(1) $\Rightarrow$ (2). Let $\mathcal{A}$ be an open covering of X. Let $\mathcal{B}$ be an open refinement of $\mathcal{A}$ that covers X and is countably locally finite; let

$$\mathcal{B} = \bigcup \mathcal{B}_n$$

where each $\mathcal{B}_n$ is locally finite.

Now we apply essentially the same sort of shrinking trick we have used before to make sets from different $\mathcal{B}_n$'s disjoint. Given i, let

$$V_i = \bigcup_{U \in \mathcal{B}_i} U.$$

Then for each $n \in \mathbb{Z}_+$ and each element U of $\mathcal{B}_n$, define

$$S_n(U) = U - \bigcup_{i<n} V_i.$$

[Note that $S_n(U)$ is not necessarily open, nor closed.] Let

$$\mathcal{C}_n = \{S_n(U) \mid U \in \mathcal{B}_n\}.$$

Then $\mathcal{C}_n$ is a refinement of $\mathcal{B}_n$, because $S_n(U) \subset U$ for each $U \in \mathcal{B}_n$.

Let $\mathcal{C} = \bigcup \mathcal{C}_n$. We assert that $\mathcal{C}$ is the required locally finite refinement of $\mathcal{A}$, covering X.

Let x be a point of X. We wish to prove that x lies in an element of $\mathcal{C}$, and that x has a neighborhood intersecting only finitely many elements of $\mathcal{C}$. Consider the covering $\mathcal{B} = \bigcup \mathcal{B}_n$; let N be the smallest integer such that x lies in an element of $\mathcal{B}_N$. Let U be an element of $\mathcal{B}_N$ containing x. First, note that since x lies in no element of $\mathcal{B}_i$ for $i < N$, the point x lies in the element $S_N(U)$ of $\mathcal{C}$. Second, note that since each collection $\mathcal{B}_n$ is locally finite, we can choose for each $n = 1, \ldots, N$ a neighborhood W_n of x that intersects only finitely many elements of $\mathcal{B}_n$. Now if W_n intersects the element $S_n(V)$ of $\mathcal{C}_n$, it must intersect the element V of $\mathcal{B}_n$, since $S_n(V) \subset V$. Therefore, W_n intersects only finitely many elements of $\mathcal{C}_n$. Furthermore, because U is in $\mathcal{B}_N$, U intersects no element of $\mathcal{C}_n$ for $n > N$. As a result, the neighborhood

$$W_1 \cap W_2 \cap \cdots \cap W_N \cap U$$

of x intersects only finitely many elements of $\mathcal{C}$.

(2) $\Rightarrow$ (3). Let $\mathcal{A}$ be an open covering of X. Let $\mathcal{B}$ be the collection of all open sets U of X such that $\bar{U}$ is contained in an element of $\mathcal{A}$. By regularity, $\mathcal{B}$ covers X. Using (2), we can find a refinement $\mathcal{C}$ of $\mathcal{B}$ that covers X and is locally finite. Let

$$\mathcal{D} = \{\bar{C} \mid C \in \mathcal{C}\}.$$

Then $\mathcal{D}$ also covers X; it is locally finite by Lemma 39.1; and it refines $\mathcal{A}$.

(3) $\Rightarrow$ (4). Let $\mathcal{A}$ be an open covering of X. Using (3), choose $\mathcal{B}$ to be a refinement of $\mathcal{A}$ that covers X and is locally finite. (We can take $\mathcal{B}$ to be a closed refinement if we like, but that is irrelevant.) We seek to expand each element B of $\mathcal{B}$ slightly to

Definition. Let $\{U_\alpha\}_{\alpha \in J}$ be an indexed open covering of X. An indexed family of continuous functions

$$\phi_\alpha : X \to [0, 1]$$

is said to be a **partition of unity** on X, dominated by $\{U_\alpha\}$, if:
 (1) (Support ϕ_α) $\subset U_\alpha$ for each α.
 (2) The indexed family $\{$Support $\phi_\alpha\}$ is locally finite.
 (3) $\sum \phi_\alpha(x) = 1$ for each x.

Condition (2) implies that each $x \in X$ has a neighborhood on which the function ϕ_α vanishes identically for all but finitely many values of α. Thus we can make sense of the "sum" indicated in (3); we interpret it to mean the sum of the terms $\phi_\alpha(x)$ that do not equal zero.

We now construct a partition of unity on an arbitrary paracompact Hausdorff space. We begin by proving a "shrinking lemma," just as we did for the finite case in §36.

*Lemma 41.6. *Let X be a paracompact Hausdorff space; let $\{U_\alpha\}_{\alpha \in J}$ be an indexed family of open sets covering X. Then there exists a locally finite indexed family $\{V_\alpha\}_{\alpha \in J}$ of open sets covering X such that $\bar{V}_\alpha \subset U_\alpha$ for each α.*

The condition that $\bar{V}_\alpha \subset U_\alpha$ for each α is sometimes expressed by saying that the family $\{\bar{V}_\alpha\}$ is a **precise refinement** of the family $\{U_\alpha\}$.

Proof. Let $\mathcal{A}$ be the collection of all open sets A such that $\bar{A}$ is contained in some element of the collection $\{U_\alpha\}$. Regularity of X implies that $\mathcal{A}$ covers X. Since X is paracompact, we can find a locally finite collection $\mathcal{B}$ of open sets covering X that refines $\mathcal{A}$. Let us index $\mathcal{B}$ bijectively with some index set K; then the general element of $\mathcal{B}$ can be denoted B_β, for $\beta \in K$, and $\{B_\beta\}_{\beta \in K}$ is a locally finite indexed family. Since $\mathcal{B}$ refines $\mathcal{A}$, we can define a function $f : K \to J$ by choosing, for each β in K, an element $f(\beta) \in J$ such that

$$\bar{B}_\beta \subset U_{f(\beta)}.$$

Then for each $\alpha \in J$, we define V_α to be the union of the elements of the collection

$$\mathcal{B}_\alpha = \{B_\beta \mid f(\beta) = \alpha\}.$$

(Note that V_α is empty if there exists no index β such that $f(\beta) = \alpha$.) For each element B_β of the collection $\mathcal{B}_\alpha$ we have $\bar{B}_\beta \subset U_\alpha$ by definition. Because the collection $\mathcal{B}_\alpha$ is locally finite, $\bar{V}_\alpha$ equals the union of the closures of the elements of $\mathcal{B}_\alpha$, so that $\bar{V}_\alpha \subset U_\alpha$.

Finally, we check local finiteness. Given $x \in X$, choose a neighborhood W of x such that W intersects B_β for only finitely many values of β, say $\beta = \beta_1, \ldots, \beta_K$. Then W can intersect V_α only if α is one of the indices $f(\beta_1), \ldots, f(\beta_K)$. $\blacksquare$

*Theorem 41.7. *Let X be a paracompact Hausdorff space; let $\{U_\alpha\}_{\alpha \in J}$ be an indexed open covering of X. Then there exists a partition of unity on X dominated by $\{U_\alpha\}$.*

Proof. We begin by applying the shrinking lemma twice, to find locally finite indexed familes of open sets $\{W_\alpha\}$ and $\{V_\alpha\}$ covering X, such that $\overline{W}_\alpha \subset V_\alpha$ and $\overline{V}_\alpha \subset U_\alpha$ for each α. Since X is normal, we may choose, for each α, a continuous function $\psi_\alpha : X \to [0, 1]$ such that $\psi_\alpha(\overline{W}_\alpha) = \{1\}$ and $\psi_\alpha(X - V_\alpha) = \{0\}$. Since ψ_α is nonzero only at points of V_α, we have

$$(\text{Support } \psi_\alpha) \subset \overline{V}_\alpha \subset U_\alpha.$$

Furthermore, the indexed family $\{\overline{V}_\alpha\}$ is locally finite (since an open set intersects $\overline{V}_\alpha$ only if it intersects V_α); hence the indexed family $\{\text{Support } \psi_\alpha\}$ is also locally finite. Note that because $\{W_\alpha\}$ covers X, for any given x at least one of the functions ψ_α is positive at x.

We can now make sense of the formally infinite sum

$$\Psi(x) = \sum_\alpha \psi_\alpha(x).$$

Since each $x \in X$ has a neighborhood W_x that intersects the set $(\text{Support } \psi_\alpha)$ for only finitely many values of α, we can interpret this infinite sum to mean the sum of its (finitely many) nonzero terms. It follows that the restriction of Ψ to W_x equals a finite sum of continuous functions, and is thus continuous. Then since Ψ is continuous on W_x for each x, it is continuous on X. It is also positive. We now define

$$\phi_\alpha(x) = \psi_\alpha(x)/\Psi(x)$$

to obtain our desired partition of unity. ∎

Partitions of unity are most often used in mathematics to "patch together" functions that are defined locally so as to obtain a function that is defined globally. Their use in §36 illustrates this process. Here is another such illustration:

*Theorem 41.8. *Let X be a paracompact Hausdorff space; let $\mathcal{C}$ be a collection of subsets of X; for each $C \in \mathcal{C}$, let ϵ_C be a positive number. If $\mathcal{C}$ is locally finite, there is a continuous function $f : X \to \mathbb{R}$ such that $f(x) > 0$ for all x, and $f(x) \leq \epsilon_C$ for $x \in C$.*

Proof. Cover X by open sets each of which intersects at most finitely many elements of $\mathcal{C}$; index this collection of open sets so that it becomes an indexed family $\{U_\alpha\}_{\alpha \in J}$. Choose a partition of unity $\{\phi_\alpha\}$ on X dominated by $\{U_\alpha\}$. Given α, let δ_α be the minimum of the numbers ϵ_C, as C ranges over all those elements of $\mathcal{C}$ that intersect the support of ϕ_α; if there are no such elements of C, set $\delta_\alpha = 1$. Then define

$$f(x) = \sum \delta_\alpha \phi_\alpha(x).$$

Because all the numbers δ_α are positive, so is f. We show that $f(x) \leq \epsilon_C$ for $x \in C$. It will suffice to show that for $x \in C$ and arbitrary α, we have

$$(*) \qquad\qquad \delta_\alpha \phi_\alpha(x) \leq \epsilon_C \phi_\alpha(x);$$

then the desired inequality follows by summing, as $\sum \phi_\alpha(x) = 1$. If $x \notin \text{Support } \phi_\alpha$, then inequality $(*)$ is trivial because $\phi_\alpha(x) = 0$. And if $x \in \text{Support } \phi_\alpha$ and $x \in C$, then C intersects the support of ϕ_α, so that $\delta_\alpha \leq \epsilon_C$ by construction; thus $(*)$ holds. ∎

Exercises

1. Give an example to show that if X is paracompact, it does not follow that for every open covering $\mathcal{A}$ of X, there is a locally finite *subcollection* of $\mathcal{A}$ that covers X.

2. (a) Show that the product of a paracompact space and a compact space is paracompact. [*Hint:* Use the tube lemma.]
   (b) Conclude that S_Ω is not paracompact.

3. Is every locally compact Hausdorff space paracompact?

4. (a) Show that if X has the discrete topology, then X is paracompact.
   (b) Show that if $f : X \to Y$ is continuous and X is paracompact, the subspace $f(X)$ of Y need not be paracompact.

5. Let X be paracompact. We proved a "shrinking lemma" for arbitrary indexed open coverings of X. Here is an "expansion lemma" for arbitrary locally finite indexed families in X.
   Lemma.   *Let $\{B_\alpha\}_{\alpha \in J}$ be a locally finite indexed family of subsets of the paracompact Hausdorff space X. Then there is a locally finite indexed family $\{U_\alpha\}_{\alpha \in J}$ of open sets in X such that $B_\alpha \subset U_\alpha$ for each α.*

6. (a) Let X be a regular space. If X is a countable union of compact subspaces of X, then X is paracompact.
   (b) Show $\mathbb{R}^\infty$ is paracompact as a subspace of $\mathbb{R}^\omega$ in the box topology.

*7. Let X be a regular space.
   (a) If X is a finite union of closed paracompact subspaces of X, then X is paracompact.
   (b) If X is a countable union of closed paracompact subspaces of X whose interiors cover X, show X is paracompact.

8. Let $p : X \to Y$ be a perfect map. (See Exercise 7 of §31.)
   (a) Show that if Y is paracompact, so is X. [*Hint:* If $\mathcal{A}$ is an open covering of X, find a locally finite open covering of Y by sets B such that $p^{-1}(B)$ can be covered by finitely many elements of $\mathcal{A}$; then intersect $p^{-1}(B)$ with these elements of $\mathcal{A}$.]
   (b) Show that if X is a paracompact Hausdorff space, then so is Y. [*Hint:* If $\mathcal{B}$ is a locally finite closed covering of X, then $\{p(B) \mid B \in \mathcal{B}\}$ is a locally finite closed covering of Y.]

9. Let G be a locally compact, connected topological group. Show that G is para-compact. [*Hint:* Let U_1 be a neighborhood of e having compact closure. In general, define $U_{n+1} = \bar{U}_n \cdot U_1$. Show the union of the sets $\bar{U}_n$ is both open and closed in G.]

This result holds without assuming G is connected, but the proof requires more effort.

10. *Theorem.*   *If X is a Hausdorff space that is locally compact and paracompact, then each component of X has a countable basis.*

Proof. If X_0 is a component of X, then X_0 is locally compact and paracompact. Let $\mathcal{C}$ be a locally finite covering of X_0 by sets open in X_0 that have compact closures. Let U_1 be a nonempty element of $\mathcal{C}$, and in general let U_n be the union of all elements of $\mathcal{C}$ that intersect $\bar{U}_{n-1}$. Show $\bar{U}_n$ is compact, and the sets U_n cover X_0.

§42   The Smirnov Metrization Theorem

The Nagata-Smirnov metrization theorem gives one set of necessary and sufficient conditions for metrizability of a space. In this section we prove a theorem that gives another such set of conditions. It is a corollary of the Nagata-Smirnov theorem and was first proved by Smirnov.

Definition.   A space X is ***locally metrizable*** if every point x of X has a neighborhood U that is metrizable in the subspace topology.

Theorem 42.1 (Smirnov metrization theorem).   *A space X is metrizable if and only if it is a paracompact Hausdorff space that is locally metrizable.*

Proof.   Suppose that X is metrizable. Then X is locally metrizable; it is also para-compact, by Theorem 41.4.

Conversely, suppose that X is a paracompact Hausdorff space that is locally metrizable. We shall show that X has a basis that is countably locally finite. Since X is regular, it will then follow from the Nagata-Smirnov theorem that X is metrizable.

The proof is an adaptation of the last part of the proof of Theorem 40.3. Cover X by open sets that are metrizable; then choose a locally finite open refinement $\mathcal{C}$ of this covering that covers X. Each element C of $\mathcal{C}$ is metrizable; let the function $d_C :$ $C \times C \to \mathbb{R}$ be a metric that gives the topology of C. Given $x \in C$, let $B_C(x, \epsilon)$ denote the set of all points y of C such that $d_C(x, y) < \epsilon$. Being open in C, the set $B_C(x, \epsilon)$ is also open in X.

Given $m \in \mathbb{Z}_+$, let $\mathcal{A}_m$ be the covering of X by all these open balls of radius $1/m$; that is, let

$$\mathcal{A}_m = \{B_C(x, 1/m) \mid x \in C \text{ and } C \in \mathcal{C}\}.$$

Let $\mathcal{D}_m$ be a locally finite open refinement of $\mathcal{A}_m$ that covers X. (Here we use paracompactness.) Let $\mathcal{D}$ be the union of the collections $\mathcal{D}_m$. Then $\mathcal{D}$ is countably locally finite. We assert that $\mathcal{D}$ is a basis for X; our theorem follows.

Let x be a point of X and let U be a neighborhood of x. We seek to find an element D of $\mathcal{D}$ such that $x \in D \subset U$. Now x belongs to only finitely many elements of $\mathcal{C}$, say to $C_1, \ldots, C_k$. Then $U \cap C_i$ is a neighborhood of x in the set C_i, so there is an $\epsilon_i > 0$ such that

$$B_{C_i}(x, \epsilon) \subset (U \cap C_i).$$

Choose m so that $2/m < \min\{\epsilon_1, \ldots, \epsilon_k\}$. Because the collection $\mathcal{D}_m$ covers X, there must be an element D of $\mathcal{D}_m$ containing x. Because $\mathcal{D}_m$ refines $\mathcal{A}_m$, there must be an element $B_C(y, 1/m)$ of $\mathcal{A}_m$, for some $C \in \mathcal{C}$ and some $y \in C$, that contains D. Because

$$x \in D \subset B_C(y, 1/m),$$

the point x belongs to C, so that C must be one of the sets $C_1, \ldots, C_k$. Say $C = C_i$. Since $B_C(y, 1/m)$ has diameter at most $2/m < \epsilon_i$, it follows that

$$x \in D \subset B_{C_i}(y, 1/m) \subset B_{C_i}(x, \epsilon_i) \subset U,$$

as desired.   ∎

Exercises

1. Compare Theorem 42.1 with Exercises 7 and 8 of §34.

2. (a) Show that for each $x \in S_\Omega$, the section of S_Ω by x has a countable basis and hence is metrizable.

   (b) Conclude that S_Ω is not paracompact.

Chapter 7

Complete Metric Spaces
and Function Spaces

The concept of completeness for a metric space is one you may have seen already. It is basic for all aspects of analysis. Although completeness is a metric property rather than a topological one, there are a number of theorems involving complete metric spaces that are topological in character. In this chapter, we shall study the most important examples of complete metric spaces and shall prove some of these theorems.

The most familiar example of a complete metric space is euclidean space in either of its usual metrics. Another example, just as important, is the set $\mathcal{C}(X, Y)$ of all continuous functions mapping a space X into a metric space Y. This set has a metric called the *uniform metric*, analogous to the uniform metric defined for $\mathbb{R}^J$ in §20. If Y is a complete metric space, then $\mathcal{C}(X, Y)$ is complete in the uniform metric. This we demonstrate in §43. As an application, we construct in §44 the well-known *Peano space-filling curve*.

One theorem of topological character concerning complete metric spaces is a theorem relating compactness of a space to completeness. We prove it in §45. An immediate corollary is a theorem concerning compact subspaces of the function space $\mathcal{C}(X, \mathbb{R}^n)$; it is the classical version of a famous theorem called *Ascoli's theorem*.

There are other useful topologies on the function space $\mathcal{C}(X, Y)$ besides the one derived from the uniform metric. We study some of them in §46, leading to a proof of a general version of Ascoli's theorem in §47.

§43   Complete Metric Spaces

In this section we define the notion of completeness and show that if Y is a complete metric space, then the function space $\mathcal{C}(X, Y)$ is complete in the uniform metric. We also show that every metric space can be imbedded isometrically in a complete metric space.

Definition.   Let (X, d) be a metric space. A sequence (x_n) of points of X is said to be a *Cauchy sequence* in (X, d) if it has the property that given $\epsilon > 0$, there is an integer N such that

$$d(x_n, x_m) < \epsilon \quad \text{whenever } n, m \geq N.$$

The metric space (X, d) is said to be *complete* if every Cauchy sequence in X converges.

Any convergent sequence in X is necessarily a Cauchy sequence, of course; completeness requires that the converse hold.

Note that a closed subset A of a complete metric space (X, d) is necessarily complete in the restricted metric. For a Cauchy sequence in A is also a Cauchy sequence in X, hence it converges in X. Because A is a closed subset of X, the limit must lie in A.

Note also that if X is complete under the metric d, then X is complete under the standard bounded metric

$$\bar{d}(x, y) = \min\{d(x, y), 1\}$$

corresponding to d, and conversely. For a sequence (x_n) is a Cauchy sequence under $\bar{d}$ if and only if it is a Cauchy sequence under d. And a sequence converges under $\bar{d}$ if and only if it converges under d.

A useful criterion for a metric space to be complete is the following:

Lemma 43.1.   *A metric space X is complete if every Cauchy sequence in X has a convergent subsequence.*

Proof.   Let (x_n) be a Cauchy sequence in (X, d). We show that if (x_n) has a subsequence (x_{n_i}) that converges to a point x, then the sequence (x_n) itself converges to x.

Given $\epsilon > 0$, first choose N large enough that

$$d(x_n, x_m) < \epsilon/2$$

for all $n, m \geq N$ [using the fact that (x_n) is a Cauchy sequence]. Then choose an integer i large enough that $n_i \geq N$ and

$$d(x_{n_i}, x) < \epsilon/2$$

[using the fact that $n_1 < n_2 < \ldots$ is an increasing sequence of integers and x_{n_i} converges to x]. Putting these facts together, we have the desired result that for $n \geq N$,

$$d(x_n, x) \leq d(x_n, x_{n_i}) + d(x_{n_i}, x) < \epsilon. \qquad \blacksquare$$

Theorem 43.2. *Euclidean space $\mathbb{R}^k$ is complete in either of its usual metrics, the euclidean metric d or the square metric ρ.*

Proof. To show the metric space $(\mathbb{R}^k, \rho)$ is complete, let (x_n) be a Cauchy sequence in $(\mathbb{R}^k, \rho)$. Then the set $\{x_n\}$ is a bounded subset of $(\mathbb{R}^k, \rho)$. For if we choose N so that

$$\rho(x_n, x_m) \leq 1$$

for all $n, m \geq N$, then the number

$$M = \max\{\rho(x_1, \mathbf{0}), \ldots, \rho(x_{N-1}, \mathbf{0}), \rho(x_N, \mathbf{0}) + 1\}$$

is an upper bound for $\rho(x_n, \mathbf{0})$. Thus the points of the sequence (x_n) all lie in the cube $[-M, M]^k$. Since this cube is compact, the sequence (x_n) has a convergent subsequence, by Theorem 28.2. Then $(\mathbb{R}^k, \rho)$ is complete.

To show that $(\mathbb{R}^k, d)$ is complete, note that a sequence is a Cauchy sequence relative to d if and only if it is a Cauchy sequence relative to ρ, and a sequence converges relative to d if and only if it converges relative to ρ. $\qquad \blacksquare$

Now we deal with the product space $\mathbb{R}^\omega$. We need a lemma about sequences in a product space.

Lemma 43.3. *Let X be the product space $X = \prod X_\alpha$; let $\mathbf{x}_n$ be a sequence of points of X. Then $\mathbf{x}_n \to \mathbf{x}$ if and only if $\pi_\alpha(\mathbf{x}_n) \to \pi_\alpha(\mathbf{x})$ for each α.*

Proof. This result was given as an exercise in §19; we give a proof here. Because the projection mapping $\pi_\alpha : X \to X_\alpha$ is continuous, it preserves convergent sequences; the "only if" part of the lemma follows. To prove the converse, suppose $\pi_\alpha(\mathbf{x}_n) \to \pi_\alpha(\mathbf{x})$ for each $\alpha \in J$. Let $U = \prod U_\alpha$ be a basis element for X that contains $\mathbf{x}$. For each α for which U_α does *not* equal the entire space X_α, choose N_α so that $\pi_\alpha(\mathbf{x}_n) \in U_\alpha$ for $n \geq N_\alpha$. Let N be the largest of the numbers N_α; then for all $n \geq N$, we have $\mathbf{x}_n \in U$. $\qquad \blacksquare$

Theorem 43.4. *There is a metric for the product space $\mathbb{R}^\omega$ relative to which $\mathbb{R}^\omega$ is complete.*

Proof. Let $\bar{d}(a, b) = \min\{|a - b|, 1\}$ be the standard bounded metric on $\mathbb{R}$. Let D be the metric on $\mathbb{R}^\omega$ defined by

$$D(\mathbf{x}, \mathbf{y}) = \sup\{\bar{d}(x_i, y_i)/i\}.$$

Then D induces the product topology on $\mathbb{R}^\omega$; we verify that $\mathbb{R}^\omega$ is complete under D. Let $\mathbf{x}_n$ be a Cauchy sequence in $(\mathbb{R}^\omega, D)$. Because

$$\bar{d}(\pi_i(\mathbf{x}), \pi_i(\mathbf{y})) \le i D(\mathbf{x}, \mathbf{y}),$$

we see that for fixed i the sequence $\pi_i(\mathbf{x}_n)$ is a Cauchy sequence in $\mathbb{R}$, so it converges, say to a_i. Then the sequence $\mathbf{x}_n$ converges to the point $\mathbf{a} = (a_1, a_2, \ldots)$ of $\mathbb{R}^\omega$. $\blacksquare$

EXAMPLE 1.   An example of a noncomplete metric space is the space $\mathbb{Q}$ of rational numbers in the usual metric $d(x, y) = |x - y|$. For instance, the sequence

$$1.4, 1.41, 1.414, 1.4142, 1.41421, \ldots$$

of finite decimals converging (in $\mathbb{R}$) to $\sqrt{2}$ is a Cauchy sequence in $\mathbb{Q}$ that does not converge (in $\mathbb{Q}$).

EXAMPLE 2.   Another noncomplete space is the open interval $(-1, 1)$ in $\mathbb{R}$, in the metric $d(x, y) = |x - y|$. In this space the sequence (x_n) defined by

$$x_n = 1 - 1/n$$

is a Cauchy sequence that does not converge. This example shows that completeness is not a topological property, that is, it is not preserved by homeomorphisms. For $(-1, 1)$ is homeomorphic to the real line $\mathbb{R}$, and $\mathbb{R}$ is complete in its usual metric.

Although both the product spaces $\mathbb{R}^n$ and $\mathbb{R}^\omega$ have metrics relative to which they are complete, one cannot hope to prove the same result for the product space $\mathbb{R}^J$ in general, because $\mathbb{R}^J$ is not even metrizable if J is uncountable (see §21). There is, however, another topology on the set $\mathbb{R}^J$, the one given by the uniform metric. Relative to this metric, $\mathbb{R}^J$ *is* complete, as we shall see.

We define the uniform metric in general as follows:

Definition.   Let (Y, d) be a metric space; let $\bar{d}(a, b) = \min\{d(a, b), 1\}$ be the standard bounded metric on Y derived from d. If $\mathbf{x} = (x_\alpha)_{\alpha \in J}$ and $\mathbf{y} = (y_\alpha)_{\alpha \in J}$ are points of the cartesian product Y^J, let

$$\bar{\rho}(\mathbf{x}, \mathbf{y}) = \sup\{\bar{d}(x_\alpha, y_\alpha) \mid \alpha \in J\}.$$

It is easy to check that ρ is a metric; it is called the ***uniform metric*** on Y^J corresponding to the metric d on Y.

Here we have used the standard "tuple" notation for the elements of the cartesian product Y^J. Since the elements of Y^J are simply functions from J to Y, we could also use functional notation for them. In this chapter, functional notation will be more convenient than tuple notation, so we shall use it throughout. In this notation, the definition of the uniform metric takes the following form: If $f, g : J \to Y$, then

$$\bar{\rho}(f, g) = \sup\{\bar{d}(f(\alpha), g(\alpha)) \mid \alpha \in J\}.$$

Theorem 43.5. *If the space Y is complete in the metric d, then the space Y^J is complete in the uniform metric $\bar{\rho}$ corresponding to d.*

Proof. Recall that if (Y, d) is complete, so is $(Y, \bar{d})$, where $\bar{d}$ is the bounded metric corresponding to d. Now suppose that $f_1, f_2, \ldots$ is a sequence of points of Y^J that is a Cauchy sequence relative to $\bar{\rho}$. Given α in J, the fact that

$$\bar{d}(f_n(\alpha), f_m(\alpha)) \leq \bar{\rho}(f_n, f_m)$$

for all n, m means that the sequence $f_1(\alpha), f_2(\alpha), \ldots$ is a Cauchy sequence in $(Y, \bar{d})$. Hence this sequence converges, say to a point y_α. Let $f : J \to Y$ be the function defined by $f(\alpha) = y_\alpha$. We assert that the sequence (f_n) converges to f in the metric $\bar{\rho}$.

Given $\epsilon > 0$, first choose N large enough that $\bar{\rho}(f_n, f_m) < \epsilon/2$ whenever $n, m \geq N$. Then, in particular,

$$\bar{d}(f_n(\alpha), f_m(\alpha)) < \epsilon/2$$

for $n, m \geq N$ and $\alpha \in J$. Letting n and α be fixed, and letting m become arbitrarily large, we see that

$$\bar{d}(f_n(\alpha), f(\alpha)) \leq \epsilon/2.$$

This inequality holds for all α in J, provided merely that $n \geq N$. Therefore,

$$\bar{\rho}(f_n, f) \leq \epsilon/2 < \epsilon$$

for $n \geq N$, as desired. ∎

Now let us specialize somewhat, and consider the set Y^X where X is a *topological space* rather than merely a set. Of course, this has no effect on what has gone before; the topology of X is irrelevant when considering the set of *all* functions $f : X \to Y$. But suppose that we consider the subset $\mathcal{C}(X, Y)$ of Y^X consisting of all *continuous* functions $f : X \to Y$. It turns out that if Y is complete, this subset is also complete in the uniform metric. The same holds for the set $\mathcal{B}(X, Y)$ of all bounded functions $f : X \to Y$. (A function f is said to be **bounded** if its image $f(X)$ is a bounded subset of the metric space (Y, d).)

Theorem 43.6. *Let X be a topological space and let (Y, d) be a metric space. The set $\mathcal{C}(X, Y)$ of continuous functions is closed in Y^X under the uniform metric. So is the set $\mathcal{B}(X, Y)$ of bounded functions. Therefore, if Y is complete, these spaces are complete in the uniform metric.*

Proof. The first part of this theorem is just the uniform limit theorem (Theorem 21.6) in a new guise. First, we show that if a sequence of elements f_n of Y^X converges to the element f of Y^X relative to the metric $\bar{\rho}$ on Y^X, then it converges to f uniformly in the sense defined in §21, relative to the metric $\bar{d}$ on Y. Given $\epsilon > 0$, choose an integer N such that

$$\bar{\rho}(f, f_n) < \epsilon$$

for all $n > N$. Then for all $x \in X$ and all $n \geq N$,

$$\bar{d}(f_n(x), f(x)) \leq \bar{\rho}(f_n, f) < \epsilon.$$

Thus (f_n) converges uniformly to f.

Now we show that $\mathcal{C}(X, Y)$ is closed in Y^X relative to the metric $\bar{\rho}$. Let f be an element of Y^X that is a limit point of $\mathcal{C}(X, Y)$. Then there is a sequence (f_n) of elements of $\mathcal{C}(X, Y)$ converging to f in the metric $\bar{\rho}$. By the uniform limit theorem, f is continuous, so that $f \in \mathcal{C}(X, Y)$.

Finally, we show that $\mathcal{B}(X, Y)$ is closed in Y^X. If f is a limit point of $\mathcal{B}(X, Y)$, there is a sequence of elements f_n of $\mathcal{B}(X, Y)$ converging to f. Choose N so large that $\bar{\rho}(f_N, f) < 1/2$. Then for $x \in X$, we have $\bar{d}(f_N(x), f(x)) < 1/2$, which implies that $d(f_N(x), f(x)) < 1/2$. It follows that if M is the diameter of the set $f_N(X)$, then $f(X)$ has diameter at most $M + 1$. Hence $f \in \mathcal{B}(X, Y)$.

We conclude that $\mathcal{C}(X, Y)$ and $\mathcal{B}(X, Y)$ are complete in the metric $\bar{\rho}$ if Y is complete in d. ∎

Definition. If (Y, d) is a metric space, one can define another metric on the set $\mathcal{B}(X, Y)$ of bounded functions from X to Y by the equation

$$\rho(f, g) = \sup\{d(f(x), g(x)) \mid x \in X\}.$$

It is easy to see that ρ is well-defined, for the set $f(X) \cup g(X)$ is bounded if both $f(X)$ and $g(X)$ are. The metric ρ is called the **sup metric**.

There is a simple relation between the sup metric and the uniform metric. Indeed, if $f, g \in \mathcal{B}(X, Y)$, then

$$\bar{\rho}(f, g) = \min\{\rho(f, g), 1\}.$$

For if $\rho(f, g) > 1$, then $d(f(x_0), g(x_0)) > 1$ for at least one $x_0 \in X$, so that $\bar{d}(f(x_0), g(x_0)) = 1$ and $\bar{\rho}(f, g) = 1$ by definition. On the other hand, if $\rho(f, g) \leq 1$, then $\bar{d}(f(x), g(x)) = d(f(x), g(x)) \leq 1$ for all x, so that $\bar{\rho}(f, g) = \rho(f, g)$. Thus on $\mathcal{B}(X, Y)$, the metric $\bar{\rho}$ is just the standard bounded metric derived from the metric ρ. That is the reason we introduced the notation $\bar{\rho}$ for the uniform metric, back in §20!

If X is a compact space, then every continuous function $f : X \to Y$ is bounded; hence the sup metric is defined on $\mathcal{C}(X, Y)$. If Y is complete under d, then $\mathcal{C}(X, Y)$ is complete under the corresponding uniform metric $\bar{\rho}$, so it is also complete under the sup metric ρ. We often use the sup metric rather than the uniform metric in this situation.

We now prove a classical theorem, to the effect that every metric space can be imbedded isometrically in a complete metric space. (A different proof, somewhat more direct, is outlined in Exercise 9.) Although we shall not need this theorem, it is useful in other parts of mathematics.

Theorem 43.7.   *Let (X, d) be a metric space. There is an isometric imbedding of X into a complete metric space.*

Proof.   Let $\mathcal{B}(X, \mathbb{R})$ be the set of all bounded functions mapping X into $\mathbb{R}$. Let x_0 be a fixed point of X. Given $a \in X$, define $\phi_a : X \to \mathbb{R}$ by the equation

$$\phi_a(x) = d(x, a) - d(x, x_0).$$

We assert that ϕ_a is bounded. For it follows, from the inequalities

$$d(x, a) \leq d(x, b) + d(a, b),$$
$$d(x, b) \leq d(x, a) + d(a, b),$$

that

$$|d(x, a) - d(x, b)| \leq d(a, b).$$

Setting $b = x_0$, we conclude that $|\phi_a(x)| \leq d(a, x_0)$ for all x.

Define $\Phi : X \to \mathcal{B}(X, \mathbb{R})$ by setting

$$\Phi(a) = \phi_a.$$

We show that Φ is an isometric imbedding of (X, d) into the complete metric space $(\mathcal{B}(X, \mathbb{R}), \rho)$. That is, we show that for every pair of points $a, b \in X$,

$$\rho(\phi_a, \phi_b) = d(a, b).$$

By definition,

$$\rho(\phi_a, \phi_b) = \sup\{|\phi_a(x) - \phi_b(x)|; \; x \in X\}$$
$$= \sup\{|d(x, a) - d(x, b)|; \; x \in X\}.$$

We conclude that

$$\rho(\phi_a, \phi_b) \leq d(a, b).$$

On the other hand, this inequality cannot be strict, for when $x = a$,

$$|d(x, a) - d(x, b)| = d(a, b). \qquad \blacksquare$$

Definition.   Let X be a metric space. If $h : X \to Y$ is an isometric imbedding of X into a complete metric space Y, then the subspace $\overline{h(X)}$ of Y is a complete metric space. It is called the *completion* of X.

The completion of X is uniquely determined up to an isometry. See Exercise 10.

Exercises

1. Let X be a metric space.
   (a) Suppose that for some $\epsilon > 0$, every ϵ-ball in X has compact closure. Show that X is complete.
   (b) Suppose that for each $x \in X$ there is an $\epsilon > 0$ such that the ball $B(x, \epsilon)$ has compact closure. Show by means of an example that X need not be complete.

2. Let (X, d_X) and (Y, d_Y) be metric spaces; let Y be complete. Let $A \subset X$. Show that if $f : A \to Y$ is uniformly continuous, then f can be uniquely extended to a continuous function $g : \bar{A} \to Y$, and g is uniformly continuous.

3. Two metrics d and d' on a set X are said to be **metrically equivalent** if the identity map $i : (X, d) \to (X, d')$ and its inverse are both uniformly continuous.
   (a) Show that d is metrically equivalent to the standard bounded metric $\bar{d}$ derived from d.
   (b) Show that if d and d' are metrically equivalent, then X is complete under d if and only if it is complete under d'.

4. Show that the metric space (X, d) is complete if and only if for every nested sequence $A_1 \supset A_2 \supset \cdots$ of nonempty closed sets of X such that diam $A_n \to 0$, the intersection of the sets A_n is nonempty.

5. If (X, d) is a metric space, recall that a map $f : X \to X$ is called a *contraction* if there is a number $\alpha < 1$ such that

$$d(f(x), f(y)) \le \alpha d(x, y)$$

   for all $x, y \in X$. Show that if f is a contraction of a complete metric space, then there is a unique point $x \in X$ such that $f(x) = x$. Compare Exercise 7 of §28.

6. A space X is said to be **topologically complete** if there exists a metric for the topology of X relative to which X is complete.
   (a) Show that a closed subspace of a topologically complete space is topologically complete.
   (b) Show that a countable product of topologically complete spaces is topologically complete (in the product topology).
   (c) Show that an open subspace of a topologically complete space is topologically complete. [*Hint:* If $U \subset X$ and X is complete under the metric d, define $\phi : U \to \mathbb{R}$ by the equation

$$\phi(x) = 1/d(x, X - U).$$

   Imbed U in $X \times \mathbb{R}$ by setting $f(x) = x \times \phi(x)$.]
   (d) Show that if A is a G_δ set in a topologically complete space, then A is topologically complete. [*Hint:* Let A be the intersection of the open sets U_n, for $n \in \mathbb{Z}_+$. Consider the diagonal imbedding $f(a) = (a, a, \ldots)$ of A into $\prod U_n$.] Conclude that the irrationals are topologically complete.

7. Show that the set of all sequences $(x_1, x_2, \ldots)$ such that $\sum x_i^2$ converges is complete in the ℓ^2-metric. (See Exercise 8 of §20.)

8. If X and Y are spaces, define

$$e : X \times \mathcal{C}(X, Y) \to Y$$

by the equation $e(x, f) = f(x)$; the map e is called the **evaluation map**. Show that if d is a metric for Y and $\mathcal{C}(X, Y)$ has the corresponding uniform topology, then e is continuous. We shall generalize this result in §46.

9. Let (X, d) be a metric space. Show that there is an isometric imbedding h of X into a complete metric space (Y, D), as follows: Let $\tilde{X}$ denote the set of all Cauchy sequences

$$\mathbf{x} = (x_1, x_2, \ldots)$$

of points of X. Define $\mathbf{x} \sim \mathbf{y}$ if

$$d(x_n, y_n) \longrightarrow 0.$$

Let $[\mathbf{x}]$ denote the equivalence class of $\mathbf{x}$; and let Y denote the set of these equivalence classes. Define a metric D on Y by the equation

$$D([\mathbf{x}], [\mathbf{y}]) = \lim_{n \to \infty} d(x_n, y_n).$$

(a) Show that $\sim$ is an equivalence relation, and show that D is a well-defined metric.

(b) Define $h : X \to Y$ by letting $h(x)$ be the equivalence class of the constant sequence $(x, x, \ldots)$:

$$h(x) = [(x, x, \ldots)].$$

Show that h is an isometric imbedding.

(c) Show that $h(X)$ is dense in Y; indeed, given $\mathbf{x} = (x_1, x_2, \ldots) \in \tilde{X}$, show the sequence $h(x_n)$ of points of Y converges to the point $[\mathbf{x}]$ of Y.

(d) Show that if A is a dense subset of a metric space (Z, ρ), and if every Cauchy sequence in A converges in Z, then Z is complete.

(e) Show that (Y, D) is complete.

10. *Theorem* (*Uniqueness of the completion*). *Let* $h : X \to Y$ *and* $h' : X \to Y'$ *be isometric imbeddings of the metric space* (X, d) *in the complete metric spaces* (Y, D) *and* (Y', D'), *respectively. Then there is an isometry of* $(\overline{h(X)}, D)$ *with* $(\overline{h'(X)}, D')$ *that equals* $h' h^{-1}$ *on the subspace* $h(X)$.

*§44   A Space-Filling Curve

As an application of the completeness of the metric space $\mathcal{C}(X, Y)$ in the uniform metric when Y is complete, we shall construct the famous "Peano space-filling curve."

Theorem 44.1. *Let $I = [0, 1]$. There exists a continuous map $f : I \to I^2$ whose image fills up the entire square I^2.*

The existence of this path violates one's naive geometric intuition in much the same way as does the existence of the continuous nowhere-differentiable function (which we shall come to later).

Proof.   *Step 1.* We shall construct the map f as the limit of a sequence of continuous functions f_n. First we describe a particular operation on paths, which will be used to generate the sequence f_n.

Begin with an arbitrary closed interval $[a, b]$ in the real line and an arbitrary square in the plane with sides parallel to the coordinate axes, and consider the triangular path g pictured in Figure 44.1. It is a continuous map of $[a, b]$ into the square. The operation we wish to describe replaces the path g by the path g' pictured in Figure 44.2. It is made up of four triangular paths, each half the size of g. Note that g and g' have the same initial point and the same final point. You can write the equations for g and g' if you like.

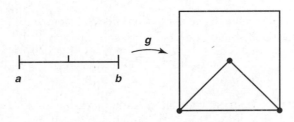

Figure 44.1

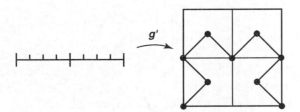

Figure 44.2

This same operation can also be applied to any triangular path connecting two adjacent corners of the square. For instance, when applied to the path h pictured in Figure 44.3, it gives the path h'.

Step 2. Now we define a sequence of functions $f_n : I \to I^2$. The first function, which we label f_0 for convenience, is the triangular path pictured in Figure 44.1, letting $a = 0$ and $b = 1$. The next function f_1 is the function obtained by applying the operation described in Step 1 to the function f_0; it is pictured in Figure 44.2. The next function f_2 is the function obtained by applying this same operation to each of the four

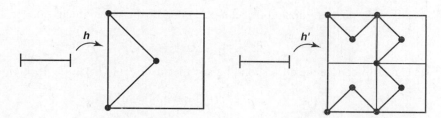

Figure 44.3

triangular paths that make up f_1. It is pictured in Figure 44.4. The next function f_3 is obtained by applying the operation to each of the 16 triangular paths that make up f_2; it is pictured in Figure 44.5. And so on. At the general step, f_n is a path made up of 4^n triangular paths of the type considered in Step 1, each lying in a square of edge length $1/2^n$. The function f_{n+1} is obtained by applying the operation of Step 1 to these triangular paths, replacing each one by four smaller triangular paths.

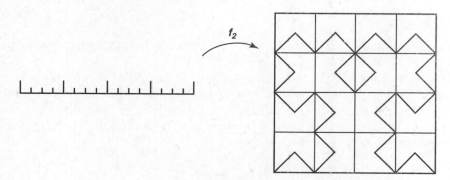

Figure 44.4

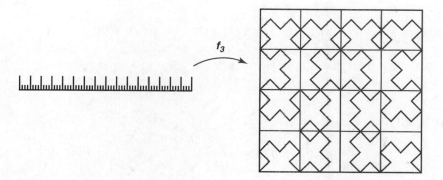

Figure 44.5

Step 3. For purposes of this proof, let $d(\mathbf{x}, \mathbf{y})$ denote the square metric on $\mathbb{R}^2$,

$$d(\mathbf{x}, \mathbf{y}) = \max\{|x_1 - y_1|, |x_2 - y_2|\}.$$

Then we can let ρ denote the corresponding sup metric on $\mathcal{C}(I, I^2)$:

$$\rho(f, g) = \sup\{d(f(t), g(t)) \mid t \in I\}.$$

Because I^2 is closed in $\mathbb{R}^2$, it is complete in the square metric; then $\mathcal{C}(I, I^2)$ is complete in the metric ρ.

We assert that the sequence of functions (f_n) defined in Step 2 is a Cauchy sequence under ρ. To prove this fact, let us examine what happens when we pass from f_n to f_{n+1}. Each of the small triangular paths that make up f_n lies in a square of edge length $1/2^n$. The operation by which we obtain f_{n+1} replaces each such triangular path by four triangular paths that lie in the same square. Therefore, in the square metric on I^2, the distance between $f_n(t)$ and $f_{n+1}(t)$ is at most $1/2^n$. As a result, $\rho(f_n, f_{n+1}) \leq 1/2^n$. It follows that (f_n) is a Cauchy sequence, since

$$\rho(f_n, f_{n+m}) \leq 1/2^n + 1/2^{n+1} + \cdots + 1/2^{n+m-1} < 2/2^n$$

f٠ all n and m.

Step 4. Because $\mathcal{C}(I, I^2)$ is complete, the sequence f_n converges to a continuous function $f : I \to I^2$. We prove that f is surjective.

Let $\mathbf{x}$ be a point of I^2; we show that $\mathbf{x}$ belongs to $f(I)$. First we note that, given n, the path f_n comes within a distance of $1/2^n$ of the point $\mathbf{x}$. For the path f_n touches each of the little squares of edge length $1/2^n$ into which we have divided I^2.

Using this fact, we shall prove that, given $\epsilon > 0$, the ϵ-neighborhood of $\mathbf{x}$ intersects $f(I)$. Choose N large enough that

$$\rho(f_N, f) < \epsilon/2 \quad \text{and} \quad 1/2^N < \epsilon/2.$$

By the result of the previous paragraph, there is a point $t_0 \in I$ such that $d(\mathbf{x}, f_N(t_0)) \leq 1/2^N$. Then since $d(f_N(t), f(t)) < \epsilon/2$ for all t, it follows that

$$d(\mathbf{x}, f(t_0)) < \epsilon,$$

so the ϵ-neighborhood of $\mathbf{x}$ intersects $f(I)$.

It follows that $\mathbf{x}$ belongs to the closure of $f(I)$. But I is compact, so $f(I)$ is compact and is therefore closed. Hence $\mathbf{x}$ lies in $f(I)$, as desired.   ∎

Exercises

1. Given n, show there is a continuous surjective map $g : I \to I^n$. [*Hint:* Consider $f \times f : I \times I \to I^2 \times I^2$.]

2. Show there is a continuous surjective map $f : \mathbb{R} \to \mathbb{R}^n$.

3. (a) If $\mathbb{R}^\omega$ is given the product topology, show there is no continuous surjective map $f : \mathbb{R} \to \mathbb{R}^\omega$. [*Hint:* Show that $\mathbb{R}^\omega$ is not a countable union of compact subspaces.]

   (b) If $\mathbb{R}^\omega$ is given the product topology, determine whether or not there is a continuous surjective map of $\mathbb{R}$ onto the subspace $\mathbb{R}^\infty$.

   (c) What happens to the statements in (a) and (b) if $\mathbb{R}^\omega$ is given the uniform topology or the box topology?

4. (a) Let X be a Hausdorff space. Show that if there is a continuous surjective map $f : I \to X$, then X is compact, connected, weakly locally connected, and metrizable. [*Hint:* Show f is a perfect map.]

   (b) The converse of the result in (a) is a famous theorem of point-set topology called the *Hahn-Mazurkiewicz theorem* (see [H-Y], p. 129). Assuming this theorem, show there is a continuous surjective map $f : I \to I^\omega$.

   A Hausdorff space that is the continuous image of the closed unit interval is often called a **Peano space**.

§45   Compactness in Metric Spaces

We have already shown that compactness, limit point compactness, and sequential compactness are equivalent for metric spaces. There is still another formulation of compactness for metric spaces, one that involves the notion of completeness. We study it in this section. As an application, we shall prove a theorem characterizing those subspaces of $\mathcal{C}(X, \mathbb{R}^n)$ that are compact in the uniform topology.

How is compactness of a metric space X related to completeness of X? It follows from Lemma 43.1 that every compact metric space is complete. The converse does not hold—a complete metric space need not be compact. It is reasonable to ask what extra condition one needs to impose on a complete space to be assured of its compactness. Such a condition is the one called *total boundedness*.

Definition.   A metric space (X, d) is said to be **totally bounded** if for every $\epsilon > 0$, there is a finite covering of X by ϵ-balls.

EXAMPLE 1.   Total boundedness clearly implies boundedness. For if $B(x_1, 1/2), \ldots ,$ $B(x_n, 1/2)$ is a finite covering of X by open balls of radius $1/2$, then X has diameter at most $1 + \max\{d(x_i, x_j)\}$. The converse does not hold, however. For example, in the metric $\bar{d}(a, b) = \min\{1, |a - b|\}$, the real line $\mathbb{R}$ is bounded but not totally bounded.

EXAMPLE 2.   Under the metric $d(a, b) = |a - b|$, the real line $\mathbb{R}$ is complete but not totally bounded, while the subspace $(-1, 1)$ is totally bounded but not complete. The subspace $[-1, 1]$ is both complete and totally bounded.

Theorem 45.1.   *A metric space (X, d) is compact if and only if it is complete and totally bounded.*

Proof.   If X is a compact metric space, then X is complete, as noted above. The fact that X is totally bounded is a consequence of the fact that the covering of X by all open ϵ-balls must contain a finite subcovering.

Conversely, let X be complete and totally bounded. We shall prove that X is sequentially compact. This will suffice.

Let (x_n) be a sequence of points of X. We shall construct a subsequence of (x_n) that is a Cauchy sequence, so that it necessarily converges. First cover X by finitely many balls of radius 1. At least one of these balls, say B_1, contains x_n for infinitely many values of n. Let J_1 be the subset of $\mathbb{Z}_+$ consisting of those indices n for which $x_n \in B_1$.

Next, cover X by finitely many balls of radius $1/2$. Because J_1 is infinite, at least one of these balls, say B_2, must contain x_n for infinitely many values of n in J_1. Choose J_2 to be the set of those indices n for which $n \in J_1$ and $x_n \in B_2$. In general, given an infinite set J_k of positive integers, choose J_{k+1} to be an infinite subset of J_k such that there is a ball B_{k+1} of radius $1/(k+1)$ that contains x_n for all $n \in J_{k+1}$.

Choose $n_1 \in J_1$. Given n_k, choose $n_{k+1} \in J_{k+1}$ such that $n_{k+1} > n_k$; this we can do because J_{k+1} is an infinite set. Now for $i, j \geq k$, the indices n_i and n_j both belong to J_k (because $J_1 \supset J_2 \supset \cdots$ is a nested sequence of sets). Therefore, for all $i, j \geq k$, the points x_{n_i} and x_{n_j} are contained in a ball B_k of radius $1/k$. It follows that the sequence (x_{n_i}) is a Cauchy sequence, as desired.   ∎

We now apply this result to find the compact subspaces of the space $\mathcal{C}(X, \mathbb{R}^n)$, in the uniform topology. We know that a subspace of $\mathbb{R}^n$ is compact if and only if it is closed and bounded. One might hope that an analogous result holds for $\mathcal{C}(X, \mathbb{R}^n)$. But it does not, even if X is compact. One needs to assume that the subspace of $\mathcal{C}(X, \mathbb{R}^n)$ satisfies an additional condition, called *equicontinuity*. We consider that notion now.

Definition.   Let (Y, d) be a metric space. Let $\mathcal{F}$ be a subset of the function space $\mathcal{C}(X, Y)$. If $x_0 \in X$, the set $\mathcal{F}$ of functions is said to be ***equicontinuous at x_0*** if given $\epsilon > 0$, there is a neighborhood U of x_0 such that for all $x \in U$ and all $f \in \mathcal{F}$,

$$d(f(x), f(x_0)) < \epsilon.$$

If the set $\mathcal{F}$ is equicontinuous at x_0 for each $x_0 \in X$, it is said simply to be ***equicontinuous***.

Continuity of the function f at x_0 means that given f and given $\epsilon > 0$, there exists a neighborhood U of x_0 such that $d(f(x), f(x_0)) < \epsilon$ for $x \in U$. Equicontinuity of $\mathcal{F}$ means that a single neighborhood U can be chosen that will work for all the functions f in the collection $\mathcal{F}$.

Note that equicontinuity depends on the specific metric d rather than merely on the topology of Y.

Lemma 45.2. *Let X be a space; let (Y, d) be a metric space. If the subset $\mathcal{F}$ of $\mathcal{C}(X, Y)$ is totally bounded under the uniform metric corresponding to d, then $\mathcal{F}$ is equicontinuous under d.*

Proof. Assume $\mathcal{F}$ is totally bounded. Given $0 < \epsilon < 1$, and given x_0, we find a neighborhood U of x_0 such that $d(f(x), f(x_0)) < \epsilon$ for $x \in U$ and $f \in \mathcal{F}$.

Set $\delta = \epsilon/3$; cover $\mathcal{F}$ by finitely many open δ-balls

$$B(f_1, \delta), \ldots, B(f_n, \delta)$$

in $\mathcal{C}(X, Y)$. Each function f_i is continuous; therefore, we can choose a neighborhood U of x_0 such that for $i = 1, \ldots, n$,

$$d(f_i(x), f_i(x_0)) < \delta$$

whenever $x \in U$.

Let f be an arbitrary element of $\mathcal{F}$. Then f belongs to at least one of the above δ-balls, say to $B(f_i, \delta)$. Then for $x \in U$, we have

$$\bar{d}(f(x), f_i(x)) < \delta,$$
$$d(f_i(x), f_i(x_0)) < \delta,$$
$$\bar{d}(f_i(x_0), f(x_0)) < \delta.$$

The first and third inequalities hold because $\bar{\rho}(f, f_i) < \delta$, and the second holds because $x \in U$. Since $\delta < 1$, the first and third also hold if $\bar{d}$ is replaced by d; then the triangle inequality implies that for all $x \in U$, we have $d(f(x), f(x_0)) < \epsilon$, as desired. ∎

Now we prove the classical version of Ascoli's theorem, which concerns compact subspaces of the function space $\mathcal{C}(X, \mathbb{R}^n)$. A more general version, whose proof does not depend on this one, is given in §47. The general version, however, relies on the Tychonoff theorem, whereas this one does not.

We begin by proving a partial converse to the preceding lemma, which holds when X and Y are compact.

*Lemma 45.3. *Let X be a space; let (Y, d) be a metric space; assume X and Y are compact. If the subset $\mathcal{F}$ of $\mathcal{C}(X, Y)$ is equicontinuous under d, then $\mathcal{F}$ is totally bounded under the uniform and sup metrics corresponding to d.*

Proof. Since X is compact, the sup metric ρ is defined on $\mathcal{C}(X, Y)$. Total boundedness under ρ is equivalent to total boundedness under $\bar{\rho}$, for whenever $\epsilon < 1$, every ϵ-ball under ρ is also an ϵ-ball under $\bar{\rho}$, and conversely. Therefore, we may as well use the metric ρ throughout.

Assume $\mathcal{F}$ is equicontinuous. Given $\epsilon > 0$, we cover $\mathcal{F}$ by finitely many sets that are open ϵ-balls in the metric ρ.

Set $\delta = \epsilon/3$. Given any $a \in X$, there is a corresponding neighborhood U_a of a such that $d(f(x), f(a)) < \delta$ for all $x \in U_a$ and all $f \in \mathcal{F}$. Cover X by finitely many such neighborhoods U_a, for $a = a_1, \dots, a_k$; denote U_{a_i} by U_i. Then cover Y by finitely many open sets $V_1, \dots, V_m$ of diameter less than δ.

Let J be the collection of all functions $\alpha : \{1, \dots, k\} \to \{1, \dots, m\}$. Given $\alpha \in J$, if there exists a function f of $\mathcal{F}$ such that $f(a_i) \in V_{\alpha(i)}$ for each $i = 1, \dots, k$, choose one such function and label it f_α. The collection $\{f_\alpha\}$ is indexed by a subset J' of the set J and is thus finite. We assert that the open balls $B_\rho(f_\alpha, \epsilon)$, for $\alpha \in J'$, cover $\mathcal{F}$.

Let f be an element of $\mathcal{F}$. For each $i = 1, \dots, k$, choose an integer $\alpha(i)$ such that $f(a_i) \in V_{\alpha(i)}$. Then the function α is in J'. We assert that f belongs to the ball $B_\rho(f_\alpha, \epsilon)$.

Let x be a point of X. Choose i so that $x \in U_i$. Then

$$d(f(x), f(a_i)) < \delta,$$
$$d(f(a_i), f_\alpha(a_i)) < \delta,$$
$$d(f_\alpha(a_i), f_\alpha(x)) < \delta.$$

The first and third inequalities hold because $x \in U_i$, and the second holds because $f(a_i)$ and $f_\alpha(a_i)$ are in $V_{\alpha(i)}$. We conclude that $d(f(x), f_\alpha(x)) < \epsilon$. Because this inequality holds for every $x \in X$,

$$\rho(f, f_\alpha) = \max\{d(f(x), f_\alpha(x))\} < \epsilon.$$

Thus f belongs to $B_\rho(f_\alpha, \epsilon)$, as asserted.   ∎

Definition.   If (Y, d) is a metric space, a subset $\mathcal{F}$ of $\mathcal{C}(X, Y)$ is said to be **pointwise bounded** under d if for each $x \in X$, the subset

$$\mathcal{F}_a = \{f(a) \mid f \in \mathcal{F}\}$$

of Y is bounded under d.

*Theorem 45.4 (Ascoli's theorem, classical version).   *Let X be a compact space; let $(\mathbb{R}^n, d)$ denote euclidean space in either the square metric or the euclidean metric; give $\mathcal{C}(X, \mathbb{R}^n)$ the corresponding uniform topology. A subspace $\mathcal{F}$ of $\mathcal{C}(X, \mathbb{R}^n)$ has compact closure if and only if $\mathcal{F}$ is equicontinuous and pointwise bounded under d.*

Proof.   Since X is compact, the sup metric ρ is defined on $\mathcal{C}(X, \mathbb{R}^n)$ and gives the uniform topology on $\mathcal{C}(X, \mathbb{R}^n)$. Throughout, let $\mathcal{G}$ denote the closure of $\mathcal{F}$ in $\mathcal{C}(X, \mathbb{R}^n)$.

Step 1.   We show that if $\mathcal{G}$ is compact, then $\mathcal{G}$ is equicontinuous and pointwise bounded under d. Since $\mathcal{F} \subset \mathcal{G}$, it follows that $\mathcal{F}$ is also equicontinuous and pointwise bounded under d. This proves the "only if" part of the theorem.

Compactness of $\mathcal{G}$ implies that $\mathcal{G}$ is totally bounded under ρ and $\bar{\rho}$ by Theorem 45.1; this in turn implies that $\mathcal{G}$ is equicontinuous under d, by Lemma 45.2. Compactness of $\mathcal{G}$ also implies that $\mathcal{G}$ is bounded under ρ; this in turn implies that $\mathcal{G}$ is pointwise bounded under d. For if $\rho(f, g) \leq M$ for all $f, g \in \mathcal{G}$, then in particular $d(f(a), g(a)) \leq M$ for $f, g \in \mathcal{G}$, so that $\mathcal{G}_a$ has diameter at most M.

Step 2. We show that if $\mathcal{F}$ is equicontinuous and pointwise bounded under d, then so is $\mathcal{G}$.

First, we check equicontinuity. Given $x_0 \in X$ and given $\epsilon > 0$, choose a neighborhood U of x_0 such that $d(f(x), f(x_0)) < \epsilon/3$ for all $x \in U$ and $f \in \mathcal{F}$. Given $g \in \mathcal{G}$, choose $f \in \mathcal{F}$ so that $\rho(f, g) < \epsilon/3$. The triangle inequality implies that $d(g(x), g(x_0)) < \epsilon$ for all $x \in U$. Since g is arbitrary, equicontinuity of $\mathcal{G}$ at x_0 follows.

Second, we verify pointwise boundedness. Given a, choose M so that diam $\mathcal{F}_a \leq M$. Then, given $g, g' \in \mathcal{G}$, choose $f, f' \in \mathcal{F}$ such that $\rho(f, g) < 1$ and $\rho(f', g') < 1$. Since $d(f(a), f'(a)) \leq M$, it follows that $d(g(a), g'(a)) \leq M + 2$. Then since g and g' are arbitrary, it follows that diam $\mathcal{G}_a \leq M + 2$.

Step 3. We show that if $\mathcal{G}$ is equicontinuous and pointwise bounded, then there is a compact subspace Y of $\mathbb{R}^n$ that contains the union of the sets $g(X)$, for $g \in \mathcal{G}$.

Choose, for each $a \in X$, a neighborhood U_a of a such that $d(g(x), g(a)) < 1$ for $x \in U_a$ and $g \in \mathcal{G}$. Since X is compact, we can cover X by finitely many such neighborhoods, say for $a = a_1, \ldots, a_k$. Because the sets $\mathcal{G}_{a_i}$ are bounded, their union is also bounded; suppose it lies in the ball of radius N in $\mathbb{R}^n$ centered at the origin. Then for all $g \in \mathcal{G}$, the set $g(X)$ is contained in the ball of radius $N + 1$ centered at the origin. Let Y be the closure of this ball.

Step 4. We prove the "if" part of the theorem. Assume that $\mathcal{F}$ is equicontinuous and pointwise bounded under d. We show that $\mathcal{G}$ is complete and totally bounded under ρ; then Theorem 45.1 implies that $\mathcal{G}$ is compact.

Completeness is easy, for $\mathcal{G}$ is a closed subspace of the complete metric space $(\mathcal{C}(X, \mathbb{R}^n), \rho)$.

We verify total boundedness. First, Step 2 implies that $\mathcal{G}$ is equicontinuous and pointwise bounded under d; then Step 3 tells us that there is a compact subspace Y of $\mathbb{R}^n$ such that $\mathcal{G} \subset \mathcal{C}(X, Y)$. Equicontinuity of $\mathcal{G}$ now implies, by Lemma 45.3, that $\mathcal{G}$ is totally bounded under ρ, as desired.   ∎

*Corollary 45.5. *Let X be compact; let d denote either the square metric or the euclidean metric on $\mathbb{R}^n$; give $\mathcal{C}(X, \mathbb{R}^n)$ the corresponding uniform topology. A subspace $\mathcal{F}$ of $\mathcal{C}(X, \mathbb{R}^n)$ is compact if and only if it is closed, bounded under the sup metric ρ, and equicontinuous under d.*

Proof. If $\mathcal{F}$ is compact, it must be closed and bounded; the preceding theorem implies that it is also equicontinuous. Conversely, if $\mathcal{F}$ is closed, it equals its closure $\mathcal{G}$; if it is bounded under ρ, it is pointwise bounded under d; and if it is also equicontinuous, the preceding theorem implies that it is compact.   ∎

Exercises

1. If X_n is metrizable with metric d_n, then

$$D(\mathbf{x}, \mathbf{y}) = \sup\{\bar{d}_i(x_i, y_i)/i\}$$

   is a metric for the product space $X = \prod X_n$. Show that X is totally bounded under D if each X_n is totally bounded under d_n. Conclude without using the Tychonoff theorem that a countable product of compact metrizable spaces is compact.

2. Let (Y, d) be a metric space; let $\mathcal{F}$ be a subset of $\mathcal{C}(X, Y)$.
   (a) Show that if $\mathcal{F}$ is finite, then $\mathcal{F}$ is equicontinuous.
   (b) Show that if f_n is a sequence of elements of $\mathcal{C}(X, Y)$ that converges uniformly, then the collection $\{f_n\}$ is equicontinuous.
   (c) Suppose that $\mathcal{F}$ is a collection of differentiable functions $f : \mathbb{R} \to \mathbb{R}$ such that each $x \in \mathbb{R}$ lies in a neighborhood U on which the derivatives of the functions in $\mathcal{F}$ are uniformly bounded. [This means that there is an M such that $|f'(x)| \leq M$ for all f in $\mathcal{F}$ and all $x \in U$.] Show that $\mathcal{F}$ is equicontinuous.

3. Prove the following:
   Theorem (Arzela's theorem).   *Let X be compact; let $f_n \in \mathcal{C}(X, \mathbb{R}^k)$. If the collection $\{f_n\}$ is pointwise bounded and equicontinuous, then the sequence f_n has a uniformly convergent subsequence.*

4. (a) Let $f_n : I \to \mathbb{R}$ be the function $f_n(x) = x^n$. The collection $\mathcal{F} = \{f_n\}$ is pointwise bounded but the sequence (f_n) has no uniformly convergent subsequence; at what point or points does $\mathcal{F}$ fail to be equicontinuous?
   (b) Repeat (a) for the functions f_n of Exercise 9 of §21.

5. Let X be a space. A subset $\mathcal{F}$ of $\mathcal{C}(X, \mathbb{R})$ is said to ***vanish uniformly at infinity*** if given $\epsilon > 0$, there is a compact subspace C of X such that $|f(x)| < \epsilon$ for $x \in X - C$ and $f \in \mathcal{F}$. If $\mathcal{F}$ consists of a single function f, we say simply that f ***vanishes at infinity***. Let $\mathcal{C}_0(X, \mathbb{R})$ denote the set of continuous functions $f : X \to \mathbb{R}$ that vanish at infinity.
   Theorem.   *Let X be locally compact Hausdorff; give $\mathcal{C}_0(X, \mathbb{R})$ the uniform topology. A subset $\mathcal{F}$ of $\mathcal{C}_0(X, \mathbb{R})$ has compact closure if and only if it is pointwise bounded, equicontinuous, and vanishes uniformly at infinity.*
   [*Hint:* Let Y denote the one-point compactification of X. Show that $\mathcal{C}_0(X, \mathbb{R})$ is isometric with a closed subspace of $\mathcal{C}(Y, \mathbb{R})$ if both are given the sup metric.]

6. Show that our proof of Ascoli's theorem goes through if $\mathbb{R}^n$ is replaced by any metric space in which all closed bounded subspaces are compact.

*7. Let (X, d) be a metric space. If $A \subset X$ and $\epsilon > 0$, let $U(A, \epsilon)$ be the ϵ-neighborhood of A. Let $\mathcal{H}$ be the collection of all (nonempty) closed, bounded subsets of X. If $A, B \in \mathcal{H}$, define

$$D(A, B) = \inf\{\epsilon \mid A \subset U(B, \epsilon) \text{ and } B \subset U(A, \epsilon)\}.$$

(a) Show that D is a metric on $\mathcal{H}$; it is called the ***Hausdorff metric***.
(b) Show that if (X, d) is complete, so is $(\mathcal{H}, D)$. [*Hint:* Let A_n be a Cauchy sequence in $\mathcal{H}$; by passing to a subsequence, assume $D(A_n, A_{n+1}) < 1/2^n$. Define A to be the set of all points x that are the limits of sequences $x_1, x_2, \ldots$ such that $x_i \in A_i$ for each i and $d(x_i, x_{i+1}) < 1/2^i$. Show $A_n \to \bar{A}$.]
(c) Show that if (X, d) is totally bounded, so is $(\mathcal{H}, D)$. [*Hint:* Given ϵ, choose $\delta < \epsilon$ and let S be a finite subset of X such that the collection $\{B_d(x, \delta) \mid x \in S\}$ covers X. Let $\mathcal{A}$ be the collection of all nonempty subsets of S; show that $\{B_D(A, \epsilon) \mid A \in \mathcal{A}\}$ covers $\mathcal{H}$.]
(d) *Theorem.   If X is compact in the metric d, then the space $\mathcal{H}$ is compact in the Hausdorff metric D.*

*8. Let (X, d_X) and (Y, d_Y) be metric spaces; give $X \times Y$ the corresponding square metric; let $\mathcal{H}$ denote the collection of all nonempty closed, bounded subsets of $X \times Y$ in the resulting Hausdorff metric. Consider the space $\mathcal{C}(X, Y)$ in the uniform metric; let $\mathrm{gr} : \mathcal{C}(X, Y) \to \mathcal{H}$ be the function that assigns, to each continuous function $f : X \to Y$, its graph

$$G_f = \{x \times f(x) \mid x \in X\}.$$

(a) Show that the map gr is injective and uniformly continuous.
(b) Let $\mathcal{H}_0$ denote the image set of the map gr; let $g : \mathcal{C}(X, Y) \to \mathcal{H}_0$ be the surjective map obtained from gr. Show that if $f : X \to Y$ is uniformly continuous, then the map g^{-1} is continuous at the point G_f.
(c) Give an example where g^{-1} is not continuous at the point G_f.
(d) *Theorem.   If X is compact, then $\mathrm{gr} : \mathcal{C}(X, Y) \to \mathcal{H}$ is an imbedding.*

§46   Pointwise and Compact Convergence

There are other useful topologies on the spaces Y^X and $\mathcal{C}(X, Y)$ in addition to the uniform topology. We shall consider three of them here; they are called the *topology of pointwise convergence*, the *topology of compact convergence*, and the *compact-open topology*.

Definition.   Given a point x of the set X and an open set U of the space Y, let

$$S(x, U) = \{f \mid f \in Y^X \text{ and } f(x) \in U\}.$$

The sets $S(x, U)$ are a subbasis for topology on Y^X, which is called the ***topology of pointwise convergence*** (or the ***point-open topology***).

The general basis element for this topology is a finite intersection of subbasis elements $S(x, U)$. Thus a typical basis element about the function f consists of all functions g that are "close" to f at finitely many points. Such a neighborhood is

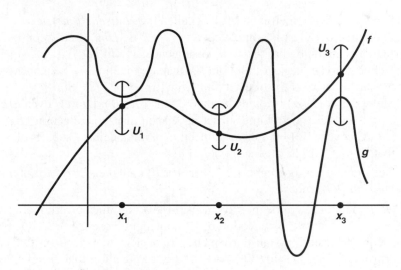

Figure 46.1

illustrated in Figure 46.1; it consists of all functions g whose graphs intersect the three vertical intervals pictured.

The topology of pointwise convergence on Y^X is nothing new. It is just the product topology we have already studied. If we replace X by J and denote the general element of J by α to make it look more familiar, then the set $S(\alpha, U)$ of all functions $\mathbf{x} : J \to Y$ such that $\mathbf{x}(\alpha) \in U$ is just the subset $\pi_\alpha^{-1}(U)$ of Y^J, which is the standard subbasis element for the product topology.

The reason for calling it the topology of pointwise convergence comes from the following theorem:

Theorem 46.1.   *A sequence f_n of functions converges to the function f in the topology of pointwise convergence if and only if for each x in X, the sequence $f_n(x)$ of points of Y converges to the point $f(x)$.*

Proof.   This result is just a reformulation, in function space notation, of a standard result about the product topology proved as Lemma 43.3.   ∎

EXAMPLE 1.   Consider the space $\mathbb{R}^I$, where $I = [0, 1]$. The sequence (f_n) of continuous functions given by $f_n(x) = x^n$ converges in the topology of pointwise convergence to the function f defined by

$$f(x) = \begin{cases} 0 & \text{for } 0 \le x < 1, \\ 1 & \text{for } x = 1. \end{cases}$$

This example shows that the subspace $\mathcal{C}(I, \mathbb{R})$ of continuous functions is not closed in $\mathbb{R}^I$ in the topology of pointwise convergence.

We know that a sequence (f_n) of continuous functions that converges in the uniform topology has a continuous limit, and the preceding example shows that a sequence that converges only in the topology of pointwise convergence need not. One can ask whether there is a topology intermediate between these two that will suffice to ensure that the limit of a convergent sequence of continuous functions is continuous. The answer is "yes"; assuming the (fairly mild) restriction that the space X be compactly generated, it will suffice if f_n converges to f in the topology of compact convergence, which we now define.

Definition.   Let (Y, d) be a metric space; let X be a topological space. Given an element f of Y^X, a compact subspace C of X, and a number $\epsilon > 0$, let $B_C(f, \epsilon)$ denote the set of all those elements g of Y^X for which

$$\sup\{d(f(x), g(x)) \mid x \in C\} < \epsilon.$$

The sets $B_C(f, \epsilon)$ form a basis for a topology on Y^X. It is called the **topology of compact convergence** (or sometimes the "topology of uniform convergence on compact sets").

It is easy to show that the sets $B_C(f, \epsilon)$ satisfy the conditions for a basis. The crucial step is to note that if $g \in B_C(f, \epsilon)$, then for

$$\delta = \epsilon - \sup\{d(f(x), g(x)) \mid x \in C\},$$

we have $B_C(g, \delta) \subset B_C(f, \epsilon)$.

The topology of compact convergence differs from the topology of pointwise convergence in that the general basis element containing f consists of functions that are "close" to f not just at finitely many points, but at all points of some compact set.

The justification for the choice of terminology comes from the following theorem, whose proof is immediate.

Theorem 46.2.   *A sequence $f_n : X \to Y$ of functions converges to the function f in the topology of compact convergence if and only if for each compact subspace C of X, the sequence $f_n|C$ converges uniformly to $f|C$.*

Definition.   A space X is said to be **compactly generated** if it satisfies the following condition: A set A is open in X if $A \cap C$ is open in C for each compact subspace C of X.

This condition is equivalent to requiring that a set B be closed in X if $B \cap C$ is closed in C for each compact C. It is a fairly mild restriction on the space; many familiar spaces are compactly generated. For instance:

Lemma 46.3.   *If X is locally compact, or if X satisfies the first countability axiom, then X is compactly generated.*

Proof. Suppose that X is locally compact. Let $A \cap C$ be open in C for every compact subspace C of X. We show A is open in X. Given $x \in A$, choose a neighborhood U of x that lies in a compact subspace C of X. Since $A \cap C$ is open in C by hypothesis, $A \cap U$ is open in U, and hence open in X. Then $A \cap U$ is a neighborhood of x contained in A, so that A is open in X.

Suppose that X satisfies the first countability axiom. If $B \cap C$ is closed in C for each compact subspace C of X, we show that B is closed in X. Let x be a point of $\bar{B}$; we show that $x \in B$. Since X has a countable basis at x, there is a sequence (x_n) of points of B converging to x. The subspace

$$C = \{x\} \cup \{x_n \mid n \in \mathbb{Z}_+\}$$

is compact, so that $B \cap C$ is by assumption closed in C. Since $B \cap C$ contains x_n for every n, it contains x as well. Therefore, $x \in B$, as desired. ∎

The crucial fact about compactly generated spaces is the following:

Lemma 46.4. *If X is compactly generated, then a function $f : X \to Y$ is continuous if for each compact subspace C of X, the restricted function $f|C$ is continuous.*

Proof. Let V be an open subset of Y; we show that $f^{-1}(V)$ is open in X. Given any subspace C of X,

$$f^{-1}(V) \cap C = (f|C)^{-1}(V).$$

If C is compact, this set is open in C because $f|C$ is continuous. Since X is compactly generated, it follows that $f^{-1}(V)$ is open in X. ∎

Theorem 46.5. *Let X be a compactly generated space: let (Y, d) be a metric space. Then $\mathcal{C}(X, Y)$ is closed in Y^X in the topology of compact convergence.*

Proof. Let $f \in Y^X$ be a limit point of $\mathcal{C}(X, Y)$; we wish to show f is continuous. It suffices to show that $f|C$ is continuous for each compact subspace C of X. For each n, consider the neighborhood $B_C(f, 1/n)$ of f; it intersects $\mathcal{C}(X, Y)$, so we can choose a function $f_n \in \mathcal{C}(X, Y)$ lying in this neighborhood. The sequence of functions $f_n|C : C \to Y$ converges uniformly to the function $f|C$, so that by the uniform limit theorem, $f|C$ is continuous. ∎

Corollary 46.6. *Let X be a compactly generated space; let (Y, d) be a metric space. If a sequence of continuous functions $f_n : X \to Y$ converges to f in the topology of compact convergence, then f is continuous.*

Now we have three topologies for the function space Y^X when Y is metric. The relation between them is stated in the following theorem, whose proof is straightforward.

Theorem 46.7. *Let X be a space; let (Y, d) be a metric space. For the function space Y^X, one has the following inclusions of topologies:*

$$(\text{uniform}) \supset (\text{compact convergence}) \supset (\text{pointwise convergence}).$$

If X is compact, the first two coincide, and if X is discrete, the second two coincide.

Now the definitions of the uniform topology and the compact convergence topology made specific use of the metric d for the space Y. But the topology of pointwise convergence did not; in fact, it is defined for any space Y. It is natural to ask whether either of these other topologies can be extended to the case where Y is an arbitrary topological space. There is no satisfactory answer to this question for the space Y^X of *all* functions mapping X into Y. But for the subspace $\mathcal{C}(X, Y)$ of continuous functions, one *can* prove something. It turns out that there is in general a topology on $\mathcal{C}(X, Y)$, called the *compact-open topology*, that coincides with the compact convergence topology when Y is a metric space. This topology is important in its own right, as we shall see.

Definition. Let X and Y be topological spaces. If C is a compact subspace of X and U is an open subset of Y, define

$$S(C, U) = \{f \mid f \in \mathcal{C}(X, Y) \text{ and } f(C) \subset U\}.$$

The sets $S(C, U)$ form a subbasis for a topology on $\mathcal{C}(X, Y)$ that is called the ***compact-open topology***.

It is clear from the definition that the compact-open topology is finer than the pointwise convergence topology. The compact-open topology can in fact be defined on the entire function space Y^X. It is, however, of interest only for the subspace $\mathcal{C}(X, Y)$, so we shall consider it only for that space.

Theorem 46.8. *Let X be a space and let (Y, d) be a metric space. On the set $\mathcal{C}(X, Y)$, the compact-open topology and the topology of compact convergence coincide.*

Proof. If A is a subset of Y and $\epsilon > 0$, let $U(A, \epsilon)$ be the ϵ-neighborhood of A. If A is compact and V is an open set containing A, then there is an $\epsilon > 0$ such that $U(A, \epsilon) \subset V$. Indeed, the minimum value of the function $d(a, X - V)$ is the required ϵ.

We first prove that the topology of compact convergence is finer than the compact-open topology. Let $S(C, U)$ be a subbasis element for the compact-open topology, and let f be an element of $S(C, U)$. Because f is continuous, $f(C)$ is a compact subset of the open set U. Therefore, we can choose ϵ so that ϵ-neighborhood of $f(C)$ lies in U. Then, as desired,

$$B_C(f, \epsilon) \subset S(C, U).$$

Now we prove that the compact-open topology is finer than the topology of compact convergence. Let $f \in \mathcal{C}(X, Y)$. Given an open set about f in the topology of compact convergence, it contains a basis element of the form $B_C(f, \epsilon)$. We shall find a basis element for the compact-open topology that contains f and lies in $B_C(f, \epsilon)$.

Each point x of X has a neighborhood V_x such that $f(\bar{V}_x)$ lies in an open set U_x of Y having diameter less than ϵ. [For example, choose V_x so that $f(V_x)$ lies in the $\epsilon/4$-neighborhood of $f(x)$. Then $f(\bar{V}_x)$ lies in the $\epsilon/3$-neighborhood of $f(x)$, which has diameter at most $2\epsilon/3$.] Cover C by finitely many such sets V_x, say for $x = x_1, \ldots, x_n$. Let $C_x = \bar{V}_x \cap C$. Then C_x is compact, and the basis element

$$S(C_{x_1}, U_{x_1}) \cap \cdots \cap S(C_{x_n}, U_{x_n})$$

contains f and lies in $B_C(f, \epsilon)$, as desired.   ∎

Corollary 46.9.   *Let Y be a metric space. The compact convergence topology on $\mathcal{C}(X, Y)$ does not depend on the metric of Y. Therefore if X is compact, the uniform topology on $\mathcal{C}(X, Y)$ does not depend on the metric of Y.*

The fact that the definition of the compact-open topology does not involve a metric is just one of its useful features. Another is the fact that it satisfies the requirement of "joint continuity." Roughly speaking, this means that the expression $f(x)$ is continuous not only in the single "variable" x, but is continuous jointly in both the "variables" x and f. More precisely, one has the following theorem:

Theorem 46.10.   *Let X be locally compact Hausdorff; let $\mathcal{C}(X, Y)$ have the compact-open topology. Then the map*

$$e : X \times \mathcal{C}(X, Y) \to Y$$

defined by the equation

$$e(x, f) = f(x)$$

is continuous.

The map e is called the **evaluation map**.

Proof.   Given a point (x, f) of $X \times \mathcal{C}(X, Y)$ and an open set V in Y about the image point $e(x, f) = f(x)$, we wish to find an open set about (x, f) that e maps into V. First, using the continuity of f and the fact that X is locally compact Hausdorff, we can choose an open set U about x having compact closure $\bar{U}$, such that f carries $\bar{U}$ into V. Then consider the open set $U \times S(\bar{U}, V)$ in $X \times \mathcal{C}(X, Y)$. It is an open set containing (x, f). And if (x', f') belongs to this set, then $e(x', f') = f'(x')$ belongs to V, as desired.   ∎

A consequence of this theorem is the theorem that follows. It is useful in algebraic topology.

Definition. Given a function $f : X \times Z \to Y$, there is a corresponding function $F : Z \to \mathcal{C}(X, Y)$, defined by the equation

$$(F(z))(x) = f(x, z).$$

Conversely, given $F : Z \to \mathcal{C}(X, Y)$, this equation defines a corresponding function $f : X \times Z \to Y$. We say that F is the map of Z into $\mathcal{C}(X, Y)$ that is ***induced*** by f.

*Theorem 46.11. *Let X and Y be spaces; give $\mathcal{C}(X, Y)$ the compact-open topology. If $f : X \times Z \to Y$ is continuous, then so is the induced function $F : Z \to \mathcal{C}(X, Y)$. The converse holds if X is locally compact Hausdorff.*

Proof. Suppose first that F is continuous and that X is locally compact Hausdorff. It follows that f is continuous, since f equals the composite

$$X \times Z \xrightarrow{i_X \times F} X \times \mathcal{C}(X, Y) \xrightarrow{e} Y,$$

where i_X is the identity map of X.

Now suppose that f is continuous. To prove continuity of F, we take a point z_0 of Z and a subbasis element $S(C, U)$ for $\mathcal{C}(X, Y)$ containing $F(z_0)$, and find a neighborhood W of z_0 that is mapped by F into $S(C, U)$. This will suffice.

The statement that $F(z_0)$ lies in $S(C, U)$ means simply that $(F(z_0))(x) = f(x, z_0)$ is in U for all $x \in C$. That is, $f(C \times z_0) \subset U$. Continuity of f implies that $f^{-1}(U)$ is an open set in $X \times Z$ containing $C \times z_0$. Then

$$f^{-1}(U) \cap (C \times Z)$$

is an open set in the subspace $C \times Z$ containing the slice $C \times z_0$. The tube lemma of §26 implies that there is a neighborhood W of z_0 in Z such that the entire tube $C \times W$ lies in $f^{-1}(U)$. See Figure 46.2. Then for $z \in W$ and $x \in C$, we have $f(x, z) \in U$. Hence $F(W) \subset S(C, U)$, as desired. ∎

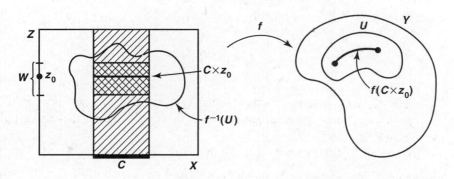

Figure 46.2

We discuss briefly the connections between the compact-open topology and the concept of *homotopy*, which arises in algebraic topology.

If f and g are continuous maps of X into Y, we say that f and g are *homotopic* if there is a continuous map

$$h : X \times [0, 1] \longrightarrow Y$$

such that $h(x, 0) = f(x)$ and $h(x, 1) = g(x)$ for each $x \in X$. The map h is called a *homotopy* between f and g.

Roughly speaking, a homotopy is a "continuous one-parameter family" of maps from X to Y. More precisely, we note that a homotopy h gives rise to a map

$$H : [0, 1] \longrightarrow \mathcal{C}(X, Y)$$

that assigns, to each parameter value t in $[0, 1]$, the corresponding continuous map from X to Y. Assuming that X is locally compact Hausdorff, we see that h is continuous if and only if H is continuous. This means that a homotopy h between f and g corresponds precisely to a *path* in the function space $\mathcal{C}(X, Y)$ from the point f of $\mathcal{C}(X, Y)$ to the point g.

We shall return to a more detailed study of homotopy in Part II of the book.

Exercises

1. Show that the sets $B_C(f, \epsilon)$ form a basis for a topology on Y^X.

2. Prove Theorem 46.7.

3. Show that the set $\mathcal{B}(\mathbb{R}, \mathbb{R})$ of bounded functions $f : \mathbb{R} \to \mathbb{R}$ is closed in $\mathbb{R}^{\mathbb{R}}$ in the uniform topology, but not in the topology of compact convergence.

4. Consider the sequence of continuous functions $f_n : \mathbb{R} \to \mathbb{R}$ defined by

$$f_n(x) = x/n.$$

In which of the three topologies of Theorem 46.7 does this sequence converge? Answer the same question for the sequence given in Exercise 9 of §21.

5. Consider the sequence of functions $f_n : (-1, 1) \to \mathbb{R}$, defined by

$$f_n(x) = \sum_{k=1}^{n} kx^k.$$

   (a) Show that (f_n) converges in the topology of compact convergence; conclude that the limit function is continuous. (This is a standard fact about power series.)
   (b) Show that (f_n) does not converge in the uniform topology.

6. Show that in the compact-open topology, $\mathcal{C}(X, Y)$ is Hausdorff if Y is Hausdorff, and regular if Y is regular. [*Hint:* If $\bar{U} \subset V$, then $\overline{S(C, U)} \subset S(C, V)$.]

7. Show that if Y is locally compact Hausdorff, then composition of maps

$$\mathcal{C}(X, Y) \times \mathcal{C}(Y, Z) \longrightarrow \mathcal{C}(X, Z)$$

is continuous, provided the compact-open topology is used throughout. [*Hint:* If $g \circ f \in S(C, U)$, find V such that $f(C) \subset V$ and $g(\bar{V}) \subset U$.]

8. Let $\mathcal{C}'(X, Y)$ denote the set $\mathcal{C}(X, Y)$ in some topology $\mathcal{T}$. Show that if the evaluation map

$$e : X \times \mathcal{C}'(X, Y) \longrightarrow Y$$

is continuous, then $\mathcal{T}$ contains the compact-open topology. [*Hint:* The induced map $E : \mathcal{C}'(X, Y) \to \mathcal{C}(X, Y)$ is continuous.]

9. Here is an (unexpected) application of Theorem 46.11 to quotient maps. (Compare Exercise 11 of §29.)

Theorem. If $p : A \to B$ is a quotient map and X is locally compact Hausdorff, then $i_X \times p : X \times A \to X \times B$ is a quotient map.

   Proof.

  (a) Let Y be the quotient space induced by $i_X \times p$; let $q : X \times A \to Y$ be the quotient map. Show there is a bijective continuous map $f : Y \to X \times B$ such that $f \circ q = i_X \times p$.

  (b) Let $g = f^{-1}$. Let $G : B \to \mathcal{C}(X, Y)$ and $Q : A \to \mathcal{C}(X, Y)$ be the maps induced by g and q, respectively. Show that $Q = G \circ p$.

  (c) Show that Q is continuous; conclude that G is continuous, so that g is continuous.

*10. A space is locally compact if it can be covered by open sets each of which is contained in a compact subspace of X. It is said to be **σ-compact** if it can be covered by countably many such open sets.

  (a) Show that if X is locally compact and second-countable, it is σ-compact.

  (b) Let (Y, d) be a metric space. Show that if X is σ-compact, there is a metric for the topology of compact convergence on Y^X such that if (Y, d) is complete, Y^X is complete in this metric. [*Hint:* Let $A_1, A_2, \ldots$ be a countable collection of compact subspaces of X whose interiors cover X. Let Y_i denote the set of all functions from A_i to Y, in the uniform topology. Define a homeomorphism of Y^X with a closed subspace of the product space $Y_1 \times Y_2 \times \cdots$.]

11. Let (Y, d) be a metric space; let X be a space. Define a topology on $\mathcal{C}(X, Y)$ as follows: Given $f \in \mathcal{C}(X, Y)$, and given a positive continuous function $\delta : X \to \mathbb{R}_+$ on X, let

$$B(f, \delta) = \{g \mid d(f(x), g(x)) < \delta(x) \text{ for all } x \in X\}.$$

  (a) Show that the sets $B(f, \delta)$ form a basis for a topology on $\mathcal{C}(X, Y)$. We call it the *fine topology*.

  (b) Show that the fine topology contains the uniform topology.

(c) Show that if X is compact, the fine and uniform topologies agree.
(d) Show that if X is discrete, then $\mathcal{C}(X, Y) = Y^X$ and the fine and box topologies agree.

§47   Ascoli's Theorem

Now we prove a more general version of Ascoli's theorem. It characterizes the compact subspaces of $\mathcal{C}(X, Y)$ in the topology of compact convergence. The proof, however, involves all three of our standard function space topologies: the topology of pointwise convergence, the topology of compact convergence, and the uniform topology.

Theorem 47.1 (Ascoli's theorem).   *Let X be a space and let (Y, d) be a metric space. Give $\mathcal{C}(X, Y)$ the topology of compact convergence; let $\mathcal{F}$ be a subset of $\mathcal{C}(X, Y)$.*
  (a) *If $\mathcal{F}$ is equicontinuous under d and the set*

$$\mathcal{F}_a = \{ f(a) \mid f \in \mathcal{F} \}$$

  has compact closure for each $a \in X$, then $\mathcal{F}$ is contained in a compact subspace of $\mathcal{C}(X, Y)$.
  (b) *The converse holds if X is locally compact Hausdorff.*

Proof of (a).   Throughout, we give Y^X the product topology, which is the same as the topology of pointwise convergence. Then Y^X is a Hausdorff space. The space $\mathcal{C}(X, Y)$, which has the topology of compact convergence, is *not* a subspace of Y^X. Let $\mathcal{G}$ be the closure of $\mathcal{F}$ in Y^X.

Step 1. We show that $\mathcal{G}$ is a compact subspace of Y^X. Given $a \in X$, let C_a denote the closure of $\mathcal{F}_a$ in Y; by hypothesis, C_a is a compact subspace of Y. The set $\mathcal{F}$ is contained in the product space

$$\prod_{a \in X} C_a,$$

since this product by definition consists of all functions $f : X \to Y$ satisfying the condition $f(a) \in C_a$ for all a. This product space is compact, by the Tychonoff theorem; it is a closed subspace of the product space Y^X. Because $\mathcal{G}$ equals the closure of $\mathcal{F}$ in Y^X, $\mathcal{G}$ is contained in $\prod C_a$; being closed, $\mathcal{G}$ is therefore compact.

Step 2. We show that each function belonging to $\mathcal{G}$ is continuous, and indeed that $\mathcal{G}$ itself is equicontinuous under d.
  Given $x_0 \in X$ and $\epsilon > 0$, choose a neighborhood U of x_0 such that

$(*)$ $\qquad\qquad d(f(x), f(x_0)) < \epsilon/3 \qquad$ for all $f \in \mathcal{F}$ and all $x \in U$.

We shall show that $d(g(x), g(x_0)) < \epsilon$ for all $g \in \mathcal{G}$ and all $x \in U$; it follows that $\mathcal{G}$ is equicontinuous.

Let $g \in \mathcal{G}$ and let x be a point of U. Define V_x to be the subset of Y^X, open in Y^X, consisting of all elements h of Y^X such that

$(**)$ $d(h(x), g(x)) < \epsilon/3$ and $d(h(x_0), g(x_0)) < \epsilon/3$.

Because g belongs to the closure of $\mathcal{F}$, the neighborhood V_x of g must contain an element f of $\mathcal{F}$. Applying the triangle inequality to $(*)$ and $(**)$, it follows that $d(g(x), g(x_0)) < \epsilon$, as desired.

Step 3. We show that the product topology on Y^X and the compact convergence topology on $\mathcal{C}(X, Y)$ coincide on the subset $\mathcal{G}$.

In general, the compact convergence topology is finer than the product topology. We prove that the reverse holds for the subset $\mathcal{G}$. Let g be an element of $\mathcal{G}$, and let $B_C(g, \epsilon)$ be a basis element for the compact convergence topology on Y^X that contains g. We find a basis element B for the pointwise convergence topology on Y^X that contains g such that

$$[B \cap \mathcal{G}] \subset [B_C(g, \epsilon) \cap \mathcal{G}].$$

Using equicontinuity of $\mathcal{G}$ and compactness of C, we can cover C by finitely many open sets $U_1, \ldots, U_n$ of X, containing points $x_1, \ldots, x_n$, respectively, such that for each i, we have

$$d(g(x), g(x_i)) < \epsilon/3$$

for $x \in U_i$ and $g \in \mathcal{G}$. Then we define B to be the basis element for Y^X defined by the equation

$$B = \{h \mid h \in Y^X \text{ and } d(h(x_i), g(x_i)) < \epsilon/3 \text{ for } i = 1, \ldots, n\}.$$

We show that if h is an element of $B \cap \mathcal{G}$, then h belongs to $B_C(g, \epsilon)$. That is, we show that $d(h(x), g(x)) < \epsilon$ for $x \in C$. Given $x \in C$, choose i so that $x \in U_i$. Then

$$d(h(x), h(x_i)) < \epsilon/3 \quad \text{and}$$
$$d(g(x), g(x_i)) < \epsilon/3$$

because $x \in U_i$ and $g, h \in \mathcal{G}$, while

$$d(h(x_i), g(x_i)) < \epsilon/3$$

because $h \in B$. It follows from the triangle inequality that $d(h(x), g(x)) < \epsilon$, as desired.

Step 4. We complete the proof. The set $\mathcal{G}$ contains $\mathcal{F}$ and is contained in $\mathcal{C}(X, Y)$. It is compact as a subspace of Y^X in the product topology. By the result just proved, it is also compact as a subspace of $\mathcal{C}(X, Y)$ in the compact convergence topology.

Proof of (b). Let $\mathcal{H}$ be a compact subspace of $\mathcal{C}(X, Y)$ that contains $\mathcal{F}$. We show that $\mathcal{H}$ is equicontinuous and that $\mathcal{H}_a$ is compact for each $a \in X$. It follows that $\mathcal{F}$ is equicontinuous (since $\mathcal{F} \subset \mathcal{H}$), and that $\mathcal{F}_a$ lies in the compact subspace $\mathcal{H}_a$ of Y, so that $\tilde{\mathcal{F}}_a$ is compact.

To show $\mathcal{H}_a$ is compact, consider the composite of the map

$$j : \mathcal{C}(X, Y) \to X \times \mathcal{C}(X, Y)$$

defined by $j(f) = a \times f$, and the evaluation map

$$e : X \times \mathcal{C}(X, Y) \to Y,$$

given by the equation $e(x \times f) = f(x)$. The map j is obviously continuous, and the map e is continuous by Theorems 46.8 and 46.10. The composite $e \circ j$ maps $\mathcal{H}$ to $\mathcal{H}_a$; since $\mathcal{H}$ is compact, so is $\mathcal{H}_a$.

Now we show that $\mathcal{H}$ is equicontinuous at a, relative to the metric d. Let A be a compact subspace of X that contains a neighborhood of a. It suffices to show that the subset

$$\mathcal{R} = \{f|A ; \ f \in \mathcal{H}\}$$

of $\mathcal{C}(A, Y)$ is equicontinuous at a.

Give $\mathcal{C}(A, Y)$ the compact convergence topology. We show that the restriction map

$$r : \mathcal{C}(X, Y) \to \mathcal{C}(A, Y)$$

is continuous. Let f be an element of $\mathcal{C}(X, Y)$ and let $B = B_C(f|A, \epsilon)$ be a basis element for $\mathcal{C}(A, Y)$ containing $f|A$, where C is a compact subspace of A. Then C is a compact subspace of X, and r maps the neighborhood $B_C(f, \epsilon)$ of f in $\mathcal{C}(X, Y)$ into B.

The map r maps $\mathcal{H}$ onto $\mathcal{R}$; because $\mathcal{H}$ is compact, so is $\mathcal{R}$. Now $\mathcal{R}$ is a subspace of $\mathcal{C}(A, Y)$; because A is compact, the compact convergence and the uniform topologies on $\mathcal{C}(A, Y)$ coincide. It follows from Theorem 45.1 that $\mathcal{R}$ is totally bounded in the uniform metric on $\mathcal{C}(A, Y)$; then Lemma 45.2 implies that $\mathcal{R}$ is equicontinuous relative to d. ∎

An even more general version of Ascoli's theorem may be found in [K] or [Wd]. There it is not assumed that Y is a metric space, but only that it has what is called a *uniform structure*, which is a generalization of the notion of metric.

Ascoli's theorem has many applications in analysis, but these lie outside the scope of this book. See [K-F] for several such applications.

Exercises

1. Which of the following subsets of $\mathcal{C}(\mathbb{R}, \mathbb{R})$ are pointwise bounded? Which are equicontinuous?

   (a) The collection $\{f_n\}$, where $f_n(x) = x + \sin nx$.

(b) The collection $\{g_n\}$, where $g_n(x) = n + \sin x$.

(c) The collection $\{h_n\}$, where $h_n(x) = |x|^{1/n}$.

(d) The collection $\{k_n\}$, where $k_n(x) = n \sin(x/n)$.

2. Prove the following:

   Theorem. *If X is a locally compact Hausdorff space, then a subspace $\mathcal{F}$ of $\mathcal{C}(X, \mathbb{R}^n)$ in the topology of compact convergence has compact closure if and only if $\mathcal{F}$ is pointwise bounded and equicontinuous under either of the standard metrics on $\mathbb{R}^n$.*

3. Show that the general version of Ascoli's theorem implies the classical version (Theorem 45.4) when X is Hausdorff.

4. Prove the following:

   Theorem (Arzela's theorem, general version). *Let X be a Hausdorff space that is σ-compact; let f_n be a sequence of functions $f_n : X \to \mathbb{R}^k$. If the collection $\{f_n\}$ is pointwise bounded and equicontinuous, then the sequence f_n has a subsequence that converges, in the topology of compact convergence, to a continuous function.*

   [*Hint:* Show $\mathcal{C}(X, \mathbb{R}^k)$ is first-countable.]

5. Let (Y, d) be a metric space; let $f_n : X \to Y$ be a sequence of continuous functions; let $f : X \to Y$ be a function (not necessarily continuous). Suppose f_n converges to f in the topology of pointwise convergence. Show that if $\{f_n\}$ is equicontinuous, then f is continuous and f_n converges to f in the topology of compact convergence.

Chapter 8

Baire Spaces and Dimension Theory

In this chapter, we introduce a class of topological spaces called the *Baire spaces*. The defining condition for a Baire space is a bit complicated to state, but it is often useful in the applications, in both analysis and topology. Most of the spaces we have been studying are Baire spaces. For instance, a Hausdorff space is a Baire space if it is compact, or even locally compact. And a metrizable space X is a Baire space if it is topologically complete, that is, if there is a metric for X relative to which X is complete.

It follows that, since the space $\mathcal{C}(X, \mathbb{R}^n)$ of all continuous functions from a space X to $\mathbb{R}^n$ is complete in the uniform metric, it is a Baire space in the uniform topology. This fact has a number of interesting applications.

One application is the proof we give in §49 of the existence of a continuous nowhere-differentiable real-valued function.

Another application arises in that branch of topology called *dimension theory*. In §50, we define a topological notion of dimension, due to Lebesgue. And we prove the classical theorem that every compact metrizable space of topological dimension m can be imbedded in euclidean space $\mathbb{R}^N$ of dimension $N = 2m + 1$. It follows that every compact m-manifold can be imbedded in $\mathbb{R}^{2m+1}$. This generalizes the imbedding theorem proved in §36.

Throughout the chapter, we assume familiarity with complete metric spaces (§43). When we study dimension theory, we shall make use of §36, Imbeddings of Manifolds, as well as a bit of linear algebra.

§48   Baire Spaces

The defining condition for a Baire space is probably as "unnatural looking" as any condition we have yet introduced in this book. But bear with us awhile.

In this section, we shall define Baire spaces and shall show that two important classes of spaces—the complete metric spaces and the compact Hausdorff spaces— are contained in the class of Baire spaces. Then we shall give some applications, which, even if they do not make the Baire condition seem any more natural, will at least show what a useful tool it can be. In fact, it turns out to be a very useful and fairly sophisticated tool in both analysis and topology.

Definition.   Recall that if A is a subset of a space X, the *interior* of A is defined as the union of all open sets of X that are contained in A. To say that A has ***empty interior*** is to say then that A contains no open set of X other than the empty set. Equivalently, A has empty interior if every point of A is a limit point of the complement of A, that is, if the complement of A is dense in X.

EXAMPLE 1.   The set $\mathbb{Q}$ of rationals has empty interior as a subset of $\mathbb{R}$, but the interval $[0, 1]$ has nonempty interior. The interval $[0, 1] \times 0$ has empty interior as a subset of the plane $\mathbb{R}^2$, and so does the subset $\mathbb{Q} \times \mathbb{R}$.

Definition.   A space X is said to be a ***Baire space*** if the following condition holds: Given any countable collection $\{A_n\}$ of closed sets of X each of which has empty interior in X, their union $\bigcup A_n$ also has empty interior in X.

EXAMPLE 2.   The space $\mathbb{Q}$ of rationals is not a Baire space. For each one-point set in $\mathbb{Q}$ is closed and has empty interior in $\mathbb{Q}$; and $\mathbb{Q}$ is the countable union of its one-point subsets.

The space $\mathbb{Z}_+$, on the other hand, does form a Baire space. Every subset of $\mathbb{Z}_+$ is open, so that there exist no subsets of $\mathbb{Z}_+$ having empty interior, except for the empty set. Therefore, $\mathbb{Z}_+$ satisfies the Baire condition vacuously.

More generally, every closed subspace of $\mathbb{R}$, being a complete metric space, is a Baire space. Somewhat surprising is the fact that the irrationals in $\mathbb{R}$ also form a Baire space; see Exercise 6.

The terminology originally used by R. Baire for this concept involved the word "category." A subset A of a space X was said to be of the *first category* in X if it was contained in the union of a countable collection of closed sets of X having empty interiors in X; otherwise, it was said to be of the *second category* in X. Using this terminology, we can say the following:

A space X is a Baire space if and only if every nonempty open set in X is of the second category.

We shall not use the terms "first category" and "second category" in this book.

The preceding definition is the "closed set definition" of a Baire space. There is also a formulation involving open sets that is frequently useful. It is given in the following lemma.

Lemma 48.1.   *X is a Baire space if and only if given any countable collection $\{U_n\}$ of open sets in X, each of which is dense in X, their intersection $\bigcap U_n$ is also dense in X.*

Proof.   Recall that a set C is dense in X if $\bar{C} = X$. The theorem now follows at once from the two remarks:

(1) A is closed in X if and only if $X - A$ is open in X.

(2) B has empty interior in X if and only if $X - B$ is dense in X.   ∎

There are a number of theorems giving conditions under which a space is a Baire space. The most important is the following:

Theorem 48.2 (Baire category theorem).   *If X is a compact Hausdorff space or a complete metric space, then X is a Baire space.*

Proof.   Given a countable collection $\{A_n\}$ of closed set of X having empty interiors, we want to show that their union $\bigcup A_n$ also has empty interior in X. So, given the nonempty open set U_0 of X, we must find a point x of U_0 that does not lie in any of the sets A_n.

Consider the first set A_1. By hypothesis, A_1 does not contain U_0. Therefore, we may choose a point y of U_0 that is not in A_1. Regularity of X, along with the fact that A_1 is closed, enables us to choose a neighborhood U_1 of y such that

$$\bar{U}_1 \cap A_1 = \varnothing,$$
$$\bar{U}_1 \subset U_0.$$

If X is metric, we also choose U_1 small enough that its diameter is less than 1.

In general, given the nonempty open set U_{n-1}, we choose a point of U_{n-1} that is not in the closed set A_n, and then we choose U_n to be a neighborhood of this point such that

$$\bar{U}_n \cap A_n = \varnothing,$$
$$\bar{U}_n \subset U_{n-1},$$
$$\text{diam}\, U_n < 1/n \quad \text{in the metric case.}$$

We assert that the intersection $\bigcap \bar{U}_n$ is nonempty. From this fact, our theorem will follow. For if x is a point of $\bigcap \bar{U}_n$, then x is in U_0 because $\bar{U}_1 \subset U_0$. And for each n, the point x is not in A_n because $\bar{U}_n$ is disjoint from A_n.

The proof that $\bigcap \bar{U}_n$ is nonempty splits into two parts, depending on whether X is compact Hausdorff or complete metric. If X is compact Hausdorff, we consider the nested sequence $\bar{U}_1 \supset \bar{U}_2 \supset \cdots$ of nonempty subsets of X. The collection $\{\bar{U}_n\}$ has the finite intersection property; since X is compact, the intersection $\bigcap \bar{U}_n$ must be nonempty.

If X is complete metric, we apply the following lemma.   ∎

Lemma 48.3. *Let $C_1 \supset C_2 \supset \cdots$ be a nested sequence of nonempty closed sets in the complete metric space X. If diam $C_n \to 0$, then $\bigcap C_n \neq \varnothing$.*

Proof. We gave this as an exercise in §43. Here is a proof: Choose $x_n \in C_n$ for each n. Because $x_n, x_m \in C_N$ for $n, m \geq N$, and because diam C_N can be made less than any given ϵ by choosing N large enough, the sequence (x_n) is a Cauchy sequence. Suppose that it converges to x. Then for given k, the subsequence $x_k, x_{k+1}, \ldots$ also converges to x. Thus x necessarily belongs to $\bar{C}_k = C_k$. Then $x \in \bigcap C_k$, as desired. ∎

Here is one application of the theory of Baire spaces; we shall give further applications in the sections that follow. This application is perhaps more amusing than profound. It concerns a question that a student might ask concerning convergent sequences of continuous functions.

Let $f_n : [0, 1] \to \mathbb{R}$ be a sequence of continuous functions such that $f_n(x) \to f(x)$ for each $x \in [0, 1]$. There are examples that show the limit function f need not be continuous. But one might wonder just how discontinuous f can be: Could it be discontinuous everywhere, for instance? The answer is "no." We shall show that f must be continuous at infinitely many points of $[0, 1]$. In fact, the set of points at which f is continuous is dense in $[0, 1]$!

To prove this result, we need the following lemma:

*Lemma 48.4. *Any open subspace Y of a Baire space X is itself a Baire space.*

Proof. Let A_n be a countable collection of closed sets of Y that have empty interiors in Y. We show that $\bigcup A_n$ has empty interior in Y.

Let $\bar{A}_n$ be the closure of A_n in X; then $\bar{A}_n \cap Y = A_n$. The set $\bar{A}_n$ has empty interior in X. For if U is a nonempty open set of X contained in $\bar{A}_n$, then U must intersect A_n. Then $U \cap Y$ is a nonempty open set of Y contained in A_n, contrary to hypothesis.

If the union of the sets A_n contains the nonempty open set W of Y, then the union of the sets $\bar{A}_n$ also contains the set W, which is open in X because Y is open in X. But each set $\bar{A}_n$ has empty interior in X, contradicting the fact that X is a Baire space. ∎

*Theorem 48.5. *Let X be a space; let (Y, d) be a metric space. Let $f_n : X \to Y$ be a sequence of continuous functions such that $f_n(x) \to f(x)$ for all $x \in X$, where $f : X \to Y$. If X is a Baire space, the set of points at which f is continuous is dense in X.*

Proof. Given a positive integer N and given $\epsilon > 0$, define $A_N(\epsilon) = d^{-1}\left([0, \epsilon]\right)$

$$A_N(\epsilon) = \{x \mid d(f_n(x), f_m(x)) \leq \epsilon \text{ for all } n, m \geq N\}.$$

Note that $A_N(\epsilon)$ is closed in X. For the set of those x for which $d(f_n(x), f_m(x)) \leq \epsilon$ is closed in X, by continuity of f_n and f_m, and $A_N(\epsilon)$ is the intersection of these sets for all $n, m \geq N$.

For fixed ϵ, consider the sets $A_1(\epsilon) \subset A_2(\epsilon) \subset \cdots$. The union of these sets is all of X. For, given $x_0 \in X$, the fact that $f_n(x_0) \to f(x_0)$ implies that the sequence $f_n(x_0)$ is a Cauchy sequence; hence $x_0 \in A_N(\epsilon)$ for some N.

Now let

$$U(\epsilon) = \bigcup_{N \in \mathbb{Z}_+} \operatorname{Int} A_N(\epsilon).$$

[handwritten: $X = \bigcup_{n \in \mathbb{N}} A_n(\varepsilon)$]

We shall prove two things:

(1) $U(\epsilon)$ is open and dense in X.

[handwritten: $V \cap A_n(\varepsilon)$ is closed]

(2) The function f is continuous at each point of the set

[handwritten: $\bigcup_{n=1}^{\infty} V \cap A_n(\varepsilon)$ is countable]

$$C = U(1) \cap U(1/2) \cap U(1/3) \cap \cdots .$$

[handwritten: union of closed sets $= V \cap X$]

Our theorem then follows from the fact that X is a Baire space.

[handwritten: is open since V is open. Use contrapositive of Baire's theorem.]

To show that $U(\epsilon)$ is dense in X, it suffices to show that for any nonempty open set V of X, there is an N such that the set $V \cap \operatorname{Int} A_N(\epsilon)$ is nonempty. For this purpose, we note first that for each N, the set $V \cap A_N(\epsilon)$ is <u>closed in</u> V. Because V is a Baire space, by the preceding lemma at least one of these sets, say $V \cap A_M(\epsilon)$, must contain a nonempty open set W of V. Because V is open in X, the set W is open in X; therefore, it is contained in $\operatorname{Int} A_M(\epsilon)$.

Now we show that if $x_0 \in C$, then f is continuous at x_0. Given $\epsilon > 0$, we shall find a neighborhood W of x_0 such that $d(f(x), f(x_0)) < \epsilon$ for $x \in W$.

First, choose k so that $1/k < \epsilon/3$. Since $x_0 \in C$, we have $x_0 \in U(1/k)$; therefore, there is an N such that $x_0 \in \operatorname{Int} A_N(1/k)$. Finally, continuity of the function f_N enables us to choose a neighborhood W of x_0, contained in $A_N(1/k)$, such that

(*) $$d(f_N(x), f_N(x_0)) < \epsilon/3 \quad \text{for } x \in W.$$

The fact that $W \subset A_N(1/k)$ implies that

$$d(f_n(x), f_N(x)) \le 1/k \quad \text{for } n \ge N \text{ and } x \in W.$$

Letting $n \to \infty$, we obtain the inequality

(**) $$d(f(x), f_N(x)) \le 1/k < \epsilon/3 \quad \text{for } x \in W.$$

In particular, since $x_0 \in W$, we have

(***) $$d(f(x_0), f_N(x_0)) < \epsilon/3.$$

Applying the triangle inequality to (*), (**), and (***) gives us our desired result. ∎

Exercises

1. Let X equal the countable union $\bigcup B_n$. Show that if X is a nonempty Baire space, at least one of the sets $\bar{B}_n$ has a nonempty interior.

2. The Baire category theorem implies that $\mathbb{R}$ cannot be written as a countable union of closed subsets having empty interiors. Show this fails if the sets are not required to be closed.

3. Show that every locally compact Hausdorff space is a Baire space.

4. Show that if every point x of X has a neighborhood that is a Baire space, then X is a Baire space. [*Hint:* Use the open set formulation of the Baire condition.]

5. Show that if Y is a G_δ set in X, and if X is compact Hausdorff or complete metric, then Y is a Baire space in the subspace topology. [*Hint:* Suppose that $Y = \bigcap W_n$, where W_n is open in X, and that B_n is closed in Y and has empty interior in Y. Given U_0 open in X with $U_0 \cap Y \neq \varnothing$, find a sequence of open sets U_n of X with $U_n \cap Y$ nonempty, such that

$$\bar{U}_n \subset U_{n-1},$$
$$\bar{U}_n \cap \bar{B}_n = \varnothing,$$
$$\text{diam } U_n < 1/n \quad \text{in the metric case,}$$
$$\bar{U}_n \subset W_n.]$$

6. Show that the irrationals are a Baire space.

7. Prove the following:
   Theorem. *If D is a countable dense subset of $\mathbb{R}$, there is no function $f : \mathbb{R} \to \mathbb{R}$ that is continuous precisely at the points of D.*
      Proof.
   (a) Show that if $f : \mathbb{R} \to \mathbb{R}$, then the set C of points at which f is continuous is a G_δ set in $\mathbb{R}$. [*Hint:* Let U_n be the union of all open sets U of $\mathbb{R}$ such that diam $f(U) < 1/n$. Show that $C = \bigcap U_n$.]
   (b) Show that D is not a G_δ set in $\mathbb{R}$. [*Hint:* Suppose $D = \bigcap W_n$, where W_n is open in $\mathbb{R}$. For $d \in D$, set $V_d = \mathbb{R} - \{d\}$. Show W_n and V_d are dense in $\mathbb{R}$.]

8. If f_n is a sequence of continuous functions $f_n : \mathbb{R} \to \mathbb{R}$ such that $f_n(x) \to f(x)$ for each $x \in \mathbb{R}$, show that f is continuous at uncountably many points of $\mathbb{R}$.

9. Let $g : \mathbb{Z}_+ \to \mathbb{Q}$ be a bijective function; let $x_n = g(n)$. Define $f : \mathbb{R} \to \mathbb{R}$ as follows:

$$f(x_n) = 1/n \quad \text{for } x_n \in \mathbb{Q},$$
$$f(x) = 0 \quad \text{for } x \notin \mathbb{Q}.$$

Show that f is continuous at each irrational and discontinuous at each rational. Can you find a sequence of continuous functions f_n coverging to f?

10. Prove the following:
    Theorem (*Uniform boundedness principle*). *Let X be a complete metric space, and let $\mathcal{F}$ be a subset of $\mathcal{C}(X, \mathbb{R})$ such that for each $a \in X$, the set*

$$\mathcal{F}_a = \{f(a) \mid f \in \mathcal{F}\}$$

is bounded. Then there is a nonempty open set U of X on which the functions in $\mathcal{F}$ are uniformly bounded, that is, there is a number M such that $|f(x)| \leq M$ for all $x \in U$ and all $f \in \mathcal{F}$. [*Hint:* Let $A_N = \{x; |f(x)| \leq N$ for all $f \in \mathcal{F}\}$.]

11. Determine whether or not $\mathbb{R}_\ell$ is a Baire space

12. Show that $\mathbb{R}^J$ is a Baire space in the box, product, and uniform topologies.

*13. Let X be a topological space; let Y be a complete metric space. Show that $\mathcal{C}(X, Y)$ is a Baire space in the fine topology (see Exercise 11 of §46). [*Hint:* Given basis elements $B(f_i, \delta_i)$ such that $\delta_1 \leq 1$ and $\delta_{i+1} \leq \delta_i/3$ and $f_{i+1} \in B(f_i, \delta_i/3)$, show that

$$\bigcap B(f_i, \delta_i) \neq \varnothing.]$$

*§49 A Nowhere-Differentiable Function

We prove the following result from analysis:

Theorem 49.1. *Let $h : [0, 1] \to \mathbb{R}$ be a continuous function. Given $\epsilon > 0$, there is a function $g : [0, 1] \to \mathbb{R}$ with $|h(x) - g(x)| < \epsilon$ for all x, such that g is continuous and nowhere differentiable.*

Proof. Let $I = [0, 1]$. Consider the space $\mathcal{C} = \mathcal{C}(I, \mathbb{R})$ of continuous maps from I to $\mathbb{R}$, in the metric

$$\rho(f, g) = \max\{|f(x) - g(x)|\}.$$

This space is a complete metric space and, therefore, is a Baire space. We shall define, for each n, a certain subset U_n of $\mathcal{C}$ that is open in $\mathcal{C}$ and dense in $\mathcal{C}$, and has the property that the functions belonging to the intersection

$$\bigcap_{n \in \mathbb{Z}_+} U_n$$

are nowhere differentiable. Because $\mathcal{C}$ is a Baire space, this intersection is dense in $\mathcal{C}$, by Lemma 48.1. Therefore, given h and ϵ, this intersection must contain a function g such that $\rho(h, g) < \epsilon$. The theorem follows.

The tricky part is to define the set U_n properly. We first take a function f and consider its difference quotients. Given $x \in I$ and given $0 < h \leq \frac{1}{2}$, consider the expressions

$$\left| \frac{f(x + h) - f(x)}{h} \right| \quad \text{and} \quad \left| \frac{f(x - h) - f(x)}{-h} \right|.$$

Since $h \leq \frac{1}{2}$, at least one of the numbers $x + h$ and $x - h$ belongs to I, so that at least one of these expressions is defined. Let $\Delta f(x, h)$ denote the larger of the two if both are defined; otherwise, let it denote the one that is defined. If the derivative $f'(x)$ of f at x exists, it equals the limit of these difference quotients, so that

$$|f'(x)| = \lim_{h \to 0} \Delta f(x, h).$$

We seek to find a continuous function for which this limit does not exist. To be specific, we shall construct f so that given x, there is a sequence of numbers h_n converging to 0 for which the numbers $\Delta f(x, h_n)$ become arbitrarily large.

This gives us the idea for defining the set U_n. Given any positive number $h \le 1/2$, let

U_n *contains no where differentiable functions*

$$\Delta_h f = \inf\{\Delta f(x, h) \mid x \in I\}.$$

$\Delta f(x,h)$ *is bd below by 0*

Then for $n \ge 2$, we define U_n by declaring that a function f belongs to U_n if and only if for some positive number $h \le 1/n$, we have $\Delta_h f > n$. $|f(x+h) - f(x)| > 1$

EXAMPLE 1.   Let $\alpha > 0$ be given. The function $f : [0, 1] \to \mathbb{R}$ given by the equation $f(x) = 4\alpha x(1 - x)$, whose graph is a parabola, satisfies the condition $\Delta f(x, h) \ge \alpha$ for $h = 1/4$ and all x, as you can check. Geometrically speaking, what this says is that for each x, at least one of the indicated secant lines of the parabola in Figure 49.1 has slope of absolute value at least α. Hence if $\alpha > 4$, the function f belongs to U_4. The function g pictured in Figure 49.1 satisfies the condition $\Delta g(x, h) \ge \alpha$ for *any* $h \le 1/4$; hence g belongs to U_n provided $\alpha > n$. The function k satisfies the condition $k(x, h) \ge \alpha$ for any $h \le 1/8$; hence k belongs to U_n if $\alpha > n$.

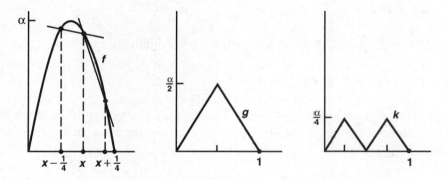

Figure 49.1

Now we prove the following facts about the set U_n:

(1) $\bigcap U_n$ *consists of nowhere-differentiable functions.* Let $f \in \bigcap U_n$. We shall prove that given x in $[0, 1]$, the limit

$$\lim \Delta f(x, h)$$

does not exist: Given n, the fact that f belongs to U_n means that we can find a number h_n with $0 < h_n \le 1/n$ such that

$$\Delta f(x, h_n) > n.$$

Then the sequence (h_n) converges to zero, but the sequence $(\Delta f(x, h_n))$ does not converge. As a result, f is not differentiable at x.

(2) *U_n is open in $\mathcal{C}$.* Suppose that $f \in U_n$; we find a δ-neighborhood of f that is contained in U_n. Because $f \in U_n$, there is a number h with $0 < h \le 1/n$ such that $\Delta_h f > n$. Set $M = \Delta_h f$, and let

$$\delta = h(M - n)/4.$$

We assert that if g is a function with $\rho(f, g) < \delta$, then

$$\Delta g(x, h) \ge \tfrac{1}{2}(M + n) > n$$

for all $x \in I$, so that $g \in U_n$.

To prove the assertion, let us first assume that $\Delta f(x, h)$ is equal to the quotient $|f(x + h) - f(x)|/h$. We compute

$$\left| \frac{f(x + h) - f(x)}{h} - \frac{g(x + h) - g(x)}{h} \right| =$$
$$(1/h)|[f(x + h) - g(x + h)] - [f(x) - g(x)]| \le 2\delta/h = (M - n)/2.$$

If the first difference quotient is at least M in absolute value, then the second is in absolute value at least

$$M - \tfrac{1}{2}(M - n) = \tfrac{1}{2}(M + n).$$

A similar remark applies if $\Delta f(x, h)$ equals the other difference quotient.

(3) *U_n is dense in $\mathcal{C}$.* We must show that given f in $\mathcal{C}$, given $\epsilon > 0$, and given n, we can find an element g of U_n within ϵ of f.

Choose $\alpha > n$. We shall construct g as a "piecewise-linear" function, that is, a function whose graph is a broken line segment; each line segment in the graph of g will have slope at least α in absolute value. It follows at once that such a function g belongs to U_n. For let

$$0 = x_0 < x_1 < x_2 < \cdots < x_k = 1$$

be a partition of the interval $[0, 1]$ such that the restriction of g to each subinterval $I_i = [x_{i-1}, x_i]$ is a linear function. Then choose h so that $h \le 1/n$ and

$$h \le \tfrac{1}{2} \min\{|x_i - x_{i-1}|; \ i = 1, \ldots, k\}.$$

If x is in $[0, 1]$, then x belongs to some subinterval I_i. If x belongs to the first half of the subinterval I_i, then $x + h$ belongs to I_i and $(g(x + h) - g(x))/h$ equals the slope of the linear function $g|I_i$. Similarly, if x belongs to the second half of I_i, then $x - h$ belongs to I_i and $(g(x - h) - g(x))/(-h)$ equals the slope of $g|I_i$. In either case, $\Delta g(x, h) \ge \alpha$, so $g \in U_n$, as desired.

Now given f, ϵ, and α, we must show how to construct the desired piecewise-linear function g. First, we use uniform continuity of f to choose a partition of the interval

$$0 = t_0 < t_1 < \cdots < t_m = 1$$

having the property that f varies by at most $\epsilon/4$ on each subinterval $[t_{i-1}, t_i]$ of this partition. For each $i = 1, \ldots, m$, choose a point $a_i \in (t_{i-1}, t_i)$. We then define a piecewise-linear function g_1 by the equations

$$g_1(x) = \begin{cases} f(t_{i-1}) & \text{for } x \in [t_{i-1}, a_i], \\ f(t_{i-1}) + m_i(x - a_i) & \text{for } x \in [a_i, t_i], \end{cases}$$

where $m_i = (f(t_i) - f(t_{i-1}))/(t_i - a_i)$. The graphs of f and g_1 are pictured in Figure 49.2.

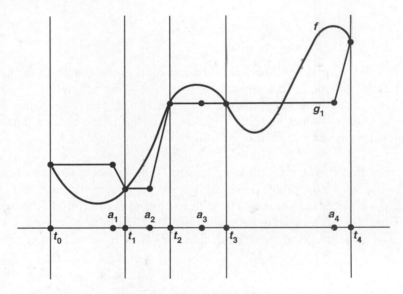

Figure 49.2

We have some freedom of choice in choosing the point a_i. If $f(t_i) \neq f(t_{i-1})$, we require a_i to be close enough to t_i that

$$t_i - a_i < \frac{|f(t_i) - f(t_{i-1})|}{\alpha}.$$

Then the graph of g_1 will consist entirely of line segments of slope zero and line segments of slope at least α in absolute value.

Furthermore, we assert that $\rho(g_1, f) \leq \epsilon/2$: On the interval I_i, both $g_1(x)$ and $f(x)$ vary by at most $\epsilon/4$ from $f(t_{i-1})$; therefore, they are within $\epsilon/2$ of each other. Then $\rho(g_1, f) = \max\{|g_1(x) - f(x)|\} \leq \epsilon/2$.

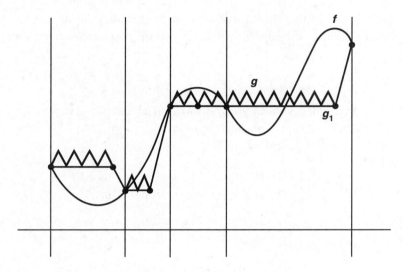

Figure 49.3

The function g_1 is not yet the function we want. We now define a function g by replacing each ɦorizontal line segment in the graph of g_1 by a "sawtooth" graph that lies within $\epsilon/2$ of the graph of g_1 and has the property that each edge of the sawtooth has slope at least α in absolute value. We leave this part of the construction to you. The result is the desired piecewise-linear function g. See Figure 49.3. ∎

You may find this proof frustrating, in that it seems so abstract and nonconstructive. Implicit in the proof, however, is a procedure for constructing a specific sequence f_n of piecewise-linear functions that converges uniformly to the nowhere-differentiable function f. And defining the function f in this way is just as constructive as the usual definition of the sine function, for instance, as the limit of an infinite series.

Exercises

1. Check the stated properties of the functions f, g, and k of Example 1.
2. Given n and ϵ, define a continuous function $f : I \to \mathbb{R}$ such that $f \in U_n$ and $|f(x)| \leq \epsilon$ for all x.

§50 Introduction to Dimension Theory

Ve showed in §36 that if X is a compact manifold, then X can be imbedded in $\mathbb{R}^N$ or some positive integer N. In this section, we generalize this theorem to arbitrary compact metrizable spaces.

We shall define, for an arbitrary topological space X, a notion of topological dimension. It is the "covering dimension" originally defined by Lebesgue. We shall prove that each compact subset of $\mathbb{R}^m$ has topological dimension at most m. We shall also prove that the topological dimension of any compact m-manifold is at most m. (It is, in fact, precisely m, but this we shall not prove.)

The major theorem of this section is the theorem, due to K. Menger and G. Nöbeling, that any compact metrizable space of topological dimension m can be imbedded in $\mathbb{R}^N$ for $N = 2m + 1$. The proof is an application of the Baire theorem. It follows that every compact m-manifold can be imbedded in $\mathbb{R}^{2m+1}$. It follows also that a compact metrizable space can be imbedded in $\mathbb{R}^N$ for some N if and only if it has finite topological dimension.

Much of what we shall do holds without requiring the space in question to be compact. But we shall restrict ourselves to that case whenever it is convenient to do so. Generalizations to the noncompact case are given in the exercises.

Definition.   A collection $\mathcal{A}$ of subsets of the space X is said to have **order** $m + 1$ if some point of X lies in $m + 1$ elements of $\mathcal{A}$, and no point of X lies in more than $m + 1$ elements of $\mathcal{A}$.

Now we define what we mean by the *topological dimension* of a space X. Recall that given a collection $\mathcal{A}$ of subsets of X, a collection $\mathcal{B}$ is said to *refine* $\mathcal{A}$, or to be a *refinement* of $\mathcal{A}$, if for each element B of $\mathcal{B}$ there is an element A of $\mathcal{A}$ such that $B \subset A$.

Definition.   A space X is said to be *finite dimensional* if there is some integer m such that for every open covering $\mathcal{A}$ of X, there is an open covering $\mathcal{B}$ of X that refines $\mathcal{A}$ and has order at most $m + 1$. The *topological dimension* of X is defined to be the smallest value of m for which this statement holds; we denote it by $\dim X$.

EXAMPLE 1.   *Any compact subspace X of $\mathbb{R}$ has topological dimension at most 1.* We begin by defining an open covering of $\mathbb{R}$ of order 2. Let $\mathcal{A}_1$ denote the collection of all open intervals of the form $(n, n + 1)$ in $\mathbb{R}$, where n is an integer. Let $\mathcal{A}_0$ denote the collection of all open intervals of the form $(n - 1/2, n + 1/2)$, for n an integer. Then $\mathcal{A} = \mathcal{A}_0 \cup \mathcal{A}_1$ is an open covering of $\mathbb{R}$ by sets of diameter one. Because no two elements of $\mathcal{A}_0$ intersect, and no two elements of $\mathcal{A}_1$ intersect, $\mathcal{A}$ has order 2.

Now let X be a compact subspace of $\mathbb{R}$. Given a covering $\mathcal{C}$ of X by sets open in X, this covering has a positive Lebesgue number δ. This means that any collection of subsets of X that have diameter less than δ is automatically a refinement of $\mathcal{C}$. Consider the homeomorphism $f : \mathbb{R} \to \mathbb{R}$ defined by $f(x) = (\frac{1}{2}\delta)x$. The images under f of the elements of the collection $\mathcal{A}$ form an open covering of $\mathbb{R}$ of order 2 whose elements have diameter $\frac{1}{2}\delta$; their intersections with X form the required open covering of X.

EXAMPLE 2.   *The interval $X = [0, 1]$ has topological dimension 1.* We know that $\dim X \leq 1$. To show equality holds, let $\mathcal{A}$ be the covering of X by the sets $[0, 1)$ and $(0, 1]$. We show that if $\mathcal{B}$ is any open covering of X that refines $\mathcal{A}$, then $\mathcal{B}$ has order at least 2. Since $\mathcal{B}$ refines $\mathcal{A}$, it must contain more than one element. Let U be one of the elements of $\mathcal{B}$ and let V be the union of the others. If $\mathcal{B}$ had order 1, then the sets U and V would be disjoint and would thus form a separation of X. We conclude that $\mathcal{B}$ has order at least 2.

EXAMPLE 3.   *Any compact subspace X of $\mathbb{R}^2$ has topological dimension at most* 2. To prove this fact, we construct a certain open covering $\mathcal{A}$ of $\mathbb{R}^2$ that has order 3. We begin by defining $\mathcal{A}_2$ to be the collection of all open unit squares in $\mathbb{R}^2$ of the following form:

$$\mathcal{A}_2 = \{(n, n+1) \times (m, m+1) \mid n, m \text{ integers}\}.$$

Note that the elements of $\mathcal{A}_2$ are disjoint. Then, we define a collection $\mathcal{A}_1$ by taking each (open) edge e of one of these squares,

$$e = \{n\} \times (m, m+1) \quad \text{or} \quad e = (n, n+1) \times \{m\},$$

and expanding it slightly to an open set U_e of $\mathbb{R}^2$, being careful to ensure that if $e \neq e'$, the sets U_e and $U_{e'}$ are disjoint. We also choose each U_e so that its diameter is at most 2. Finally, we define $\mathcal{A}_0$ to be the collection consisting of all open balls of radius $\frac{1}{2}$ about the points $n \times m$. See Figure 50.1.

The collection of open sets $\mathcal{A} = \mathcal{A}_2 \cup \mathcal{A}_1 \cup \mathcal{A}_0$ covers $\mathbb{R}^2$. Each of its elements has diameter at most 2. And it has order 3, since no point of $\mathbb{R}^2$ can lie in more than one set from each $\mathcal{A}_i$.

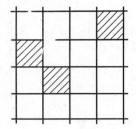 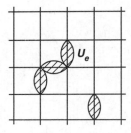 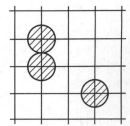

Figure 50.1

Now let X be a compact subspace of $\mathbb{R}^2$. Given an open covering of X, it has a positive Lebesgue number δ. Consider the homeomorphism $f : \mathbb{R}^2 \to \mathbb{R}^2$ defined by the equation $f(x) = (\delta/3)x$. The images under f of the open sets of the collection $\mathcal{A}$ form an open covering of $\mathbb{R}^2$ by sets of diameter less than δ; their intersections with X form the required open covering of X.

We shall generalize this result to compact subsets of $\mathbb{R}^n$ shortly.

Some basic facts about topological dimension are given in the following theorems:

Theorem 50.1.   *Let X be a space having finite dimension. If Y is a closed subspace of X, then Y has finite dimension and $\dim Y \leq \dim X$.*

Proof.   Let $\dim X = m$. Let $\mathcal{A}$ be a covering of Y by sets open in Y. For each $A \in \mathcal{A}$, choose an open set A' of X such that $A' \cap Y = A$. Cover X by the open sets A', along with the open set $X - Y$. Let $\mathcal{B}$ be a refinement of this covering that is an open covering of X and has order at most $m + 1$. Then the collection

$$\{B \cap Y \mid B \in \mathcal{B}\}$$

is a covering of Y by sets open in Y, it has order at most $m + 1$, and it refines $\mathcal{A}$. ∎

Theorem 50.2. *Let $X = Y \cup Z$, where Y and Z are closed subspaces of X having finite topological dimension. Then*

$$\dim X = \max\{\dim Y, \dim Z\}.$$

Proof. Let $m = \max\{\dim Y, \dim Z\}$. We shall show that X is finite dimensional and has topological dimension at most m. It then follows from the preceding theorem that X has topological dimension precisely m.

Step 1. If $\mathcal{A}$ is an open covering of X, we say that $\mathcal{A}$ has order at most $m + 1$ *at points of* Y provided no point of Y lies in more than $m + 1$ elements of $\mathcal{A}$.

We show that if $\mathcal{A}$ is an open covering of X, then there is an open covering of X that refines $\mathcal{A}$ and has order at most $m + 1$ at points of Y.

To prove this fact, consider the collection

$$\{A \cap Y \mid A \in \mathcal{A}\}.$$

It is an open covering of Y, so it has a refinement $\mathcal{B}$ that is an open covering of Y and has order at most $m + 1$. Given $B \in \mathcal{B}$, choose an open set U_B of X such that $U_B \cap Y = B$. Choose also an element A_B of $\mathcal{A}$ such that $B \subset A_B$. Let $\mathcal{C}$ be the collection consisting of all the sets $U_B \cap A_B$, for $B \in \mathcal{B}$, along with all the sets $A - Y$, for $A \in \mathcal{A}$. Then $\mathcal{C}$ is the desired open covering of X.

Step 2. Now let $\mathcal{A}$ be an open covering of X. We construct an open covering $\mathcal{D}$ of X that refines $\mathcal{A}$ and has order at most $m + 1$. Let $\mathcal{B}$ be an open covering of X refining $\mathcal{A}$ that has order at most $m + 1$ at points of Y. Then let $\mathcal{C}$ be an open covering of X refining $\mathcal{B}$ that has order at most $m + 1$ at points of Z.

We form a new covering $\mathcal{D}$ of X as follows: Define $f : \mathcal{C} \to \mathcal{B}$ by choosing for each $C \in \mathcal{C}$ an element $f(C)$ of $\mathcal{B}$ such that $C \subset f(C)$. Given $B \in \mathcal{B}$, define $D(B)$ to be the union of all those elements C of $\mathcal{C}$ for which $f(C) = B$. (Of course, $D(B)$ is empty if B is not in the image of f.) Let $\mathcal{D}$ be the collection of all the sets $D(B)$, for $B \in \mathcal{B}$.

Now $\mathcal{D}$ refines $\mathcal{B}$, because $D(B) \subset B$ for each B; therefore, $\mathcal{D}$ refines $\mathcal{A}$. Also, $\mathcal{D}$ covers X because $\mathcal{C}$ covers X and $C \subset D(f(C))$ for each $C \in \mathcal{C}$. We show that $\mathcal{D}$ has order at most $m + 1$. Suppose $x \in D(B_1) \cap \cdots \cap D(B_k)$, where the sets $D(B_i)$ are distinct. We wish to prove that $k \leq m + 1$. Note that the sets $B_1, \ldots, B_k$ must be distinct because the sets $D(B_i)$ are. Because $x \in D(B_i)$, we can choose for each i, a set $C_i \in \mathcal{C}$ such that $x \in C_i$ and $f(C_i) = B_i$. The sets C_i are distinct because the sets B_i are. Furthermore,

$$x \in [C_1 \cap \cdots \cap C_k] \subset [D(B_1) \cap \cdots \cap D(B_k)] \subset [B_1 \cap \cdots \cap B_k].$$

If x happens to lie in Y, then $k \leq m + 1$ because $\mathcal{B}$ has order at most $m + 1$ at points of Y; and if x is in Z, then $k \leq m + 1$ because $\mathcal{C}$ has order at most $m + 1$ at points of Z. ∎

Corollary 50.3. *Let* $X = Y_1 \cup \cdots \cup Y_k$, *where each* Y_i *is a closed subspace of* X *and is finite dimensional. Then*

$$\dim X = \max\{\dim Y_1, \ldots, \dim Y_k\}.$$

EXAMPLE 4.   *Every compact* 1*-manifold* X *has topological dimension* 1. The space X can be written as a finite union of spaces that are homeomorphic to the unit interval $[0, 1]$; then the preceding corollary applies.

EXAMPLE 5.   *Every compact* 2*-manifold* X *has topological dimension at most* 2. The space X can be written as a finite union of spaces that are homeomorphic to the closed unit ball in $\mathbb{R}^2$; then the preceding corollary applies.

An obvious question occurs at this point: Does a compact 2-manifold have topological dimension precisely 2? The answer is "yes," but the proof is not easy; it requires the tools of algebraic topology. We will prove in Part II of this book that every closed triangular region in $\mathbb{R}^2$ has topological dimension at least 2. (See §55.) It then follows that any compact subspace of $\mathbb{R}^2$ that contains a closed triangular region has topological dimension 2, from which it follows that every compact 2-manifold has topological dimension 2.

EXAMPLE 6.   An ***arc*** A is a space homeomorphic to the closed unit interval; the ***end points*** of A are the points p and q such that $A - \{p\}$ and $A - \{q\}$ are connected. A (finite) ***linear graph*** G is a Hausdorff space that is written as the union of finitely many arcs, each pair of which intersect in at most a common end point. The arcs in the collection are called the ***edges*** of G, and the end points of the arcs are called the ***vertices*** of G. Each edge of G, being compact, is closed in G; the preceding corollary tells us that G has topological dimension 1.

Two particular linear graphs are sketched in Figure 50.2. The first is a diagram of the familiar "gas-water-electricity problem"; the second is called the "complete graph on five vertices." Neither of them can be imbedded in $\mathbb{R}^2$. Although this fact is "intuitively obvious," it is highly nontrivial to prove. We shall give a proof in §64.

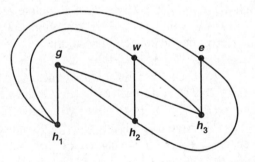

Figure 50.2

EXAMPLE 7.   *Every finite linear graph can be imbedded in* $\mathbb{R}^3$. The proof involves the notion of "general position." A set S of points of $\mathbb{R}^3$ is said to be in *general position* if no three of the points of S are collinear and no four of them are coplanar. It is easy to find such a set of points. For example, the points of the curve

$$S = \{(t, t^2, t^3) \mid t \in \mathbb{R}\}$$

are in general position. For if four of these points belonged to a single plane $Ax + By + Cz = D$, then the polynomial equation

$$At + Bt^2 + Ct^3 = D$$

would have four distinct real roots! And if three of these points belonged to a single line, we could take an additional point of S and obtain four points that lie on a plane.

Now, given a finite linear graph G, with vertices $v_1, \ldots, v_n$, let us choose a set $\{z_1, \ldots, z_n\}$ of points of $\mathbb{R}^3$ that is in general position. Define a map $f : G \to \mathbb{R}^3$ by letting f map the vertex v_i to the point z_i, and map the edge joining v_i and v_j homeomorphically onto the line segment joining z_i and z_j. Now each edge of G is closed in G. It follows that f is continuous, by the pasting lemma. We show that f is injective, from which it follows that f is an imbedding. Let $e = v_i v_j$ and $e' = v_k v_m$ be two edges of G. If they have no vertex in common, then the line segments $f(e)$ and $f(e')$ are disjoint, for otherwise the points z_i, z_j, z_k, z_m would be coplanar. And if e and e' have a vertex in common, so that $i = k$, say, then the line segments $f(e)$ and $f(e')$ intersect only in the point $z_i = z_k$, for otherwise z_i, z_j, and z_m would be collinear.

Now we prove our general imbedding theorem, to the effect that every compact metrizable space of topological dimension m can be imbedded in $\mathbb{R}^{2m+1}$. This theorem is another "deep" theorem; it is not at all obvious, for instance, why $2m + 1$ should be the crucial dimension. That will come out in the course of the proof.

To prove the imbedding theorem, we shall need to generalize the notion of general position to $\mathbb{R}^N$. This involves a bit of the analytic geometry of $\mathbb{R}^N$, which is nothing more than the usual linear algebra of $\mathbb{R}^N$ translated into somewhat different language.

Definition.   A set $\{x_0, \ldots, x_k\}$ of points of $\mathbb{R}^N$ is said to be *geometrically independent*, or *affinely independent*, if the equations

$$\sum_{i=0}^{k} a_i x_i = 0 \quad \text{and} \quad \sum_{i=0}^{k} a_i = 0$$

hold only if each $a_i = 0$.

Obviously, a set consisting of only one point is geometrically independent. But what does geometric independence mean in general? If we solve the second equation for a_0 and plug the answer into the first equation, we see that this definition is equivalent to the statement that the equation

$$\sum_{i=1}^{k} a_i (x_i - x_0) = 0$$

holds only if each $a_i = 0$. This is just the definition of *linear independence* for the set of vectors $x_1 - x_0, \ldots, x_k - x_0$ of the vector space $\mathbb{R}^N$. This gives us something to visualize: Any two distinct points form a geometrically independent set. Three points form a geometrically independent set if they are not collinear. Four points in $\mathbb{R}^3$ form a geometrically independent set if they are not coplanar. And so on.

It follows from these remarks that the points

$$\mathbf{0} = (0, 0, \ldots, 0),$$
$$\epsilon_1 = (1, 0, \ldots, 0),$$
$$\ldots$$
$$\epsilon_N = (0, 0, \ldots, 1)$$

are geometrically independent in $\mathbb{R}^N$. It also follows that any geometrically independent set of points in $\mathbb{R}^N$ contains no more than $N + 1$ points.

Definition. Let $\{\mathbf{x}_0, \ldots, \mathbf{x}_k\}$ be a set of points of $\mathbb{R}^N$ that is geometrically independent. The *plane P determined by these points* is defined to be the set of all points $\mathbf{x}$ of $\mathbb{R}^N$ such that

$$\mathbf{x} = \sum_{i=0}^{k} t_i \mathbf{x}_i, \quad \text{where } \sum_{i=0}^{k} t_i = 1.$$

It is simple algebra to check that P can also be expressed as the set of all points $\mathbf{x}$ such that

$$(*) \qquad \mathbf{x} = \mathbf{x}_0 + \sum_{i=1}^{k} a_i (\mathbf{x}_i - \mathbf{x}_0)$$

for some scalars $a_1, \ldots, a_k$. Thus P can be described not only as "the plane determined by the points $\mathbf{x}_0, \ldots, \mathbf{x}_k$," but also as "the plane passing through the point $\mathbf{x}_0$ parallel to the vectors $\mathbf{x}_1 - \mathbf{x}_0, \ldots, \mathbf{x}_k - \mathbf{x}_0$."

Consider now the homeomorphism $T : \mathbb{R}^N \to \mathbb{R}^N$ defined by the equation $T(\mathbf{x}) = \mathbf{x} - \mathbf{x}_0$. It is called a *translation* of $\mathbb{R}^N$. Expression $(*)$ shows that this map carries the plane P onto the vector subspace V^k of $\mathbb{R}^N$ having as basis the vectors $\mathbf{x}_1 - \mathbf{x}_0, \ldots, \mathbf{x}_k - \mathbf{x}_0$. For this reason, we often call P a *k-plane* in $\mathbb{R}^N$.

Two facts follow at once: First, if $k < N$, the k-plane P necessarily has empty interior in $\mathbb{R}^N$ (because V^k does). And second, if $\mathbf{y}$ is any point of $\mathbb{R}^N$ not lying in P, then the set

$$\{\mathbf{x}_0, \ldots, \mathbf{x}_k, \mathbf{y}\}$$

is geometrically independent. For if $\mathbf{y} \notin P$, then $T(\mathbf{y}) = \mathbf{y} - \mathbf{x}_0$ is not in V^k. By a standard theorem of linear algebra, the vectors $\{\mathbf{x}_1 - \mathbf{x}_0, \ldots, \mathbf{x}_k - \mathbf{x}_0, \mathbf{y} - \mathbf{x}_0\}$ are linearly independent, from which our result follows.

Definition. A set A of points of $\mathbb{R}^N$ is said to be in *general position in $\mathbb{R}^N$* if every subset of A containing $N + 1$ or fewer points is geometrically independent.

In the case of $\mathbb{R}^3$, this is the same as the definition given earlier, as you can check.

Lemma 50.4. *Given a finite set $\{x_1, \ldots, x_n\}$ of points of $\mathbb{R}^N$ and given $\delta > 0$, there exists a set $\{y_1, \ldots, y_n\}$ of points of $\mathbb{R}^N$ in general position in $\mathbb{R}^N$, such that $|x_i - y_i| < \delta$ for all i.*

Proof.   We proceed by induction. Set $y_1 = x_1$. Suppose that we are given $y_1, \ldots, y_p$ in general position in $\mathbb{R}^N$. Consider the set of all planes in $\mathbb{R}^N$ determined by subsets of $\{y_1, \ldots, y_p\}$ that contain N or fewer elements. Every such subset is geometrically independent and determines a k-plane of $\mathbb{R}^N$ for some $k \le N-1$. Each of these planes has empty interior in $\mathbb{R}^N$. Because there are only finitely many of them, their union also has empty interior in $\mathbb{R}^N$. (Recall that $\mathbb{R}^N$ is a Baire space.) Choose y_{p+1} to be a point of $\mathbb{R}^N$ within δ of x_{p+1} that does not lie in any of these planes. It follows at once that the set

$$C = \{y_1, \ldots, y_p, y_{p+1}\}$$

is in general position in $\mathbb{R}^N$. For let D be any subset of C containing $N + 1$ or fewer elements. If D does not contain y_{p+1}, then D is geometrically independent by the induction hypothesis. If D does contain y_{p+1}, then $D - \{y_{p+1}\}$ contains N or fewer points and y_{p+1} is not in the plane determined by these points, by construction. Then as noted above, D is geometrically independent.   ∎

Theorem 50.5 (The imbedding theorem).   *Every compact metrizable space X of topological dimension m can be imbedded in $\mathbb{R}^{2m+1}$.*

Proof.   Let $N = 2m + 1$. Let us denote the square metric for $\mathbb{R}^N$ by

$$|x - y| = \max\{|x_i - y_i| \, ; \, i = 1, \ldots, N\}.$$

Then we can use ρ to denote the corresponding sup metric on the space $\mathcal{C}(X, \mathbb{R}^N)$;

$$\rho(f, g) = \sup\{|f(x) - g(x)| \, ; \, x \in X\}.$$

The space $\mathcal{C}(X, \mathbb{R}^N)$ is complete in the metric ρ, since $\mathbb{R}^N$ is complete in the square metric.

Choose a metric d for the space X; because X is compact, d is bounded. Given a continuous map $f : X \to \mathbb{R}^N$, let us define

$$\Delta(f) = \sup\{\text{diam } f^{-1}(\{z\}) \mid z \in f(X)\}.$$

The number $\Delta(f)$ measures how far f "deviates" from being injective; if $\Delta(f) = 0$, each set $f^{-1}(\{z\})$ consists of exactly one point, so f is injective.

Now, given $\epsilon > 0$, define U_ϵ to be the set of all those continuous maps $f : X \to \mathbb{R}^N$ for which $\Delta(f) < \epsilon$; it consists of all those maps that "deviate" from being injective by less than ϵ. We shall show that U_ϵ is both open and dense in $\mathcal{C}(X, \mathbb{R}^N)$. It follows that the intersection

$$\bigcap_{n \in \mathbb{Z}_+} U_{1/n}$$

is dense in $C(X, \mathbb{R}^N)$ and is in particular nonempty.

If f is an element of this intersection, then $\Delta(f) < 1/n$ for every n. Therefore, $\Delta(f) = 0$ and f is injective. Because X is compact, f is an imbedding. Thus, the imbedding theorem is proved.

(1) U_ϵ is open in $C(X, \mathbb{R}^N)$. Given an element f of U_ϵ, we wish to find some ball $B_\rho(f, \delta)$ about f that is contained in U_ϵ. First choose a number b such that $\Delta(f) < b < \epsilon$. Note that if $f(x) = f(y) = z$, then x and y belong to the set $f^{-1}(\{z\})$, so that $d(x, y)$ must be less than b. It follows that if we let A be the following subset of $X \times X$,

$$A = \{x \times y \mid d(x, y) \geq b\}, \quad \text{otherwise} \quad x, y \in f^{-1}(\{z\}) \Rightarrow d(x,y) < b$$

then the function $|f(x) - f(y)|$ is positive on A. Now A is closed in $X \times X$ and therefore compact; hence the function $|f(x) - f(y)|$ has a positive minimum on A. Let

$$\delta = \tfrac{1}{2} \min\{|f(x) - f(y)| \,;\, x \times y \in A\}.$$

We assert that this value of δ will suffice.

Suppose that g is a map such that $\rho(f, g) < \delta$. If $x \times y \in A$, then $|f(x) - f(y)| \geq 2\delta$ by definition; since $g(x)$ and $g(y)$ are within δ of $f(x)$ and $f(y)$, respectively, we must have $|g(x) - g(y)| > 0$. Hence the function $|g(x) - g(y)|$ is positive on A. As a result, if x and y are two points such that $g(x) = g(y)$, then necessarily $d(x, y) < b$. We conclude that $\Delta g \leq b < \epsilon$, as desired.

(2) U_ϵ is dense in $C(X, \mathbb{R}^N)$. This is the difficult part of the proof. We need to use the analytic geometry of $\mathbb{R}^N$ discussed earlier. Let $f \in C(X, \mathbb{R}^N)$. Given $\epsilon > 0$ and given $\delta > 0$, we wish to find a function $g \in C(X, \mathbb{R}^N)$ such that $g \in U_\epsilon$ and $\rho(f, g) < \delta$.

Let us cover X by finitely many open sets $\{U_1, \ldots, U_n\}$ such that

(1) diam $U_i < \epsilon/2$ in X,

(2) diam $f(U_i) < \delta/2$ in $\mathbb{R}^N$,

(3) $\{U_1, \ldots, U_n\}$ has order $\leq m + 1$.

Let $\{\phi_i\}$ be a partition of unity dominated by $\{U_i\}$ (see §36). For each i, choose a point $x_i \in U_i$. Then choose, for each i, a point $\mathbf{z}_i \in \mathbb{R}^N$ such that $\mathbf{z}_i$ is within $\delta/2$ of the point $f(x_i)$, and such that the set $\{\mathbf{z}_1, \ldots, \mathbf{z}_n\}$ is in general position in $\mathbb{R}^N$. Finally, define $g : X \to \mathbb{R}^N$ by the equation

$$g(x) = \sum_{i=1}^{n} \phi_i(x)\mathbf{z}_i.$$

We assert that g is the desired function.

First, we show that $\rho(f, g) < \delta$. Note that

$$g(x) - f(x) = \sum_{i=1}^{n} \phi_i(x)\mathbf{z}_i - \sum_{i=1}^{n} \phi_i(x)f(x);$$

here we use the fact that $\sum \phi_i(x) = 1$. Then

$$g(x) - f(x) = \sum \phi_i(x)(\mathbf{z}_i - f(x_i)) + \sum \phi_i(x)(f(x_i) - f(x)).$$

Now $|\mathbf{z}_i - f(x_i)| < \delta/2$ for each i, by choice of the points $\mathbf{z}_i$. And if i is an index such that $\phi_i(x) \neq 0$, then $x \in U_i$; because we have diam $f(U_i) < \delta/2$, it follows that $|f(x_i) - f(x)| < \delta/2$. Since $\sum \phi_i(x) = 1$, we conclude that $|g(x) - f(x)| < \delta$. Therefore, $\rho(g, f) < \delta$, as desired.

Second, we show that $g \in U_\epsilon$. We shall prove that if $x, y \in X$ and $g(x) = g(y)$, then x and y belong to one of the open sets U_i, so that necessarily $d(x, y) < \epsilon/2$ (since diam $U_i < \epsilon/2$). As a result, $\Delta(g) \leq \epsilon/2 < \epsilon$, as desired.

So suppose $g(x) = g(y)$. Then

$$\sum_{i=1}^{n} [\phi_i(x) - \phi_i(y)]\mathbf{z}_i = \mathbf{0}.$$

Because the covering $\{U_i\}$ has order at most $m+1$, at most $m+1$ of the numbers $\phi_i(x)$ are nonzero, and at most $m+1$ of the numbers $\phi_i(y)$ are nonzero. Thus, the sum $\sum [\phi_i(x) - \phi_i(y)]\mathbf{z}_i$ has at most $2m+2$ nonzero terms. Note that the sum of the coefficients vanishes because

$$\sum [\phi_i(x) - \phi_i(y)] = 1 - 1 = 0.$$

The points $\mathbf{z}_i$ are in general position in $\mathbb{R}^N$, so that any subset of them having $N+1$ or fewer elements is geometrically independent. And by hypothesis $N+1 = 2m+2$. (Aha!) Therefore, we conclude that

$$\phi_i(x) - \phi_i(y) = 0$$

for all i.

Now $\phi_i(x) > 0$ for some i, so that $x \in U_i$. Since $\phi_i(y) = \phi_i(x)$, we have $y \in U_i$ also, as asserted. ∎

To give some content to the imbedding theorem, we need some more examples of spaces that are finite dimensional. We prove the following theorem:

Theorem 50.6. *Every compact subspace of $\mathbb{R}^N$ has topological dimension at most N.*

Proof. The proof is a generalization of the proof given in Example 3 for $\mathbb{R}^2$. Let ρ be the square metric on $\mathbb{R}^N$.

Step 1. We begin by breaking $\mathbb{R}^N$ up into "unit cubes." Define $\mathcal{J}$ to be the following collection of open intervals in $\mathbb{R}$:

$$\mathcal{J} = \{(n, n+1) \mid n \in \mathbb{Z}\},$$

and define $\mathcal{K}$ to be the following collection of one-point sets in $\mathbb{R}$:

$$\mathcal{K} = \{\{n\} \mid n \in \mathbb{Z}\}.$$

If M is an integer such that $0 \le M \le N$, let $\mathcal{C}_M$ denote the set of all products

$$C = A_1 \times A_2 \times \cdots \times A_N,$$

where exactly M of the sets A_i belong to $\mathcal{J}$, and the remainder belong to $\mathcal{K}$. If $M > 0$, then C is homeomorphic to the product $(0, 1)^M$ and will be called an **M-cube**. If $M = 0$, then C consists of a single point and will be called a **0-cube**.

Let $\mathcal{C} = \mathcal{C}_0 \cup \mathcal{C}_1 \cup \cdots \cup \mathcal{C}_N$. Note that each point $\mathbf{x}$ of $\mathbb{R}^N$ lies in precisely one element of $\mathcal{C}$ because each real number x_i lies in precisely one element of $\mathcal{J} \cup \mathcal{K}$. We shall expand each element C of $\mathcal{C}$ slightly to an open set $U(C)$ of $\mathbb{R}^N$ of diameter at most $3/2$, in such a way that if C and D are two different M-cubes, then $U(C)$ and $U(D)$ are disjoint.

Let $\mathbf{x} = (x_1, \ldots, x_N)$ be a point of the M-cube C. We show that there is a number $\epsilon(\mathbf{x}) > 0$ such that the $\epsilon(\mathbf{x})$-neighborhood of $\mathbf{x}$ intersects no M-cube other than C. If C is a 0-cube, we set $\epsilon(\mathbf{x}) = 1/2$ and we are finished. Otherwise, $M > 0$, and exactly M of the numbers x_i are not integers. Choose $\epsilon \le 1/2$ so that for each x_i that is not an integer, the interval $(x_i - \epsilon, x_i + \epsilon)$ contains no integer. If $\mathbf{y} = (y_1, \ldots, y_N)$ is a point lying in the ϵ-neighborhood of $\mathbf{x}$, then y_i is nonintegral whenever x_i is nonintegral. This means that $\mathbf{y}$ either belongs to the same M-cube as $\mathbf{x}$ does, or $\mathbf{y}$ belongs to some L-cube for $L > M$. In either case, the ϵ-neighborhood of $\mathbf{x}$ intersects no M-cube other than C.

Given an M-cube C, we define the neighborhood $U(C)$ of C to be the union of the $\epsilon(\mathbf{x})/2$-neighborhoods of $\mathbf{x}$ for all $\mathbf{x} \in C$. It is then immediate that if C and D are different M-cubes, $U(C)$ and $U(D)$ are disjoint. Furthermore, if $\mathbf{z}$ is a point of $U(C)$, then $d(\mathbf{z}, \mathbf{x}) < \epsilon(\mathbf{x})/2 < 1/4$ for some point $\mathbf{x}$ of C. Since C has diameter 1, the set $U(C)$ has diameter at most $3/2$.

Step 2. Given M with $0 \le M \le N$, define $\mathcal{A}_M$ to be the collection of all sets $U(C)$, where $C \in \mathcal{C}_M$. The elements of $\mathcal{A}_M$ are disjoint, and each has diameter at most $3/2$. The remainder of the proof is a copy of the proof given in Example 3 for $\mathbb{R}^2$. ∎

Corollary 50.7. *Every compact m-manifold has topological dimension at most m.*

Corollary 50.8. *Every compact m-manifold can be imbedded in $\mathbb{R}^{2m+1}$.*

Corollary 50.9. *Let X be a compact metrizable space. Then X can be imbedded in some euclidean space $\mathbb{R}^N$ if and only if X has finite topological dimension.*

As mentioned earlier, much of what we have proved holds without assumption of compactness. We ask you to prove the appropriate generalizations in the exercises that follow.

One thing we do *not* ask you to prove is the fact that the topological dimension of an m-manifold is precisely m. And for good reason; the proof requires the tools of algebraic topology.

Nor do we ask you to prove that $N = 2m + 1$ is the smallest value of N such that every compact metrizable space of topological dimension m can be imbedded in $\mathbb{R}^N$. The reason is the same. Even in the case of a linear graph, where $m = 1$, the proof is nontrivial, as we remarked earlier.

For further results in dimension theory, the reader is referred to the classical book of Hurewicz and Wallman [H-W]. In particular, this book discusses another, entirely different, definition of topological dimension, due to Menger and Urysohn. It is an inductive definition. The empty set has dimension -1. And a space has dimension at most n if there is a basis for its topology such that for each basis element B, the boundary of B has dimension at most $n - 1$. The dimension of a space is the smallest value of n for which this condition holds. This notion of dimension agrees with ours for compact metrizable spaces.

Exercises

1. Show that any discrete space has dimension 0.

2. Show that any connected T_1 space having more than one point has dimension at least 1.

3. Show that the topologist's sine curve has dimension 1.

4. Show that the points $\mathbf{0}$, ϵ_1, ϵ_2, ϵ_3, and $(1, 1, 1)$ are in general position in $\mathbb{R}^3$. Sketch the corresponding imbedding into $\mathbb{R}^3$ of the complete graph on five vertices.

5. Examine the proof of the imbedding theorem in the case $m = 1$ and show that the map g of part (2) actually maps X onto a linear graph in $\mathbb{R}^3$.

6. Prove the following:

    Theorem.   *Let X be a locally compact Hausdorff space with a countable basis, such that every compact subspace of X has topological dimension at most m. Then X is homeomorphic to a closed subspace of $\mathbb{R}^{2m+1}$.*

    Proof. If $f : X \to \mathbb{R}^N$ is a continuous map, we say $f(x) \to \infty$ as $x \to \infty$ if given n, there is a compact subspace C of X such that $f(x) > n$ for $x \in X - C$.

    (a) Let $\bar{\rho}$ be the uniform metric on $\mathcal{C}(X, \mathbb{R}^N)$. Show that if $f(x) \to \infty$ as $x \to \infty$ and $\bar{\rho}(f, g) < 1$, then $g(x) \to \infty$ as $x \to \infty$.

    (b) Show that if $f(x) \to \infty$ as $x \to \infty$, then f extends to a continuous map of one-point compactifications. Conclude that if f is injective as well, then f is a homeomorphism of X with a closed subspace of $\mathbb{R}^N$.

    (c) Given $f : X \to \mathbb{R}^N$ and given a compact subspace C of X, let

    $$U_\epsilon(C) = \{f \mid \Delta(f|C) < \epsilon\}.$$

    Show that $U_\epsilon(C)$ is open in $\mathcal{C}(X, \mathbb{R}^N)$.

    (d) Show that if $N = 2m + 1$, then $U_\epsilon(C)$ is dense in $\mathcal{C}(X, \mathbb{R}^N)$. [*Hint:* Given f and given $\epsilon, \delta > 0$, choose $g : C \to \mathbb{R}^N$ so that $d(f(x), g(x)) < \delta$ for

$x \in C$, and $\Delta(g) < \epsilon$. Extend $f - g$ to $h : X \rightarrow [-\delta, \delta]^N$ using the Tietze theorem.]

(e) Show there exists a map $f : X \rightarrow \mathbb{R}$ such that $f(x) \rightarrow \infty$ as $x \rightarrow \infty$. [*Hint:* Write X as the union of compact subspaces C_n such that $C_n \subset$ Int C_{n+1} for each n.]

(f) Let C_n be as in (e). Use the fact that $\bigcap U_{1/n}(C_n)$ is dense in $\mathcal{C}(X, \mathbb{R}^N)$ to complete the proof.

7. Corollary. *Every m-manifold can be imbedded in $\mathbb{R}^{2m+1}$ as a closed subspace.*

8. Recall that X is said to be σ-*compact* if there is a countable collection of compact subspaces of X whose interiors cover X.

Theorem. *Let X be a σ-compact Hausdorff space. If every compact subspace of X has topological dimension at most m, then so does X.*

Proof. Let $\mathcal{A}$ be an open cover of X. Find an open cover $\mathcal{B}$ of X refining $\mathcal{A}$ that has order at most $m + 1$, as follows:

(a) Show that $X = \bigcup X_n$, where X_n is compact and $X_n \subset$ Int X_{n+1} for each n. Let $X_0 = \varnothing$.

(b) Find an open covering $\mathcal{B}_0$ of X refining $\mathcal{A}$ such that for each n, each element of $\mathcal{B}_0$ that intersects X_n lies in X_{n+1}.

(c) Suppose $n \geq 0$ and $\mathcal{B}_n$ is an open covering of X refining $\mathcal{B}_0$ such that $\mathcal{B}_n$ has order at most $m + 1$ at points of X_n. Choose an open covering $\mathcal{C}$ of X refining $\mathcal{B}_n$ that has order at most $m + 1$ at points of X_{n+1}. Choose $f : \mathcal{C} \rightarrow \mathcal{B}_n$ so that $C \subset f(C)$. For $B \in \mathcal{B}_n$, let $D(B)$ be the union of those C for which $f(C) = B$. Let $\mathcal{B}_{n+1}$ consist of all sets $B \in \mathcal{B}_n$ for which $B \cap X_{n-1} \neq \varnothing$, along with all sets $D(B)$ for which $B \in \mathcal{B}_n$ and $B \cap X_{n-1} = \varnothing$. Show that $\mathcal{B}_{n+1}$ is an open covering of X that refines $\mathcal{B}_n$ and has order at most $m + 1$ at points of X_{n+1}.

(d) Define $\mathcal{B}$ as follows: Given a set B, it belongs to $\mathcal{B}$ if there is an N such that $B \in \mathcal{B}_n$ for all $n \geq N$.

9. Corollary. *Every m-manifold has topological dimension at most m.*

10. Corollary. *Every closed subspace of $\mathbb{R}^N$ has topological dimension at most N.*

11. Corollary. *A space X can be imbedded as a closed subspace of $\mathbb{R}^N$ for some N if and only if X is locally compact and Hausdorff with a countable basis, and has finite topological dimension.*

*Supplementary Exercises: Locally Euclidean Spaces

A space X is said to be *locally m-euclidean* if for each $x \in X$, there is a neighborhood of x that is homeomorphic to an open set of $\mathbb{R}^m$. Such a space X automatically satisfies the T_1 axiom, but it need not be Hausdorff. (See the exercises of §36.) However, if X is Hausdorff and has a countable basis, then X is called an *m-manifold*.

Throughout these exercises, let X be a space that is locally m-euclidean.

1. Show that X is locally compact and locally metrizable.

2. Consider the following conditions on X:
   (i) X is compact Hausdorff.
   (ii) X is an m-manifold.
   (iii) X is metrizable.
   (iv) X is normal.
   (v) X is Hausdorff.
   Show that (i) $\Rightarrow$ (ii) $\Rightarrow$ (iii) $\Rightarrow$ (iv) $\Rightarrow$ (v).

3. Show that $\mathbb{R}$ is locally 1-euclidean and satisfies (ii) but not (i).

4. Show that $\mathbb{R} \times \mathbb{R}$ in the dictionary order topology is locally 1-euclidean and satisfies (iii) but not (ii).

5. Show that the long line is locally 1-euclidean and satisfies (iv) but not (iii). (See the exercises of §24.)

*6. There is a space that is locally 2-euclidean and satisfies (v) but not (iv). It is constructed as follows. Let A be the following subspace of $\mathbb{R}^3$:

$$A = \{(x, y, 0) \mid x > 0\}.$$

Given c real, let B_c be the following subspace of $\mathbb{R}^3$:

$$B_c = \{(x, y, c) \mid x \leq 0\}.$$

Let X be the set that is the union of A and all the spaces B_c, for c real. Topologize X by taking as a basis all sets of the following three types:
   (i) U, where U is open in A.
   (ii) V, where V is open in the subspace of B_c consisting of points with $x < 0$.
   (iii) For each open interval $I = (a, b)$ of $\mathbb{R}$, each real number c, and each $\epsilon > 0$, the set $A_c(I, \epsilon) \cup B_c(I, \epsilon)$, where

$$A_c(I, \epsilon) = \{(x, y, 0) \mid 0 < x < \epsilon \text{ and } c + ax < y < c + bx\},$$
$$B_c(I, \epsilon) = \{(x, y, c) \mid -\epsilon < x \leq 0 \text{ and } a < y < b\}.$$

The space X is called the "Prüfer manifold."
   (a) Sketch the sets $A_c(I, \epsilon)$ and $B_c(I, \epsilon)$.
   (b) Show the sets of types (i)–(iii) form a basis for a topology on X.
   (c) Show the map $f_c : \mathbb{R}^2 \to X$ given by

$$f_c(x, y) = \begin{cases} (x, c + xy, 0) & \text{for } x > 0, \\ (x, y, c) & \text{for } x \leq 0 \end{cases}$$

defines a homeomorphism of $\mathbb{R}^2$ with the subspace $A \cup B_c$ of X.

(d) Show that $A \cup B_c$ is open in X; conclude that X is 2-euclidean.
(e) Show that X is Hausdorff.
(f) Show that X is not normal. [*Hint:* The subspace

$$L = \{(0, 0, c) \mid c \in \mathbb{R}\}$$

of X is closed and discrete. Compare Example 3 of §31.]

7. Show that X is Hausdorff if and only if X is completely regular.

8. Show that X is metrizable if and only if X is paracompact Hausdorff.

9. Show that if X is metrizable, then each component of X is an m-manifold.

Chapter 9

The Fundamental Group

One of the basic problems of topology is to determine whether two given topological spaces are homeomorphic or not. There is no method for solving this problem in general, but techniques do exist that apply in particular cases.

Showing that two spaces *are* homeomorphic is a matter of constructing a continuous mapping from one to the other having a continuous inverse, and constructing continuous functions is a problem that we have developed techniques to handle.

Showing that two spaces are *not* homeomorphic is a different matter. For that, one must show that a continuous function with continuous inverse does *not* exist. If one can find some topological property that holds for one space but not for the other, then the problem is solved—the spaces cannot be homeomorphic. The closed interval $[0, 1]$ cannot be homeomorphic to the open interval $(0, 1)$, for instance, because the first space is compact and the second one is not. And the real line $\mathbb{R}$ cannot be homeomorphic to the "long line" L, because $\mathbb{R}$ has a countable basis and L does not. Nor can the real line $\mathbb{R}$ be homeomorphic to the plane $\mathbb{R}^2$; deleting a point from $\mathbb{R}^2$ leaves a connected space remaining, and deleting a point from $\mathbb{R}$ does not.

But the topological properties we have studied up to now do not carry us very far in solving the problem. For instance, how does one show that the plane $\mathbb{R}^2$ is not homeomorphic to three-dimensional space $\mathbb{R}^3$? As one goes down the list of topological properties—compactness, connectedness, local connectedness, metrizability, and so on—one can find no topological property that distinguishes between them. As another example, consider such surfaces as the 2-sphere S^2, the torus T (surface of a doughnut), and the double torus $T\#T$ (surface of a two-holed doughnut). None of the topological properties we have studied up to now will distinguish between them.

So we must introduce new properties and new techniques. One of the most natural such properties is that of *simple connectedness*. You probably have studied this notion already, when you studied line integrals in the plane. Roughly speaking, one says that a space X is simply connected if every closed curve in X can be shrunk to a point in X. (We shall make this more precise later.) The property of simple connectedness, it turns out, will distinguish between $\mathbb{R}^2$ and $\mathbb{R}^3$; deleting a point from $\mathbb{R}^3$ leaves a simply connected space remaining, but deleting a point from $\mathbb{R}^2$ does not. It will also distinguish between S^2 (which is simply connected) and the torus T (which is not). But it will not distinguish between T and $T\#T$; neither of them is simply connected.

There is an idea more general than the idea of simple connectedness, an idea that includes simple connectedness as a special case. It involves a certain *group* that is called the *fundamental group* of the space. Two spaces that are homeomorphic have fundamental groups that are isomorphic. And the condition of simple connectedness is just the condition that the fundamental group of X is the trivial (one-element) group. Thus, the proof that S^2 and T are not homeomorphic can be rephrased by saying that the fundamental group of S^2 is trivial and the fundamental group of T is not. The fundamental group will distinguish between more spaces than the condition of simple connectedness will. It can be used, for example, to show that T and $T\#T$ are not homeomorphic; it turns out that T has an abelian fundamental group and $T\#T$ does not.

In this chapter, we define the fundamental group and study its properties. Then we apply it to a number of problems, including the problem of showing that various spaces, such as those already mentioned, are not homeomorphic.

Other applications include theorems about fixed points and antipode-preserving maps of the sphere, as well as the well-known *fundamental theorem of algebra*, which says that every polynomial equation with real or complex coefficients has a root. Finally, there is the famous *Jordan curve theorem*, which we shall study in the next chapter; it states that every simple closed curve C in the plane separates the plane into two components, of which C is the common boundary.

Throughout, we assume familiarity with the quotient topology (§22) and local connectedness (§25).

§51 Homotopy of Paths

Before defining the fundamental group of a space X, we shall consider paths on X and an equivalence relation called *path homotopy* between them. And we shall define a certain operation on the collection of the equivalence classes that makes it into what is called in algebra a *groupoid*.

Definition.   If f and f' are continuous maps of the space X into the space Y, we say that f is **homotopic** to f' if there is a continuous map $F : X \times I \to Y$ such that

$$F(x, 0) = f(x) \quad \text{and} \quad F(x, 1) = f'(x)$$

for each x. (Here $I = [0, 1]$.) The map F is called a **homotopy** between f and f'. If f is homotopic to f', we write $f \simeq f'$. If $f \simeq f'$ and f' is a constant map, we say that f is **nulhomotopic**.

We think of a homotopy as a continuous one-parameter family of maps from X to Y. If we imagine the parameter t as representing time, then the homotopy F represents a continuous "deforming" of the map f to the map f', as t goes from 0 to 1.

Now we consider the special case in which f is a path in X. Recall that if $f : [0, 1] \to X$ is a continuous map such that $f(0) = x_0$ and $f(1) = x_1$, we say that f is a path in X from x_0 to x_1. We also say that x_0 is the **initial point**, and x_1 the **final point**, of the path f. In this chapter, we shall for convenience use the interval $I = [0, 1]$ as the domain for all paths.

If f and f' are two paths in X, there is a stronger relation between them than mere homotopy. It is defined as follows:

Definition.   Two paths f and f', mapping the interval $I = [0, 1]$ into X, are said to be **path homotopic** if they have the same initial point x_0 and the same final point x_1, and if there is a continuous map $F : I \times I \to X$ such that

$$F(s, 0) = f(s) \quad \text{and} \quad F(s, 1) = f'(s),$$
$$F(0, t) = x_0 \quad \text{and} \quad F(1, t) = x_1,$$

for each $s \in I$ and each $t \in I$. We call F a **path homotopy** between f and f'. See Figure 51.1. If f is path homotopic to f', we write $f \simeq_p f'$.

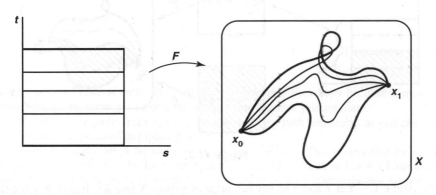

Figure 51.1

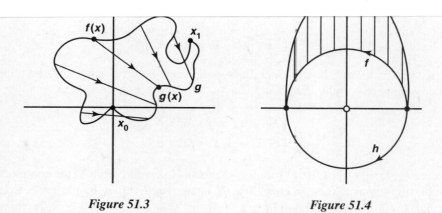

Figure 51.3   **Figure 51.4**

EXAMPLE 2.   Let X denote the **punctured plane**, $\mathbb{R}^2 - \{0\}$, which we shall denote by $\mathbb{R}^2 - \mathbf{0}$ for short. The following paths in X,

$$f(s) = (\cos \pi s, \sin \pi s),$$
$$g(s) = (\cos \pi s, 2 \sin \pi s)$$

are path homotopic; the straight-line homotopy between them is an acceptable path homotopy. But the straight-line homotopy between f and the path

$$h(s) = (\cos \pi s, - \sin \pi s)$$

is not acceptable, for its image does not lie in the space $X = \mathbb{R}^2 - \mathbf{0}$. See Figure 51.4.

Indeed, there exists *no* path homotopy in X between paths f and h. This result is hardly surprising; it is intuitively clear that one cannot "deform f past the hole at $\mathbf{0}$" without introducing a discontinuity. But it takes some work to prove. We shall return to this example later.

This example illustrates the fact that you must know what the range space is before you can tell whether two paths are path homotopic or not. The paths f and h would be path homotopic if they were paths in $\mathbb{R}^2$.

Now we introduce some algebra into this geometric situation. We define a certain operation on path-homotopy classes as follows:

The first condition says simply that F is a homotopy between f and f', and the second says that for each t, the path f_t defined by the equation $f_t(s) = F(s, t)$ is a path from x_0 to x_1. Said differently, the first condition says that F represents a continuous way of deforming the path f to the path f', and the second condition says that the end points of the path remain fixed during the deformation.

Lemma 51.1. *The relations $\simeq$ and $\simeq_p$ are equivalence relations.*

If f is a path, we shall denote its path-homotopy equivalence class by $[f]$.

Proof. Let us verify the properties of an equivalence relation.

Given f, it is trivial that $f \simeq f$; the map $F(x, t) = f(x)$ is the required homotopy. If f is a path, F is a path homotopy.

Given $f \simeq f'$, we show that $f' \simeq f$. Let F be a homotopy between f and f'. Then $G(x, t) = F(x, 1 - t)$ is a homotopy between f' and f. If F is a path homotopy, so is G.

Suppose that $f \simeq f'$ and $f' \simeq f''$. We show that $f \simeq f''$. Let F be a homotopy between f and f', and let F' be a homotopy between f' and f''. Define $G : X \times I \to Y$ by the equation

$$G(x, t) = \begin{cases} F(x, 2t) & \text{for } t \in [0, \tfrac{1}{2}], \\ F'(x, 2t - 1) & \text{for } t \in [\tfrac{1}{2}, 1]. \end{cases}$$

The map G is well defined, since if $t = \tfrac{1}{2}$, we have $F(x, 2t) = f'(x) = F'(x, 2t - 1)$. Because G is continuous on the two closed subsets $X \times [0, \tfrac{1}{2}]$ and $X \times [\tfrac{1}{2}, 1]$ of $X \times I$, it is continuous on all of $X \times I$, by the pasting lemma. Thus G is the required homotopy between f and f''.

You can check that if F and F' are path homotopies, so is G. See Figure 51.2. ∎

Definition. If f is a path in X from x_0 to x_1, and if g is a path in X from x_1 to x_2, we define the **product** $f * g$ of f and g to be the path h given by the equations

$$h(s) = \begin{cases} f(2s) & \text{for } s \in [0, \tfrac{1}{2}], \\ g(2s - 1) & \text{for } s \in [\tfrac{1}{2}, 1]. \end{cases}$$

The function h is well-defined and continuous, by the pasting lemma; it is a path in X from x_0 to x_2. We think of h as the path whose first half is the path f and whose second half is the path g.

The product operation on paths induces a well-defined operation on path-homotopy classes, defined by the equation

$$[f] * [g] = [f * g].$$

To verify this fact, let F be a path homotopy between f and f' and let G be a path homotopy between g and g'. Define

$$H(s, t) = \begin{cases} F(2s, t) & \text{for } s \in [0, \tfrac{1}{2}], \\ G(2s - 1, t) & \text{for } s \in [\tfrac{1}{2}, 1]. \end{cases}$$

Because $F(1, t) = x_1 = G(0, t)$ for all t, the map H is well-defined; it is continuous by the pasting lemma. You can check that H is the required path homotopy between $f * g$ and $f' * g'$. It is pictured in Figure 51.5.

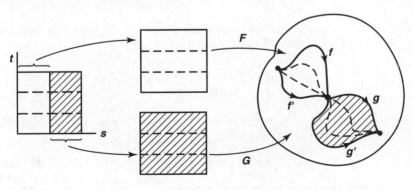

Figure 51.5

The operation $*$ on path-homotopy classes turns out to satisfy properties that look very much like the axioms for a group. They are called the *groupoid properties* of $*$. One difference from the properties of a group is that $[f] * [g]$ is not defined for every pair of classes, but only for those pairs $[f]$, $[g]$ for which $f(1) = g(0)$.

Theorem 51.2. *The operation $*$ has the following properties:*

(1) *(Associativity) If $[f] * ([g] * [h])$ is defined, so is $([f] * [g]) * [h]$, and they are equal.*

(2) *(Right and left identities) Given $x \in X$, let e_x denote the constant path $e_x : I \to X$ carrying all of I to the point x. If f is a path in X from x_0 to x_1, then*

$$[f] * [e_{x_1}] = [f] \quad and \quad [e_{x_0}] * [f] = [f].$$

(3) *(Inverse) Given the path f in X from x_0 to x_1, let $\bar{f}$ be the path defined by $\bar{f}(s) = f(1 - s)$. It is called the **reverse** of f. Then*

$$[f] * [\bar{f}] = [e_{x_0}] \quad and \quad [\bar{f}] * [f] = [e_{x_1}].$$

Proof. We shall make use of two elementary facts. The first is the fact that if $k : X \to Y$ is a continuous map, and if F is a path homotopy in X between the paths f and f', then $k \circ F$ is a path homotopy in Y between the paths $k \circ f$ and $k \circ f'$. See Figure 51.6.

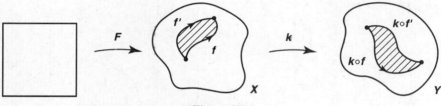

Figure 51.6

The second is the fact that if $k : X \to Y$ is a continuous map and if f and g are paths in X with $f(1) = g(0)$, then

$$k \circ (f * g) = (k \circ f) * (k \circ g).$$

This equation follows at once from the definition of the product operation $*$.

Step 1. We verify properties (2) and (3). To verify (2), we let e_0 denote the constant path in I at 0, and we let $i : I \to I$ denote the identity map, which is a path in I from 0 to 1. Then $e_0 * i$ is also a path in I from 0 to 1. (The graphs of these two paths are pictured in Figure 51.7.)

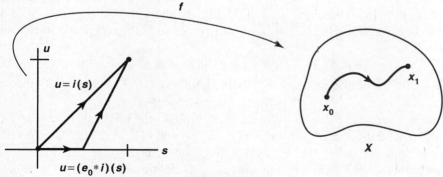

Figure 51.7

Because I is convex, there is a path homotopy G in I between i and $e_0 * i$. Then $f \circ G$ is a path homotopy in X between the paths $f \circ i = f$ and

$$f \circ (e_0 * i) = (f \circ e_0) * (f \circ i) = e_{x_0} * f.$$

An entirely similar argument, using the fact that if e_1 denotes the constant path at 1, then $i * e_1$ is path homotopic in I to the path i, shows that $[f] * [e_{x_1}] = [f]$.

To verify (3), note that the reverse of i is $\bar{i}(s) = 1 - s$. Then $i * \bar{i}$ is a path in I beginning and ending at 0, and so is the constant path e_0. (Their graphs are pictured in Figure 51.8.) Because I is convex, there is a path homotopy H in I between e_0 and $i * \bar{i}$. Then $f \circ H$ is a path homotopy between $f \circ e_0 = e_{x_0}$ and

$$(f \circ i) * (f \circ \bar{i}) = f * \bar{f}.$$

An entirely similar argument, using the fact that $\bar{i} * i$ is path homotopic in I to e_1, shows that $[\bar{f}] * [f] = [e_{x_1}]$.

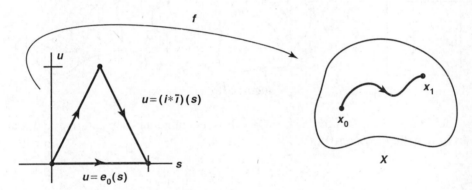

Figure 51.8

Step 2. The proof of (1), associativity, is a bit trickier. For this proof, and for later use as well, it will be convenient to describe the product $f * g$ in a different way.

If $[a, b]$ and $[c, d]$ are two intervals in $\mathbb{R}$, there is a unique map $p : [a, b] \to [c, d]$ of the form $p(x) = mx + k$ that carries a to c and b to d; we call it the **positive linear map** of $[a, b]$ to $[c, d]$ because its graph is a straight line with positive slope. Note that the inverse of such a map is another such map, and so is the composite of two such maps.

With this terminology, the product $f * g$ can be described as follows: On $[0, \frac{1}{2}]$, it equals the positive linear map of $[0, \frac{1}{2}]$ to $[0, 1]$, followed by f; and on $[\frac{1}{2}, 1]$, it equals the positive linear map of $[\frac{1}{2}, 1]$ to $[0, 1]$, followed by g.

Now we verify (1). Given paths f, g, and h in X, the products $f * (g * h)$ and $(f * g) * h$ are defined precisely when $f(1) = g(0)$ and $g(1) = h(0)$. Assuming these two conditions, we define also a "triple product" of the paths f, g, and h as follows: Choose points a and b of I so that $0 < a < b < 1$. Define a path $k_{a,b}$ in X as follows:

On $[0, a]$ it equals the positive linear map of $[0, a]$ to I followed by f; on $[a, b]$ it equals the positive linear map of $[a, b]$ to I followed by g; and on $[b, 1]$ it equals the positive linear map of $[b, 1]$ to I followed by h. The path $k_{a,b}$ depends of course on the choice of the points a and b. But its path-homotopy class does not! We show that if c and d are another pair of points of I with $0 < c < d < 1$, then $k_{c,d}$ is path homotopic to $k_{a,b}$.

Let $p : I \to I$ be the map whose graph is pictured in Figure 51.9. When restricted to $[0, a]$, $[a, b]$, and $[b, 1]$, respectively, it equals the positive linear maps of these intervals onto $[0, c]$, $[c, d]$, and $[d, 1]$, respectively. It follows at once that $k_{c,d} \circ p$ equals $k_{a,b}$. But p is a path in I from 0 to 1; and so is the identity map $i : I \to I$. Hence, there is a path homotopy P in I between p and i. Then $k_{c,d} \circ P$ is a path homotopy in X between $k_{a,b}$ and $k_{c,d}$.

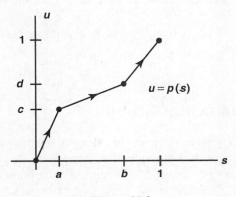

Figure 51.9

What has this to do with associativity? A great deal. For the product $f * (g * h)$ is exactly the triple product $k_{a,b}$ in the case where $a = 1/2$ and $b = 3/4$, as you can check, while the product $(f * g) * h$ equals $k_{c,d}$ in the case where $c = 1/4$ and $d = 1/2$. Therefore these two products are path homotopic. ∎

The argument just used to prove associativity goes through for any finite product of paths. Roughly speaking, it says that as far as the path-homotopy class of the result is concerned, it doesn't matter how you chop up the interval when you form the product of paths! This result will be useful to us later, so we state it formally as a theorem here:

Theorem 51.3. *Let f be a path in X, and let $a_0, \ldots, a_n$ be numbers such that $0 = a_0 < a_1 < \cdots < a_n = 1$. Let $f_i : I \to X$ be the path that equals the positive linear map of I onto $[a_{i-1}, a_i]$ followed by f. Then*

$$[f] = [f_1] * \cdots * [f_n].$$

Exercises

1. Show that if $h, h' : X \to Y$ are homotopic and $k, k' : Y \to Z$ are homotopic, then $k \circ h$ and $k' \circ h'$ are homotopic.

2. Given spaces X and Y, let $[X, Y]$ denote the set of homotopy classes of maps of X into Y.
   (a) Let $I = [0, 1]$. Show that for any X, the set $[X, I]$ has a single element.
   (b) Show that if Y is path connected, the set $[I, Y]$ has a single element.

3. A space X is said to be ***contractible*** if the identity map $i_X : X \to X$ is nulhomotopic.
   (a) Show that I and $\mathbb{R}$ are contractible.
   (b) Show that a contractible space is path connected.
   (c) Show that if Y is contractible, then for any X, the set $[X, Y]$ has a single element.
   (d) Show that if X is contractible and Y is path connected, then $[X, Y]$ has a single element.

§52   The Fundamental Group

The set of path-homotopy classes of paths in a space X does not form a group under the operation $*$ because the product of two path-homotopy classes is not always defined. But suppose we pick out a point x_0 of X to serve as a "base point" and restrict ourselves to those paths that begin and end at x_0. The set of these path-homotopy classes does form a group under $*$. It will be called the *fundamental group* of X.

In this section, we shall study the fundamental group and derive some of its properties. In particular, we shall show that the group is a topological invariant of the space X, the fact that is of crucial importance in using it to study homeomorphism problems.

Let us first review some terminology from group theory. Suppose G and G' are groups, written multiplicatively. A ***homomorphism*** $f : G \to G'$ is a map such that $f(x \cdot y) = f(x) \cdot f(y)$ for all x, y; it automatically satisfies the equations $f(e) = e'$ and $f(x^{-1}) = f(x)^{-1}$, where e and e' are the identities of G and G', respectively, and the exponent -1 denotes the inverse. The ***kernel*** of f is the set $f^{-1}(e')$; it is a subgroup of G. The image of f, similarly, is a subgroup of G'. The homomorphism f is called a ***monomorphism*** if it is injective (or equivalently, if the kernel of f consists of e alone). It is called an ***epimorphism*** if it is surjective; and it is called an ***isomorphism*** if it is bijective.

Suppose G is a group and H is a subgroup of G. Let xH denote the set of all products xh, for $h \in H$; it is called a ***left coset*** of H in G. The collection of all such cosets forms a partition of G. Similarly, the collection of all right cosets Hx of H in G forms a partition of G. We call H a ***normal subgroup*** of G if $x \cdot h \cdot x^{-1} \in H$ for each $x \in G$ and each $h \in H$. In this case, we have $xH = Hx$ for each x, so that our two partitions of G are the same. We denote this partition by G/H; if one defines

$$(xH) \cdot (yH) = (x \cdot y)H,$$

one obtains a well-defined operation on G/H that makes it a group. This group is called the **quotient** of G by H. The map $f : G \rightarrow G/H$ carrying x to xH is an epimorphism with kernel H. Conversely, if $f : G \rightarrow G'$ is an epimorphism, then its kernel N is a normal subgroup of G, and f induces an isomorphism $G/N \rightarrow G'$ that carries xN to $f(x)$ for each $x \in G$.

If the subgroup H of G is not normal, it will still be convenient to use the symbol G/H; we will use it to denote the collection of *right* cosets of H in G.

Now we define the fundamental group.

Definition. Let X be a space; let x_0 be a point of X. A path in X that begins and ends at x_0 is called a **loop** based at x_0. The set of path homotopy classes of loops based at x_0, with the operation $*$, is called the **fundamental group** of X relative to the **base point** x_0. It is denoted by $\pi_1(X, x_0)$.

It follows from Theorem 51.2 that the operation $*$, when restricted to this set, satisfies the axioms for a group. Given two loops f and g based at x_0, the product $f * g$ is always defined and is a loop based at x_0. Associativity, the existence of an identity element $[e_{x_0}]$, and the existence of an inverse $[\bar{f}]$ for $[f]$ are immediate.

Sometimes this group is called the **first homotopy group** of X, which term implies that there is a second homotopy group. There are indeed groups $\pi_n(X, x_0)$ for all $n \in \mathbb{Z}_+$, but we shall not study them in this book. They are part of the general subject called *homotopy theory*.

EXAMPLE 1.   Let $\mathbb{R}^n$ denote euclidean n-space. Then $\pi_1(\mathbb{R}^n, x_0)$ is the trivial group (the group consisting of the identity alone). For if f is a loop in $\mathbb{R}^n$ based at x_0, the straight-line homotopy is a path homotopy between f and the constant path at x_0. More generally, if X is any convex subset of $\mathbb{R}^n$, then $\pi_1(X, x_0)$ is the trivial group. In particular, the **unit ball** B^n in $\mathbb{R}^n$,

$$B^n = \{\mathbf{x} \mid x_1^2 + \cdots + x_n^2 \leq 1\},$$

has trivial fundamental group.

An immediate question one asks is the extent to which the fundamental group depends on the base point. We consider that question now.

Definition. Let α be a path in X from x_0 to x_1. We define a map

$$\hat{\alpha} : \pi_1(X, x_0) \longrightarrow \pi_1(X, x_1)$$

by the equation

$$\hat{\alpha}([f]) = [\bar{\alpha}] * [f] * [\alpha].$$

The map $\hat{\alpha}$, which we call "α-hat," is well-defined because the operation $*$ is well-defined. If f is a loop based at x_0, then $\bar{\alpha} * (f * \alpha)$ is a loop based at x_1. Hence $\hat{\alpha}$ maps $\pi_1(X, x_0)$ into $\pi_1(X, x_1)$, as desired; note that it depends only on the path-homotopy class of α. It is pictured in Figure 52.1.

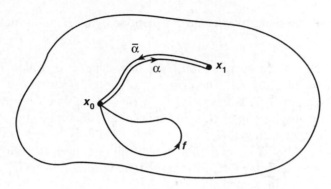

Figure 52.1

Theorem 52.1. *The map $\hat{\alpha}$ is a group isomorphism.*

Proof. To show that $\hat{\alpha}$ is a homomorphism, we compute

$$\hat{\alpha}([f]) * \hat{\alpha}([g]) = ([\bar{\alpha}] * [f] * [\alpha]) * ([\bar{\alpha}] * [g] * [\alpha])$$
$$= [\bar{\alpha}] * [f] * [g] * [\alpha]$$
$$= \hat{\alpha}([f] * [g]).$$

To show that $\hat{\alpha}$ is an isomorphism, we show that if β denotes the path $\bar{\alpha}$, which is the reverse of α, then $\hat{\beta}$ is an inverse for $\hat{\alpha}$. We compute, for each element $[h]$ of $\pi_1(X, x_1)$,

$$\hat{\beta}([h]) = [\bar{\beta}] * [h] * [\beta] = [\alpha] * [h] * [\bar{\alpha}],$$
$$\hat{\alpha}(\hat{\beta}([h])) = [\bar{\alpha}] * ([\alpha] * [h] * [\bar{\alpha}]) * [\alpha] = [h].$$

A similar computation shows that $\hat{\beta}(\hat{\alpha}([f])) = [f]$ for each $[f] \in \pi_1(X, x_0)$. ∎

Corollary 52.2. *If X is path connected and x_0 and x_1 are two points of X, then $\pi_1(X, x_0)$ is isomorphic to $\pi_1(X, x_1)$.*

Suppose that X is a topological space. Let C be the path component of X containing x_0. It is easy to see that $\pi_1(C, x_0) = \pi_1(X, x_0)$, since all loops and homotopies in X that are based at x_0 must lie in the subspace C. Thus $\pi_1(X, x_0)$ depends on only the path component of X containing x_0; it gives us no information whatever about the rest of X. For this reason, it is usual to deal with only path-connected spaces when studying the fundamental group.

If X is path connected, all the groups $\pi_1(X, x)$ are isomorphic, so it is tempting to try to "identify" all these groups with one another and to speak simply of the fundamental group of the space X, without reference to base point. The difficulty with this approach is that there is no *natural* way of identifying $\pi_1(X, x_0)$ with $\pi_1(X, x_1)$; different paths α and β from x_0 to x_1 may give rise to different isomorphisms between these groups. For this reason, omitting the base point can lead to error.

It turns out that the isomorphism of $\pi_1(X, x_0)$ with $\pi_1(X, x_1)$ is independent of path if and only if the fundamental group is abelian. (See Exercise 3.) This is a stringent requirement on the space X.

Definition.   A space X is said to be ***simply connected*** if it is a path-connected space and if $\pi_1(X, x_0)$ is the trivial (one-element) group for some $x_0 \in X$, and hence for every $x_0 \in X$. We often express the fact that $\pi_1(X, x_0)$ is the trivial group by writing $\pi_1(X, x_0) = 0$.

Lemma 52.3.   *In a simply connected space X, any two paths having the same initial and final points are path homotopic.*

Proof.   Let α and β be two paths from x_0 to x_1. Then $\alpha * \bar{\beta}$ is defined and is a loop on X based at x_0. Since X is simply connected, this loop is path homotopic to the constant loop at x_0. Then

$$[\alpha * \bar{\beta}] * [\beta] = [e_{x_0}] * [\beta],$$

from which it follows that $[\alpha] = [\beta]$.   ∎

It is intuitively clear that the fundamental group is a topological invariant of the space X. A convenient way to prove this fact formally is to introduce the notion of the "homomorphism induced by a continuous map."

Suppose that $h : X \to Y$ is a continuous map that carries the point x_0 of X to the point y_0 of Y. We often denote this fact by writing

$$h : (X, x_0) \longrightarrow (Y, y_0).$$

If f is a loop in X based at x_0, then the composite $h \circ f : I \to Y$ is a loop in Y based at y_0. The correspondence $f \to h \circ f$ thus gives rise to a map carrying $\pi_1(X, x_0)$ into $\pi_1(Y, y_0)$. We define it formally as follows:

Definition.   Let $h : (X, x_0) \to (Y, y_0)$ be a continuous map. Define

$$h_* : \pi_1(X, x_0) \longrightarrow \pi_1(Y, y_0)$$

by the equation

$$h_*([f]) = [h \circ f].$$

The map h_* is called the ***homomorphism induced by h***, relative to the base point x_0.

The map h_* is well-defined, for if F is a path homotopy between the paths f and f', then $h \circ F$ is a path homotopy between the paths $h \circ f$ and $h \circ f'$. The fact that h_* is a homomorphism follows from the equation

$$(h \circ f) * (h \circ g) = h \circ (f * g).$$

The homomorphism h_* depends not only on the map $h : X \to Y$ but also on the choice of the base point x_0. (Once x_0 is chosen, y_0 is determined by h.) So some notational difficulty will arise if we want to consider several different base points for X. If x_0 and x_1 are two different points of X, we cannot use the same symbol h_* to stand for two different homomorphisms, one having domain $\pi_1(X, x_0)$ and the other having domain $\pi_1(X, x_1)$. Even if X is path connected, so these groups are isomorphic, they are still not the same group. In such a case, we shall use the notation

$$(h_{x_0})_* : \pi_1(X, x_0) \longrightarrow \pi_1(Y, y_0)$$

for the first homomorphism and $(h_{x_1})_*$ for the second. If there is only one base point under consideration, we shall omit mention of the base point and denote the induced homomorphism merely by h_*.

The induced homomorphism has two properties that are crucial in the applications. They are called its "functorial properties" and are given in the following theorem:

Theorem 52.4. *If $h : (X, x_0) \to (Y, y_0)$ and $k : (Y, y_0) \to (Z, z_0)$ are continuous, then $(k \circ h)_* = k_* \circ h_*$. If $i : (X, x_0) \to (X, x_0)$ is the identity map, then i_* is the identity homomorphism.*

Proof. The proof is a triviality. By definition,

$$(k \circ h)_*([f]) = [(k \circ h) \circ f],$$
$$(k_* \circ h_*)([f]) = k_*(h_*([f])) = k_*([h \circ f]) = [k \circ (h \circ f)].$$

Similarly, $i_*([f]) = [i \circ f] = [f]$.   ∎

Corollary 52.5. *If $h : (X, x_0) \to (Y, y_0)$ is a homeomorphism of X with Y, then h_* is an isomorphism of $\pi_1(X, x_0)$ with $\pi_1(Y, y_0)$.*

Proof. Let $k : (Y, y_0) \to (X, x_0)$ be the inverse of h. Then $k_* \circ h_* = (k \circ h)_* = i_*$, where i is the identity map of (X, x_0); and $h_* \circ k_* = (h \circ k)_* = j_*$, where j is the identity map of (Y, y_0). Since i_* and j_* are the identity homomorphisms of the groups $\pi_1(X, x_0)$ and $\pi_1(Y, y_0)$, respectively, k_* is the inverse of h_*.   ∎

Exercises

1. A subset A of $\mathbb{R}^n$ is said to be ***star convex*** if for some point a_0 of A, all the line segments joining a_0 to other points of A lie in A.
   (a) Find a star convex set that is not convex.
   (b) Show that if A is star convex, A is simply connected.

2. Let α be a path in X from x_0 to x_1; let β be a path in X from x_1 to x_2. Show that if $\gamma = \alpha * \beta$, then $\hat{\gamma} = \hat{\beta} \circ \hat{\alpha}$.

3. Let x_0 and x_1 be points of the path-connected space X. Show that $\pi_1(X, x_0)$ is abelian if and only if for every pair α and β of paths from x_0 to x_1, we have $\hat{\alpha} = \hat{\beta}$.

4. Let $A \subset X$; suppose $r : X \to A$ is a continuous map such that $r(a) = a$ for each $a \in A$. (The map r is called a *retraction* of X onto A.) If $a_0 \in A$, show that

$$r_* : \pi_1(X, a_0) \longrightarrow \pi_1(A, a_0)$$

is surjective.

5. Let A be a subspace of $\mathbb{R}^n$; let $h : (A, a_0) \to (Y, y_0)$. Show that if h is extendable to a continuous map of $\mathbb{R}^n$ into Y, then h_* is the trivial homomorphism (the homomorphism that maps everything to the identity element).

6. Show that if X is path connected, the homomorphism induced by a continuous map is independent of base point, up to isomorphisms of the groups involved. More precisely, let $h : X \to Y$ be continuous, with $h(x_0) = y_0$ and $h(x_1) = y_1$. Let α be a path in X from x_0 to x_1, and let $\beta = h \circ \alpha$. Show that

$$\hat{\beta} \circ (h_{x_0})_* = (h_{x_1})_* \circ \hat{\alpha}.$$

This equation expresses the fact that the following diagram of maps "commutes."

$$
\begin{array}{ccc}
\pi_1(X, x_0) & \xrightarrow{(h_{x_0})_*} & \pi_1(Y, y_0) \\
\downarrow{\hat{\alpha}} & & \downarrow{\hat{\beta}} \\
\pi_1(X, x_1) & \xrightarrow{(h_{x_1})_*} & \pi_1(Y, y_1)
\end{array}
$$

7. Let G be a topological group with operation $\cdot$ and identity element x_0. Let $\Omega(G, x_0)$ denote the set of all loops in G based at x_0. If $f, g \in \Omega(G, x_0)$, let us define a loop $f \otimes g$ by the rule

$$(f \otimes g)(s) = f(s) \cdot g(s).$$

  (a) Show that this operation makes the set $\Omega(G, x_0)$ into a group.
  (b) Show that this operation induces a group operation $\otimes$ on $\pi_1(G, x_0)$.
  (c) Show that the two group operations $*$ and $\otimes$ on $\pi_1(G, x_0)$ are the same.
      [*Hint:* Compute $(f * e_{x_0}) \otimes (e_{x_0} * g)$.]
  (d) Show that $\pi_1(G, x_0)$ is abelian.

§53   Covering Spaces

We have shown that any convex subspace of $\mathbb{R}^n$ has a trivial fundamental group; we turn now to the task of computing some fundamental groups that are not trivial. One of the most useful tools for this purpose is the notion of *covering space*, which we introduce in this section. Covering spaces are also important in the study of Riemann surfaces and complex manifolds. (See [A-S].) We shall study them in more detail in Chapter 12.

Definition. Let $p : E \to B$ be a continuous surjective map. The open set U of B is said to be *evenly covered* by p if the inverse image $p^{-1}(U)$ can be written as the union of disjoint open sets V_α in E such that for each α, the restriction of p to V_α is a homeomorphism of V_α onto U. The collection $\{V_\alpha\}$ will be called a partition of $p^{-1}(U)$ into *slices*.

If U is an open set that is evenly covered by p, we often picture the set $p^{-1}(U)$ as a "stack of pancakes," each having the same size and shape as U, floating in the air above U; the map p squashes them all down onto U. See Figure 53.1. Note that if U is evenly covered by p and W is an open set contained in U, then W is also evenly covered by p.

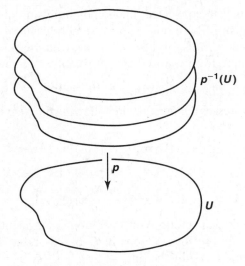

Figure 53.1

Definition. Let $p : E \to B$ be continuous and surjective. If every point b of B has a neighborhood U that is evenly covered by p, then p is called a *covering map*, and E is said to be a *covering space* of B.

Note that if $p : E \to B$ is a covering map, then for each $b \in B$ the subspace $p^{-1}(b)$ of E has the discrete topology. For each slice V_α is open in E and intersects the set $p^{-1}(b)$ in a single point; therefore, this point is open in $p^{-1}(b)$.

Note also that if $p : E \to B$ is a covering map, then p is an open map. For suppose A is an open set of E. Given $x \in p(A)$, choose a neighborhood U of x that is evenly covered by p. Let $\{V_\alpha\}$ be a partition of $p^{-1}(U)$ into slices. There is a point y of A such that $p(y) = x$; let V_β be the slice containing y. The set $V_\beta \cap A$ is open in E and hence open in V_β; because p maps V_β homeomorphically onto U, the set $p(V_\beta \cap A)$ is open in U and hence open in B; it is thus a neighborhood of x contained in $p(A)$, as desired.

EXAMPLE 1.   Let X be any space; let $i : X \to X$ be the identity map. Then i is a covering map (of the most trivial sort). More generally, let E be the space $X \times \{1, \ldots, n\}$ consisting of n disjoint copies of X. The map $p : E \to X$ given by $p(x, i) = x$ for all i is again a (rather trivial) covering map. In this case, we can picture the entire space E as a stack of pancakes over X.

In practice, one often restricts oneself to covering spaces that are path connected, to eliminate trivial coverings of the pancake-stack variety. An example of such a non-trivial covering space is the following:

Theorem 53.1.   *The map $p : \mathbb{R} \to S^1$ given by the equation*

$$p(x) = (\cos 2\pi x, \sin 2\pi x)$$

is a covering map.

One can picture p as a function that wraps the real line $\mathbb{R}$ around the circle S^1, and in the process maps each interval $[n, n+1]$ onto S^1.

Proof.   The fact that p is a covering map comes from elementary properties of the sine and cosine functions. Consider, for example, the subset U of S^1 consisting of those points having positive first coordinate. The set $p^{-1}(U)$ consists of those points x for which $\cos 2\pi x$ is positive; that is, it is the union of the intervals

$$V_n = (n - \tfrac{1}{4}, n + \tfrac{1}{4}),$$

for all $n \in \mathbb{Z}$. See Figure 53.2. Now, restricted to any closed interval $\bar{V}_n$, the map p is injective because $\sin 2\pi x$ is strictly monotonic on such an interval. Furthermore, p carries $\bar{V}_n$ surjectively onto $\bar{U}$, and V_n to U, by the intermediate value theorem. Since $\bar{V}_n$ is compact, $p|\bar{V}_n$ is a homeomorphism of $\bar{V}_n$ with $\bar{U}$. In particular, $p|V_n$ is a homeomorphism of V_n with U.

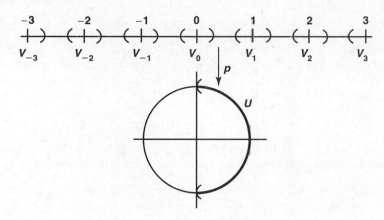

Figure 53.2

Similar arguments can be applied to the intersections of S^1 with the upper and lower open half-planes, and with the open left-hand half-plane. These open sets cover S^1, and each of them is evenly covered by p. Hence $p : \mathbb{R} \to S^1$ is a covering map. ∎

If $p : E \to B$ is a covering map, then p is a *local homeomorphism* of E with B. That is, each point e of E has a neighborhood that is mapped homeomorphically by p onto an open subset of B. The condition that p be a local homeomorphism does not suffice, however, to ensure that p is a covering map, as the following example shows.

EXAMPLE 2. The map $p : \mathbb{R}_+ \to S^1$ given by the equation

$$p(x) = (\cos 2\pi x, \sin 2\pi x)$$

is surjective, and it is a local homeomorphism. See Figure 53.3. But it is not a covering map, for the point $b_0 = (1, 0)$ has no neighborhood U that is evenly covered by p. The typical neighborhood U of b_0 has an inverse image consisting of small neighborhoods V_n of each integer n for $n > 0$, along with a small interval V_0 of the form $(0, \epsilon)$. Each of the intervals V_n for $n > 0$ is mapped homeomorphically onto U by the map p, but the interval V_0 is only imbedded in U by p.

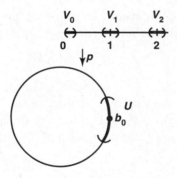

Figure 53.3

EXAMPLE 3. The preceding example might lead you to think that the real line $\mathbb{R}$ is the only connected covering space of the circle S^1. This is not so. Consider, for example, the map $p : S^1 \to S^1$ given in equations by

$$p(z) = z^2.$$

[Here we consider S^1 as the subset of the complex plane $\mathbb{C}$ consisting of those complex numbers z with $|z| = 1$.] We leave it to you to check that p is a covering map.

Example 2 shows that the map obtained by restricting a covering map may not be a covering map. Here is one situation where it *will* be a covering map:

Theorem 53.2. *Let $p : E \to B$ be a covering map. If B_0 is a subspace of B, and if $E_0 = p^{-1}(B_0)$, then the map $p_0 : E_0 \to B_0$ obtained by restricting p is a covering map.*

Proof. Given $b_0 \in B_0$, let U be an open set in B containing b_0 that is evenly covered by p; let $\{V_\alpha\}$ be a partition of $p^{-1}(U)$ into slices. Then $U \cap B_0$ is a neighborhood of b_0 in B_0, and the sets $V_\alpha \cap E_0$ are disjoint open sets in E_0 whose union is $p^{-1}(U \cap B_0)$, and each is mapped homeomorphically onto $U \cap B_0$ by p.   ∎

Theorem 53.3. *It $p : E \to B$ and $p' : E' \to B'$ are covering maps, then*

$$p \times p' : E \times E' \to B \times B'$$

is a covering map.

Proof. Given $b \in B$ and $b' \in B'$, let U and U' be neighborhoods of b and b', respectively, that are evenly covered by p and p', respectively. Let $\{V_\alpha\}$ and $\{V'_\beta\}$ be partitions of $p^{-1}(U)$ and $(p')^{-1}(U')$, respectively, into slices. Then the inverse image under $p \times p'$ of the open set $U \times U'$ is the union of all the sets $V_\alpha \times V'_\beta$. These are disjoint open sets of $E \times E'$, and each is mapped homeomorphically onto $U \times U'$ by $p \times p'$.   ∎

EXAMPLE 4.   Consider the space $T = S^1 \times S^1$; it is called the ***torus***. The product map

$$p \times p : \mathbb{R} \times \mathbb{R} \longrightarrow S^1 \times S^1$$

is a covering of the torus by the plane $\mathbb{R}^2$, where p denotes the covering map of Theorem 53.1. Each of the unit squares $[n, n+1] \times [m, m+1]$ gets wrapped by $p \times p$ entirely around the torus. See Figure 53.4.

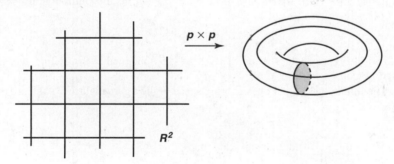

Figure 53.4

In this figure, we have pictured the torus not as the product $S^1 \times S^1$, which is a subspace of $\mathbb{R}^4$ and thus difficult to visualize, but as the familiar doughnut-shaped surface D in $\mathbb{R}^3$ obtained by rotating the circle C_1 in the xz-plane of radius $\frac{1}{3}$ centered at $(1, 0, 0)$ about the z-axis. It is not hard to see that $S^1 \times S^1$ is homeomorphic with the surface D. Let C_2 be the circle of radius 1 in the xy-plane centered at the origin. Then let us map $C_1 \times C_2$ into D by defining $f(a \times b)$ to be that point into which a is carried when one rotates the circle C_1 about the z-axis until its center hits the point b. See Figure 53.5. The map f will be a homeomorphism of $C_1 \times C_2$ with D, as you can check mentally. If you wish, you can write equations for f and check continuity, injectivity, and surjectivity directly. (Continuity of f^{-1} will follow from compactness of $C_1 \times C_2$.)

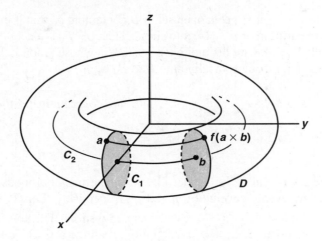

Figure 53.5

EXAMPLE 5.   Consider the covering map $p \times p$ of the preceding example. Let b_0 denote the point $p(0)$ of S^1; and let B_0 denote the subspace

$$B_0 = (S^1 \times b_0) \cup (b_0 \times S^1)$$

of $S^1 \times S^1$. Then B_0 is the union of two circles that have a point in common; we sometimes call it the **figure-eight space**. The space $E_0 = p^{-1}(B_0)$ is the "infinite grid"

$$E_0 = (\mathbb{R} \times \mathbb{Z}) \cup (\mathbb{Z} \times \mathbb{R})$$

pictured in Figure 53.4. The map $p_0 : E_0 \to B_0$ obtained by restricting $p \times p$ is thus a covering map.

The infinite grid is but one covering space of the figure eight; we shall see others later on.

EXAMPLE 6.   Consider the covering map

$$p \times i : \mathbb{R} \times \mathbb{R}_+ \longrightarrow S^1 \times \mathbb{R}_+,$$

where i is the identity map of $\mathbb{R}_+$ and p is the map of Theorem 53.1. If we take the standard homeomorphism of $S^1 \times \mathbb{R}_+$ with $\mathbb{R}^2 - 0$, sending $x \times t$ to tx, the composite gives us a covering

$$\mathbb{R} \times \mathbb{R}_+ \longrightarrow \mathbb{R}^2 - 0$$

of the punctured plane by the open upper half-plane. It is pictured in Figure 53.6. This covering map appears in the study of complex variables as the *Riemann surface* corresponding to the complex logarithm function.

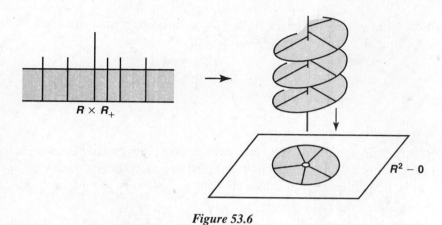

Figure 53.6

Exercises

1. Let Y have the discrete topology. Show that if $p : X \times Y \to X$ is projection on the first coordinate, then p is a covering map.

2. Let $p : E \to B$ be continuous and surjective. Suppose that U is an open set of B that is evenly covered by p. Show that if U is connected, then the partition of $p^{-1}(U)$ into slices is unique.

3. Let $p : E \to B$ be a covering map; let B be connected. Show that if $p^{-1}(b_0)$ has k elements for some $b_0 \in B$, then $p^{-1}(b)$ has k elements for every $b \in B$. In such a case, E is called a **k-fold covering** of B.

4. Let $q : X \to Y$ and $r : Y \to Z$ be covering maps; let $p = r \circ q$. Show that if $r^{-1}(z)$ is finite for each $z \in Z$, then p is a covering map.

5. Show that the map of Example 3 is a covering map. Generalize to the map $p(z) = z^n$.

6. Let $p : E \to B$ be a covering map.
   (a) If B is Hausdorff, regular, completely regular, or locally compact Hausdorff, then so is E. [*Hint:* If $\{V_\alpha\}$ is a partition of $p^{-1}(U)$ into slices, and C is a closed set of B such that $C \subset U$, then $p^{-1}(C) \cap V_\alpha$ is a closed set of E.]
   (b) If B is compact and $p^{-1}(b)$ is finite for each $b \in B$, then E is compact.

§54   The Fundamental Group of the Circle

The study of covering spaces of a space X is intimately related to the study of the fundamental group of X. In this section, we establish the crucial links between the two concepts, and compute the fundamental group of the circle.

Definition.   Let $p : E \to B$ be a map. If f is a continuous mapping of some space X into B, a **lifting** of f is a map $\tilde{f} : X \to E$ such that $p \circ \tilde{f} = f$.

The existence of liftings when p is a covering map is an important tool in studying covering spaces and the fundamental group. First, we show that for a covering space, paths can be lifted; then we show that path homotopies can be lifted as well. First, an example:

EXAMPLE 1.   Consider the covering $p : \mathbb{R} \to S^1$ of Theorem 53.1. The path $f :$ $[0, 1] \to S^1$ beginning at $b_0 = (1, 0)$ given by $f(s) = (\cos \pi s, \sin \pi s)$ lifts to the path $\tilde{f}(s) = s/2$ beginning at 0 and ending at $\frac{1}{2}$. The path $g(s) = (\cos \pi s, -\sin \pi s)$ lifts to the path $\tilde{g}(s) = -s/2$ beginning at 0 and ending at $-\frac{1}{2}$. The path $h(s) = (\cos 4\pi s, \sin 4\pi s)$ lifts to the path $\tilde{h}(s) = 2s$ beginning at 0 and ending at 2. Intuitively, h wraps the interval $[0, 1]$ around the circle twice; this is reflected in the fact that the lifted path $\tilde{h}$ begins at zero and ends at the number 2. These paths are pictured in Figure 54.1.

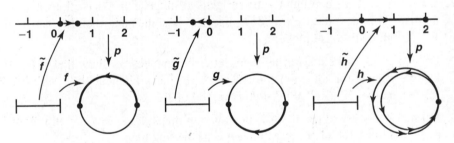

Figure 54.1

Lemma 54.1.   *Let $p : E \to B$ be a covering map, let $p(e_0) = b_0$. Any path $f : [0, 1] \to B$ beginning at b_0 has a unique lifting to a path $\tilde{f}$ in E beginning at e_0.*

Proof.   Cover B by open sets U each of which is evenly covered by p. Find a subdivision of $[0, 1]$, say $s_0, \ldots, s_n$, such that for each i the set $f([s_i, s_{i+1}])$ lies in such an open set U. (Here we use the Lebesgue number lemma.) We define the lifting $\tilde{f}$ step by step.

First, define $\tilde{f}(0) = e_0$. Then, supposing $\tilde{f}(s)$ is defined for $0 \leq s \leq s_i$, we define $\tilde{f}$ on $[s_i, s_{i+1}]$ as follows: The set $f([s_i, s_{i+1}])$ lies in some open set U that is evenly covered by p. Let $\{V_\alpha\}$ be a partition of $p^{-1}(U)$ into slices; each set V_α is mapped homeomorphically onto U by p. Now $\tilde{f}(s_i)$ lies in one of these sets, say in V_0. Define $\tilde{f}(s)$ for $s \in [s_i, s_{i+1}]$ by the equation

$$\tilde{f}(s) = (p \mid V_0)^{-1}(f(s)).$$

Because $p|V_0 : V_0 \to U$ is a homeomorphism, $\tilde{f}$ will be continuous on $[s_i, s_{i+1}]$.

Continuing in this way, we define $\tilde{f}$ on all of $[0, 1]$. Continuity of $\tilde{f}$ follows from the pasting lemma; the fact that $p \circ \tilde{f} = f$ is immediate from the definition of $\tilde{f}$.

The uniqueness of $\tilde{f}$ is also proved step by step. Suppose that $\tilde{\tilde{f}}$ is another lifting of f beginning at e_0. Then $\tilde{\tilde{f}}(0) = e_0 = \tilde{f}(0)$. Suppose that $\tilde{\tilde{f}}(s) = \tilde{f}(s)$ for all s such that $0 \leq s \leq s_i$. Let V_0 be as in the preceding paragraph; then for $s \in [s_i, s_{i+1}]$, $\tilde{f}(s)$ is defined as $(p|V_0)^{-1}(f(s))$. What can $\tilde{\tilde{f}}(s)$ equal? Since $\tilde{\tilde{f}}$ is a lifting of f, it must carry the interval $[s_i, s_{i+1}]$ into the set $p^{-1}(U) = \bigcup V_\alpha$. The slices V_α are open and disjoint; because the set $\tilde{\tilde{f}}([s_i, s_{i+1}])$ is connected, it must lie entirely in one of the sets V_α. Because $\tilde{\tilde{f}}(s_i) = \tilde{f}(s_i)$, which is in V_0, $\tilde{\tilde{f}}$ must carry all of $[s_i, s_{i+1}]$ into the set V_0. Thus, for s in $[s_i, s_{i+1}]$, $\tilde{\tilde{f}}(s)$ must equal some point y of V_0 lying in $p^{-1}(f(s))$. But there is only *one* such point y, namely, $(p|V_0)^{-1}(f(s))$. Hence $\tilde{\tilde{f}}(s) = \tilde{f}(s)$ for $s \in [s_i, s_{i+1}]$.   ∎

Lemma 54.2.   *Let $p : E \to B$ be a covering map; let $p(e_0) = b_0$. Let the map $F : I \times I \to B$ be continuous, with $F(0, 0) = b_0$. There is a unique lifting of F to a continuous map*

$$\tilde{F} : I \times I \to E$$

such that $\tilde{F}(0, 0) = e_0$. If F is a path homotopy, then $\tilde{F}$ is a path homotopy.

Proof.   Given F, we first define $\tilde{F}(0, 0) = e_0$. Next, we use the preceding lemma to extend $\tilde{F}$ to the left-hand edge $0 \times I$ and the bottom edge $I \times 0$ of $I \times I$. Then we extend $\tilde{F}$ to all of $I \times I$ as follows:

Choose subdivisions

$$s_0 < s_1 < \cdots < s_m,$$
$$t_0 < t_1 < \cdots < t_n$$

of I fine enough that each rectangle

$$I_i \times J_j = [s_{i-1}, s_i] \times [t_{j-1}, t_j]$$

is mapped by F into an open set of B that is evenly covered by p. (Use the Lebesgue number lemma.) We define the lifting $\tilde{F}$ step by step, beginning with the rectangle $I_1 \times J_1$, continuing with the other rectangles $I_i \times J_1$ in the "bottom row," then with the rectangles $I_i \times J_2$ in the next row, and so on.

In general, given i_0 and j_0, assume that $\tilde{F}$ is defined on the set A which is the union of $0 \times I$ and $I \times 0$ and all the rectangles "previous" to $I_{i_0} \times J_{j_0}$ (those rectangles $I_i \times J_j$ for which $j < j_0$ and those for which $j = j_0$ and $i < i_0$). Assume also that $\tilde{F}$ is a continuous lifting of $F|A$. We define $\tilde{F}$ on $I_{i_0} \times J_{j_0}$. Choose an open set U of B that is evenly covered by p and contains the set $F(I_{i_0} \times J_{j_0})$. Let $\{V_\alpha\}$ be a partition of $p^{-1}(U)$ into slices; each set V_α is mapped homeomorphically onto U by p. Now $\tilde{F}$ is already defined on the set $C = A \cap (I_{i_0} \times J_{j_0})$. This set is the union of the left and bottom edges of the rectangle $I_{i_0} \times J_{j_0}$, so *it is connected*. Therefore, $\tilde{F}(C)$ is connected and must lie entirely within one of the sets V_α. Suppose it lies in V_0. Then, the situation is as pictured in Figure 54.2.

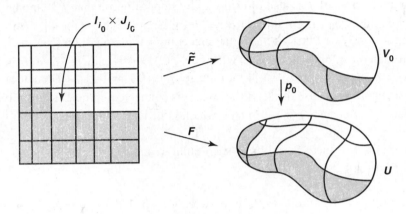

Figure 54.2

Let $p_0 : V_0 \to U$ denote the restriction of p to V_0. Since $\tilde{F}$ is a lifting of $F|A$, we know that for $x \in C$,

$$p_0(\tilde{F}(x)) = p(\tilde{F}(x)) = F(x),$$

so that $\tilde{F}(x) = p_0^{-1}(F(x))$. Hence we may extend $\tilde{F}$ by defining

$$\tilde{F}(x) = p_0^{-1}(F(x))$$

for $x \in I_{i_0} \times J_{j_0}$. The extended map will be continuous by the pasting lemma.

Continuing in this way, we define $\tilde{F}$ on all of I^2.

To check uniqueness, note that at each step of the construction of $\tilde{F}$, as we extend $\tilde{F}$ first to the bottom and left edges of I^2, and then to the rectangles $I_i \times J_j$, one by one, there is only one way to extend $\tilde{F}$ continuously. Thus, once the value of $\tilde{F}$ at $(0, 0)$ is specified, $\tilde{F}$ is completely determined.

Now suppose that F is a path homotopy. We wish to show that $\tilde{F}$ is a path homotopy. The map F carries the entire left edge $0 \times I$ of I^2 into a single point b_0 of B. Because $\tilde{F}$ is a lifting of F, it carries this edge into the set $p^{-1}(b_0)$. But this set has the discrete topology as a subspace of E. Since $0 \times I$ is connected and $\tilde{F}$ is continuous, $\tilde{F}(0 \times I)$ is connected and thus must equal a one-point set. Similarly, $\tilde{F}(1 \times I)$ must be a one-point set. Thus $\tilde{F}$ is a path homotopy. ∎

Theorem 54.3. *Let $p : E \to B$ be a covering map; let $p(e_0) = b_0$. Let f and g be two paths in B from b_0 to b_1; let $\tilde{f}$ and $\tilde{g}$ be their respective liftings to paths in E beginning at e_0. If f and g are path homotopic, then $\tilde{f}$ and $\tilde{g}$ end at the same point of E and are path homotopic.*

Proof. Let $F : I \times I \to B$ be the path homotopy between f and g. Then $F(0, 0) = b_0$. Let $\tilde{F} : I \times I \to E$ be the lifting of F to E such that $\tilde{F}(0, 0) = e_0$. By the preceding lemma, $\tilde{F}$ is a path homotopy, so that $\tilde{F}(0 \times I) = \{e_0\}$ and $\tilde{F}(1 \times I)$ is a one-point set $\{e_1\}$.

The restriction $\tilde{F}|I \times 0$ of $\tilde{F}$ to the bottom edge of $I \times I$ is a path on E beginning at e_0 that is a lifting of $F|I \times 0$. By uniqueness of path liftings, we must have $\tilde{F}(s, 0) = \tilde{f}(s)$. Similarly, $\tilde{F}|I \times 1$ is a path on E that is a lifting of $F|I \times 1$, and it begins at e_0 because $\tilde{F}(0 \times I) = \{e_0\}$. By uniqueness of path liftings, $\tilde{F}(s, 1) = \tilde{g}(s)$. Therefore, both $\tilde{f}$ and $\tilde{g}$ end at e_1, and $\tilde{F}$ is a path homotopy between them.   ∎

Definition. Let $p : E \to B$ be a covering map; let $b_0 \in B$. Choose e_0 so that $p(e_0) = b_0$. Given an element $[f]$ of $\pi_1(B, b_0)$, let $\tilde{f}$ be the lifting of f to a path in E that begins at e_0. Let $\phi([f])$ denote the end point $\tilde{f}(1)$ of $\tilde{f}$. Then ϕ is a well-defined set map

$$\phi : \pi_1(B, b_0) \to p^{-1}(b_0).$$

We call ϕ the *lifting correspondence* derived from the covering map p. It depends of course on the choice of the point e_0.

Theorem 54.4. *Let $p : E \to B$ be a covering map; let $p(e_0) = b_0$. If E is path connected, then the lifting correspondence*

$$\phi : \pi_1(B, b_0) \to p^{-1}(b_0)$$

is surjective. If E is simply connected, it is bijective.

Proof. If E is path connected, then, given $e_1 \in p^{-1}(b_0)$, there is a path $\tilde{f}$ in E from e_0 to e_1. Then $f = p \circ \tilde{f}$ is a loop in B at b_0, and $\phi([f]) = e_1$ by definition.

Suppose E is simply connected. Let $[f]$ and $[g]$ be two elements of $\pi_1(B, b_0)$ such that $\phi([f]) = \phi([g])$. Let $\tilde{f}$ and $\tilde{g}$ be the liftings of f and g, respectively, to paths in E that begin at e_0; then $\tilde{f}(1) = \tilde{g}(1)$. Since E is simply connected, there is a path homotopy $\tilde{F}$ in E between $\tilde{f}$ and $\tilde{g}$. Then $p \circ \tilde{F}$ is a path homotopy in B between f and g.   ∎

Theorem 54.5. *The fundamental group of S^1 is isomorphic to the additive group of integers.*

Proof. Let $p : \mathbb{R} \to S^1$ be the covering map of Theorem 53.1, let $e_0 = 0$, and let $b_0 = p(e_0)$. Then $p^{-1}(b_0)$ is the set $\mathbb{Z}$ of integers. Since $\mathbb{R}$ is simply connected, the lifting correspondence

$$\phi : \pi_1(S^1, b_0) \to \mathbb{Z}$$

is bijective. We show that ϕ is a homomorphism, and the theorem is proved.

Given $[f]$ and $[g]$ in $\pi_1(B, b_0)$, let $\tilde{f}$ and $\tilde{g}$ be their respective liftings to paths on $\mathbb{R}$ beginning at 0. Let $n = \tilde{f}(1)$ and $m = \tilde{g}(1)$; then $\phi([f]) = n$ and $\phi([g]) = m$, by definition. Let $\tilde{\tilde{g}}$ be the path

$$\tilde{\tilde{g}}(s) = n + \tilde{g}(s)$$

on $\mathbb{R}$. Because $p(n + x) = p(x)$ for all $x \in \mathbb{R}$, the path $\tilde{\tilde{g}}$ is a lifting of g; it begins at n. Then the product $\tilde{f} * \tilde{\tilde{g}}$ is defined, and it is the lifting of $f * g$ that begins at 0, as you can check. The end point of this path is $\tilde{\tilde{g}}(1) = n + m$. Then by definition,

$$\phi([f] * [g]) = n + m = \phi([f]) + \phi([g]). \qquad \blacksquare$$

Definition.   Let G be a group; let x be an element of G. we denote the inverse of x by x^{-1}. The symbol x^n denotes the n-fold product of x with itself, x^{-n} denotes the n-fold product of x^{-1} with itself, and x^0 denotes the identity element of G. If the set of all elements of the form x^m, for $m \in \mathbb{Z}$, equals G, then G is said to be a *cyclic* group, and x is said to be a *generator* of G.

The cardinality of a group is also called the *order* of the group. A group is cyclic of infinite order if and only if it is isomorphic to the additive group of integers; it is cyclic of order k if and only if it is isomorphic to the group $\mathbb{Z}/k$ of integers modulo k. The preceding theorem implies that the fundamental group of the circle is infinite cyclic.

Note that if x is a generator of the infinite cyclic group G, and if y is an element of the arbitrary group H, then there is a unique homomorphism h of G into H such that $h(x) = y$; it is defined by setting $h(x^n) = y^n$ for all n.

For later use, in §65 and in Chapters 13 and 14, we prove here a strengthened version of Theorem 54.4.

*Theorem 54.6.   *Let $p : E \to B$ be a covering map; let $p(e_0) = b_0$.*

(a) *The homomorphism $p_* : \pi_1(E, e_0) \to \pi_1(B, b_0)$ is a monomorphism.*

(b) *Let $H = p_*(\pi_1(E, e_0))$. The lifting correspondence ϕ induces an injective map*

$$\Phi : \pi_1(B, b_0)/H \to p^{-1}(b_0)$$

of the collection of right cosets of H into $p^{-1}(b_0)$, which is bijective if E is path connected.

(c) *If f is a loop in B based at b_0, then $[f] \in H$ if and only if f lifts to a loop in E based at e_0.*

Proof.   (a) Suppose $\tilde{h}$ is a loop in E at e_0, and $p_*([\tilde{h}])$ is the identity element. Let F be a path homotopy between $p \circ \tilde{h}$ and the constant loop. If $\tilde{F}$ is the lifting of F to E such that $\tilde{F}(0, 0) = e_0$, then $\tilde{F}$ is a path homotopy between $\tilde{h}$ and the constant loop at e_0.

(b) Given loops f and g in B, let $\tilde{f}$ and $\tilde{g}$ be liftings of them to E that begin at e_0. Then $\phi([f]) = \tilde{f}(1)$ and $\phi([g]) = \tilde{g}(1)$. We show that $\phi([f]) = \phi([g])$ if and only if $[f] \in H * [g]$.

First, suppose that $[f] \in H * [g]$. Then $[f] = [h * g]$, where $h = p \circ \tilde{h}$ for some loop $\tilde{h}$ in E based at e_0. Now the product $\tilde{h} * \tilde{g}$ is defined, and it is a lifting of $h * g$. Because $[f] = [h * g]$, the liftings $\tilde{f}$ and $\tilde{h} * \tilde{g}$, which begin at e_0, must end at the same point of E. Then $\tilde{f}$ and $\tilde{g}$ end at the same point of E, so that $\phi([f]) = \phi([g])$. See Figure 54.3.

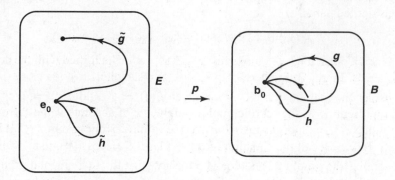

Figure 54.3

Now suppose that $\phi([f]) = \phi([g])$. Then $\tilde{f}$ and $\tilde{g}$ end at the same point of E. The product of $\tilde{f}$ and the reverse of $\tilde{g}$ is defined, and it is a loop $\tilde{h}$ in E based at e_0. By direct computation, $[\tilde{h} * \tilde{g}] = [\tilde{f}]$. If $\tilde{F}$ is a path homotopy in E between the loops $\tilde{h} * \tilde{g}$ and $\tilde{f}$, then $p \circ \tilde{F}$ is a path homotopy in B between $h * g$ and f, where $h = p \circ \tilde{h}$. Thus $[f] \in H * [g]$, as desired.

If E is path connected, then ϕ is surjective, so that Φ is surjective as well.

(c) Injectivity of Φ means that $\phi([f]) = \phi([g])$ if and only if $[f] \in H * [g]$. Applying this result in the case where g is the constant loop, we see that $\phi([f]) = e_0$ if and only if $[f] \in H$. But $\phi([f]) = e_0$ precisely when the lift of f that begins at e_0 also ends at e_0. ∎

Exercises

1. What goes wrong with the "path-lifting lemma" (Lemma 54.1) for the local homeomorphism of Example 2 of §53?

2. In defining the map $\tilde{F}$ in the proof of Lemma 54.2, why were we so careful about the order in which we considered the small rectangles?

3. Let $p : E \to B$ be a covering map. Let α and β be paths in B with $\alpha(1) = \beta(0)$; let $\tilde{\alpha}$ and $\tilde{\beta}$ be liftings of them such that $\tilde{\alpha}(1) = \tilde{\beta}(0)$. Show that $\tilde{\alpha} * \tilde{\beta}$ is a lifting of $\alpha * \beta$.

4. Consider the covering map $p : \mathbb{R} \times \mathbb{R}_+ \to \mathbb{R}^2 - \mathbf{0}$ of Example 6 of §53. Find liftings of the paths

$$f(t) = (2 - t, 0),$$
$$g(t) = ((1 + t) \cos 2\pi t, (1 + t) \sin 2\pi t)$$
$$h(t) = f * g.$$

Sketch these paths and their liftings.

5. Consider the covering map $p \times p : \mathbb{R} \times \mathbb{R} \to S^1 \times S^1$ of Example 4 of §53. Consider the path

$$f(t) = (\cos 2\pi t, \sin 2\pi t) \times (\cos 4\pi t, \sin 4\pi t)$$

in $S^1 \times S^1$. Sketch what f looks like when $S^1 \times S^1$ is identified with the doughnut surface D. Find a lifting $\tilde{f}$ of f to $\mathbb{R} \times \mathbb{R}$, and sketch it.

6. Consider the maps $g, h : S^1 \to S^1$ given by $g(z) = z^n$ and $h(z) = 1/z^n$. (Here we represent S^1 as the set of complex numbers z of absolute value 1.) Compute the induced homomorphisms g_*, h_* of the infinite cyclic group $\pi_1(S^1, b_0)$ into itself. [*Hint:* Recall the equation $(\cos \theta + i \sin \theta)^n = \cos n\theta + i \sin n\theta$.]

7. Generalize the proof of Theorem 54.5 to show that the fundamental group of the torus is isomorphic to the group $\mathbb{Z} \times \mathbb{Z}$.

8. Let $p : E \to B$ be a covering map, with E path connected. Show that if B is simply connected, then p is a homeomorphism.

§55 Retractions and Fixed Points

We now prove several classical results of topology that follow from our knowledge of the fundamental group of S^1.

Definition. If $A \subset X$, a *retraction* of X onto A is a continuous map $r : X \to A$ such that $r|A$ is the identity map of A. If such a map r exists, we say that A is a *retract* of X.

Lemma 55.1. *If A is a retract of X, then the homomorphism of fundamental groups induced by inclusion $j : A \to X$ is injective.*

Proof. If $r : X \to A$ is a retraction, then the composite map $r \circ j$ equals the identity map of A. It follows that $r_* \circ j_*$ is the identity map of $\pi_1(A, a)$, so that j_* must be injective. ∎

Theorem 55.2 (No-retraction theorem). *There is no retraction of B^2 onto S^1.*

Proof. If S^1 were a retract of B^2, then the homomorphism induced by inclusion $j : S^1 \to B^2$ would be injective. But the fundamental group of S^1 is nontrivial and the fundamental group of B^2 is trivial. ∎

Lemma 55.3. *Let $h : S^1 \to X$ be a continuous map. Then the following conditions are equivalent:*

(1) h is nulhomotopic.

(2) h extends to a continuous map $k : B^2 \to X$.

(3) h_* is the trivial homomorphism of fundamental groups.

Proof.   (1) $\Rightarrow$ (2). Let $H : S^1 \times I \to X$ be a homotopy between h and a constant map. Let $\pi : S^1 \times I \to B^2$ be the map

$$\pi(x, t) = (1 - t)x.$$

Then π is continuous, closed and surjective, so it is a quotient map; it collapses $S^1 \times 1$ to the point $\mathbf{0}$ and is otherwise injective. Because H is constant on $S^1 \times 1$, it induces, *via* the quotient map π, a continuous map $k : B^2 \to X$ that is an extension of h. See Figure 55.1.

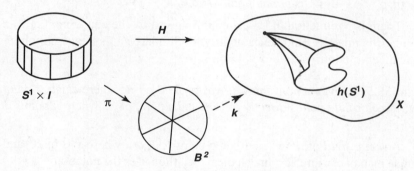

Figure 55.1

(2) $\Rightarrow$ (3). If $j : S^1 \to B^2$ is the inclusion map, then h equals the composite $k \circ j$. Hence $h_* = k_* \circ j_*$. But

$$j_* : \pi_1(S^1, b_0) \to \pi_1(B^2, b_0)$$

is trivial because the fundamental group of B^2 is trivial. Therefore h_* is trivial.

(3) $\Rightarrow$ (1). Let $p : \mathbb{R} \to S^1$ be the standard covering map, and let $p_0 : I \to S^1$ be its restriction to the unit interval. Then $[p_0]$ generates $\pi_1(S^1, b_0)$ because p_0 is a loop in S^1 whose lift to $\mathbb{R}$ begins at 0 and ends at 1.

Let $x_0 = h(b_0)$. Because h_* is trivial, the loop $f = h \circ p_0$ represents the identity element of $\pi_1(X, x_0)$. Therefore, there is a path homotopy F in X between f and the constant path at x_0. The map $p_0 \times \mathrm{id} : I \times I \to S^1 \times I$ is a quotient map, being continuous, closed, and surjective; it maps $0 \times t$ and $1 \times t$ to $b_0 \times t$ for each t, but is otherwise injective. The path homotopy F maps $0 \times I$ and $1 \times I$ and $I \times 1$ to the point x_0 of X, so it induces a continuous map $H : S^1 \times I \to X$ that is a homotopy between h and a constant map. See Figure 55.2.   ∎

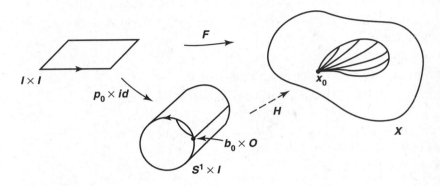

Figure 55.2

Corollary 55.4. *The inclusion map $j : S^1 \to R^2 - 0$ is not nulhomotopic. The identity map $i : S^1 \to S^1$ is not nulhomotopic.*

Proof. There is a retraction of $\mathbb{R} - 0$ onto S^1 given by the equation $r(x) = x/\|x\|$. Therefore, j_* is injective, and hence nontrivial. Similarly, i_* is the identity homomorphism, and hence nontrivial.   ■

Theorem 55.5. *Given a nonvanishing vector field on B^2, there exists a point of S^1 where the vector field points directly inward and a point of S^1 where it points directly outward.*

Proof. A ***vector field*** on B^2 is an ordered pair $(x, v(x))$, where x is in B^2 and v is a continuous map of B^2 into $\mathbb{R}^2$. In calculus, one often uses the notation

$$\mathbf{v}(x) = v_1(x)\mathbf{i} + v_2(x)\mathbf{j}$$

for the function v, where $\mathbf{i}$ and $\mathbf{j}$ are the standard unit basis vectors in $\mathbb{R}^2$. But we shall stick with simple functional notation. To say that a vector field is *nonvanishing* means that $v(x) \neq \mathbf{0}$ for every x; in such a case v actually maps B^2 into $\mathbb{R}^2 - \mathbf{0}$.

We suppose first that $v(x)$ does not point directly inward at any point x of S^1 and derive a contradiction. Consider the map $v : B^2 \to \mathbb{R}^2 - \mathbf{0}$; let w be its restriction to S^1. Because the map w extends to a map of B^2 into $\mathbb{R}^2 - \mathbf{0}$, it is nulhomotopic.

On the other hand, w is homotopic to the inclusion map $j : S^1 \to \mathbb{R}^2 - \mathbf{0}$. Figure 55.3 illustrates the homotopy; one defines it formally by the equation

$$F(x, t) = tx + (1 - t)w(x),$$

for $x \in S^1$. We must show that $F(x, t) \neq \mathbf{0}$. Clearly, $F(x, t) \neq \mathbf{0}$ for $t = 0$ and $t = 1$. If $F(x, t) = \mathbf{0}$ for some t with $0 < t < 1$, then $tx + (1 - t)w(x) = 0$, so that $w(x)$ equals a negative scalar multiple of x. But this means that $w(x)$ points directly inward at x! Hence F maps $S^1 \times I$ into $\mathbb{R}^2 - \mathbf{0}$, as desired.

It follows that j is nulhomotopic, contradicting the preceding corollary.

To show that v points directly outward at some point of S^1, we apply the result just proved to the vector field $(x, -v(x))$.   ■

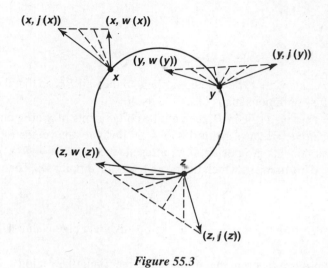

Figure 55.3

We have already seen that every continuous map $f : [0, 1] \to [0, 1]$ has a fixed point (see Exercise 3 of §24). The same is true for the ball B^2, although the proof is deeper:

Theorem 55.6 (Brouwer fixed-point theorem for the disc).   *If $f : B^2 \to B^2$ is continuous, then there exists a point $x \in B^2$ such that $f(x) = x$.*

Proof.   We proceed by contradiction. Suppose that $f(x) \neq x$ for every x in B^2. Then defining $v(x) = f(x) - x$ gives us a nonvanishing vector field $(x, v(x))$ on B^2. But the vector field v cannot point directly outward at any point x of S^1, for that would mean

$$f(x) - x = ax$$

for some *positive* real number a, so that $f(x) = (1 + a)x$ would lie outside the unit ball B^2. We thus arrive at a contradiction.   ∎

One might well wonder why fixed-point theorems are of interest in mathematics. It turns out that many problems, such as problems concerning existence of solutions for systems of equations, for instance, can be formulated as fixed-point problems. Here is one example, a classical theorem of Frobenius. We assume some knowledge of linear algebra at this point.

*Corollary 55.7.   *Let A be a 3 by 3 matrix of positive real numbers. Then A has a positive real eigenvalue (characteristic value).*

Proof.   Let $T : \mathbb{R}^3 \to \mathbb{R}^3$ be the linear transformation whose matrix (relative to the standard basis for $\mathbb{R}^3$) is A. Let B be the intersection of the 2-sphere S^2 with the first octant

$$\{(x_1, x_2, x_3) \mid x_1 \geq 0 \text{ and } x_2 \geq 0 \text{ and } x_3 \geq 0\}$$

of $\mathbb{R}^3$. It is easy to show that B is homeomorphic to the ball B^2, so that the fixed-point theorem holds for continuous maps of B into itself.

Now if $x = (x_1, x_2, x_3)$ is in B, then all the components of x are nonnegative and at least one is positive. Because all entries of A are positive, the vector $T(x)$ is a vector all of whose components are positive. As a result, the map $x \rightarrow T(x)/\|T(x)\|$ is a continuous map of B to itself, which therefore has a fixed point x_0. Then

$$T(x_0) = \|T(x_0)\|x_0,$$

so that T (and therefore the matrix A) has the positive real eigenvalue $\|T(x_0)\|$.   ∎

Finally, we prove a theorem that implies that the triangular region

$$T = \{(x, y) \mid x \geq 0 \text{ and } y \geq 0 \text{ and } x + y \leq 1\}$$

in $\mathbb{R}^2$ has topological dimension at least 2. (See §50.)

*Theorem 55.8.   *There is an $\epsilon > 0$ such that for every open covering $\mathcal{A}$ of T by sets of diameter less than ϵ, some point of T belongs to at least three elements of $\mathcal{A}$.*

Proof.   We use the fact that T is homeomorphic to B^2, so that we can apply the results proved in this section to the space T.

Choose $\epsilon > 0$ so that no set of diameter less than ϵ intersects all three edges of T. (In fact, $\epsilon = \frac{1}{2}$ will do.) We suppose that $\mathcal{A} = \{U_1, \ldots, U_n\}$ is an open covering of T by sets of diameter less than ϵ, such that no three elements of $\mathcal{A}$ intersect, and derive a contradiction.

For each $i = 1, \ldots, n$, choose a vertex v_i of T as follows: If U_i intersects two edges of T, let v_i be the vertex common to these edges. If U_i intersects only one edge of T, let v_i be one of the end points of this edge. If U_i intersects no edge of T, let v_i be any vertex of T.

Now let $\{\phi_i\}$ be a partition of unity dominated by $\{U_1, \ldots, U_n\}$. (See §36.) Define $k : T \rightarrow \mathbb{R}^2$ by the equation

$$k(x) = \sum_{i=1}^{n} \phi_i(x)v_i.$$

Then k is continuous. Given a point x of T, it lies in at most two elements of $\mathcal{A}$; hence at most two of the numbers $\phi_i(x)$ are nonzero. Then $k(x) = v_i$ if x lies in only one open set U_i, and $k(x) = tv_i + (1-t)v_j$ for some t with $0 \leq t \leq 1$ if x lies in two open sets U_i and U_j. In either case, $k(x)$ belongs to the union of the edges of T, which is Bd T. Thus k maps T into Bd T.

Furthermore, k maps each edge of T into itself. For if x belongs to the edge vw of T, any open set U_i containing x intersects this edge, so that v_i must equal either v or w. The definition of k then shows that $k(x)$ belongs to vw.

Let $h : \operatorname{Bd} T \to \operatorname{Bd} T$ be the restriction of k to $\operatorname{Bd} T$. Since h can be extended to the continuous map k, it is nulhomotopic. On the other hand, h is homotopic to the identity map of $\operatorname{Bd} T$ to itself; indeed, since h maps each edge of T into itself, the straight-line homotopy between h and the identity map of $\operatorname{Bd} T$ is such a homotopy. But the identity map i of $\operatorname{Bd} T$ is *not* nulhomotopic.   ∎

Exercises

1. Show that if A is a retract of B^2, then every continuous map $f : A \to A$ has a fixed point.

2. Show that if $h : S^1 \to S^1$ is nulhomotopic, then h has a fixed point and h maps some point x to its antipode $-x$.

3. Show that if A is a nonsingular 3 by 3 matrix having nonnegative entries, then A has a positive real eigenvalue.

4. Suppose that you are given the fact that for each n, there is no retraction $r : B^{n+1} \to S^n$. (This result can be proved using more advanced techniques of algebraic topology.) Prove the following:
   (a) The identity map $i : S^n \to S^n$ is not nulhomotopic.
   (b) The inclusion map $j : S^n \to \mathbb{R}^{n+1} - \mathbf{0}$ is not nulhomotopic.
   (c) Every nonvanishing vector field on B^{n+1} points directly outward at some point of S^n, and directly inward at some point of S^n.
   (d) Every continuous map $f : B^{n+1} \to B^{n+1}$ has a fixed point.
   (e) Every $n + 1$ by $n + 1$ matrix with positive real entries has a positive eigenvalue.
   (f) If $h : S^n \to S^n$ is nulhomotopic, then h has a fixed point and h maps some point x to its antipode $-x$.

*§56   The Fundamental Theorem of Algebra

It is a basic fact about the complex numbers that every polynomial equation

$$x^n + a_{n-1}x^{n-1} + \cdots + a_1 x + a_0 = 0$$

of degree n with real or complex coefficients has n roots (if the roots are counted according to their multiplicities). You probably first were told this fact in high school algebra, although it is doubtful that it was proved for you at that time.

The proof is, in fact, rather hard; the most difficult part is to prove that every polynomial equation of positive degree has *at least one* root. There are various ways of doing this. One can use only techniques of algebra; this proof is long and arduous. Or one can develop the theory of analytic functions of a complex variable to the point where it becomes a trivial corollary of Liouville's theorem. Or one can prove it as a relatively easy corollary of our computation of the fundamental group of the circle; this we do now.

Theorem 56.1 (The fundamental theorem of algebra).   *A polynomial equation*

$$x^n + a_{n-1}x^{n-1} + \cdots + a_1 x + a_0 = 0$$

of degree $n > 0$ *with real or complex coefficients has at least one (real or complex) root.*

Proof.   *Step 1.* Consider the map $f : S^1 \to S^1$ given by $f(z) = z^n$, where z is a complex number. We show that the induced homomorphism f_* of fundamental groups is injective.

Let $p_0 : I \to S^1$ be the standard loop in S^1,

$$p_0(s) = e^{2\pi i s} = (\cos 2\pi s, \sin 2\pi s).$$

Its image under f_* is the loop

$$f(p_0(s)) = (e^{2\pi i s})^n = (\cos 2\pi n s, \sin 2\pi n s).$$

This loop lifts to the path $s \to ns$ in the covering space $\mathbb{R}$. Therefore, the loop $f \circ p_0$ corresponds to the integer n under the standard isomorphism of $\pi_1(S^1, b_0)$ with the integers, whereas p_0 corresponds to the number 1. Thus f_* is "multiplication by n" in the fundamental group of S^1, so that in particular, f_* is injective.

Step 2. We show that if $g : S^1 \to \mathbb{R}^2 - \mathbf{0}$ is the map $g(z) = z^n$, then g is not nulhomotopic.

The map g equals the map f of Step 1 followed by the inclusion map $j : S^1 \to \mathbb{R}^2 - \mathbf{0}$. Now f_* is injective, and j_* is injective because S^1 is a retract of $\mathbb{R}^2 - \mathbf{0}$. Therefore, $g_* = j_* \circ f_*$ is injective. Thus g cannot be nulhomotopic.

Step 3. Now we prove a special case of the theorem. Given a polynomial equation

$$x^n + a_{n-1}x^{n-1} + \cdots + a_1 x + a_0 = 0,$$

we assume that

$$|a_{n-1}| + \cdots + |a_1| + |a_0| < 1$$

and show that the equation has a root lying in the unit ball B^2.

Assume it has no such root. Then we can define a map $k : B^2 \to \mathbb{R}^2 - \mathbf{0}$ by the equation

$$k(z) = z^n + a_{n-1}z^{n-1} + \cdots + a_1 z + a_0.$$

Let h be the restriction of k to S^1. Because h extends to a map of the unit ball into $\mathbb{R}^2 - \mathbf{0}$, the map h is nulhomotopic.

On the other hand, we shall define a homotopy F between h and the map g of Step 2; since g is not nulhomotopic, we have a contradiction. We define $F : S^1 \times I \to \mathbb{R}^2 - \mathbf{0}$ by the equation

$$F(z, t) = z^n + t(a_{n-1}z^{n-1} + \cdots + a_0).$$

See Figure 56.1; $F(z, t)$ never equals $\mathbf{0}$ because

$$
\begin{aligned}
|F(z, t)| &\geq |z^n| - |t(a_{n-1}z^{n-1} + \cdots + a_0)| \\
&\geq 1 - t(|a_{n-1}z^{n-1}| + \cdots + |a_0|) \\
&= 1 - t(|a_{n-1}| + \cdots + |a_0|) > 0.
\end{aligned}
$$

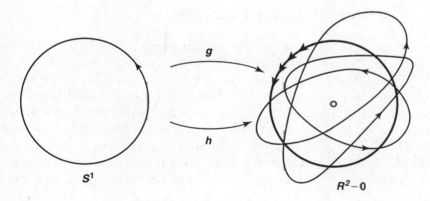

Figure 56.1

Step 4. Now we prove the general case. Given a polynomial equation

$$x^n + a_{n-1}x^{n-1} + \cdots + a_1 x + a_0 = 0,$$

let us choose a real number $c > 0$ and substitute $x = cy$. We obtain the equation

$$(cy)^n + a_{n-1}(cy)^{n-1} + \cdots + a_1(cy) + a_0 = 0$$

or

$$y^n + \frac{a_{n-1}}{c}y^{n-1} + \cdots + \frac{a_1}{c^{n-1}}y + \frac{a_0}{c^n} = 0.$$

If this equation has the root $y = y_0$, then the original equation has the root $x_0 = cy_0$. So we need merely choose c large enough that

$$\left|\frac{a_{n-1}}{c}\right| + \left|\frac{a_{n-2}}{c^2}\right| + \cdots + \left|\frac{a_1}{c^{n-1}}\right| + \left|\frac{a_0}{c^n}\right| < 1$$

to reduce the theorem to the special case considered in Step 3. ■

Exercises

1. Given a polynomial equation

$$x^n + a_{n-1}x^{n-1} + \cdots + a_1x + a_0 = 0$$

   with real or complex coefficients. Show that if $|a_{n-1}| + \cdots + |a_1| + |a_0| < 1$, then *all* the roots of the equation lie interior to the unit ball B^2. [*Hint:* Let $g(x) = 1 + a_{n-1}x + \cdots + a_1x^{n-1} + a_0x^n$, and show that $g(x) \neq 0$ for $x \in B^2$.]

2. Find a circle about the origin containing all the roots of the polynomial equation $x^7 + x^2 + 1 = 0$.

*§57   The Borsuk-Ulam Theorem

Here is a "brain-teaser" problem: Suppose you are given a bounded polygonal region A in the plane $\mathbb{R}^2$. No matter what shape A has, it is easy to show that there exists a straight line that bisects A, that is, one that cuts the area of A in half. Simply take the horizontal line $y = c$, let $f(c)$ denote the area of that part of A that lies beneath this line, note that f is a continuous function of c, and use the intermediate-value theorem to find a value of c for which $f(c)$ equals exactly half the area of A.

But now suppose instead that you are given *two* such regions A_1 and A_2, you are asked to find a single line that bisects them *both*. It is not obvious even that there exists such a line. Try to find one for an arbitrary pair of triangular regions if you have doubts!

In fact, such a line always exists. This result is a corollary of a well-known theorem called the Borsuk-Ulam theorem, to which we now turn.

Definition.   If x is a point of S^n, then its ***antipode*** is the point $-x$. A map $h : S^n \to S^m$ is said to be ***antipode-preserving*** if $h(-x) = -h(x)$ for all $x \in S^n$.

Theorem 57.1.   *If $h : S^1 \to S^1$ is continuous and antipode-preserving, then h is not nulhomotopic.*

Proof.   Let b_0 be the point $(1, 0)$ of S^1. Let $\rho : S^1 \to S^1$ be a rotation of S^1 that maps $h(b_0)$ to b_0. Since ρ preserves antipodes, so does the composite $\rho \circ h$. Furthermore, if H were a homotopy between h and a constant map, then $\rho \circ H$ would be a homotopy between $\rho \circ h$ and a constant map. Therefore, it suffices to prove the theorem under the additional hypothesis that $h(b_0) = b_0$.

Step 1. Let $q : S^1 \to S^1$ be the map $q(z) = z^2$, where z is a complex number. Or in real coordinates, $q(\cos\theta, \sin\theta) = (\cos 2\theta, \sin 2\theta)$. The map q is a quotient map, being continuous, closed, and surjective. The inverse image under q of any point of S^1 consists of two antipodal points z and $-z$ of S^1. Because $h(-z) = -h(z)$, one has the equation $q(h(-z)) = q(h(z))$. Therefore, because q is a quotient map, the map $q \circ h$ induces a continuous map $k : S^1 \to S^1$ such that $k \circ q = q \circ h$.

$$
\begin{array}{ccc}
S^1 & \xrightarrow{\ h\ } & S^1 \\
{\scriptstyle q}\downarrow & & \downarrow{\scriptstyle q} \\
S^1 & \dashrightarrow{\ k\ } & S^1
\end{array}
$$

Note that $q(b_0) = h(b_0) = b_0$, so that $k(b_0) = b_0$ as well. Also, $h(-b_0) = -b_0$.

Step 2. We show that the homomorphism k_* of $\pi_1(S^1, b_0)$ with itself is nontrivial.

For this purpose, we first show that q is a covering map. (We gave this as an exercise in §53.) The proof is similar to the proof that the standard map $p : \mathbb{R} \to S^1$ is a covering map. If, for instance, U is the subset of S^1 consisting of those points having positive second coordinate, then $p^{-1}(U)$ consist of those points of S^1 lying in the first and third quadrants of $\mathbb{R}^2$. The map q carries each of these sets homeomorphically onto U. Similar arguments apply when U is the intersection of S^1 with the open lower half-plane, or with the open right and left half-planes.

Second, we note that if $\tilde{f}$ is any path in S^1 from b_0 to $-b_0$, then the loop $f = q \circ \tilde{f}$ represents a nontrivial element of $\pi_1(S^1, b_0)$. For $\tilde{f}$ is a lifting of f to S^1 that begins at b_0 and does not end at b_0.

Finally, we show k_* is nontrivial. Let $\tilde{f}$ be a path in S^1 from b_0 to $-b_0$, and let f be the loop $q \circ \tilde{f}$. Then $k_*[f]$ is not trivial, for $k_*[f] = [k \circ (q \circ \tilde{f})] = [q \circ (h \circ \tilde{f})]$; the latter is nontrivial because $h \circ \tilde{f}$ is a path in S^1 from b_0 to $-b_0$.

Step 3. Finally, we show that the homomorphism h_* is nontrivial, so that h cannot be nulhomotopic.

The homomorphism k_* is injective, being a nontrivial homomorphism of an infinite cyclic group with itself. The homomorphism q_* is also injective; indeed, q_* corresponds to multiplication by two in the group of integers. It follows that $k_* \circ q_*$ is injective. Since $q_* \circ h_* = k_* \circ q_*$, the homomorphism h_* must be injective as well. ∎

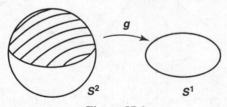

Figure 57.1

Theorem 57.2. *There is no continuous antipode-preserving map $g : S^2 \to S^1$.*

Proof. Suppose $g : S^2 \to S^1$ is continuous and antipode preserving. Let us take S^1 to be the equator of S^2. Then the restriction of g to S^1 is a continuous antipode-preserving map h of S^1 to itself. By the preceding theorem, h is not nulhomotopic. But the upper hemisphere E of S^2 is homeomorphic to the ball B^2, and g is a continuous extension of h to E! See Figure 57.1. ∎

Theorem 57.3 (Borsuk-Ulam theorem for S^2). *Given a continuous map $f : S^2 \to \mathbb{R}^2$, there is a point x of S^2 such that $f(x) = f(-x)$.*

Proof. Suppose that $f(x) \neq f(-x)$ for all $x \in S^2$. Then the map

$$g(x) = [f(x) - f(-x)]/\|f(x) - f(-x)\|$$

is a continuous map $g : S^2 \to S^1$ such that $g(-x) = -g(x)$ for all x. $\blacksquare$

Theorem 57.4 (The bisection theorem). *Given two bounded polygonal regions in $\mathbb{R}^2$, there exists a line in $\mathbb{R}^2$ that bisects each of them.*

Proof. We take two bounded polygonal regions A_1 and A_2 in the plane $\mathbb{R}^2 \times 1$ in $\mathbb{R}^3$, and show there is a line L in this plane that bisects each of them.

Given a point u of S^2, let us consider the plane P in $\mathbb{R}^3$ passing through the origin that has u as its unit normal vector. This plane divides $\mathbb{R}^3$ into two half-spaces; let $f_i(u)$ equal the area of that portion of A_i that lies on the same side of P as does the vector u.

If u is the unit vector $\mathbf{k}$, then $f_i(u) = $ area A_i; and if $u = -\mathbf{k}$, then $f_i(u) = 0$. Otherwise, the plane P intersects the plane $\mathbb{R}^2 \times 1$ in a line L that splits $\mathbb{R}^2 \times 1$ into two half-planes, and $f_i(u)$ is the area of that part of A_i that lies on one side of this line. See Figure 57.2.

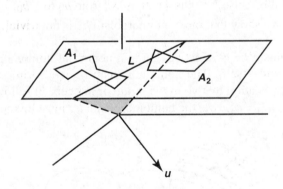

Figure 57.2

Replacing u by $-u$ gives us the same plane P, but the other half-space, so that $f_i(-u)$ is the area of that part of A_i that lies on the other side of P from u. It follows that

$$f_i(u) + f_i(-u) = \text{area } A_i.$$

Now consider the map $F : S^2 \to \mathbb{R}^2$ given by $F(u) = (f_1(u), f_2(u))$. The Borsuk-Ulam theorem gives us a point u of S^2 for which $F(u) = F(-u)$. Then $f_i(u) = f_i(-u)$ for $i = 1, 2$, that $f_i(u) = \frac{1}{2}$area A_i, as desired. $\blacksquare$

We have proved the bisection theorem for bounded polygonal regions in the plane. However, all that was needed in the proof was the existence of an additive area function for A_1 and A_2. Thus, the theorem holds for any two sets A_1 and A_2 that are "Jordan-measurable" in the sense used in analysis.

These theorems generalize to higher dimensions, but the proofs are considerably more sophisticated. The generalized version of the bisection theorem states that given n Jordan-measurable sets in $\mathbb{R}^n$, there exists a plane of dimension $n - 1$ that bisects them all. In the case $n = 3$, this result goes by the pleasant name of the "ham sandwich theorem." If one considers a ham sandwich to consist of two pieces of bread and a slab of ham, then the bisection theorem says that one can divide each of them precisely in half with a single whack of a cleaver!

Exercises

1. Prove the following "theorem of meteorology": At any given moment in time, there exists a pair of antipodal points on the surface of the earth at which both the temperature and the barometric pressure are equal.

2. Show that if $g : S^2 \to S^2$ is continuous and $g(x) \neq g(-x)$ for all x, then g is surjective. [*Hint:* If $p \in S^2$, then $S^2 - \{p\}$ is homeomorphic to $\mathbb{R}^2$.]

3. Let $h : S^1 \to S^1$ be continuous and antipode-preserving with $h(b_0) = b_0$. Show that h_* carries a generator of $\pi_1(S^1, b_0)$ to an *odd* power of itself. [*Hint:* If k is the map constructed in the proof of Theorem 57.1, show that k_* does the same.]

4. Suppose you are given the fact that for each n, no continuous antipode-preserving map $h : S^n \to S^n$ is nulhomotopic. (This result can be proved using more advanced techniques of algebraic topology.) Prove the following:
   (a) There is no retraction $r : B^{n+1} \to S^n$.
   (b) There is no continuous antipode-preserving map $g : S^{n+1} \to S^n$.
   (c) (Borsuk-Ulam theorem) Given a continuous map $f : S^{n+1} \to \mathbb{R}^{n+1}$, there is a point x of S^{n+1} such that $f(x) = f(-x)$.
   (d) If $A_1, \ldots, A_{n+1}$ are bounded measurable sets in $\mathbb{R}^{n+1}$, there exists an n-plane in $\mathbb{R}^{n+1}$ that bisects each of them.

§58   Deformation Retracts and Homotopy Type

As we have seen, one way of obtaining information about the fundamental group of a space X is to study the covering spaces of X. Another is one we discuss in this section, which involves the notion of *homotopy type*. It provides a method for reducing the problem of computing the fundamental group of a space to that of computing the fundamental group of some other space—preferably, one that is more familiar.

We begin with a lemma.

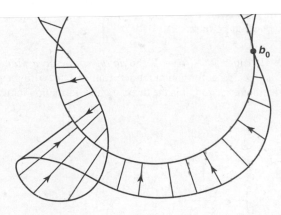

Figure 58.1

These comments lead us to formulate a more general situation in which the same procedure applies.

Definition.   Let A be a subspace of X. We say that A is a ***deformation retract*** of X if the identity map of X is homotopic to a map that carries all of X into A, such that each point of A remains fixed during the homotopy. This means that there is a continuous map $H : X \times I \to X$ such that $H(x, 0) = x$ and $H(x, 1) \in A$ for all $x \in X$, and $H(a, t) = a$ for all $a \in A$. The homotopy H is called a ***deformation retraction*** of X onto A. The map $r : X \to A$ defined by the equation $r(x) = H(x, 1)$ is a retraction of X onto A, and H is a homotopy between the identity map of X and the map $j \circ r$, where $j : A \to X$ is inclusion.

The proof of the preceding theorem generalizes immediately to prove the following:

Theorem 58.3.   *Let A be a deformation retract of X; let $x_0 \in A$. Then the inclusion map*

$$j : (A, x_0) \to (X, x_0)$$

induces an isomorphism of fundamental groups.

Lemma 58.1.   *Let $h, k : (X, x_0) \to (Y, y_0)$ be continuous maps. If h and k are homotopic, and if the image of the base point x_0 of X remains fixed at y_0 during the homotopy, then the homomorphisms h_* and k_* are equal.*

Proof.   The proof is immediate. By assumption, there is a homotopy $H : X \times I \to Y$ between h and k such that $H(x_0, t) = y_0$ for all t. It follows that if f is a loop in X based at x_0, then the composite

$$I \times I \xrightarrow{\; f \times \mathrm{id} \;} X \times I \xrightarrow{\; H \;} Y$$

is a homotopy between $h \circ f$ and $k \circ f$; it is a path homotopy because f is a loop at x_0 and H maps $x_0 \times I$ to y_0. ∎

Using this lemma, we generalize a result about the space $\mathbb{R}^2 - \mathbf{0}$ proved earlier, proving that the homomorphism induced by inclusion $j : S^1 \to \mathbb{R}^2 - \mathbf{0}$ is not only injective but surjective as well. More generally, we prove the following:

Theorem 58.2.   *The inclusion map $j : S^n \to \mathbb{R}^{n+1} - \mathbf{0}$ induces an isomorphism of fundamental groups.*

Proof.   Let $X = \mathbb{R}^{n+1} - \mathbf{0}$; let $b_0 = (1, 0, \ldots, 0)$. Let $r : X \to S^n$ be the map $r(x) = x/\|x\|$. Then $r \circ j$ is the identity map of S^n, so that $r_* \circ j_*$ is the identity homomorphism of $\pi_1(S^n, b_0)$.

Now consider the composite $j \circ r$, which maps X to itself;

$$X \xrightarrow{\; r \;} S^n \xrightarrow{\; j \;} X \; .$$

This map is not the identity map of X, but it is homotopic to the identity map. Indeed, the straight-line homotopy $H : X \times I \to X$, given by

$$H(x, t) = (1 - t)x + tx/\|x\|,$$

is a homotopy between the identity map of X and the map $j \circ r$. For $H(x, t)$ is never equal to $\mathbf{0}$, because $(1 - t) + t/\|x\|$ is a number between 1 and $1/\|x\|$. Note that the point b_0 remains fixed during the homotopy, since $\|b_0\| = 1$. It follows from the preceding lemma that the homomorphism $(j \circ r)_* = j_* \circ r_*$ is the identity homomorphism of $\pi_1(X, b_0)$. ∎

EXAMPLE 1.   Let B denote the z-axis in $\mathbb{R}^3$. Consider the space $\mathbb{R}^3 - B$. It has the punctured xy-plane $(\mathbb{R}^2 - \mathbf{0}) \times 0$ as a deformation retract. The map H defined by the equation

$$H(x, y, z, t) = (x, y, (1 - t)z)$$

is a deformation retraction; it gradually collapses each line parallel to the z-axis into the point where the line intersects the xy-plane. We conclude that the space $\mathbb{R}^3 - B$ has an infinite cyclic fundamental group.

EXAMPLE 2.   Consider $\mathbb{R}^2 - p - q$, the ***doubly punctured plane***. We assert it has the "figure eight" space as a deformation retract. Rather than writing equations, we merely sketch the deformation retraction; it is the three-stage deformation indicated in Figure 58.2.

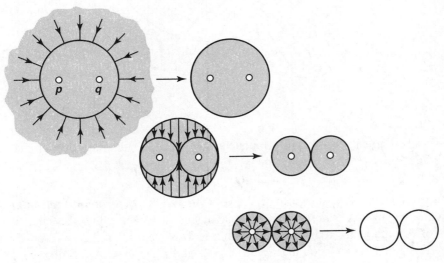

Figure 58.2

EXAMPLE 3.   Another deformation retract of $\mathbb{R}^2 - p - q$ is the "theta space"

$$\theta = S^1 \cup (0 \times [-1, 1]);$$

we leave it to you to sketch the maps involved. As a result, the figure eight and the theta space have isomorphic fundamental groups, even though neither is a deformation retract of the other.

Of course, we do not know anything about the fundamental group of the figure eight as yet. But we shall.

The example of the figure eight and the theta space suggests the possibility that there might be a more general way of showing two spaces have isomorphic fundamental groups than by showing that one is homeomorphic to a deformation retract of the other. We formulate such a notion now.

Definition.   Let $f : X \to Y$ and $g : Y \to X$ be continuous maps. Suppose that the map $g \circ f : X \to X$ is homotopic to the identity map of X, and the map $f \circ g : Y \to Y$ is homotopic to the identity map of Y. Then the maps f and g are called ***homotopy equivalences***, and each is said to be a ***homotopy inverse*** of the other.

It is straightforward to show that if $f : X \to Y$ is a homotopy equivalence of X with Y and $h : Y \to Z$ is a homotopy equivalence of Y with Z, then $h \circ f : X \to Z$ is a homotopy equivalence of X with Z. It follows that the relation of homotopy equivalence is an equivalence relation. Two spaces that are homotopy equivalent are said to have the same ***homotopy type***.

Note that if A is a deformation retract of X, then A has the same homotopy type as X. For let $j : A \to X$ be the inclusion mapping and let $r : X \to A$ be the retraction mapping. Then the composite $r \circ j$ *equals* the identity map of A, and the composite $j \circ r$ is by hypothesis homotopic to the identity map of X (and in fact each point of A remains fixed during the homotopy).

We now show that two spaces having the same homotopy type have isomorphic fundamental groups. For this purpose, we need to study what happens when we have a homotopy between two continuous maps of X into Y such that the base point of X does *not* remain fixed during the homotopy.

Lemma 58.4.   *Let $h, k : X \to Y$ be continuous maps; let $h(x_0) = y_0$ and $k(x_0) = y_1$. If h and k are homotopic, there is a path α in Y from y_0 to y_1 such that $k_* = \hat{\alpha} \circ h_*$. Indeed, if $H : X \times I \to Y$ is the homotopy between h and k, then α is the path $\alpha(t) = H(x_0, t)$.*

$$\pi_1(X, x_0) \xrightarrow{\ h_*\ } \pi_1(Y, y_0)$$
$$k_* \searrow \qquad \downarrow \hat{\alpha}$$
$$\pi_1(Y, y_1)$$

Proof.   Let $f : I \to X$ be a loop in X based at x_0. We must show that

$$k_*([f]) = \hat{\alpha}(h_*([f])).$$

This equation states that $[k \circ f] = [\bar{\alpha}] * [h \circ f] * [\alpha]$, or equivalently, that

$$[\alpha] * [k \circ f] = [h \circ f] * [\alpha].$$

This is the equation we shall verify.

To begin, consider the loops f_0 and f_1 in the space $X \times I$ given by the equations

$$f_0(s) = (f(s), 0) \quad \text{and} \quad f_1(s) = (f(s), 1).$$

Consider also the path c in $X \times I$ given by the equation

$$c(t) = (x_0, t).$$

Exercises

1. Show that if A is a deformation retract of X, and B is a deformation retract of A, then B is a deformation retract of X.

2. For each of the following spaces, the fundamental group is either trivial, infinite cyclic, or isomorphic to the fundamental group of the figure eight. Determine for each space which of the three alternatives holds.
   (a) The "solid torus," $B^2 \times S^1$.
   (b) The torus T with a point removed.
   (c) The cylinder $S^1 \times I$.
   (d) The infinite cylinder $S^1 \times \mathbb{R}$.
   (e) $\mathbb{R}^3$ with the nonnegative x, y, and z axes deleted.
   The following subsets of $\mathbb{R}^2$:
   (f) $\{x \mid \|x\| > 1\}$
   (g) $\{x \mid \|x\| \geq 1\}$
   (h) $\{x \mid \|x\| < 1\}$
   (i) $S^1 \cup (\mathbb{R}_+ \times 0)$
   (j) $S^1 \cup (\mathbb{R}_+ \times \mathbb{R})$
   (k) $S^1 \cup (\mathbb{R} \times 0)$
   (l) $\mathbb{R}^2 - (\mathbb{R}_+ \times 0)$

3. Show that given a collection $\mathcal{C}$ of spaces, the relation of homotopy equivalence is an equivalence relation on $\mathcal{C}$.

4. Let X be the figure eight and let Y be the theta space. Describe maps $f : X \to Y$ and $g : Y \to X$ that are homotopy inverse to each other.

5. Recall that a space X is said to be *contractible* if the identity map of X to itself is nulhomotopic. Show that X is contractible if and only if X has the homotopy type of a one-point space.

6. Show that a retract of a contractible space is contractible.

7. Let A be a subspace of X; let $j : A \to X$ be the inclusion map, and let $f : X \to A$ be a continuous map. Suppose there is a homotopy $H : X \times I \to X$ between the map $j \circ f$ and the identity map of X.
   (a) Show that if f is a retraction, then j_* is an isomorphism.
   (b) Show that if H maps $A \times I$ into A, then j_* is an isomorphism.
   (c) Give an example in which j_* is not an isomorphism.

*8. Find a space X and a point x_0 of X such that inclusion $\{x_0\} \to X$ is a homotopy equivalence, but $\{x_0\}$ is not a deformation retract of X. [*Hint:* Let X be the subspace of $\mathbb{R}^2$ that is the union of the line segments $(1/n) \times I$, for $n \in \mathbb{Z}_+$, the line segment $0 \times I$, and the line segment $I \times 0$; let x_0 be the point $(0, 1)$. If $\{x_0\}$ is a deformation retract of X, show that for any neighborhood U of x_0, the path component of U containing x_0 contains a neighborhood of x_0.]

9. We define the *degree* of a continuous map $h : S^1 \to S^1$ as follows:
   Let b_0 be the point $(1, 0)$ of S^1; choose a generator γ for the infinite cyclic group $\pi_1(S^1, b_0)$. If x_0 is any point of S^1, choose a path α in S^1 from b_0 to x_0,

and define $\gamma(x_0) = \hat{\alpha}(\gamma)$. Then $\gamma(x_0)$ generates $\pi_1(S^1, x_0)$. The element $\gamma(x_0)$ is independent of the choice of the path α, since the fundamental group of S^1 is abelian.

Now given $h : S^1 \to S^1$, choose $x_0 \in S^1$ and let $h(x_0) = x_1$. Consider the homomorphism

$$h_* : \pi_1(S^1, x_0) \longrightarrow \pi_1(S^1, x_1).$$

Since both groups are infinite cyclic, we have

$(*)$ \qquad\qquad $h_*(\gamma(x_0)) = d \cdot \gamma(x_1)$

for some integer d, if the group is written additively. The integer d is called the **degree** of h and is denoted by $\deg h$.

The degree of h is independent of the choice of the generator γ; choosing the other generator would merely change the sign of both sides of $(*)$.

(a) Show that d is independent of the choice of x_0.

(b) Show that if $h, k : S^1 \to S^1$ are homotopic, they have the same degree.

(c) Show that $\deg(h \circ k) = (\deg h) \cdot (\deg k)$.

(d) Compute the degrees of the constant map, the identity map, the reflection map $\rho(x_1, x_2) = (x_1, -x_2)$, and the map $h(z) = z^n$, where z is a complex number.

*(e) Show that if $h, k : S^1 \to S^1$ have the same degree, they are homotopic.

10. Suppose that to every map $h : S^n \to S^n$ we have assigned an integer, denoted by $\deg h$ and called the **degree** of h, such that:

(i) Homotopic maps have the same degree.

(ii) $\deg(h \circ k) = (\deg h) \cdot (\deg k)$.

(iii) The identity map has degree 1, any constant map has degree 0, and the reflection map $\rho(x_1, \ldots, x_{n+1}) = (x_1, \ldots, x_n, -x_{n+1})$ has degree -1.

[One can construct such a function, using the tools of algebraic topology. Intuitively, $\deg h$ measures how many times h wraps S^n about itself; the sign tells you whether h preserves orientation or not.] Prove the following:

(a) There is no retraction $r : B^{n+1} \to S^n$.

(b) If $h : S^n \to S^n$ has degree different from $(-1)^{n+1}$, then h has a fixed point. [*Hint:* Show that if h has no fixed point, then h is homotopic to the antipodal map $a(x) = -x$.]

(c) If $h : S^n \to S^n$ has degree different from 1, then h maps some point x to its antipode $-x$.

(d) If S^n has a nonvanishing tangent vector field v, then n is odd. [*Hint:* If v exists, show the identity map is homotopic to the antipodal map.]

Step 2. We prove the theorem. Let U and V be the open sets $U = S^n - p$ and $V = S^n - q$ of S^n.

Note first that for $n \geq 1$, the sphere S^n is path connected. This follows from the fact that U and V are path connected (being homeomorphic to $\mathbb{R}^n$) and have the point $(1, 0, \ldots, 0)$ of S^n in common.

Now we show that for $n \geq 2$, the sphere S^n is simply connected. The spaces U and V are simply connected, being homeomorphic to $\mathbb{R}^n$. Their intersection equals $S^n - p - q$, which is homeomorphic under stereographic projection to $\mathbb{R}^n - \mathbf{0}$. The latter space is path connected, for every point of $\mathbb{R}^n - \mathbf{0}$ can be joined to a point of S^{n-1} by a straight-line path, and S^{n-1} is path connected if $n \geq 2$. Then the preceding corollary applies. ∎

Exercises

1. Let X be the union of two copies of S^2 having a point in common. What is the fundamental group of X? Prove that your answer is correct. [Be careful! The union of two simply connected spaces having a point in common is not necessarily simply connected. See [S], p. 59.]

2. Criticize the following "proof" that S^2 is simply connected: Let f be a loop in S^2 based at x_0. Choose a point p of S^2 not lying in the image of f. Since $S^2 - p$ is homeomorphic with $\mathbb{R}^2$, and $\mathbb{R}^2$ is simply connected, the loop f is path homotopic to the constant loop.

3. (a) Show that $\mathbb{R}^1$ and $\mathbb{R}^n$ are not homeomorphic if $n > 1$.
   (b) Show that $\mathbb{R}^2$ and $\mathbb{R}^n$ are not homeomorphic if $n > 2$.
   It is, in fact, true that $\mathbb{R}^m$ and $\mathbb{R}^n$ are not homeomorphic if $n \neq m$, but the proof requires more advanced tools of algebraic topology.

4. Assume the hypotheses of Theorem 59.1.
   (a) What can you say about the fundamental group of X if j_* is the trivial homomorphism? If both i_* and j_* are trivial?
   (b) Give an example where i_* and j_* are trivial but neither U nor V have trivial fundamental groups.

§60　Fundamental Groups of Some Surfaces

Recall that a *surface* is a Hausdorff space with a countable basis, each point of which has a neighborhood that is homeomorphic with an open subset of $\mathbb{R}^2$. Surfaces are of interest in various parts of mathematics, including geometry, topology, and complex analysis. We consider here several surfaces, including the torus and double torus, and show by comparing their fundamental groups that they are not homeomorphic. In a later chapter, we shall classify up to homeomorphism all compact surfaces.

First, we consider the torus. In an earlier exercise, we asked you to compute its fundamental group using the theory of covering spaces. Here, we compute its fundamental group by using a theorem about the fundamental group of a product space.

Recall that if A and B are groups with operation $\cdot$, then the cartesian product $A \times B$ is given a group structure by using the operation

$$(a \times b) \cdot (a' \times b') = (a \cdot a') \times (b \cdot b').$$

Recall also that if $h : C \to A$ and $k : C \to B$ are group homomorphisms, then the map $\Phi : C \to A \times B$ defined by $\Phi(c) = h(c) \times k(c)$ is a group homomorphism.

Theorem 60.1. $\pi_1(X \times Y, x_0 \times y_0)$ *is isomorphic with* $\pi_1(X, x_0) \times \pi_1(Y, y_0)$.

Proof.   Let $p : X \times Y \to X$ and $q : X \times Y \to Y$ be the projection mappings. If we use the base points indicated in the statement of the theorem, we have induced homomorphisms

$$p_* : \pi_1(X \times Y, x_0 \times y_0) \longrightarrow \pi_1(X, x_0),$$
$$q_* : \pi_1(X \times Y, x_0 \times y_0) \longrightarrow \pi_1(Y, y_0).$$

We define a homomorphism

$$\Phi : \pi_1(X \times Y, x_0 \times y_0) \longrightarrow \pi_1(X, x_0) \times \pi_1(Y, y_0)$$

by the equation

$$\Phi([f]) = p_*([f]) \times q_*([f]) = [p \circ f] \times [q \circ f].$$

We shall show that Φ is an isomorphism.

The map Φ is surjective. Let $g : I \to X$ be a loop based at x_0; let $h : I \to Y$ be a loop based at y_0. We wish to show that the element $[g] \times [h]$ lies in the image of Φ. Define $f : I \to X \times Y$ by the equation

$$f(s) = g(s) \times h(s).$$

Then f is a loop in $X \times Y$ based at $x_0 \times y_0$, and

$$\Phi([f]) = [p \circ f] \times [q \circ f] = [g] \times [h],$$

as desired.

The kernel of Φ vanishes. Suppose that $f : I \to X \times Y$ is a loop in $X \times Y$ based at $x_0 \times y_0$ and $\Phi([f]) = [p \circ f] \times [q \circ f]$ is the identity element. This means that $p \circ f \simeq_p e_{x_0}$ and $q \circ f \simeq_p e_{y_0}$; let G and H be the respective path homotopies. Then the map $F : I \times I \to X \times Y$ defined by

$$F(s, t) = G(s, t) \times H(s, t)$$

is a path homotopy between f and the constant loop based at $x_0 \times y_0$.   ∎

Corollary 60.2.   *The fundamental group of the torus* $T = S^1 \times S^1$ *is isomorphic to the group* $\mathbb{Z} \times \mathbb{Z}$.

Now we define a surface called the projective plane and compute its fundamental group.

Definition.   The *projective plane* P^2 is the quotient space obtained from S^2 by identifying each point x of S^2 with its antipodal point $-x$.

The projective plane may not be a space that is familiar to you; it cannot be imbedded in $\mathbb{R}^3$ and is thus difficult to visualize. It is, however, the fundamental object of study in projective geometry, just as the euclidean plane $\mathbb{R}^2$ is in ordinary euclidean geometry. Topologists are primarily interested in it as an example of a surface.

Theorem 60.3.   *The projective plane* P^2 *is a compact surface, and the quotient map* $p : S^2 \to P^2$ *is a covering map.*

Proof.   First we show that p is an open map. Let U be open in S^2. Now the antipodal map $a : S^2 \to S^2$ given by $a(x) = -x$ is a homeomorphism of S^2; hence $a(U)$ is open in S^2. Since

$$p^{-1}(p(U)) = U \cup a(U),$$

this set also is open in S^2. Therefore, by definition, $p(U)$ is open in P^2. A similar proof shows that p is a closed map.

Now we show that p is a covering map. Given a point y of P^2, choose $x \in p^{-1}(y)$. Then choose an ϵ-neighborhood U of x in S^2 for some $\epsilon < 1$, using the euclidean metric d of $\mathbb{R}^3$. Then U contains no pair $\{z, a(z)\}$ of antipodal points of S^2, since $d(z, a(z)) = 2$. As a result, the map

$$p : U \longrightarrow p(U)$$

is bijective. Being continuous and open, it is a homeomorphism. Similarly,

$$p : a(U) \to p(a(U)) = p(U)$$

is a homeomorphism. The set $p^{-1}(p(U))$ is thus the union of the two disjoint open sets U and $a(U)$, each of which is mapped homeomorphically by p onto $p(U)$. Then $p(U)$ is a neighborhood of $p(x) = y$ that is evenly covered by p.

Since S^2 has a countable basis $\{U_n\}$, the space P^2 has a countable basis $\{p(U_n)\}$.

The fact that P^2 is Hausdorff follows from the fact that S^2 is normal and p is a closed map. (See Exercise 6 of §31.) Alternatively, one can give a direct proof: Let y_1 and y_2 be two points of P^2. The set $p^{-1}(y_1) \cup p^{-1}(y_2)$ consists of four points; let 2ϵ be the minimum distance between them. Let U_1 be the ϵ-neighborhood of one of the points of $p^{-1}(y_1)$, and let U_2 be the ϵ-neighborhood of one of the points of $p^{-1}(y_2)$. Then

$$U_1 \cup a(U_1) \quad \text{and} \quad U_2 \cup a(U_2)$$

are disjoint. It follows that $p(U_1)$ and $p(U_2)$ are disjoint neighborhoods of y_1 and y_2, respectively, in P^2.

Since S^2 is a surface and every point of P^2 has a neighborhood homeomorphic with an open subset of S^2, the space P^2 is also a surface. ∎

Corollary 60.4. *$\pi_1(P^2, y)$ is a group of order 2.*

Proof. The projection $p : S^2 \to P^2$ is a covering map. Since S^2 is simply connected, we can apply Theorem 54.4, which tells us there is a bijective correspondence between $\pi_1(P^2, y)$ and the set $p^{-1}(y)$. Since this set is a two-element set, $\pi_1(P^2, y)$ is a group of order 2.

Any group of order 2 is isomorphic to $\mathbb{Z}/2$, the integers mod 2, of course. ∎

One can proceed similarly to define P^n, for any $n \in \mathbb{Z}_+$, as the space obtained from S^n by identifying each point x with its antipode $-x$; it is called *projective n-space*. The proof of Theorem 60.3 goes through without change to prove that the projection $p : S^n \to P^n$ is a covering map. Then because S^n is simply connected for $n \geq 2$, it follows that $\pi_1(P^n, y)$ is a two-element group for $n \geq 2$. We leave it to you to figure out what happens when $n = 1$.

Now we study the double torus. We begin with a lemma about the figure eight.

Lemma 60.5. *The fundamental group of the figure eight is not abelian.*

Proof. Let X be the union of two circles A and B in $\mathbb{R}^2$ whose intersection consists of the single point x_0. We describe a certain covering space E of X.

The space E is the subspace of the plane consisting of the x-axis and the y-axis, along with tiny circles tangent to these axes, one circle tangent to the x-axis at each nonzero integer point and one circle tangent to the y-axis at each nonzero integer point.

The projection map $p : E \to X$ wraps the x-axis around the circle A and wraps the y-axis around the other circle B; in each case the integer points are mapped by p into the base point x_0. Each circle tangent to an integer point on the x-axis is mapped homeomorphically by p onto B, while each circle tangent to an integer point on the y-axis is mapped homeomorphically onto A; in each case the point of tangency is mapped onto the point x_0. We leave it to you to check mentally that the map p is indeed a covering map.

We could write this description down in equations if we wished, but the informal description seems to us easier to follow.

Now let $\tilde{f} : I \to E$ be the path $\tilde{f}(s) = s \times 0$, going along the x-axis from the origin to the point 1×0. Let $\tilde{g} : I \to E$ be the path $\tilde{g}(s) = 0 \times s$, going along the y-axis from the origin to the point 0×1. Let $f = p \circ \tilde{f}$ and $g = p \circ \tilde{g}$; then f and g are loops in the figure eight based at x_0, going around the circles A and B, respectively. See Figure 60.1.

We assert that $f * g$ and $g * f$ are not path homotopic, so that the fundamental group of the figure eight is not abelian.

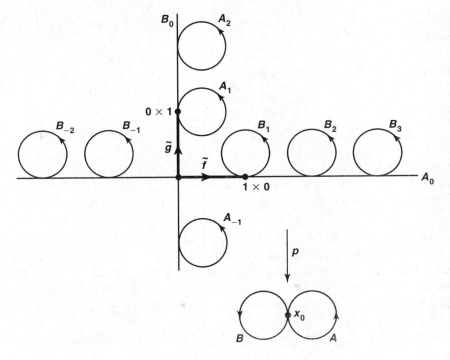

Figure 60.1

To prove this assertion, let us lift each of these to a path in E beginning at the origin. The path $f * g$ lifts to a path that goes along the x-axis from the origin to 1×0 and then goes once around the circle tangent to the x-axis at 1×0. On the other hand, the path $g * f$ lifts to a path in E that goes along the y-axis from the origin to 0×1, and then goes once around the circle tangent to the y-axis at 0×1. Since the lifted paths do not end at the same point, $f * g$ and $g * f$ cannot be path homotopic.   ∎

We shall prove later that the fundamental group of the figure eight is, in fact, the group that algebraists call the "free group on two generators."

Theorem 60.6. *The fundamental group of the double torus is not abelian.*

Proof. The double torus $T \# T$ is the surface obtained by taking two copies of the torus, deleting a small open disc from each of them, and pasting the remaining pieces together along their edges. We assert that the figure eight X is a retract of $T \# T$. This fact implies that inclusion $j : X \to T \# T$ induces a monomorphism j_*, so that $\pi_1(T \# T, x_0)$ is not abelian.

One can write equations for the retraction $r : T \# T \to X$, but it is simpler to indicate it in pictures, as we have done in Figure 60.2. Let Y be the union of two tori having a point in common. First one maps $T \# T$ onto Y by a map that collapses the dotted circle to a point but is otherwise one-to-one; it defines a homeomorphism h of

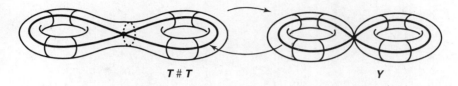

T # T   *Y*

Figure 60.2

the figure eight in $T\#T$ with the figure eight in Y. Then one retracts Y onto its figure eight by mapping each cross-sectional circle to the point where it intersects the figure eight. Then one maps the figure eight in Y back onto the figure eight in $T\#T$ by the map h^{-1}.   ∎

Corollary 60.7.   *The 2-sphere, torus, projective plane, and double torus are topologically distinct.*

Exercises

1. Compute the fundamental groups of the "solid torus" $S^1 \times B^2$ and the product space $S^1 \times S^2$.

2. Let X be the quotient space obtained from B^2 by identifying each point x of S^1 with its antipode $-x$. Show that X is homeomorphic to the projective plane P^2.

3. Let $p : E \to X$ be the map constructed in the proof of Lemma 60.5. Let E' be the subspace of E that is the union of the x-axis and the y-axis. Show that $p|E'$ is not a covering map.

4. The space P^1 and the covering map $p : S^1 \to P^1$ are familiar ones. What are they?

5. Consider the covering map indicated in Figure 60.3. Here, p wraps A_1 around A twice and wraps B_1 around B twice; p maps A_0 and B_0 homeomorphically onto A and B, respectively. Use this covering space to show that the fundamental group of the figure eight is not abelian.

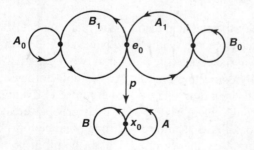

Figure 60.3

Chapter 10

Separation Theorems in the Plane

There are several difficult questions concerning the topology of the plane that arise quite naturally in the study of analysis. The answers to these questions seem geometrically quite obvious but turn out to be surprisingly hard to prove. They include the Jordan curve theorem, the Brouwer theorem on invariance of domain, and the classical theorem that the winding number of a simple closed curve is zero or ± 1. We prove them in this chapter as consequences of our study of covering spaces and the fundamental group.

§61   The Jordan Separation Theorem

We consider first one of the classical theorems of mathematics, the Jordan curve theorem. It states a fact that is geometrically quite believable, the fact that a simple closed curve in the plane always separates the plane into two pieces, its "inside" and its "outside." It was originally conjectured in 1892 by Camille Jordan, and several incorrect proofs were published, including one by Jordan himself. Eventually, a correct proof was provided by Oswald Veblen, in 1905. The early proofs were complicated, but over the years, simpler proofs have been found. If one uses the tools of modern algebraic topology, singular homology theory in particular, the proof is quite straightforward. The proof we give here is the simplest one we know that uses only results from the theory of covering spaces and the fundamental group.

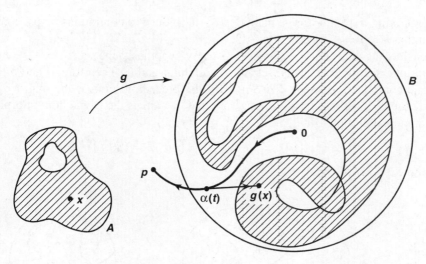

Figure 61.2

An ***arc*** A is a space homeomorphic to the unit interval $[0, 1]$. The ***end points*** of A are the two points p and q of A such that $A - p$ and $A - q$ are connected; the other points of A are called ***interior points*** of A.

A ***simple closed curve*** is a space homeomorphic to the unit circle S^1.

Theorem 61.3 (The Jordan separation theorem).   *Let C be a simple closed curve in S^2. Then C separates S^2.*

Proof.   Because $S^2 - C$ is locally path connected, its components and path components are the same. We assume that $S^2 - C$ is path connected and derive a contradiction.

Let us write C as the union of two arcs A_1 and A_2 that intersect only in their end points a and b. Let X denote the space $S^2 - a - b$. Let U be the open set $S^2 - A_1$ of X, and let V be the open set $S^2 - A_2$. Then X is the union of the sets U and V, and

$$U \cap V = S^2 - (A_1 \cup A_2) = S^2 - C,$$

which by hypothesis is path connected. Thus the hypotheses of Theorem 59.1 are satisfied.

Let x_0 be a point of $U \cap V$. We will show that the inclusions

$$i : (U, x_0) \longrightarrow (X, x_0) \quad \text{and} \quad j : (V, x_0) \longrightarrow (X, x_0)$$

induce trivial homomorphisms of the fundamental groups involved. It then follows from Theorem 59.1 that the group $\pi_1(X, x_0)$ is trivial. But $X = S^2 - a - b$, which is homeomorphic to the punctured plane $\mathbb{R}^2 - \mathbf{0}$, so its fundamental group is *not* trivial.

Let us prove that i_* is the trivial homomorphism; given a loop $f : I \to U$ based at x_0, we show that $i_*([f])$ is trivial. For this purpose, let $p : I \to S^1$ be the standard loop generating $\pi_1(S^1, b_0)$. The map $f : I \to U$ induces a continuous map $h : S^1 \to U$ such that $h \circ p = f$. See Figure 61.3.

Consider the map $i \circ h : S^1 \to S^2 - a - b$. By hypothesis, the set $i(h(S^1)) = h(S^1)$ does not intersect the connected set A_1 containing a and b. Therefore, a and b lie in the same component of $S^2 - i(h(S^1))$. By the preceding lemma, the map $i \circ h$ is nulhomotopic. It follows from Lemma 55.3 that $(i \circ h)_*$ is the trivial homomorphism of fundamental groups. But

$$(i \circ h)_*([p]) = [i \circ h \circ p] = [i \circ f] = i_*([f]).$$

Therefore, $i_*([f])$ is trivial, as desired. ∎

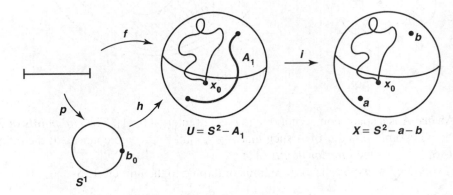

Figure 61.3

Let us examine the preceding proof. What facts did we use about the simple closed curve C? All we actually needed was the fact that C could be written as the union of the two closed connected sets A_1 and A_2, whose intersection consisted of the two points a and b. This remark leads to the following generalized version of the separation theorem, which will be useful later.

Theorem 61.4 (A general separation theorem). *Let A_1 and A_2 be closed connected subsets of S^2 whose intersection consists of precisely two points a and b. Then the set $C = A_1 \cup A_2$ separates S^2.*

Proof. We must show first that C cannot equal all of S^2. That fact was obvious in the earlier proof. In the present case, we can see that $C \neq S^2$ because $S^2 - a - b$ is connected and $C - a - b$ is not. (The sets $A_i - a - b$ form a separation of $C - a - b$.)

The remainder of the proof is a copy of the proof of the preceding theorem. ∎

Exercises

1. Give examples to show that a simple closed curve in the torus may or may not separate the torus.

2. Let A be the subset of $\mathbb{R}^2$ consisting of the union of the topologist's sine curve and the broken-line path from $(0, -1)$ to $(0, -2)$ to $(1, -2)$ to $(1, \sin 1)$. See Figure 61.4. We call A the *closed topologist's sine curve*. Show that if C is a subspace of S^2 homeomorphic to the closed topologist's sine curve, then C separates S^2.

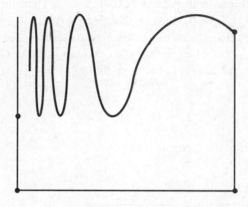

Figure 61.4

*§62   Invariance of Domain[†]

One of the theorems of topology that is truly fundamental, because it expresses an intrinsic property of euclidean space, is the theorem on "invariance of domain," proved by L. E. J. Brouwer in 1912. It states that for any open set U of $\mathbb{R}^n$ and any continuous injective mapping $f : U \to \mathbb{R}^n$, the image set $f(U)$ is open in $\mathbb{R}^n$ and the inverse function is continuous. (The Inverse Function Theorem of analysis derives this result under the additional hypothesis that the map f is continuously differentiable with non-singular Jacobian matrix.) We shall prove this theorem in the case $n = 2$.

Lemma 62.1 (Homotopy extension lemma). *Let X be a space such that $X \times I$ is normal. Let A be a closed subspace of X, and let $f : A \to Y$ be a continuous map, where Y is an open subspace of $\mathbb{R}^n$. If f is nulhomotopic, then f may be extended to a continuous map $g : X \to Y$ that is also nulhomotopic.*

Proof. Let $F : A \times I \to Y$ be a homotopy between f and a constant map. Then $F(a, 0) = f(a)$ and $F(a, 1) = y_0$ for all a. Extend F to the space $X \times 1$ by setting $F(x, 1) = y_0$ for $x \in X$. Then F is a continuous map of the closed subspace $(A \times I) \cup (X \times 1)$ of $X \times I$ into $\mathbb{R}^n$; by the Tietze extension theorem, it may be extended to a continuous map $G : X \times I \to \mathbb{R}^n$.

[†]In this section, we use the Tietze extension theorem (§35).

Now the map $x \to G(x, 0)$ is an extension of f, but it maps X into $\mathbb{R}^n$ rather than into the subspace Y. To obtain our desired map, we proceed as follows: Let U be the open subset $U = G^{-1}(Y)$ of $X \times I$. Then U contains $(A \times I) \cup (X \times 1)$. See Figure 62.1. Since I is compact, the tube lemma implies that there is an open set W of X containing A such that $W \times I \subset U$. Now the space X is itself normal, being homeomorphic to the closed subspace $X \times 0$ of $X \times I$. Therefore, we may choose a continuous function $\phi : X \to [0, 1]$ such that $\phi(x) = 0$ for $x \in A$ and $\phi(x) = 1$ for $x \in X - W$. The map $x \to x \times \phi(x)$ carries X into the subspace $(W \times I) \cup (X \times 1)$ of $X \times I$, which lies in U. Then the continuous map $g(x) = G(x, \phi(x))$ carries X into Y. And for $x \in A$, we have $\phi(x) = 0$, so that $g(x) = G(x, 0) = f(x)$. Thus g is the desired extension of f. The map $H : X \times I \to Y$ given by

$$H(x, t) = G(x, (1 - t)\phi(x) + t)$$

is a homotopy between g and a constant map. ∎

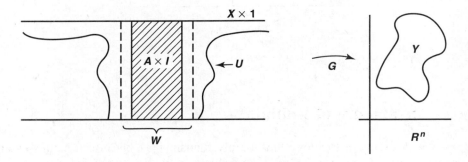

Figure 62.1

The following lemma is a partial converse to the nulhomotopy lemma of the preceding section.

Lemma 62.2 (Borsuk lemma). *Let a and b be points of S^2. Let A be a compact space, and let $f : A \to S^2 - a - b$ be a continuous injective map. If f is nulhomotopic, then a and b lie in the same component of $S^2 - f(A)$.*

Proof. Because A is compact and S^2 is Hausdorff, $f(A)$ is a compact subspace of S^2 that is homeomorphic to A. Because f is nulhomotopic, so is the inclusion mapping of $f(A)$ into $S^2 - a - b$. Hence it suffices to prove the lemma in the special case where f is simply an inclusion map. Furthermore, we can replace S^2 by $\mathbb{R}^2 \cup \{\infty\}$, letting a correspond to **0**, and b to ∞. Then our lemma reduces to the following statement:

Let A be a compact subspace of $\mathbb{R}^2 - \mathbf{0}$. If the inclusion $j : A \to \mathbb{R}^2 - \mathbf{0}$ is nulhomotopic, then $\mathbf{0}$ lies in the unbounded component of $\mathbb{R}^2 - A$.

This we now prove. Let C be the component of $\mathbb{R}^2 - A$ containing $\mathbf{0}$; we suppose C is bounded and derive a contradiction. Let D be the union of the other components of $\mathbb{R}^2 - A$, including the unbounded component. Then C and D are disjoint open sets of $\mathbb{R}^2$, and $\mathbb{R}^2 - A = C \cup D$. See Figure 62.2.

We define a continuous map $h : \mathbb{R}^2 \to \mathbb{R}^2 - \mathbf{0}$ that equals the identity outside C.

Begin with the inclusion map $j : A \to \mathbb{R}^2 - \mathbf{0}$. Since j is by hypothesis nulhomotopic, the preceding lemma implies that j can be extended to a continuous map k of $C \cup A$ into $\mathbb{R}^2 - \mathbf{0}$. Then k equals the identity at points of A. Extend k to a map $h : \mathbb{R}^2 \to \mathbb{R}^2 - \mathbf{0}$ by setting $h(x) = x$ for $x \in D \cup A$; then h is continuous by the pasting lemma.

Now we derive a contradiction. Let B be the closed ball in $\mathbb{R}^2$ of radius M centered at the origin, where M is so large that Int B contains $C \cup A$. (Here, we use the fact that C is bounded.) If we restrict h to B, we obtain a map $g : B \to \mathbb{R}^2 - \mathbf{0}$ such that $g(x) = x$ for $x \in \mathrm{Bd}\, B$. If we follow g by the standard retraction $x \to Mx/\|x\|$ of $\mathbb{R}^2 - \mathbf{0}$ onto Bd B, we obtain a retraction of B onto Bd B. Such a retraction does not exist. ∎

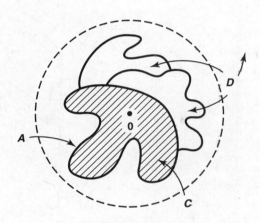

Figure 62.2

Theorem 62.3 (Invariance of domain). *If U is an open subset of $\mathbb{R}^2$ and $f : U \to \mathbb{R}^2$ is continuous and injective, then $f(U)$ is open in $\mathbb{R}^2$ and the inverse function $f^{-1} : f(U) \to U$ is continuous.*

Proof.   As usual, we can replace $\mathbb{R}^2$ by S^2. We show that if U is an open subset of $\mathbb{R}^2$ and $f : U \to S^2$ is continuous and injective, then $f(U)$ is open in S^2 and the inverse function is continuous.

Step 1. We show that if B is any closed ball in $\mathbb{R}^2$ contained in U, then $f(B)$ does not separate S^2.

Let a and b be two points of $S^2 - f(B)$. Because the identity map $i : B \to B$ is nulhomotopic, the map $h : B \to S^2 - a - b$ obtained by restricting f is nulhomotopic. The Borsuk lemma then implies that a and b lie in the same component of $S^2 - h(B) = S^2 - f(B)$.

Step 2. We show that if B is any closed ball of $\mathbb{R}^2$ lying in U, then $f(\text{Int } B)$ is open in S^2.

The space $C = f(\text{Bd } B)$ is a simple closed curve in S^2, so it separates S^2. Let V be the component of $S^2 - C$ that contains the connected set $f(\text{Int } B)$, and let W be the union of the others. Because S^2 is locally connected, V and W are open in S^2. We show $V = f(\text{Int } B)$, and we are through.

We suppose a is a point of V that is not in $f(\text{Int } B)$ and derive a contradiction. Let b be a point of W. Since the set $D = f(B)$ does not separate S^2, the set $S^2 - D$ is a connected set containing a and b. This set is contained in $S^2 - C$ (since $D \supset C$); it follows that a and b lie in the same component of $S^2 - C$, contrary to construction. See Figure 62.3.

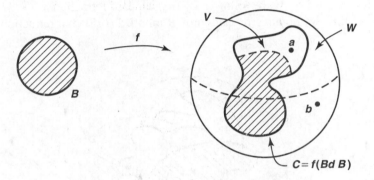

Figure 62.3

Step 3. We prove the theorem. Since, for any ball B contained in U, the set $f(\text{Int } B)$ is open in S^2, the map $f : U \to S^2$ is an open map. It follows that $f(U)$ is open in S^2 and f^{-1} is continuous. ∎

Exercises

1. Give an example to show that the conclusion of the Borsuk lemma need not hold if f is not injective.

2. Let A be a compact contractible subspace of S^2. Show that A does not separate S^2.

3. Let X be a space such that $X \times I$ is normal. Let A be a closed subspace of X; let $f : A \to Y$ be a continuous map, where Y is an open subspace of $\mathbb{R}^n$. If f is homotopic to a map that is extendable to a continuous map $h : X \to Y$, then f itself is extendable to a continuous map $g : X \to Y$, such that $g \simeq h$.

4. Let C be a simple closed curve in $\mathbb{R}^2 - \mathbf{0}$; let $j : C \to \mathbb{R}^2 - \mathbf{0}$ be the inclusion mapping. Show that j_* is trivial if $\mathbf{0}$ lies in the unbounded component of $\mathbb{R}^2 - C$, and is nontrivial otherwise. (In fact, j_* is an *isomorphism* in the latter case, as we shall prove in §65.)

5. **Theorem.** *Let U be a simply connected open set in $\mathbb{R}^2$. If C is a simple closed curve lying in U, then each bounded component of $\mathbb{R}^2 - C$ also lies in U.*

(This condition actually characterizes the simply connected open sets of $\mathbb{R}^2$. See [RW]. The space $\mathbb{R}^2 - C$ has, of course, only one bounded component, as we shall prove in the next section.)

6. Suppose you are given that there is no retraction of B^n onto S^{n-1}.
   (a) Show the Borsuk lemma holds for S^n.
   (b) Show that no compact contractible subspace of S^n separates S^n.
   (c) Suppose you are given also that any subspace of S^n homeomorphic to S^{n-1} separates S^n. Prove the invariance of domain theorem in dimension n.

§63   The Jordan Curve Theorem

The special case of the Seifert-van Kampen theorem that we used in proving the Jordan separation theorem tells us something about the fundamental group of the space $X = U \cup V$ in the case where the intersection $U \cap V$ is path connected. In the next theorem, we examine what happens when $U \cap V$ is *not* path connected. This result will enable us to complete the proof of the Jordan curve theorem.

Theorem 63.1. *Let X be the union of two open sets U and V, such that $U \cap V$ can be written as the union of two disjoint open sets A and B. Assume that there is a path α in U from a point a of A to a point b of B, and that there is a path β in V from b to a. Let f be the loop $f = \alpha * \beta$.*

(a) *The path-homotopy class $[f]$ generates an infinite cyclic subgroup of $\pi_1(X, a)$.*

(b) If $\pi_1(X, a)$ is itself infinite cyclic, it is generated by $[f]$.[†]

(c) *Assume there is a path γ in U from a to the point a' of A, and that there is a path δ in V from a' to a. Let g be the loop $g = \gamma * \delta$. Then the subgroups of $\pi_1(X, a)$ generated by $[f]$ and $[g]$ intersect in the identity element alone.*

Proof.   The proof is in many ways an imitation of the proof in §54 that the fundamental group of the circle is infinite cyclic. As in that proof, the crucial step is to find an appropriate covering space E for the space X.

Step 1. (Construction of E). We construct E by pasting together copies of the subspaces U and V. Let us take countably many copies of U and countably many copies of V, all disjoint, say

$$U \times (2n) \quad \text{and} \quad V \times (2n + 1)$$

for all $n \in \mathbb{Z}$, where $\mathbb{Z}$ denotes the integers. Let Y denote the union of these spaces; Y is a subspace of $X \times \mathbb{Z}$. Now we form a new space E as a quotient space of Y by

---

[†]This result uses Theorem 54.6, and will be used only when we deal with winding numbers in §65.

identifying the points

$$x \times (2n) \quad \text{and} \quad x \times (2n - 1) \quad \text{for } x \in A$$

and by identifying the points

$$x \times (2n) \quad \text{and} \quad x \times (2n + 1) \quad \text{for } x \in B.$$

Let $\pi : Y \to E$ be the quotient map.

Now the map $\rho : Y \to X$ defined by $\rho(x \times m) = x$ induces a map $p : E \to X$; the map p is continuous because E has the quotient topology. The map p is also surjective. We shall show that p is a covering map. See Figure 63.1.

First let us show that the map π is an open map. Since Y is the union of the disjoint open sets $\{U \times (2n)\}$ and $\{V \times (2n + 1)\}$, it will suffice to show that $\pi|(U \times 2n)$ and $\pi|(V \times (2n + 1))$ are open maps. And this is easy. Take an open set in $U \times 2n$, for example; it will be of the form $W \times 2n$, where W is open in U. Then

$$\pi^{-1}(\pi(W \times 2n)) = [W \times 2n] \cup [(W \cap B) \times (2n + 1)]$$
$$\cup [(W \cap A) \times (2n - 1)],$$

which is the union of three open sets of Y and hence open in Y. By definition of the quotient topology, $\pi(W \times 2n)$ is open in E, as desired.

Now we prove that p is a covering map; we show that the open sets U and V are evenly covered by p. Consider U, for example. The set $p^{-1}(U)$ is the union of the disjoint sets $\pi(U \times 2n)$ for $n \in \mathbb{Z}$. Each of these sets is open in E because π is an open map. Let π_{2n} denote the restriction of π to the open set $U \times 2n$, mapping it onto $\pi(U \times 2n)$. It is a homeomorphism because it is bijective, continuous, and open. Then when restricted to $\pi(U \times 2n)$, the map p is just the composite of the two homeomorphisms

$$\pi(U \times 2n) \xrightarrow{\pi_{2n}^{-1}} U \times 2n \xrightarrow{\rho} U$$

and is thus a homeomorphism. Therefore, $p|\pi(U \times 2n)$ maps this set homeomorphically onto U, as desired.

Step 2. Now we define a family of liftings of the loop $f = \alpha * \beta$.

For each integer n, let e_n be the point $\pi(a \times 2n)$ of E. Then the points e_n are distinct, and they constitute the set $p^{-1}(a)$. We define a lifting $\tilde{f}_n$ of f that begins at e_n and ends at e_{n+1}.

Since α and β are paths in U and V, respectively, we can define

$$\tilde{\alpha}_n(s) = \pi(\alpha(s) \times 2n),$$
$$\tilde{\beta}_n(s) = \pi(\beta(s) \times (2n + 1));$$

then $\tilde{\alpha}_n$ and $\tilde{\beta}_n$ are liftings of α and β, respectively. (The case $n = 0$ is illustrated in Figure 63.1.) The product $\tilde{\alpha}_n * \tilde{\beta}_n$ is defined, since $\tilde{\alpha}_n$ ends at $\pi(b \times 2n)$ and $\tilde{\beta}_n$ begins at

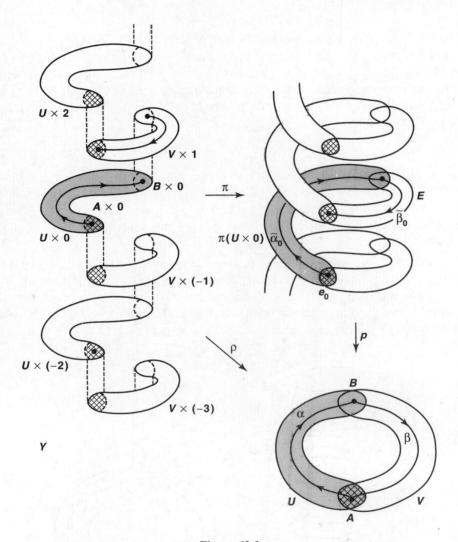

Figure 63.1

$\pi(b \times (2n+1))$. We set $\tilde{f}_n = \tilde{\alpha}_n * \tilde{\beta}_n$, and note that $\tilde{f}_n$ begins at $\tilde{\alpha}_n(0) = \pi(a \times 2n) = e_n$ and ends at $\tilde{\beta}_n(1) = \pi(a \times (2n+1)) = \pi(a \times (2n+2)) = e_{n+1}$.

Step 3. We show that $[f]$ generates an infinite cyclic subgroup of $\pi_1(X, a)$. It suffices to show that if m is a positive integer, then $[f]^m$ is not the identity element. But this is easy. For the product

$$\tilde{h} = \tilde{f}_0 * (\tilde{f}_1 * (\cdots * \tilde{f}_{m-1}))$$

is defined and is a lifting of the m-fold product

$$h = f * (f * (\cdots * f)).$$

Because $\tilde{h}$ begins at e_0 and ends at e_m, the class $[h] = [f]^m$ cannot be trivial.

Step 4. Now we show that if $\pi_1(X, a)$ is infinite cyclic, it is generated by $[f]$. Consider the lifting correspondence $\phi : \pi_1(X, a) \to p^{-1}(a)$. We showed in Step 3 that for each positive integer m, the correspondence ϕ carries $[f]^m$ to the point e_m of $p^{-1}(a)$. A similar argument shows that it carries $[f]^{-m}$ to e_{-m}. Thus ϕ is surjective. Now by Theorem 54.6, ϕ induces an injective map

$$\Phi : \pi_1(X, a)/H \longrightarrow p^{-1}(a),$$

where $H = p_*(\pi_1(E, e_0))$; the map Φ is surjective because ϕ is surjective. It follows that H is the trivial group, since the quotient of an infinite cyclic group by any non-trivial subgroup is finite. Then the lifting correspondence ϕ itself is bijective; since it maps the subgroup generated by $[f]$ *onto* $p^{-1}(a)$, this subgroup must equal all of $\pi_1(X, a)$.

Step 5. Now we prove (c). The picture in Figure 63.1 may mislead you into thinking that the element $[g]$ of $\pi_1(X, a)$ considered in part (c) is in fact trivial. But that figure is rather special. Figure 63.2 illustrates what can occur when A is itself the union of two disjoint nonempty open sets. In this case (which will be useful to us shortly) both $[f]$ and $[g]$ generate infinite cyclic subgroups of $\pi_1(X, a)$.

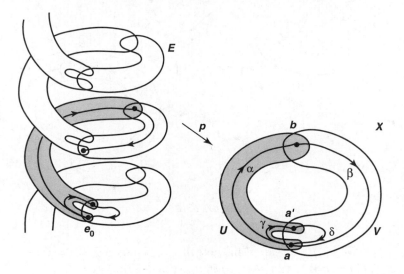

Figure 63.2

Given $g = \gamma * \delta$, we define a lifting of g to E as follows: Since γ is a path in U, we can define

$$\tilde{\gamma}(s) = \pi(\gamma(s) \times 0);$$

since δ is a path in V, we can define

$$\tilde{\delta}(s) = \pi(\delta(s) \times (-1)).$$

Then $\tilde{\gamma}$ and $\tilde{\delta}$ are liftings of γ and δ. The product $\tilde{\gamma} = \tilde{\gamma} * \tilde{\delta}$ is defined, since $\tilde{\gamma}$ ends at $\pi(a' \times 0)$ and $\tilde{\delta}$ begins at $\pi(a' \times (-1))$; and it is a lifting of g. Note that $\tilde{g}$ is a *loop* in E, for it begins and ends at $\pi(a \times 0) = \pi(a \times (-1)) = e_0$.

It follows that the subgroups generated by $[f]$ and $[g]$ have only the identity element in common. For the m-fold product of f with itself lifts to a path that begins at e_0 and ends at e_m, while every product of g with itself lifts to a path beginning and ending at e_0. Hence $[f]^m \neq [g]^k$ for every nonzero m and k. ∎

Theorem 63.2 (A nonseparation theorem).   *Let D be an arc in S^2. Then D does not separate S^2.*

Proof.   We give two proofs of this theorem. The first uses the results of the preceding section, and the second does not.

First proof. Because D is contractible, the identity map $i : D \to D$ is nulhomotopic. Hence if a and b are any two points of S^2 not in D, the inclusion $j : D \to S^2 - a - b$ is nulhomotopic. The Borsuk lemma then implies that a and b lie in the same component of $S^2 - D$.

Second Proof. Let us write D as the union of two arcs D_1 and D_2 that intersect in a single point d. Let a and b be points not in D. We show that if a and b can be joined by paths in $S^2 - D_1$ and in $S^2 - D_2$, then they can be joined by a path in $S^2 - D$. Figure 63.3 illustrates the fact that this assertion is not entirely trivial.

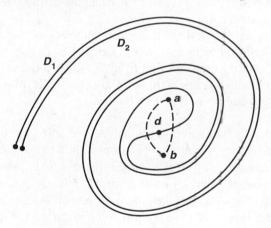

Figure 63.3

We suppose that a and b cannot be joined by a path in $S^2 - D$ and derive a contradiction. We apply Theorem 63.1. Let X be the space $S^2 - d$. Let U and V be the open sets

$$U = S^2 - D_1 \quad \text{and} \quad V = S^2 - D_2.$$

Then $X = U \cup V$, and $U \cap V = S^2 - D$. By hypothesis, a and b are points of $S^2 - D$ that cannot be joined by a path in $S^2 - D$. Therefore, $U \cap V$ is not path connected.

Let A be the path component of $U \cap V$ containing a; let B be the union of the other path components of $U \cap V$. Since $U \cap V$ is locally path connected (being open in S^2), the path components of $U \cap V$ are open; hence A and B are open in X. We are given that a and b can be joined by paths in $U = S^2 - D_1$ and $V = S^2 - D_2$. We conclude from Theorem 63.1 that $\pi_1(X, a)$ is not trivial. But $X = S^2 - d$, so its fundamental group *is* trivial.

Now we prove the theorem. Given the arc D and the points a and b of $S^2 - D$, we suppose that a and b cannot be joined by a path in $S^2 - D$ and derive a contradiction. Choose a homeomorphism $h : [0, 1] \rightarrow D$; let $D_1 = h([0, 1/2])$ and $D_2 = h([1/2, 1])$. The result of the preceding paragraph shows that since a and b cannot be joined by a path in $S^2 - D$, they cannot be joined by paths in both $S^2 - D_1$ and $S^2 - D_2$. To be definite, suppose that a and b cannot be joined by a path in $S^2 - D_1$.

Now repeat the argument, breaking D_1 up into two arcs $E_1 = h([0, 1/4])$ and $E_2 = h([1/4, 1/2])$. We conclude, as before, that a and b cannot be joined by paths in both $S^2 - E_1$ and $S^2 - E_2$.

Continue similarly. In this way we define a sequence

$$I \supset I_1 \supset I_2 \supset \cdots$$

of closed intervals such that I_n has length $(1/2)^n$ and such that for each n, the points a and b cannot be joined by a path in $S^2 - h(I_n)$. Compactness of the unit interval guarantees there is a point x in $\bigcap I_n$; since the lengths of the intervals converge to zero, there is only one such point.

Consider the space $S^2 - h(x)$. Since this space is homeomorphic to $\mathbb{R}^2$, the points a and b can be joined by a path α in $S^2 - h(x)$. Because $\alpha(I)$ is compact, it is closed, so some ϵ-neighborhood of $h(x)$ is disjoint from $\alpha(I)$. Then because h is continuous, there is some m such that $h(I_m)$ lies in this ϵ-neighborhood. It follows that α is a path in $S^2 - h(I_m)$ joining a and b, contrary to hypothesis. ∎

Both proofs of this theorem are interesting. As we noted in §62, the first generalizes to show that no compact contractible subspace of S^2 separates S^2. The second generalizes in another direction. Let us examine this second proof, and ask ourselves what properties of the sets D_1 and D_2 made it work? One readily sees that all that was needed was the fact that D_1 and D_2 were closed subsets of S^2 and that $S^2 - (D_1 \cap D_2)$ was simply connected. Hence we have the following result, which we shall use later:

Theorem 63.3 (A general nonseparation theorem). *Let D_1 and D_2 be closed subsets of S^2 such that $S^2 - D_1 \cap D_2$ is simply connected. If neither D_1 nor D_2 separates S^2, then $D_1 \cup D_2$ does not separate S^2.*

Now we prove the Jordan curve theorem.

Theorem 63.4 (The Jordan curve theorem). *Let C be a simple closed curve in S^2. Then C separates S^2 into precisely two components W_1 and W_2. Each of the sets W_1 and W_2 has C as its boundary; that is, $C = \overline{W_i} - W_i$ for $i = 1, 2$.*

Proof.   Step 1. We first prove that $S^2 - C$ has precisely two components. Write C as the union of two arcs C_1 and C_2 that intersect in a two-point set $\{p, q\}$. Let X be the space $S^2 - p - q$, and let U and V be the open sets

$$U = S^2 - C_1 \quad \text{and} \quad V = S^2 - C_2.$$

Then $X = U \cup V$, and $U \cap V = S^2 - C$. The space $U \cap V$ has at least two components, by the Jordan separation theorem.

We suppose that $U \cap V$ has more than two components and derive a contradiction. Let A_1 and A_2 be two of the components of $U \cap V$, and let B be the union of the others. Because $S^2 - C$ is locally connected, each of these sets is open. Let $a \in A_1$ and $a' \in A_2$ and $b \in B$. Because the arcs C_1 and C_2 do not separate S^2, there are paths α and γ in U from a to b and from a to a', respectively, and there are paths β and δ in V from b to a and from a' to a, respectively. Consider the loops $f = \alpha * \beta$ and $g = \gamma * \delta$. Writing $U \cap V$ as the union of the open sets $A_1 \cup A_2$ and B, we see that Theorem 63.1 implies that $[f]$ is a nontrivial element of $\pi_1(X, a)$. Writing $U \cap V$ as the union of the disjoint open sets A_1 and $A_2 \cup B$, we see that $[g]$ is also a nontrivial element of $\pi_1(X, a)$. Since $\pi_1(X, a)$ is infinite cyclic, we must have $[f]^m = [g]^k$ for some nonzero integers m and k. This result contradicts (c) of Theorem 63.1.

Step 2. Now we show that C is the common boundary of W_1 and W_2

Because S^2 is locally connected, each of the components W_1 and W_2 of $S^2 - C$ is open in S^2. In particular, neither contains a limit point of the other, so that both the sets $\overline{W}_1 - W_1$ and $\overline{W}_2 - W_2$ must be contained in C.

To prove the reverse inclusion, we show that if x is a point of C, every neighborhood U of x intersects the closed set $\overline{W}_1 - W_1$. It follows that x is in the set $\overline{W}_1 - W_1$.

So let U be a neighborhood of x. Because C is homeomorphic to the circle S^1, we can break C up into two arcs C_1 and C_2 that intersect in only their end points, such that C_1 is small enough that it lies inside U. See Figure 63.4.

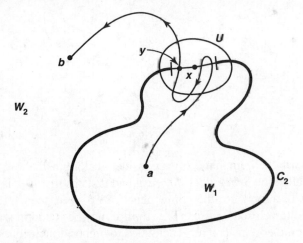

Figure 63.4

Let a and b be points of W_1 and W_2, respectively. Because C_2 does not separate S^2, we can find a path α in $S^2 - C_2$ joining a and b. The set $\alpha(I)$ must contain a point y of the set $\overline{W}_1 - W_1$, because otherwise $\alpha(I)$ would be a connected set lying in the union of the disjoint open sets W_1 and $S^2 - \overline{W}_1$, and intersecting each of them. The point y belongs to the closed curve C, since $(\overline{W}_1 - W_1) \subset C$. Because the path α does not intersect the arc C_2, the point y must therefore lie in the arc C_1, which in turn lies in the open set U. Thus, U intersects $\overline{W}_1 - W_1$ in the point y, as desired. ∎

Just as with the earlier theorems, we now ask ourselves what made the proof of this theorem work. Examining Step 1 of the proof, we see that all we used were the facts that C_1 and C_2 were closed connected sets, that $C_1 \cap C_2$ consisted of two points, and that neither C_1 nor C_2 separated S^2. The first two facts implied that $C_1 \cup C_2$ separated S^2 into at least two components; the third implied that there were *only* two components. Hence one has, with no further effort, the following result:

Theorem 63.5. *Let C_1 and C_2 be closed connected subsets of S^2 whose intersection consists of two points. If neither C_1 nor C_2 separates S^2, then $C_1 \cup C_2$ separates S^2 into precisely two components.*

EXAMPLE 1.   The second half of the Jordan curve theorem, to the effect that C is the common boundary of W_1 and W_2, may seem so obvious as hardly to require comment. But it depends crucially on the fact that C is homeomorphic to S^1.

For instance, consider the space indicated in Figure 63.5. It is the union of two arcs whose intersection consists of two points, so it separates S^2 into two components W_1 and W_2 just as the circle does, by Theorem 63.5. But C does not equal the common boundary of W_1 and W_2 in this case.

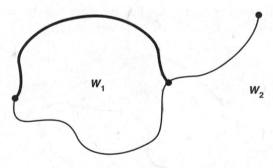

Figure 63.5

There is a fourth theorem that is often considered along with these three separation theorems. It is called the *Schoenflies theorem*, and it states that if C is a simple closed curve in S^2 and U and V are the components of $S^2 - C$, then $\overline{U}$ and $\overline{V}$ are each homeomorphic to the closed unit ball B^2. A proof may be found in [H-S].

The separation theorems can be generalized to higher dimensions as follows:

(1) Any subspace C of S^n homeomorphic to S^{n-1} separates S^n.

(2) No subspace A of S^n homeomorphic to $[0, 1]$ or to some ball B^m separates S^n.

(3) Any subspace C of S^n homeomorphic to S^{n-1} separates S^n into two components, of which C is the common boundary.

These theorems can be proved quite readily once one has studied singular homology groups in algebraic topology. (See [Mu], p. 202.) The Brouwer theorem on invariance of domain for $\mathbb{R}^n$ follows as a corollary.

The Schoenflies theorem, however, does not generalize to higher dimensions without some restrictions on the way the space C is imbedded in S^n. This is shown by the famous example of the "Alexander horned sphere," a homeomorphic image of S^2 in S^3, one of whose complementary domains is not simply connected! (See [H-Y], p. 176.)

The separation theorems can be generalized even further than this. The definitive theorem along these lines is the famous *Alexander-Pontryagin duality theorem*, a rather deep theorem of algebraic topology, which we shall not attempt to state here. (See [Mu].) It implies that if the closed subspace C separates S^n into k components, so does any subspace of S^n that is homeomorphic to C (or even homotopy equivalent to C). The separation theorems (1)–(3) are immediate corollaries.

Exercises

1. Let C_1 and C_2 be disjoint simple closed curves in S^2.
   (a) Show that $S^2 - C_1 - C_2$ has precisely three components. [*Hint:* If W_1 is the component of $S^2 - C_1$ disjoint from C_2, and if W_2 is the component of $S^2 - C_2$ disjoint from C_1, show that $\overline{W}_1 \cup \overline{W}_2$ does not separate S^2.]
   (b) Show that these three components have boundaries C_1 and C_2 and $C_1 \cup C_2$, respectively.

2. Let D be a closed connected subspace of S^2 that separates S^2 into n components.
   (a) If A is an arc in S^2 whose intersection with D consists of one of its end points, show that $D \cup A$ separates S^2 into n components.
   (b) If A is an arc in S^2 whose intersection with D consists of its end points, show that $D \cup A$ separates S^2 into $n + 1$ components.
   (c) If C is a simple closed curve in S^2 that intersects D in a single point, show $D \cup C$ separates S^2 into $n + 1$ components.

*3. (a) Let D be a subspace of S^2 homeomorphic to the topologist's sine curve $\bar{S}$. (See §24.) Show that D does not separate S^2. [*Hint:* Let $h : \bar{S} \to D$ be the homeomorphism. Given $0 < c < 1$, let $\bar{S}_c$ equal the intersection of $\bar{S}$ with the set $\{(x, y) \mid x \le c\}$. Show that given $a, b \in S^2 - D$, there is, for some value of c, a path in $S^2 - h(\bar{S}_c)$ from a to b. Conclude that there is a path in $S^2 - D$ from a to b.]
   (b) Let C be a subspace of S^2 homeomorphic to the closed topologist's sine curve. Show that C separates S^2 into precisely two components, of which C is the common boundary. [*Hint:* Let h be the homeomorphism of the closed topologist's sine curve with C. Let $C_0 = h(0 \times [-1, 1])$. Show first, using

the argument of Theorem 63.4, that each point of $C - C_0$ lies in the boundary of each component of $S^2 - C$.]

§64   Imbedding Graphs in the Plane

A (finite) ***linear graph*** G is a Hausdorff space that is written as the union of finitely many arcs, each pair of which intersect in at most a common end point. The arcs are called the ***edges*** of the graph, and the end points of the arcs are called the ***vertices*** of the graph.

Linear graphs are used in mathematics to model many real-life phenomena; however, we shall look at them simply as interesting spaces that in some sense are generalizations of simple closed curves.

Note that any graph is determined completely (up to homeomorphism) by listing its vertices and specifying which pairs of vertices have an edge joining them.

EXAMPLE 1.   If G contains exactly n vertices, and if for every pair of distinct vertices of G there is an edge of G joining them, then G is called the ***complete graph on n vertices*** and is denoted G_n. Several such graphs are pictured in Figure 64.1. Note that the first three of these graphs are pictured as subspaces of $\mathbb{R}^2$, but the fourth is pictured instead as a subspace of $\mathbb{R}^3$. A little experimentation will convince you that this graph *cannot* in fact be imbedded in $\mathbb{R}^2$. We shall prove this result shortly.

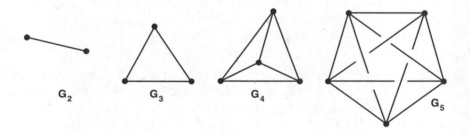

Figure 64.1

EXAMPLE 2.   Another interesting graph arises in considering the classical puzzle: "Given three houses, h_1, h_2, and h_3, and three utilities, g (for gas), w (for water), and e (for electricity), can you connect each utility to each house without letting any of the connecting lines cross?" Formulated mathematically, this is just the question whether the graph pictured in Figure 64.2, which is called the ***utilities graph***, can be imbedded in $\mathbb{R}^2$. Again, a little experimentation will convince you that it cannot, a fact that we shall prove shortly.

Definition.   A ***theta space*** X is a Hausdorff space that is written as the union of three arcs A, B, and C, each pair of which intersect precisely in their end points. (The space X is of course homeomorphic to the Greek letter theta.)

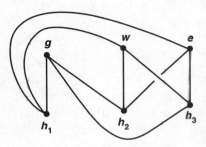

Figure 64.2

Note that as it stands, a theta space X is not a linear graph, for the arcs in question intersect in more than a common end point. One can write it as a graph, however, by breaking each of the arcs A, B, and C up into two arcs with an end point in common.

Lemma 64.1.   *Let X be a theta space that is a subspace of S^2; let A, B, and C be the arcs whose union is X. Then X separates S^2 into three components, whose boundaries are $A \cup B$, $B \cup C$, and $A \cup C$, respectively. The component having $A \cup B$ as its boundary equals one of the components of $S^2 - A \cup B$.*

Proof.   Let a and b be the end points of the arcs A, B, and C. Consider the simple closed curve $A \cup B$; it separates S^2 into two components U and U', each of which is open in S^2 and has boundary $A \cup B$. See Figure 64.3.

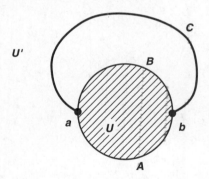

Figure 64.3

The space $C - a - b$ is connected, so it is contained in one of these components, say in U'. Then consider the two spaces $\bar{U} = U \cup A \cup B$ and C; each is connected. Neither separates S^2, for C is an arc, and the complement of $\bar{U}$ is the connected set U'. Since the intersection of these two sets consists of the two points a and b, their union separates S^2 into two components V and W, by Theorem 63.5. It follows that $S^2 - (A \cup B \cup C)$ is the union of the three disjoint connected sets U, V, and W; because they are open in S^2, they are the components of $S^2 - (A \cup B \cup C)$. The component U has $A \cup B$ as its boundary. Symmetry implies that the other two have $B \cup C$ and

$A \cup C$ as their boundaries. ∎

Theorem 64.2. *Let X be the utilities graph. Then X cannot be imbedded in the plane.*

Proof. If X can be imbedded in the plane, then it can be imbedded in S^2. So suppose X is a subspace of S^2. We derive a contradiction.

We use the notation of Example 2, where g, w, e, h_1, h_2, and h_3 are the vertices of X. Let A, B, and C be the following arcs contained in X:

$$A = gh_1w,$$
$$B = gh_2w,$$
$$C = gh_3w.$$

Each pair of these arcs intersect in their end points g and w alone; hence $Y = A \cup B \cup C$ is a theta space. The space Y separates S^2 into three components U, V, and W, whose boundaries are $A \cup B$, $B \cup C$, and $A \cup C$, respectively. See Figure 64.4.

Now the vertex e of X lies in one of these three components, so that the arcs eh_1 and eh_2 and eh_3 of X lie in the closure of that component. That component cannot be U, for $\bar{U}$ is contained in $U \cup A \cup B$, a set that does not contain the point h_3. Similarly, the component containing e cannot be V or W, because $\bar{V}$ does not contain h_1, and $\bar{W}$ does not contain h_2. Thus, we have reached a contradiction. ∎

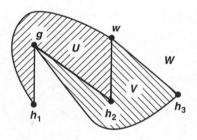

Figure 64.4

Lemma 64.3. *Let X be a subspace of S^2 that is a complete graph on four vertices a_1, a_2, a_3, and a_4. Then X separates S^2 into four components. The boundaries of these components are the sets X_1, X_2, X_3, and X_4, where X_i is the union of those edges of X that do not have a_i as a vertex.*

Proof. Let Y be the union of all the arcs of X different from the arc a_2a_4. Then we can write Y as a theta space by setting

$$A = a_1a_2a_3,$$
$$B = a_1a_3,$$
$$C = a_1a_4a_3.$$

See Figure 64.5. The arcs A, B, and C intersect in their end points a_1 and a_3 alone, and their union is Y.

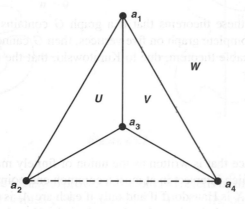

Figure 64.5

The space Y separates S^2 into three components U, V, and W, whose boundaries are $A \cup B$, $B \cup C$, and $A \cup C$, respectively. The space $a_2 a_4 - a_2 - a_4$, being connected, must lie in one of them. It cannot lie in U, because $A \cup B$ does not contain a_4. And it cannot lie in V because $B \cup C$ does not contain a_2. Hence it must lie in W.

Now $\bar{U} \cup \bar{V}$ is connected because $\bar{U}$ and $\bar{V}$ are connected and have nonempty intersection B. Furthermore, the set $\bar{U} \cup \bar{V}$ does not separate S^2, because its complement is W. Similarly, the arc $a_2 a_4$ is connected and does not separate S^2. And the sets $a_2 a_4$ and $\bar{U} \cup \bar{V}$ intersect in the points a_2 and a_4 alone. It follows from Theorem 63.5 that $a_2 a_4 \cup \bar{U} \cup \bar{V}$ separates S^2 into two components W_1 and W_2. Then $S^2 - Y$ is the union of the four disjoint connected sets U, V, W_1, and W_2. Since these sets are open, they are the components of $S^2 - Y$.

Now one of these components, namely U, has the graph $A \cup B = X_4$ as its boundary. Symmetry implies that the other three have X_1, X_2, and X_3 as their respective boundaries. ■

Theorem 64.4. *The complete graph on five vertices cannot be imbedded in the plane.*

Proof.   Suppose that G is a subspace of S^2 that is a complete graph on the five vertices a_1, a_2, a_3, a_4, and a_5. Let X be the union of those edges of G that do not have a_5 as a vertex; then X is a complete graph on four vertices. The space X separates S^2 into four components, whose respective boundaries are the graphs $X_1, \ldots, X_4$, where X_i consists of those edges of X that do not have a_i as a vertex. Now the point a_5 must lie in one of these four components. It follows that the connected space

$$a_1 a_5 \cup a_2 a_5 \cup a_3 a_5 \cup a_4 a_5,$$

which is the union of those edges of G that have a_5 as a vertex, must lie in the closure of this component. Then all the vertices $a_1, \ldots, a_4$ lie in the boundary of this component.

$j_* : \pi_1(C, x) \to \pi_1(X, x)$ is surjective, so that j_* must be an isomorphism (since the groups involved are infinite cyclic). See Figure 65.3.

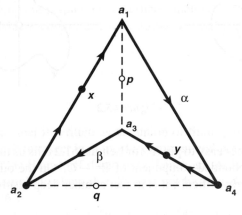

Figure 65.3

Let D_1 and D_2 be the arcs

$$D_1 = pa_3a_2q \quad \text{and} \quad D_2 = qa_4a_1p,$$

and let $U = S^2 - D_1$ and $V = S^2 - D_2$. See Figure 65.4. Then $X = U \cup V$, and $U \cap V$ equals $S^2 - D$, where D is the simple closed curve $D = D_1 \cup D_2$. Hence, $U \cap V$ has two components, by the Jordan curve theorem. Furthermore, since D equals the simple closed curve $a_1a_3a_2a_4a_1$, the result of (a) implies that the points x and y, which lie interior to the other two edges of the graph G, lie in different components of $S^2 - D$.

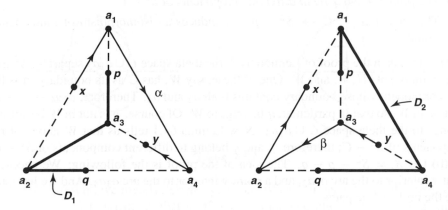

Figure 65.4

The hypotheses of Theorem 63.1 are thus satisfied. The path α is a path in U from x to y, while β is a path in V from y to x. Because the fundamental group of X

is infinite cyclic, the loop $\alpha * \beta$ represents a generator of this group.   ■

Now we prove our main theorem.

Theorem 65.2. *Let C be a simple closed curve in S^2; let p and q lie in different components of $S^2 - C$. Then the inclusion mapping $j : C \to S^2 - p - q$ induces an isomorphism of fundamental groups.*

Proof. The proof involves constructing a complete graph on four vertices that contains C as a subgraph.

Step 1. Let a, b, and c be three distinct points of $\mathbb{R}^2$. If A is an arc with end points points a and b, and if B is an arc with end points b and c, then there exists an arc contained in $A \cup B$ with end points a and c.

Choose paths $f : I \to A$ from a to b, and $g : I \to B$ from b to c, such that f and g are homeomorphisms. Let t_0 be a smallest point of I such that $f(t_0) \in B$; and let t_1 be the point of I such that $g(t_1) = f(t_0)$. Then the set $f([0, t_0]) \cup g([t_1, 1])$ is the required arc. (If $t_0 = 0$ or $t_1 = 1$, one of these sets consists of a single point.) See Figure 65.5.

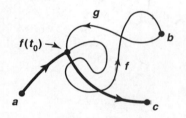

Figure 65.5

Step 2. We show that if U is an open set of $\mathbb{R}^2$, any two points of U that can be connected by a path in U are the end points of an arc lying in U.

If $x, y \in U$, set $x \sim y$ if $x = y$ or if there is an arc in U with end points x and y. The result of Step 1 shows that this is an equivalence relation. The equivalence classes are open, for if the ϵ-neighborhood of x lies in U, it consists of points equivalent to x. Since U is connected, there is only one such equivalence class.

Step 3. Let C be a simple closed curve in $\mathbb{R}^2$. We construct a subspace G of $\mathbb{R}^2$ that is a complete graph on four vertices $a_1, \ldots, a_4$ such that C equals the subgraph $a_1 a_2 a_3 a_4 a_1$.

For convenience, we assume that 0 lies in the bounded component of $\mathbb{R}^2 - C$. Consider the x-axis $\mathbb{R} \times 0$ in $\mathbb{R}^2$; let a_1 be the largest point on the negative x-axis that lies in C, and let a_3 be the smallest point on the positive x-axis that lies in C. Then the line segment $a_1 a_3$ lies in the closure of the bounded component of $\mathbb{R}^2 - C$.

Let us write C as the union of two arcs C_1 and C_2 with end points a_1 and a_3. Let a be a point of the unbounded component of $\mathbb{R}^2 - C$. Since C_1 and C_2 do not separate $\mathbb{R}^2$, we can choose paths $\alpha : I \to \mathbb{R}^2 - C_1$ and $\beta : I \to \mathbb{R}^2 - C_2$ from a

to $\mathbf{0}$; in view of Step 2, we may assume that α and β are injective. Let $a_2 = \alpha(t_0)$, where t_0 is the smallest number such that $\alpha(t_0) \in C$; then a_2 is a point interior to C_2. Similarly, let $a_4 = \beta(t_1)$, where t_1 is the smallest number such that $\beta(t_1) \in C$; then a_4 is an interior point of C_1. Then $\alpha([0, t_0])$ and $\beta([0, t_1])$ are arcs joining a to a_2 and a_4, respectively; by Step 2, their union contains an arc with end points a_2 and a_4; this arc intersects C only in these two points. This arc, along with the line segment $a_1 a_3$ and the curve C, forms the desired graph. See Figure 65.6.

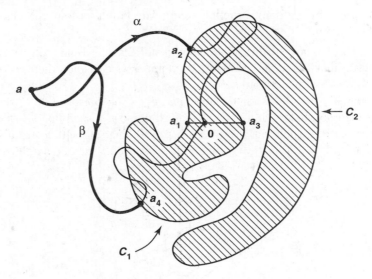

Figure 65.6

Step 4. It follows from the result of Step 3 and the preceding lemma that for *some* pair of points p, q lying in different components of $S^2 - C$, the inclusion $j : C \rightarrow S^2 - p - q$ induces an isomorphism of fundamental groups. To complete the proof, we need only show that the same holds for *any* pair p, q of points lying in different components of $S^2 - C$. For that purpose, it suffices to prove the following:

Let D be a simple closed curve in $\mathbb{R}^2$; suppose $\mathbf{0}$ lies in the bounded component of $\mathbb{R}^2 - D$. Let p be another point of this component. If inclusion $j : D \rightarrow \mathbb{R}^2 - \mathbf{0}$ induces an isomorphism of fundamental groups, then so does the inclusion $k : D \rightarrow \mathbb{R}^2 - p$.

Let $f : \mathbb{R}^2 - p \rightarrow \mathbb{R}^2 - \mathbf{0}$ be the homeomorphism $f(x) = x - p$. It suffices to show that the map

$$ D \xrightarrow{\ k\ } \mathbb{R}^2 - p \xrightarrow{\ f\ } \mathbb{R}^2 - \mathbf{0} $$

indices an isomorphism of fundamental groups. Let α be a path in $\mathbb{R}^2 - D$ from $\mathbf{0}$ to p, and let $F : D \times I \rightarrow \mathbb{R}^2 - \mathbf{0}$ be the map $F(x, t) = x - \alpha(t)$. Then F is a homotopy between j and $f \circ k$; since j induces an isomorphism, so does $f \circ k$. (See Corollary 58.5). ∎

This theorem is a special case of a rather deep theorem of algebraic topology, concerning the "linking number" of two disjoint subspaces of S^{m+n+1}, one homeomorphic to an m-sphere and the other homeomorphic to an n-sphere; it is related to the Alexander duality theorem. (See [Mu], p. 433.) The special case of our theorem is that of a 0-sphere (i.e., a two-point space) and a 1-sphere (i.e., a simple closed curve) in S^2.

§66   The Cauchy Integral Formula

One of the central theorems in the study of functions of a complex variable is the one concerning the Cauchy integral formula for analytic functions. For the classical version of this theorem, one needs to assume not only the Jordan curve theorem, but also the winding-number theorem of the last section. There is, however, a reformulation of the Cauchy integral theorem that avoids using these results; this version of the theorem, although it is rather less natural, is the one now commonly found in texts on the subject.

Since we have the Jordan curve theorem at our disposal, we shall set ourselves the task of deriving the Cauchy integral formula in its classical version from the reformulated version.

We begin by introducing the notion of "winding number" more formally.

Definition.   Let f be a loop in $\mathbb{R}^2$, and let a be a point not in the image of f. Set

$$g(s) = [f(s) - a]/\|f(s) - a\|;$$

then g is a loop in S^1. Let $p : \mathbb{R} \to S^1$ be the standard covering map, and let $\tilde{g}$ be a lifting of g to S^1. Because g is a loop, the difference $\tilde{g}(1) - \tilde{g}(0)$ is an integer. This integer is called the **winding number of f with respect to a**, and is denoted $n(f, a)$.

Note that $n(f, a)$ is independent of the choice of the lifting of g. For if $\tilde{g}$ is one lifting of g, then uniqueness of liftings implies that any other lifting of g has the form $\tilde{g}(s) + m$ for some integer m.

Definition.   Let $F : I \times I \to X$ be a continuous map such that $F(0, t) = F(1, t)$ for all t. Then for each t, the map $f_t(s) = F(s, t)$ is a loop in X. The map F is called a **free homotopy** between the loops f_0 and f_1. It is a homotopy of loops in which the base point of the loop is allowed to move during the homotopy.

Lemma 66.1.   *Let f be a loop in $\mathbb{R}^2 - a$.*

(a) *If $\bar{f}$ is the reverse of f, then $n(\bar{f}, a) = -n(f, a)$.*

(b) *If f is freely homotopic to f', through loops lying in $\mathbb{R}^2 - a$, then $n(f, a) = n(f', a)$.*

(c) *If a and b lie in the same component of $\mathbb{R}^2 - f(I)$, then $n(f, a) = n(f, b)$.*

Proof. (a) To compute $n(\bar{f}, a)$, one replace s by $1 - s$ throughout the definition. This has the effect of changing $\tilde{g}(1) - \tilde{g}(0)$ by a sign.

(b) Let F be a free homotopy between f and f'. Define $G : I \times I \to S^1$ by the equation

$$G(s, t) = [F(s, t) - a]/\|F(s, t) - a\|.$$

Let $\tilde{G}$ be a lifting of G to $\mathbb{R}$. Then $\tilde{G}(1, t) - \tilde{G}(0, t)$ is an integer for each t; being continuous, it is constant.

(c) Let α be a path in $\mathbb{R}^2 - f(I)$ from a to b. Note that by definition, $n(f, a) = n(f - a, \mathbf{0})$. Since $f(s) - \alpha(t)$ is a free homotopy in $\mathbb{R}^2 - \mathbf{0}$ between $f - a$ and $f - b$, our result follows. ∎

Definition. Let f be a loop in X. We call f a **simple loop** provided $f(s) = f(s')$ only if $s = s'$ or if one of the points s, s' is 0 and the other is 1. If f is a simple loop, its image set is a simple closed curve in X.

Theorem 66.2. *Let f be a simple loop in $\mathbb{R}^2$. If a lies in the unbounded component of $\mathbb{R}^2 - f(I)$, then $n(f, a) = 0$; while if a lies in the bounded component, $n(f, a) = \pm 1$.*

Proof. Since $n(f, a) = n(f - a, \mathbf{0})$, we may restrict ourselves to the case $a = \mathbf{0}$. Furthermore, we may assume that the base point of f lies on the positive x-axis. For one can gradually rotate $\mathbb{R}^2 - \mathbf{0}$ until the base point of f is such a point; this modifies f by a free homotopy, so it does not affect the conclusion of the theorem.

So let f be a simple loop in $X = \mathbb{R}^2 - \mathbf{0}$ based at a point x_0 of the positive x-axis. Let C be the simple closed curve $f(I)$. We show that if $\mathbf{0}$ lies in the bounded component of $\mathbb{R}^2 - C$, then $[f]$ generates $\pi_1(X, x_0)$, while if $\mathbf{0}$ lies in the unbounded component, $[f]$ is trivial.

The map f induces, *via* the standard quotient map $p : I \to S^1$, a homeomorphism $h : S^1 \to C$. The element $[p]$ generates the fundamental group of S^1, so $h_*[p]$ generates the fundamental group of C. If $\mathbf{0}$ lies in the bounded component of $\mathbb{R}^2 - C$, Theorem 65.2 tells us that $j_*h_*[p] = [f]$ generates the fundamental group of $\mathbb{R}^2 - \mathbf{0}$, where $j : C \to \mathbb{R}^2 - \mathbf{0}$ is the inclusion. On the other hand, if $\mathbf{0}$ lies in the unbounded component of $\mathbb{R}^2 - C$, then $j \circ h$ is nulhomotopic by Lemma 61.2, so that $[f]$ is trivial.

Now we show that if $[f]$ generates $\pi_1(X, x_0)$, then $n(f, \mathbf{0}) = \pm 1$, while if $[f]$ is trivial, $n(f, \mathbf{0}) = 0$. Since the retraction $x \to x/\|x\|$ of $\mathbb{R}^2 - \mathbf{0}$ onto S^1 induces an isomorphism of fundamental groups, the loop $g(s) = f(s)/\|f(s)\|$ represents a generator of $\pi_1(S^1, b_0)$ in the first case, and the identity element in the second case. If we examine the isomorphism $\phi : \pi_1(S^1, b_0) \to \mathbb{Z}$ constructed in the proof of Theorem 54.5, we see this means that when we lift g to a path $\tilde{g}$ in $\mathbb{R}$ beginning at 0, the path $\tilde{g}$ ends at ± 1 in the first case, and at 0 in the second. ∎

Definition. Let f be a simple loop in $\mathbb{R}^2$. We say f is a **counterclockwise** loop if $n(f, a) = +1$ for some a (and hence for every a) in the bounded component of

$\mathbb{R}^2 - f(I)$. We say it is a ***clockwise*** loop if $n(f, a) = -1$. The standard loop $p(s) = (\cos 2\pi s, \sin 2\pi s)$ is thus a counterclockwise loop.

Application to complex variables

We now relate winding numbers to complex line integrals.

Lemma 66.3.   *Let f be a piecewise-differentiable loop in the complex plane; let a be a point not in the image of f. Then*

$$n(f, a) = \frac{1}{2\pi i} \int_f \frac{dz}{z - a}.$$

This equation is often used as the *definition* of the winding number of f.

Proof.   The proof is a simple exercise in computation. Let $p : \mathbb{R} \to S^1$ be the standard covering map. Let $r(s) = \| f(s) - a \|$ and $g(s) = [f(s) - a]/r(s)$. Let $\tilde{g}$ be a lifting of g to $\mathbb{R}$. Set $\theta(s) = 2\pi \tilde{g}(s)$. Then $f(s) - a = r(s) \exp(i\theta(s))$, so that

$$\int_f \frac{dz}{z - a} = \int_0^1 [(r'e^{i\theta} + ir\theta'e^{i\theta})/re^{i\theta}]\, ds$$
$$= [\log r(s) + i\theta(s)]_0^1$$
$$= i[\theta(1) - \theta(0)]$$
$$= 2\pi i[\tilde{g}(1) - \tilde{g}(0)]. \qquad \blacksquare$$

Theorem 66.4 (Cauchy integral formula-classical version).   *Let C be a simple closed piecewise-differentiable curve in the complex plane. Let B be the bounded component of $\mathbb{R}^2 - C$. If $F(z)$ is analytic in an open set Ω that contains B and C, then for each point a of B,*

$$F(a) = \pm\frac{1}{2\pi i} \int_C \frac{F(z)}{z - a}\, dz.$$

The sign is $+$ if C is oriented counterclockwise, and $-$ otherwise.

Proof.   We derive this formula from the version of it proved in Ahlfors [A], which is the following:

Let F be analytic in a region Ω. Let f be a piecewise-differentiable loop in Ω. Assume that $n(f, b) = 0$ for each b not in Ω. If $a \in \Omega$ and a is not in the image of f, then

$$n(f, a) \cdot F(a) = \frac{1}{2\pi i} \int_f \frac{F(z)}{z - a}\, dz.$$

We apply this result to a piecewise-differentiable parametrization f of our simple closed curve C. The condition $n(f, b) = 0$ holds for each b not in Ω, since any such b lies in the unbounded component of $\mathbb{R}^2 - C$. Furthermore, $n(f, a) = \pm 1$ whenever a is in B, the sign depending on the orientation of C, by Theorem 66.2. The theorem follows.   ∎

Note that one cannot even state the classical version of the Cauchy integral theorem without knowing the Jordan curve theorem. To prove it requires even more, namely, knowledge of the winding number of a simple closed curve. It is of interest to note that this latter result can be proved (at least in the differentiable case) by an entirely different method, using the general version of *Green's Theorem*, proved in analysis. This proof is outlined in Exercise 2.

Exercises

1. Let f be a loop in $\mathbb{R}^2 - a$; let $g(s) = [f(s) - a]/\|f(s) - a\|$ The map g induces, *via* the standard quotient map $p : I \to S^1$, a continuous map $h : S^1 \to S^1$. Show that $n(f, a)$ equals the *degree* of h, as defined in Exercise 9 of §58.

2. This exercise assumes some familiarity with analysis on manifolds.

    Theorem. *Let C be a simple closed curve in $\mathbb{R}^2$ that is a smooth submanifold of $\mathbb{R}^2$; let $f : I \to C$ be a simple loop smoothly parameterizing C. If $\mathbf{0}$ is a point of the bounded component of $\mathbb{R}^2 - C$, then $n(f, \mathbf{0}) = \pm 1$.*

    Proof. Let U be the bounded component of $\mathbb{R}^2 - C$. Let B be a closed ϵ-ball centered at $\mathbf{0}$ that lies in U; let $S = \operatorname{Bd} B$. Let M equal the closure of $U - B$.

    (a) Show M is a smooth 2-manifold with boundary $C \cup S$.

    (b) Apply Green's theorem to show that $\int_C dz/z = \pm \int_S dz/z$, the sign depending on the orientations of S and C. [*Hint:* Set $P = -y/(x^2 + y^2)$ and $Q = x/(x^2 + y^2)$.]

    (c) Show that the second integral equals $\pm 2\pi i$.

Chapter 11

The Seifert-van Kampen Theorem

§67   Direct Sums of Abelian Groups

In this section, we shall consider only groups that are abelian. As is usual, we shall write such groups additively. Then 0 denotes the identity element of the group, $-x$ denotes the inverse of x, and nx denotes the n-fold sum $x + \cdots + x$.

Suppose G is an abelian group, and $\{G_\alpha\}_{\alpha \in J}$ is an indexed family of subgroups of G. We say that the groups G_α **generate** G if every element x of G can be written as a finite sum of elements of the groups G_α. Since G is abelian, we can always rearrange such a sum to group together terms that belong to a single G_α; hence we can always write x in the form

$$x = x_{\alpha_1} + \cdots + x_{\alpha_n},$$

where the indices α_i are distinct. In this case, we often write x as the formal sum $x = \sum_{\alpha \in J} x_\alpha$, where it is understood that $x_\alpha = 0$ if α is not one of the indices $\alpha_1, \ldots, \alpha_n$.

If the groups G_α generate G, we often say that G is the **sum** of the groups G_α, writing $G = \sum_{\alpha \in J} G_\alpha$ in general, or $G = G_1 + \cdots + G_n$ in the case of the finite index set $\{1, \ldots, n\}$.

Now suppose that the groups G_α generate G, and that for each $x \in G$, the expression $x = \sum x_\alpha$ for x is *unique*. That is, suppose that for each $x \in G$, there is only one

J-tuple $(x_\alpha)_{\alpha \in J}$ with $x_\alpha = 0$ for all but finitely many α such that $x = \sum x_\alpha$. Then G is said to be the **direct sum** of the groups G_α, and we write

$$G = \bigoplus_{\alpha \in J} G_\alpha,$$

or in the finite case, $G = G_1 \oplus \cdots \oplus G_n$.

    EXAMPLE 1.   The cartesian product $\mathbb{R}^\omega$ is an abelian group under the operation of coordinate-wise addition. The set G_n consisting of those tuples (x_i) such that $x_i = 0$ for $i \neq n$ is a subgroup isomorphic to $\mathbb{R}$. The groups G_n generate the subgroup $\mathbb{R}^\infty$ of $\mathbb{R}^\omega$; indeed, $\mathbb{R}^\infty$ is their direct sum.

    A useful characterization of direct sums is given in the following lemma; we call it the **extension condition** for direct sums:

Lemma 67.1.   *Let G be an abelian group; let $\{G_\alpha\}$ be a family of subgroups of G. If G is the direct sum of the groups G_α, then G satisfies the following condition:*

(∗)   *Given any abelian group H and any family of homomorphisms $h_\alpha : G_\alpha \to H$, there exists a homomorphism $h : G \to H$ whose restriction to G_α equals h_α, for each α.*

Furthermore, h is unique. Conversely, if the groups G_α generate G and the extension condition (∗) holds, then G is the direct sum of the groups G_α.

Proof.   We show first that if G has the stated extension property, then G is the direct sum of the G_α. Suppose $x = \sum x_\alpha = \sum y_\alpha$; we show that for any particular index β, we have $x_\beta = y_\beta$. Let H denote the group G_β; and let $h_\alpha : G_\alpha \to H$ be the trivial homomorphism for $\alpha \neq \beta$, and the identity homomorphism for $\alpha = \beta$. Let $h : G \to H$ be the hypothesized extension of the homomorphisms h_α. Then

$$h(x) = \sum h_\alpha(x_\alpha) = x_\beta,$$
$$h(x) = \sum h_\alpha(y_\alpha) = y_\beta,$$

so that $x_\beta = y_\beta$.

    Now we show that if G is the direct sum of the G_α, then the extension condition holds. Given homomorphisms h_α, we define $h(x)$ as follows: If $x = \sum x_\alpha$, set $h(x) = \sum h_\alpha(x_\alpha)$. Because this sum is finite, it makes sense; because the expression for x is unique, h is well-defined. One checks readily that h is the desired homomorphism. Uniqueness follows by noting that h *must* satisfy this equation if it is a homomorphism that equals h_α on G_α for each α.   ∎

    This lemma makes a number of results about direct sums quite easy to prove:

Corollary 67.2.   *Let $G = G_1 \oplus G_2$. Suppose G_1 is the direct sum of subgroups H_α for $\alpha \in J$, and G_2 is the direct sum of subgroups H_β for $\beta \in K$, where the index sets J and K are disjoint. Then G is the direct sum of the subgroups H_γ, for $\gamma \in J \cup K$.*

Proof. If $h_\alpha : H_\alpha \to H$ and $h_\beta : H_\beta \to H$ are families of homomorphisms, they extend to homomorphisms $h_1 : G_1 \to H$ and $h_2 : G_2 \to H$ by the preceding lemma. Then h_1 and h_2 extend to a homomorphism $h : G \to H$. ∎

This corollary implies, for example, that

$$(G_1 \oplus G_2) \oplus G_3 = G_1 \oplus G_2 \oplus G_3 = G_1 \oplus (G_2 \oplus G_3).$$

Corollary 67.3. *If $G = G_1 \oplus G_2$, then G/G_2 is isomorphic to G_1.*

Proof. Let $H = G_1$, let $h_1 : G_1 \to H$ be the identity homomorphism, and let $h_2 : G_2 \to H$ be the trivial homomorphism. Let $h : G \to H$ be their extension to G. Then h is surjective with kernel G_2. ∎

In many situations, one is given a family of abelian groups $\{G_\alpha\}$ and one wishes to find a group G that contains subgroups G'_α isomorphic to the groups G_α, such that G is the direct sum of these subgroups. This can in fact always be done; it leads to a notion called the *external direct sum.*

Definition. Let $\{G_\alpha\}_{\alpha \in J}$ be an indexed family of abelian groups. Suppose that G is an abelian group, and that $i_\alpha : G_\alpha \to G$ is a family of monomorphisms, such that G is the direct sum of the groups $i_\alpha(G_\alpha)$. Then we say that G is the *external direct sum* of the groups G_α, relative to the monomorphisms i_α.

The group G is not unique, of course; we show later that it is unique up to isomorphism. Here is one way of constructing G:

Theorem 67.4. *Given a family of abelian groups $\{G_\alpha\}_{\alpha \in J}$, there exists an abelian group G and a family of monomorphisms $i_\alpha : G_\alpha \to G$ such that G is the direct sum of the groups $i_\alpha(G_\alpha)$.*

Proof. Consider first the cartesian product

$$\prod_{\alpha \in J} G_\alpha;$$

it is an abelian group if we add two J-tuples by adding them coordinate-wise. Let G denote the subgroup of the cartesian product consisting of those tuples $(x_\alpha)_{\alpha \in J}$ such that $x_\alpha = 0_\alpha$, the identity element of G_α, for all but finitely many values of α. Given an index β, define $i_\beta : G_\beta \to G$ by letting $i_\beta(x)$ be the tuple that has x as its βth coordinate and 0_α as its αth coordinate for all $\alpha \neq \beta$. It is immediate that i_β is a monomorphism. It is also immediate that since each element $\mathbf{x}$ of G has only finitely many nonzero coordinates, $\mathbf{x}$ can be written uniquely as a finite sum of elements from the groups $i_\beta(G_\beta)$. ∎

The extension condition that characterizes ordinary direct sums translates immediately into an extension condition for external direct sums:

Lemma 67.5. *Let $\{G_\alpha\}_{\alpha \in J}$ be an indexed family of abelian groups; let G be an abelian group; let $i_\alpha : G_\alpha \to G$ be a family of homomorphisms. If each i_α is a monomorphism and G is the direct sum of the groups $i_\alpha(G_\alpha)$, then G satisfies the following extension condition:*

(∗)　　*Given any abelian group H and any family of homomorphisms $h_\alpha : G_\alpha \to H$, there exists a homomorphism $h : G \to H$ such that $h \circ i_\alpha = h_\alpha$ for each α.*

Furthermore, h is unique. Conversely, suppose the groups $i_\alpha(G_\alpha)$ generate G and the extension condition (∗) holds. Then each i_α is a monomorphism, and G is the direct sum of the groups $i_\alpha(G_\alpha)$.

Proof. The only part that requires proof is the statement that if the extension condition holds, then each i_α is a monomorphism. That is proved as follows. Given an index β, set $H = G_\beta$ and let $h_\alpha : G_\alpha \to H$ be the identity homomorphism if $\alpha = \beta$, and the trivial homomorphism if $\alpha \neq \beta$. Let $h : G \to H$ be the hypothesized extension. Then in particular, $h \circ i_\beta = h_\beta$; it follows that i_β is injective. ∎

An immediate consequence is a uniqueness theorem for direct sums:

Theorem 67.6 (Uniqueness of direct sums). *Let $\{G_\alpha\}_{\alpha \in J}$ be a family of abelian groups. Suppose G and G' are abelian groups and $i_\alpha : G_\alpha \to G$ and $i'_\alpha : G_\alpha \to G'$ are families of monomorphisms, such that G is the direct sum of the groups $i_\alpha(G_\alpha)$ and G' is the direct sum of the groups $i'_\alpha(G_\alpha)$. Then there is a unique isomorphism $\phi : G \to G'$ such that $\phi \circ i_\alpha = i'_\alpha$ for each α.*

Proof. We apply the preceding lemma (four times!). Since G is the external direct sum of the G_α and $\{i'_\alpha\}$ is a family of homomorphisms, there exists a unique homomorphism $\phi : G \to G'$ such that $\phi \circ i_\alpha = i'_\alpha$ for each α. Similarly, since G' is the external direct sum of the G_α and $\{i_\alpha\}$ is a family of homomorphisms, there exists a unique homomorphism $\psi : G' \to G$ such that $\psi \circ i'_\alpha = i_\alpha$ for each α. Now $\psi \circ \phi : G \to G$ has the property that $\psi \circ \phi \circ i_\alpha = i_\alpha$ for each α; since the identity map of G has the same property, the uniqueness part of the lemma shows that $\psi \circ \phi$ must equal the identity map of G. Similarly, $\phi \circ \psi$ must equal the identity map of G'. ∎

If G is the external direct sum of the groups G_α, relative to the monomorphisms i_α, we sometimes abuse notation and write $G = \bigoplus G_\alpha$, even though the groups G_α are not subgroups of G. That is, we identify each group G_α with its image under i_α, and treat G as an ordinary direct sum rather than an external direct sum. In each case, the context will make the meaning clear.

Now we discuss free abelian groups.

Definition.   Let G be an abelian group and let $\{a_\alpha\}$ be an indexed family of elements of G; let G_α be the subgroup of G generated by a_α. If the groups G_α generate G, we also say that the *elements* a_α generate G. If each group G_α is infinite cyclic, and if G is the *direct* sum of the groups G_α, then G is said to be a *free abelian group* having the elements $\{a_\alpha\}$ as a *basis*.

The extension condition for direct sums implies the following extension condition for free abelian groups:

Lemma 67.7.   *Let G be an abelian group; let $\{a_\alpha\}_{\alpha \in J}$ be a family of elements of G that generates G. Then G is a free abelian group with basis $\{a_\alpha\}$ if and only if for any abelian group H and any family $\{y_\alpha\}$ of elements of H, there is a homomorphism h of G into H such that $h(a_\alpha) = y_\alpha$ for each α. In such case, h is unique.*

Proof.   Let G_α denote the subgroup of G generated by a_α. Suppose first that the extension property holds. We show first that each group G_α is infinite cyclic. Suppose that for some index β, the element a_β generates a finite cyclic subgroup of G. Then if we set $H = \mathbb{Z}$, there is no homomorphism $h : G \to H$ that maps each a_α to the number 1. For a_β has finite order and 1 does not! To show that G is the direct sum of the groups G_α, we merely apply Lemma 67.1.

Conversely, if G is free abelian with basis $\{a_\alpha\}$, then given the elements $\{y_\alpha\}$ of H, there are homomorphisms $h_\alpha : G_\alpha \to H$ such that $h_\alpha(a_\alpha) = y_\alpha$ (because G_α is infinite cyclic). Then Lemma 67.1 applies.   ∎

Theorem 67.8.   *If G is a free abelian group with basis $\{a_1, \ldots, a_n\}$, then n is uniquely determined by G.*

Proof.   The group G is isomorphic to the n-fold product $\mathbb{Z} \times \cdots \times \mathbb{Z}$; the subgroup $2G$ corresponds to the product $(2\mathbb{Z}) \times \cdots \times (2\mathbb{Z})$. Then the quotient group $G/2G$ is in bijective correspondence with the set $(\mathbb{Z}/2\mathbb{Z}) \times \cdots \times (\mathbb{Z}/2\mathbb{Z})$, so that $G/2G$ has cardinality 2^n. Thus n is uniquely determined by G.   ∎

If G is a free abelian group with a finite basis, the number of elements in a basis for G is called the *rank* of G.

Exercises

1. Suppose that $G = \sum G_\alpha$. Show this sum is direct if and only if the equation
$$x_{\alpha_1} + \cdots + x_{\alpha_n} = 0$$
implies that each x_{α_i} equals 0. (Here $x_{\alpha_i} \in G_{\alpha_i}$ and the indices α_i are distinct.)

2. Show that if G_1 is a subgroup of G, there may be no subgroup G_2 of G such that $G = G_1 \oplus G_2$. [*Hint:* Set $G = \mathbb{Z}$ and $G_1 = 2\mathbb{Z}$.]

3. If G is free abelian with basis $\{x, y\}$, show that $\{2x + 3y, x - y\}$ is also a basis for G.

4. The *order* of an element a of an abelian group G is the smallest positive integer m such that $ma = 0$, if such exists; otherwise, the order of a is said to be infinite. The order of a thus equals the order of the subgroup generated by a.

   (a) Show the elements of finite order in G form a subgroup of G, called its *torsion subgroup*.

   (b) Show that if G is free abelian, it has no elements of finite order.

   (c) Show the additive group of rationals has no elements of finite order, but is not free abelian. [*Hint:* If $\{a_\alpha\}$ is a basis, express $\frac{1}{2}a_\alpha$ in terms of this basis.]

5. Give an example of a free abelian group G of rank n having a subgroup H of rank n for which $H \neq G$.

6. Prove the following:

   Theorem. *If A is a free abelian group of rank n, then any subgroup B of A is a free abelian group of rank at most n.*

   Proof. We can assume $A = \mathbb{Z}^n$, the n-fold cartesian product of $\mathbb{Z}$ with itself. Let $\pi_i : \mathbb{Z}^n \to \mathbb{Z}$ be projection on the ith coordinate. Given $m \leq n$, let B_m consist of all elements $\mathbf{x}$ of B such that $\pi_i(\mathbf{x}) = 0$ for $i > m$. Then B_m is a subgroup of B.

   Consider the subgroup $\pi_m(B_m)$ of $\mathbb{Z}$. If this subgroup is nontrivial, choose $\mathbf{x}_m \in B_m$ so that $\pi_m(\mathbf{x}_m)$ is a generator of this subgroup. Otherwise, set $\mathbf{x}_m = \mathbf{0}$.

   (a) Show $\{\mathbf{x}_1, \ldots, \mathbf{x}_m\}$ generates B_m, for each m.

   (b) Show the nonzero elements of $\{\mathbf{x}_1, \ldots, \mathbf{x}_m\}$ form a basis for B_m, for each m.

   (c) Show that $B_n = B$ is free abelian with rank at most n.

§68   Free Products of Groups

We now consider groups G that are not necessarily abelian. In this case, we write G multiplicatively. We denote the identity element of G by 1, and the inverse of the element x by x^{-1}. The symbol x^n denotes the n-fold product of x with itself, x^{-n} denotes the n-fold product of x^{-1} with itself, and x^0 denotes 1.

In this section, we study a concept that plays a role for arbitrary groups similar to that played by the direct sum for abelian groups. It is called the *free product* of groups.

Let G be a group. If $\{G_\alpha\}_{\alpha \in J}$ is a family of subgroups of G, we say (as before) that these groups *generate* G if every element x of G can be written as a finite product of elements of the groups G_α. This means that there is a finite sequence $(x_1, \ldots, x_n)$ of elements of the groups G_α such that $x = x_1 \cdots x_n$. Such a sequence is called a *word* (of length n) in the groups G_α; it is said to *represent* the element x of G.

Note that because we lack commutativity, we cannot rearrange the factors in the expression for x so as to group together factors that belong to a single one of the groups G_α. However, if x_i and x_{i+1} both belong to the same group G_α, we *can* group them together, thereby obtaining the word

$$(x_1, \ldots, x_{i-1}, x_i x_{i+1}, x_{i+2}, \ldots, x_n),$$

of length $n - 1$, which also represents x. Furthermore, if any x_i equals 1, we can delete x_i from the sequence, again obtaining a shorter word that represents x.

Applying these reduction operations repeatedly, one can in general obtain a word representing x of the form $(y_1, \ldots, y_m)$, where no group G_α contains both y_i and y_{i+1}, and where $y_i \neq 1$ for all i. Such a word is called a ***reduced word***. This discussion does not apply, however, if x is the identity element of G. For in that case, one might represent x by a word such as (a, a^{-1}), which reduces successively to the word (aa^{-1}) of length one, and then disappears altogether! Accordingly, we make the convention that the empty set is considered to be a reduced word (of length zero) that represents the identity element of G. With this convention, it is true that if the groups G_α generate G, then every element of G can be represented by a reduced word in the elements of the groups G_α.

Note that if $(x_1, \ldots, x_n)$ and $(y_1, \ldots, y_m)$ are words representing x and y, respectively, then $(x_1, \ldots, x_n, y_1, \ldots, y_m)$ is a word representing xy. Even if the first two words are reduced words, however, the third will not be a reduced word unless none of the groups G_α contains both x_n and y_1.

Definition. Let G be a group, let $\{G_\alpha\}_{\alpha \in J}$ be a family of subgroups of G that generates G. Suppose that $G_\alpha \cap G_\beta$ consists of the identity element alone whenever $\alpha \neq \beta$. We say that G is the ***free product*** of the groups G_α if for each $x \in G$, there is only one reduced word in the groups G_α that represents x. In this case, we write

$$G = \prod_{\alpha \in J}^{*} G_\alpha,$$

or in the finite case, $G = G_1 * \cdots * G_n$.

Let G be the free product of the groups G_α, and let $(x_1, \ldots, x_n)$ be a word in the groups G_α satisfying the condition $x_i \neq 1$ for all i. Then, for each i, there is a unique index α_i such that $x_i \in G_{\alpha_i}$; to say the word is a reduced word is to say simply that $\alpha_i \neq \alpha_{i+1}$ for each i.

Suppose the groups G_α generate G, where $G_\alpha \cap G_\beta = \{1\}$ for $\alpha \neq \beta$. In order for G to be the free product of these groups, it suffices to know that the representation of 1 by the empty word is unique. For suppose this weaker condition holds, and suppose that $(x_1, \ldots, x_n)$ and $(y_1, \ldots, y_m)$ are two reduced words that represent the same element x of G. Let α_i and β_i be the indices such that $x_i \in G_{\alpha_i}$ and $y_i \in G_{\beta_i}$. Since

$$x_1 \cdots x_n = x = y_1 \cdots y_m,$$

the word

$$(y_m^{-1}, \ldots, y_1^{-1}, x_1, \ldots, x_n)$$

is not the identity element of G_{α_i}. We define the empty set to be the unique reduced word of length zero. Note that we are not given a group G that contains all the G_α as subgroups, so we cannot speak of a word "representing" an element of G.

Let W denote the set of all reduced words in the elements of the groups G_α. Let $P(W)$ denote the set of all bijective functions $\pi : W \to W$. Then $P(W)$ is itself a group, with composition of functions as the group operation. We shall obtain our desired group G as a subgroup of $P(W)$.

Step 1. For each index α and each $x \in G_\alpha$, we define a set map $\pi_x : W \to W$. It will satisfy the following conditions:

(1) If $x = 1_\alpha$, the identity element of G_α, then π_x is the identity map of W.

(2) If $x, y \in G_\alpha$ and $z = xy$, then $\pi_z = \pi_x \circ \pi_y$.

We proceed as follows: Let $x \in G_\alpha$. For notational purposes, let $w = (x_1, \ldots, x_n)$ denote the general nonempty element of W, and let α_1 denote the index such that $x_1 \in G_{\alpha_1}$. If $x \neq 1_\alpha$, define π_x as follows:

(i) $\qquad \pi_x(\varnothing) = (x)$,

(ii) $\qquad \pi_x(w) = (x, x_1, \ldots, x_n)$ $\qquad$ if $\alpha_1 \neq \alpha$,

(iii) $\qquad \pi_x(w) = (xx_1, \ldots, x_n)$ $\qquad$ if $\alpha_1 = \alpha$ and $x_1 \neq x^{-1}$,

(iv) $\qquad \pi_x(w) = (x_2, \ldots, x_n)$ $\qquad$ if $\alpha_1 = \alpha$ and $x_1 = x^{-1}$.

If $x = 1_\alpha$, define π_x to be the identity map of W.

Note that the value of π_x is in each case a reduced word, that is, an element of W. In cases (i) and (ii), the action of π_x increases the length of the word; in case (iii) it leaves the length unchanged, and in case (iv) it reduces the length of the word. When case (iv) applies to a word w of length one, it maps w to the empty word.

Step 2. We show that if $x, y \in G_\alpha$ and $z = xy$, then $\pi_z = \pi_x \circ \pi_y$.

The result is trivial if either x or y equals 1_α, since in that case π_x or π_y is the identity map. So let us assume henceforth that $x \neq 1_\alpha$ and $y \neq 1_\alpha$. We compute the values of π_z and of $\pi_x \circ \pi_y$ on the reduced word w. There are four cases to consider.

(i) Suppose w is the empty word. We have $\pi_y(\varnothing) = (y)$. If $z = 1_\alpha$, then $y = x^{-1}$ and $\pi_x \pi_y(\varnothing) = \varnothing$ by (iv), while $\pi_z(\varnothing)$ equals the same thing because π_z is the identity map. If $z \neq 1_\alpha$, then

$$\pi_x \pi_y(\varnothing) = (xy) = (z) = \pi_z(\varnothing).$$

In the remaining cases, we assume $w = (x_1 \ldots, x_n)$, with $x_1 \in G_{\alpha_1}$.

(ii) Suppose $\alpha \neq \alpha_1$. Then $\pi_y(w) = (y, x_1, \ldots, x_n)$. If $z = 1_\alpha$, then $y = x^{-1}$ and $\pi_x \pi_y(w) = (x_1, \ldots, x_n)$ by (iv), while $\pi_z(w)$ equals the same because π_z is the identity map. If $z \neq 1_\alpha$, then

$$\pi_x \pi_y(w) = (xy, x_1, \ldots, x_n)$$
$$= (z, x_1, \ldots, x_n) = \pi_z(w).$$

(iii) Suppose $\alpha = \alpha_1$ and $yx_1 \neq 1_\alpha$. Then $\pi_y(w) = (yx_1, x_2, \ldots, x_n)$. If $xyx_1 = 1_\alpha$, then $\pi_x \pi_y(w) = (x_2, \ldots, x_n)$, while $\pi_z(w)$ equals the same thing because $zx_1 = xyx_1 = 1_\alpha$. If $xyx_1 \neq 1_\alpha$, then

$$\pi_x \pi_y(w) = (xyx_1, x_2, \ldots, x_n)$$
$$= (zx_1, x_2, \ldots, x_n) = \pi_z(w).$$

(iv) Finally, suppose $\alpha = \alpha_1$ and $yx_1 = 1_\alpha$. Then $\pi_y(w) = (x_2, \ldots, x_n)$, which is empty if $n = 1$. We compute

$$\pi_x \pi_y(w) = (x, x_2, \ldots, x_n)$$
$$= (x(yx_1), x_2, \ldots, x_n)$$
$$= (zx_1, x_2, \ldots, x_n) = \pi_z(w).$$

Step 3. The map π_x is an element of $p(W)$, and the map $i_\alpha : G_\alpha \to P(W)$ defined by $i_\alpha(x) = \pi_x$ is a monomorphism.

To show that π_x is bijective, we note that if $y = x^{-1}$, then conditions (1) and (2) imply that $\pi_y \circ \pi_x$ and $\pi_x \circ \pi_y$ equal the identity map of W. Hence π_x belongs to $P(W)$. The fact that i_α is a homomorphism is a consequence of condition (2). To show that i_α is a monomorphism, we note that if $x \neq 1_\alpha$, then $\pi_x(\varnothing) = (x)$, so that π_x is not the identity map of W.

Step 4. Let G be the subgroup of $P(W)$ generated by the groups $G'_\alpha = i_\alpha(G_\alpha)$. We show that G is the free product of the groups G'_α.

First, we show that $G'_\alpha \cap G'_\beta$ consists of the identity alone if $\alpha \neq \beta$. Let $x \in G_\alpha$ and $y \in G_\beta$; we suppose that neither π_x nor π_y is the identity map of W and show that $\pi_x \neq \pi_y$. But this is easy, for $\pi_x(\varnothing) = (x)$ and $\pi_y(\varnothing) = (y)$, and these are different words.

Second, we show that no nonempty reduced word

$$w' = (\pi_{x_1}, \ldots, \pi_{x_n})$$

in the groups G'_α represents the identity element of G. Let α_i be the index such that $x_i \in G_{\alpha_i}$; then $\alpha_i \neq \alpha_{i+1}$ and $x_i \neq 1_{\alpha_i}$ for each i. We compute

$$\pi_{x_1}(\pi_{x_2}(\cdots (\pi_{x_n}(\varnothing)))) = (x_1, \ldots, x_n),$$

so the element of G represented by w' is not the identity element of $P(W)$.   ∎

Although this proof of the existence of free products is certainly correct, it has the disadvantage that it doesn't provide us with a convenient way of thinking about the elements of the free product. For many purposes this doesn't matter, for the extension condition is the crucial property that is used in the applications. Nevertheless, one would be more comfortable having a more concrete model for the free product.

For the external direct sum, one had such a model. The external direct sum of the abelian groups G_α consisted of those elements (x_α) of the cartesian product $\prod G_\alpha$

carries N_1 to the identity element, so that it induces a homomorphism

$$i_1 : G_1/N_1 \longrightarrow (G_1 * G_2)/N.$$

Similarly, the composite of the inclusion and projection homomorphisms induces a homomorphism

$$i_2 : G_2/N_2 \longrightarrow (G_1 * G_2)/N.$$

We show that the extension condition of Lemma 68.5 holds with respect to i_1 and i_2; it follows that i_1 and i_2 are monomorphisms and that $(G_1 * G_2)/N$ is the external free product of G_1/N_1 and G_2/N_2 relative to these monomorphisms.

So let $h_1 : G_1/N_1 \to H$ and $h_2 : G_2/N_2 \to H$ be arbitrary homomorphisms. The extension condition for $G_1 * G_2$ implies that there is a homomorphism of $G_1 * G_2$ into H that equals the composite

$$G_i \longrightarrow G_i/N_i \longrightarrow H$$

of the projection map and h_i on G_i, for $i = 1, 2$. This homomorphism carries the elements of N_1 and N_2 to the identity element, so its kernel contains N. Therefore it induces a homomorphism $h : (G_1 * G_2)/N \to H$ that satisfies the conditions $h_1 = h \circ i_1$ and $h_2 = h \circ i_2$.   ∎

Corollary 68.8. *If N is the least normal subgroup of $G_1 * G_2$ that contains G_1, then $(G_1 * G_2)/N \cong G_2$.*

The notion of "least normal subgroup" is a concept that will appear frequently as we proceed. Obviously, if N is the least normal subgroup of G containing the subset S of G, then N contains S and all conjugates of elements of S. For later use, we now verify that these elements actually *generate* N.

Lemma 68.9. *Let S be a subset of the group G. If N is the least normal subgroup of G containing S, then N is generated by all conjugates of elements of S.*

Proof. Let N' be the subgroup of G generated by all conjugates of elements of S. We know that $N' \subset N$; to verify the reverse inclusion, we need merely show that N' is normal in G. Given $x \in N'$ and $c \in G$, we show that $cxc^{-1} \in N'$.

We can write x in the form $x = x_1 x_2 \cdots x_n$, where each x_i is conjugate to an element s_i of S. Then cx_ic^{-1} is also conjugate to s_i. Because

$$cxc^{-1} = (cx_1c^{-1})(cx_2c^{-1}) \cdots (cx_nc^{-1}),$$

cxc^{-1} is a product of conjugates of elements of S, so that $cxc^{-1} \in N'$, as desired.   ∎

Exercises

1. Check the details of Example 1.

2. Let $G = G_1 * G_2$, where G_1 and G_2 are nontrivial groups.
   (a) Show G is not abelian.
   (b) If $x \in G$, define the *length* of x to be the length of the unique reduced word in the elements of G_1 and G_2 that represents x. Show that if x has even length (at least 2), then x does not have finite order. Show that if x has odd length, then x is conjugate to an element of shorter length.
   (c) Show that the only elements of G that have finite order are the elements of G_1 and G_2 that have finite order, and their conjugates.

3. Let $G = G_1 * G_2$. Given $c \in G$, let cG_1c^{-1} denote the set of all elements of the form cxc^{-1}, for $x \in G_1$. It is a subgroup of G; show that its intersection with G_2 consists of the identity alone.

4. Prove Theorem 68.4.

§69   Free Groups

Let G be a group; let $\{a_\alpha\}$ be a family of elements of G, for $\alpha \in J$. We say the elements $\{a_\alpha\}$ **generate** G if every element of G can be written as a product of powers of the elements a_α. If the family $\{a_\alpha\}$ is finite, we say G is **finitely generated**.

Definition.   Let $\{a_\alpha\}$ be a family of elements of a group G. Suppose each a_α generates an infinite cyclic subgroup G_α of G. If G is the free product of the groups $\{G_\alpha\}$, then G is said to be a *free group*, and the family $\{a_\alpha\}$ is called a *system of free generators* for G.

In this case, for each element x of G, there is a unique reduced word in the elements of the groups G_α that represents x. This says that if $x \neq 1$, then x can be written uniquely in the form

$$x = (a_{\alpha_1})^{n_1} \cdots (a_{\alpha_k})^{n_k},$$

where $\alpha_i \neq \alpha_{i+1}$ and $n_i \neq 0$ for each i. (Of course, n_i may be negative.)

Free groups are characterized by the following extension property:

Lemma 69.1.   *Let G be a group; let $\{a_\alpha\}_{\alpha \in J}$ be a family of elements of G. If G is a free group with system of free generators $\{a_\alpha\}$, then G satisfies the following condition:*

(∗)   *Given any group H and any family $\{y_\alpha\}$ of elements of H, there is a homomorphism $h : G \to H$ such that $h(a_\alpha) = y_\alpha$ for each α.*

Furthermore, h is unique. Conversely, if the extension condition (∗) holds, then G is a free group with system of free generators $\{a_\alpha\}$.

The properties of free groups are in many ways similar to those of free abelian groups. For instance, if H is a subgroup of a free abelian group G, then H itself is a free abelian group. (The proof in the case where G has finite rank is outlined in Exercise 6 of §67; the proof in the general case is similar.) The analogous result holds for free groups, but the proof is considerably more difficult. We shall give a proof in Chapter 14 that is based on the theory of covering spaces.

In other ways, free groups are very different from free abelian groups. Given a free abelian group of rank n, the rank of any subgroup is at most n; but the analogous result for free groups does *not* hold. If G is a free group with a system of n free generators, then the cardinality of a system of free generators for a subgroup of G may be greater than n; it may even be infinite! We shall explore this situation later.

Generators and relations

A basic problem in group theory is to determine, for two given groups, whether or not they are isomorphic. For free abelian groups, the problem is solved; two such groups are isomorphic if and only if they have bases with the same cardinality. Similarly, two free groups are isomorphic if and only if their systems of free generators have the same cardinality. (We have proved these facts in the case of finite cardinality.)

For arbitrary groups, however the answer is not so simple. Only in the case of an abelian group that is finitely generated is there a clear-cut answer.

If G is abelian and finitely generated, then there is a fundamental theorem to the effect that G is the direct sum of two subgroups, $G = H \oplus T$, where H is free abelian of finite rank, and T is the subgroup of G consisting of all elements of finite order. (We call T the **torsion subgroup** of G.) The rank of H is uniquely determined by G, since it equals the rank of the quotient of G by its torsion subgroup. This number is often called the **betti number** of G. Furthermore, the subgroup T is itself a direct sum; it is the direct sum of a finite number of finite cyclic groups whose orders are powers of primes. The orders of these groups are uniquely determined by T (and hence by G), and are called the **elementary divisors** of G. Thus the isomorphism class of G is completely determined by specifying its betti number and its elementary divisors.

If G is not abelian, matters are not nearly so satisfactory, even if G is finitely generated. What can we specify that will determine G? The best we can do is the following:

Given G, suppose we are given a family $\{a_\alpha\}_{\alpha \in J}$ of generators for G. Let F be the free group on the elements $\{a_\alpha\}$. Then the obvious map $h(a_\alpha) = a_\alpha$ of these elements into G extends to a homomorphism $h : F \to G$ that is surjective. If N equals the kernel of h, then $F/N \cong G$. So one way of specifying G is to give a family $\{a_\alpha\}$ of generators for G, and somehow to specify the subgroup N. Each element of N is called a **relation** on F, and N is called the **relations subgroup**. We can specify N by giving a set of generators for N. But since N is normal in F, we can also specify N by a smaller set. Specifically, we can specify N by giving a family $\{r_\beta\}$ of elements of F such that these elements *and their conjugates* generate N, that is, such that N is the least normal subgroup of F that contains the elements r_β. In this case, we call the family $\{r_\beta\}$ a **complete set of relations** for G.

Each element of N belongs to F, so it can of course be represented uniquely by a reduced word in powers of the generators $\{a_\alpha\}$. When we speak of a *relation* on the generators of G, we sometimes refer to this reduced word, rather than to the element of N it represents. The context will make the meaning clear.

Definition. If G is a group, a **presentation** of G consists of a family $\{a_\alpha\}$ of generators for G, along with a complete set $\{r_\beta\}$ of relations for G, where each r_β is an element of the free group on the set $\{a_\alpha\}$. If the family $\{a_\alpha\}$ is finite, then G is finitely generated, of course. If both the families $\{a_\alpha\}$ and $\{r_\beta\}$ are finite, then G is said to be **finitely presented**, and these families form what is called a **finite presentation** for G.

This procedure for specifying G is far from satisfactory. A presentation for G does determine G uniquely, up to isomorphism; but two completely different presentations can lead to groups that are isomorphic. Furthermore, even in the finite case there is no effective procedure for determining, from two different presentations, whether or not the groups they determine are isomorphic. This result is known as the "unsolvability of the isomorphism problem" for groups.

Unsatisfactory as it is, this is the best we can do!

Exercises

1. If $G = G_1 * G_2$, show that
$$G/[G, G] \cong (G_1/[G_1, G_1]) \oplus (G_2/[G_2, G_2]).$$

   [*Hint:* Use the extension condition for direct sums and free products to define homomorphisms
   $$G/[G, G] \rightleftarrows (G_1/[G_1, G_1]) \oplus (G_2/[G_2, G_2])$$
   that are inverse to each other.]

2. Generalize the result of Exercise 1 to arbitrary free products.

3. Prove the following:
   Theorem. *Let $G = G_1 * G_1$, where G_1 and G_2 are cyclic of orders m and n, respectively. Then m and n are uniquely determined by G.*
   Proof.
   (a) Show $G/[G, G]$ has order mn.
   (b) Determine the largest integer k such that G has an element of order k. (See Exercise 2 of §68.)
   (c) Prove the theorem.

4. Show that if $G = G_1 \oplus G_2$, where G_1 and G_2 are cyclic of orders m and n, respectively, then m and n are not uniquely determined by G in general. [*Hint:* If m and n are relatively prime, show that G is cyclic of order mn.]

First, we show that σ is an extension of ρ. If f is a *loop* based at x_0 lying in either U or V, then

$$L(f) = e_{x_0} * (f * e_{x_0})$$

because α_{x_0} is the constant path at x_0. Then $L(f)$ is path homotopic to f in either U or V, so that $\rho(L(f)) = \rho(f)$ by condition (1) for ρ. Hence $\sigma(f) = \rho(f)$.

To check condition (1), let f and g be paths that are path homotopic in U or in V. Then the loops $L(f)$ and $L(g)$ are also path homotopic either in U or in V, so condition (1) for ρ applies. To check (2), let f and g be arbitrary paths in U or in V such that $f(1) = g(0)$. We have

$$L(f) * L(g) = (\alpha_x * (f * \bar{\alpha}_y)) * (\alpha_y * (g * \bar{\alpha}_z))$$

for appropriate points x, y, and z; this loop is path homotopic in U or V to $L(f * g)$. Then

$$\rho(L(f * g)) = \rho(L(f) * L(g)) = \rho(L(f)) \cdot \rho(L(g))$$

by conditions (1) and (2) for ρ. Hence $\sigma(f * g) = \sigma(f) \cdot \sigma(g)$.

Step 3. Finally, we extend σ to a set map τ that assigns, to an *arbitrary* path f of X, an element of H. It will satisfy the following conditions:

(1) If $[f] = [g]$, then $\tau(f) = \tau(g)$.
(2) $\tau(f * g) = \tau(f) \cdot \tau(g)$ if $f * g$ is defined.

Given f, choose a subdivision $s_0 < \cdots < s_n$ of $[0, 1]$ such that f maps each of the subintervals $[s_{i-1}, s_i]$ into U or V. Let f_i denote the positive linear map of $[0, 1]$ onto $[s_{i-1}, s_i]$, followed by f. Then f_i is a path in U or in V, and

$$[f] = [f_1] * \cdots * [f_n].$$

If τ is to be an extension of σ and satisfy (1) and (2), we must have

$$(*) \qquad \tau(f) = \sigma(f_1) \cdot \sigma(f_2) \cdots \sigma(f_n).$$

So we shall use this equation as our definition of τ.

We show that this definition is independent of the choice of subdivision. It suffices to show that the value of $\tau(f)$ remains unchanged if we adjoin a single additional point p to the subdivision. Let i be the index such that $s_{i-1} < p < s_i$. If we compute $\tau(f)$ using this new subdivision, the only change in formula $(*)$ is that the factor $\sigma(f_i)$ disappears and is replaced by the product $\sigma(f_i') \cdot \sigma(f_i'')$, where f_i' and f_i'' equal the positive linear maps of $[0, 1]$ to $[s_{i-1}, p]$ and to $[p, s_i]$, respectively, followed by f. But f_i is path homotopic to $f_i' * f_i''$ in U or V, so that $\sigma(f_i) = \sigma(f_i') \cdot \sigma(f_i'')$, by conditions (1) and (2) for σ. Thus τ is well-defined.

It follows that τ is an extension of σ. For if f already lies in U or V, we can use the trivial partition of $[0, 1]$ to define $\tau(f)$; then $\tau(f) = \sigma(f)$ by definition.

Step 4. We prove condition (1) for the set map τ. This part of the proof requires some care.

We first verify this condition in a special case. Let f and g be paths in X from x to y, say, and let F be a path homotopy between them. Let us assume the additional hypothesis that there exists a subdivision $s_0, \ldots, s_n$ of $[0, 1]$ such that F carries each rectangle $R_i = [s_{i-1}, s_i] \times I$ into either U or V. We show in this case that $\tau(f) = \tau(g)$.

Given i, consider the positive linear map of $[0, 1]$ onto $[s_{i-1}, s_i]$ followed by f or by g; and call these two paths f_i and g_i, respectively. The restriction of F to the rectangle R_i gives us a homotopy between f_i and g_i that takes place in either U or V, but it is not a path homotopy because the end points of the paths may move during the homotopy. Let us consider the paths traced out by these end points during the homotopy. We define β_i to be the path $\beta_i(t) = F(s_i, t)$. Then β_i is a path in X from $f(s_i)$ to $g(s_i)$. The paths β_0 and β_n are the constant paths at x and y, respectively. See Figure 70.2. We show that for each i,

$$f_i * \beta_i \simeq_p \beta_{i-1} * g_i,$$

with the path homotopy taking place in U or in V.

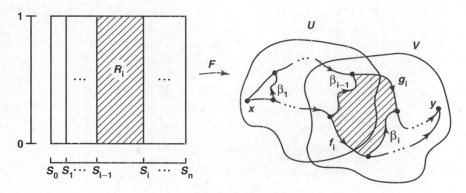

Figure 70.2

In the rectangle R_i, take the broken-line path that runs along the bottom and right edges of R_i, from $s_{i-1} \times 0$ to $s_i \times 0$ to $s_i \times 1$; if we follow this path by the map F, we obtain the path $f_i * \beta_i$. Similarly, if we take the broken-line path along the left and top edges of R_i and follow it by F, we obtain the path $\beta_{i-1} * g_i$. Because R_i is convex, there is a path homotopy in R_i between these two broken-line paths; if we follow by F, we obtain a path homotopy between $f_i * \beta_i$ and $\beta_{i-1} * g_i$ that takes place in either U or V, as desired.

It follows from conditions (1) and (2) for σ that

$$\sigma(f_i) \cdot \sigma(\beta_i) = \sigma(\beta_{i-1}) \cdot \sigma(g_i),$$

so that

(**) $$\sigma(f_i) = \sigma(\beta_{i-1}) \cdot \sigma(g_i) \cdot \sigma(\beta_i)^{-1}.$$

It follows similarly that since β_0 and β_n are constant paths, $\sigma(\beta_0) = \sigma(\beta_n) = 1$. (For the fact that $\beta_0 * \beta_0 = \beta_0$ implies that $\sigma(\beta_0) \cdot \sigma(\beta_0) = \sigma(\beta_0)$.)

We now compute as follows:

$$\tau(f) = \sigma(f_1) \cdot \sigma(f_2) \cdots \sigma(f_n).$$

Substituting (∗∗) in this equation and simplifying, we have the equation

$$\tau(f) = \sigma(g_1) \cdot \sigma(g_2) \cdots \sigma(g_n)$$
$$= \tau(g).$$

Thus, we have proved condition (1) in our special case.

Now we prove condition (1) in the general case. Given f and g and a path homotopy F between them, let us choose subdivisions $s_0, \ldots, s_n$ and $t_0, \ldots, t_m$ of $[0, 1]$ such that F maps each subrectangle $[s_{i-1}, s_i] \times [t_{j-1}, t_j]$ into either U or V. Let f_j be the path $f_j(s) = F(s, t_j)$; then $f_0 = f$ and $f_m = g$. The pair of paths f_{j-1} and f_j satisfy the requirements of our special case, so that $\tau(f_{j-1}) = \tau(f_j)$ for each j. It follows that $\tau(f) = \tau(g)$, as desired.

Step 5. Now we prove condition (2) for the set map τ. Given a path $f * g$ in X, let us choose a subdivision $s_0 < \cdots < s_n$ of $[0, 1]$ containing the point $1/2$ as a subdivision point, such that $f * g$ carries each subinterval into either U or V. Let k be the index such that $s_k = 1/2$.

For $i = 1, \ldots, k$, the positive linear map of $[0, 1]$ to $[s_{i-1}, s_i]$, followed by $f * g$, is the same as the positive linear map of $[0, 1]$ to $[2s_{i-1}, 2s_i]$ followed by f; call this map f_i. Similarly, for $i = k + 1, \ldots, n$, the positive linear map of $[0, 1]$ to $[s_{i-1}, s_i]$, followed by $f * g$, is the same as the positive linear map of $[0, 1]$ to $[2s_{i-1} - 1, 2s_i - 1]$ followed by g; call this map g_{i-k}. Using the subdivision $s_0, \ldots, s_n$ for the domain of the path $f * g$, we have

$$\tau(f * g) = \sigma(f_1) \cdots \sigma(f_k) \cdot \sigma(g_1) \cdots \sigma(g_{n-k}).$$

Using the subdivision $2s_0, \ldots, 2s_k$ for the path f, we have

$$\tau(f) = \sigma(f_1) \cdots \sigma(f_k).$$

And using the subdivision $2s_k - 1, \ldots, 2s_n - 1$ for the path g, we have

$$\tau(g) = \sigma(g_1) \cdots \sigma(g_{n-k}).$$

Thus (2) holds trivially.

Step 6. The theorem follows. For each loop f in X based at x_0, we define

$$\Phi([f]) = \tau(f).$$

Conditions (1) and (2) show that Φ is a well-defined homomorphism.

Let us show that $\Phi \circ j_1 = \phi_1$. If f is a loop in U, then

$$\Phi(j_1([f]_U)) = \Phi([f])$$
$$= \tau(f)$$
$$= \rho(f) = \phi_1([f]_U),$$

as desired. The proof that $\Phi \circ j_2 = \phi_2$ is similar. ∎

The preceding theorem is the modern formulation of the Seifert-van Kampen theorem. We now turn to the classical version, which involves the free product of two groups. Recall that if G is the external free product $G = G_1 * G_2$, we often treat G_1 and G_2 as if they were subgroups of G, for simplicity of notation.

Theorem 70.2 (Seifert-van Kampen theorem, classical version). *Assume the hypotheses of the preceding theorem. Let*

$$j : \pi_1(U, x_0) * \pi_1(V, x_0) \longrightarrow \pi_1(X, x_0)$$

be the homomorphism of the free product that extends the homomorphisms j_1 and j_2 induced by inclusion. Then j is surjective, and its kernel is the least normal subgroup N of the free product that contains all elements represented by words of the form

$$(i_1(g)^{-1}, i_2(g)),$$

for $g \in \pi_1(U \cap V, x_0)$.

Said differently, the kernel of j is generated by all elements of the free product of the form $i_1(g)^{-1}i_2(g)$, and their conjugates.

Proof.   The fact that $\pi_1(X, x_0)$ is generated by the images of j_1 and j_2 implies that j is surjective.

We show that $N \subset \ker j$. Since $\ker j$ is normal, it is enough to show that $i_1(g)^{-1}i_2(g)$ belongs to $\ker j$ for each $g \in \pi_1(U \cap V, x_0)$. If $i : U \cap V \to X$ is the inclusion mapping, then

$$ji_1(g) = j_1i_1(g) = i_*(g) = j_2i_2(g) = ji_2(g).$$

Then $i_1(g)^{-1}i_2(g)$ belongs to the kernel of j.

It follows that j induces an epimorphism

$$k : \pi_1(U, x_0) * \pi_1(V, x_0)/N \longrightarrow \pi_1(X, x_0).$$

We show that N equals $\ker j$ by showing that k is injective. It suffices to show that k has a left inverse.

Let H denote the group $\pi_1(U, x_0) * \pi_1(V, x_0)/N$. Let $\phi_1 : \pi_1(U, x_0) \to H$ equal the inclusion of $\pi_1(U, x_0)$ into the free product followed by projection of the free product onto its quotient by N. Let $\phi_2 : \pi_1(V, x_0) \to H$ be defined similarly. Consider the diagram

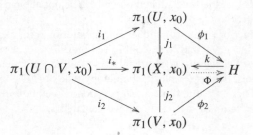

It is easy to see that $\phi_1 \circ i_1 = \phi_2 \circ i_2$. For if $g \in \pi_1(U \cap V, x_0)$, then $\phi_1(i_1(g))$ is the coset $i_1(g)N$ in H, and $\phi_2(i_2(g))$ is the coset $i_2(g)N$. Because $i_1(g)^{-1}i_2(g) \in N$, these cosets are equal.

It follows from Theorem 70.1 that there is a homomorphism $\Phi : \pi_1(X, x_0) \to H$ such that $\Phi \circ j_1 = \phi_1$ and $\Phi \circ j_2 = \phi_2$. We show that Φ is a left inverse for k. It suffices to show that $\Phi \circ k$ acts as the identity on any generator of H, that is, on any coset of the form gN, where g is in $\pi_1(U, x_0)$ or $\pi_1(V, x_0)$. But if $g \in \pi_1(U, x_0)$, we have

$$k(gN) = j(g) = j_1(g),$$

so that

$$\Phi(k(gN)) = \Phi(j_1(g)) = \phi_1(g) = gN,$$

as desired. A similar remark applies if $g \in \pi_1(V, x_0)$. ∎

Corollary 70.3. *Assume the hypotheses of the Seifert-van Kampen theorem. If $U \cap V$ is simply connected, then there is an isomorphism*

$$k : \pi_1(U, x_0) * \pi_1(V, x_0) \longrightarrow \pi_1(X, x_0).$$

Corollary 70.4. *Assume the hypotheses of the Seifert-van Kampen theorem. If V is simply connected, there is an isomorphism*

$$k : \pi_1(U, x_0)/N \longrightarrow \pi_1(X, x_0),$$

where N is the least normal subgroup of $\pi_1(U, x_0)$ containing the image of the homomorphism

$$i_1 : \pi_1(U \cap V, x_0) \to \pi_1(U, x_0).$$

EXAMPLE 1.   Let X be a theta-space. Then X is a Hausdorff space that is the union of three arcs A, B, and C, each pair of which intersect precisely in their end points p and q. We showed earlier that the fundamental group of X is not abelian. We show here that this group is in fact a free group on two generators.

Let a be an interior point of A and let b be an interior point of B. Write X as the union of the open sets $U = X - a$ and $V = X - b$. See Figure 70.3. The space $U \cap V = X - a - b$ is simply connected because it is contractible. Furthermore, U and V have infinite cyclic fundamental groups, because U has the homotopy type of $B \cup C$ and V has the homotopy type of $A \cup C$. Therefore, the fundamental group of X is the free product of two infinite cyclic groups, that is, it is a free group on two generators.

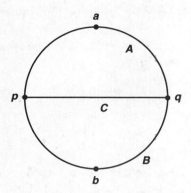

Figure 70.3

Exercises

In the following exercises, assume the hypotheses of the Seifert-van Kampen theorem.

1. Suppose that the homomorphism i_* induced by inclusion $i : U \cap V \to X$ is trivial.

    (a) Show that j_1 and j_2 induce an epimorphism

    $$h : (\pi_1(U, x_0)/N_1) * (\pi_1(V, x_0)/N_2) \longrightarrow \pi_1(X, x_0),$$

    where N_1 is the least normal subgroup of $\pi_1(U, x_0)$ containing image i_1, and N_2 is the least normal subgroup of $\pi_1(V, x_0)$ containing image i_2.

    (b) Show that h is an isomorphism. [*Hint:* Use Theorem 70.1 to define a left inverse for h.]

2. Suppose that i_2 is surjective.

    (a) Show that j_1 induces an epimorphism

    $$h : \pi_1(U, x_0)/M \longrightarrow \pi_1(X, x_0),$$

    where M is the least normal subgroup of $\pi_1(U, x_0)$ containing $i_1(\ker i_2)$. [*Hint:* Show j_1 is surjective.]

    (b) Show that h is an isomorphism. [*Hint:* Let $H = \pi_1(U, x_0)/M$. Let $\phi_1 : \pi_1(U, x_0) \to H$ be the projection. Use the fact that $\pi_1(U \cap V, x_0)/\ker i_2$ is isomorphic to $\pi_1(V, x_0)$ to define a homomorphism $\phi_2 : \pi_1(V, x_0) \to H$. Use Theorem 70.1 to define a left inverse for h.]

3. (a) Show that if G_1 and G_2 have finite presentations, so does $G_1 * G_2$.

    (b) Show that if $\pi_1(U \cap V, x_0)$ is finitely generated and $\pi_1(U, x_0)$ and $\pi_1(V, x_0)$ have finite presentations, then $\pi_1(X, x_0)$ has a finite presentation. [*Hint:* If N' is a normal subgroup of $\pi_1(U, x_0) * \pi_1(V, x_0)$ that contains the elements $i_1(g_i)^{-1}i_2(g_i)$ where g_i runs over a set of generators for $\pi_1(U \cap V, x_0)$, then N' contains $i_1(g)^{-1}i_2(g)$ for arbitrary g.]

§71 The Fundamental Group of a Wedge of Circles

In this section, we define what we mean by a *wedge of circles*, and we compute its fundamental group.

Definition. Let X be a Hausdorff space that is the union of the subspaces $S_1, \ldots, S_n$, each of which is homeomorphic to the unit circle S^1. Assume that there is a point p of X such that $S_i \cap S_j = \{p\}$ whenever $i \neq j$. Then X is called the *wedge of the circles* $S_1, \ldots, S_n$.

Note that each space S_i, being compact, is closed in X. Note also that X can be imbedded in the plane; if C_i denotes the circle of radius i in $\mathbb{R}^2$ with center at $(i, 0)$, then X is homeomorphic to $C_1 \cup \cdots \cup C_n$.

Theorem 71.1. *Let X be the wedge of the circles $S_1, \ldots, S_n$; let p be the common point of these circles. Then $\pi_1(X, p)$ is a free group. If f_i is a loop in S_i that represents a generator of $\pi_1(S_i, p)$, then the loops $f_1, \ldots, f_n$ represent a system of free generators for $\pi_1(X, p)$.*

Proof. The result is immediate if $n = 1$. We proceed by induction on n. The proof is similar to the one given in Example 1 of the preceding section.

Let X be the wedge of the circles $S_1, \ldots, S_n$, with p the common point of these circles. Choose a point q_i of S_i different from p, for each i. Set $W_i = S_i - q_i$, and let

$$U = S_1 \cup W_2 \cup \cdots \cup W_n \quad \text{and} \quad V = W_1 \cup S_2 \cup \cdots \cup S_n.$$

Then $U \cap V = W_1 \cup \cdots \cup W_n$. See Figure 71.1. Each of the spaces U, V, and $U \cap V$ is path connected, being the union of path-connected spaces having a point in common.

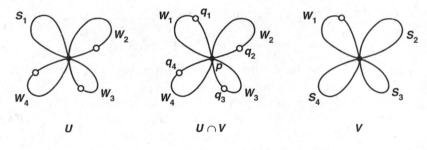

Figure 71.1

The space W_i is homeomorphic to an open interval, so it has the point p as a deformation retract; let $F_i : W_i \times I \to W_i$ be the deformation retraction. The maps F_i fit together to define a map $F : (U \cap V) \times I \to U \cap V$ that is a deformation retraction of $U \cap V$ onto p. (To show that F is continuous, we note that because S_i is a closed subspace of X, the space $W_i = S_i - q_i$ is a closed subspace of $U \cap V$, so that $W_i \times I$

is a closed subspace of $(U \cap V) \times I$. Then the pasting lemma applies.) It follows that $U \cap V$ is simply connected, so that $\pi_1(X, p)$ is the free product of the groups $\pi_1(U, p)$ and $\pi_1(V, p)$, relative to the monomorphisms induced by inclusion.

A similar argument shows that S_1 is a deformation retract of U and $S_2 \cup \cdots \cup S_n$ is a deformation retract of V. It follows that $\pi_1(U, p)$ is infinite cyclic, and the loop f_1 represents a generator. It also follows, using the induction hypothesis, that $\pi_1(V, p)$ is a free group, with the loops $f_2, \ldots, f_n$ representing a system of free generators. Our theorem now follows from Theorem 69.2. ∎

We generalize this result to a space X that is the union of *infinitely* many circles having a point in common. Here we must be careful about the topology of X.

Definition. Let X be a space that is the union of the subspaces X_α, for $\alpha \in J$. The topology of X is said to be **coherent** with the subspaces X_α provided a subset C of X is closed in X if $C \cap X_\alpha$ is closed in X_α for each α. An equivalent condition is that a set be open in X if its intersection with each X_α is open in X_α.

If X is the union of finitely many closed subspaces $X_1, \ldots, X_n$, then the topology of X is automatically coherent with these subspaces, since if $C \cap X_i$ is closed in X_i, it is closed in X, and C is the finite union of the sets $C \cap X_i$.

Definition. Let X be a space that is the union of the subspaces S_α, for $\alpha \in J$, each of which is homeomorphic to the unit circle. Assume there is a point p of X such that $S_\alpha \cap S_\beta = \{p\}$ whenever $\alpha \neq \beta$. If the topology of X is coherent with the subspaces S_α, then X is called the **wedge of the circles** S_α.

In the finite case, the definition involved the Hausdorff condition instead of the coherence condition; in that case the coherence condition followed. In the infinite case, this would no longer be true, so we included the coherence condition as part of the definition. We would include the Hausdorff condition as well, but that is no longer necessary, for it follows from the coherence condition:

Lemma 71.2. *Let X be the wedge of the circles S_α, for $\alpha \in J$. Then X is normal. Furthermore, any compact subspace of X is contained in the union of finitely many circles S_α.*

Proof. It is clear that one-point sets are closed in X. Let A and B be disjoint closed subsets of X; assume that B does not contain p. Choose disjoint subsets U_α and V_α of S_α that are open in S_α and contain $\{p\} \cup (A \cap S_\alpha)$ and $B \cap S_\alpha$, respectively. Let $U = \bigcup U_\alpha$ and $V = \bigcup V_\alpha$; then U and V are disjoint. Now $U \cap S_\alpha = U_\alpha$ because all the sets U_α contain p, and $V \cap S_\alpha = V_\alpha$ because no set V_α contains p. Hence U and V are open in X, as desired. Thus X is normal.

Now let C be a compact subspace of X. For each α for which it is possible, choose a point x_α of $C \cap (S_\alpha - p)$. The set $D = \{x_\alpha\}$ is closed in X, because its intersection with each space S_α is a one-point set or is empty. For the same reason, each *subset* of D is closed in X. Thus D is a closed discrete subspace of X contained in C; since C is limit point compact, D must be finite.   ∎

Theorem 71.3. *Let X be the wedge of the circles S_α, for $\alpha \in J$; let p be the common point of these circles. Then $\pi_1(X, p)$ is a free group. If f_α is a loop in S_α representing a generator of $\pi_1(S_\alpha, p)$, then the loops $\{f_\alpha\}$ represent a system of free generators for $\pi_1(X, p)$.*

Proof. Let $i_\alpha : \pi_1(S_\alpha, p) \to \pi_1(X, p)$ be the homomorphism induced by inclusion; let G_α be the image of i_α.

Note that if f is any loop in X based at p, then the image set of f is compact, so that f lies in some finite union of subspaces S_α. Furthermore, if f and g are two loops that are path homotopic in X, then they are actually path homotopic in some finite union of the subspaces S_α.

It follows that the groups $\{G_\alpha\}$ generate $\pi_1(X, p)$. For if f is a loop in X, then f lies in $S_{\alpha_1} \cup \cdots \cup S_{\alpha_n}$ for some finite set of indices; then Theorem 71.1 implies that $[f]$ is a product of elements of the groups $G_{\alpha_1}, \ldots, G_{\alpha_n}$. Similarly, it follows that i_β is a monomorphism. For if f is a loop in S_β that is path homotopic in X to a constant, then f is path homotopic to a constant in some finite union of spaces S_α, so that Theorem 71.1 implies that f is path homotopic to a constant in S_β.

Finally, suppose there is a reduced nonempty word

$$w = (g_{\alpha_1} \ldots, g_{\alpha_n})$$

in the elements of the groups G_α that represents the identity element of $\pi_1(X, p)$. Let f be a loop in X whose path-homotopy class is represented by w. Then f is path homotopic to a constant in X, so it is path homotopic to a constant in some finite union of subspaces S_α. This contradicts Theorem 71.1.   ∎

The preceding theorem depended on the fact that the topology of X was coherent with the subspaces S_α. Consider the following example:

EXAMPLE 1.   Let C_n be the circle of radius $1/n$ in $\mathbb{R}^2$ with center at the point $(1/n, 0)$. Let X be the subspace of $\mathbb{R}^2$ that is the union of these circles; then X is the union of a countably infinite collection of circles, each pair of which intersect in the origin p. However, X is *not* the wedge of the circles C_n; we call X (for convenience) the ***infinite earring***.

One can verify directly that X does not have the topology coherent with the subspaces C_n; the intersection of the positive x-axis with X contains exactly one point from each circle C_n, but it is not closed in X. Alternatively, for each n, let f_n be a loop in C_n that represents a generator of $\pi_1(C_n, p)$; we show that $\pi_1(X, p)$ is *not* a free group with $\{[f_n]\}$ as a system of free generators. Indeed, we show the elements $[f_i]$ do not even *generate* the group $\pi_1(X, p)$.

Consider the loop g in X defined as follows: For each n, define g on the interval $[1/(n + 1), 1/n]$ to be the positive linear map of this interval onto $[0, 1]$ followed by f_n. This specifies g on $(0, 1]$; define $g(0) = p$. Because X has the subspace topology derived from $\mathbb{R}^2$, it is easy to see that g is continuous. See Figure 71.2. We show that given n, the element $[g]$ does not belong to the subgroup G_n of $\pi_1(X, p)$ generated by $[f_1], \ldots, [f_n]$.

Choose $N > n$, and consider the map $h : X \to C_N$ defined by setting $h(x) = x$ for $x \in C_N$ and $h(x) = p$ otherwise. Then h is continuous, and the induced homomorphism $h_* : \pi_1(X, p) \to \pi_l(C_N, p)$ carries each element of G_n to the identity element. On the other hand, $h \circ g$ is the loop in C_N that is constant outside $[1/(N + 1), 1/N]$ and on this interval equals the positive linear map of this interval onto $[0, 1]$ followed by f_N. Therefore, $h_*([g]) = [f_N]$, which *generates* $\pi_1(C_N, p)$! Thus $[g] \notin G_n$.

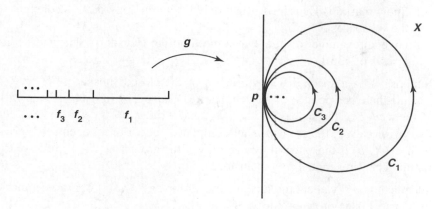

Figure 71.2

In the preceding theorem, we calculated the fundamental group of a space that is an infinite wedge of circles. For later use, we now show that such spaces do exist! (We shall use this result in Chapter 14.)

*Lemma 71.4.   *Given an index set J, there exists a space X that is a wedge of circles S_α for $\alpha \in J$.*

Proof.   Give the set J the discrete topology, and let E be the product space $S^1 \times J$. Choose a point $b_0 \in S^1$, and let X be the quotient space obtained from E by collapsing the closed set $P = b_0 \times J$ to a point p. Let $\pi : E \to X$ be the quotient map; let $S_\alpha = \pi(S^1 \times \alpha)$. We show that each S_α is homeomorphic to S^1 and X is the wedge of the circles S_α.

Note that if C is closed in $S^1 \times \alpha$, then $\pi(C)$ is closed in X. For $\pi^{-1}\pi(C) = C$ if the point $b_0 \times \alpha$ is not in C, and $\pi^{-1}\pi(C) = C \cup P$ otherwise. In either case, $\pi^{-1}\pi(C)$ is closed in $S^1 \times J$, so that $\pi(C)$ is closed in X.

It follows that S_α is itself closed in X, since $S^1 \times \alpha$ is closed in $S^1 \times J$, and that π maps $S^1 \times \alpha$ homeomorphically onto S_α. Let π_α be this homeomorphism.

To show that X has the topology coherent with the subspaces S_α, let $D \subset X$ and suppose that $D \cap S_\alpha$ is closed in S_α for each α. Now

$$\pi^{-1}(D) \cap (S^1 \times \alpha) = \pi_\alpha^{-1}(D \cap S_\alpha);$$

the latter set is closed in $S^1 \times \alpha$ because π_α is continuous. Then $\pi^{-1}(D)$ is closed in $S^1 \times J$, so that D is closed in X by definition of the quotient topology.   ∎

Exercises

1. Let X be a space that is the union of subspaces $S_1, \ldots, S_n$, each of which is homeomorphic to the unit circle. Assume there is a point p of X such that $S_i \cap S_j = \{p\}$ for $i \neq j$.

   (a) Show that X is Hausdorff if and only if each space S_i is closed in X.

   (b) Show that X is Hausdorff if and only if the topology of X is coherent with the subspaces S_i.

   (c) Give an example to show that X need not be Hausdorff. [*Hint:* See Exercises 5 of §36.]

2. Suppose X is a space that is the union of the closed subspaces $X_1, \ldots, X_n$; assume there is a point p of X such that $X_i \cap X_j = \{p\}$ for $i \neq j$. Then we call X the **wedge** of the spaces $X_1, \ldots, X_n$, and write $X = X_1 \vee \cdots \vee X_n$. Show that if for each i, the point p is a deformation retract of an open set W_i of X_i, then $\pi_1(X, p)$ is the external free product of the groups $\pi_1(X_i, p)$ relative to the monomorphisms induced by inclusion.

3. What can you say about the fundamental group of $X \vee Y$ if X is homeomorphic to S^1 and Y is homeomorphic to S^2?

4. Show that if X is an infinite wedge of circles, then X does not satisfy the first countability axiom.

5. Let S_n be the circle of radius n in $\mathbb{R}^2$ whose center is at the point $(n, 0)$. Let Y be the subspace of $\mathbb{R}^2$ that is the union of these circles; let p be their common point.

   (a) Show that Y is not homeomorphic to a countably infinite wedge X of circles, nor to the bouquet of circles of Example 1.

   (b) Show, however, that $\pi_1(Y, p)$ is a free group with $\{[f_n]\}$ as a system of free generators, where f_n is a loop representing a generator of $\pi_1(S_n, p)$.

§72 Adjoining a Two-cell

We have computed the fundamental group of the torus $T = S^1 \times S^1$ in two ways. One involved considering the standard covering map $p \times p : \mathbb{R} \times \mathbb{R} \to S^1 \times S^1$ and using the lifting correspondence. Another involved a basic theorem about the fundamental group of a product space. Now we compute the fundamental group of the torus in yet another way.

If one restricts the covering map $p \times p$ to the unit square, one obtains a quotient map $\pi : I^2 \to T$. It maps Bd I^2 onto the subspace $A = (S^1 \times b_0) \cup (b_0 \times S^1)$, which is the wedge of two circles, and it maps the rest of I^2 bijectively onto $T - A$. Thus, T can be thought of as the space obtained by pasting the edges of the square I^2 onto the space A.

The process of constructing a space by pasting the edges of a polygonal region in the plane onto another space is quite useful. We show here how to compute the fundamental group of such a space. The applications will be many and fruitful.

Theorem 72.1. *Let X be a Hausdorff space; let A be a closed path-connected subspace of X. Suppose that there is a continuous map $h : B^2 \to X$ that maps Int B^2 bijectively onto $X - A$ and maps $S^1 = \mathrm{Bd}\ B^2$ into A. Let $p \in S^1$ and let $a = h(p)$; let $k : (S^1, p) \to (A, a)$ be the map obtained by restricting h. Then the homomorphism*

$$i_* : \pi_1(A, a) \longrightarrow \pi_1(X, a)$$

induced by inclusion is surjective, and its kernel is the least normal subgroup of $\pi_1(A, a)$ containing the image of $k_* : \pi_1(S^1, p) \to \pi_1(A, a)$.

We sometimes say that the fundamental group of X is obtained from the fundamental group of A by "killing off" the class $k_*[f]$, where $[f]$ generates $\pi_1(S^1, p)$.

Proof.   *Step 1.* The origin $\mathbf{0}$ is the center point of B^2; let x_0 be the point $h(\mathbf{0})$ of X. If U is the open set $U = X - x_0$ of X, we show that A is a deformation retract of U. See Figure 72.1.

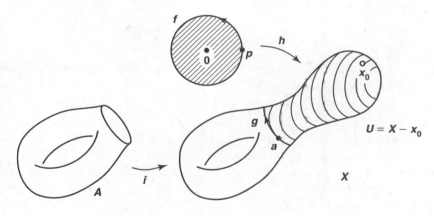

Figure 72.1

Let $C = h(B^2)$, and let $\pi : B^2 \to C$ be the map obtained by restricting the range of h. Consider the map

$$\pi \times \mathrm{id} : B^2 \times I \longrightarrow C \times I;$$

it is a closed map because $B^2 \times I$ is compact and $C \times I$ is Hausdorff; therefore, it is a quotient map. Its restriction

$$\pi' : (B^2 - \mathbf{0}) \times I \longrightarrow (C - x_0) \times I$$

is also a quotient map, since its domain is open in $B^2 \times I$ and is saturated with respect to $\pi \times \mathrm{id}$. There is a deformation retraction of $B^2 - \mathbf{0}$ onto S^1; it induces, *via* the quotient map π', a deformation retraction of $C - x_0$ onto $\pi(S^1)$. We extend this deformation retraction to all of $U \times I$ by letting it keep each point of A fixed during the deformation. Thus A is a deformation retract of U.

It follows that the inclusion of A into U induces an isomorphism of fundamental groups. Our theorem then reduces to proving the following statement:

Let f be a loop whose class generates $\pi_1(S^1, p)$. Then the inclusion of U into X induces an epimorphism

$$\pi_1(U, a) \longrightarrow \pi_1(X, a)$$

whose kernel is the least normal subgroup containing the class of the loop $g = h \circ f$.

Step 2. In order to prove this result, it is convenient to consider first the homomorphism $\pi_1(U, b) \to \pi_1(X, b)$ induced by inclusion relative to a base point b that does *not* belong to A.

Let b be any point of $U - A$. Write X as the union of the open sets U and $V = X - A = \pi(\text{Int } B^2)$. Now U is path connected, since it has A as a deformation retract. Because π is a quotient map, its restriction to Int B^2 is also a quotient map and hence a homeomorphism; thus V is simply connected. The set $U \cap V = V - x_0$ is homeomorphic to Int $B^2 - \mathbf{0}$, so it is path connected and its fundamental group is infinite cyclic. Since b is a point of $U \cap V$, Corollary 70.4 implies that the homomorphism

$$\pi_1(U, b) \longrightarrow \pi_1(X, b)$$

induced by inclusion is surjective, and its kernel is the least normal subgroup containing the image of the infinite cyclic group $\pi_1(U \cap V, b)$.

Step 3. Now we change the base point back to a, proving the theorem.

Let q be the point of B^2 that is the midpoint of the line segment from $\mathbf{0}$ to p, and let $b = h(q)$; then b is a point of $U \cap V$. Let f_0 be a loop in Int $B^2 - \mathbf{0}$ based at q that represents a generator of the fundamental group of this space; then $g_0 = h \circ f_0$ is a loop in $U \cap V$ based at b that represents a generator of the fundamental group of $U \cap V$. See Figure 72.2.

Step 2 tells us that the homomorphism $\pi_1(U, b) \to \pi_1(X, b)$ induced by inclusion is surjective and its kernel is the least normal subgroup containing the class of the loop $g_0 = h \circ f_0$. To obtain the analogous result with base point a we proceed as follows:

Let γ be the straight-line path in B^2 from q to p; let δ be the path $\delta = h \circ \gamma$ in U from b to a. The isomorphisms induced by the path δ (both of which we denote by $\hat{\delta}$) commute with the homomorphisms induced by inclusion in the following diagram:

$$
\begin{array}{ccc}
\pi_1(U, b) & \longrightarrow & \pi_1(X, b) \\
\downarrow{\scriptstyle \hat{\delta}} & & \downarrow{\scriptstyle \hat{\delta}} \\
\pi_1(U, a) & \longrightarrow & \pi_1(X, a)
\end{array}
$$

Therefore, the homomorphism of $\pi_1(U, a)$ into $\pi_1(X, a)$ induced by inclusion is surjective, and its kernel is the least normal subgroup containing the element $\hat{\delta}([g_0])$.

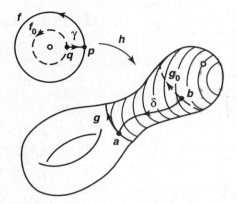

Figure 72.2

The loop f_0 represents a generator of the fundamental group of Int $B^2 - 0$ based at q. Then the loop $\bar{\gamma} * (f_0 * \gamma)$ represents a generator of the fundamental group of $B^2 - 0$ based at p. Therefore, it is path homotopic either to f or its reverse; suppose the former. Following this path homotopy by the map h, we see that $\bar{\delta} * (g_0 * \delta)$ is path homotopic in U to g. Then $\hat{\delta}([g_0]) = [g]$, and the theorem follows. ∎

There is nothing special in this theorem about the unit ball B^2. The same result holds if we replace B^2 by any space B homeomorphic to B^2, if we denote by Bd B the subspace corresponding to S^1 under the homeomorphism. Such a space B is called a *2-cell*. The space X of this theorem is thought of as having been obtained by "adjoining a 2-cell" to A. We shall treat this situation more formally later.

Exercises

1. Let X be a Hausdorff space; let A be a closed path-connected subspace. Suppose that $h : B^n \to X$ is a continuous map that maps S^{n-1} into A and maps Int B^n bijectively onto $X - A$. Let a be a point of $h(S^{n-1})$. If $n > 2$, what can you say about the homomorphism of $\pi_1(A, a)$ into $\pi_1(X, a)$ induced by inclusion?

2. Let X be the adjunction space formed from the disjoint union of the normal, path-connected space A and the unit ball B^2 by means of a continuous map $f : S^1 \to A$. (See Exercise 8 of §35.) Show that X satisfies the hypotheses of Theorem 72.1. Where do you use the fact that A is normal?

3. Let G be a group; let x be an element of G; let N be the least normal subgroup of G containing x. Show that if there is a normal, path-connected space whose fundamental group is isomorphic to G, then there is a normal, path-connected space whose fundamental group is isomorphic to G/N.

§73   The Fundamental Groups of the Torus and the Dunce Cap

We now apply the results of the preceding section to compute two fundamental groups, one of which we already know and the other of which we do not. The techniques involved will be important later.

Theorem 73.1.   *The fundamental group of the torus has a presentation consisting of two generators α, β and a single relation $\alpha\beta\alpha^{-1}\beta^{-1}$.*

Proof.   Let $X = S^1 \times S^1$ be the torus, and let $h : I^2 \to X$ be obtained by restricting the standard covering map $p \times p : \mathbb{R} \times \mathbb{R} \to S^1 \times S^1$. Let p be the point $(0, 0)$ of Bd I^2, let $a = h(p)$, and let $A = h(\text{Bd } I^2)$. Then the hypotheses of Theorem 72.1 are satisfied.

The space A is the wedge of two circles, so the fundamental group of A is free. Indeed, if we let a_0 be the path $a_0(t) = (t, 0)$ and b_0 be the path $b_0(t) = (0, t)$ in Bd I^2, then the paths $\alpha = h \circ a_0$ and $\beta = h \circ b_0$ are loops in A such that $[\alpha]$ and $[\beta]$ form a system of free generators for $\pi_1(A, a)$. See Figure 73.1.

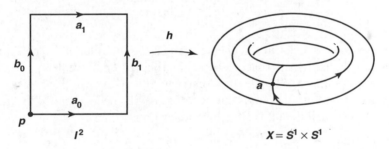

Figure 73.1

Now let a_1 and b_1 be the paths $a_1(t) = (t, 1)$ and $b_1(t) = (1, t)$ in Bd I^2. Consider the loop f in Bd I^2 defined by the equation

$$f = a_0 * (b_1 * (\bar{a}_1 * \bar{b}_0)).$$

Then f represents a generator of $\pi_1(\text{Bd } I^2, p)$; and the loop $g = h \circ f$ equals the product $\alpha * (\beta * (\bar{\alpha} * \bar{\beta}))$. Theorem 72.1 tells us that $\pi_1(X, a)$ is the quotient of the free group on the free generators $[\alpha]$ and $[\beta]$ by the least normal subgroup containing the element $[\alpha][\beta][\alpha]^{-1}[\beta]^{-1}$.   ∎

Corollary 73.2.   *The fundamental group of the torus is a free abelian group of rank* 2.

Proof.   Let G be the free group on generators α, β; and let N be the least normal subgroup containing the element $\alpha\beta\alpha^{-1}\beta^{-1}$. Because this element is a commutator, N is contained in the commutator subgroup $[G, G]$ of G. On the other hand, G/N

is abelian; for it is generated by the cosets αN and βN, and these elements of G/N commute. Therefore N contains the commutator subgroup of G.

It follows from Theorem 69.4 that G/N is a free abelian group of rank 2.   ∎

Definition.   Let n be a positive integer with $n > 1$. Let $r : S^1 \to S^1$ be rotation through the angle $2\pi/n$, mapping the point $(\cos\theta, \sin\theta)$ to the point $(\cos(\theta + 2\pi/n), \sin(\theta + 2\pi/n))$. Form a quotient space X from the unit ball B^2 by identifying each point x of S^1 with the points $r(x), r^2(x), \ldots, r^{n-1}(x)$. We shall show that X is a compact Hausdorff space; we call it the *n-fold dunce cap*.

Let $\pi : B^2 \to X$ be the quotient map; we show that π is a closed map. In order to do this, we must show that if C is a closed set of B^2, then $\pi^{-1}\pi(C)$ is also closed in B^2; it then will follow from the definition of the quotient topology that $\pi(C)$ is closed in X. Let $C_0 = C \cap S^1$; it is closed in B^2. The set $\pi^{-1}\pi(C)$ equals the union of C and the sets $r(C_0), r^2(C_0), \ldots, r^{n-1}(C_0)$, all of which are closed in B^2 because r is a homeomorphism. Hence $\pi^{-1}\pi(C)$ is closed in B^2, as desired.

Because π is continuous, X is compact. The fact that X is Hausdorff is a consequence of the following lemma, which was given as an exercise in §31.

Lemma 73.3.   *Let $\pi : E \to X$ be a closed quotient map. If E is normal, then so is X.*

Proof.   Assume E is normal. One-point sets are closed in X because one-point sets are closed in E. Now let A and B be disjoint closed sets of X. Then $\pi^{-1}(A)$ and $\pi^{-1}(B)$ are disjoint closed sets of E. Choose disjoint open sets U and V of E containing $\pi^{-1}(A)$ and $\pi^{-1}(B)$, respectively. It is tempting to assume that $\pi(U)$ and $\pi(V)$ are the open sets about A and B that we are seeking. But they are not. For they need not be open (π is not necessarily an open map), and they need not be disjoint! See Figure 73.2.

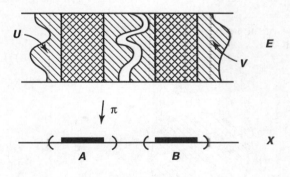

Figure 73.2

So we proceed as follows: Let $C = E - U$ and let $D = E - V$. Because C and D are closed sets of E, the sets $\pi(C)$ and $\pi(D)$ are closed in X. Because C contains no point of $\pi^{-1}(A)$, the set $\pi(C)$ is disjoint from A. Then $U_0 = X - \pi(C)$ is an open set of X containing A. Similarly, $V_0 = X - \pi(D)$ is an open set of X containing B. Furthermore, U_0 and V_0 are disjoint. For if $x \in U_0$, then $\pi^{-1}(x)$ is disjoint from C, so that it is contained in U. Similarly, if $x \in V_0$, then $\pi^{-1}(x)$ is contained in V. Since U and V are disjoint, so are U_0 and V_0. ∎

Let us note that the 2-fold dunce cap is a space we have seen before; it is homeomorphic to the projective plane P^2. To verify this fact, recall that P^2 was defined to be the quotient space obtained from S^2 by identifying x with $-x$ for each x. Let $p : S^2 \to P^2$ be the quotient map. Let us take the standard homeomorphism i of B^2 with the upper hemisphere of S^2, given by the equation

$$i(x, y) = (x, y, (1 - x^2 - y^2)^{1/2}),$$

and follow it by the map p. We obtain a map $\pi : B^2 \to P^2$ that is continuous, closed, and surjective. On Int B it is injective, and for each $x \in S^1$, it maps x and $-x$ to the same point. Hence it induces a homeomorphism of the 2-fold dunce cap with P^2.

The fundamental group of the n-fold dunce cap is just what you might expect from our computation for P^2.

Theorem 73.4. *The fundamental group of the n-fold dunce cap is a cyclic group of order n.*

Proof. Let $h : B^2 \to X$ be the quotient map, where X is the n-fold dunce cap. Set $A = h(S^1)$. Let $p = (1, 0) \in S^1$ and let $a = h(p)$. Then h maps the arc C of S^1 running from p to $r(p)$ onto A; it identifies the end points of C but is otherwise injective. Therefore, A is homeomorphic to a circle, so its fundamental group is infinite cyclic. Indeed, if γ is the path

$$\gamma(t) = (\cos(2\pi t/n), \sin(2\pi t/n))$$

in S^1 from p to $r(p)$, then $\alpha = h \circ \gamma$ represents a generator of $\pi_1(A, a)$. See Figure 73.3.

Now the class of the loop

$$f = \gamma * ((r \circ \gamma) * ((r^2 \circ \gamma) * \cdots * (r^{n-1} \circ \gamma)))$$

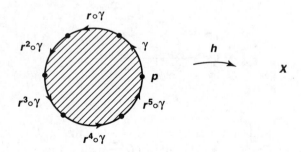

Figure 73.3

generates $\pi_1(S^1, p)$. Since $h(r^m(x)) = h(x)$ for all x and m, the loop $h \circ f$ equals the n-fold product $\alpha * (\alpha * (\cdots * \alpha))$. The theorem follows. ∎

Exercises

1. Find spaces whose fundamental groups are isomorphic to the following groups. (Here $\mathbb{Z}/n$ denotes the additive group of integers modulo n.)
   (a) $\mathbb{Z}/n \times \mathbb{Z}/m$.
   (b) $\mathbb{Z}/n_1 \times \mathbb{Z}/n_2 \times \cdots \times \mathbb{Z}/n_k$.
   (c) $\mathbb{Z}/n * \mathbb{Z}/m$. (See Exercise 2 of §71.)
   (d) $\mathbb{Z}/n_1 * \mathbb{Z}/n_2 * \cdots * \mathbb{Z}/n_k$.

2. Prove the following:
   Theorem. If G is a finitely presented group, then there is a compact Hausdorff space X whose fundamental group is isomorphic to G.
   Proof. Suppose G has a presentation consisting of n generators and m relations. Let A be the wedge of n circles; form an adjunction space X from the union of A and m copies $B_1, \ldots, B_m$ of the unit ball by means of a continuous map $f : \bigcup \operatorname{Bd} B_i \to A$.
   (a) Show that X is Hausdorff.
   (b) Prove the theorem in the case $m = 1$.
   (c) Proceed by induction on m, using the algebraic result stated in the following exercise.
      The construction outlined in this exercise is a standard one in algebraic topology; the space X is called a two-dimensional **CW complex**.

3. *Lemma.   Let $f : G \to H$ and $g : H \to K$ be homomorphisms; assume f is surjective. If $x_0 \in G$, and if $\ker g$ is the least normal subgroup of H containing $f(x_0)$, then $\ker(g \circ f)$ is the least normal subgroup N of G containing $\ker f$ and x_0.*
   Proof. Show that $f(N)$ is normal; conclude that $\ker(g \circ f) = f^{-1}(\ker g) \subset f^{-1}f(N) = N$.

4. Show that the space constructed in Exercise 2 is in fact metrizable. [*Hint:* The quotient map is a perfect map.]

Chapter 12

Classification of Covering Spaces

Up to this point, we have used covering spaces primarily as a tool for computing fundamental groups. Now we turn things around and use the fundamental group as a tool for studying covering spaces.

To do this in any reasonable way, we must restrict ourselves to the case where B is locally path connected. Once we have done this, we may as well require B to be path connected as well, since B breaks up into the disjoint open sets B_α that are its path components, and the maps $p^{-1}(B_\alpha) \to B_\alpha$ obtained by restricting p are covering maps, by Theorem 53.2. We may as well assume also that E is path connected. For if E_α is a path component of $p^{-1}(B_\alpha)$, then the map $E_\alpha \to B_\alpha$ obtained by restricting p is also a covering map. (See Lemma 75.1.) Therefore, one can determine all coverings of the locally path-connected space B merely by determining all path-connected coverings of each path component of B!

For this reason, we make the following:

Convention. *Throughout this chapter, the statement that $p : E \to B$ is a covering map will include the assumption that E and B are locally path connected and path connected, unless specifically stated otherwise.*

With this convention, we now describe the connection between covering spaces of B and the fundamental group of B.

If $p : E \to B$ is a covering map, with $p(e_0) = b_0$, then the induced homomorphism p_* is injective, by Theorem 54.6, so that

$$H_0 = p_*(\pi_1(E, e_0))$$

is a subgroup of $\pi_1(B, b_0)$ isomorphic to $\pi_1(E, e_0)$. It turns out that the subgroup H_0 determines the covering p completely, up to a suitable notion of equivalence of coverings. This we shall prove in §74. Furthermore, under a (fairly mild) additional "local niceness" condition on B, there exists, for each subgroup H_0 of $\pi_1(B, b_0)$, a covering $p : E \to B$ of B whose corresponding subgroup is H_0. This we shall prove in §77.

Roughly speaking, these results show that one can determine all covering spaces of B merely by examining the collection of all subgroups of $\pi_1(B, b_0)$. This is the classical procedure of algebraic topology; one "solves" a problem of topology by reducing it to a problem of algebra, hopefully one that is more tractable.

Throughout the chapter, we assume the general lifting correspondence theorem, Theorem 54.6.

§74 Equivalence of Covering Spaces

In this section, we show that the subgroup H_0 of $\pi_1(B, b_0)$ determines the covering $p : E \to B$ completely, up to a suitable notion of equivalence of coverings.

Definition. Let $p : E \to B$ and $p' : E' \to B$ be covering maps. They are said to be *equivalent* if there exists a homeomorphism $h : E \to E'$ such that $p = p' \circ h$. The homeomorphism h is called an *equivalence of covering maps* or an *equivalence of covering spaces*.

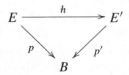

Given two covering maps $p : E \to B$ and $p' : E' \to B$ whose corresponding subgroups H_0 and H_0' are equal, we shall prove that there exists an equivalence $h : E \to E'$. For this purpose, we need to generalize the lifting lemmas of §54.

Lemma 74.1 (The general lifting lemma). *Let $p : E \to B$ be a covering map; let $p(e_0) = b_0$. Let $f : Y \to B$ be a continuous map, with $f(y_0) = b_0$. Suppose Y is path connected and locally path connected. The map f can be lifted to a map $\tilde{f} : Y \to E$ such that $\tilde{f}(y_0) = e_0$ if and only if*

$$f_*(\pi_1(Y, y_0)) \subset p_*(\pi_1(E, e_0)).$$

Furthermore, if such a lifting exists, it is unique.

Proof. If the lifting $\tilde{f}$ exists, then

$$f_*(\pi_1(Y, Y_0)) = p_*(\tilde{f}_*(\pi_1(Y, y_0))) \subset p_*(\pi_1(E, e_0)).$$

This proves the "only if" part of the theorem.

Now we prove that if $\tilde{f}$ exists, it is unique. Given $y_1 \in Y$, choose a path α in Y from y_0 to y_1. Take the path $f \circ \alpha$ in B and lift it to a path γ in E beginning at e_0. If a lifting $\tilde{f}$ of f exists, then $\tilde{f}(y_1)$ must equal the end point $\gamma(1)$ of γ, for $\tilde{f} \circ \alpha$ is a lifting of $f \circ \alpha$ that begins at e_0, and path liftings are unique.

Finally, we prove the "if" part of the theorem. The uniqueness part of the proof gives us a clue how to proceed. Given $y_1 \in Y$, choose a path α in Y from y_0 to y_1. Lift the path $f \circ \alpha$ to a path γ in E beginning at e_0, and define $\tilde{f}(y_1) = \gamma(1)$. See Figure 74.1. It is a certain amount of work to show that $\tilde{f}$ is well-defined, independent of the choice of α. Once we prove that, continuity of $\tilde{f}$ is proved easily, as we now show.

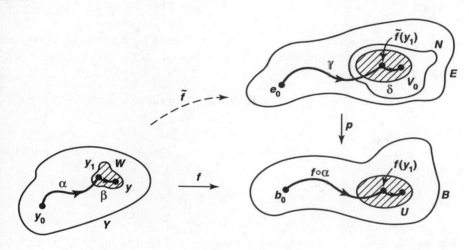

Figure 74.1

To prove continuity of $\tilde{f}$ at the point y_1 of Y, we show that, given a neighborhood N of $\tilde{f}(y_1)$, there is a neighborhood W of y_1 such that $\tilde{f}(W) \subset N$. To begin, choose a path-connected neighborhood U of $f(y_1)$ that is evenly covered by p. Break $p^{-1}(U)$ up into slices, and let V_0 be the slice that contains the point $\tilde{f}(y_1)$. Replacing U by a smaller neighborhood of $f(y_1)$ if necessary, we can assume that $V_0 \subset N$. Let $p_0 : V_0 \to U$ be obtained by restricting p; then p_0 is a homeomorphism. Because f is continuous at y_1 and Y is locally path connected, we can find a path-connected neighborhood W of y_1 such that $f(W) \subset U$. We shall show that $\tilde{f}(W) \subset V_0$; then our result is proved.

Given $y \in W$, choose a path β in W from y_1 to y. Since $\tilde{f}$ is well defined, $\tilde{f}(y)$ can be obtained by taking the path $\alpha * \beta$ from y_0 to y, lifting the path $f \circ (\alpha * \beta)$ to a path in E beginning at e_0, and letting $\tilde{f}(y)$ be the end point of this lifted path. Now γ is a lifting of α that begins at e_0. Since the path $f \circ \beta$ lies in U, the path $\delta = p_0^{-1} \circ f \circ \beta$

is a lifting of it that begins at $\tilde{f}(y_1)$. Then $\gamma * \delta$ is a lifting of $f \circ (\alpha * \beta)$ that begins at e_0; it ends at the point $\delta(1)$ of V_0. Hence $\tilde{f}(W) \subset V_0$, as desired.

Finally, we show $\tilde{f}$ is well defined. Let α and β be two paths in Y from y_0 to y_1. We must show that if we lift $f \circ \alpha$ and $f \circ \beta$ to paths in E beginning at e_0, then these lifted paths end at the same point of E.

First, we lift $f \circ \alpha$ to a path γ in E beginning at e_0; then we lift $f \circ \bar{\beta}$ to a path δ in E beginning at the end point $\gamma(1)$ of γ. Then $\gamma * \delta$ is a lifting of the loop $f \circ (\alpha * \bar{\beta})$. Now by hypothesis,

$$f_*(\pi_1(Y, y_0)) \subset p_*(\pi_1(E, e_0)).$$

Hence $[f \circ (\alpha * \bar{\beta})]$ belongs to the image of p_*. Theorem 54.6 now implies that its lift $\gamma * \delta$ is a *loop* in E.

It follows that $\tilde{f}$ is well defined. For $\bar{\delta}$ is a lifting of $f \circ \beta$ that begins at e_0, and γ is a lifting of $f \circ \alpha$ that begins at e_0, and both liftings end at the same point of E.   ∎

Theorem 74.2. *Let $p : E \to B$ and $p' : E' \to B$ be covering maps; let $p(e_0) = p'(e'_0) = b_0$. There is an equivalence $h : E \to E'$ such that $h(e_0) = e'_0$ if and only if the groups*

$$H_0 = p_*(\pi_1(E, e_0)) \quad \text{and} \quad H'_0 = p'_*(\pi_1(E', e'_0))$$

are equal. If h exists, it is unique.

Proof.   We prove the "only if" part of the theorem. Given h, the fact that h is a homeomorphism implies that

$$h_*(\pi_1(E, e_0)) = \pi_1(E', e'_0).$$

Since $p' \circ h = p$, we have $H_0 = H'_0$.

Now we prove the "if" part of the theorem; we assume that $H_0 = H'_0$ and show that h exists. We shall apply the preceding lemma (four times!). Consider the maps

$$
\begin{array}{ccc}
 & & E' \\
 & & \downarrow p' \\
E & \xrightarrow{\ p\ } & B.
\end{array}
$$

Because p' is a covering map and E is path connected and locally path connected, there exists a map $h : E \to E'$ with $h(e_0) = e'_0$ that is a lifting of p (that is, such that $p' \circ h = p$). Reversing the roles of E and E' in this argument, we see there is a map $k : E' \to E$ with $k(e'_0) = e_0$ such that $p \circ k = p'$. Now consider the maps

$$
\begin{array}{ccc}
 & & E \\
 & & \downarrow p \\
E & \xrightarrow{\ p\ } & B.
\end{array}
$$

The map $k \circ h : E \to E$ is a lifting of p (since $p \circ k \circ h = p' \circ h = p$), with $p(e_0) = e_0$. The identity map i_E of E is another such lifting. The uniqueness part of the preceding lemma implies that $k \circ h = i_E$. A similar argument shows that $h \circ k$ equals the identity map of E'. ∎

We seem to have solved our equivalence problem. But there is a somewhat subtle point we have overlooked. We have obtained a necessary and sufficient condition for there to exist an equivalence $h : E \to E'$ that carries the point e_0 to the point e_0'. But we have not yet determined under what conditions there exists an equivalence in general. It is possible that there may be no equivalence carrying e_0 to e_0' but that there *is* an equivalence carrying e_0 to some other point e_1' of $(p')^{-1}(b_0)$. Can we determine whether this is the case merely by examining the subgroups H_0 and H_0'? We consider this problem now.

If H_1 and H_2 are subgroups of a group G, you may recall from algebra that they are said to be ***conjugate*** subgroups if $H_2 = \alpha \cdot H_1 \cdot \alpha^{-1}$ for some element α of G. Said differently, they are conjugate if the isomorphism of G with itself that maps x to $\alpha \cdot x \cdot \alpha^{-1}$ carries the group H_1 onto the group H_2. It is easy to check that conjugacy is an equivalence relation on the collection of subgroups of G. The equivalence class of the subgroup H is called the ***conjugacy class*** of H.

Lemma 74.3. *Let $p : E \to B$ be a covering map. Let e_0 and e_1 be points of $p^{-1}(b_0)$, and let $H_i = p_*(\pi_1(E, e_i))$.*

(a) If γ is a path in E from e_0 to e_1, and α is the loop $p \circ \gamma$ in B, then the equation $[\alpha] * H_1 * [\alpha]^{-1} = H_0$ holds; hence H_0 and H_1 are conjugate.

(b) Conversely, given e_0, and given a subgroup H of $\pi_1(B, b_0)$ conjugate to H_0, there exists a point e_1 of $p^{-1}(b_0)$ such that $H_1 = H$.

Proof. (a) First, we show that $[\alpha] * H_1 * [\alpha]^{-1} \subset H_0$. Given an element $[h]$ of H_1, we have $[h] = p_*([\tilde{h}])$ for some loop $\tilde{h}$ in E based at e_1. Let $\tilde{k}$ be the path $\tilde{k} = (\gamma * \tilde{h}) * \bar{\gamma}$; it is a loop in E based at e_0, and

$$p_*([\tilde{k}]) = [(\alpha * h) * \bar{\alpha}] = [\alpha] * [h] * [\alpha]^{-1},$$

so the latter element belongs to $p_*(\pi_1(E, e_0)) = H_0$, as desired. See Figure 74.2.

Now we show that $[\alpha] * H_1 * [\alpha]^{-1} \supset H_0$. Note that $\bar{\gamma}$ is a path from e_1 to e_0 and $\bar{\alpha}$ equals the loop $p \circ \bar{\gamma}$. By the result just proved, we have

$$[\bar{\alpha}] * H_0 * [\bar{\alpha}]^{-1} \subset H_1,$$

which implies out desired result.

(b) To prove the converse, let e_0 be given and let H be conjugate to H_0. Then $H_0 = [\alpha] * H * [\alpha]^{-1}$ for some loop α in B based at b_0. Let γ be the lifting of α to a path in E beginning at e_0, and let $e_1 = \gamma(1)$. Then (a) implies that $H_0 = [\alpha] * H_1 * [\alpha]^{-1}$. We conclude that $H = H_1$. ∎

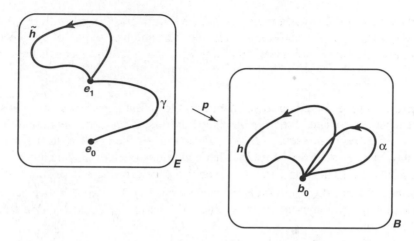

Figure 74.2

Theorem 74.4. *Let $p : E \to B$ and $p' : E' \to B$ be covering maps; let $p(e_0) = p'(e'_0) = b_0$. The covering maps p and p' are equivalent if and only if the subgroups*

$$H_0 = p_*(\pi_1(E, e_0)) \quad \text{and} \quad H'_0 = p'_*(\pi_1(E', e'_0))$$

of $\pi_1(B, b_0)$ are conjugate.

Proof. If $h : E \to E'$ is an equivalence, let $e'_1 = h(e_0)$, and let $H'_1 = p_*(\pi_1(E', e'_1))$. Theorem 74.2 implies that $H_0 = H'_1$, while the preceding lemma tells us that H'_1 is conjugate to H'_0.

Conversely, if the groups H_0 and H'_0 are conjugate, the preceding lemma implies there is a point e'_1 of E' such that $H'_1 = H_0$. Theorem 74.2 then gives us an equivalence $h : E \to E'$ such that $h(e_0) = e'_1$.   ∎

EXAMPLE 1.   Consider covering spaces of the circle $B = S^1$. Because $\pi_1(B, b_0)$ is abelian, two subgroups of $\pi_1(B, b_0)$ are conjugate if and only if they are equal. Therefore two coverings of B are equivalent if and only if they correspond to the same subgroup of $\pi_1(B, b_0)$.

Now $\pi_1(B, b_0)$ is isomorphic to the integers $\mathbb{Z}$. What are the subgroups of $\mathbb{Z}$? It is standard theorem of modern algebra that, given a nontrivial subgroup of $\mathbb{Z}$, it must be the group G_n consisting of all multiples of n, for some $n \in \mathbb{Z}_+$.

We have studied one covering space of the circle, the covering $p : \mathbb{R} \to S^1$. It must correspond to the trivial subgroup of $\pi_1(S^1, b_0)$, because $\mathbb{R}$ is simply connected. We have also considered the covering $p : S^1 \to S^1$ defined by $p(z) = z^n$, where z is a complex number. In this case, the map p_* carries a generator of $\pi_1(S^1, b_0)$ into n times itself. Therefore, the group $p_*(\pi_1(S^1, b_0))$ corresponds to the subgroup G_n of $\mathbb{Z}$ under the standard isomorphism of $\pi_1(S^1, b_0)$ with $\mathbb{Z}$.

We conclude from the preceding theorem that every path-connected covering space of S^1 is equivalent to one of these coverings.

Exercises

1. Show that if $n > 1$, every continuous map $f : S^n \to S^1$ is nulhomotopic. [*Hint:* Use the lifting lemma.]

2. (a) Show that every continuous map $f : P^2 \to S^1$ is nulhomotopic.
   (b) Find a continuous map of the torus into S^1 that is not nulhomotopic.

3. Let $p : E \to B$ be a covering map; let $p(e_0) = b_0$. Show that $H_0 = p_*(\pi_1(E, e_0))$ is a normal subgroup of $\pi_1(B, b_0)$ if and only if for every pair of points e_1, e_2 of $p^{-1}(b_0)$, there is an equivalence $h : E \to E$ with $h(e_1) = e_2$.

4. Let $T = S^1 \times S^1$, the torus. There is an isomorphism of $\pi_1(T, b_0 \times b_0)$ with $\mathbb{Z} \times \mathbb{Z}$ induced by projections of T onto its two factors.
   (a) Find a covering space of T corresponding to the subgroup of $\mathbb{Z} \times \mathbb{Z}$ generated by the element $m \times 0$, where m is a positive integer.
   (b) Find a covering space of T corresponding to the trivial subgroup of $\mathbb{Z} \times \mathbb{Z}$.
   (c) Find a covering space of T corresponding to the subgroup of $\mathbb{Z} \times \mathbb{Z}$ generated by $m \times 0$ and $0 \times n$, where m and n are positive integers.

*5. Let $T = S^1 \times S^1$ be the torus; let $x_0 = b_0 \times b_0$.
   (a) Prove the following:

   Theorem. *Every isomorphism of $\pi_1(T, x_0)$ with itself is induced by a homeomorphism of T with itself that maps x_0 to x_0.*

   [*Hint:* Let $p : \mathbb{R}^2 \to T$ be the usual covering map. If A is a 2×2 matrix with integer entries, the linear map $T_A : \mathbb{R}^2 \to \mathbb{R}^2$ with matrix A induces a continuous map $f : T \to T$. Furthermore, f is a homeomorphism if A is invertible over the integers.]

   (b) Prove the following:

   Theorem. *If E is a covering space of T, then E is homeomorphic either to $\mathbb{R}^2$, or to $S^1 \times \mathbb{R}$, or to T.*

   [*Hint:* You may use the following result from algebra: If F is a free abelian group of rank 2 and N is a nontrivial subgroup, then there is a basis a_1, a_2 for F such that either (1) ma_1 is a basis for N, for some positive integer m, or (2) ma_1, na_2 is a basis for N, where m and n are positive integers.]

*6. Prove the following:

   Theorem. *Let G be a topological group with multiplication operation $m : G \times G \to G$ and identity element e. Assume $p : \tilde{G} \to G$ is a covering map. Given $\tilde{e}$ with $p(\tilde{e}) = e$, there is a unique multiplication operation on $\tilde{G}$ that makes it into a topological group such that $\tilde{e}$ is the identity element and p is a homomorphism.*
   Proof. Recall that, by our convention, G and $\tilde{G}$ are path connected and locally path connected.

   (a) Let $I : G \to G$ be the map $I(g) = g^{-1}$. Show there exist unique maps $\tilde{m} : \tilde{G} \times \tilde{G} \to \tilde{G}$ and $\tilde{I} : \tilde{G} \to \tilde{G}$ with $\tilde{m}(\tilde{e} \times \tilde{e}) = \tilde{e}$ and $\tilde{I}(\tilde{e}) = \tilde{e}$ such that $p \circ \tilde{m} = m \circ (p \times p)$ and $p \circ \tilde{I} = I \circ p$.

   (b) Show the maps $\tilde{G} \to \tilde{G}$ given by $\tilde{g} \to \tilde{m}(\tilde{e} \times \tilde{g})$ and $\tilde{g} \to \tilde{m}(\tilde{g} \times \tilde{e})$ equal the identity map of $\tilde{G}$. [*Hint:* Use the uniqueness part of Lemma 74.1.]

(c) Show the maps $\tilde{G} \to \tilde{G}$ given by $\tilde{g} \to \tilde{m}(\tilde{g} \times \tilde{I}(\tilde{g}))$ and $\tilde{g} \to \tilde{m}(\tilde{I}(\tilde{g}) \times \tilde{g})$ map $\tilde{G}$ to $\tilde{e}$.

(d) Show the maps $\tilde{G} \times \tilde{G} \times \tilde{G} \to \tilde{G}$ given by

$$\tilde{g} \times \tilde{g}' \times \tilde{g}'' \to \tilde{m}(\tilde{g} \times \tilde{m}(\tilde{g}' \times \tilde{g}''))$$
$$\tilde{g} \times \tilde{g}' \times \tilde{g}'' \to \tilde{m}(\tilde{m}(\tilde{g} \times \tilde{g}') \times \tilde{g}'')$$

are equal.

(e) Complete the proof.

7. Let $p : \tilde{G} \to G$ be a homomorphism of topological groups that is a covering map. Show that if G is abelian, so is $\tilde{G}$.

§75 The Universal Covering Space

Suppose $p : E \to B$ is a covering map, with $p(e_0) = b_0$. If E is simply connected, then E is called a ***universal covering space*** of B. Since $\pi_1(E, e_0)$ is trivial, this covering space corresponds to the trivial subgroup of $\pi_1(B, b_0)$ under the correspondence defined in the preceding section. Theorem 74.4 thus implies that any two universal covering spaces of B are equivalent. For this reason, we often speak of "the" universal covering space of a given space B. Not every space has a universal covering space, as we shall see. For the moment, we shall simply assume that B has a universal covering space and derive some consequences of this assumption.

We prove two preliminary lemmas:

Lemma 75.1. *Let B be path connected and locally path connected. Let $p : E \to B$ be a covering map in the former sense (so that E is not required to be path connected). If E_0 is a path component of E, then the map $p_0 : E_0 \to B$ obtained by restricting p is a covering map.*

Proof. We first show p_0 is surjective. Since the space E is locally homeomorphic to B, it is locally path connected. Therefore E_0 is open in E. It follows that $p(E_0)$ is open in B. We show that $p(E_0)$ is also closed in B, so that $p(E_0) = B$.

Let x be a point of B belonging to the closure of $p(E_0)$. Let U be a path-connected neighborhood of x that is evenly covered by p. Since U contains a point of $p(E_0)$, some slice V_α of $p^{-1}(U)$ must intersect E_0. Since V_α is homeomorphic to U, it is path connected; therefore it must be contained in E_0. Then $p(V_\alpha) = U$ is contained in $p(E_0)$, so that in particular, $x \in p(E_0)$.

Now we show $p_0 : E_0 \to B$ is a covering map. Given $x \in B$, choose a neighborhood U of x as before. If V_α is a slice of $p^{-1}(U)$, then V_α is path connected; if it intersects E_0, it lies in E_0. Therefore, $p_0^{-1}(U)$ equals the union of those slices V_α of $p^{-1}(U)$ that intersect E_0; each of these is open in E_0 and is mapped homeomorphically by p_0 onto U. Thus U is evenly covered by p_0. ∎

Lemma 75.2. *Let p, q, and r be continuous maps with $p = r \circ q$, as in the following diagram:*

(a) *If p and r are covering maps, so is q.*

*(b) *If p and q are covering maps, so is r.*

Proof. By our convention, X, Y, and Z are path connected and locally path connected. Let $x_0 \in X$; set $y_0 = q(x_0)$ and $z_0 = p(x_0)$.

(a) Assume that p and r are covering maps. We show first that q is surjective. Given $y \in Y$, choose a path $\tilde{\alpha}$ in Y from y_0 to y. Then $\alpha = r \circ \tilde{\alpha}$ is a path in Z beginning at z_0; let $\tilde{\tilde{\alpha}}$ be a lifting of α to a path in X beginning at x_0. Then $q \circ \tilde{\tilde{\alpha}}$ is a lifting of α to Y that begins at y_0. By uniqueness of path liftings, $\tilde{\alpha} = q \circ \tilde{\tilde{\alpha}}$. Then q maps the end point of $\tilde{\tilde{\alpha}}$ to the end point y of $\tilde{\alpha}$. Thus q is surjective.

Given $y \in Y$, we find a neighborhood of y that is evenly covered by q. Let $z = r(y)$. Since p and r are covering maps, we can find a path-connected neighborhood U of z that is evenly covered by both p and r. Let V be the slice of $r^{-1}(U)$ that contains the point y; we show V is evenly covered by q. Let $\{U_\alpha\}$ be the collection of slices of $p^{-1}(U)$. Now q maps each set U_α into the set $r^{-1}(U)$; because U_α is connected, it must be mapped by q into a single one of the slices of $r^{-1}(U)$. Therefore, $q^{-1}(V)$ equals the union of those slices U_α that are mapped by q into V. It is easy to see that each such U_α is mapped homeomorphically *onto* V by q. For let p_0, q_0, r_0 be the maps obtained by restricting p, q, and r, respectively, as indicated in the following diagram:

Because p_0 and r_0 are homeomorphisms, so is $q_0 = r_0^{-1} \circ p_0$.

*(b) We shall use this result only in the exercises. Assume that p and q are covering maps. Because $p = r \circ q$ and p is surjective, r is also surjective.

Given $z \in Z$, let U be a path-connected neighborhood of z that is evenly covered by p. We show that U is also evenly covered by r. Let $\{V_\beta\}$ be the collection of path components of $r^{-1}(U)$; these sets are disjoint and open in Y. We show that for each β, the map r carries V_β homeomorphically onto U.

Let $\{U_\alpha\}$ be the collection of slices of $p^{-1}(U)$; they are disjoint, open, and path connected, so they are the path components of $p^{-1}(U)$. Now q maps each U_α into the set $r^{-1}(U)$; because U_α is connected, it must be mapped by q into one of the sets V_β. Therefore $q^{-1}(V_\beta)$ equals the union of a subcollection of the collection $\{U_\alpha\}$. Theorem 53.2 and Lemma 75.1 together imply that if U_{α_0} is any one of the path components of $q^{-1}(V_\beta)$ then the map $q_0 : U_{\alpha_0} \to V_\beta$ obtained by restricting q is a covering map.

In particular, q_0 is surjective. Hence q_0 is a homeomorphism, being continuous, open, and injective as well. Consider the maps

$$
\begin{array}{ccc}
U_{\alpha_0} & \xrightarrow{\ q_0\ } & \\
p_0 \downarrow & \searrow & V_\beta \\
U & \xleftarrow{\ r_0\ } &
\end{array}
$$

obtained by restricting p, q, and r. Because p_0 and q_0 are homeomorphisms, so is r_0. ∎

Theorem 75.3. *Let $p : E \to B$ be a covering map, with E simply connected. Given any covering map $r : Y \to B$, there is a covering map $q : E \to Y$ such that $r \circ q = p$.*

$$
\begin{array}{ccc}
E & \xrightarrow{\ q\ } & \\
p \downarrow & \searrow & Y \\
B & \xleftarrow{\ r\ } &
\end{array}
$$

This theorem shows why E is called a *universal* covering space of B; it covers every other covering space of B.

Proof. Let $b_0 \in B$; choose e_0 and y_0 so that $p(e_0) = b_0$ and $r(y_0) = b_0$. We apply Lemma 74.1 to construct q. The map r is a covering map, and the condition

$$
p_*(\pi_1(E, e_0)) \subset r_*(\pi_1(Y, y_0))
$$

is satisfied trivially because E is simply connected. Therefore, there is a map $q : E \to Y$ such that $r \circ q = p$ and $q(e_0) = y_0$. It follows from the preceding lemma that q is a covering map. ∎

Now we give an example of a space that has no universal covering space. We need the following lemma.

Lemma 75.4. *Let $p : E \to B$ be a covering map; let $p(e_0) = b_0$. If E is simply connected, then b_0 has a neighborhood U such that inclusion $i : U \to B$ induces the trivial homomorphism*

$$
i_* : \pi_1(U, b_0) \longrightarrow \pi_1(B, b_0).
$$

Proof. Let U be a neighborhood of b_0 that is evenly covered by p; break $p^{-1}(U)$ up into slices; let U_α be the slice containing e_0. Let f be a loop in U based at b_0. Because p defines a homeomorphism of U_α with U, the loop f lifts to a *loop* $\tilde{f}$ in U_α based at e_0. Since E is simply connected, there is a path homotopy $\tilde{F}$ in E between $\tilde{f}$ and a constant loop. Then $p \circ \tilde{F}$ is a path homotopy in B between f and a constant loop. ∎

EXAMPLE 1.   Let X be our familiar "infinite earring" in the plane; if C_n is the circle of radius $1/n$ in the plane with center at the point $(1/n, 0)$, then X is the union of the circles C_n. Let b_0 be the origin; we show that if U is any neighborhood of b_0 in X, then the homomorphism of fundamental groups induced by inclusion $i : U \to X$ is not trivial.

Given n, there is a retraction $r : X \to C_n$ obtained by letting r map each circle C_i for $i \neq n$ to the point b_0. Choose n large enough that C_n lies in U. Then in the following diagram of homomorphisms induced by inclusion, j_* is injective; hence i_* cannot be trivial.

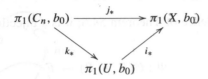

It follows that even though X is path connected and locally path connected, it has no universal covering space.

Exercise

1. Let $q : X \to Y$ and $r : Y \to Z$ be maps; let $p = r \circ q$.
   (a) Let q and r be covering maps. Show that if Z has a universal covering space, then p is a covering map. Compare Exercise 4 of §53.
   *(b) Give an example where q and r are covering maps but p is not.

*§76   Covering Transformations

Given a covering map $p : E \to B$, it is of some interest to consider the set of all equivalences of this covering space with *itself.* Such an equivalence is called a ***covering transformation***. Composites and inverses of covering transformations are covering transformations, so this set forms a group; it is called the ***group of covering transformations*** and denoted $\mathcal{C}(E, p, B)$.

Throughout this section, we shall assume that $p : E \to B$ is a covering map with $p(e_0) = b_0$; and we shall let $H_0 = p_*(\pi_1(E, e_0))$. We shall show that the group $\mathcal{C}(E, p, B)$ is completely determined by the group $\pi_1(B, b_0)$ and the subgroup H_0. Specifically, we shall show that if $N(H_0)$ is the largest subgroup of $\pi_1(B, b_0)$ of which H_0 is a normal subgroup, then $\mathcal{C}(E, p, B)$ is isomorphic to $N(H_0)/H_0$.

We define $N(H_0)$ formally as follows:

Definition.   If H is a subgroup of the group G, then the ***normalizer*** of H in G is the subset of G defined by the equation

$$N(H) = \{g \mid gHg^{-1} = H\}.$$

It is easy to see that $N(H)$ is a subgroup of G. It follows from the definition that it contains H as a normal subgroup and is the largest such subgroup of G.

In general, if $h : E \to E$ is a covering transformation, then any loop in the base space that lifts to a loop in E at e_0 also lifts to a loop when the lift begins at $h(e_0)$. In the present case, a loop that generates the fundamental group of A lifts to a non-loop when the lift is based at e_0 and lifts to a loop when it is based at any other point of $p^{-1}(b_0)$ lying on the y-axis. Similarly, a loop that generates the fundamental group of B lifts to a non-loop beginning at e_0 and to a loop beginning at any other point of $p^{-1}(b_0)$ lying on the x-axis. It follows that $h(e_0) = e_0$, so that h is the identity map.

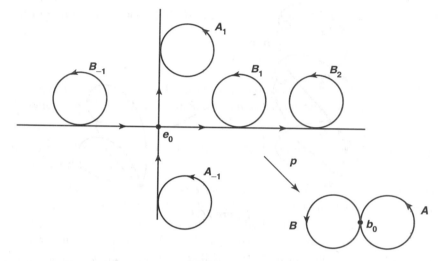

Figure 76.2

There is a method for constructing covering spaces that automatically leads to a covering that is regular; and in fact every regular covering space can be constructed by this method. It involves the *action* of a group G on a space X.

Definition. Let X be a space, and let G be a subgroup of the group of homeomorphisms of X with itself. The *orbit space* X/G is defined to be the quotient space obtained from X by means of the equivalence relation $x \sim g(x)$ for all $x \in X$ and all $g \in G$. The equivalence class of x is called the *orbit* of x.

Definition. If G is a group of homeomorphisms of X, the action of G on X is said to be *properly discontinuous* if for every $x \in X$ there is a neighborhood U of x such that $g(U)$ is disjoint from U whenever $g \neq e$. (Here e is the identity element of G.) It follows that $g_0(U)$ and $g_1(U)$ are disjoint whenever $g_0 \neq g_1$, for otherwise U and $g_0^{-1} g_1(U)$ would not be disjoint.

Theorem 76.5. *Let X be path connected and locally path connected; let G be a group of homeomorphisms of X. The quotient map $\pi : X \to X/G$ is a covering map if and only if the action of G is properly discontinuous. In this case, the covering map π is regular and G is its group of covering transformations.*

Proof. We show π is an open map. If U is open in X, then $\pi^{-1}\pi(U)$ is the union of the open sets $g(U)$ of X, for $g \in G$. Hence $\pi^{-1}\pi(U)$ is open in X, so that $\pi(U)$ is open in X/G by definition. Thus π is open.

Step 1. We suppose that the action of G is properly discontinuous and show that π is a covering map. Given $x \in X$, let U be a neighborhood of x such that $g_0(U)$ and $g_1(U)$ are disjoint whenever $g_0 \neq g_1$. Then $\pi(U)$ is evenly covered by π. Indeed, $\pi^{-1}\pi(U)$ equals the union of the disjoint open sets $g(U)$, for $g \in G$, each of which contains at most one point of each orbit. Therefore, the map $g(U) \to \pi(U)$ obtained by restricting π is bijective; being continuous and open, it is a homeomorphism. The sets $g(U)$, for $g \in G$, thus form a partition of $\pi^{-1}\pi(U)$ into slices.

Step 2. We suppose now that π is a covering map and show that the action of G is properly discontinuous. Given $x \in X$, let V be a neighborhood of $\pi(x)$ that is evenly covered by π. Partition $\pi^{-1}(V)$ into slices; let U_α be the slice containing x. Given $g \in G$ with $g \neq e$, the set $g(U_\alpha)$ must be disjoint from U_α, for otherwise, two points of U_α would belong to the same orbit and the restriction of π to U_α would not be injective. It follows that the action of G is properly discontinuous.

Step 3. We show that if π is a covering map, then G is its group of covering transformations and π is regular. Certainly any $g \in G$ is a covering transformation, for $\pi \circ g = \pi$ because the orbit of $g(x)$ equals the orbit of x. On the other hand, let h be a covering transformation with $h(x_1) = x_2$, say. Because $\pi \circ h = \pi$, the points x_1 and x_2 map to the same point under π; therefore there is an element $g \in G$ such that $g(x_1) = x_2$. The uniqueness part of Theorem 74.2 then implies that $h = g$.

It follows that π is regular. Indeed, for any two points x_1 and x_2 lying in the same orbit, there is an element $g \in G$ such that $g(x_1) = x_2$. Then Corollary 76.3 applies. ∎

Theorem 76.6. *If $p : X \to B$ is a regular covering map and G is its group of covering transformations, then there is a homeomorphism $k : X/G \to B$ such that $p = k \circ \pi$, where $\pi : X \to X/G$ is the projection.*

$$
\begin{array}{ccc}
X & = & X \\
\big\downarrow \scriptstyle \pi & & \big\downarrow \scriptstyle p \\
X/G & \xrightarrow{\ k\ } & B
\end{array}
$$

Proof. If g is a covering transformation, then $p(g(x)) = p(x)$ by definition. Hence p is constant on each orbit, so it induces a continuous map k of the quotient space X/G into B. On the other hand, p is a quotient map because it is continuous, surjective, and open. Because p is regular, any two points of $p^{-1}(b)$ belong to the same orbit under the action of G. Therefore, π induces a continuous map $B \to X/G$ that is an inverse for k.   ∎

EXAMPLE 3.   Let X be the cylinder $S^1 \times I$; let $h : X \to X$ be the homeomorphism $h(x, t) = (-x, t)$; and let $k : X \to X$ be the homeomorphism $k(x, t) = (-x, 1 - t)$. The groups $G_1 = \{e, h\}$ and $G_2 = \{e, k\}$ are isomorphic to the integers modulo 2; both

(a) Show that h generates a subgroup G of the homeomorphism group of S^3 that is cyclic of order n, and that only the identity element of G has a fixed point. The orbit space S^3/G is called the **lens space** $L(n, k)$.

(b) Show that if $L(n, k)$ and $L(n', k')$ are homeomorphic, then $n = n'$. [It is a theorem that $L(n, k)$ and $L(n', k')$ are homeomorphic if and only if $n = n'$ and either $k \equiv k' \pmod{n}$ or $kk' \equiv 1 \pmod{n}$. The proof is decidedly nontrivial.]

(c) Show that $L(n, k)$ is a compact 3-manifold.

6. Prove the following:

Theorem. *Let X be a locally compact Hausdorff space; let G be a group of homeomorphisms of X such that the action of G is fixed-point free. Suppose that for each compact subspace C of X, there are only finitely many elements g of G such that the intersection $C \cap g(C)$ is nonempty. Then the action of G is properly discontinuous, and X/G is locally compact Hausdorff.*

Proof.

(a) For each compact subspace C of X, show that the union of the sets $g(C)$, for $g \in G$, is closed in X. [*Hint:* If U is a neighborhood of x with $\bar{U}$ compact, then $\bar{U} \cup C$ intersects $g(\bar{U} \cup C)$ for only finitely many g.]

(b) Show X/G is Hausdorff.

(c) Show the action of G is properly discontinuous.

(d) Show X/G is locally compact.

§77 Existence of Covering Spaces

We have shown that corresponding to each covering map $p : E \to B$ is a conjugacy class of subgroups of $\pi_1(B, b_0)$, and that two such covering maps are equivalent if and only if they correspond to the same such class. Thus, we have an injective correspondence from equivalence classes of coverings of B to conjugacy classes of subgroups of $\pi_1(B, b_0)$. Now we ask the question whether this correspondence is surjective, that is, whether for every conjugacy class of subgroups of $\pi_1(B, b_0)$, there exists a covering of B that corresponds to this class.

The answer to this question is "no," in general. In §75, we gave an example of a path-connected, locally path-connected space B that had no simply connected covering space, that is, that had no covering space corresponding to the class of the trivial subgroup. This example relied on Lemma 75.4, which gave a condition that any space having a simply connected covering space must satisfy. We now introduce this condition formally.

Definition. A space B is said to be **semilocally simply connected** if for each $b \in B$, there is a neighborhood U of b such that the homomorphism

$$i_* : \pi_1(U, b) \to \pi_1(B, b)$$

induced by inclusion is trivial.

Note that if U satisfies this condition, then so does any smaller neighborhood of b, so that b has "arbitrarily small" neighborhoods satisfying this condition. Note also that this condition is weaker than true local simple connectedness, which would require that within each neighborhood of b there should exist a neighborhood U of b that is itself simply connected.

Semilocal simple connectedness of B is both necessary and sufficient for there to exist, for every conjugacy class of subgroups of $\pi_1(B, b_0)$, a corresponding covering space of B. Necessity was proved in Lemma 75.4; sufficiency is proved in this section.

Theorem 77.1. *Let B be path connected, locally path connected, and semilocally simply connected. Let $b_0 \in B$. Given a subgroup H of $\pi_1(B, b_0)$, there exists a covering map $p : E \to B$ and a point $e_0 \in p^{-1}(b_0)$ such that*

$$p_*(\pi_1(E, e_0)) = H.$$

Proof. Step 1. Construction of E. The procedure for constructing E is reminiscent of the procedure used in complex analysis for constructing Riemann surfaces. Let $\mathscr{P}$ denote the set of all paths in B beginning at b_0. Define an equivalence relation on $\mathscr{P}$ by setting $\alpha \sim \beta$ if α and β end at the same point of B and

$$[\alpha * \bar{\beta}] \in H.$$

This relation is easily seen to be an equivalence relation. We will denote the equivalence class of the path α by $\alpha^{\#}$.

Let E denote the collection of equivalence classes, and define $p : E \to B$ by the equation

$$p(\alpha^{\#}) = \alpha(1).$$

Since B is path connected, p is surjective. We shall topologize E so that p is a covering map.

We first note two facts:
(1) If $[\alpha] = [\beta]$, then $\alpha^{\#} = \beta^{\#}$.
(2) If $\alpha^{\#} = \beta^{\#}$, then $(\alpha * \delta)^{\#} = (\beta * \delta)^{\#}$ for any path δ in B beginning at $\alpha(1)$.

The first follows by noting that if $[\alpha] = [\beta]$, then $[\alpha * \bar{\beta}]$ is the identity element, which belongs to H. The second follows by noting that $\alpha * \delta$ and $\beta * \delta$ end at the same point of B, and

$$[(\alpha * \delta) * \overline{(\beta * \delta)}] = [(\alpha * \delta) * (\bar{\delta} * \bar{\beta})] = [\alpha * \bar{\beta}],$$

which belongs to H by hypothesis.

Step 2. Topologizing E. One way to topologize E is to give $\mathscr{P}$ the compact-open topology (see Chapter 7) and E the corresponding quotient topology. But we can topologize E directly as follows:

Let α be any element of $\mathcal{P}$, and let U be any path-connected neighborhood of $\alpha(1)$. Define

$$B(U, \alpha) = \{(\alpha * \delta)^{\#} \mid \delta \text{ is a path in } U \text{ beginning at } \alpha(1)\}.$$

Note that $\alpha^{\#}$ is an element of $B(U, \alpha)$, since if $b = \alpha(1)$, then $\alpha^{\#} = (\alpha * e_b)^{\#}$; this element belongs to $B(U, \alpha)$ by definition. We assert that the sets $B(U, \alpha)$ form a basis for a topology on E.

First, we show that if $\beta^{\#} \in B(U, \alpha)$, then $\alpha^{\#} \in B(U, \beta)$ and $B(U, \alpha) = B(U, \beta)$. If $\beta^{\#} \in B(U, \alpha)$, then $\beta^{\#} = (\alpha * \delta)^{\#}$ for some path δ in U. Then

$$(\beta * \bar{\delta})^{\#} = ((\alpha * \delta) * \bar{\delta})^{\#} \qquad \text{by (2)}$$
$$= \alpha^{\#} \qquad\qquad\qquad \text{by (1)},$$

so that $\alpha^{\#} \in B(U, \beta)$ by definition. See Figure 77.1. We show first that $B(U, \beta) \subset B(U, \alpha)$. Note that the general element of $B(U, \beta)$ is of the form $(\beta * \gamma)^{\#}$, where γ is a path in U. Then note that

$$(\beta * \gamma)^{\#} = ((\alpha * \delta) * \gamma)^{\#}$$
$$= (\alpha * (\delta * \gamma))^{\#},$$

which belongs to $B(U, \alpha)$ by definition. Symmetry gives the inclusion $B(U, \alpha) \subset B(U, \beta)$ as well.

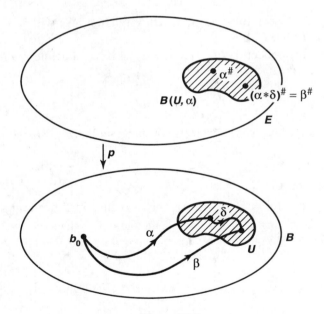

Figure 77.1

Now we show the sets $B(U, \alpha)$ form a basis. If $\beta^{\#}$ belongs to the intersection $B(U_1, \alpha_1) \cap B(U_2, \alpha_2)$, we need merely choose a path-connected neighborhood V

of $\beta(1)$ contained in $U_1 \cap U_2$. The inclusion

$$B(V, \beta) \subset B(U_1, \beta) \cap B(U_2, \beta)$$

follows from the definition of these sets, and the right side of the equation equals $B(U_1, \alpha_1) \cap B(U_2, a_2)$ by the result just proved.

Step 3. The map p is continuous and open. It is easy to see that p is open, for the image of the basis element $B(U, \alpha)$ is the open subset U of B: Given $x \in U$, we choose a path δ in U from $\alpha(1)$ to x; then $(\alpha * \delta)^\#$ is in $B(U, \alpha)$ and $p((\alpha * \delta)^\#) = x$.

To show that p is continuous, let us take an element $\alpha^\#$ of E and a neighborhood W of $p(\alpha^\#)$. Choose a path-connected neighborhood U of the point $p(\alpha^\#) = \alpha(1)$ lying in W. Then $B(U, \alpha)$ is a neighborhood of $\alpha^\#$ that p maps into W. Thus p is continuous at $\alpha^\#$.

Step 4. Every point of B has a neighborhood that is evenly covered by p. Given $b_1 \in B$, choose U to be a path-connected neighborhood of b_1 that satisfies the further condition that the homomorphism $\pi_1(U, b_1) \to \pi_1(B, b_1)$ induced by inclusion is trivial. We assert that U is evenly covered by p.

First, we show that $p^{-1}(U)$ equals the union of the sets $B(U, \alpha)$, as α ranges over all paths in B from b_0 to b_1. Since p maps each set $B(U, \alpha)$ onto U, it is clear that $p^{-1}(U)$ contains this union. On the other hand, if $\beta^\#$ belongs to $p^{-1}(U)$, then $\beta(1) \in U$. Choose a path δ in U from b_1 to $\beta(1)$ and let α be the path $\beta * \bar{\delta}$ from b_0 to b_1. Then $[\beta] = [\alpha * \delta]$, so that $\beta^\# = (\alpha * \delta)^\#$, which belongs to $B(U, \alpha)$. Thus $p^{-1}(U)$ is contained in the union of the sets $B(U, \alpha)$.

Second, note that distinct sets $B(U, \alpha)$ are disjoint. For if $\beta^\#$ belongs to $B(U, \alpha_1) \cap B(U, \alpha_2)$, then $B(U, \alpha_1) = B(U, \beta) = B(U, \alpha_2)$, by Step 2.

Third, we show that p defines a bijective map of $B(U, \alpha)$ with U. It follows that $p|B(U, \alpha)$ is a homeomorphism, being bijective and continuous and open. We already know that p maps $B(U, \alpha)$ onto U. To prove injectivity, suppose that

$$p((\alpha * \delta_1)^\#) = p((\alpha * \delta_2)^\#),$$

where δ_1 and δ_2 are paths in U. Then $\delta_1(1) = \delta_2(1)$. Because the homomorphism $\pi_1(U, b_1) \to \pi_1(B, b_1)$ induced by inclusion is trivial, $\delta_1 * \bar{\delta}_2$ is path homotopic in B to the constant loop. Then $[\alpha * \delta_1] = [\alpha * \delta_2]$, so that $(\alpha * \delta_1)^\# = (\alpha * \delta_2)^\#$, as desired.

It follows that $p : E \to B$ is a covering map in the sense used in earlier chapters. To show it is a covering map in the sense used in this chapter, we must show E is path connected. This we shall do shortly.

Step 5. Lifting a path in B. Let e_0 denote the equivalence class of the constant path at b_0; then $p(e_0) = b_0$ by definition. Given a path α in B beginning at b_0, we calculate its lift to a path in E beginning at e_0 and show that this lift ends at $\alpha^\#$.

To begin, given $c \in [0, 1]$, let $\alpha_c : I \to B$ denote the path defined by the equation

$$\alpha_c(t) = \alpha(tc) \quad \text{for} \quad 0 \leq t \leq 1.$$

Then α_c is the "portion" of α that runs from $\alpha(0)$ to $\alpha(c)$. In particular, α_0 is the constant path at b_0, and α_1 is the path α itself. We define $\tilde{\alpha} : I \to E$ by the equation

$$\tilde{\alpha}(c) = (\alpha_c)^\#$$

and show that $\tilde{\alpha}$ is continuous. Then $\tilde{\alpha}$ is a lift of α, since $p(\tilde{\alpha}(c)) = \alpha_c(1) = \alpha(c)$; furthermore, $\tilde{\alpha}$ begins at $(\alpha_0)^\# = e_0$ and ends at $(\alpha_1)^\# = \alpha^\#$.

To verify continuity, we introduce the following notation. Given $0 \le c < d \le 1$, let $\delta_{c,d}$ denote the path that equals the positive linear map of I onto $[c, d]$ followed by α. Note that the paths α_d and $\alpha_c * \delta_{c,d}$ are path homotopic because one is just a reparametrization of the other. See Figure 77.2.

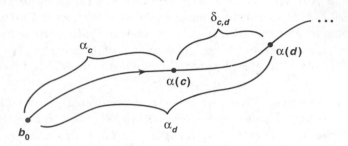

Figure 77.2

We now verify continuity of $\tilde{\alpha}$ at the point c of $[0, 1]$. Let W be a basis element in E about the point $\tilde{\alpha}(c)$. Then W equals $B(U, \alpha_c)$ for some path-connected neighborhood U of $\alpha(c)$. Choose $\epsilon > 0$ so that for $|c - t| < \epsilon$, the point $\alpha(t)$ lies in U. We show that if d is a point of $[0, 1]$ with $|c - d| < \epsilon$, then $\tilde{\alpha}(d) \in W$; this proves continuity of $\tilde{\alpha}$ at c.

So suppose $|c - d| < \epsilon$. Take first the case where $d > c$. Set $\delta = \delta_{c,d}$; then since $[\alpha_d] = [\alpha_c * \delta]$, we have

$$\tilde{\alpha}(d) = (\alpha_d)^\# = (\alpha_c * \delta)^\#.$$

Since δ lies in U, we have $\tilde{\alpha}(d) \in B(U, \alpha_c)$, as desired. If $d < c$, set $\delta = \delta_{d,c}$ and proceed similarly.

Step 6. The map $p : E \to B$ is a covering map. We need only verify that E is path connected, and this is easy. For if $\alpha^\#$ is any point of E, then the lift $\tilde{\alpha}$ of the path α is a path in E from e_0 to $\alpha^\#$.

Step 7. Finally, $H = p_*(\pi_1(E, e_0)$. Let α be a loop in B at b_0. Let $\tilde{\alpha}$ be its lift to E beginning at e_0. Theorem 54.6 tells us that $[\alpha] \in p_*(\pi_1(E, e_0))$ if and only if $\tilde{\alpha}$ is a *loop* in E. Now the final point of $\tilde{\alpha}$ is the point $\alpha^\#$, and $\alpha^\# = e_0$ if and only if α is equivalent to the constant path at b_0, i.e., if and only if $[\alpha * \bar{e}_{b_0}] \in H$. This occurs precisely when $[\alpha] \in H$. ∎

Corollary 77.2. *The space B has a universal covering space if and only if B is path connected, locally path connected, and semilocally simply connected.*

Exercises

1. Show that a simply connected space is semilocally simply connected.

2. Let X be the infinite earring in $\mathbb{R}^2$. (See Example 1 of §75.) Let $C(X)$ be the subspace of $\mathbb{R}^3$ that is the union of all line segments joining points of $X \times 0$ to the point $p = (0, 0, 1)$. It is called the ***cone*** on X. Show that $C(X)$ is simply connected, but is not locally simply connected at the origin.

*Supplementary Exercises: Topological Properties and π_1

The results of the preceding section tell us that the appropriate hypotheses for classifying the covering spaces of B are that B is path connected, locally path connected, and semilocally simply connected. We now show that they are also the correct hypotheses for studying the relation between various topological properties of B and the fundamental group of B.

1. Let X be a space; let $\mathcal{A}$ be an open covering of X. Under what conditions does there exist an open covering $\mathcal{B}$ of X refining $\mathcal{A}$ such that for each pair B, B' of elements of $\mathcal{B}$ that have nonempty intersection, the union $B \cup B'$ lies in an element of $\mathcal{A}$?

   (a) Show that such a covering $\mathcal{B}$ exists if X is metrizable. [*Hint:* Choose $\epsilon(x)$ so $B(x, 3\epsilon(x))$ lies in an element of $\mathcal{A}$. Let $\mathcal{B}$ consist of the open sets $B(x, \epsilon(x))$.]

   (b) Show that such a covering exists if X is compact Hausdorff. [*Hint:* Let $A_1, \ldots, A_n$ be a finite subcollection of $\mathcal{A}$ that covers X. Choose an open covering $C_1, \ldots, C_n$ of X such that $\bar{C}_i \subset A_i$ for each i. For each nonempty subset J of $\{1, \ldots, n\}$, consider the set

   $$B_J = \bigcap_{j \in J} A_j - \bigcup_{j \notin J} \bar{C}_j.]$$

2. Prove the following:

   Theorem. *Let X be a space that is path connected, locally path connected, and semilocally simply connected. If X is regular with a countable basis, then $\pi_1(X, x_0)$ is countable.*

   Proof. Let $\mathcal{A}$ be a covering of X by path-connected open sets A such that for each $A \in \mathcal{A}$ and each $a \in A$, the homomorphism $\pi_1(A, a) \to \pi_1(X, a)$ induced by inclusion is trivial. Let $\mathcal{B}$ be a countable open covering of X by nonempty path-connected sets that satisfies the conditions of Exercise 1. Choose a point $p(B) \in B$ for each $B \in \mathcal{B}$. For each pair B, B' of elements of $\mathcal{B}$ for which $B \cap B' \neq \varnothing$, choose a path $g(B, B')$ in $B \cup B'$ from $p(B)$ to $p(B')$. We call the path $g(B, B')$ a *select path*.

Let B_0 be a fixed element of $\mathcal{B}$; let $x_0 = p(B_0)$. Show that if f is a loop in X based at x_0, then f is path homotopic to a product of select paths, as follows:

(a) Show that there is a subdivision

$$0 = t_0 < \cdots < t_n = 1$$

of $[0, 1]$ such that f maps $[t_{n-1}, t_n]$ into B_0, and for each $i = 1, \ldots, n-1$, f maps $[t_{i-1}, t_i]$ into an element B_i of $\mathcal{B}$. Set $B_n = B_0$.

(b) Let f_i be the positive linear map of $[0, 1]$ onto $[t_{i-1}, t_i]$ followed by f. Let $g_i = g(B_{i-1}, B_i)$. Choose a path α_i in B_i from $f(t_i)$ to $p(B_i)$; if $i = 0$ or n, let α_i be the constant path at x_0. Show that

$$[f_i] * [\alpha_i] = [\alpha_{i-1}] * [g_i].$$

(c) Show that $[f] = [g_1] * \cdots * [g_n]$.

3. Let $p : E \to X$ be a covering map such that $\pi_1(X, x_0)$ is countable. Show that if X is regular with a countable basis, so is E. [*Hint:* Let $\mathcal{B}$ be a countable basis for X consisting of path-connected sets. Let $\mathcal{C}$ be the collection of path components of $p^{-1}(B)$, for $B \in \mathcal{B}$. Compare Exercise 6 of §53.]

4. Prove the following:

Theorem. *Let X be a space that is path connected, locally path connected, and semilocally simply connected. If X is compact Hausdorff, then $\pi_1(X, x_0)$ is finitely generated, and hence countable.*

Proof. Repeat the proof outlined in Exercise 2, choosing $\mathcal{B}$ to be finite. One has the equation

$$[f] = [g_1] * \cdots * [g_n],$$

as before. Choose, for each $x \in X$, a path β_x from x_0 to x; let β_{x_0} be the constant path. If $g = g(B, B')$, define

$$L(g) = \beta_x * (g * \bar{\beta}_y),$$

where $x = p(B)$ and $y = p(B')$. Show that

$$[f] = [L(g_1)] * \cdots * [L(g_n)].$$

5. Let X be the infinite earring (see Example 1 of §75). Show that X is a compact Hausdorff space with a countable basis whose fundamental group is uncountable. [*Hint:* Let $r_n : X \to C_n$ be a retraction. Given a sequence $a_1, a_2, \ldots$ of zeros and ones, show there exists a loop f in X such that, for each n, the element $(r_n)_*[f]$ is trivial if and only if $a_n = 0$.]

Chapter 13

Classification of Surfaces

One of the earliest successes of algebraic topology was its role in solving the problem of classifying compact surfaces up to homeomorphism. "Solving" this problem means giving a list of compact surfaces such that no two surfaces on the list are homeomorphic, and such that every compact surface is homeomorphic to one of them. This is the problem we tackle in this chapter.

§78   Fundamental Groups of Surfaces

In this section, we show how to construct a number of compact connected surfaces, and we compute their fundamental groups. We shall construct each of these surfaces as the quotient space obtained from a polygonal region in the plane by "pasting its edges together."

To treat this pasting process formally requires some care. First, let us define precisely what we shall mean by a "polygonal region in the plane." Given a point c of $\mathbb{R}^2$, and given $a > 0$, consider the circle of radius a in $\mathbb{R}^2$ with center at c. Given a finite sequence $\theta_0 < \theta_1 < \cdots < \theta_n$ of real numbers, where $n \geq 3$ and $\theta_n = \theta_0 + 2\pi$, consider the points $p_i = c + a(\cos\theta_i, \sin\theta_i)$, which lie on this circle. They are numbered in counterclockwise order around the circle, and $p_n = p_0$. The line through p_{i-1} and p_i splits the plane into two closed half-planes; let H_i be the one that contains all the points p_k. Then the space

$$P = H_1 \cap \cdots \cap H_n$$

is called the ***polygonal region*** determined by the points p_i. The points p_i are called the ***vertices*** of P; the line segment joining p_{i-1} and p_i is called an ***edge*** of P; the union of the edges of P is denoted Bd P; and $P - $ Bd P is denoted Int P. It is not hard to show that if p is any point of Int P, then P is the union of all line segments joining p and points of Bd P, and that two such line segments intersect only in the point p.

Given a line segment L in $\mathbb{R}^2$, an ***orientation*** of L is simply an ordering of its end points; the first, say a, is called the ***initial point***, and the second, say b, is called the ***final point***, of the oriented line segment. We often say that L is oriented ***from a to b***; and we picture the orientation by drawing an arrow on L that points from a towards b. If L' is another line segment, oriented from c to d, then the ***positive linear map*** of L onto L' is the homeomorphism h that carries the point $x = (1 - s)a + sb$ of L to the point $h(x) = (1 - s)c + sd$ of L'.

If two polygonal regions P and Q have the same number of vertices, $p_0, \ldots, p_n$ and $q_0, \ldots, q_n$, respectively, with $p_0 = p_n$ and $q_0 = q_n$, then there is an obvious homeomorphism h of Bd P with Bd Q that carries the line segment from p_{i-1} to p_i by a positive linear map onto the line segment from q_{i-1} to q_i. If p and q are fixed points of Int P and Int Q, respectively, then this homeomorphism may be extended to a homeomorphism of P with Q by letting it map the line segment from p to the point x of Bd P linearly onto the line segment from q to $h(x)$. See Figure 78.1.

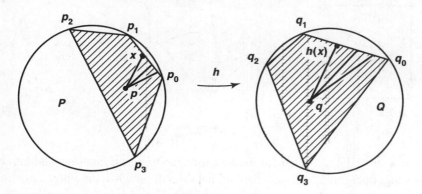

Figure 78.1

Definition.   Let P be a polygonal region in the plane. A ***labelling*** of the edges of P is a map from the set of edges of P to a set S called the set of ***labels***. Given an orientation of each edge of P, and given a labelling of the edges of P, we define an equivalence relation on the points of P as follows: Each point of Int P is equivalent only to itself. Given any two edges of P that have the same label, let h be the positive linear map of one onto the other, and define each point x of the first edge to be equivalent to the point $h(x)$ of the second edge. This relation generates an equivalence relation on P. The quotient space X obtained from this equivalence relation is said to have been obtained by **pasting the edges of P together** according to the given orientations and labelling.

EXAMPLE 1.   Consider the orientations and labelling of the edges of the triangular region pictured in Figure 78.2. The figure indicates how one can show that the resulting quotient space is homeomorphic to the unit ball.

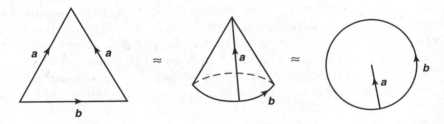

Figure 78.2

EXAMPLE 2.   The orientations and labelling of the edges of the square pictured in Figure 78.3 give rise to a space that is homeomorphic to the sphere S^2.

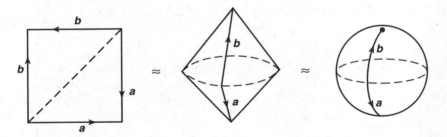

Figure 78.3

We now describe a convenient method for specifying orientations and labels for the edges of a polygonal region, a method that does not involve drawing a picture.

Definition.   Let P be a polygonal region with successive vertices $p_0, \ldots, p_n$, where $p_0 = p_n$. Given orientations and a labelling of the edges of P, let $a_1, \ldots, a_m$ be the distinct labels that are assigned to the edges of P. For each k, let a_{i_k} be the label assigned to the edge $p_{k-1}p_k$, and let $\epsilon_k = +1$ or -1 according as the orientation assigned to this edge goes from p_{k-1} to p_k or the reverse. Then the number of edges of P, the orientations of the edges, and the labelling are completely specified by the symbol

$$w = (a_{i_1})^{\epsilon_1}(a_{i_2})^{\epsilon_2} \cdots (a_{i_n})^{\epsilon_n}.$$

We call this symbol a ***labelling scheme of length n*** for the edges of P; it is simply a sequence of labels with exponents $+1$ or -1.

We normally omit the exponents that equal $+1$ when giving a labelling scheme. Then the orientations and labelling of Example 1 can be specified by the labelling scheme $a^{-1}ba$, if we take p_0 to be the top vertex of the triangle. If we take one of the other vertices to be p_0, then we obtain one of the labelling schemes baa^{-1} or $aa^{-1}b$.

Similarly, the orientations and labelling indicated in Example 2 can be specified (if we begin at the lower left corner of the square) by the symbol $aa^{-1}bb^{-1}$.

It is clear that a cyclic permutation of the terms in a labelling scheme will change the space X formed by using the scheme only up to homeomorphism. Later we will consider other modifications one can make to a labelling scheme that will leave the space X unchanged up to homeomorphism.

EXAMPLE 3.   We have already showed how the torus can be expressed as a quotient space of the unit square by means of the quotient map $p \times p : I \times I \to S^1 \times S^1$. This same quotient space can be specified by the orientations and labelling of the edges of the square indicated in Figure 78.4. It can be specified also by the scheme $aba^{-1}b^{-1}$.

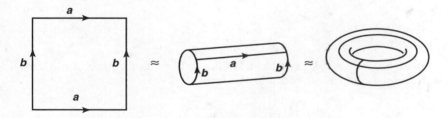

Figure 78.4

EXAMPLE 4.   The projective plane P^2 is homeomorphic to the quotient space of the unit ball B^2 obtained by identifying x with $-x$ for each $x \in S^1$. Because the unit square is homeomorphic to the unit ball, this space can also be specified by the orientations and labelling of the edges of the unit square indicated in Figure 78.5. It can be specified by the scheme $abab$.

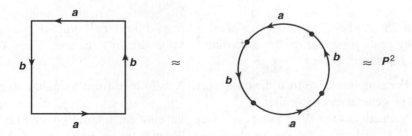

Figure 78.5

Now there is no reason to restrict oneself to a single polygonal region when forming a space by pasting edges together. Given a finite number $P_1, \ldots, P_k$ of disjoint polygonal regions, along with orientations and a labelling of their edges, one can form a quotient space X in exactly the same way as for a single region, by pasting the edges of these regions together. Also, one specifies orientations and a labelling in a similar way, by means of k labelling schemes. Depending on the particular schemes, the space X one obtains may or may not be connected.

EXAMPLE 5.   Figure 78.6 indicates a labelling of the edges of two squares for which the resulting quotient space is connected; it is the space called the *Möbius band*. Of course, this space could also be obtained from a single square by using the labelling scheme $abac$, as you can check.

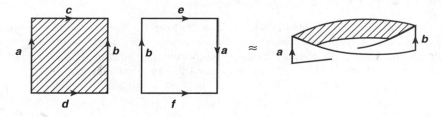

Figure 78.6

EXAMPLE 6.   Figure 78.7 indicates a labelling scheme for the edges of two squares for which the resulting quotient space is not connected.

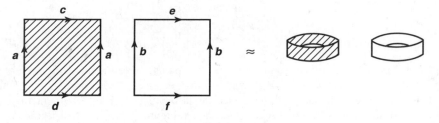

Figure 78.7

Theorem 78.1.   *Let X be the space obtained from a finite collection of polygonal regions by pasting edges together according to some labelling scheme. Then X is a compact Hausdorff space.*

Proof.   For simplicity, we treat the case where X is formed from a single polygonal region. The general case is similar.

It is immediate that X is compact, since the quotient map is continuous. To show X is Hausdorff, it suffices to show that the quotient map π is a closed map. (See Lemma 73.3.) For this purpose, we must show that for each closed set C of P, the set $\pi^{-1}\pi(C)$ is closed in P. Now $\pi^{-1}\pi(C)$ consists of the points of C and all points of P that are pasted to points of C by the map π. These points are easy to determine. For each edge e of P, let C_e denote the compact subspace $C \cap e$ of P. If e_i is an edge of P that is pasted to e, and if $h_i : e_i \to e$ is the pasting homeomorphism, then the set $D_e = \pi^{-1}\pi(C) \cap e$ contains the space $h_i(C_{e_i})$. Indeed, D_e equals the union of C_e and the spaces $h_i(C_{e_i})$, as e_i ranges over all edges of P that are pasted to e. This union is compact; therefore, it is closed in e and in P.

Since $\pi^{-1}\pi(C)$ is the union of the set C and the sets D_e, as e ranges over all edges of P, it is closed in P, as desired.   ∎

Now we note that if X is obtained by pasting the edges of a polygonal region together, the quotient map π may map all the vertices of the polygonal region to a single point of X, or it may not. In the case of the torus of Example 3, the quotient map does satisfy this condition, while in the case of the ball and sphere of Examples 1 and 2, it does not. We are especially happy when π satisfies this condition, for in this case one can readily compute the fundamental group of X:

Theorem 78.2. *Let P be a polygonal region; let*

$$w = (a_{i_1})^{\epsilon_1} \cdots (a_{i_n})^{\epsilon_n}$$

be a labelling scheme for the edges of P. Let X be the resulting quotient space; let $\pi : P \to X$ be the quotient map. If π maps all the vertices of P to a single point x_0 of X, and if $a_1, \ldots, a_k$ are the distinct labels that appear in the labelling scheme, then $\pi_1(X, x_0)$ is isomorphic to the quotient of the free group on k generators $\alpha_1, \ldots, \alpha_k$ by the least normal subgroup containing the element

$$(\alpha_{i_1})^{\epsilon_1} \cdots (\alpha_{i_n})^{\epsilon_n}.$$

Proof. The proof is similar to the proof we gave for the torus in §73. Because π maps all vertices of P to a single point of X, the space $A = \pi(\text{Bd } P)$ is a wedge of k circles. For each i, choose an edge of P that is labelled a_i; let f_i be the positive linear map of I onto this edge oriented counterclockwise; and let $g_i = \pi \circ f_i$. Then the loops $g_1, \ldots, g_k$ represent a set of free generators for $\pi_1(A, x_0)$. The loop f running around Bd P once in the counterclockwise direction generates the fundamental group of Bd P, and the loop $\pi \circ f$ equals the loop

$$(g_{i_1})^{\epsilon_1} * \cdots * (g_{i_n})^{\epsilon_n}$$

The theorem now follows from Theorem 72.1.   ∎

Definition. Consider the space obtained from a $4n$-sided polygonal region P by means of the labelling scheme

$$(a_1 b_1 a_1^{-1} b_1^{-1})(a_2 b_2 a_2^{-1} b_2^{-1}) \cdots (a_n b_n a_n^{-1} b_n^{-1}).$$

This space is called the ***n-fold connected sum of tori***, or simply the ***n-fold torus***, and denoted $T \# \cdots \# T$.

The 2-fold torus is pictured in Figure 78.8. If we split the polygonal region P along the indicated line c, each of the resulting pieces represents a torus with an open disc removed. If we paste these pieces together along the curve c, we obtain the space we introduced in §60 and called there the ***double torus***. A similar argument shows that the 3-fold torus $T\#T\#T$ can be pictured as the surface in Figure 78.9.

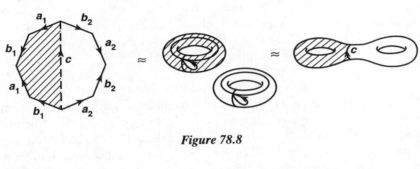

Figure 78.8

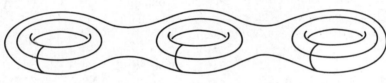

Figure 78.9

Theorem 78.3. *Let X denote the n-fold torus. Then $\pi_1(X, x_0)$ is isomorphic to the quotient of the free group on the $2n$ generators $\alpha_1, \beta_1, \ldots, \alpha_n, \beta_n$ by the least normal subgroup containing the element*

$$[\alpha_1, \beta_1][\alpha_2, \beta_2] \cdots [\alpha_n, \beta_n],$$

where $[\alpha, \beta] = \alpha\beta\alpha^{-1}\beta^{-1}$, as usual.

Proof. In order to apply Theorem 78.2, one must show that under the labelling scheme for X, all the vertices of the polygonal region belong to the same equivalence class. We leave this to you to check. ∎

Definition. Let $m > 1$. Consider the space obtained from a $2m$-sided polygonal region P in the plane by means of the labelling scheme

$$(a_1 a_1)(a_2 a_2) \cdots (a_m a_m)$$

This space is called the ***m-fold connected sum of projective planes***, or simply the ***m-fold projective plane***, and denoted $P^2\# \cdots \#P^2$.

The 2-fold projective plane $P^2\#P^2$ is pictured in Figure 78.10. The figure indicates how this space can be obtained from two copies of the projective plane by deleting an open disc from each and pasting the resulting spaces together along the boundaries of the deleted discs. As with P^2 itself, we have no convenient way for picturing the m-fold projective plane as a surface in $\mathbb{R}^3$, for in fact it cannot be imbedded in $\mathbb{R}^3$. Sometimes, however, we can picture it in $\mathbb{R}^3$ as a surface that intersects itself. (We then speak of an *immersed* surface rather than an imbedded one.) We explore this topic in the exercises.

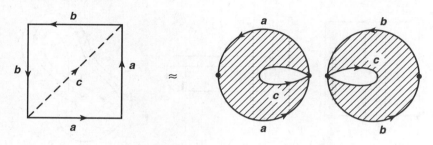

Figure 78.10

Theorem 78.4. *Let X denote the m-fold projective plane. Then $\pi_1(X, x_0)$ is isomorphic to the quotient of the free group on m generators $\alpha_1, \ldots, \alpha_m$ by the least normal subgroup containing the element*

$$(\alpha_1)^2 (\alpha_2)^2 \cdots (\alpha_m)^2.$$

Proof. One needs only to check that under the labelling scheme for X, all the vertices of the polygonal region belong to the same equivalence class. This we leave to you. ∎

There exist many other ways to form compact surfaces. One can for instance delete an open disc from each of the spaces P^2 and T, and paste the resulting spaces together along the boundaries of the deleted discs. You can check that this space can be obtained from a 6-sided polygonal region by means of the labelling scheme $aabcb^{-1}c^{-1}$. But we shall stop at this point. For it turns out that we have already obtained a complete list of the compact connected surfaces. This is the basic *classification theorem for surfaces*, which we shall consider shortly.

Exercises

1. Find a presentation for the fundamental group of $P^2 \# T$.

2. Consider the space X obtained from a seven-sided polygonal region by means of the labelling scheme $abaaab^{-1}a^{-1}$. Show that the fundamental group of X is the free product of two cyclic groups. [*Hint:* See Theorem 68.7.]

3. The **Klein bottle** K is the space obtained from a square by means of the labelling scheme $aba^{-1}b$. Figure 78.11 indicates how K can be pictured as an immersed surface in $\mathbb{R}^3$.
   (a) Find a presentation for the fundamental group of K.
   (b) Find a double covering map $p : T \to K$, where T is the torus. Describe the induced homomorphism of fundamental groups.

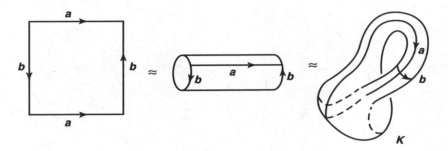

Figure 78.11

4. (a) Show that the Klein bottle is homeomorphic to $P^2 \# P^2$. [*Hint:* Split the square in Figure 78.11 along a diagonal, flip one of the resulting triangular pieces over, and paste the two pieces together along the edge labelled b.]
   (b) Show how to picture the 4-fold projective plane as an immersed surface in $\mathbb{R}^3$.

5. The Möbius band M is not a surface, but what is called a "surface with boundary". Show that M is homeomorphic to the space obtained by deleting an open disc from P^2.

6. If $n > 1$, show that the fundamental group of the n-fold torus is not abelian. [*Hint:* Let G be the free group on the set $\{\alpha_1, \beta_1, \ldots, \alpha_n, \beta_n\}$; let F be the free group on the set $\{\gamma, \delta\}$. Consider the homomorphism of G onto F that sends α_1 and β_1 to γ and all other α_i and β_i to δ.]

7. If $m > 1$, show the fundamental group of the m-fold projective plane is not abelian. [*Hint:* There is a homomorphism mapping this group onto the group $\mathbb{Z}/2 * \mathbb{Z}/2$.]

§79 Homology of Surfaces

Although we have succeeded in obtaining presentations for the fundamental groups of a number of surfaces, we now pause to ask ourselves what we have actually accomplished. Can we conclude from our computations, for instance, that the double torus and the triple torus are topologically distinct? Not immediately. For, as we know, we lack an effective procedure for determining from the presentations for two groups whether or not these groups are isomorphic. Matters are much more satisfactory if we pass to the abelian group $\pi_1/[\pi_1, \pi_1]$, where $\pi_1 = \pi_1(X, x_0)$. For then we have some known invariants to work with. We explore this situation in this section.

We know that if X is a path-connected space, and if α is a path in X from x_0 to x_1, then there is an isomorphism $\hat{\alpha}$ of the fundamental group based at x_0 with the fundamental group based at x_1, but the isomorphism depends on the choice of the path α. A stronger result holds for the group $\pi_1/[\pi_1, \pi_1]$. In this case, the isomorphism of the "abelianized fundamental group" based at x_0 with the one based at x_1, induced by α, is in fact *independent* of the choice of the path α.

To verify this fact, it suffices to show that if α and β are two paths from x_0 to x_1, then the path $g = \alpha * \bar{\beta}$ induces the identity isomorphism of $\pi_1/[\pi_1, \pi_1]$ with itself. And this is easy. If $[f] \in \pi_1(X, x_0)$, we have

$$\hat{g}[f] = [\bar{g} * f * g] = [g]^{-1} * [f] * [g].$$

When we pass to the cosets in the abelian group $\pi_1/[\pi_1, \pi_1]$, we see that $\hat{g}$ induces the identity map.

Definition.   If X is a path-connected space, let

$$H_1(X) = \pi_1(X, x_0)/[\pi_1(X, x_0), \pi_1(X, x_0)].$$

We call $H_1(X)$ the **first homology group** of X. We omit the base point from the notation because there is a unique path-induced isomorphism between the abelianized fundamental groups based at two different points.

If you study algebraic topology further, you will see an entirely different definition of $H_1(X)$. In fact, you will see groups $H_n(X)$ called the **homology groups** of X that are defined for all $n \geq 0$. These are abelian groups that are topological invariants of X; they are of fundamental importance in applying results of algebra to problems of topology. A theorem due to W. Hurewicz establishes a connection between these groups and the homotopy groups of X. It implies in particular that for a path-connected space X, the first homology group $H_1(X)$ of X is isomorphic to the abelianized fundamental group of X. This theorem motivates our choice of notation for the abelianized fundamental group.

To compute $H_1(X)$ for the surfaces considered earlier, we need the following result:

Theorem 79.1.   *Let F be a group; let N be a normal subgroup of F; let $q : F \rightarrow F/N$ be the projection. The projection homomorphism*

$$p : F \rightarrow F/[F, F]$$

induces an isomorphism

$$\phi : q(F)/[q(F), q(F)] \rightarrow p(F)/p(N).$$

This theorem states, roughly speaking, that if one divides F by N and then abelianizes the quotient, one obtains the same result as if one first abelianizes F and then divides by the image of N in this abelianization.

Proof. One has projection homomorphisms p, q, r, s, as in the following diagram, where $q(F) = F/N$ and $p(F) = F/[F, F]$.

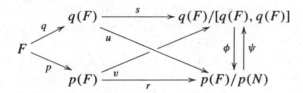

Because $r \circ p$ maps N to 1, it induces a homomorphism $u : q(F) \to p(F)/p(N)$. Then because $p(F)/p(N)$ is abelian, the homomorphism u induces a homomorphism ϕ of $q(F)/[q(F), q(F)]$. On the other hand, because $s \circ q$ maps F into an abelian group, it induces a homomorphism $v : p(F) \to q(F)/[q(F), q(F)]$. Because $s \circ q$ carries N to 1, so does $v \circ p$; hence v induces a homomorphism ψ of $p(F)/p(N)$.

The homomorphism ϕ can be described as follows: Given an element y of the group $q(F)/[q(F), q(F)]$, choose an element x of F such that $s(q(x)) = y$; then $\phi(y) = r(p(x))$. The homomorphism ψ can be described similarly. It follows that ϕ and ψ are inverse to each other. ∎

Corollary 79.2. *Let F be a free group with free generators $\alpha_1, \ldots, \alpha_n$; let N be the least normal subgroup of F containing the element x of F; let $G = F/N$. Let $p : F \to F/[F, F]$ be projection. Then $G/[G, G]$ is isomorphic to the quotient of $F/[F, F]$, which is free abelian with basis $p(\alpha_1), \ldots, p(\alpha_n)$, by the subgroup generated by $p(x)$.*

Proof. Note that because N is generated by x and all its conjugates, the group $p(N)$ is generated by $p(x)$. The corollary then follows from the preceding theorem. ∎

Theorem 79.3. *If X is the n-fold connected sum of tori, then $H_1(X)$ is a free abelian group of rank $2n$.*

Proof. In view of the preceding corollary, Theorem 78.3 implies that $H_1(X)$ is isomorphic to the quotient of the free abelian group F' on the set $\alpha_1, \beta_1, \ldots, \alpha_n, \beta_n$ by the subgroup generated by the element $[\alpha_1, \beta_1] \cdots [\alpha_n, \beta_n]$, where $[\alpha, \beta] = \alpha\beta\alpha^{-1}\beta^{-1}$ as usual. Because the group F' is abelian, this element equals the identity element. ∎

Theorem 79.4. *If X is the m-fold connected sum of projective planes, then the torsion subgroup $T(X)$ of $H_1(X)$ has order 2, and $H_1(X)/T(X)$ is a free abelian group of rank $m - 1$.*

Proof. In view of the preceding corollary, Theorem 78.4 implies that $H_1(X)$ is isomorphic to the quotient of the free abelian group F' on the set $\alpha_1, \ldots, \alpha_m$ by the subgroup generated by $(\alpha_1)^2 \cdots (\alpha_m)^2$. If we switch to additive notation (which is usual when dealing with abelian groups), this is the subgroup generated by the element $2(\alpha_1 + \cdots + \alpha_m)$. Let us change bases in the group F'. If we let $\beta = \alpha_1 + \cdots + \alpha_m$, then the elements $\alpha_1, \ldots, \alpha_{m-1}, \beta$ form a basis for F'; any element of F' can be written uniquely in terms of these elements. The group $H_1(X)$ is isomorphic to the quotient of the free abelian group on $\alpha_1, \ldots, \alpha_{m-1}, \beta$ by the subgroup generated by 2β. Said differently, $H_1(X)$ is isomorphic to the quotient of the m-fold cartesian product $\mathbb{Z} \times \cdots \times \mathbb{Z}$ by the subgroup $0 \times \cdots \times 0 \times 2\mathbb{Z}$. The theorem follows. ∎

Theorem 79.5. *Let T_n and P_m denote the n-fold connected sum of tori and the m-fold connected sum of projective planes, respectively. Then the surfaces S^2; T_1, T_2, $\ldots$; P_1, P_2, $\ldots$ are topologically distinct.*

Exercises

1. Calculate $H_1(P^2 \# T)$. Assuming that the list of compact surfaces given in Theorem 79.5 is a complete list, to which of these surfaces is $P^2 \# T$ homeomorphic?

2. If K is the Klein bottle, calculate $H_1(K)$ directly.

3. Let X be the quotient space obtained from an 8-sided polygonal region P by pasting its edges together according to the labelling scheme $acadbcb^{-1}d$.
    (a) Check that all vertices of P are mapped to the same point of the quotient space X by the pasting map.
    (b) Calculate $H_1(X)$.
    (c) Assuming X is homeomorphic to one of the surfaces given in Theorem 79.5 (which it is), which surface is it?

*4. Let X be the quotient space obtained from an 8-sided polygonal region P by means of the labelling scheme $abcdad^{-1}cb^{-1}$. Let $\pi : P \to X$ be the quotient map.
    (a) Show that π does not map all the vertices of P to the same point of X.
    (b) Determine the space $A = \pi(\operatorname{Bd} P)$ and calculate its fundamental group.
    (c) Calculate $\pi_1(X, x_0)$ and $H_1(X)$.
    (d) Assuming X is homeomorphic to one of the surfaces given in Theorem 79.5, which surface is it?

§80   Cutting and Pasting

To prove the classification theorem, we need to use certain geometric arguments involving what are called "cut-and-paste" techniques. These techniques show how to take a space X that is obtained by pasting together the edges of one or more polygonal regions according to some labelling scheme and to represent X by a different collection of polygonal regions and a different labelling scheme.

First, let us consider what it means to "cut apart" a polygonal region. Let P be a polygonal region with successive vertices $p_0, \ldots, p_n = p_0$, as usual. Given k with $1 < k < n - 1$, let us consider the polygonal regions Q_1, with successive vertices $p_0, p_1, \ldots, p_k, p_0$, and Q_2, with successive vertices $p_0, p_k, \ldots, p_n = p_0$. These regions have the edge $p_0 p_k$ in common, and the region P is their union.

Let us move Q_1 by a translation of $\mathbb{R}^2$ so as to obtain a polygonal region Q_1' that is disjoint from Q_2; then Q_1' has successive vertices $q_0, q_1, \ldots, q_k, q_0$, where q_i is the image of p_i under the translation. The regions Q_1' and Q_2 are said to have been obtained by **cutting P apart** along the line from p_0 to p_k. The region P is homeomorphic to the quotient space of Q_1' and Q_2 obtained by pasting the edge of Q_1' going from q_0 to q_k to the edge of Q_2 going from p_0 to p_k, by the positive linear map of one edge onto the other. See Figure 80.1.

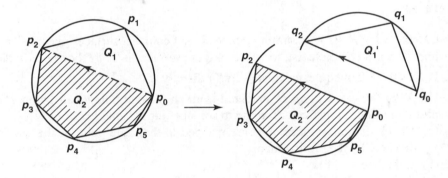

Figure 80.1

Now let us consider how we can reverse this process. Suppose we are given two disjoint polygonal regions Q_1' with successive vertices $q_0, \ldots, q_k, q_0$, and Q_2, with successive vertices $p_0, p_k, \ldots, p_n = p_0$. And suppose we form a quotient space by pasting the edge of Q_1' from q_0 to q_k onto the edge of Q_2 by p_0 to p_k, by the positive linear map of one edge onto the other. We wish to represent this space by a polygonal region P.

This task is accomplished as follows: The points of Q_2 lie on a circle and are arranged in counterclockwise fashion. Let us choose points $p_1, \ldots, p_{k-1}$ on this same circle in such a way that $p_0, p_1, \ldots, p_{k-1}, p_k$ are arranged in counterclockwise order, and let Q_1 be the polygonal region with these as successive vertices. There is a homeomorphism of Q_1' onto Q_1 that carries q_i to p_i for each i and maps the edge $q_0 q_k$ of Q_1' linearly onto the edge $p_0 p_k$ of Q_2. Therefore, the quotient space in question is homeomorphic to the region P that is the union of Q_1 and Q_2. We say that P is obtained by **pasting Q_1' and Q_2 together** along the indicated edges. See Figure 80.2.

Now we ask the following question: If a polygonal region has a labelling scheme, what effect does cutting the region apart have on this labelling scheme? More pre-

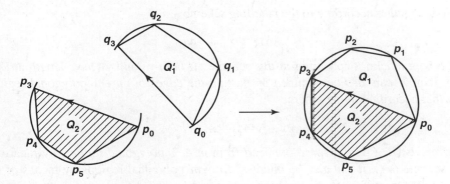

Figure 80.2

cisely, suppose we have a collection of disjoint polygonal regions $P_1, \ldots, P_m$ and a labelling scheme for these regions, say $w_1, \ldots, w_m$, where w_i is a labelling scheme for the edges of P_i. Suppose that X is the quotient space obtained from this labelling scheme. If we cut P_1 apart along the line from p_0 to p_k, what happens? We obtain $m + 1$ polygonal regions $Q'_1, Q_2, P_2, \ldots, P_m$; to obtain the space X from *these* regions, we need one additional edge pasting. We indicate the additional pasting that is required by introducing a new label that is to be assigned to the edges $q_0 q_k$ and $p_0 p_k$ that we introduced. Because the orientation from p_0 to p_k is counterclockwise for Q_2, and the orientation from q_0 to q_k is clockwise for Q'_1, this label will have exponent $+1$ when it appears in the scheme for Q_2 and exponent -1 when it appears in the scheme for Q'_1.

Let us be more specific. We can write the labelling scheme w_1 for P_1 in the form $w_1 = y_0 y_1$, where y_0 consists of the first k terms of w_1 and y_1 consists of the remainder. Let c be a label that does not appear in any of the schemes $w_1, \ldots, w_m$. Then give Q'_1 the labelling scheme $y_0 c^{-1}$, give Q_2 the labelling scheme $c y_1$, and for $i > 1$ give the region P_i its old scheme w_i.

It is immediate that the space X can be obtained from the regions $Q'_1, Q_2, P_2, \ldots, P_m$ by means of this labelling scheme. For the composite of quotient maps is a quotient map, so it does not matter whether we paste all the edges together at once, or instead paste the edge $p_0 p_k$ to the edge $q_0 q_k$ before pasting the others!

One can of course apply this procedure in reverse. If X is represented by a labelling scheme for the regions $Q'_1, Q_2, P_2, \ldots, P_m$ and if the labelling scheme indicates that an edge of the first is to be pasted to an edge of the second (*and no other edge is to be pasted to these*), we can actually carry out the pasting so as to represent X by a labelling scheme for the m regions $P_1, \ldots, P_m$.

We state this fact formally as a theorem:

Theorem 80.1. *Suppose X is the space obtained by pasting the edges of m polygonal* regions together according to the labelling scheme

$(*)$ $\qquad\qquad\qquad\qquad\qquad y_0 y_1, w_2, \ldots, w_m.$

Let c be a label not appearing in this scheme. If both y_0 and y_1 have length at least two, then X can also be obtained by pasting the edges of $m + 1$ polygonal regions together according to the scheme

$(**)$ $\qquad\qquad\qquad\qquad\qquad y_0 c^{-1}, c y_1, w_2, \ldots, w_m.$

Conversely, if X is the space obtained from $m + 1$ polygonal regions by means of the scheme $(**)$, it can also be obtained from m polygonal regions by means of the scheme $(*)$, providing that c does not appear in scheme $(*)$.

Elementary operations on schemes

We now list a number of elementary operations that can be performed on a labelling scheme $w_1, \ldots, w_m$ without affecting the resulting quotient space X. The first two arise from the theorem just stated.

(i) *Cut.* One can replace the scheme $w_1 = y_0 y_1$ by the scheme $y_0 c^{-1}$ and $c y_1$, provided c does not appear elsewhere in the total scheme and y_0 and y_1 have length at least two.

(ii) *Paste.* One can replace the scheme $y_0 c^{-1}$ and $c y_1$ by the scheme $y_0 y_1$, provided c does not appear elsewhere in the total scheme.

(iii) *Relabel.* One can replace all occurrences of any given label by some other label that does not appear elsewhere in the scheme. Similarly, one can change the sign of the exponent of all occurrences of a given label a; this amounts to reversing the orientations of all the edges labelled "a". Neither of these alterations affects the pasting map.

(iv) *Permute.* One can replace any one of the schemes w_i by a cyclic permutation of w_i. Specifically, if $w_i = y_0 y_1$, we can replace w_i by $y_1 y_0$. This amount to renumbering the vertices of the polygonal region P_i so as to begin with a different vertex; it does not affect the resulting quotient space.

(v) *Flip.* One can replace the scheme

$$w_i = (a_{i_1})^{\epsilon_1} \cdots (a_{i_n})^{\epsilon_n}$$

by its formal inverse

$$w_i^{-1} = (a_{i_n})^{-\epsilon_n} \cdots (a_{i_1})^{-\epsilon_1}.$$

This amounts simply to "flipping the polygonal region P_i over.". The order of the vertices is reversed, and so is the orientation of each edge. The quotient space X is not affected.

(vi) *Cancel.* One can replace the scheme $w_i = y_0 a a^{-1} y_1$ by the scheme $y_0 y_1$, provided a does not appear elsewhere in the total scheme and both y_0 and y_1 have length at least two.

This last result follows from the three-step argument indicated in Figure 80.3, only one step of which is new. Letting b and c be labels that do not appear elsewhere in the total scheme, one first replaces $y_0 a a^{-1} y_1$ by the scheme $y_0 a b$ and $b^{-1} a^{-1} y_1$, using the cutting operation (i). Then one combines the edges labelled a and b in each polygonal region into a single edge, with a new label. This is the step that is new. The result is the scheme $y_0 c$ and $c^{-1} y_1$, which one can replace by the single scheme $y_0 y_1$, using the pasting operation (ii).

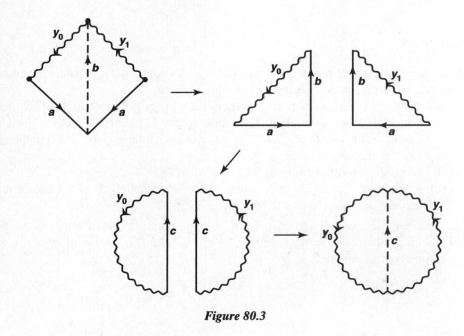

Figure 80.3

(vii) *Uncancel.* This is the reverse of operation (vi). It replaces the scheme $y_0 y_1$ by the scheme $y_0 a a^{-1} y_1$, where a is a label that does not appear elsewhere in the total scheme. We shall not actually have occasion to use this operation.

Definition.   We define two labelling schemes for collections of polygonal regions to be ***equivalent*** if one can be obtained from the other by a sequence of elementary scheme operations. Since each elementary operation has as its inverse another such operation, this is an equivalence relation.

EXAMPLE 1.   The Klein bottle K is the space obtained from the labelling scheme $aba^{-1}b$. In the exercises of §78, you were asked to show that K is homeomorphic to the 2-fold projective plane $P^2 \# P^2$. The geometric argument suggested there in fact consists of the following elementary operations:

$$aba^{-1}b \longrightarrow abc^{-1} \text{ and } ca^{-1}b \qquad \text{by cutting}$$

$$\longrightarrow c^{-1}ab \text{ and } b^{-1}ac^{-1} \qquad \text{by permuting the first}$$
and flipping the second

$$\longrightarrow c^{-1}aac^{-1} \qquad \text{by pasting}$$

$$\longrightarrow aacc \qquad \text{by permuting and relabelling.}$$

Exercises

1. Consider the quotient space X obtained from two polygonal regions by means of the labelling scheme $w_1 = acbc^{-1}$ and $w_2 = cdba^{-1}d$.
    (a) If one pastes these regions together along the edges labelled "a," one can represent X as the quotient space of a single 7-sided region P. What is a labelling scheme for P? What sequence of elementary operations is involved in obtaining this scheme?
    (b) Repeat (a), pasting along the edges labelled "b".
    (c) Explain why one cannot paste along the edges labelled "c" to obtain the scheme $acbdba^{-1}d$ as a way of representing X.

2. Consider the space X obtained from two polygonal regions by means of the labelling scheme $w_1 = abcc$ and $w_2 = c^{-1}c^{-1}ab$. The following sequence of elementary operations:

$$abcc \text{ and } c^{-1}c^{-1}ab \longrightarrow ccab \text{ and } b^{-1}a^{-1}cc \qquad \text{by permuting}$$
and flipping

$$\longrightarrow ccaa^{-1}cc \qquad \text{by pasting}$$

$$\longrightarrow cccc \qquad \text{by cancelling}$$

indicates that X is homeomorphic to the four-fold dunce cap. The sequence of operations

$$abcc \text{ and } c^{-1}c^{-1}ab \longrightarrow abcc^{-1}ab \qquad \text{by pasting}$$

$$\longrightarrow abab \qquad \text{by cancelling}$$

indicates that X is homeomorphic to P^2. But these two spaces are *not* homeomorphic. Which (if either) argument is correct?

§81   The Classification Theorem

We prove in this section the geometric part of our classification theorem for surfaces. We show that every space obtained by pasting the edges of a polygonal region together in pairs is homeomorphic either to S^2, to the n-fold torus T_n, or to the m-fold projective plane P_m. Later we discuss the problem of showing that every compact surface can be obtained in this way.

Suppose $w_1, \ldots, w_k$ is a labelling scheme for the polygonal regions $P_1, \ldots, P_k$. If each label appears exactly *twice* in this scheme, we call it a ***proper*** labelling scheme. Note the following important fact:

If one applies any elementary operation to a proper scheme, one obtains another proper scheme.

Definition.   Let w be a proper labelling scheme for a single polygonal region. We say that w is of ***torus type*** if each label in it appears once with exponent $+1$ and once with exponent -1. Otherwise, we say w is of ***projective type***.

We begin by considering a scheme w of projective type. We will show that w is equivalent to a scheme (of the same length) in which all labels having the same exponent are paired and appear at the beginning of the scheme. That is, w is equivalent to a scheme of the form

$$(a_1a_1)(a_2a_2) \cdots (a_ka_k)w_1,$$

where w_1 is of torus type or is empty.

Because w is of projective type, there is at least one label, say a, such that both occurrences of a in the scheme w have the same exponent. Therefore, we can assume that w has the form

$$w = y_0ay_1ay_2,$$

where some of the y_i may be empty. We shall insert brackets in this expression for visual convenience, writing it in the form

$$w = [y_0]a[y_1]a[y_2].$$

We have the following result:

Lemma 81.1.   *Let w be a proper scheme of the form*

$$w = [y_0]a[y_1]a[y_2],$$

where some of the y_i may be empty. Then one has the equivalence

$$w \sim aa[y_0y_1^{-1}y_2]$$

where y_1^{-1} denotes the formal inverse of y_1.

Proof.   *Step 1.* We first consider the case where y_0 is empty. We show that

$$a[y_1]a[y_2] \sim aa[y_1^{-1}y_2].$$

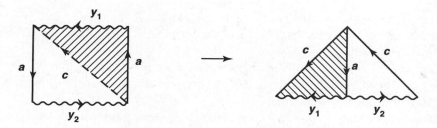

Figure 81.1

If y_1 is empty, this result is immediate, while if y_2 is empty, it follows from flipping, permuting, and relabelling. If neither is empty, we apply the cutting and pasting argument indicated in Figure 81.1, followed by a relabelling. We leave it to you to write down the sequence of elementary operations involved.

Step 2. Now we consider the general case. Let $w = [y_0]a[y_1]a[y_2]$, where y_0 is not empty. If both y_1 and y_2 are empty, the lemma follows by permuting. Otherwise, we apply the cutting and pasting argument indicated in Figure 81.2 to show that

$$w \sim b[y_2]b[y_1 y_0^{-1}].$$

It follows that

$$
\begin{aligned}
w &\sim bb[y_2^{-1} y_1 y_0^{-1}] && \text{by Step 1} \\
&\sim [y_0 y_1^{-1} y_2]b^{-1}b^{-1} && \text{by flipping} \\
&\sim aa[y_0 y_1^{-1} y_2] && \text{by permuting and relabelling.} \quad \blacksquare
\end{aligned}
$$

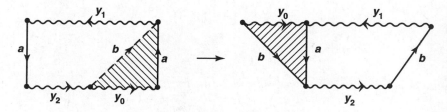

Figure 81.2

Corollary 81.2. *If w is a scheme of projective type, then w is equivalent to a scheme of the same length having the form*

$$(a_1 a_1)(a_2 a_2) \cdots (a_k a_k)w_1,$$

where $k \geq 1$ and w_1 is either empty or of torus type.

Proof.   The scheme w can be written in the form

$$w = [y_0]a[y_1]a[y_2];$$

then the preceding lemma implies that w is equivalent to a scheme of the form $w' = aaw_1$ that has the same length as w. If w_1 is of torus type, we are finished; otherwise, we can write w' in the form

$$w' = aa[z_0]b[z_1]b[z_2] = [aaz_0]b[z_1]b[z_2].$$

Applying the preceding lemma again, we conclude that w' is equivalent to a scheme w'' of the form

$$w'' = bb[aaz_0 z_1^{-1} z_2] = bbaaw_2,$$

where w'' has the same length as w. If w_2 is of torus type, we are finished; otherwise, we continue the argument similarly.   ∎

It follows from the preceding corollary that if w is a proper labelling scheme for a polygonal region, then either (1) w is of torus type, or (2) w is equivalent to a scheme of the form $(a_1 a_1) \ldots (a_k a_k) w_1$, where w_1 is of torus type, or (3) w is equivalent to a scheme of the form $(a_1 a_1) \ldots (a_k a_k)$. In case (3), we are finished, for such a scheme represents a connected sum of projective planes. So let us consider cases (1) and (2).

At this point, we note that if w is a scheme of length greater than four of the form indicated in case (1) or case (2), and if w contains two adjacent terms having the same label but opposite exponents, then the cancelling operation may be applied to reduce w to a shorter scheme that is also of the form indicated in cases (1), (2), or (3). Therefore, we can reduce w either to a scheme of length four, or to a scheme that does not contain two such adjacent terms.

Schemes of length four are easy to deal with, as we shall see later, so let us assume that w does not contain two adjacent terms having the same label but opposite exponents. In that case, we show that w is equivalent to a scheme w', of the same length as w, having the form

$$w' = aba^{-1}b^{-1}w'' \qquad \text{in case (1) or}$$
$$w' = (a_1 a_1) \cdots (a_k a_k) aba^{-1}b^{-1}w'' \quad \text{in case (2),}$$

where w'' is of torus type or is empty. This is the substance of the following lemma:

Lemma 81.3.   *Let w be a proper scheme of the form $w = w_0 w_1$, where w_1 is a scheme of torus type that does not contain two adjacent terms having the same label. Then w is equivalent to a scheme of the form $w_0 w_2$, where w_2 has the same length as w_1 and has the form*

$$w_2 = aba^{-1}b^{-1}w_3,$$

where w_3 is of torus type or is empty.

Proof.   This is the most elaborate proof of this section; three cuttings and pastings are involved. We show first that, switching labels and exponents if necessary, w can be written in the form

$(*)$ $\qquad\qquad\qquad w = w_0[y_1]a[y_1]b[y_3]a^{-1}[y_4]b^{-1}[y_5],$

where some of the y_i may be empty.

Among the labels appearing in w_1, let a be one whose two occurrences (with opposite exponents of course) are as close together as possible. These occurrences are nonadjacent, by hypothesis. Switching exponents if necessary, we can assume that the term a occurs first and the term a^{-1} occurs second. Let b be any label appearing between a and a^{-1}; we can assume its exponent is $+1$. Now the term b^{-1} appears in w_1, but cannot occur between a and a^{-1} because these two are as close together as possible. If b^{-1} appears following a^{-1}, we are finished. If it appears preceding a, then all we need to do is to switch exponents on the b terms, and then switch the labels a and b, to obtain a scheme of the desired form.

So let us assume that w has the form $(*)$.

First cutting and pasting. We show that w is equivalent to the scheme

$$w' = w_0a[y_2]b[y_3]a^{-1}[y_1y_4]b^{-1}[y_5].$$

To prove this result, we rewrite w in the form

$$w = w_0[y_1]a[y_2by_3]a^{-1}[y_4b^{-1}y_5].$$

We then apply the cutting and pasting argument indicated in Figure 81.3 to conclude that

$$w \sim w_0c[y_2by_3]c^{-1}[y_1y_4b^{-1}y_5]$$
$$\sim w_0a[y_2]b[y_3]a^{-1}[y_1y_4]b^{-1}[y_5],$$

by relabelling. Note that the cut at c can be made because both the resulting polygons have at least three sides.

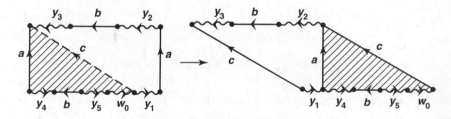

Figure 81.3

Second cutting and pasting. Given

$$w' = w_0a[y_2]b[y_3]a^{-1}[y_1y_4]b^{-1}[y_5],$$

we show that w' is equivalent to the scheme

$$w'' = w_0 a[y_1 y_4 y_3] b a^{-1} b^{-1} [y_2 y_5].$$

If all the schemes y_1, y_4, y_5, and w_0 are empty, then the argument is easy, since in that case

$$w' = a[y_2]b[y_3]a^{-1}b^{-1},$$
$$\sim b[y_3]a^{-1}b^{-1}a[y_2] \qquad \text{by permuting}$$
$$\sim a[y_3]ba^{-1}b^{-1}[y_2] \qquad \text{by relabelling}$$
$$= w''.$$

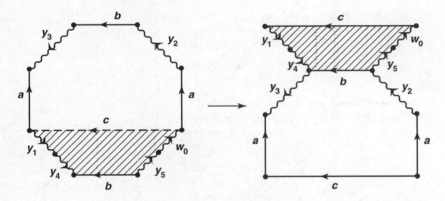

Figure 81.4

Otherwise, we apply the argument indicated in Figure 81.4 to conclude that

$$w' = w_0 a[y_2]b[y_3]a^{-1}[y_1 y_4]b^{-1}[y_5]$$
$$\sim w_0 c[y_1 y_4 y_3]a^{-1}c^{-1}a[y_2 y_5]$$
$$\sim w_0 a[y_1 y_4 y_3]ba^{-1}b^{-1}[y_2 y_5],$$

by relabelling.

Third cutting and pasting. We complete the proof. Given

$$w'' = w_0 a[y_1 y_4 y_3]ba^{-1}b^{-1}[y_2 y_5],$$

we show that w'' is equivalent to the scheme

$$w''' = w_0 aba^{-1}b^{-1}[y_1 y_4 y_3 y_2 y_5].$$

If the schemes w_0, y_5, and y_2 are empty, the argument is easy, since in that case

$$w'' = a[y_1 y_4 y_3]ba^{-1}b^{-1}$$
$$\sim ba^{-1}b^{-1}a[y_1 y_4 y_3] \qquad \text{by permuting}$$
$$\sim aba^{-1}b^{-1}[y_1 y_4 y_3] \qquad \text{by relabelling}$$
$$= w'''.$$

Otherwise, we apply the argument indicated in Figure 81.5 to conclude that

$$w'' = w_0 a [y_1 y_4 y_3] b a^{-1} b^{-1} [y_2 y_5]$$
$$\sim w_0 c a^{-1} c^{-1} a [y_1 y_4 y_3 y_2 y_5]$$
$$\sim w_0 a b a^{-1} b^{-1} [y_1 y_4 y_3 y_2 y_5],$$

by relabelling, as desired. ∎

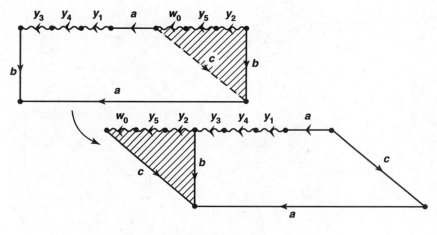

Figure 81.5

The final step of our classification procedure involves showing that a connected sum of projective planes and tori is equivalent to a connected sum of projective planes alone.

Lemma 81.4. *Let w be a proper scheme of the form*

$$w = w_0 (cc)(aba^{-1}b^{-1})w_1.$$

Then w is equivalent to the scheme

$$w' = w_0 (aabbcc)w_1.$$

Proof. Recall Lemma 81.1, which states that for proper schemes we have

(∗) $$[y_0] a [y_1] a [y_2] \sim aa[y_0 y_1^{-1} y_2].$$

We proceed as follows:

$$w \sim (cc)(aba^{-1}b^{-1})w_1w_0 \qquad \text{by permuting}$$
$$= cc[ab][ba]^{-1}[w_1w_0]$$
$$\sim [ab]c[ba]c[w_1w_0] \qquad \text{by } (*) \text{ read backwards}$$
$$= [a]b[c]b[acw_1w_0]$$
$$\sim bb[ac^{-1}acw_1w_0] \qquad \text{by } (*)$$
$$= [bb]a[c]^{-1}a[cw_1w_0]$$
$$\sim aa[bbccw_1w_0] \qquad \text{by } (*)$$
$$\sim w_0aabbccw_1 \qquad \text{by permuting.} \qquad \blacksquare$$

Theorem 81.5 (The classification theorem). *Let X be the quotient space obtained from a polygonal region in the plane by pasting its edges together in pairs. Then X is homeomorphic either to S^2, to the n-fold torus T_n, or to the m-fold projective plane P_m.*

Proof. Let w be the labelling scheme by which one forms the space X from the polygonal region P. Then w is a proper scheme of length least 4. We show that w is equivalent to one of the following schemes:

(1) $aa^{-1}bb^{-1}$,

(2) $abab$,

(3) $(a_1a_1)(a_2a_2)\cdots(a_ma_m)$ with $m \geq 2$,

(4) $(a_1b_1a_1^{-1}b_1^{-1})(a_2b_2a_2^{-1}b_2^{-1})\cdots(a_nb_na_n^{-1}b_n^{-1})$ with $n \geq 1$.

The first scheme gives rise to the space S^2, and the second, to the space P^2, as we noted in Examples 2 and 4 of §78. The third leads to the space P_m and the fourth to the space T_n.

Step 1. Let w be a proper scheme of torus type. We show that w is equivalent either to scheme (1) or to a scheme of type (4).

It w has length four, then it can be written in one of the forms

$$aa^{-1}bb^{-1} \quad \text{or} \quad aba^{-1}b^{-1}.$$

The first is of type (1) and the second of type (4).

We proceed by induction on the length of w. Assume w has length greater than four. If w is equivalent to a shorter scheme of torus type, then the induction hypothesis applies. Otherwise, we know that w contains no pair of adjacent terms having the same label. We apply Lemma 81.3 (with w_0 empty) to conclude that w is equivalent to a scheme having the same length as w, of the form

$$aba^{-1}b^{-1}w_3,$$

where w_3 is of torus type. Note that w_3 is not empty because w has length greater than four. Again, w_3 cannot contain two adjacent terms having the same label, since

w is not equivalent to a shorter scheme of torus type. Applying the lemma again, with $w_0 = aba^{-1}b^{-1}$, we conclude that w is equivalent to a scheme of the form

$$(aba^{-1}b^{-1})(cdc^{-1}d^{-1})w_4,$$

where w_4 is empty or of torus type. If w_4 is empty, we are finished; otherwise we apply the lemma again. Continue similarly.

Step 2. Now let w be a proper scheme of projective type. We show that w is equivalent either to scheme (2) or to a scheme of type (3).

If w has length four, Corollary 81.2 implies that w is equivalent to one of the schemes $aabb$ or $aab^{-1}b$. The first is of type (3). The second can be written in the form $aay_1^{-1}y_2$, with $y_1 = y_2 = b$; then Lemma 81.1 implies that it is equivalent to the scheme $ay_1ay_2 = abab$, which is of type (2).

We proceed by induction on the length of w. Assume w has length greater than four. Corollary 81.2 tells us that w is equivalent to a scheme of the form

$$w' = (a_1a_1) \cdots (a_ka_k)w_1,$$

where $k \geq 1$ and w_1 is of torus type or empty. If w_1 is empty, we are finished. If w_1 has two adjacent terms having the same label, then w' is equivalent to a shorter scheme of projective type and the induction hypothesis applies. Otherwise, Lemma 81.3 tells us that w' is equivalent to a scheme of the form

$$w'' = (a_1a_1) \cdots (a_ka_k)aba^{-1}b^{-1}w_2,$$

where w_2 is either empty or of torus type. Then we apply Lemma 81.4 to conclude that w'' is equivalent to the scheme

$$(a_1a_1) \cdots (a_ka_k)aabbw_2.$$

We continue similarly. Eventually we reach a scheme of type (3). ∎

Exercises

1. Let X be a space obtained by pasting the edges of a polygonal region together in pairs.
   (a) Show that X is homeomorphic to exactly one of the spaces in the following list: S^2, P^2, K, T_n, $T_n \# P^2$, $T_n \# K$, where K is the Klein bottle and $n \geq 1$.
   (b) Show that X is homeomorphic to exactly one of the spaces in the following list: S^2, T_n, P^2, K_m, $P^2 \# K_m$, where K_m is the m-fold connected sum of K with itself and $m \geq 1$.

2. (a) Write down the sequence of elementary operations required to carry out the arguments indicated in Figures 81.1 and 81.2.
   (b) Write down the sequence of elementary operations required to carry out the arguments indicated in Figures 81.3, 81.4, and 81.5.

3. The proof of the classification theorem provides an algorithm for taking a proper labelling scheme for a polygonal region and reducing it to one of the four standard forms indicated in the theorem. The appropriate equivalences are the following:

(i) $[y_0]a[y_1]a[y_2] \sim aa[y_0 y_1^{-1} y_2]$.

(ii) $[y_0]aa^{-1}[y_1] \sim [y_0 y_1]$ if $y_0 y_1$ has length at least 4.

(iii) $w_0[y_1]a[y_2]b[y_3]a^{-1}[y_4]b^{-1}[y_5] \sim w_0 aba^{-1}b^{-1}[y_1 y_4 y_3 y_2 y_5]$.

(iv) $w_0(cc)(aba^{-1}b^{-1})w_1 \sim w_0 aabbccw_1$.

Using this algorithm, reduce each of the following schemes to one of the standard forms.

(a) $abacb^{-1}c^{-1}$.

(b) $abca^{-1}cb$.

(c) $abbca^{-1}ddc^{-1}$.

(d) $abcda^{-1}b^{-1}c^{-1}d^{-1}$.

(e) $abcda^{-1}c^{-1}b^{-1}d^{-1}$.

(f) $aabcdc^{-1}b^{-1}d^{-1}$.

(g) $abcdabdc$.

(h) $abcdabcd$.

4. Let w be a proper labelling scheme for a 10-sided polygonal region. If w is of projective type, which of the list of spaces in Theorem 81.5 can it represent? What if w is of torus type?

§82   Constructing Compact Surfaces

To complete our classification of the compact surfaces, we must show that every compact connected surface can be obtained by pasting together in pairs the edges of a polygonal region. We shall actually prove something slightly weaker than this, for we shall assume that the surface in question has what is called a *triangulation*. We define this notion as follows:

Definition. Let X be a compact Hausdorff space. A *curved triangle* in X is a subspace A of X and a homeomorphism $h : T \to A$, where T is a closed triangular region in the plane. If e is an edge of T, then $h(e)$ is is said to be an *edge* of A; if v is a vertex of T, then $h(v)$ is said to be a *vertex* of A. A *triangulation* of X is a collection of curved triangles $A_1, \ldots, A_n$ in X whose union is X such that for $i \neq j$, the intersection $A_i \cap A_j$ is either empty, or a vertex of both A_i and A_j, or an edge of both. Furthermore, if $h_i : T_i \to A_i$ is the homeomorphism associated with A_i, we require that when $A_i \cap A_j$ is an edge e of both, then the map $h_j^{-1}h_i$ defines a linear homeomorphism of the edge $h_i^{-1}(e)$ of T_i with the edge $h_j^{-1}(e)$ of T_j. If X has a triangulation, it is said to be *triangulable*.

It is a basic theorem that every compact surface is triangulable. The proof is long but not exceedingly difficult. (See [A-S] or [D-M].)

Theorem 82.1. *If X is a compact triangulable surface, then X is homeomorphic to the quotient space obtained from a collection of disjoint triangular regions in the plane by pasting their edges together in pairs.*

Proof. Let $A_1, \ldots, A_n$ be a triangulation of X, with corresponding homeomorphisms $h_i : T_i \to A_i$. We assume the triangles T_i are disjoint; then the maps h_i combine to define a map $h : E = T_1 \cup \cdots \cup T_n \to X$ that is automatically a quotient map. (E is compact and X is Hausdorff.) Furthermore, because the map $h_j^{-1} \circ h_i$ is linear whenever A_i and A_j intersect in an edge, h pastes the edges of T_i and T_j together by a linear homeomorphism.

We have two things to prove. First, we must show that for each edge e of a triangle A_i, there is exactly one other triangle A_j such that $A_i \cap A_j = e$. This will show that the quotient map h pastes the edges of the triangles T_i together *in pairs*.

The second is a bit less obvious. We must show that if the intersection $A_i \cap A_j$ equals a vertex v of each, then there is a sequence of triangles having v as a vertex, beginning with A_i and ending with A_j, such that the intersection of each triangle of the sequence with its successor equals an edge of each. See Figure 82.1.

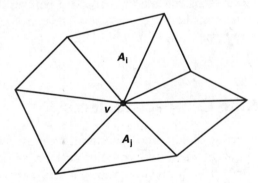

Figure 82.1

If this were not the case, one might have a situation such as that pictured in Figure 82.2. Here, one cannot specify the quotient map h merely by specifying how the edges of the triangles T_i are to be pasted together, but one must also indicate how the vertices are to be identified when that identification is not forced by the pasting of edges.

Step 1. Let us tackle the second problem first. We show that because the space X is a surface, a situation such as that indicated in Figure 82.2 cannot occur.

Given v, let us define two triangles A_i and A_j having v as a vertex to be *equivalent* if there is a sequence of triangles having v as a vertex, beginning with A_i and ending with A_j, such that the intersection of each triangle with its successor is an edge of each. If there is more than one equivalence class, let B be the union of the triangles in one

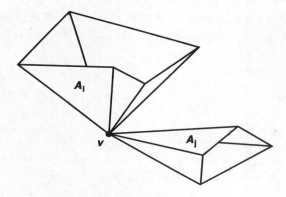

Figure 82.2

class and let C be the union of the others. The sets B and C intersect in v alone because no triangle in B has an edge in common with a triangle in C. We conclude that *for every sufficiently small neighborhood W of v in X, the space $W - v$ is nonconnected.*

On the other hand, if X is a surface, then v has a neighborhood homeomorphic to an open 2-ball. In this case, v has arbitrarily small neighborhoods W such that $W - v$ is connected.

Step 2. Now we tackle the first question. This is a bit more work. First, we show that, given an edge e of the triangle A_i, there is *at least one* additional triangle A_j having e as an edge. This is a consequence of the following result:

If X is a triangular region in the plane and if x is a point interior to one of the edges of X, then x does not have a neighborhood in X homeomorphic to an open 2-ball.

To prove this fact, we note that x has arbitrarily small neighborhoods W for which $W - x$ is simply connected. Indeed, if W is the ϵ-neighborhood of x in X, for ϵ small, then it is easy to see that $W - x$ is contractible to a point. See Figure 82.3.

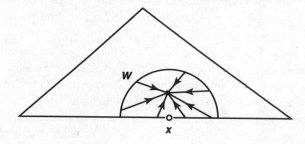

Figure 82.3

On the other hand, suppose there is a neighborhood U of x that is homeomorphic to an open ball in $\mathbb{R}^2$, with the homeomorphism carrying x to $\mathbf{0}$. We show that x does *not* have arbitrarily small neighborhoods W such that $W - x$ is simply connected.

Indeed, let B be the open unit ball in $\mathbb{R}^2$ centered at the origin, and suppose V is any neighborhood of $\mathbf{0}$ that is contained in B. Choose ϵ so that the open ball B_ϵ of radius ϵ centered at $\mathbf{0}$ lies in V, and consider the inclusion mappings

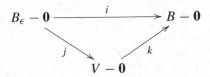

The inclusion i is homotopic to the homeomorphism $h(x) = x/\epsilon$, so it induces an isomorphism of fundamental groups. Therefore, k_* is surjective; it follows that $V - \mathbf{0}$ cannot be simply connected. See Figure 82.4.

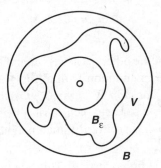

Figure 82.4

Step 3. Now we show that given an edge e of the triangle A_i, there is *no more than one* additional triangle A_j having e as an edge. This is a consequence of the following result:

Let X be the union of k triangles in $\mathbb{R}^3$, each pair of which intersect in the common edge e. Let x be an interior point of e. If $k \geq 3$, then x does not have a neighborhood in X homeomorphic to an open 2-ball.

We show that there is no neighborhood W of x in X such that $W - x$ has abelian fundamental group. It follows that no neighborhood of x is homeomorphic to an open 2-ball.

To begin, we show that if A is the union of all the edges of the triangles of X that are different from e, then the fundamental group of A is not abelian. The space A is the union of a collection of k arcs, each pair of which intersect in their end points. If B is the union of three of the arcs that make up A, then there is a retraction r of A onto B, obtained by mapping each of the arcs not in B homeomorphically onto one of the arcs in B, keeping the end points fixed. Then r_* is an epimorphism. Since the fundamental group of B is not abelian (by Example 1 of §70 or Example 3 of §58), neither is the fundamental group of A.

It follows that the fundamental group of $X - x$ is not abelian, for it is easy to see that A is a deformation retract of $X - x$. See Figure 82.5.

Now we prove our result. For convenience, assume x is the origin in $\mathbb{R}^3$. If W is an arbitrary neighborhood of $\mathbf{0}$, we can find a "shrinking map" $f(x) = \epsilon x$ that carries X

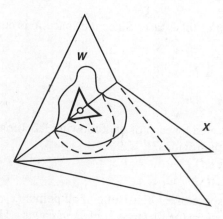

Figure 82.5

into W. The space $X_\epsilon = f(X)$ is a copy of X lying inside W. Consider the inclusions

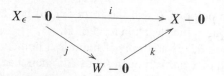

The inclusion i is homotopic to the homeomorphism $h(x) = x/\epsilon$, so it induces an iso-morphism of fundamental groups. It follows that k_* is surjective, so the fundamental group of $W - \mathbf{0}$ cannot be abelian. ∎

Theorem 82.2. *If X is a compact connected triangulable surface, then X is homeo-morphic to a space obtained from a polygonal region in the plane by pasting the edges together in pairs.*

Proof. It follows from the preceding theorem that there is a collection $T_1, \ldots, T_n$ of triangular regions in the plane, and orientations and a labelling of the edges of these regions, where each label appears exactly twice in the total labelling scheme, such that X is homeomorphic to the quotient space obtained from these regions by means of this labelling scheme.

We apply the pasting operation of §80. If two triangular regions have edges bear-ing the same label, we can (after flipping one of the regions if necessary) paste the regions together along these two edges. The result is to replace the two triangular re-gions by a single four-sided polygonal region, whose edges still bear orientations and labels. We continue similarly. As long as we have two regions having edges bearing the same label, the process can be continued.

Eventually one reaches the situation where either one has a single polygonal re-gion, in which case the theorem is proved, or one has several polygonal regions, no two of which have edges bearing the same label. In such a case, the space formed by carrying out the indicated pasting of edges is not connected; in fact, each of the regions gives rise to a component of this space. Since the space X is connected, this situation cannot occur. ∎

Exercises

1. What space is indicated by each of the following labelling schemes for a collection of four triangular regions?
   (a) abc, dae, bef, cdf.
   (b) abc, cba, def, dfe^{-1}.

2. Let H^2 be the subspace of $\mathbb{R}^2$ consisting of all points (x_1, x_2) with $x_2 \geq 0$. A 2-*manifold with boundary* (or *surface with boundary*) is a Hausdorff space X with a countable basis such that each point x of X has a neighborhood homeomorphic with an open set of $\mathbb{R}^2$ or H^2. The **boundary** of X (denoted ∂X) consists of those points x such that x has no neighborhood homeomorphic with an open set of $\mathbb{R}^2$.
   (a) Show that no point of H^2 of the form $(x_1, 0)$ has a neighborhood (in H^2) that is homeomorphic to an open set of $\mathbb{R}^2$.
   (b) Show that $x \in \partial X$ if and only if there is a homeomorphism h mapping a neighborhood of x onto an open set of H^2 such that $h(x) \in \mathbb{R} \times 0$.
   (c) Show that ∂X is a 1-manifold.

3. Show that the closed unit ball in $\mathbb{R}^2$ is a 2-manifold with boundary.

4. Let X be a 2-manifold; let $U_1, \ldots, U_k$ be a collection of disjoint open sets in X; and suppose that for each i, there is a homeomorphism h_i of the open unit ball B^2 with U_i. Let $\epsilon = 1/2$ and let B_ϵ be the open ball of radius ϵ. Show that the space $Y = X - \bigcup h_i(B_\epsilon)$ is a 2-manifold with boundary, and that ∂Y has k components. The space Y is called "X-with-k-holes."

5. Prove the following:
   Theorem. *Given a compact connected triangulable 2-manifold Y with boundary, such that ∂Y has k components, then Y is homeomorphic to X-with-k-holes, where X is either S^2 or the n-fold torus T_n or the m-fold projective plane P_m.*
   [*Hint:* Each component of ∂Y is homeomorphic to a circle.]

Bibliography

[A]   L. V. Ahlfors. *Complex Analysis, 3rd edition*. McGraw-Hill Book Company, New York, 1979.

[A-S]   L. V. Ahlfors and L. Sario. *Riemann Surfaces*. Princeton University Press, Princeton, N.J., 1960.

[C]   P. J. Campbell. The origin of "Zorn's lemma". *Historia Mathematica*, 5:77–89, 1978.

[D-M]   P. H. Doyle and D.A. Moran. A short proof that compact 2-manifolds can be triangulated. *Inventiones Math.*, 5:160–162, 1968.

[D]   J. Dugundji. *Topology*. Allyn and Bacon, Boston, 1966.

[F]   M. Fuchs. A note on mapping cylinders. *Michigan Mathematical Journal*, 18:289–290, 1971.

[G-P]   V. Guillemin and A. Pollack. *Differential Topology*. Prentice Hall, Inc., Englewood Cliffs, N.J., 1974.

[H]   P. R. Halmos. *Naive Set Theory*. Van Nostrand Reinhold Co., New York, 1960.

[H-S] D. W. Hall and G. L. Spencer. *Elementary Topology*. John Wiley & Sons, Inc., New York, 1955.

[H-W] W. Hurewicz and H. Wallman. *Dimension Theory*. Princeton University Press, Princeton, New Jersey, 1974.

[H-Y] J. G. Hocking and G. S. Young. *Topology*. Addison-Wesley Publishing Company, Inc., Reading, Mass., 1961.

[K]   J. L. Kelley. *General Topology*. Springer-Verlag, New York, 1991.

[K-F] A. N. Kolmogorov and S. V. Fomin. *Elements of the Theory of Functions and Functional Analysis, vol. 1*. Graylock Press, Rochester, New York, 1957.

[M]   W. S. Massey. *Algebraic Topology: An Introduction*. Springer-Verlag, New York, 1990.

[Mo]   G. H. Moore. *Zermelo's Axiom of Choice*. Springer-Verlag, New York, 1982.

[Mu]   J. R. Munkres. *Elements of Algebraic Topology*. Perseus Books, Reading, Mass., 1993.

[M-Z] D. Montgomery and L. Zippin. *Topological Transformation Groups*. Interscience Publishers, Inc., New York, 1955.

[RM]   M. E. Rudin. The box product of countably many compact metric spaces. *General Topology and Its Applications*, 2:293–298, 1972.

[RW]   W. Rudin. *Real and Complex Analysis, 3rd edition*. McGraw-Hill Book Company, New York, 1987.

[S-S] L. A. Steen and J. A. Seebach Jr. *Counterexamples in Topology*. Holt, Rinehart & Winston, Inc., New York, 1970.

[Sm]   R. M. Smullyan. The continuum hypothesis. In *The Mathematical Sciences, A Collection of Essays*. The M.I.T. Press, Cambridge, Mass., 1969.

[S]   E. H. Spanier. *Algebraic Topology*. McGraw-Hill Book Company, New York, 1966.

[T]   J. Thomas. A regular space, not completely regular. *American Mathematical Monthly*, 76:181–182, 1969.

[W]   R. L. Wilder. *Introduction to the Foundations of Mathematics*. John Wiley and Sons, Inc., New York, 1965.

[Wd]   S. Willard. *General Topology*. Addison-Wesley Publishing Company, Inc., Reading, Mass., 1970.

Index

Continuity, 100–102, 104, 106–109, 114, 127–128, 130, 132–133, 135, 145, 154–155, 161, 165, 167, 170, 173–174, 188, 208, 215, 238, 249, 274, 284–285, 295–296, 301, 335, 339, 445, 464
Continuous function, 100, 102, 106–108, 110, 129, 145, 165, 173, 205, 209–211, 213, 217, 220–221, 224, 237–239, 248, 257, 266, 268, 272, 279, 287, 291, 298–299, 302, 317, 352, 378
Convergence, 129–130, 132–133, 169, 279–291
Coordinates, 14, 28, 57, 61, 130–131, 196–197, 352, 405
Cosine, 109, 333
Counting, 38
Cubes, 147, 311–312